Ephesians 5:19 and 20:
Sing psalms and hymns and inspired songs among yourselves,
singing and chanting to the Lord in your hearts, always and everywhere giving
thanks to God who is our Father in the name of our Lord Jesus Christ.

THE DIVINE HOURS™

PRAYERS FOR AUTUMN
AND WINTERTIME

THE
DIVINE HOURS™

PRAYERS FOR AUTUMN
AND WINTERTIME

Compiled and with a Preface by
Phyllis Tickle

Doubleday
New York London Toronto Sydney Auckland

PUBLISHED BY DOUBLEDAY
a division of Random House, Inc.
1540 Broadway, New York, New York 10036

DOUBLEDAY and the portrayal of an anchor with a dolphin are trademarks
of Doubleday, a division of Random House, Inc.

The Divine Hours™ Tickle, Inc.

BOOK DESIGN BY RENATO STANISIC

Library of Congress Cataloging-in-Publication Data
Divine hours: prayers for autumn and wintertime / compiled and with a preface by
Phyllis Tickle.—1st ed.
p.   cm.
Includes index.
1. Prayers.   2. Winter—Prayer-books and devotions—English.
I. Tickle, Phyllis.
BV135.W56 D58 2000
264'.15—dc21   99-046160

ISBN 0-385-49757-1

PRINTED IN THE UNITED STATES OF AMERICA

First Edition, September 2000
10 9 8 7 6

Contents

An Introduction to This Manual

From the beginning two things have been the necessary form and mystery of Christian spirituality. Two things, even before the closing events of resurrection, ascension, and commission, wove disparate and often renegade believers into an inspirited body of the whole, connected to God and each other.

Like a double helix rendered elegant by complexity and splendid by authority, the amalgam of gospel and shared meal with the discipline of fixed-hour prayer were, and have remained, the chain of golden connection tying Christian to Christ and Christian to Christian across history, across geography, and across idiosyncrasies of faith. The former is known as the food and sustenance of the Church, the latter as its work. *The Divine Hours* is about the second part of this double strand, the work; it is a manual for the contemporary exercise of fixed-hour prayer.

Although designed primarily for private use by individuals or by small groups, *The Divine Hours* may certainly be employed by larger and/or more public communities. Likewise, though designed primarily for lay use, it can as well be employed by the ordained in either private or corporate prayer.

Those already familiar with fixed-hour prayer (variously referred to as "The Liturgy of the Hours" or "keeping the hours" or "saying the offices") and with its tools (the breviaries of monastic worship and the Book of Hours manuals for laity that date from medieval times) will find some modifications and innovations here. They may wish to scan what follows for explication of these changes. Others, especially those for whom keeping the hours is a new practice, may wish to read the remainder of this introduction more thoroughly.

A Brief History of Fixed-Hour Prayer

The Age of the Apostles

Fixed-hour prayer, while it is with the Eucharist the oldest surviving form of Christian spirituality, actually had its origins in the Judaism out of which Christianity came. Centuries before the birth of Jesus of Nazareth, the Hebrew psalmist wrote that "Seven times a day do I praise you" (Ps. 119:164). Although scholars do not agree on the hours of early Judaism's set prayers (they were probably adjusted and readjusted many times), we do know that by the first century a.d. the ritual of daily prayer had assumed two characteristics that would travel down the millennia to us: The prayers had been set or fixed into something very close to their present-day schedule, and they had begun to assume something very close to their present-day intention.

By the beginning of the common era, Judaism and its adherents, already thoroughly accustomed to fixed hours for prayer, were scattered across the Roman Empire. It was an empire whose efficiency and commerce depended in no small part upon the orderly and organized conduct of each business day. In the cities of the Empire, the forum bell rang the beginning of that day at six o'clock each morning (prime or "first" hour); noted the day's progress by striking again at nine o'clock (terce or third hour); sounded the lunch break at noon (sext or sixth hour); called citizens back to work by striking at three o'clock (none or ninth hour); and closed the day's markets by sounding again at six o'clock in the afternoon (vespers or evening hour). Every part of daily life within Roman culture eventually came, to some greater or lesser extent, to be ordered by the ringing of the forum bells, including Jewish prayer and, by natural extension, Christian prayer as well.

The first detailed miracle of the apostolic Church, the healing of the lame man on the Temple steps by Sts. Peter and John (Acts 3:1), occurred when and where it did because two devout Jews (who did not yet know they were Christians as such) were on their way to ninth-hour (three o'clock) prayers. Not many years later, one of the great defining events of Christianity—St. Peter's vision of the descending sheet filled with both clean and unclean animals—was to occur at noon on a rooftop because he had gone there to observe the sixth-hour prayers.

The directive Peter received during his noon devotion—i.e., to accept all that God had created as clean—was pivotal because it became the basis of the ecumenism that rapidly thereafter expanded Church fellowship beyond Jewry. Peter was on the roof, however, not by some accident of having been in that spot when the noon bell caught him but by his own intention. In Joppa and far from Jerusalem and the Temple, Peter had sought out the solitude of his host's rooftop as a substitute site for keeping the appointed time of prayer.

Such readiness to accommodate circumstance was to become a characteristic of fixed-hour prayer. So too were some of the words Peter must have used. We know, for instance, that from its very earliest days, the Christian community incorporated the Psalms in their prayers (Acts 4:23–30); and the Psalter has remained as the living core of the daily offices ever since. Likewise, by c. 60 a.d., the author of the first known manual of Christian practice, the Didache, was teaching the inclusion of the Lord's Prayer at least three times each day, a usage that was to expand quickly to include all the offices.

From the Apostles to the Early Fathers

As Christianity grew and, thanks to Peter's rooftop vision, as it spread, so too did the practice of formalized daily prayer. The process by which the fixed-hour prayers of the first century slowly recast themselves as the Divine Hours or Daily Offices of later Christians is blurred in some of its particulars, though we can attest to the approximate date and agency of many of them.

We know from their writings that by the second and third centuries the great Fathers of the Church—Clement (c. 150–215 a.d.), Origen (c. 185–254 a.d.), Tertullian (c. 160–225 a.d.), etc.—assumed as normative the observance of prayers in the morning and at night as well as for the so-called "little hours" of terce, sext, and none . . . or in modern parlance, nine a.m., noon, and three p.m. These daily prayers were often said or observed alone, though they could be offered by families or in small groups.

Regardless of whether or not the fixed-hour prayers were said alone or in community, however, they were never individualistic in nature. Rather, they employed the time-honored and time-polished prayers and recitations of the faith. Every Christian was to observe the prayers; none was empowered to create them.

Within the third century, the Desert Fathers, the earliest monastics of the Church, began to pursue the universal Christian desideratum of living out St. Paul's admonition to "pray without ceasing" (I Th. 5:17). To accomplish this, they devised the stratagem of having one group of monks pass the praying of an office on seamlessly to another group of monks waiting to commence the next office. The result was the introduction into Christian thinking of the concept of a continuous cascade of prayer before the throne of God. That concept was to remain into our own time as a realized grace for many, many Christians, both monastic and lay.

Christians today, wherever they practice the discipline of fixed-hour prayer, frequently find themselves filled with a conscious awareness that they are handing their worship, at its final "Amen," on to other Christians in the next time zone. Like relay runners passing a lighted torch, those who do the work of fixed-hour prayer create thereby a continuous cascade of praise before the throne of God. To participate in such a regimen with such an awareness is to pray, as did the Desert Fathers, from within the spiritual community of shared texts as well as within the company of innumerable other Christians, unseen but present, who have preceded one across time or who, in time, will follow one.

From St. Benedict to the Middle Ages

Once the notion of unbroken and uninterrupted prayer had entered monastic practice, so too, almost by default, did much longer prayers enter there. Yet for all their lengthiness and growing complexity and cumbersomeness, the monks' fixed-hour prayers became normative for the religious in both the Eastern and the Western branches of the Church. By the fourth century, certainly, the principal characteristics of the daily offices as we know them today were plainly in place, and their organization would be more or less recognizable as such to us today.

Meanwhile for secular (i.e., nonmonastic) clergy and for the laity, the prayers appointed for the fixed hours were of necessity much, much shorter, often confined to something not unlike the brief minutes of present-day observance. There were also many public churches or basilicas that, despite their uncloistered nature, were pastored by monastic orders, and in these there was some, almost inevitable, blending of the two forms—i.e., of the cumbersome monastic and the far more economical lay practices. St. Benedict, for example, fashioned his famous Rule after the offices as they were observed by monastics in the open basilicas of Rome.

It was, of course, St. Benedict whose ordering of the prayers was to become a kind of master template against which all subsequent observance and structuring of the Divine Hours was to be tested. It was also Benedict who first said, "*Orare est laborare, laborare est orare.*" "To pray is to work, to work is to pray." In so doing he gave form to another of the great, informing concepts of Christian spirituality—the inseparability of spiritual life from physical life. He also formalized the concept of "divine work."

"Office" as a word comes into modern usage from the Latin word *opus,* or "work." For most English speakers, it immediately connotes a place, rather than an activity. Yet those same speakers quite as naturally refer to professional functions— political ones, for example—as "offices," as in "He is running for office." Most of them readily refer to the voluntary giving up of the product of work as "offering" or "an offering." And those who govern or regulate work are routinely referred to as "officers" of a corporation or a civic unit. Thus in an earlier time that was much closer than we to the original possibilities of *opus,* it was entirely fitting that "office" should become the denominator for "the work of God."

For Benedict, as for many before him and almost all after him, fixed-hour prayer was and will always be *opus dei,* "the work of God," "the offices." As for the hours on whose striking the prayers are done, those belong to God and are, as a result, "divine." And the work is real—as fixed in its understanding of itself as it is in its timing.

Prayer is as variform as any other human activity. The Liturgy of the Hours, or the Divine Offices, is but one of those forms, yet it is the only one consistently referred to as "the work of God." The Divine Hours are prayers of praise offered as a sacrifice of thanksgiving and faith to God and as a sweet-smelling incense of the human soul before the throne of God. To offer them is to serve before that throne as part of the priesthood of all believers. It is to assume the "office" of attendant upon the Divine.

While the words and ordering of the prayers of the Divine Hours have changed and changed again over the centuries, that purpose and that characterization have remained constant. Other prayers may be petitionary or intercessory or valedictory or any number of other things, but the Liturgy of the Hours remains an act of offering . . . offering by the creature to the Creator. The fact that the creature grows strong and his or her faith more sinewy and efficacious as a result of keeping the hours is a by-product (albeit a desirable one) of that practice and not its purpose.

From the Middle Ages to Us

As the keeping of the hours grew in importance to become the organizing principle of both Christian spirituality and the Christian day, so too did the elaboration of the offices. By the eleventh century, saying an office required a veritable stack of books . . . a Psalter from which to sing the Psalms appointed for that day and hour, a lectionary from which to ascertain the appointed scripture reading, a sacred text from which to read the scripture thus discovered, a hymnal for singing, etc. As the growth of small communities took the laity away from the great cathedral centers where such tools and their ordering were available, it also created a need for some kind of unification of all the pieces and parts into a more manageable and more portable form. The result was the creation of a set of mnemonics, a kind of master list or, in Latin, *breviarium*, of how the fixed-hour prayers were to be observed and of the texts to be used.

From the less cumbersome listings of the *breviarium*, it was a short leap to incorporating into a book at least the first few words (and sometimes the whole) of all the texts required by the listing. This the officiants of the Papal Chapel did in the twelfth century, and the modern breviary was born. Breviaries, or manuals of prayer for keeping the daily offices, have varied over the subsequent centuries from order to order, from church to church, and from communion to communion within Christianity. So too has the ordering and number of the offices to be observed and even, in some cases, the setting of the appointed hours themselves.

The Anglican communion, for example, as one of its first acts of defiance in the time of the Reformation, created a new prayer book to govern the thinking and the practice of Christians in the new Church of England. That manual was given the intentionally populist name of *The Book of Common Prayer*. More often referred to affectionately today simply as the BCP, the manual has gone through many updates and revisions that have adjusted its language and even its theology to changing times and sensibilities. Despite those changes, however, and perhaps as a result of them, the BCP still orders, through one edition or another, the spiritual and religious lives of millions of Christians, many of them not Anglican by profession and all save a few of them certainly not English.

As one of its more "reforming" amendments, the first and subsequent editions of the BCP reduced or collapsed the Daily Offices into only two obligatory observances—morning prayer and evensong. Almost four hundred and fifty years later, in 1979, the U.S. (or Episcopal) Church bowed to the centuries and the yearning of many remembering hearts by restoring the noon office to its rightful place in the American BCP. In doing so, the Episcopal Church in the United States also acted within another abiding consistency of fixed-hour prayer—the enduring sense that the so-called Little Hours of terce, sext, and none, even when collapsed into one noontime observance, are as integral as are morning and evening prayer to the offices and to daily Christian practice, be it private or public.

Episcopal practice was not the first to undergo restructuring in the closing years of the twentieth century. In 1971 in accord with the work of the Second Vatican

Council, Pope Paul VI issued The Liturgy of the Hours, which modified the offices to an ordering very similar to the one the American BCP would assume eight years later. Four offices were now suggested to laity and required of monastics, secular clergy, and those under orders: a morning office called still by its Latin name of Lauds; a noon office that allows the individual Christian to choose the hour of his or her workday (either terce, sext or none) in which to pray the office and, as a result of that first choice, which of the three possible texts will be prayed; the early evening office of vespers; and before retiring, the simple, consoling office of compline. Under Paul VI's rubrics, there is also an obligatory Office of Readings that may be observed at any time of the believer's day as is most convenient.

Despite all the diversity that centuries and evolving doctrine have laid upon them, the Divine Hours have none the less remained absolute in their adherence to certain principles that have become their definition. The Daily Offices and the manuals that effect them are, as a result of that defining constancy, dedicated: to the exercise of praise as the work of God and the core of the offices; to the informing concept of a cascade of prayer being lifted ceaselessly by Christians around the world; to the recognition for every observant of an exultant membership with other observants in a communion of saints across both time and space; to the centrality of the Psalms as the informing text of all the offices (a centrality made doubly intense by the fact that theirs are the words, rhythms, and understandings that Jesus of Nazareth himself used in his own devotions while on earth); to the establishment in every breviary or manual of a fixed cycle that provides for the reading of at least some portion of all save three of the Psalms in the Hebrew/Christian Psalter (the present manual employs a six-week cycle and some portion of every Psalm); to the necessity of fixed components like the Our Father; to the formal ordering of each office's conduct; and to the efficacy of the repetition of prayers, creeds, and sacred texts in spiritual growth and exercise. It is on these principles and within the scope of these purposes that *The Divine Hours* is built.

Notes for the Use of This Manual

The Divine Hours: Prayers for Autumn and Wintertime, like most variations and revisions of established forms, is born out of contemporary need. In particular the manual strives for simplicity or familiarity of wording and ease of use. Not only will such an approach reassure those Christians who have not yet begun the practice of keeping the hours, but it will also provide even the liturgically accomplished with what one observer referred to as "a welcome lack of so many ribbons." With few exceptions, the entire text for each office is printed within that office, and the rubrics or headers of each part of each office are in contemporary rather than ecclesial English. The first evidence of this approach is in the manual's title itself. *Prayers for Autumn and Wintertime* uses the assignations of the physical year rather than those of the liturgical one. The rough correspondence in this case is between what common speech conceives of as two seasons and calls autumn and wintertime, and what the Western Church conceives of as a period of several seasons and designates by several liturgical or religious names, principal among them in wintertime the seasons of Advent, Christmas, and Epiphany.

Advent, four Sundays in duration, is a time of heightened devotion and of spiritual preparation for the coming (advent) of the Christ Child. Christmas, for the Church if not for the culture at large, lasts for the twelve days that extend from Christmas Day to January 6, that being the length of time tradition says it took the Wise Men first to see the Christmas star in the east and then to follow it to Bethlehem's manger. Epiphany commences on January 6 and extends through the rest of the month into some or all of February.

The liturgical calendar of the Church is filled, as is the secular calendar, with observances and seasons that both acknowledge and give exercise to the rhythms of life. Almost all of these feasts and celebrations are like Christmas and the saints' days; that is, they are tied to specific dates of the physical calendar. The season of Advent is also tied to a specific date, albeit a bit more indirectly: Advent begins each year on the first Sunday after November 30. In addition, that first Sunday of Advent, called Advent I, is also the first day of the new liturgical year. (For many Christians, having to hold esoteric dates in memory is bothersome. They may be reassured that there are numerous reminders of Advent's approach within the texts of the November offices.)

The Daily Offices in this manual are appointed, as is often done now, not by the date of an individual day nor by the week of the liturgical year, but rather they are dated from the Sunday of each week of the physical calendar. The Church has long assigned certain prayers, readings, and intentions to certain days of the week. Thus, Friday is normally regarded as a penitential day, Saturday as a day of preparation for corporate worship, Sunday as a Sabbath. Ordering the offices by calendar dates rather than from the first Sunday of each calendar week obscures these historic rhythms. Any system of ordering, however, including this one, must also accommodate the changing seasons of the Church's year. For that reason, this manual adheres to established tradition also in dating the Advent offices according to the individual weeks of Advent and in dating the first eight days of Christmas by their specific place in the physical calendar.

Following current Church practice, the offices appointed for each day are four in number: morning, noon, vespers, and compline. Following the ancient principle of accommodation, there is flexibility about the hour or half hour within which each may be observed. The morning and vespers or evening prayers adhere to the general configurations of their antecedents, and the noon office is an amalgam of the Little Hours of terce, sext, and none into one whole. The fourth—compline—is frequently referred to as "the dear office." Unlike the others, compline is fixed by the individual and not by the clock, for it is observed just before retiring.

Because compline is indeed the dear office of rest and because it is freer in its timing, it is also more repetitive or fixed here in its structure. Likewise, there is only one week of compline texts for each month of the manual. Thus the compline for the first Monday in October is the compline for each Monday in October. The only variance from this pattern is in the month of December, when there is one set of compline prayers for Advent and another for Christmas.

Each month's texts are preceded by a prefatory page that gives the page number for that month's compline texts; the physical or calendar date of saints' days and observances for the month; and the text of the Gloria and the Our Father. Most Christians are so absolutely familiar with both of these fixed prayers as to need no assistance in praying them. For that reason, they are the only parts of the daily offices not reproduced here within the texts of each office. On the other hand, new Christians or those just commencing the practice of the offices may find it reassuring to know that these two integral components are immediately available at the head of each month.

The Feasts and saints' days of the Church are so numerous as to be only rarely incorporated *in toto* by any breviary or manual. Rather, each selects for inclusion those holy days which are the major observances of the Church as well as some of those that seem most applicable to the volume's intended communion. Although this manual lists on each month's header the exact date of observation for each selected observance, it follows the pattern of celebrating the saint or feast on the Monday of the week within which the occasion falls. This system allows the user the flexibility to choose between precise commemoration or that of the memorializing week in general. In the event, as in the first week of January, that there are two observances in one week, the later one is celebrated on Thursday. The one exception to this pattern occurs in the first week of November, when the twinned holy days of All Saints and All Souls are commemorated in tandem.

To facilitate the Church's increasing emphasis on sacred texts, *The Divine Hours* incorporates readings into three offices—morning, noon, and compline. To make such incorporation feasible as well as possible, hymns are primary here only in the vespers office. In much the same way, some of the more repetitive practices of earlier manuals have been omitted. The list, which follows below, of the symbols and conventions used in this manual will enrich the user's understanding of some of the other particulars of *The Divine Hours* as well.

The Symbols and Conventions Used in This Manual

Except where otherwise indicated, the texts for the sacred readings in this manual are taken from *The New Jerusalem Bible*. Thus, the conventions of that translation obtain here as well. For example, the italicizing of a segment within a reading, both in the NJB and in the readings taken from it for use here, indicates that those words or phrases have also occurred elsewhere in scripture and probably constitute a direct quotation or incorporation by the current speaker.

On those few occasions when a sacred reading is from the King James Version rather than *The New Jerusalem*, that change is noted at the reading's conclusion by the notation, "KJV." The texts for all save a handful of the Psalms and Psalm hymns employed here are from the Psalter of *The Book of Common Prayer*. These departures are marked with the appropriate citing words with only two exceptions. Because of frequency and for aesthetic reasons, the symbol ❖ is used to indicate a medley or hymning of the canonical Psalms as assembled by Dr. Fred Bassett (c.f.,

Acknowledgments). For similar reasons, the symbol § indicates that compline's closing petition is from the work of St. Augustine.

Unless otherwise indicated, the appointed prayers are taken from the BCP. Many of them have been adapted, however, for use here. Such texts are indicated by the symbol †. Principally, the user already familiar with the BCP will note that many of the first-person plural pronouns of "us, we, our" have been changed to the singular ones of "me, I, my." The sensibility informing these adaptations has been the desire to make each more immediately personal. Whether the offices as they are produced here are said in private (as will be by far the greater use) or in public, each observant prays both as an individual and as a participant in a praying community. Where the pronominal singulars of "me, I, my" are employed, the attention should be directed toward the individual. Where the plurals are employed, attention and intention are toward the larger community of the Church.

The Psalms are poetry, albeit a poetry that does not work on a poetics familiar to most English speakers. Few translations of that great body of devotion have come so close, however, as has the Psalter of the BCP to exposing and celebrating the rhythms, images, and aesthetic force of the originals; and it is for that reason that they have been used here. The BCP Psalter, like every other, has its own conventions, and they are followed here. This is particularly obvious in the presentations of the name of God. Long a problem for translators as well as readers, the presence in the Psalms of three different terms for the divine name requires carefully chosen English wording as well as a clearly defined rationale for the application of each term chosen. This rationale, while too lengthy for inclusion here, may be found in the prefatory material to the BCP Psalter.

The Psalms as reproduced here retain as well the *, or asterisks, that indicate the poetic breaks in the original Hebrew poem. Whether one is reading or chanting the Psalm, there should be a pause at this point in order for the rhythm of the poetry to be realized fully. Many Christians will want to chant the Psalms, since that most ancient of practices still extends to the observant the greatest and purest spiritual benefit personally. For the more chary, reading aloud will offer a similar benefit, since it too involves the body as well as the intellect in the keeping of the office.

Most contemporary observants, be they lay or ordained, keep the Hours during the work day, a circumstance that means that the noon office in particular is observed within a space that is not only secular, but frequently populated. While one may withdraw to some removed space like a lounge or a car, one still is rarely sufficiently secluded to be comfortable chanting or reading aloud. By contrast, for weekend days and for the offices of morning and evening, chanting or oral reading may be both possible and desirable.

Chanting an office is a complex exercise with an equally complex and intricate history. Those who are already informed in the art will find that the asterisks here furnish the necessary pointing. For those who have not previously chanted the offices but wish to add that exercise to their spiritual discipline and for those who are new observants, a few simple principles may be sufficient for basic proficiency.

In general, Psalms are sung or chanted along one single note or tone, one that is chosen by the observant as pleasing and comfortable to maintain over the course of the text. The pacing is natural, neither hurried nor pretentiously extended. By chanting, the observant is weaving in yet another part of the bouquet of prayer that is being offered to God, and a constant remembrance of this purpose will do much to make the discipline acceptable and pleasing. Each verse of the Psalm, by and large, constitutes a poetic unit and is interrupted or pointed by an asterisk. The asterisk signals not only the poetic break in the verse but also the point at which the chanter is to raise his or her tone one note. That raising occurs on the last accented syllable nearest to the asterisk. At the end of the second half of the verse—i.e., the sequence of words after the asterisk—the chanter lowers by one note the final accented syllable. Pronouns like "me, he, thee," etc., are never elevated or lowered. The ear and the throat will soon show the new chanter as well that many English words are trisyllabic, having their accent on the first syllable. When such a word is the last one before an asterisk or a verse end, the first unaccented syllable goes up or down a note or half note as the case may be, and the second unaccented syllable goes up or down another similar gradation.

From such basic premises, the intrigued or impassioned chanter will discover rather quickly ways to elaborate the office to a rendering pleasing to him or her. Such elaborations, the chanter should be assured, have probably already been tried through the centuries by other Christians and may well be in full, current use by many of them. So also is there a range of options for rendering the prose or unpointed portions of each office. Readings or appointed prayers, for example, if chanted, are normally offered in a monotone with a lengthening of the final syllable of each breath pause or sentence unit. The Our Father is frequently the exception to this principle, being offered silently by many worshipers.

The only necessary principle, in fact, is really to remember the words of St. Augustine: "Whoever sings, prays twice." In so saying, Augustine spoke to the attitude as well as the benefit of chanting the Psalms: That which deepens the observant's contemplation and that which increases the beauty of our devotion are, by definition, appropriate and good.

THE DIVINE HOURS™
PRAYERS FOR AUTUMN AND WINTERTIME

The Gloria

Glory be to God the Father, God the Son, and God the Holy Spirit. As it was in the beginning, so it is now and so it shall ever be, world without end. Alleluia. *Amen.*

The Lord's Prayer

Our Father, who art in heaven, hallowed be your Name.
May your kingdom come, and your will be done, on earth as in heaven.
Give us today our daily bread.
Forgive us our sins as we forgive those who sin against us.
Lead us not into temptation, but deliver us from evil;
for yours are the kingdom and the power and the glory
forever and ever. *Amen.*

Compline Prayers for October Are Located on Page 133.

The Following Holy Days Occur in October:
The Feast of St. Francis of Assisi: *October 4*
The Feast of St. Luke the Evangelist: *October 18*
The Feast of St. James of Jerusalem: *October 23*
The Feast of St. Simon and St. Jude: *October 28*

October

The Morning Office   To Be Observed on the Hour or Half Hour
Between 6 and 9 a.m.

The Call to Prayer

Praise God from whom all blessings flow; Praise Him all creatures here below;
Praise him above, you heavenly hosts; Praise Father, Son, and Holy Ghost.

Traditional Doxology

The Request for Presence

Hear, O Shepherd of Israel, leading Joseph like a flock;* shine forth, you that are
enthroned upon the cherubim.

Psalm 80:1

The Greeting

The LORD lives! Blessed is my Rock!* Exalted is the God of my salvation!
Glory to God the Father, God the Son, and God the Holy Spirit. As it was in the
beginning, so it is now and so shall ever be, world without end. Alleluia. *Amen.*

Psalm 18:46; Gloria

The Refrain for the Morning Lessons

My heart is firmly fixed, O God, my heart is fixed;* I will sing and make melody.

Psalm 108:1

A Reading

Jesus taught us, saying: "Everyone who comes to me and listens to my words and
acts on them—I will show you what such a person is like. Such a person is like
the man who, when he built a house, dug, and dug deep, and laid the foundations on rock; when the river was in flood it bore down on that house but could
not shake it, it was so well built. But someone who listens and does nothing is
like the man who built a house on soil, with no foundations; as soon as the
river bore down on it, it collapsed; and what a ruin that house became!"

Luke 6:47–49

The Refrain

My heart is firmly fixed, O God, my heart is fixed;* I will sing and make melody.

The Morning Psalm   *In the Beginning, O LORD*

In the beginning, O LORD, you laid the foundations of the earth,* and the heavens
are the work of your hands;
They shall perish, but you will endure; they all shall wear out like a garment;* as
clothing you will change them, and they shall be changed;
But you are always the same,* and your years will never end.
The children of your servants shall continue,* and their offspring shall stand fast
in your sight.

Psalm 102:25–28

The Refrain

My heart is firmly fixed, O God, my heart is fixed;* I will sing and make melody.

The Small Verse
The people that walked in darkness have seen a great light; on those who live in a land of deep shadow a light has shone.

Isaiah 9:1

The Lord's Prayer

The Prayer Appointed for the Week
Almighty and everlasting God, you are always more ready to hear than we to pray, and to give more than we either desire or deserve: Pour upon your church the abundance of your mercy, forgiving us those things of which our conscience is afraid, and giving us those good things for which we are not worthy to ask, except through the merits and mediation of Jesus Christ our Savior; who lives and reigns with you and the Holy Spirit, one God, for ever and ever. *Amen.*✝

The Concluding Prayer of the Church
Lord God, almighty and everlasting Father, you have brought me in safety to this new day: Preserve me with your mighty power, that I may not fall into sin, nor be overcome by adversity; and in all I do direct me to the fulfilling of your purpose; through Jesus Christ my Lord. *Amen.*✝

The Midday Office   **To Be Observed on the Hour or Half Hour**
Between 11 a.m. and 2 p.m.

The Call to Prayer
Proclaim with me the greatness of the LORD;* let us exalt his Name together.

Psalm 34:3

The Request for Presence
LORD, hear my prayer, and let my cry come before you.
Incline your ear to me;* when I call, make haste to answer me.

Psalm 102:1ff

The Greeting
Let all who seek you rejoice and be glad in you;* let those who love your salvation say for ever, "Great is the LORD!"

Psalm 70:4

The Refrain for the Midday Lessons
I will give thanks to you, O LORD, with my whole heart;* I will tell of all your marvelous works.

Psalm 9:1

A Reading

We have been given possession of an unshakable kingdom. Let us therefore be
grateful and use our gratitude to worship God in the way that pleases him, in
reverence and fear. For our *God* is a *consuming fire.*

Hebrews 12:28–29

The Refrain

I will give thanks to you, O Lord, with my whole heart;* I will tell of all your marvelous works.

The Midday Psalm   *We Will Not Fear, Though the Earth Be Moved*

God is our refuge and strength,* a very present help in trouble.
Therefore we will not fear, though the earth be moved,* and though the
mountains be toppled into the depths of the sea;
Though its waters rage and foam,* and though the mountains tremble at its
tumult.
The Lord of hosts is with us;* the God of Jacob is our stronghold.
There is a river whose streams make glad the city of God,* the holy habitation of
the Most High.

Psalm 46:1–5

The Refrain

I will give thanks to you, O Lord, with my whole heart;* I will tell of all your marvelous works.

The Gloria

The Lord's Prayer

The Prayer Appointed for the Week

Almighty and everlasting God, you are always more ready to hear than we to
pray, and to give more than we either desire or deserve: Pour upon your
church the abundance of your mercy, forgiving us those things of which our
conscience is afraid, and giving us those good things for which we are not worthy to ask, except through the merits and mediation of Jesus Christ our Savior;
who lives and reigns with you and the Holy Spirit, one God, for ever and ever.
Amen.†

The Concluding Prayer of the Church

Lord, my God, King of heaven and of earth, for this day please direct and sanctify,
set right and govern my heart and my body, my sentiments, my words and my
actions in conformity with Your law and Your commandments. Thus I shall be
able to attain salvation and deliverance, in time and in eternity, by Your help, O
Savior of the world, who lives and reigns forever. *Amen.*

adapted from Divine Office, II

The Vespers Office   To Be Observed on the Hour or Half Hour
                                          Between 5 and 8 p.m.

The Call to Prayer
Behold now, bless the LORD, all you servants of the LORD,* you that stand by night
in the house of the LORD.

Psalm 134:1

The Request for Presence
For God alone my soul in silence waits;* truly, my hope is in him.

Psalm 62:6

The Greeting
I remember your Name in the night, O LORD,* and dwell upon your law.

Psalm 119:55

The Hymn   *Prayer of St. Francis of Assisi*
    Lord, make me an instrument of Thy peace;
    Where there is hatred let me sow love;
    Where there is injury, pardon;
    Where there is despair, hope;
    Where there is darkness, light;
    And where there is sadness, joy.
    O Divine Master, grant that
    I may not so much seek
    To be consoled, as to console;
    To be understood, as to understand;
    To be loved, as to love;
    For it is in giving that we receive,
    It is in pardoning that we are pardoned,
    And it is in dying that we are born to eternal life.

                            St. Francis of Assisi

The Refrain for the Vespers Lessons
Behold, he who keeps watch over Israel* shall neither slumber nor sleep.

Psalm 121:4

The Vespers Psalm   *The Just Shall See His Face*
The LORD is in his holy temple;* the LORD's throne is in heaven.
His eyes behold the inhabited world;* his piercing eye weighs our worth.
The LORD weighs the righteous as well as the wicked,* but those who delight in
    violence he abhors.
Upon the wicked he shall rain coals of fire and burning sulfur;* a scorching wind
    shall be their lot.
For the LORD is righteous; he delights in righteous deeds;* and the just shall see his
    face.

Psalm 11:4–8

The Refrain
Behold, he who keeps watch over Israel* shall neither slumber nor sleep.

The Gloria

The Lord's Prayer

The Prayer Appointed for the Week
Almighty and everlasting God, you are always more ready to hear than we to
pray, and to give more than we either desire or deserve: Pour upon your
church the abundance of your mercy, forgiving us those things of which our
conscience is afraid, and giving us those good things for which we are not worthy to ask, except through the merits and mediation of Jesus Christ our Savior;
who lives and reigns with you and the Holy Spirit, one God, for ever and ever.
Amen.†

The Concluding Prayer of the Church
Protect me, Lord, as I stay awake; watch over me as I sleep, that awake I may
watch with Christ, and asleep, rest in peace. *Amen.*

The Morning Office   To Be Observed on the Hour or Half Hour
Between 6 and 9 a.m.

The Call to Prayer
Come, let us sing to the LORD;* let us shout for joy to the Rock of our salvation.
Let us come before his presence with thanksgiving* and raise a loud shout to him
with psalms.

Psalm 95:1–2

The Request for Presence
LORD, God of hosts, hear my prayer;* hearken, O God of Jacob.

Psalm 84:7

The Greeting
The LORD lives! Blessed is my Rock!* Exalted is the God of my salvation!
Therefore will I extol you among the nations, O LORD,* and sing praises to your
Name.

Psalm 18:46ff

The Refrain for the Morning Lessons
The heaven of heavens is the LORD's,* but he entrusted the earth to its peoples.

Psalm 115:16

A Reading   *On October 4, the Church remembers with gratitude and affection
the life of St. Francis of Assisi, powerful witness to his Lord and
advocate for the oppressed.*

Jesus taught us, saying: "How blessed are the poor in spirit: the kingdom of
heaven is theirs. Blessed are the gentle: they shall have the earth as inheritance.
Blessed are those who mourn: they shall be comforted. Blessed are those who

hunger and thirst for uprightness: they shall have their fill. Blessed are the merciful: they shall have mercy shown them. Blessed are the pure in heart: they shall see God. Blessed are the peacemakers: they shall be recognized as children of God. Blessed are those who are persecuted in the cause of uprightness: the kingdom of heaven is theirs."

Matthew 5:3–10

The Refrain
The heaven of heavens is the Lord's,* but he entrusted the earth to its peoples.

The Morning Psalm   *Like a Child Upon Its Mother's Breast*
O Lord, I am not proud;* I have no haughty looks.
I do not occupy myself with great matters,* or with things that are too hard for me.
But I still my soul and make it quiet, like a child upon its mother's breast;* my soul is quieted within me.

Psalm 131:1–3

The Refrain
The heaven of heavens is the Lord's,* but he entrusted the earth to its peoples.

The Small Verse
Show us your mercy, O Lord; and grant us your salvation.
Clothe your ministers with righteousness; let your people sing with joy.
Give peace, O Lord, in all the world; for only in you can we live in safety.

The Lord's Prayer

The Prayer Appointed for the Week
Almighty and everlasting God, you are always more ready to hear than we to pray, and to give more than we either desire or deserve: Pour upon your church the abundance of your mercy, forgiving us those things of which our conscience is afraid, and giving us those good things for which we are not worthy to ask, except through the merits and mediation of Jesus Christ our Savior; who lives and reigns with you and the Holy Spirit, one God, for ever and ever. *Amen.*†

Concluding Prayers of the Church
Heavenly Father, Shepherd of your people, I thank you for your servant Francis, who was faithful in the care and nurture of your flock; and I pray that, following his example and the teaching of his holy life, I may by your grace grow into the stature of the fullness of our Lord Jesus Christ; who lives and reigns with you and the Holy Spirit, one God, for ever and ever. *Amen.*†

Lord God, almighty and everlasting Father, you have brought me in safety to this new day: Preserve me with your mighty power, that I may not fall into sin, nor be overcome by adversity; and in all I do direct me to the fulfilling of your purpose; through Jesus Christ my Lord. *Amen.*†

The Midday Office   To Be Observed on the Hour or Half Hour
                                     Between 11 a.m. and 2 p.m.

The Call to Prayer
All who take refuge in you will be glad;* they will sing out their joy forever.
You will shelter them,* so that those who love your Name may exult in you.
For you, O LORD, will bless the righteous;* you will defend them with your favor
    as with a shield.

Psalm 5:13–15

The Request for Presence
You are the LORD; do not withhold your compassion from me;* let your love and
    your faithfulness keep me safe for ever.

Psalm 40:12

The Greeting
O LORD, what are we that you should care for us?* mere mortals that you should
    think of us?
We are like a puff of wind;* our days are like a passing shadow.

Psalm 144:3–4

The Refrain for the Midday Lessons
Protect my life and deliver me;* let me not be put to shame, for I have trusted in
    you.
Let integrity and uprightness preserve me,* for my hope is in you.

Psalm 25:19–20

A Reading
After all, brothers, you were called to be free; do not use your freedom as an open-
    ing for self-indulgence, but be servants to one another in love, since the whole
    of the Law is summarized in one commandment: *You must love your neighbor as
    yourself.* If you go snapping off at one another and tearing one another to
    pieces, take care: you will be eaten up by one another.

Galatians 5:13–15

The Refrain
Protect my life and deliver me;* let me not be put to shame, for I have trusted in
    you.
Let integrity and uprightness preserve me,* for my hope is in you.

The Midday Psalm   *Behold, I Did Not Restrain My Lips*
I proclaimed righteousness in the great congregation;* behold, I did not restrain
    my lips; and that, O LORD, you know.
Your righteousness have I not hidden in my heart; I have spoken of your
    faithfulness and your deliverance;* I have not concealed your love and
    faithfulness from the great congregation.

Psalm 40:10–11

The Refrain
Protect my life and deliver me;* let me not be put to shame, for I have trusted in you.
Let integrity and uprightness preserve me,* for my hope is in you.

The Cry of the Church
O God, come to my assistance! O Lord, make haste to help me!

The Lord's Prayer

The Prayer Appointed for the Week
Almighty and everlasting God, you are always more ready to hear than we to pray, and to give more than we either desire or deserve: Pour upon your church the abundance of your mercy, forgiving us those things of which our conscience is afraid, and giving us those good things for which we are not worthy to ask, except through the merits and mediation of Jesus Christ our Savior; who lives and reigns with you and the Holy Spirit, one God, for ever and ever. Amen.†

The Concluding Prayer of the Church
O God, whose blessed Son became poor that we through his poverty might be rich: Deliver us from the inordinate love of this world, that we, inspired by the devotion of your servant Francis, may serve you with singleness of heart, and attain to the riches of the age to come; through Jesus Christ our Lord, who lives and reigns with you and the Holy Spirit, one God, now and for ever. Amen.†

The Vespers Office To Be Observed on the Hour or Half Hour
Between 5 and 8 p.m.

The Call to Prayer
Open my lips, O Lord,* and my mouth shall proclaim your praise.
Had you desired it, I would have offered sacrifice,* but you take no delight in burnt-offerings.
The sacrifice of God is a troubled spirit;* and a broken and contrite heart, O God, you will not despise.

Psalm 51:16–18

The Request for Presence
Give ear, O Lord, to my prayer,* and attend to the voice of my supplications.

Psalm 86:6

The Greeting
I give you thanks, O God, I give you thanks,* calling upon your Name and declaring all your wonderful deeds.

adapted from Psalm 75:1

The Hymn   *The Canticle of Brother Sun*

Most high, omnipotent, good, Lord,
To You alone, most High, do all belong,
And there is no one worthy to mention You.
Praised be my Lord,
by means of all Your creatures,
and most especially by Sir Brother Sun,
Who makes the day and illumines us by his light:
For he is beautiful and radiant with great splendor,
And is a symbol of You, God most high.
Praised be my Lord,
by means of Sister Moon and all the stars:
For in heaven You have placed them,
clear, precious, and fair.
Praised be my Lord, by means of Brother Wind,
And by means of the air, the clouds,
and the clear sky and every kind of weather,
through which You give Your creatures nourishment.
Praised be my Lord, by means of Sister Water:
For she is very useful, humble, precious and chaste.
Praised be my Lord, by means of Brother Fire,
By whom You do illumine the night:
For he is fair and gay and mighty and strong.
Praised be my Lord, by means of our sister Mother Earth,
Which sustains us and keeps us,
And brings forth varied fruits
with colored flowers and leaves.
Praised be my Lord,
through those who give pardon for love of You,
And suffer infirmity and tribulation.
Blessed are they who endure all in peace,
For they, O God most high, will be crowned by You.
Praised be my Lord, through our sister Bodily Death,
From whom no living person can escape.
Woe to those who die in mortal sin!
But blessed are those found in Your most holy will,
For the second death will do them no harm.
Praise and bless my Lord,
And thank Him, and serve Him with great humility.

St. Francis of Assisi

The Refrain for the Vespers Lessons
For you are my hope, O Lord God,* my confidence since I was young.

Psalm 71:5

The Vespers Psalm   *Praise Him, All His Host*

Hallelujah! Praise the Lord from the heavens;* praise him in the heights.

Praise him, all you angels of his;* praise him, all his host.

Praise him, sun and moon;* praise him, all you shining stars.

Praise him, heaven of heavens,* and you waters above the heavens.

Let them praise the Name of the Lord;* for he commanded, and they were
  created.

He made them stand fast for ever and ever;* he gave them a law which shall not
  pass away.

Praise the Lord from the earth,* you sea-monsters and all deeps;

Fire and hail, snow and fog,* tempestuous wind, doing his will;

Mountains and all hills,* fruit trees and all cedars;

Wild beasts and all cattle,* creeping things and winged birds;

Kings of the earth and all peoples,* princes and all rulers of the world;

Young men and maidens,* old and young together.

Let them praise the Name of the Lord,* for his Name only is exalted, his splendor
  is over earth and heaven.

He has raised up strength for his people and praise for all his loyal servants,* the
  children of Israel, a people who are near him. Hallelujah!

Psalm 148:1–14

The Refrain

For you are my hope, O Lord God,* my confidence since I was young.

The Small Verse

The Lord is my shepherd and nothing is wanting to me. In green pastures He has
  settled me.

The Short Breviary

The Lord's Prayer

The Prayer Appointed for the Week

Almighty and everlasting God, you are always more ready to hear than we to
  pray, and to give more than we either desire or deserve: Pour upon your
  church the abundance of your mercy, forgiving us those things of which our
  conscience is afraid, and giving us those good things for which we are not worthy to ask, except through the merits and mediation of Jesus Christ our Savior;
  who lives and reigns with you and the Holy Spirit, one God, for ever and ever.
  Amen.†

The Concluding Prayer of the Church

Almighty God, you gave to your servant Francis special gifts of grace to understand
  and teach the truth as it is in Christ Jesus: Grant that by this teaching I may know
  you, the one true God, and Jesus Christ whom you have sent; who lives and
  reigns with you and the Holy Spirit, one God, for ever and ever. *Amen.*†

The Morning Office   To Be Observed on the Hour or Half Hour
                                  Between 6 and 9 a.m.

The Call to Prayer
Sing praise to the LORD who dwells in Zion;* proclaim to the peoples the things he
    has done.

Psalm 9:11

The Request for Presence
May God be merciful to us and bless us,* show us the light of his countenance and
    come to us.

Psalm 67:1

The Greeting
Awesome things will you show us in your righteousness, O God of our salvation,*
    O Hope of all the ends of the earth and of the seas that are far away.

Psalm 65:5

The Refrain for the Morning Lessons
From this day forward all generations will call me blessed, for the Almighty has
    done great things for me.

Luke 1:48

A Reading
Jesus taught us, saying: "I am the Way; I am Truth and Life. No one can come to
    the Father except through me. If you know me, you will know my Father too.
    From this moment you know him and have seen him."

John 14:6–7

The Refrain
From this day forward all generations will call me blessed, for the Almighty has
    done great things for me.

The Morning Psalm   *O Israel, If You Would but Listen to Me*
Hear, O my people, and I will admonish you:* O Israel, if you would but listen to
    me!
There shall be no strange god among you;* you shall not worship a foreign god.
I am the LORD your God, who brought you out of the land of Egypt and said,*
    "Open your mouth wide, and I will fill it."

Psalm 81:8–10

The Refrain
From this day forward all generations will call me blessed, for the Almighty has
    done great things for me.

The Cry of the Church
O God, come to my assistance! O Lord, make haste to help me!

The Lord's Prayer

The Prayer Appointed for the Week

Almighty and everlasting God, you are always more ready to hear than we to pray, and to give more than we either desire or deserve: Pour upon your church the abundance of your mercy, forgiving us those things of which our conscience is afraid, and giving us those good things for which we are not worthy to ask, except through the merits and mediation of Jesus Christ our Savior; who lives and reigns with you and the Holy Spirit, one God, for ever and ever. *Amen.*✝

The Concluding Prayer of the Church

Lord God, almighty and everlasting Father, you have brought me in safety to this new day: Preserve me with your mighty power, that I may not fall into sin, nor be overcome by adversity; and in all I do direct me to the fulfilling of your purpose; through Jesus Christ my Lord. *Amen.*✝

The Midday Office	To Be Observed on the Hour or Half Hour
	Between 11 a.m. and 2 p.m.

The Call to Prayer

Know this, the LORD himself is God;* he himself has made us, and we are his; we are his people and the sheep of his pasture.

Psalm 100:2

The Request for Presence

Open my eyes, that I may see* the wonders of your law.

Psalm 119:18

The Greeting

I restrain my feet from every evil way,* that I may keep your word.

Psalm 119:101

The Refrain for the Midday Lessons

Blessed be God, who has not rejected my prayer,* nor withheld his love from me.

Psalm 66:18

A Reading

I pray that the God of peace, *who brought back* from the dead our Lord Jesus, the great *Shepherd of the sheep, by the blood that sealed an eternal covenant,* may prepare you to do his will in every kind of good action; effecting in us all whatever is acceptable to himself through Jesus Christ, to whom be glory for ever and ever, Amen.

Hebrews 13:20–21

The Refrain

Blessed be God, who has not rejected my prayer,* nor withheld his love from me.

The Midday Psalm   *We Flourish Like a Flower of the Field*
Our days are like the grass;* we flourish like a flower of the field;
When the wind goes over it, it is gone,* and its place shall know it no more.
But the merciful goodness of the LORD endures for ever on those who fear him,*
    and his righteousness on children's children.

Psalm 103:15–17

The Refrain
Blessed be God, who has not rejected my prayer,* nor withheld his love from me.

The Small Verse
Create in me a clean heart, O God,* and renew a right spirit within me.
Cast me not away from your presence* and take not your holy Spirit from me.
Give me the joy of your saving help again* and sustain me with your bountiful
    spirit.

Psalm 51:11–13

The Lord's Prayer

The Prayer Appointed for the Week
Almighty and everlasting God, you are always more ready to hear than we to
    pray, and to give more than we either desire or deserve: Pour upon your
    church the abundance of your mercy, forgiving us those things of which our
    conscience is afraid, and giving us those good things for which we are not wor-
    thy to ask, except through the merits and mediation of Jesus Christ our Savior;
    who lives and reigns with you and the Holy Spirit, one God, for ever and ever.
    Amen.†

The Concluding Prayer of the Church   *The Privilege Is Ours to Share in the Loving*
Almighty God, our heavenly Father, the privilege is ours to share in the loving,
    healing, reconciling mission of your Son Jesus Christ, our Lord, in this age and
    wherever we are. Since without you we can do no good thing,
    May your Spirit make us wise;
    May your Spirit guide us;
    May your Spirit renew us;
    May your Spirit strengthen us;
So that we will be:
    Strong in faith,
    Discerning in proclamation,
    Courageous in witness,
    Persistent in good deeds.
    This we ask through the name of the Father.

Church of the Province of the West Indies

The Vespers Office   To Be Observed on the Hour or Half Hour
                                              Between 5 and 8 p.m.

The Call to Prayer
Come, let us bow down, and bend the knee,* and kneel before the LORD our
    Maker.
For he is our God, and we are the people of his pasture and the sheep of his hand.
                                                                              Psalm 95:6–7

The Request for Presence
To you I lift up my eyes,* to you enthroned in the heavens.
                                                              Psalm 123:1

The Greeting
How priceless is your love, O God!* your people take refuge under the shadow of
    your wings.
They feast upon the abundance of your house;* you give them drink from the
    river of your delights.
For with you is the well of life,* and in your light we see light.
                                                                      Psalm 36:7–9

The Hymn   *O God, Our Help in Ages Past*

O God, our help in ages past,   A thousand ages, in your sight,
Our hope for years to come,   Are like an evening gone;
Our shelter from the stormy blast,   Short as the watch that ends the night,
And our eternal home.   Before the rising sun.

Under the shadow of your throne,   Time, like an ever rolling stream,
Still may we dwell secure;   Bears all who breathe away;
Sufficient is your arm alone,   They fly forgotten, as a dream
And our defense is sure.   Dies at the opening day.

Before the hills in order stood,   O God, our help in ages past,
Or earth received her frame,   Our hope for years to come,
From everlasting, you are God,   Be now our guide while life shall last,
To endless years the same.   And our eternal home.
                                                              Isaac Watts

The Refrain for the Vespers Lessons
Come and listen, all you who fear God,* and I will tell you what he has done for
    me.
                                                              Psalm 66:14

The Vespers Psalm   *He Strengthens Those in Whose Way He Delights*
Our steps are directed by the LORD;* he strengthens those in whose way he
    delights.
If they stumble, they shall not fall headlong,* for the LORD holds them by the hand.

I have been young and now I am old,* but never have I seen the righteous
forsaken, or their children begging bread.

Psalm 37:24–26

The Refrain
Come and listen, all you who fear God,* and I will tell you what he has done for
me.

The Small Verse
Have mercy on me, Lord, have mercy.
Lord, show me your love and mercy; for I put my trust in you.
In you, Lord, is my hope; and I shall never hope in vain.

The Lord's Prayer

The Prayer Appointed for the Week
Almighty and everlasting God, you are always more ready to hear than we to
pray, and to give more than we either desire or deserve: Pour upon your
church the abundance of your mercy, forgiving us those things of which our
conscience is afraid, and giving us those good things for which we are not worthy to ask, except through the merits and mediation of Jesus Christ our Savior;
who lives and reigns with you and the Holy Spirit, one God, for ever and ever.
Amen.†

The Concluding Prayer of the Church
Blessed be God, who has not rejected my prayer,* nor withheld his love from me.

Psalm 66:18

The Morning Office

To Be Observed on the Hour or Half Hour
Between 6 and 9 a.m.

The Call to Prayer
I will call upon God* and the Lord will deliver me.
In the evening, in the morning, and at the noonday, I will complain and lament,*
and he will hear my voice.
He will bring me safely back . . . God, who is enthroned of old, will hear me.

Psalm 55:17ff

The Request for Presence
Show us the light of your countenance, O God,* and come to us.

based on Psalm 67:1

The Greeting
In you, O Lord, have I taken refuge; let me never be put to shame;* deliver me in
your righteousness.

Psalm 31:1

The Refrain for the Morning Lessons
The same stone that the builders rejected* has become the chief cornerstone.

Psalm 118:22

A Reading
Jesus taught us, saying: "For the Son of man is going to come in the glory of his
Father with his angels and then he will reward each one according to his
behavior."

Matthew 16:27

The Refrain
The same stone that the builders rejected* has become the chief cornerstone.

The Morning Psalm   *A Canticle of the Messiah*
The Lord said to my Lord, "Sit at my right hand,* until I make your enemies your
footstool."
The Lord will send the scepter of your power out of Zion,* saying, "Rule over
your enemies round about you.
Princely state has been yours from the day of your birth;* in the beauty of holiness
have I begotten you, like dew from the womb of the morning."
The Lord has sworn and he will not recant:* "You are a priest for ever after the
order of Melchizedek."

Psalm 110:1–4

The Refrain
The same stone that the builders rejected* has become the chief cornerstone.

The Cry of the Church
O God, come to my assistance! O Lord, make haste to help me!

The Lord's Prayer

The Prayer Appointed for the Week
Almighty and everlasting God, you are always more ready to hear than we to
pray, and to give more than we either desire or deserve: Pour upon your
church the abundance of your mercy, forgiving us those things of which our
conscience is afraid, and giving us those good things for which we are not worthy to ask, except through the merits and mediation of Jesus Christ our Savior;
who lives and reigns with you and the Holy Spirit, one God, for ever and ever.
Amen.†

The Concluding Prayer of the Church
Lord God, almighty and everlasting Father, you have brought me in safety to this
new day: Preserve me with your mighty power, that I may not fall into sin, nor
be overcome by adversity; and in all I do direct me to the fulfilling of your purpose; through Jesus Christ my Lord. *Amen.*†

The Midday Office · · · · · · · · · · · · · · · · · To Be Observed on the Hour or Half Hour
Between 11 a.m. and 2 p.m.

The Call to Prayer
Know this: The Lord himself is God;* he himself has made us, and we are his.

Psalm 100:2

The Request for Presence
May God be merciful to us and bless us,* show us the light of his countenance and
come to us.

Psalm 67:1

The Greeting
I will confess you among the peoples, O Lord;* I will sing praise to you among the
nations.
For your loving-kindness is greater than the heavens,* and your faithfulness
reaches to the clouds.

Psalm 57:9–10

The Refrain for the Midday Lessons
Whoever is wise will ponder these things,* and consider well the mercies of the
Lord.

Psalm 107:43

A Reading
Let me sing my beloved the song of my friend for his vineyard.
My beloved had a vineyard on a fertile hillside. He dug it, cleared it of stones, and
planted it with red grapes. In the middle he built a tower, he hewed a press
there too. He expected it to yield fine grapes: wild grapes were all it yielded.
And now, citizens of Jerusalem and people of Judah, I ask you to judge
between me and my vineyard. What more could I have done for my vineyard
that I have not done? Why, when I expected it to yield fine grapes, has it
yielded wild ones?
Very well, I shall tell you what I am going to do to my vineyard: I shall take away
its hedge, for it to be grazed on, and knock down its wall, for it to be trampled
on. I shall let it go to waste, unpruned, undug, overgrown by brambles and
thorn-bushes, and I shall command the clouds to rain no rain on it. Now the
vineyard of Yahweh Sabaoth is the House of Israel, and the people of Judah the
plant he cherished. He expected fair judgement, but found injustice, uprightness, but found cries of distress.

Isaiah 5:1–7

The Refrain
Whoever is wise will ponder these things,* and consider well the mercies of the
Lord.

The Midday Psalm   *Behold and Tend This Vine, O God of Hosts*
Restore us, O God of hosts;* show the light of your countenance, and we shall be
    saved.
You have brought a vine out of Egypt;* you cast out the nations and planted it.
You prepared the ground for it;* it took root and filled the land.
The mountains were covered by its shadow* and the towering cedar trees by its
    boughs.
You stretched out its tendrils to the Sea* and its branches to the River.
Why have you broken down its wall,* so that all who pass by pluck off its grapes?
The wild boar of the forest has ravaged it,* and the beasts of the field have grazed
    upon it.
Turn now, O God of hosts, look down from heaven; behold and tend this vine;*
    preserve what your right hand has planted.

Psalm 80:7–14

The Refrain
Whoever is wise will ponder these things,* and consider well the mercies of the
    LORD.

The Small Verse
Truth shall spring up from the earth,* and righteousness shall look down from
    heaven.

Psalm 85:11

The Lord's Prayer

The Prayer Appointed for the Week
Almighty and everlasting God, you are always more ready to hear than we to
    pray, and to give more than we either desire or deserve: Pour upon your
    church the abundance of your mercy, forgiving us those things of which our
    conscience is afraid, and giving us those good things for which we are not wor-
    thy to ask, except through the merits and mediation of Jesus Christ our Savior;
    who lives and reigns with you and the Holy Spirit, one God, for ever and ever.
    Amen.†

The Concluding Prayer of the Church
Lord God Almighty, you have made all the peoples of the earth for your glory, to
    serve you in freedom and in peace: Give to the people of our country a zeal for
    justice and the strength of forbearance, that we may use our liberty in accor-
    dance with your gracious will; through Jesus Christ our Lord, who lives and
    reigns with you and the Holy Spirit, one God, for ever and ever. *Amen.*†

The Vespers Office

To Be Observed on the Hour or Half Hour
Between 5 and 8 p.m.

The Call to Prayer
Know that the LORD does wonders for the faithful;* when I call upon the LORD, he
will hear me.
Tremble, then, and do not sin;* speak to your heart in silence upon your bed.
Offer the appointed sacrifices* and put your trust in the LORD.

Psalm 4:3–5

The Request for Presence
O LORD, do not forsake me;* be not far from me, O my God.
Make haste to help me,* O Lord of my salvation.

Psalm 38:21–22

The Greeting
As the deer longs for the water-brooks,* so longs my soul for you, O God.

Psalm 42:1

The Hymn   *Breathe on Me, Breath of God*

Breathe on me, Breath of God,
Fill me with life anew,
That I may love what you do love,
And do what you would do.

Breathe on me, Breath of God,
Until my heart is pure,
Until with you I will one will,
To do and to endure.

Breathe on me, Breath of God,
Till I am wholly thine,
Till all this earthly part of me
Glows with your fire divine.

Breathe on me, Breath of God,
So shall I never die,
But live with you the perfect life
Of your eternity.

Edwin Hatch

The Refrain for the Vespers Lessons
Turn again to your rest, O my soul,* for the LORD has treated you well.
For you have rescued my life from death,* my eyes from tears, and my feet from
stumbling.

Psalm 116:6–7

The Vespers Psalm   *One Thing I Seek*
One thing have I asked of the LORD; one thing I seek;* that I may dwell in the
house of the LORD all the days of my life;
To behold the fair beauty of the LORD* and to seek him in his temple.

Psalm 27:5–6

The Refrain
Turn again to your rest, O my soul,* for the LORD has treated you well.
For you have rescued my life from death,* my eyes from tears, and my feet from
stumbling.

The Small Verse
Lord, let your way be known upon the earth; Your saving health among all
nations.
Let not the needy, O Lord, be forgotten; Nor the hope of the poor be taken away.
Create in me a clean heart, O God; And sustain me in your Holy Spirit.

The Lord's Prayer

The Prayer Appointed for the Week
Almighty and everlasting God, you are always more ready to hear than we to
pray, and to give more than we either desire or deserve: Pour upon your
church the abundance of your mercy, forgiving us those things of which our
conscience is afraid, and giving us those good things for which we are not worthy to ask, except through the merits and mediation of Jesus Christ our Savior;
who lives and reigns with you and the Holy Spirit, one God, for ever and ever.
Amen.†

The Concluding Prayer of the Church
Lord Jesus, stay with me, for evening is at hand and the day is past; be my companion in the way, kindle my heart, and awaken hope, that I may know you as
you are revealed in Scripture and the breaking of bread. Grant this for the sake
of your love. *Amen.*†

The Morning Office   **To Be Observed on the Hour or Half Hour**
Between 6 and 9 a.m.

The Call to Prayer
Let us bless the LORD* from this time forth for evermore. Hallelujah!
adapted from Psalm 115:18

The Request for Presence
Turn to me and have mercy upon me;* . . . save the child of your handmaid.
Psalm 86:16

The Greeting
You are my hiding-place . . . * you surround me with shouts of deliverance.
Psalm 32:8

The Refrain for the Morning Lessons
Behold, God is my helper;* it is the Lord who sustains my life.
Psalm 54:4

A Reading
Now it happened that when all the people had been baptized and while Jesus
after his own baptism was at prayer, heaven opened and the Holy Spirit
descended on him in a physical form, like a dove. And a voice came down
from heaven, *"You are my Son; today have I fathered you."*
Luke 3:21–22

The Refrain
Behold, God is my helper;* it is the Lord who sustains my life.

The Morning Psalm   *Show the Light of Your Countenance, and We Shall Be Saved*
Hear, O Shepherd of Israel, leading Joseph like a flock;* shine forth, you that are
    enthroned upon the cherubim.
In the presence of Ephraim, Benjamin, and Manasseh,* stir up your strength and
    come to help us.
Restore us, O God of hosts;* show the light of your countenance, and we shall be
    saved.

Psalm 80:1–3

The Refrain
Behold, God is my helper;* it is the Lord who sustains my life.

The Gloria

The Lord's Prayer

The Prayer Appointed for the Week
Almighty and everlasting God, you are always more ready to hear than we to
    pray, and to give more than we either desire or deserve: Pour upon your
    church the abundance of your mercy, forgiving us those things of which our
    conscience is afraid, and giving us those good things for which we are not wor-
    thy to ask, except through the merits and mediation of Jesus Christ our Savior;
    who lives and reigns with you and the Holy Spirit, one God, for ever and ever.
    Amen.†

The Concluding Prayer of the Church
Lord God, almighty and everlasting Father, you have brought me in safety to this
    new day: Preserve me with your mighty power, that I may not fall into sin, nor
    be overcome by adversity; and in all I do direct me to the fulfilling of your pur-
    pose; through Jesus Christ my Lord. *Amen.*†

The Midday Office   **To Be Observed on the Hour or Half Hour**
                                        Between 11 a.m. and 2 p.m.

The Call to Prayer
Sing to the Lord, you servants of his;* give thanks for the remembrance of his holi-
    ness.
For his wrath endures but the twinkling of an eye,* his favor for a lifetime.

Psalm 30:4–5

The Request for Presence
Look upon your covenant;* the dark places of the earth are haunts of violence.

Psalm 74:19

The Greeting
O LORD, your love endures for ever;* do not abandon the works of your hands.

Psalm 138:9

The Refrain for the Midday Lessons
He has not dealt with us according to our sins,* nor rewarded us according to our wickedness.

Psalm 103:10

A Reading
We ought, then, to turn our minds more attentively than before to what we have been taught, so that we do not drift away . . . we shall certainly not go unpunished if we neglect this salvation that is promised to us. The promise was first announced by the Lord himself, and is guaranteed to us by those who heard him; God himself confirmed their witness with signs and marvels and miracles of all kinds, and by freely giving the gifts of the Holy Spirit in the various ways he wills.

Hebrews 2:1–4

The Refrain
He has not dealt with us according to our sins,* nor rewarded us according to our wickedness.

The Midday Psalm   *How Exalted Is Your Name*
O LORD our Governor,* how exalted is your Name in all the world!
Out of the mouths of infants and children* your majesty is praised above the heavens.
You have set up a stronghold against your adversaries,* to quell the enemy and the avenger.
When I consider your heavens, the work of your fingers,* the moon and the stars you have set in their courses,
What is man that you should be mindful of him?* the son of man that you should seek him out?
You have made him but little lower than the angels;* you adorn him with glory and honor;
You give him mastery over the works of your hands;* you put all things under his feet:
All sheep and oxen,* even the wild beasts of the field,
The birds of the air, the fish of the sea,* and whatsoever walks in the paths of the sea.
O LORD our Governor,* how exalted is your Name in all the world!

Psalm 8

The Refrain
He has not dealt with us according to our sins,* nor rewarded us according to our
wickedness.

The Gloria

The Lord's Prayer

The Prayer Appointed for the Week
Almighty and everlasting God, you are always more ready to hear than we to
pray, and to give more than we either desire or deserve: Pour upon your
church the abundance of your mercy, forgiving us those things of which our
conscience is afraid, and giving us those good things for which we are not worthy to ask, except through the merits and mediation of Jesus Christ our Savior;
who lives and reigns with you and the Holy Spirit, one God, for ever and ever.
Amen.†

The Concluding Prayer of the Church
Almighty God, to whom our needs are known before we ask. Help me to ask only
what accords with your will; and those good things which I dare not, or in my
blindness cannot ask, grant for the sake of your Son Jesus Christ our Lord.
Amen.†

The Vespers Office   To Be Observed on the Hour or Half Hour
                                          Between 5 and 8 p.m.

The Call to Prayer
O tarry and await the LORD's pleasure; be strong, and he shall comfort your heart;*
wait patiently for the LORD.

Psalm 27:18

The Request for Presence
Open my eyes, that I may see* the wonders of your law.
Psalm 119:18

The Greeting
Your statutes have been like songs to me* wherever I have lived as a stranger.
I remember your Name in the night, O LORD,* and dwell upon your law.
This is how it has been with me,* because I have kept your commandments.
Psalm 119:54–56

The Hymn   *Standing on the Promises*
   Standing on the promises of Christ my King,
   Through eternal ages let his praises ring;
   Glory in the highest, I will shout and sing,
   Standing on the promises of God.

Standing on the promises that cannot fail,
When the howling storms of doubt and fear assail,
By the living Word of God I shall prevail,
Standing on the promises of God.

Standing on the promises of Christ the Lord,
Bound to him eternally by love's strong cord,
Overcoming daily with the Spirit's sword,
Standing on the promises of God.

Standing on the promises I cannot fall,
Listening to every moment of the Spirit's call,
Resting in my Savior as my all in all,
Standing on the promises of God.

R. Kelso Carter

The Refrain for the Vespers Lessons
'I am the Alpha and the Omega,' says the Lord God, who is, who was, and who is
to come, the Almighty.

Revelation 1:8

The Vespers Psalm   *The LORD Is My Shepherd*
The LORD is my shepherd;* I shall not be in want.
He makes me lie down in green pastures* and leads me beside still waters.
He revives my soul* and guides me along right pathways for his Name's sake.
Though I walk through the valley of the shadow of death, I shall fear no evil;* for
you are with me; your rod and your staff, they comfort me.
You spread a table before me in the presence of those who trouble me;* you have
anointed my head with oil, and my cup is running over.
Surely your goodness and mercy shall follow me all the days of my life,* and I will
dwell in the house of the LORD for ever.

Psalm 23:1–6

The Refrain
'I am the Alpha and the Omega,' says the Lord God, who is, who was, and who is
to come, the Almighty.

The Gloria

The Lord's Prayer

The Prayer Appointed for the Week
Almighty and everlasting God, you are always more ready to hear than we to
pray, and to give more than we either desire or deserve: Pour upon your
church the abundance of your mercy, forgiving us those things of which our
conscience is afraid, and giving us those good things for which we are not worthy to ask, except through the merits and mediation of Jesus Christ our Savior;
who lives and reigns with you and the Holy Spirit, one God, for ever and ever.
Amen.†

The Concluding Prayer of the Church
Lord Jesus Christ, you said to your apostles, "Peace I give to you; my own peace I
leave with you": Regard not my sins, but my faith, and give to me a place in the
peace and unity of that heavenly City, where with the Father and the Holy
Spirit you live and reign, now and forever. *Amen.*†

The Morning Office   **To Be Observed on the Hour or Half Hour**
                                          Between 6 and 9 a.m.

The Call to Prayer
Sing to the LORD a new song,* for he has done marvelous things.
With his right hand and his holy arm* has he won for himself the victory.
Psalm 98:1–2

The Request for Presence
Let your loving-kindness be my comfort,* as you have promised to your servant.
Let your compassion come to me, that I may live,* for your law is my delight.
Psalm 119:76–77

The Greeting
I will confess you among the peoples, O LORD;* I will sing praises to you among
the nations.
For your loving-kindness is greater than the heavens,* and your faithfulness
reaches to the clouds.
Psalm 108:3–4

The Refrain for the Morning Lessons
So teach us to number our days* that we may apply our hearts to wisdom.
Psalm 90:12

A Reading
Jesus taught us, saying: "Which of you, with a servant plowing or minding sheep,
would say to him when he returned from the fields, 'Come and have your meal
at once'? Would he not be more likely to say, 'Get my supper ready; fasten your
belt and wait on me while I eat and drink. You yourself can eat and drink afterwards'? Must he be grateful to the servant for doing what he was told? So with
you: when you have done all you have been told to do, say, 'We are useless servants: we have done no more than our duty.' "
Luke 17:7–10

The Refrain
So teach us to number our days* that we may apply our hearts to wisdom.

The Morning Psalm   *He Will Make Our Righteousness Clear*
Put your trust in the LORD and do good;* dwell in the land and feed on its riches.
Take delight in the LORD,* and he shall give you your heart's desire.
Commit your way to the LORD and put your trust in him,* and he will bring it to
pass.

He will make your righteousness as clear as the light* and your just dealing as the
noonday.
Be still before the LORD* and wait patiently for him.
Do not fret yourself over the one who prospers,* the one who succeeds in evil
schemes.
Refrain from anger, leave rage alone;* do not fret yourself; it leads only to evil.
For evildoers shall be cut off,* but those who wait upon the LORD shall possess the
land.

Psalm 37:3–10

The Refrain
So teach us to number our days* that we may apply our hearts to wisdom.

The Small Verse
Let me seek the Lord while he may still be found.
I will call upon his name while he is near.

Traditional

The Lord's Prayer

The Prayer Appointed for the Week
Almighty and everlasting God, you are always more ready to hear than we to
pray, and to give more than we either desire or deserve: Pour upon your
church the abundance of your mercy, forgiving us those things of which our
conscience is afraid, and giving us those good things for which we are not worthy to ask, except through the merits and mediation of Jesus Christ our Savior;
who lives and reigns with you and the Holy Spirit, one God, for ever and ever.
Amen.†

The Concluding Prayer of the Church
Lord God, almighty and everlasting Father, you have brought me in safety to this
new day: Preserve me with your mighty power, that I may not fall into sin, nor
be overcome by adversity; and in all I do direct me to the fulfilling of your purpose; through Jesus Christ my Lord. *Amen.*†

The Midday Office   **To Be Observed on the Hour or Half Hour**
                                     Between 11 a.m. and 2 p.m.

The Call to Prayer
God is the LORD; he has shined upon us;* form a procession with branches up to
the horns of the altar.

Psalm 118:27

The Request for Presence
Set watch before my mouth, O LORD, and guard the door of my lips . . .

Psalm 141:3

The Greeting
Remember your word to your servant,* because you have given me hope.
This is my comfort in my trouble,* that your promise gives me life.

Psalm 119:49–50

The Refrain for the Midday Lessons
For God alone my soul in silence waits;* from him comes my salvation.

Psalm 62:1

A Reading
Thus says the High and Exalted One who lives eternally and whose name is holy,
   'I live in the holy heights but I am with the contrite and humble, to revive the
   spirit of the humble, to revive the heart of the contrite.
'For I do not want to be forever accusing nor always to be angry, or the spirit
   would fail under my onslaught, the souls that I myself have made.'

Isaiah 57:15–16

The Refrain
For God alone my soul in silence waits;* from him comes my salvation.

The Midday Psalm   *With You Is the Well of Life*
Your love, O LORD, reaches to the heavens,* and your faithfulness to the clouds.
Your righteousness is like the strong mountains, your justice like the great deep;*
   you save both man and beast, O LORD.
How priceless is your love, O God!* your people take refuge under the shadow of
   your wings.
Continue your loving-kindness to those who know you,* and your favor to those
   who are true of heart.

Psalm 36:5–7, 10

The Refrain
For God alone my soul in silence waits;* from him comes my salvation.

The Cry of the Church
In the evening, in the morning, and at noonday, I will complain and lament,* and
   he will hear my voice.

Psalm 55:18

The Lord's Prayer

The Prayer Appointed for the Week
Almighty and everlasting God, you are always more ready to hear than we to
   pray, and to give more than we either desire or deserve: Pour upon your
   church the abundance of your mercy, forgiving us those things of which our
   conscience is afraid, and giving us those good things for which we are not worthy to ask, except through the merits and mediation of Jesus Christ our Savior;
   who lives and reigns with you and the Holy Spirit, one God, for ever and ever.
   Amen.†

The Concluding Prayer of the Church

Almighty God, whose most dear Son went not up to the joy before he first suffered pain, and did not enter into glory before he was crucified: Mercifully grant that I, walking in the way of the cross, may find it to be none other than the way of life and peace; through Jesus Christ your Son my Lord. *Amen.*†

The Vespers Office　　　　　　**To Be Observed on the Hour or Half Hour**

Between 5 and 8 p.m.

The Call to Prayer

May these words of mine please him;* I will rejoice in the LORD.

Psalm 104:35

The Request for Presence

Remember not our past sins;* let your compassion be swift to meet us . . .

Help us, O God our Savior, for the glory of your Name;* deliver us and forgive us our sins, for your Name's sake.

Psalm 79:8–9

The Greeting

You are to be praised, O God, in Zion . . .

To you that hear prayer shall all flesh come,* because of their transgressions.

Psalm 65:1–2

The Hymn　　　　　*There's a Wideness in God's Mercy*

There's a wideness in God's mercy　　　For the love of God is broader
Like the wideness of the sea;　　　　　Than the measure of our mind;
There's a kindness in God's justice,　　And the heart of the Eternal
Which is more than liberty.　　　　　　Is most wonderfully kind.

Fredrick Faber

If our love were but more simple,
We should rest upon God's word;
And our lives would be illumined
By the presence of our Lord.

The Refrain for the Vespers Lessons

Remember not the sins of my youth and my transgressions;* remember me according to your love and for the sake of your goodness, O LORD.

Psalm 25:6

The Vespers Psalm　　　　　*Cleanse Me from My Secret Faults*

Who can tell how often he offends?* cleanse me from my secret faults.

Above all, keep your servant from presumptuous sins; let them not get dominion over me;* then shall I be whole and sound, and innocent of a great offense.

Psalm 19:12–13

The Refrain
Remember not the sins of my youth and my transgressions;* remember me
according to your love and for the sake of your goodness, O LORD.

The Cry of the Church
Lord, have mercy on us. Christ, have mercy on us. Lord, have mercy on us.

The Lord's Prayer

The Prayer Appointed for the Week
Almighty and everlasting God, you are always more ready to hear than we to
pray, and to give more than we either desire or deserve: Pour upon your
church the abundance of your mercy, forgiving us those things of which our
conscience is afraid, and giving us those good things for which we are not worthy to ask, except through the merits and mediation of Jesus Christ our Savior,
who lives and reigns with you and the Holy Spirit, one God, for ever and ever.
Amen.†

Concluding Prayers of the Church
Almighty God, who has promised to hear the petitions of those who ask in your
Son's Name: I beseech you mercifully to incline your ear to me who have made
my prayers and supplications to you; and grant that those things which I have
faithfully asked according to your will may effectually be obtained, to the relief
of my necessity, and to the setting forth of your glory; through Jesus Christ my
Lord. *Amen.†*

May the souls of the faithful departed, through the mercy of God, rest in eternal
peace. *Amen.*

The Morning Office   **To Be Observed on the Hour or Half Hour**
                                    Between 6 and 9 a.m.

The Call to Prayer
Let us give thanks to the LORD for his mercy* and the wonders he does for his children.
For he satisfies the thirsty* and fills the hungry with good things.
based on Psalm 107:8–9

The Request for Presence
Give ear to my words, O LORD;* consider my meditation.
Psalm 5:1

The Greeting
Out of the mouths of infants and children, O LORD,* your majesty is praised above
the heavens.
based on Psalm 8:2

The Refrain for the Morning Lessons
I am small and of little account* yet I do not forget your commandments.

Psalm 119:141

A Reading
At this time the disciples came to Jesus and said, 'Who is the greatest in the kingdom of heaven?' So he called a little child to him whom he set among them. Then he said, 'In truth I tell you, unless you change and become like little children you will never enter the kingdom of Heaven. And so, one who makes himself as little as this little child is the greatest in the kingdom of Heaven.'

Matthew 18:1–4

The Refrain
I am small and of little account* yet I do not forget your commandments.

The Morning Psalm   *Renew a Right Spirit Within Me*
Create in me a clean heart, O God,* and renew a right spirit within me.
Cast me not away from your presence* and take not your holy Spirit from me.
Give me the joy of your saving help again* and sustain me with your bountiful
Spirit.
I shall teach your ways to the wicked,* and sinners shall return to you.

Psalm 51:11–14

The Refrain
I am small and of little account* yet I do not forget your commandments.

The Cry of the Church
O Lamb of God, that takes away the sins of the world, have mercy upon me.
O Lamb of God, that takes away the sins of the world, have mercy upon me.
O Lamb of God, that takes away the sins of the world, grant me your peace.

The Lord's Prayer

The Prayer Appointed for the Week
Almighty and everlasting God, you are always more ready to hear than we to
pray, and to give more than we either desire or deserve: Pour upon your
church the abundance of your mercy, forgiving us those things of which our
conscience is afraid, and giving us those good things for which we are not worthy to ask, except through the merits and mediation of Jesus Christ our Savior;
who lives and reigns with you and the Holy Spirit, one God, for ever and ever.
Amen.†

The Concluding Prayer of the Church
Lord God, almighty and everlasting Father, you have brought me in safety to this
new day: Preserve me with your mighty power, that I may not fall into sin, nor
be overcome by adversity; and in all I do direct me to the fulfilling of your purpose; through Jesus Christ my Lord. *Amen.*†

The Midday Office   To Be Observed on the Hour or Half Hour
                                              Between 11 a.m. and 2 p.m.

The Call to Prayer
Bless God in the congregation;* bless the LORD, you that are of the fountain of Israel.

Psalm 68:26

The Request for Presence
I call upon you, O God, for you will answer me;* incline your ear to me and hear
   my words.

Psalm 17:6

The Greeting
You are my God, and I will thank you;* you are my God, and I will exalt you.

Psalm 118:28

The Refrain for the Midday Lessons
The LORD, the God of gods, has spoken;* he has called the earth from the rising of
   the sun to its setting.

Psalm 50:1

A Reading
The apostle wrote, saying: "When we told you about the power and the coming of
   our Lord Jesus Christ, we were not slavishly repeating cleverly invented
   myths; no, we had seen his majesty with our own eyes. He was honored and
   glorified by God the Father, when a voice came to him from transcendent
   Glory, *This is my Son, the Beloved; he enjoys my favor.* We ourselves heard this
   voice from heaven, when we were with him on the holy mountain."

2 Peter 1:16–18

The Refrain
The LORD, the God of gods, has spoken;* he has called the earth from the rising of
   the sun to its setting.

The Midday Psalm   *Kingship Belongs to the LORD*
All the ends of the earth shall remember and turn to the LORD,* and all the families
   of the nations shall bow before him.
For kingship belongs to the LORD;* he rules over the nations.
To him alone all who sleep in the earth bow down in worship;* who go down to
   the dust fall before him.
My soul shall live for him; my descendants shall serve him;* they shall be known
   as the LORD's for ever.
They shall come and make known to a people yet unborn* the saving deeds that
   he has done.

Psalm 22:26–30

The Refrain
The LORD, the God of gods, has spoken;* he has called the earth from the rising of
   the sun to its setting.

The Gloria

The Lord's Prayer

The Prayer Appointed for the Week
Almighty and everlasting God, you are always more ready to hear than we to
pray, and to give more than we either desire or deserve: Pour upon your
church the abundance of your mercy, forgiving us those things of which our
conscience is afraid, and giving us those good things for which we are not worthy to ask, except through the merits and mediation of Jesus Christ our Savior;
who lives and reigns with you and the Holy Spirit, one God, for ever and ever.
Amen.†

The Concluding Prayer of the Church
O God, the source of eternal light: Shed forth your unending day upon all of us
who watch for you, that our lips may praise you, our lives may bless you, and
our worship may give you glory; through Jesus Christ our Lord. *Amen.*†

The Vespers Office   **To Be Observed on the Hour or Half Hour**
Between 5 and 8 p.m.

The Call to Prayer
Taste and see that the Lord is good;* happy are they who trust in him!
Psalm 34:8

The Request for Presence
. . . come to me speedily, O God,* . . .
Psalm 70:5

The Greeting
Blessed be the Lord GOD, the God of Israel,* . . . may all the earth be filled with his
glory. Amen. Amen.
Psalm 72:18–19

The Hymn   *Day Is Dying in the West*

Day is dying in the west;
Heaven is touching earth with rest;
Wait and worship while the night
Sets the evening lamps alight
Through all the sky.

Lord of life, beneath the dome
Of the universe, Your home,
Gather us who seek Your face
To the fold of Your embrace,
For You are nigh.

While the deepening shadows fall,
Heart of love enfolding all,
Through the glory and the grace
Of the stars that veil your face,
Our hearts ascend.

When forever from our sight
Pass the stars, the days, the night,
Lord of angels, on our eyes
Let eternal morning rise
And shadows end.

Mary Lathbury

The Refrain for the Vespers Lessons
Let all peoples know that you, whose Name is YAHWEH,* you alone are the Most
   High over all the earth.

Psalm 83:18

The Vespers Psalm   *My Soul Is Content, as with Marrow and Fatness*
. . . your loving-kindness is better than life itself;* my lips shall give you praise.
So will I bless you as long as I live* and lift up my hands in your Name.
My soul is content, as with marrow and fatness,* and my mouth praises you with
   joyful lips,
When I remember you upon my bed,* and meditate on you in the night watches.
For you have been my helper,* and under the shadow of your wings I will rejoice.
My soul clings to you;* your right hand holds me fast.

Psalm 63:3–8

The Refrain
Let all peoples know that you, whose Name is YAHWEH,* you alone are the Most
   High over all the earth.

The Small Verse
From the rising of the sun to the place of its going down, let the name of the Lord
   be praised henceforth and forever more.

The Lord's Prayer

The Prayer Appointed for the Week
Almighty and everlasting God, you are always more ready to hear than we to
   pray, and to give more than we either desire or deserve: Pour upon your
   church the abundance of your mercy, forgiving us those things of which our
   conscience is afraid, and giving us those good things for which we are not worthy to ask, except through the merits and mediation of Jesus Christ our Savior,
   who lives and reigns with you and the Holy Spirit, one God, for ever and ever.
   Amen.†

The Concluding Prayer of the Church
Glory to the Father, who has woven garments of glory for the resurrection; wor-
   ship to the Son, who was clothed in them at his rising; thanksgiving to the
   Spirit, who keeps them for all the Saints; one nature in three, to him be praise.

Syrian Orthodox

The Morning Office   To Be Observed on the Hour or Half Hour
                                                       Between 6 and 9 a.m.

The Call to Prayer
Sing to the LORD, you servants of his;* give thanks for the remembrance of his holiness.
For his wrath endures but the twinkling of an eye,* his favor for a lifetime.

Psalm 30:4–5

The Request for Presence
I cry out to you, O LORD;* I say, "You are my refuge, my portion in the land of the living."

Psalm 142:5

The Greeting
Glory to God in the highest,
and peace to his people on earth.
Lord God, heavenly King,
almighty God and Father,
we worship you, we give you thanks,
we praise you for your glory.
Lord Jesus Christ, only Son of the Father,
Lord God, Lamb of God,
you take away the sins of the world:
have mercy on us;
you are seated at the right hand of the Father:
receive our prayer.
For you alone are the Holy One,
you alone are the Lord,
you alone are the Most High,
Jesus Christ,
with the Holy Spirit,
in the glory of God the Father. *Amen.*

Gloria in Excelsis

The Refrain for the Morning Lessons
"I will appoint a time," says God;* "I will judge with equity . . ."

Psalm 75:2

A Reading
Jesus said to them: "Your father Abraham rejoiced to think that he would see my Day; he saw it and was glad." The Jews then said, "You are not fifty yet, and you have seen Abraham!" Jesus replied: "In all truth I tell you, before Abraham ever was, I am."

John 8:56–58

The Refrain
"I will appoint a time," says God;* "I will judge with equity . . ."

The Morning Psalm   *So That a People Yet Unborn May Praise the* LORD

Let this be written for a future generation,* so that a people yet unborn may praise
the LORD.

For the LORD looked down from his holy place on high;* from the heavens he
beheld the earth;

That he might hear the groan of the captive* and set free those condemned to die;

That they may declare in Zion the Name of the LORD,* and his praise in Jerusalem;

When the peoples are gathered together,* and the kingdoms also, to serve the
LORD.

Psalm 102:18–22

The Refrain

"I will appoint a time," says God;* "I will judge with equity . . ."

The Gloria

The Lord's Prayer

The Prayer Appointed for the Week

Lord, I pray that your grace may always precede and follow me, that I may continually be given to good works; through Jesus Christ my Lord, who lives and
reigns with you and the Holy Spirit, one God, now and for ever. *Amen.*†

The Concluding Prayer of the Church

Lord God, almighty and everlasting Father, you have brought me in safety to this
new day: Preserve me with your mighty power, that I may not fall into sin, nor
be overcome by adversity; and in all I do direct me to the fulfilling of your purpose; through Jesus Christ my Lord. *Amen.*†

The Midday Office   **To Be Observed on the Hour or Half Hour**
                                     Between 11 a.m. and 2 p.m.

The Call to Prayer

Sing to the LORD and bless his Name;* proclaim the good news of his salvation
from day to day.

Declare his glory among the nations* and his wonders among all peoples.

Psalm 96:2–3

The Request for Presence

Let my cry come before you, O LORD;* give me understanding, according to your
word.

Psalm 119:169

The Greeting

Lord, you have been our refuge* from one generation to another.

Before the mountains were brought forth, or the land and the earth were born,*
from age to age you are God.

Psalm 90:1–2

The Refrain for the Midday Lessons
Let me announce the decree of the LORD;* he said to me, "You are my son; this day
have I begotten you. . . ."

Psalm 2:7

A Reading
. . . In the presence of the whole assembly David blessed YAHWEH. David said:
'May you be blessed, YAHWEH, God of Israel our ancestor, for ever and for ever!
Yours, YAHWEH, is the greatness, the power, the splendor, length of days and
glory, everything in heaven and on earth is yours. Yours is the sovereignty,
YAHWEH; you are exalted, supreme over all. Wealth and riches come from you,
you are ruler of all, in your hand lie strength and power, and you bestow greatness and might on whomsoever you please. So now, our God, we give thanks
to you and praise your majestic name.'

1 Chronicles 29:10–13

The Refrain
Let me announce the decree of the LORD;* he said to me, "You are my son; this day
have I begotten you. . . ."

The Midday Psalm   *He Declares His Word to Jacob*
Worship the LORD, O Jerusalem;* praise your God, O Zion;
For he has strengthened the bars of your gates;* he has blessed your children
within you.
He has established peace on your borders;* he satisfies you with the finest wheat.
He sends out his command to the earth,* and his word runs very swiftly.
He gives snow like wool;* he scatters hoarfrost like ashes.
He scatters his hail like bread crumbs;* who can stand against his cold?
He sends forth his word and melts them;* he blows with his wind, and the waters
flow.
He declares his word to Jacob,* his statutes and his judgments to Israel.
He has not done so to any other nation;* to them he has not revealed his
judgments. Hallelujah!

Psalm 147:13–21

The Refrain
Let me announce the decree of the LORD;* he said to me, "You are my son; this day
have I begotten you. . . ."

The Small Verse
Let us bless the Lord. And all that is within me, forget not his benefits.

The Lord's Prayer

The Prayer Appointed for the Week
Lord, I pray that your grace may always precede and follow me, that I may continually be given to good works; through Jesus Christ my Lord, who lives and
reigns with you and the Holy Spirit, one God, now and for ever. *Amen.*✝

The Concluding Prayer of the Church

O God, you make me glad with the weekly remembrance of the glorious resurrection of your Son my Lord: Give me this day such blessing through my worship
of you, that the week to come may be spent in your favor; through Jesus Christ
our Lord. *Amen.*†

The Vespers Office   To Be Observed on the Hour or Half Hour
                                            Between 5 and 8 p.m.

The Call to Prayer

Let the Name of the LORD be blessed,* from this time forth for evermore.
From the rising of the sun to its going down* let the Name of the LORD be praised.
                                            Psalm 113:2–3

The Request for Presence

As the eyes of servants look to the hand of their masters,* and the eyes of a maid to
the hand of her mistress,
So our eyes look to you, O LORD our God.
                                            adapted from Psalm 123:2–3

The Greeting

Blessed is the LORD!* for he has heard the voice of my prayer.
                                            Psalm 28:7

The Hymn

O Trinity of blessed light,   Hear Thou our prayer, Almighty King!
O Unity of princely might,   Hear Thou our praises while we sing,
The fiery sun now goes his way;   Adoring with the heavenly host
Shed Thou within our hearts Thy ray.   The Father, Son, and Holy Ghost.
                                            THE SHORT BREVIARY

To Thee our morning song of praise
To Thee our evening prayer we raise;
Thy glory suppliant we adore
For ever and for evermore.

The Refrain for the Vespers Lessons

For you, O LORD, are good and forgiving,* and great is your love toward all who
call upon you.
                                            Psalm 86:5

The Vespers Psalm   *More Than Watchmen for the Morning*

I wait for the LORD; my soul waits for him;* in his word is my hope.
My soul waits for the LORD, more than watchmen for the morning,* more than
watchmen for the morning.
                                            Psalm 130:4–5

The Refrain
For you, O Lord, are good and forgiving,* and great is your love toward all who
call upon you.

The Cry of the Church
Lord, have mercy on us. Christ, have mercy on us. Lord, have mercy on us.

The Lord's Prayer

The Prayer Appointed for the Week
Lord, I pray that your grace may always precede and follow me, that I may continually be given to good works; through Jesus Christ my Lord, who lives and
reigns with you and the Holy Spirit, one God, now and for ever. *Amen.*†

The Concluding Prayer of the Church
In truth God has heard me;* he has attended to the voice of my prayer.
Blessed be God, who has not rejected my prayer,* nor withheld his love from me.

Psalm 66:17–18

The Morning Office **To Be Observed on the Hour or Half Hour**
Between 6 and 9 a.m.

The Call to Prayer
Bless the Lord, you angels of his, you mighty ones who do his bidding,* and hear-
ken to the voice of his word.
Bless the Lord, all you his hosts,* you ministers of his who do his will.
Bless the Lord, all you works of his, in all places of his dominion;* bless the Lord,
O my soul.

Psalm 103:20–22

The Request for Presence
Let those who seek you rejoice and be glad in you;* let those who love your salvation say forever, "Great is the Lord!"

Psalm 70:4

The Greeting
O Lord my God, I cried out to you,* and you restored me to health.
You brought me up, O Lord, from the dead;* you restored my life as I was going
down to the grave.

Psalm 30:2–3

The Refrain for the Morning Lessons
May you be blessed by the Lord, the maker of heaven and earth.

A Reading   On October 18, the Church celebrates the life of St. Luke, the Evangelist.
A physician by profession, he accompanied St. Paul on many mission-
ary journeys and was the author of the Book of Acts, as well as the
third gospel.

Seeing that many others have undertaken to draw up accounts of the events that
have reached their fulfillment among us, as these were handed down to us by
those who from the outset were eyewitnesses and ministers of the word, I in
my turn, after carefully going over the whole story from the beginning, have
decided to write an ordered account for you, Theophilus, so that your
Excellency may learn how well founded the teaching is that you have received.

Luke 1:1–4

The Refrain
May you be blessed by the LORD, the maker of heaven and earth.

The Morning Psalm   His Work Is Full of Majesty
Hallelujah! I will give thanks to the LORD with my whole heart,* in the assembly of
the upright, in the congregation.
Great are the deeds of the LORD!* they are studied by all who delight in them.
His work is full of majesty and splendor,* and his righteousness endures for ever.
He makes his marvelous works to be remembered;* the LORD is gracious and full
of compassion.
The works of his hands are faithfulness and justice;* all his commandments are
sure.
They stand fast for ever and ever,* because they are done in truth and equity.
He sent redemption to his people; he commanded his covenant for ever;* holy and
awesome is his Name.

Psalm 111:1–4, 7–9

The Refrain
May you be blessed by the LORD, the maker of heaven and earth.

The Small Verse
Open, Lord, my eyes that I may see.
Open, Lord, my ears that I may hear.
Open, Lord, my heart and my mind that I may understand.
So shall I turn to you and be healed.

Traditional

The Lord's Prayer

The Prayer Appointed for the Week
Lord, I pray that your grace may always precede and follow me, that I may continually be given to good works; through Jesus Christ my Lord, who lives and
reigns with you and the Holy Spirit, one God, now and for ever. *Amen.*†

Concluding Prayers of the Church
Almighty God, who inspired your servant Luke the physician to set forth in the
Gospel the love and healing power of your Son: Graciously continue in your

Church this love and power to heal, to the praise and glory of your Name; through Jesus Christ our Lord, who lives and reigns with you, in the unity of the Holy Spirit, one God, now and for ever. *Amen.*†

Lord God, almighty and everlasting Father, you have brought me in safety to this new day: Preserve me with your mighty power, that I may not fall into sin, nor be overcome by adversity; and in all I do direct me to the fulfilling of your purpose; through Jesus Christ my Lord. *Amen.*†

The Midday Office

To Be Observed on the Hour or Half Hour Between 11 a.m. and 2 p.m.

The Call to Prayer

Let us make a vow to the LORD our God and keep it;* let all around him bring gifts to him who is worthy to be feared.

adapted from Psalm 76:11

The Request for Presence

Let the peoples praise you, O God;* let all the peoples praise you.

Psalm 67:3

The Greeting

Happy are the people whose strength is in you!* whose hearts are set on the pilgrims' way.

Psalm 84:4

The Refrain for the Midday Lessons

All the nations you have made will come and worship you, O LORD,* and glorify your Name.

Psalm 86:9

A Reading

Treat the doctor with the honor that is his due, in consideration of his services; for he too has been created by the Lord. Healing itself comes from the Most High, like a gift received from a king. The doctor's learning keeps his head high, and the great regard him with awe. The Lord has brought forth medicinal herbs from the grounds, and no one sensible will despise them . . .
He has also given some people knowledge, so that they may draw credit from his mighty works. He uses these for healing and relieving pain; the druggist makes up a mixture from them. Thus, there is no end to his activities; thanks to him, well-being exists throughout the world. My child, when you are ill, do not rebel, but pray to the Lord and he will heal you. Renounce your faults, keep your hands unsoiled, and cleanse your heart from all sin . . .
Then let the doctor take over—the Lord created him too—do not let him leave you, for you need him. There are times when good health depends on doctors. For they, in their turn, will pray the Lord to grant them the grace to relieve and to heal, and so prolong your life.

Ecclesiasticus 38:1ff

The Refrain
All the nations you have made will come and worship you, O LORD,* and glorify
  your Name.

The Midday Psalm   *Great Is Our LORD*
Hallelujah! How good it is to sing praises to our God!* how pleasant it is to honor
  him with praise!
The LORD rebuilds Jerusalem;* he gathers the exiles of Israel.
He heals the brokenhearted* and binds up their wounds.
He counts the number of the stars* and calls them all by their names.
Great is our LORD and mighty in power;* there is no limit to his wisdom.
The LORD lifts up the lowly,* but casts the wicked to the ground.
Sing to the LORD with thanksgiving;* make music to our God upon the harp.
                                                          Psalm 147:1–7

The Refrain
All the nations you have made will come and worship you, O LORD,* and glorify
  your Name.

The Small Verse
Give thanks to the LORD, for he is good,* for his mercy endures for ever.
Give thanks to the God of gods,* for his mercy endures for ever.
Give thanks to the Lord of lords,* for his mercy endures for ever.
                                                          Psalm 136:1–3

The Lord's Prayer

The Prayer Appointed for the Week
Lord, I pray that your grace may always precede and follow me, that I may continually be given to good works; through Jesus Christ my Lord, who lives and
  reigns with you and the Holy Spirit, one God, now and for ever. *Amen.*†

Concluding Prayers of the Church
O God, by your Holy Spirit you give to some the word of wisdom, to others the
  word of knowledge, and to others the word of faith: I praise your Name for the
  gifts of grace manifested in your servant Luke, and pray that your Church may
  never be destitute of such gifts; through Jesus Christ our Lord, who with you
  and the Holy Spirit lives and reigns, one God, for ever and ever. *Amen.*†

Let us bless the Lord God living and true! Let us always render him praise, glory,
  honor, blessing, and all good things! Amen. Amen. So be it! So be it!
                                                      St. Francis of Assisi

The Vespers Office   To Be Observed on the Hour or Half Hour
                                              Between 5 and 8 p.m.

The Call to Prayer
Taste and see that the LORD is good;* happy are those who trust in him!
                                                          Psalm 34:8

The Request for Presence
Lord, hear my prayer, and let my cry come before you;* hide not your face from
　me in the day of my trouble.

Psalm 102:1

The Greeting
To you, O LORD, I lift up my soul;* my God I put my trust in you . . .

Psalm 25:1

The Hymn

Now let the earth with joy resound
And heaven the chant re-echo round;
Nor heaven nor earth too high can raise
The great Apostles' glorious praise!

Sickness and health your voice obey,
At your command they go or stay;
From sin's disease our souls restore,
In good confirm us more and more.

So when the world is at its end
And Christ to judgment shall descend,
May we be called those joys to see
Prepared from all eternity.

Praise to the Father, with the Son
And Paraclete for ever one:
To Thee, O holy Trinity
Be praise for all eternity.

THE SHORT BREVIARY

The Refrain for the Vespers Lessons
Some put their trust in chariots and some in horses,* but we will call upon the
　Name of the LORD our God.

Psalm 20:7

The Vespers Psalm　　　　　　　　　　　　*Glorious Things Are Spoken of You*
On the holy mountain stands the city he has founded;* the LORD loves the gates of
　Zion more than all the dwellings of Jacob.
Glorious things are spoken of you,* O city of our God.
I count Egypt and Babylon among those who know me;* behold Philistia, Tyre,
　and Ethiopia: in Zion were they born.
Of Zion it shall be said, "Everyone was born in her,* and the Most High himself
　shall sustain her."
The LORD will record as he enrolls the peoples,* "These also were born there."
The singers and the dancers will say,* "All my fresh springs are in you."

Psalm 87

The Refrain
Some put their trust in chariots and some in horses,* but we will call upon the
　Name of the LORD our God.

The Cry of the Church
Lord, have mercy on us. Christ, have mercy on us. Lord, have mercy on us.

The Lord's Prayer

The Prayer Appointed for the Week
Lord, I pray that your grace may always precede and follow me, that I may continually be given to good works; through Jesus Christ my Lord, who lives and
reigns with you and the Holy Spirit, one God, now and for ever. *Amen.*†

Concluding Prayers of the Church
O God, you have brought us near to an innumerable company of angels, and to
the spirits of just men made perfect: Grant me during my earthly pilgrimage to
abide in their fellowship, and in your heavenly country to become partakers of
their joy; through Jesus Christ our Lord, who lives and reigns with you and the
Holy Spirit, one God, now and for ever. *Amen.*†

Stay, O Lord, with those who wake, or watch, or weep tonight, and give your
angels and saints charge over those who sleep.

The Morning Office   To Be Observed on the Hour or Half Hour
                                          Between 6 and 9 a.m.

The Call to Prayer
Come, let us sing to the LORD;* let us shout for joy to the Rock of our salvation.
Let us come before his presence with thanksgiving* and raise a loud shout to him
with psalms.
                                                            Psalm 95:1–2

The Request for Presence
Early in the morning I cry out to you,* for in your word is my trust.
                                          Psalm 119:147

The Greeting
I put my trust in your mercy;* my heart is joyful because of your saving help.
                                          Psalm 13:5

The Refrain for the Morning Lessons
Yours are the heavens; the earth also is yours;* you laid the foundations of the
world and all that is in it.
                                          Psalm 89:11

A Reading
Jesus taught us, saying: "There is no need to be afraid, little flock, for it has pleased
your Father to give you the kingdom."
                                          Luke 12:32

The Refrain
Yours are the heavens; the earth also is yours;* you laid the foundations of the
world and all that is in it.

The Morning Psalm   *Wait Upon the* LORD
Wait upon the LORD and keep his way;* he will raise you up to possess the land,
and when the wicked are cut off, you will see it.

I have seen the wicked in their arrogance,* flourishing like a tree in full leaf.

I went by, and behold, they were not there;* I searched for them, but they could not be found.

Mark those who are honest; observe the upright;* for there is a future for the peaceable.

Transgressors shall be destroyed, one and all;* the future of the wicked is cut off.

But the deliverance of the righteous comes from the LORD;* he is their stronghold in time of trouble.

The LORD will help them and rescue them;* he will rescue them from the wicked and deliver them, because they seek refuge in him.

Psalm 37:36–42

The Refrain

Yours are the heavens; the earth also is yours;* you laid the foundations of the world and all that is in it.

The Gloria

The Lord's Prayer

The Prayer Appointed for the Week

Lord, I pray that your grace may always precede and follow me, that I may continually be given to good works; through Jesus Christ my Lord, who lives and reigns with you and the Holy Spirit, one God, now and for ever. *Amen.*†

The Concluding Prayer of the Church

Lord God, almighty and everlasting Father, you have brought me in safety to this new day: Preserve me with your mighty power, that I may not fall into sin, nor be overcome by adversity; and in all I do direct me to the fulfilling of your purpose; through Jesus Christ my Lord. *Amen.*†

The Midday Office
To Be Observed on the Hour or Half Hour
Between 11 a.m. and 2 p.m.

The Call to Prayer

Clap your hands all you peoples;* shout to God with a cry of joy.

Psalm 47:1

The Request for Presence

Accept, O LORD, the willing tribute of my lips,* and teach me your judgments.

Psalm 119:108

The Greeting

I will offer you the sacrifice of thanksgiving* and call upon the Name of the LORD.

Psalm 116:15

The Refrain for the Midday Lessons
He shall say to the Lord, "You are my refuge and my stronghold,* my God in
   whom I put my trust."

Psalm 91:2

A Reading
The apostle wrote, saying:
"I am writing to you, children,
because your sins have been forgiven through his name.
I am writing to you, fathers,
because you have come to know the One who has existed since the beginning.
I am writing to you, young people,
because you have overcome the Evil One.
I have written to you, children,
because you have come to know the Father.
I have written to you, parents,
because you have come to know the One who has existed since the beginning.
I have written to you, young people,
because you are strong,
and God's word remains in you,
and you have overcome the Evil One.
Do not love the world
or what is in the world.
But whoever does the will of God
remains for ever."

1 John 2:12–14, 17

The Refrain
He shall say to the Lord, "You are my refuge and my stronghold,* my God in
   whom I put my trust."

The Midday Psalm   *He Guides the Humble in Doing Right*
Gracious and upright is the Lord;* therefore he teaches sinners in his way.
He guides the humble in doing right* and teaches his way to the lowly.
All the paths of the Lord are love and faithfulness* to those who keep his
   covenant and his testimonies.

Psalm 25:7–9

The Refrain
He shall say to the Lord, "You are my refuge and my stronghold,* my God in
   whom I put my trust."

The Gloria

The Lord's Prayer

The Prayer Appointed for the Week
Lord, I pray that your grace may always precede and follow me, that I may continually be given to good works; through Jesus Christ my Lord, who lives and reigns with you and the Holy Spirit, one God, now and for ever. *Amen.*†

The Concluding Prayer of the Church
Almighty and everlasting God, by whose Spirit the whole body of your faithful people is governed and sanctified: Receive my supplications and prayers which I offer before you for all members of your holy Church, that in our vocation and ministry we all may truly and godly serve you, through our Lord and Savior Jesus Christ. *Amen.*

The Vespers Office   **To Be Observed on the Hour or Half Hour**
                                       Between 5 and 8 p.m.

The Call to Prayer
Sing to the LORD, you servants of his;* give thanks for the remembrance of his holiness.
For his wrath endures but the twinkling of an eye,* his favor for a lifetime.

Psalm 30:4–5

The Request for Presence
Hear my prayer, O LORD, and give ear to my cry* . . .
For I am but a sojourner with you,* a wayfarer, as all my forbears were.

Psalm 39:13–14

The Greeting
O God, when you went forth before your people* when you marched through the wilderness,
The earth shook, and the skies poured down rain, at the presence of God, the God of Sinai* at the presence of God, the God of Israel.
You sent a gracious rain, O God, upon your inheritance;* you refreshed the land when it was weary.
The Lord gave the word;* great was the company of women who bore the tidings.

Psalm 68:7ff

The Hymn   *Now Thank We All Our God*
Now thank we all our God, with hearts and hands and voices,
Who wonderous things has done, in whom the world rejoices;
Who from our mothers' arms has blessed us on our way
With countless gifts of love, and still is ours today.

O may this bounteous God through all our life be near us,
With ever joyful hearts and blessed peace to cheer us;
And keep us still in grace, and guide us when perplexed;
And free us from all ills, in this world and the next.

All praise and thanks to God the Father now be given;
The Son, and him who reigns with them in highest heaven;
The one eternal God, whom earth and heaven adore;
For thus it was, is now, and shall be evermore.

Martin Rinkart

The Refrain for the Vespers Lessons

Weeping may spend the night,* but joy comes in the morning.

Psalm 30:6

The Vespers Psalm   Blessed Be the LORD

Blessed be the LORD!* he has not given us over to be a prey for their teeth.
We have escaped like a bird from the snare of the fowler;* the snare is broken, and
    we have escaped.
Our help is in the Name of the LORD,* the maker of heaven and earth.

Psalm 124:6–8

The Refrain

Weeping may spend the night,* but joy comes in the morning.

The Gloria

The Lord's Prayer

The Prayer Appointed for the Week

Lord, I pray that your grace may always precede and follow me, that I may contin-
    ually be given to good works; through Jesus Christ my Lord, who lives and
    reigns with you and the Holy Spirit, one God, now and for ever. *Amen.*†

The Concluding Prayer of the Church

Hear, O Lord, your servants, offering evening praises to your Name. Through the
    silent hours of the night deign to watch over us, whom You have protected in
    all dangers of the day. Through Jesus Christ our Lord. *Amen.*

Anglo-Saxon, Traditional

The Morning Office   To Be Observed on the Hour or Half Hour
                                              Between 6 and 9 a.m.

The Call to Prayer

Bless our God, you peoples;* make the voice of his praise to be heard;
Who holds our souls in life,* and will not allow our feet to slip.

Psalm 66:7–8

The Request for Presence

. . . come to me speedily, O God.
You are my helper and my deliverer;* O LORD, do not tarry.

Psalm 70:5–6

The Greeting
You are my hope, O Lord GOD,* my confidence since I was young.
I have been sustained by you ever since I was born; from my mother's womb you
have been my strength;* my praise shall be always of you.

Psalm 71:5–6

The Refrain for the Morning Lessons
"Be still, then, and know that I am God;* I will be exalted among the nations; I will
be exalted in the earth."

Psalm 46:11

A Reading
Jesus looked round and said to his disciples, 'How hard it is for those who have
riches to enter the kingdom of God!' The disciples were astounded by these
words, but Jesus insisted, 'My children,' he said to them, 'how hard it is to
enter the kingdom of God! It is easier for a camel to pass through the eye of a
needle than for someone rich to enter the kingdom of God.' They were more
astonished than ever, saying to one another, 'In that case, who can be saved?'
Jesus gazed at them and said, 'By human resources it is impossible, but not for
God: because for God everything is possible.'

Mark 10:23–27

The Refrain
"Be still, then, and know that I am God;* I will be exalted among the nations; I will
be exalted in the earth."

The Morning Psalm   *A Thousand Years Are Like a Watch in the Night*
Lord, you have been our refuge* from one generation to another.
Before the mountains were brought forth, or the land and the earth were born,*
from age to age you are God.
You turn us back to the dust and say,* "Go back, O child of earth."
For a thousand years in your sight are like yesterday when it is past* and like a
watch in the night.
You sweep us away like a dream;* we fade away suddenly like the grass.
In the morning it is green and flourishes;* in the evening it is dried up and
withered.
For we consume away in your displeasure;* we are afraid because of your
wrathful indignation.
Our iniquities you have set before you,* and our secret sins in the light of your
countenance.
So teach us to number our days* that we may apply our hearts to wisdom.

Psalm 90:1–8, 12

The Refrain
"Be still, then, and know that I am God;* I will be exalted among the nations; I will
be exalted in the earth."

The Cry of the Church
Lord, have mercy on us. Christ, have mercy on us. Lord, have mercy on us.

The Lord's Prayer

The Prayer Appointed for the Week
Lord, I pray that your grace may always precede and follow me, that I may continually be given to good works; through Jesus Christ my Lord, who lives and reigns with you and the Holy Spirit, one God, now and for ever. *Amen.*†

The Concluding Prayer of the Church
Lord God, almighty and everlasting Father, you have brought me in safety to this new day: Preserve me with your mighty power, that I may not fall into sin, nor be overcome by adversity; and in all I do direct me to the fulfilling of your purpose; through Jesus Christ my Lord. *Amen.*†

The Midday Office   **To Be Observed on the Hour or Half Hour**
Between 11 a.m. and 2 p.m.

The Call to Prayer
Sing praise to the LORD who dwells in Zion;* proclaim to the peoples the things he has done.

Psalm 9:11

The Request for Presence
Send out your light and your truth, that they may lead me,* and bring me to your holy hill and to your dwelling.

Psalm 43:3

The Greeting
How glorious you are!* more splendid than the everlasting mountains!

Psalm 76:4

The Refrain for the Midday Lessons
Away from me, you wicked!* I will keep the commandments of my God.

Psalm 119:115

A Reading
On this mountain, for all peoples, YAHWEH Sabaoth is preparing a banquet of rich food, a banquet of fine wines, of succulent food, of well-strained wines. On this mountain, he has destroyed the veil which used to veil all peoples, the pall enveloping all nations; he has destroyed death for ever. Lord YAHWEH has wiped away the tears from every cheek; he has taken his people's shame away from everywhere on earth, for YAHWEH has spoken.
And on that day, it will be said, 'Look, that is our God, in him we put our hope that he should save us, this is YAHWEH, we put our hope in him. Let us exult and rejoice since he has saved us.' For YAHWEH's hand will rest on the moun-

tain, and Moab will be trodden under his feet as straw is trodden into the dung-heap.

Isaiah 25:6–10

The Refrain

Away from me, you wicked!* I will keep the commandments of my God.

The Midday Psalm   *Give Praise, You Servants of the LORD*

Hallelujah! Give praise, you servants of the LORD;* praise the Name of the LORD.

Let the Name of the LORD be blessed,* from this time forth for evermore.

From the rising of the sun to its going down* let the Name of the LORD be praised.

The LORD is high above all nations,* and his glory above the heavens.

Who is like the LORD our God, who sits enthroned on high* but stoops to behold
    the heavens and the earth?

He takes up the weak out of the dust* and lifts up the poor from the ashes.

He sets them with the princes,* with the princes of his people.

He makes the woman of a childless house* to be a joyful mother of children.

Psalm 113

The Refrain

Away from me, you wicked!* I will keep the commandments of my God.

The Gloria

The Lord's Prayer

The Prayer Appointed for the Week

Lord, I pray that your grace may always precede and follow me, that I may contin-
    ually be given to good works; through Jesus Christ my Lord, who lives and
    reigns with you and the Holy Spirit, one God, now and for ever. *Amen.*†

The Concluding Prayer of the Church

May our sons be like plants well nurtured from their youth,* and our daughters
    like sculptured corners of a palace.

May our barns be filled to overflowing with all manner of crops;* may the flocks
    in our pastures increase by thousands and tens of thousands; may our cattle be
    fat and sleek.

May there be no breaching of the walls, no going into exile,* no wailing in the pub-
    lic square.

Happy are the people of whom this is so!* happy are the people whose God is the
    LORD!

Psalm 144:13–16

The Vespers Office   **To Be Observed on the Hour or Half Hour**
                                      Between 5 and 8 p.m.

The Call to Prayer

Give thanks to the LORD, for he is good;* his mercy endures for ever.

Psalm 118:29

The Request for Presence
As the eyes of servants look to the hand of their masters,* and the eyes of a maid to
    the hand of her mistress,
So my eyes look to you, O LORD my God.

adapted from Psalm 123:2–3

The Greeting
My heart sings to you without ceasing;* O LORD my God, I will give you thanks
    for ever.

Psalm 30:13

The Hymn   *Come, Holy Ghost, Our Hearts Inspire*

Come, Holy Ghost, our hearts inspire,
let us your influence prove;
source of the old prophetic fire,
fountain of life and love.

Expand your wings, celestial Dove,
brood over our nature's night;
on our disordered spirits move,
and let there now be light.

Come, Holy Ghost (for moved by you
the prophets wrote and spoke),
unlock the truth, yourself the key,
unseal the sacred book.

God, through the Spirit we shall know
if you within us shine,
and sound, with all your saints below,
the depths of love divine.

Charles Wesley

The Refrain for the Vespers Lessons
But you, O LORD, are gracious and full of compassion,* slow to anger, and full of
    kindness and truth.

Psalm 86:15

The Vespers Psalm   *I Tell of Your Wonderful Works*
But I shall always wait in patience,* and shall praise you more and more.
My mouth shall recount your mighty acts and saving deeds all day long;* though I
    cannot know the number of them.
I will begin with the mighty works of the Lord GOD;* I will recall your
    righteousness, yours alone.
O God, you have taught me since I was young,* and to this day I tell of your
    wonderful works.

Psalm 71:14–17

The Refrain
But you, O LORD, are gracious and full of compassion,* slow to anger, and full of
    kindness and truth.

The Cry of the Church
Lord, have mercy on us. Christ, have mercy on us. Lord, have mercy on us.

The Lord's Prayer

The Prayer Appointed for the Week
Lord, I pray that your grace may always precede and follow me, that I may continually be given to good works; through Jesus Christ my Lord, who lives and reigns with you and the Holy Spirit, one God, now and for ever. *Amen.*†

The Concluding Prayer of the Church
I thank you, my God, for your care and protection this day, keeping me from physical harm and spiritual ignorance. I now place the work of the day into Your hands, trusting that You will redeem my mistakes, and transform my accomplishments into works of praise. And now I ask that You will work within me while I sleep, using the hours of my rest to create in me a new mind and heart and soul. May my mind, which during the day was directed to my work and activities, through the night be directed wholly to You.

Jacob Boehme

The Morning Office   To Be Observed on the Hour or Half Hour
                                              Between 6 and 9 a.m.

The Call to Prayer
Come, let us sing to the LORD; . . .
For the LORD is a great God,* and a great King above all gods.
Psalm 95:1, 3

The Request for Presence
Gladden the soul of your servant,* for to you, O LORD, I lift up my soul.
Psalm 86:4

The Greeting
Exalt yourself above the heavens, O God,* and your glory over all the earth.
Psalm 57:6

The Refrain for the Morning Lessons
Let not those who hope in you be put to shame through me, Lord GOD of hosts;*
let not those who seek you be disgraced because of me, O God of Israel.
Psalm 69:7

A Reading
Jesus also said, 'This is what the kingdom of God is like. A man scatters seed on the land. Night and day, while he sleeps, when he is awake, the seed is sprouting and growing; how, he does not know. Of its own accord the land produces first the shoot, then the ear, then the full grain in the ear. And when the crop is ready, at once he starts to reap because the harvest has come.'
Mark 4:26–29

The Refrain
Let not those who hope in you be put to shame through me, Lord GOD of hosts;*
let not those who seek you be disgraced because of me, O God of Israel.

The Morning Psalm   *Your Throne, O God, Endures For Ever and Ever*

My heart is stirring with a noble song; let me recite what I have fashioned for the
    king;* my tongue shall be the pen of a skilled writer.

You are the fairest of men;* grace flows from your lips, because God has blessed
    you for ever.

Strap your sword upon your thigh, O mighty warrior,* in your pride and in your
    majesty.

Ride out and conquer in the cause of truth* and for the sake of justice.

Your right hand will show you marvelous things;* your arrows are very sharp, O
    mighty warrior.

The peoples are falling at your feet,* and the king's enemies are losing heart.

Your throne, O God, endures for ever and ever,* a scepter of righteousness is the
    scepter of your kingdom; you love righteousness and hate iniquity.

Therefore God, your God, has anointed you* with the oil of gladness above your
    fellows.

Psalm 45:1–8

The Refrain

Let not those who hope in you be put to shame through me, Lord God of hosts;*
    let not those who seek you be disgraced because of me, O God of Israel.

The Gloria

The Lord's Prayer

The Prayer Appointed for the Week

Lord, I pray that your grace may always precede and follow me, that I may contin-
    ually be given to good works; through Jesus Christ my Lord, who lives and
    reigns with you and the Holy Spirit, one God, now and for ever. *Amen.*†

The Concluding Prayer of the Church

Lord God, almighty and everlasting Father, you have brought me in safety to this
    new day: Preserve me with your mighty power, that I may not fall into sin, nor
    be overcome by adversity; and in all I do direct me to the fulfilling of your pur-
    pose; through Jesus Christ my Lord. *Amen.*†

The Midday Office   **To Be Observed on the Hour or Half Hour**
                                         Between 11 a.m. and 2 p.m.

The Call to Prayer

Open my lips, O Lord,* and my mouth shall proclaim your praise.

Psalm 51:16

The Request for Presence

Bow down your ear, O Lord, and answer me . . .
Keep watch over my life, for I am faithful.

Psalm 86:1–2

The Greeting
I will offer you the sacrifice of thanksgiving* and call upon the Name of the LORD.
Psalm 116:15

The Refrain for the Midday Lessons
The angel of the LORD encompasses those who fear him,* and he will deliver them.
Psalm 34:7

A Reading
For the high priest we have is not incapable of feeling our weaknesses with us, but
has been put to the test in exactly the same way as ourselves, apart from sin.
Let us, then, have no fear in approaching the throne of grace to receive mercy
and to find grace when we are in need of help.
Hebrews 4:15–16

The Refrain
The angel of the LORD encompasses those who fear him,* and he will deliver them.

The Midday Psalm   *Your Love, O LORD, Upheld Me*
If the LORD had not come to my help,* I should soon have dwelt in the land of
silence.
As often as I said, "My foot has slipped,"* your love, O LORD, upheld me.
When many cares fill my mind,* your consolations cheer my soul.
Psalm 94:17–19

The Refrain
The angel of the LORD encompasses those who fear him,* and he will deliver them.

The Cry of the Church
O God, come to my assistance! O Lord, make haste to help me!

The Lord's Prayer

The Prayer Appointed for the Week
Lord, I pray that your grace may always precede and follow me, that I may continually be given to good works; through Jesus Christ my Lord, who lives and
reigns with you and the Holy Spirit, one God, now and for ever. *Amen.*†

The Concluding Prayer of the Church
Most gracious God and Father, you are with me as I make my journey throughout
this day. Help me to look lovingly upon all people and events that come into
my life today and to walk gently upon this land. Grant this through Jesus who
lives and walks among us ever present at each moment. *Amen.*†

The Vespers Office   To Be Observed on the Hour or Half Hour
                                              Between 5 and 8 p.m.

The Call to Prayer
Bless our God, you peoples;* make the voice of his praise to be heard;
Who holds our souls in life,* and will not allow our feet to slip.

Psalm 66:7–8

The Request for Presence
Show me the light of your countenance, O God, and come to me.

adapted from Psalm 67:1

The Greeting
Whom have I in heaven but you?* and having you I desire nothing upon earth.

Psalm 73:25

The Refrain for the Vespers Lessons
I have been sustained by you ever since I was born; from my mother's womb you
have been my strength;* my praise shall be always of you.

Psalm 71:6

The Hymn   *There Is a Balm in Gilead*
There is a balm in Gilead to make the wounded whole;
there is a balm in Gilead to heal the sin-sick soul.
Sometimes I feel discouraged, and think my work's in vain,
but then the Holy Spirit revives my soul again.

There is a balm in Gilead to make the wounded whole;
there is a balm in Gilead to heal the sin-sick soul.
Don't ever feel discouraged, for Jesus is your friend,
and if you look for knowledge he'll never refuse to lend.

There is a balm in Gilead to make the wounded whole;
there is a balm in Gilead to heal the sin-sick soul.
If you can't preach like Peter, if you can't pray like Paul,
just tell the love of Jesus, and say he died for all.

African-American Spiritual

The Refrain for the Vespers Lessons
I have been sustained by you ever since I was born; from my mother's womb you
have been my strength;* my praise shall be always of you.

The Vespers Psalm   *How Shall We Sing the LORD's Song Upon an Alien Soil*
By the waters of Babylon we sat down and wept,* when we remembered you,
O Zion.
As for our harps, we hung them up* on the trees in the midst of that land.
For those who led us away captive asked us for a song, and our oppressors called
for mirth:* "Sing us one of the songs of Zion."
How shall we sing the LORD's song* upon an alien soil.

If I forget you, O Jerusalem,* let my right hand forget its skill.
Let my tongue cleave to the roof of my mouth if I do not remember you,* if I do
not set Jerusalem above my highest joy.

Psalm 137:1–6

The Refrain
I have been sustained by you ever since I was born; from my mother's womb you
have been my strength;* my praise shall be always of you.

The Cry of the Church
O God, come to my assistance! O Lord, make haste to help me!

The Lord's Prayer

The Prayer Appointed for the Week
Lord, I pray that your grace may always precede and follow me, that I may continually be given to good works; through Jesus Christ my Lord, who lives and
reigns with you and the Holy Spirit, one God, now and for ever. *Amen.*†

The Concluding Prayer of the Church
Almighty Father, you have given us strength to work throughout this day. Receive
our evening sacrifice of praise in thanksgiving for your countless gifts. We ask
this through our Lord Jesus Christ, your Son, who lives and reigns with you
and the Holy Spirit, one God, for ever and ever. *Amen.*

THE LITURGY OF THE HOURS, VOL. III

The Morning Office · To Be Observed on the Hour or Half Hour
Between 6 and 9 a.m.

The Call to Prayer
Taste and see that the LORD is good;* happy are those who trust in him!

Psalm 34:8

The Request for Presence
Be my strong rock, a castle to keep me safe;* you are my crag and my stronghold.

Psalm 71:3

The Greeting
O LORD, I cry to you for help;* in the morning my prayer comes before you.

Psalm 88:14

The Refrain for the Morning Lessons
God is a righteous judge;* God sits in judgment every day.

Psalm 7:12

A Reading
Jesus taught us, saying: "Alas for you when everyone speaks well of you! This is
how their ancestors treated the false prophets."

Luke 6:26

The Refrain
God is a righteous judge;* God sits in judgment every day.

The Morning Psalm   *Teach Us to Number Our Days*
The span of our life is seventy years, perhaps in strength even eighty;* yet the sum
     of them is but labor and sorrow, for they pass away quickly and we are gone.
Who regards the power of your wrath?* who rightly fears your indignation?
So teach us to number our days* that we may apply our hearts to wisdom.

Psalm 90:10–12

The Refrain
God is a righteous judge;* God sits in judgment every day.

The Cry of the Church
O God, come to my assistance! O Lord, make haste to help me!

The Lord's Prayer

The Prayer Appointed for the Week
Lord, I pray that your grace may always precede and follow me, that I may contin-
     ually be given to good works; through Jesus Christ my Lord, who lives and
     reigns with you and the Holy Spirit, one God, now and for ever. *Amen.*†

The Concluding Prayer of the Church
Lord God, almighty and everlasting Father, you have brought me in safety to this
     new day: Preserve me with your mighty power, that I may not fall into sin, nor
     be overcome by adversity; and in all I do direct me to the fulfilling of your pur-
     pose; through Jesus Christ my Lord. *Amen.*†

The Midday Office   **To Be Observed on the Hour or Half Hour**
                                                 Between 11 a.m. and 2 p.m.

The Call to Prayer
Sing to God, O kingdoms of the earth;* sing praises to the Lord.
He rides in the heavens, the ancient heavens;* he sends forth his voice, his mighty
     voice.

Psalm 68:33–34

The Request for Presence
May God be merciful to us and bless us,* show us the light of his countenance and
     come to us.
Let your ways be known upon the earth,* your saving health among all nations.

Psalm 67:1–2

The Greeting
Exalt yourself above the heavens, O God,* and your glory over all the earth.
So that those who are dear to you may be delivered,* save with your right hand
     and answer me.

Psalm 108:5–6

The Refrain for the Midday Lessons
Righteousness and justice are the foundations of your throne;* love and truth go
before your face.

Psalm 89:14

A Reading
Blessed be God the Father of our Lord Jesus Christ, who has blessed us with all the
spiritual blessings of heaven in Christ. Thus he chose us in Christ before the
world was made to be holy and faultless before him in love, marking us out for
himself beforehand, to be adopted sons, through Jesus Christ. Such was his
purpose and good pleasure, to the praise of the glory of his grace, his free gift
to us in the Beloved . . .

Ephesians 1:3–6

The Refrain
Righteousness and justice are the foundations of your throne;* love and truth go
before your face.

The Midday Psalm   *Your Wonders Are More Than I Can Count*
Great things are they that you have done, O LORD my God! how great your
wonders and your plans for us!* there is none who can be compared with you.
Oh, that I could make them known and tell them!* but they are more than I can
count.

Psalm 40:5–6

The Refrain
Righteousness and justice are the foundations of your throne;* love and truth go
before your face.

The Cry of the Church
O God, come to my assistance! O Lord, make haste to help me!

The Lord's Prayer

The Prayer Appointed for the Week
Lord, I pray that your grace may always precede and follow me, that I may continually be given to good works; through Jesus Christ my Lord, who lives and
reigns with you and the Holy Spirit, one God, now and for ever. *Amen.*†

The Concluding Prayer of the Church
Almighty God, whose most dear Son went not up to joy before he first suffered
pain, and did not enter into glory before he was crucified: Mercifully grant that
I, walking in the way of the cross, may find it to be none other than the way of
life and peace; through Jesus Christ your son my Lord. *Amen.*†

The Vespers Office   To Be Observed on the Hour or Half Hour
                                      Between 5 and 8 p.m.

The Call to Prayer
O tarry and await the LORD's pleasure; be strong, and he shall comfort your heart;*
    wait patiently for the LORD.

                                                        Psalm 27:18

The Request for Presence
Out of the depths have I called to you, O LORD; LORD, hear my voice;* let your ears
    consider well the voice of my supplication.

                                                        Psalm 130:1

The Greeting
For your Name's sake, O LORD,* forgive my sin, for it is great.

                                                        Psalm 25:10

The Hymn   *Come, Christians, Join to Sing*
    Come, Christians, join to sing: Alleluia! Amen!
    Loud praise to Christ our King: Alleluia! Amen!
    Let all, with heart and voice,
    before his throne rejoice;
    praise is his gracious choice. Alleluia! Amen!

    Come, lift your hearts on high: Alleluia! Amen!
    Let praises fill the sky: Alleluia! Amen!
    He is our guide and friend;
    to us he'll condescend;
    his love shall never end: Alleluia! Amen!

    Praise yet the Lord again: Alleluia! Amen!
    Life shall not end the strain: Alleluia! Amen!
    On heaven's blissful shore
    his goodness we'll adore,
    singing for evermore: Alleluia! Amen!
                            Christian H. Bateman

The Refrain for the Vespers Lessons
Let not those who hope in you be put to shame through me, Lord GOD of hosts;*
    let not those who seek you be disgraced because of me, O God of Israel.

                                                        Psalm 69:7

The Vespers Psalm   *This God Is Our God For Ever and Ever*
We have waited in silence on your loving-kindness, O God,* in the midst of your
    temple.
Your praise, like your Name, O God, reaches to the world's end;* your right hand
    is full of justice.
Let Mount Zion be glad and the cities of Judah rejoice,* because of your
    judgments.

Make the circuit of Zion; walk round about her;* count the number of her towers.
Consider well her bulwarks; examine her strongholds;* that you may tell those
who come after.
This God is our God for ever and ever;* he shall be our guide for evermore.

Psalm 48:8–13

The Refrain
Let not those who hope in you be put to shame through me, Lord GOD of hosts;*
let not those who seek you be disgraced because of me, O God of Israel.

The Cry of the Church
Lord, have mercy on us. Christ, have mercy on us. Lord, have mercy on us.

The Lord's Prayer

The Prayer Appointed for the Week
Lord, I pray that your grace may always precede and follow me, that I may continually be given to good works; through Jesus Christ my Lord, who lives and
reigns with you and the Holy Spirit, one God, now and for ever. *Amen.*†

Concluding Prayers of the Church
Almighty God, who has promised to hear the petitions of those who ask in your
Son's Name: I beseech you mercifully to incline your ear to me who have made
my prayers and supplications to you; and grant that those things which I have
faithfully asked according to your will, may effectually be obtained, to the
relief of my necessity, and to the setting forth of your glory; through Jesus
Christ my Lord. *Amen.*†

May the souls of the faithful departed, through the mercy of God, rest in eternal
peace. *Amen.*

The Morning Office   **To Be Observed on the Hour or Half Hour**
Between 6 and 9 a.m.

The Call to Prayer
Let us come before his presence with thanksgiving* and raise a loud shout to him
with psalms.

Psalm 95:2

The Request for Presence
LORD God of hosts, hear my prayer;* hearken, O God of Jacob.

Psalm 84:7

The Greeting
My heart is firmly fixed, O God, my heart is fixed;* I will sing and make melody.
Wake up, my spirit; awake, lute and harp;* I myself will awaken the dawn.
I will confess you among the peoples, O LORD;* I will sing praise to you among the
nations.

For your loving-kindness is greater than the heavens,* and your faithfulness
reaches to the clouds.
Exalt yourself above the heavens, O God,* and your glory over all the earth.

Psalm 57:7–11

The Refrain for the Morning Lessons
On this day the LORD has acted;* we will rejoice and be glad in it.

Psalm 118:24

A Reading
Jesus taught us, saying: "I am the good shepherd; I know my own and my own
know me, just as the Father knows me and I know the Father; and I lay down
my life for my sheep. And there are other sheep I have that are not of this fold,
and I must lead these too. They too listen to my voice, and there will be only
one flock, one shepherd. The Father loves me, because I lay down my life in
order to take it up again."

John 10:14–17

The Refrain
On this day the LORD has acted;* we will rejoice and be glad in it.

The Morning Psalm   *The LORD Woke*
Then the LORD woke as though from sleep,* like a warrior refreshed with wine.
He chose instead the tribe of Judah* and Mount Zion, which he loved.
He built his sanctuary like the heights of heaven,* like the earth which he founded
for ever.
He chose David his servant,* and took him away from the sheepfolds.
He brought him from following the ewes,* to be a shepherd over Jacob his people
and over Israel his inheritance.
So he shepherded them with a faithful and true heart* and guided them with the
skillfulness of his hands.

Psalm 78:65, 68–72

The Refrain
On this day the LORD has acted;* we will rejoice and be glad in it.

The Small Verse
The LORD is a great God,* and a great King above all gods.
In his hand are the caverns of the earth,* and the heights of the hills are his also.
The sea is his, for he made it,* and his hands have molded the dry land.

Psalm 95:3–5

The Lord's Prayer

The Prayer Appointed for the Week
Lord, I pray that your grace may always precede and follow me, that I may continually be given to good works; through Jesus Christ my Lord, who lives and
reigns with you and the Holy Spirit, one God, now and for ever. *Amen.*✝

The Concluding Prayer of the Church
Lord God, almighty and everlasting Father, you have brought me in safety to this
new day: Preserve me with your mighty power, that I may not fall into sin, nor
be overcome by adversity; and in all I do direct me to the fulfilling of your purpose; through Jesus Christ my Lord. *Amen.*†

The Midday Office   To Be Observed on the Hour or Half Hour
                                      Between 11 a.m. and 2 p.m.

The Call to Prayer
Let the righteous be glad and rejoice before God;* let them be merry and joyful.
Psalm 68:3

The Request for Presence
You are the LORD; do not withhold your compassion from me;* let your love and
your faithfulness keep me safe forever.
Psalm 40:12

The Greeting
Therefore I will praise you upon the lyre for your faithfulness, O my God;* I will
sing to you with the harp, O Holy One of Israel.
Psalm 71:22

The Refrain for the Midday Lessons
For the LORD God is both sun and shield;* he will give grace and glory.
Psalm 84:10

A Reading
We have then, brothers, complete confidence through the blood of Jesus in entering the sanctuary, by a new way which he has opened for us, a living opening
through the curtain, that is to say, his flesh. And we have the *high priest* over all
the *sanctuary of God.* So as we go in, let us be sincere in heart and filled with
faith, our hearts sprinkled and free from any trace of bad conscience, and our
bodies washed with pure water.
Hebrews 10:19–22

The Refrain
For the LORD God is both sun and shield;* he will give grace and glory.

The Midday Psalm   *Your Love, O LORD, For Ever Will I Sing*
Your love, O LORD, for ever will I sing;* from age to age my mouth will proclaim
your faithfulness.
For I am persuaded that your love is established for ever;* you have set your
faithfulness firmly in the heavens.
Psalm 89:1–2

The Refrain
For the LORD God is both sun and shield;* he will give grace and glory.

The Gloria

The Lord's Prayer

The Prayer Appointed for the Week
Lord, I pray that your grace may always precede and follow me, that I may continually be given to good works; through Jesus Christ my Lord, who lives and
reigns with you and the Holy Spirit, one God, now and for ever. *Amen.*†

The Concluding Prayer of the Church
Almighty God, who after the creation of the world rested from all works and sanctified a day of rest for all your creatures: Grant that I, putting away all earthly
anxieties, may be duly prepared for the service of public worship, and grant as
well that my Sabbath upon earth may be a preparation for the eternal rest
promised to your people in heaven; through Jesus Christ our Lord. *Amen.*†

The Vespers Office   **To Be Observed on the Hour or Half Hour**
Between 5 and 8 p.m.

The Call to Prayer
The LORD is my strength and my shield;* my heart trusts him, and I have been
helped;
Therefore my heart dances for joy,* and in my song I will praise him.
                                                        Psalm 28:8–9

The Request for Presence
Hear, O LORD, and have mercy upon me;* O LORD, be my helper.
                                                        Psalm 30:11

The Greeting
Your righteousness, O God, reaches to the heavens;* you have done great things;
who is like you, O God?
                                                        Psalm 71:19

The Hymn   *Bringing in the Sheaves*
Sowing in the morning, sowing seeds of kindness,
Sowing in the noontide and the dewy eve;
Waiting for the harvest, and the time of reaping,
We shall come rejoicing, bringing in the sheaves.

Sowing in the sunshine, sowing in the shadows;
Fearing neither clouds nor winter's chilling breeze;
By and by the harvest and the labor ended,
We shall come rejoicing, bringing in the sheaves.

Going forth with weeping, sowing for the Master,
Though the loss sustained our spirit often grieves;
When our weeping's over, He will bid us welcome,
We shall come rejoicing, bringing in the sheaves.

Knowles Shaw

The Refrain for the Vespers Lessons
Remember me, O Lord, with the favor you have for your people,* and visit me
with your saving help.

Psalm 106:4

The Vespers Psalm   *Who Can Ascend the Hill of the Lord*
The earth is the Lord's and all that is in it,* the world and all who dwell therein.
For it is he who founded it upon the seas* and made it firm upon the rivers of the
deep.
"Who can ascend the hill of the Lord?* and who can stand in his holy place?"
"Those who have clean hands and a pure heart,* who have not pledged
themselves to falsehood, nor sworn by what is a fraud.
They shall receive a blessing from the Lord* and a just reward from the God of
their salvation."
Such is the generation of those who seek him,* of those who seek your face, O God
of Jacob.

Psalm 24:1–6

The Refrain
Remember me, O Lord, with the favor you have for your people,* and visit me
with your saving help.

The Gloria

The Lord's Prayer

The Prayer Appointed for the Week
Lord, I pray that your grace may always precede and follow me, that I may continually be given to good works; through Jesus Christ my Lord, who lives and
reigns with you and the Holy Spirit, one God, now and for ever. *Amen.*†

The Concluding Prayer of the Church
Give me courage to resist, patience to endure, constancy to persevere. Grant, in
place of all consolations of the world, the most sweet unction of Thy Spirit, and
in place of carnal love, pour into me the love of Thy Name.

St. Thomas à Kempis

The Morning Office   To Be Observed on the Hour or Half Hour
                                          Between 6 and 9 a.m.

The Call to Prayer
Let the peoples praise you, O God;* let all the peoples praise you.
Let the nations be glad and sing for joy,* for you judge the peoples with equity and
      guide all nations upon the earth.
Let the peoples praise you, O God;* let all the peoples praise you.

Psalm 67:3–5

The Request for Presence
Hear my voice, O Lord, according to your loving-kindness;* according to your
      judgments, give me life.

Psalm 119:149

The Greeting
Hosanna, Lord, hosanna!* Lord, send us now success.
Blessed is he who comes in the name of the Lord;* we bless you from the house of
      the Lord.

Psalm 118:25–26

The Refrain for the Morning Lessons
I was glad when they said to me,* "Let us go to the house of the Lord."

Psalm 122:1

A Reading
Jesus taught his disciples, saying: "You know that among the gentiles those they
      call their rulers lord it over them, and their great men make their authority felt.
      Among you this is not to happen. No, anyone who wants to become great
      among you must be your servant, and anyone who wants to be first among
      you must be slave to all. For the Son of man himself came not to be served but
      to serve, and to give his life as a ransom for many."

Mark 10:42–45

The Refrain
I was glad when they said to me,* "Let us go to the house of the Lord."

The Morning Psalm   *The Lord Has Ordained a Blessing*
Oh, how good and pleasant it is,* when brethren live together in unity!
It is like fine oil upon the head* that runs down upon the beard,
Upon the beard of Aaron,* and runs down upon the collar of his robe.
It is like the dew of Hermon* that falls upon the hills of Zion.
For there the Lord has ordained the blessing:* life for evermore.

Psalm 133

The Refrain
I was glad when they said to me,* "Let us go to the house of the Lord."

The Cry of the Church
O God, come to my assistance! O Lord, make haste to help me!

The Lord's Prayer

The Prayer Appointed for the Week
Almighty and everlasting God, in Christ you have revealed your glory among the
nations: Preserve the works of your mercy, that your Church throughout the
world may persevere with steadfast faith in the confession of your Name;
through Jesus Christ our Lord, who lives and reigns with you and the Holy
Spirit, one God, for ever and ever. *Amen.*†

The Concluding Prayer of the Church
Lord God, almighty and everlasting Father, you have brought me in safety to this
new day: Preserve me with your mighty power, that I may not fall into sin, nor
be overcome by adversity; and in all I do direct me to the fulfilling of your purpose; through Jesus Christ my Lord. *Amen.*†

The Midday Office   **To Be Observed on the Hour or Half Hour**
                                             Between 11 a.m. and 2 p.m.

The Call to Prayer
Let us give thanks to the LORD for his mercy* and the wonders he does for his children.
For he satisfies the thirsty* and fills the hungry with good things.
adapted from Psalm 107:8–9

The Request for Presence
Let all who seek you rejoice in you and be glad;* let those who love your salvation
continually say, "Great is the LORD!"
Though I am poor and afflicted,* the LORD will have regard for me.
You are my helper and my deliverer,* do not tarry, O my God.
Psalm 40:17ff

The Greeting
I love you, O LORD my strength,* O LORD my stronghold, my crag, and my haven.
My God, my rock in whom I put my trust,* my shield, the horn of my salvation,
and my refuge; you are worthy of praise.
Psalm 18:1–2

The Refrain for the Midday Lessons
I will fulfill my vows to the LORD* in the presence of all his people.
Psalm 116:16

A Reading
The word of God is something alive and active: it cuts more incisively than any
two-edged sword: it can seek out the place where soul is divided from spirit, or
joints from marrow; it can pass judgment on secret emotions and thoughts. No
created thing is hidden from him; everything is uncovered and stretched fully
open to the eyes of the one to whom we must give account of ourselves.
Hebrews 4:12–13

The Refrain
I will fulfill my vows to the LORD* in the presence of all his people.

The Midday Psalm   *The Fool Has Said, "There Is No God"*
The fool has said in his heart, "There is no God."* All are corrupt and commit
    abominable acts; there is none who does any good.
God looks down from heaven upon us all,* to see if there is any who is wise, if
    there is one who seeks after God.
Every one has proved faithless; all alike have turned bad;* there is none who does
    good; no, not one.
Have they no knowledge, those evildoers* who eat up my people like bread and
    do not call upon God?
See how greatly they tremble, such trembling as never was;* for God has scattered
    the bones of the enemy; they are put to shame, because God has rejected them.
Oh, that Israel's deliverance would come out of Zion!* when God restores the
    fortunes of his people Jacob will rejoice and Israel be glad.

Psalm 53

The Refrain
I will fulfill my vows to the LORD* in the presence of all his people.

The Cry of the Church
Even so, come, Lord Jesus!

The Lord's Prayer

The Prayer Appointed for the Week
Almighty and everlasting God, in Christ you have revealed your glory among the
    nations: Preserve the works of your mercy, that your Church throughout the
    world may persevere with steadfast faith in the confession of your Name;
    through Jesus Christ our Lord, who lives and reigns with you and the Holy
    Spirit, one God, for ever and ever. *Amen.*†

The Concluding Prayer of the Church
O God, you make me and your whole church glad with the weekly remembrance
    of the glorious resurrection of your Son our Lord: Give me this day such bless-
    ing through my worship of you, that the week to come may be spent in your
    favor; through Jesus Christ our Lord. *Amen.*†

The Vespers Office   **To Be Observed on the Hour or Half Hour**
                                      Between 5 and 8 p.m.

The Call to Prayer
Bless the LORD, O my soul,* and all that is within me, bless his holy Name.
Bless the LORD, O my soul,* and forget not all his benefits.

Psalm 103:1–2

The Request for Presence

The LORD will hear the desire of the humble;* you will strengthen their heart and your ears shall hear.

Psalm 10:18

The Greeting

I will confess you among the peoples, O LORD;* I will sing praise to you among the nations.

Psalm 57:9

The Hymn

Blessed feasts of blessed martyrs, holy women, holy men,
With affection's recollections greet we your return again.
Worthy deeds they wrought, and wonders, worthy of the Name they bore;
We, with meetest praise and sweetest, honor them for evermore.

Faith prevailing, hope unfailing, loving Christ with single heart,
Thus they, glorious and victorious, bravely bore the martyrs' part,
By contempt of every anguish, by unyielding battle done;
Victors at the last, they triumph, with the host of angels one.

Therefore, you that reign in glory, fellow heirs with Christ on high,
Join to ours your supplication when before him we draw nigh,
Praying that, this life completed, all its fleeting moments past,
By his grace we may be worthy of eternal bliss at last.

Latin, 12th Century

The Refrain for the Vespers Lessons

The LORD has heard my supplication;* the LORD accepts my prayer.

Psalm 6:9

The Vespers Psalm   *I Am with Him in Trouble*

Because he is bound to me in love, therefore will I deliver him;* I will protect him, because he knows my Name.
He shall call upon me, and I will answer him;* I am with him in trouble; I will rescue him and bring him to honor.
With long life will I satisfy him,* and show him my salvation.

Psalm 91:14–16

The Refrain

The LORD has heard my supplication;* the LORD accepts my prayer.

The Small Verse

The Lord is my shepherd and nothing is wanting to me. In green pastures He has settled me.

THE SHORT BREVIARY

The Lord's Prayer

The Prayer Appointed for the Week
Almighty and everlasting God, in Christ you have revealed your glory among the
    nations: Preserve the works of your mercy, that your Church throughout the
    world may persevere with steadfast faith in the confession of your Name;
    through Jesus Christ our Lord, who lives and reigns with you and the Holy
    Spirit, one God, for ever and ever. *Amen.*†

Concluding Prayers of the Church
O God, our heavenly Father, who raised up your faithful servant, James, to be a
    bishop in your Church and to feed your flock: Give abundantly to all bishops
    and ministers the gifts of your Holy Spirit, that they may minister in your
    household as true servants of Christ and stewards of your divine mysteries;
    through Jesus Christ our Lord, who lives and reigns with you and the Holy
    Spirit, one God, for ever and ever. *Amen.*†

Lord God, whose Son our savior Jesus Christ, triumphed over the power of death
    and prepared for us our place in the new Jerusalem: Grant that I, who have this
    day given thanks for his resurrection, may praise you in the City of which he is
    the light, and where he lives and reigns for ever and ever. *Amen.*†

The Morning Office   To Be Observed on the Hour or Half Hour
                                                                         Between 6 and 9 a.m.

The Call to Prayer
Let my mouth be full of your praise* and your glory all the day long.
Do not cast me off in my old age;* forsake me not when my strength fails.
                                                                         Psalm 71:8–9

The Request for Presence
O LORD, my God, my Savior,* by day and night I cry to you.
Let my prayer enter into your presence.
                                                                         Psalm 88:1–2

The Greeting
Show me your ways, O LORD,* and teach me your paths.
Lead me in your truth and teach me,* for you are the God of my salvation; in you
    have I trusted all the day long.
                                                                         Psalm 25:3–4

The Refrain for the Morning Lessons
Deliverance belongs to the LORD.* Your blessing be upon your people!
                                                                         Psalm 3:8

A Reading   *St. James of Jerusalem, brother of Jesus, was the Bishop of Jerusalem
                   who led the early church and directed its expansion to the gentiles.
                   He was stoned to death on October 23 c. 62 c.e.*

When Jesus had finished these parables he left the district; and, coming to his
    home town, he taught the people in their synagogue in such a way that they

were astonished and said, 'Where did the man get this wisdom and these miraculous powers? This is the carpenter's son, surely? Is not his mother the woman called Mary, and his brothers James and Joseph and Simon and Jude? His sisters, too, are they not all here with us? So where did the man get it all?' And they would not accept him. But Jesus said to them, 'A prophet is despised only in his own country and in his own house,' and he did not work many miracles there because of their lack of faith.

Matthew 13:53–58

The Refrain
Deliverance belongs to the LORD.* Your blessing be upon your people!

The Morning Psalm　　　　　　　　　*The LORD Knows the Way of the Righteous*
Happy are they who have not walked in the counsel of the wicked,* nor lingered
　in the way of sinners, nor sat in the seats of the scornful!
Their delight is in the law of the LORD,* and they meditate on his law day and
　night.
They are like trees planted by streams of water, bearing fruit in due season, with
　leaves that do not wither;* everything they do shall prosper.
It is not so with the wicked;* they are like chaff which the wind blows away.
Therefore the wicked shall not stand upright when judgment comes,* nor the
　sinner in the council of the righteous.
For the LORD knows the way of the righteous,* but the way of the wicked is
　doomed.

Psalm 1

The Refrain
Deliverance belongs to the LORD.* Your blessing be upon your people!

The Gloria

The Lord's Prayer

The Prayer Appointed for the Week
Almighty and everlasting God, in Christ you have revealed your glory among the
　nations: Preserve the works of your mercy, that your Church throughout the
　world may persevere with steadfast faith in the confession of your Name;
　through Jesus Christ our Lord, who lives and reigns with you and the Holy
　Spirit, one God, for ever and ever. *Amen.*†

Concluding Prayers of the Church
Grant, O God, that, following the example of your servant James, the brother of
　our Lord, your Church may give itself continually to prayer and to the recon-
　ciliation of all who are at variance and enmity; through Jesus Christ our Lord,
　who lives and reigns with you and the Holy Spirit, one God, now and for ever.
　Amen.†

Lord God, almighty and everlasting Father, you have brought me in safety to this
　new day: Preserve me with your mighty power, that I may not fall into sin, nor

be overcome by adversity; and in all I do direct me to the fulfilling of your purpose; through Jesus Christ my Lord. *Amen.*†

The Midday Office   **To Be Observed on the Hour or Half Hour**
                                         Between 11 a.m. and 2 p.m.

The Call to Prayer
Bless our God, you peoples;* make the voice of his praise to be heard;
Who holds our souls in life,* and will not allow our feet to slip.
                                                    Psalm 66:7–8

The Request for Presence
Show us the light of your countenance, O God,* and come to us.
                                            based on Psalm 67:1

The Greeting
Happy are the people whose strength is in you!* whose hearts are set on the pilgrims' way.
                                                    Psalm 84:4

The Refrain for the Midday Lessons
Happy are they who fear the LORD,* and who follow in his ways!
                                                    Psalm 128:1

A Reading
The tradition I handed on to you in the first place, a tradition which I myself
    received, was that Christ died for our sins, in accordance with the scriptures,
    and that he was buried; and that on the third day, he was raised to life, in accordance with the scriptures, and that he appeared to Cephas; and later to the
    Twelve; and next he appeared to more than five hundred of the brothers at the
    same time, most of whom are still with us, though some have fallen asleep;
    then he appeared to James, and then to all the apostles. Last of all he appeared
    to me too, as though I was a child born abnormally.
                                            1 Corinthians 15:3–8

The Refrain
Happy are they who fear the LORD,* and who follow in his ways!

The Midday Psalm   *Protect My Life from Fear*
Hear my voice, O God, when I complain;* protect my life from fear of the enemy.
Hide me from the conspiracy of the wicked,* from the mob of evildoers.
They say, "Who will see us? who will find out our crimes?* we have thought out a
    perfect plot."
The human mind and heart are a mystery;* but God will loose an arrow at them,
    and suddenly they will be wounded.
He will make them trip over their tongues,* and all who see them will shake their
    heads.
Everyone will stand in awe and declare God's deeds;* they will recognize his works.

The righteous will rejoice in the Lord and put their trust in him,* and all who are true of heart will glory.

Psalm 64:1–2, 6–10

The Refrain

Happy are they who fear the Lord,* and who follow in his ways!

The Small Verse

Blessed be the Name of the Lord and blessed be the people who are called by it.

The Lord's Prayer

The Prayer Appointed for the Week

Almighty and everlasting God, in Christ you have revealed your glory among the nations: Preserve the works of your mercy, that your Church throughout the world may persevere with steadfast faith in the confession of your Name; through Jesus Christ our Lord, who lives and reigns with you and the Holy Spirit, one God, for ever and ever. *Amen.*†

Concluding Prayers of the Church

Almighty God, by your Holy Spirit you have made us one with your saints in heaven and on earth: Grant that in my earthly pilgrimage I may always be supported by this fellowship of love and prayer, and know myself to be surrounded by their witness to your power and mercy. I ask this for the sake of Jesus Christ, in whom all my intercessions are acceptable through the Spirit, and who lives and reigns for ever and ever. *Amen.*†

Lord, my God, King of heaven and of earth, for this day please direct and sanctify, set right and govern my heart and my body, my sentiments, my words and my actions in conformity with Your law and Your commandments. Thus I shall be able to attain salvation and deliverance, in time and in eternity, by Your help, O Savior of the world, who lives and reigns forever. *Amen.*

adapted from Divine Office, II

The Vespers Office   To Be Observed on the Hour or Half Hour
                              Between 5 and 8 p.m.

The Call to Prayer

The Lord is in his holy temple.* Let all the earth keep silence before him.

based on Psalms 11:4

The Request for Presence

O Lord, I call to you; come to me quickly* hear my voice when I cry to you.
Let my prayer be set forth in your sight as incense,* the lifting up of my hands as the evening sacrifice.

Psalm 141:1–2

The Greeting

O Lamb of God, that takes away the sins of the world, have mercy on us.
O Lamb of God, that takes away the sins of the world, have mercy on us.
O Lamb of God, that takes away the sins of the world, grant us your peace.

The Hymn

King of the martyrs' noble band,
Crown of the true of every land,
Strength of the pilgrim on the way,
Beacon by night and cloud by day:

Dying, through you they overcame;
Living, were faithful to your Name.
Turn our rebellious hearts, and thus
Win a like victory in us.

Hear us as now we celebrate
Faith undeterred by cruel hate;
Hear and forgive us, sinners who
Are burdened by the wrong we do.

Glory to God the Father be;
Glory to Christ, who set us free;
And to the Spirit, Living flame,
Glory unceasing we proclaim.

Traditional

The Refrain for the Vespers Lessons

He who dwells in the shelter of the Most High,* abides under the shadow of the
Almighty.
He shall say to the Lord, "You are my refuge and my stronghold,* my God in
whom I put my trust."

Psalm 91:1–2

The Vespers Psalm   *Holiness Adorns Your House, O Lord*

The Lord is King; he has put on splendid apparel;* the Lord has put on his
apparel and girded himself with strength.
He has made the whole world so sure* that it cannot be moved;
Ever since the world began, your throne has been established;* you are from
everlasting.
The waters have lifted up, O Lord, the waters have lifted up their voice;* the
waters have lifted up their pounding waves.
Mightier than the sound of many waters, mightier than the breakers of the sea,*
mightier is the Lord who dwells on high.
Your testimonies are very sure,* and holiness adorns your house, O Lord, for ever
and for evermore.

Psalm 93

The Refrain

He who dwells in the shelter of the Most High,* abides under the shadow of the
Almighty.
He shall say to the Lord, "You are my refuge and my stronghold,* my God in
whom I put my trust."

The Gloria

The Lord's Prayer

The Prayer Appointed for the Week

Almighty and everlasting God, in Christ you have revealed your glory among the nations: Preserve the works of your mercy, that your Church throughout the world may persevere with steadfast faith in the confession of your Name; through Jesus Christ our Lord, who lives and reigns with you and the Holy Spirit, one God, for ever and ever. *Amen.*†

Concluding Prayers of the Church

Almighty and everlasting God, who kindled the flame of your love in the heart of your holy martyr James: Grant me, your humble servant, a like faith and power of love, that I who rejoice in his triumph may profit by his example; through Jesus Christ our Lord, who lives and reigns with you and the Holy Spirit, one God, for ever and ever. *Amen.*†

Father, as you made springs to form streams between mountains, so you made living streams of grace to flow from the apostles that their teaching may bring salvation to all nations. May I have practical knowledge of their doctrine, be obedient to their commands, obtain remission of sins through their prayers, and finally receive the reward of eternal happiness. *Amen.*

THE LITURGY OF THE HOURS, VOL. III

The Morning Office   To Be Observed on the Hour or Half Hour
                                      Between 6 and 9 a.m.

The Call to Prayer
Search for the LORD and his strength;* continually seek his face.

Psalm 105:4

The Request for Presence
Show your goodness, O LORD, to those who are good* and to those who are true of heart.

Psalm 125:4

The Greeting
Seven times a day do I praise you,* because of your righteous judgments.

Psalm 119:164

The Refrain for the Morning Lessons
Our days are like the grass;* we flourish like a flower of the field;
When the wind goes over it, it is gone,* and its place shall know it no more.

Psalm 103:15–16

A Reading
Jesus taught us, saying: "I tell you, if anyone openly declares himself for me in the presence of human beings, the Son of man will declare himself for him in the presence of God's angels. But anyone who disowns me in the presence of human beings will be disowned in the presence of God's angels."

Luke 12:8–9

The Refrain
Our days are like the grass;* we flourish like a flower of the field;
When the wind goes over it, it is gone,* and its place shall know it no more.

The Morning Psalm   *With God We Will Do Valiant Deeds*
God spoke from his holy place and said:* "I will exult and parcel out Shechem; I
    will divide the valley of Succoth.
Gilead is mine and Manasseh is mine;* Ephraim is my helmet and Judah my
    scepter.
Moab is my wash-basin, on Edom I throw down my sandal to claim it,* and over
    Philistia will I shout in triumph."
Who will lead me into the strong city?* who will bring me into Edom?
Have you not cast us off, O God?* you no longer go out, O God, with our armies.
Grant us your help against the enemy,* for vain is the help of man.
With God we will do valiant deeds,* and he shall tread our enemies under foot.

Psalm 60:6–12

The Refrain
Our days are like the grass;* we flourish like a flower of the field;
When the wind goes over it, it is gone,* and its place shall know it no more.

The Small Verse
Lord, have mercy; Christ, have mercy; Lord, have mercy.

The Lord's Prayer

The Prayer Appointed for the Week
Almighty and everlasting God, in Christ you have revealed your glory among the
    nations: Preserve the works of your mercy, that your Church throughout the
    world may persevere with steadfast faith in the confession of your Name;
    through Jesus Christ our Lord, who lives and reigns with you and the Holy
    Spirit, one God, for ever and ever. *Amen.*†

The Concluding Prayer of the Church
Lord God, almighty and everlasting Father, you have brought me in safety to this
    new day: Preserve me with your mighty power, that I may not fall into sin, nor
    be overcome by adversity; and in all I do direct me to the fulfilling of your pur-
    pose; through Jesus Christ my Lord. *Amen.*†

The Midday Office   To Be Observed on the Hour or Half Hour
                                        Between 11 a.m. and 2 p.m.

The Call to Prayer
Worship the Lord in the beauty of holiness;* let the whole earth tremble before
    him.
Tell it among the nations: "The Lord is King!* He has made the world so firm that
    it cannot be moved; he will judge the peoples with equity."

Psalm 96:9–10

The Request for Presence
Be my strong rock, a castle to keep me safe,* for you are my crag and my stronghold; for the sake of your Name, lead me and guide me.

Psalm 31:3

The Greeting
I love you, O Lord of my strength,* O Lord my stronghold, my crag, and my haven.
My God, my rock in whom I put my trust,* my shield, the horn of my salvation,
and my refuge; you are worthy of praise.

Psalm 18:1–2

The Refrain for the Midday Lessons
Into your hands I commend my spirit.

Psalm 31:5

A Reading
Concerning the Messiah, the prophet wrote: "Who has given credence to what we
have heard? And who has seen in it a revelation of Yahweh's arm? Like a
sapling he grew up before him, like a root in arid ground. He had no form or
charm to attract us, no beauty to win our hearts; he was despised, the lowest of
men, a man of sorrows, familiar with suffering, one from whom, as it were, we
averted our gaze, despised, for whom we had no regard."

Isaiah 53:1–3

The Refrain
Into your hands I commend my spirit.

The Midday Psalm   *He Turns the Flint-stone into a Flowing Spring*
Hallelujah! When Israel came out of Egypt,* the house of Jacob from a people of
strange speech,
Judah became God's sanctuary* and Israel his dominion.
The sea beheld it and fled;* Jordan turned and went back.
The mountains skipped like rams,* and the little hills like young sheep.
What ailed you, O sea, that you fled?* O Jordan, that you turned back?
You mountains, that you skipped like rams?* you little hills like young sheep?
Tremble, O earth, at the presence of the Lord,* at the presence of the God of Jacob,
Who turned the hard rock into a pool of water* and flint-stone into a flowing spring.

Psalm 114

The Refrain
Into your hands I commend my spirit.

The Small Verse
I will bless the Lord at all times
And his praise shall be always in my mouth.
Glory to the Father and the Son
And the eternal Spirit.

Traditional

The Lord's Prayer

The Prayer Appointed for the Week
Almighty and everlasting God, in Christ you have revealed your glory among the
nations: Preserve the works of your mercy, that your Church throughout the
world may persevere with steadfast faith in the confession of your Name;
through Jesus Christ our Lord, who lives and reigns with you and the Holy
Spirit, one God, for ever and ever. *Amen.*†

The Concluding Prayer of the Church
Heavenly Father, you have promised to hear what we ask in the Name of your
Son: Accept and fulfill my petitions, I pray, not as I ask in my ignorance, nor as
I deserve in my sinfulness, but as you know and love me in your Son Jesus
Christ our Lord. *Amen.*†

The Vespers Office   To Be Observed on the Hour or Half Hour
                                                    Between 5 and 8 p.m.

The Call to Prayer
Taste and see that the LORD is good;* happy are those who trust in him!
Psalm 34:8

The Request for Presence
O Lamb of God, that takes away the sins of the world, have mercy upon me.
O Lamb of God, that takes away the sins of the world, have mercy upon me.
O Lamb of God, that takes away the sins of the world, grant me your peace.

The Greeting
Happy are those whom you choose and draw to your courts to dwell there!* they
will be satisfied by the beauty of your house, by the holiness of your temple.
Psalm 65:4

The Hymn   *Let There Be Light*
Let there be light, Lord God of hosts,
Let there be wisdom on the earth!
Let broad humanity have birth;
Let there be deeds, instead of boasts.

Within our impassioned hearts instill
The calm that ends our strain and strife;
Make us your ministers of life;
Purge us from lusts that curse and kill.

Give us the peace of vision clear.
To see in a brother's good our own,
To joy and suffer not alone—
The love that casts out all our fear!

Let woe and waste of warfare cease,
That useful labor yet may build
Its homes with love and laughter filled:
God, give your wayward children peace!

William Vories

The Refrain for the Vespers Lessons
Light shines in the darkness for the upright;* the righteous are merciful and full of
compassion.

Psalm 112:4

The Vespers Psalm   *He Gives His Beloved Sleep*
Unless the LORD builds the house,* their labor is in vain who build it.
Unless the LORD watches over the city,* in vain the watchman keeps his vigil.
It is in vain that you rise so early and go to bed so late;* vain, too, to eat the bread
of toil, for he gives to his beloved sleep.

Psalm 127:1–3

The Refrain
Light shines in the darkness for the upright;* the righteous are merciful and full of
compassion.

The Cry of the Church
In the evening, in the morning, and at noonday, I will complain and lament,* and
he will hear my voice.

Psalm 55:18

The Lord's Prayer

The Prayer Appointed for the Week
Almighty and everlasting God, in Christ you have revealed your glory among the
nations: Preserve the works of your mercy, that your Church throughout the
world may persevere with steadfast faith in the confession of your Name;
through Jesus Christ our Lord, who lives and reigns with you and the Holy
Spirit, one God, for ever and ever. *Amen.*†

Concluding Prayer of the Church
Almighty Father,
you have given me the strength
to work throughout this day.
Receive my evening sacrifice of praise
in thanksgiving for your countless gifts.
I ask this through my Lord Jesus Christ, your Son,
who lives and reigns with you and the Holy Spirit,
one God, for ever and ever.

The Liturgy of the Hours, vol. III

The Morning Office   To Be Observed on the Hour or Half Hour
Between 6 and 9 a.m.

The Call to Prayer
Hallelujah! Give praise, you servants of the LORD;* praise the Name of the LORD.
Psalm 113:1

The Request for Presence
Test me, O LORD, and try me;* examine my heart and mind.
Psalm 26:2

The Greeting
All your works praise you, O LORD,* and your faithful servants bless you.
They make known the glory of your kingdom* and speak of your power;
Psalm 145:10–11

The Refrain for the Morning Lessons
Those who sowed with tears* will reap with songs of joy.
Those who go out weeping, carrying the seed,* will come again with joy, shoul-
dering their sheaves.
Psalm 126:6–7

A Reading
When Jesus spoke to the people again, he said: "I am the light of the world; anyone who follows me will not be walking in the dark but will have the light of
life."
John 8:12–13

The Refrain
Those who sowed with tears* will reap with songs of joy.
Those who go out weeping, carrying the seed,* will come again with joy, shoul-
dering their sheaves.

The Morning Psalm   *Who Is Like You, O God?*
Your righteousness, O God, reaches to the heavens;* you have done great things;
who is like you, O God?
You have showed me great troubles and adversities,* but you will restore my life
and bring me up again from the deep places of the earth.
You strengthen me more and more;* you enfold and comfort me,
Therefore I will praise you upon the lyre for your faithfulness, O my God;* I will
sing to you with the harp, O Holy One of Israel.
My lips will sing with joy when I play to you,* and so will my soul, which you
have redeemed.
My tongue will proclaim your righteousness all day long,* for they are ashamed
and disgraced who sought to do me harm.
Psalm 71:19–24

The Refrain

Those who sowed with tears* will reap with songs of joy.
Those who go out weeping, carrying the seed,* will come again with joy, shoul-
    dering their sheaves.

The Cry of the Church

In the evening, in the morning, and at noonday, I will complain and lament,* and
    he will hear my voice.

Psalm 55:18

The Lord's Prayer

The Prayer Appointed for the Week

Almighty and everlasting God, in Christ you have revealed your glory among the
    nations: Preserve the works of your mercy, that your Church throughout the
    world may persevere with steadfast faith in the confession of your Name;
    through Jesus Christ our Lord, who lives and reigns with you and the Holy
    Spirit, one God, for ever and ever. *Amen.*†

The Concluding Prayer of the Church

Lord God, almighty and everlasting Father, you have brought me in safety to this
    new day: Preserve me with your mighty power, that I may not fall into sin, nor
    be overcome by adversity; and in all I do direct me to the fulfilling of your pur-
    pose; through Jesus Christ my Lord. *Amen.*†

The Midday Office   To Be Observed on the Hour or Half Hour
                                              Between 11 a.m. and 2 p.m.

The Call to Prayer

Search for the LORD and his strength;* continually seek his face.
Remember the marvels he has done,* his wonders and the judgments of his
    mouth.

Psalm 105:4–5

The Request for Presence

Teach me your way, O LORD, and I will walk in your truth;* knit my heart to you
    that I may fear your Name.

Psalm 86:11

The Greeting

My mouth shall recount your mighty acts and saving deeds all the day long;*
    though I cannot know the number of them.

Psalm 71:15

The Refrain for the Midday Lessons

I will confess you among the peoples, O LORD;* I will sing praises to you among
    the nations.

Psalm 108:3

A Reading

Bulls' blood and goats' blood are incapable of taking away your sins, and that is
    why he said, on coming into this world: *"You wanted no sacrifice or cereal offering,
    but you gave me a body. You took no pleasure in burnt offering or sacrifice or sin; then I
    said, 'Here I am, I am coming,' in the scroll of the book it is written of me, to do your
    will, God."*

Hebrews 10:5–7

The Refrain

I will confess you among the peoples, O LORD;* I will sing praises to you among
    the nations.

The Midday Psalm   *A Song of the Messiah*

O God, give to the king Your judgment,* and to the son of the king Your justice,
To judge Your people with justice,* and Your poor with judgment.
Let the mountains bring peace to the people* and the hills bring righteousness.

Psalm 72:1–7, adapted from THE SHORT BREVIARY

The Refrain

I will confess you among the peoples, O LORD;* I will sing praises to you among
    the nations.

The Small Verse

The Lord is my shepherd and nothing is wanting to me. In green pastures He has
    settled me.

THE SHORT BREVIARY

The Lord's Prayer

The Prayer Appointed for the Week

Almighty and everlasting God, in Christ you have revealed your glory among the
    nations: Preserve the works of your mercy, that your Church throughout the
    world may persevere with steadfast faith in the confession of your Name;
    through Jesus Christ our Lord, who lives and reigns with you and the Holy
    Spirit, one God, for ever and ever. *Amen.*†

The Concluding Prayer of the Church

O Lord my God, to you and your service I devote myself, body, soul, and spirit.
    Fill my memory with the record of your mighty works; enlighten my under-
    standing with the light of your Holy Spirit; and may all the desires of my heart
    and will center in what you would have me do. Make me an instrument of
    your salvation for the people entrusted to my care, and let me by my life and
    speaking set forth your true and living Word. Be always with me in carrying
    out the duties of my salvation; in praises heighten my love and gratitude; in
    speaking of You give me readiness of thought and expression; and grant that,
    by the clearness and brightness of your holy Word, all the world may be drawn
    to your blessed kingdom. All this I ask for the sake of your Son my Savior Jesus
    Christ. *Amen.*†

The Vespers Office   To Be Observed on the Hour or Half Hour
                                            Between 5 and 8 p.m.

The Call to Prayer
Let us give thanks to the LORD for his mercy* and the wonders he does for his chil-
    dren.

Psalm 107:8

The Request for Presence
You are good and you bring forth good;* instruct me in your statutes.

Psalm 119:68

The Greeting
You are the LORD, most high over all the earth;* you are exalted far above all gods.

Psalm 97:9

The Hymn   *Immortal, Invisible*
    Immortal, invisible, God only wise,
    In light inaccessible hid from our eyes,
    Most blessed, most glorious, the Ancient of Days,
    Almighty, victorious, your great name we praise.

    Unresting, unhasting, and silent as light,
    Nor wanting, nor wasting, you rule us in might;
    Your justice like mountains high soaring above
    Your clouds which are fountains of goodness and love.

    All reigning in glory; all dwelling in light;
    Your angels adore you, while veiling their sight;
    All laud we would render: O help us to see
    It's only the splendor of light that blinds us from thee.
                            Walter Smith (adapted)

The Refrain for the Vespers Lessons
The LORD, the God of gods, has spoken;* he has called the earth from the rising of
    the sun to its setting.

Psalm 50:1

The Vespers Psalm   *O Mighty LORD, Your Faithfulness Is All Around You*
Who is like you, LORD God of hosts?* O mighty LORD, your faithfulness is all
    around you.
You rule the raging of the sea* and still the surging of its waves.
You have crushed Rahab of the deep with a deadly wound;* you have scattered
    your enemies with your mighty arm.
Yours are the heavens; the earth also is yours;* you laid the foundations of the
    world and all that is in it.
You have made the north and the south;* Tabor and Hermon rejoice in your Name.
You have a mighty arm;* strong is your hand and high is your right hand.

Righteousness and justice are the foundations of your throne;* love and truth go before your face.

Psalm 89:8–14

The Refrain

The LORD, the God of gods, has spoken;* he has called the earth from the rising of the sun to its setting.

The Gloria

The Lord's Prayer

The Prayer Appointed for the Week

Almighty and everlasting God, in Christ you have revealed your glory among the nations: Preserve the works of your mercy, that your Church throughout the world may persevere with steadfast faith in the confession of your Name; through Jesus Christ our Lord, who lives and reigns with you and the Holy Spirit, one God, for ever and ever. *Amen.†*

The Concluding Prayer of the Church

God our Father in Heaven have mercy on us.
God the Son, Redeemer of the world have mercy on us.
God the Holy Spirit have mercy on us.
Holy Trinity, one God have mercy on us.

Traditional

The Morning Office   To Be Observed on the Hour or Half Hour
                                Between 6 and 9 a.m.

The Call to Prayer

Open my lips, O Lord,* and my mouth shall proclaim your praise.

Psalm 51:16

The Request for Presence

Send out your light and your truth, that they may lead me,* and bring me to your holy hill and to your dwelling.

Psalm 43:3

The Greeting

Who is like you, LORD God of hosts?* O mighty LORD, your faithfulness is all around you.
Righteousness and justice are the foundations of your throne;* love and truth go before your face.

Psalm 89:8ff

The Refrain for the Morning Lessons

I will walk in the presence of the LORD* in the land of the living.

Psalm 116:8

A Reading

Jesus was at a feast when: "he said to his host, 'When you give a lunch or a dinner, do not invite your friends and brothers or your relations or rich neighbors, in case they invite you back and repay you. No; when you have a party, invite the poor, the crippled, the lame, the blind; then you will be blessed, for they have no means to repay you and so you will be repaid when the upright rise again.' "

Luke 14:12–14

The Refrain

I will walk in the presence of the LORD* in the land of the living.

The Morning Psalm   *Let the Righteous Be Joyful*

But let the righteous be glad and rejoice before God;* let them also be merry and joyful.

Sing to God, sing praises to his Name; exalt him who rides upon the heavens;*
YAHWEH is his Name, rejoice before him!

Father of orphans, defender of widows,* God in his holy habitation!

Psalm 68:3–5

The Refrain

I will walk in the presence of the LORD* in the land of the living.

The Cry of the Church

In the evening, in the morning, and at noonday, I will complain and lament,* and he will hear my voice.

Psalm 55:18

The Lord's Prayer

The Prayer Appointed for the Week

Almighty and everlasting God, in Christ you have revealed your glory among the nations: Preserve the works of your mercy, that your Church throughout the world may persevere with steadfast faith in the confession of your Name; through Jesus Christ our Lord, who lives and reigns with you and the Holy Spirit, one God, for ever and ever. *Amen.*†

The Concluding Prayer of the Church

Lord God, almighty and everlasting Father, you have brought me in safety to this new day: Preserve me with your mighty power, that I may not fall into sin, nor be overcome by adversity; and in all I do direct me to the fulfilling of your purpose; through Jesus Christ my Lord. *Amen.*†

The Midday Office   To Be Observed on the Hour or Half Hour
                                      Between 11 a.m. and 2 p.m.

The Call to Prayer

Come, let us sing to the LORD;* let us shout for joy to the Rock of our salvation.

Psalm 95:1

The Request for Presence

May God be merciful to us and bless us,* show us the light of his countenance and
come to us.

Psalm 67:1

The Greeting

Splendor and honor and kingly power are yours by right, O Lord our God, for you
created everything that is, and by your will they were created and have their
being.

Revelation 4:11

The Refrain for the Midday Lessons

I have been young and now I am old,* but never have I seen the righteous forsaken,
or their children begging bread.

Psalm 37:26

A Reading

The only thing you should owe to anyone is love for one another, for to love the
other person is to fulfill the law. All these: *You shall not commit adultery, You shall
not kill, You shall not steal, You shall not covet,* and all the other commandments
that there are, are summed up in this single phrase: *You must love your neighbor*
as yourself. Love can cause no harm to your neighbor, and so love is the fulfillment of the Law.

Romans 13:8–10

The Refrain

I have been young and now I am old,* but never have I seen the righteous forsaken,
or their children begging bread.

The Midday Psalm   *Happy Are They Who Consider the Poor and Needy*

Happy are they who consider the poor and needy!* the Lord will deliver them in
the time of trouble.

The Lord preserves them and keeps them alive, so that they may be happy in the
land;* he does not hand them over to the will of their enemies.

The Lord sustains them on their sickbed* and ministers to them in their illness.

Psalm 41:1–3

The Refrain

I have been young and now I am old,* but never have I seen the righteous forsaken,
or their children begging bread.

The Gloria

The Lord's Prayer

The Prayer Appointed for the Week

Almighty and everlasting God, in Christ you have revealed your glory among the
nations: Preserve the works of your mercy, that your Church throughout the
world may persevere with steadfast faith in the confession of your Name;

through Jesus Christ our Lord, who lives and reigns with you and the Holy
Spirit, one God, for ever and ever. *Amen.*†

The Concluding Prayer of the Church
You gather us together in faith, O God, as a loving mother and a gentle father.
   Help us to remember that your dwelling place is built upon love and peace,
   and that to bring about your reign on earth we must follow your way of peace.
   We pray for all governments and legislatures that they may be mindful of the
   rights of all peoples of this world to live in peace and dignity. Grant this in the
   name of Jesus. *Amen.*

THE NEW COMPANION TO THE BREVIARY

The Vespers Office   **To Be Observed on the Hour or Half Hour**
                                          Between 5 and 8 p.m.

The Call to Prayer
Exalt him who rides upon the heavens;* YAHWEH is his Name, rejoice before him!

Psalm 68:4

The Request for Presence
Hearken to my voice, O LORD, when I call;* have mercy on me and answer me.
You speak in my heart and say, "Seek my face."* Your face, LORD, will I seek.

Psalm 27:10–11

The Greeting
O gracious Light,
pure brightness of the everlasting Father in heaven,
O Jesus Christ, holy and blessed!

Now as we come to the setting of the sun,
and our eyes behold the vesper light,
we sing praises, O God: Father, Son and Holy Spirit.

You are worthy at all times to be praised by happy voices,
O Son of God, O giver of life,
and to be glorified through all the worlds.

Phos Hilaron

The Hymn   *All Glory, Laud, and Honor*
   All glory, laud, and honor, to Thee, Redeemer, King,
   To whom the lips of children made sweet hosannas ring:
   You are the King of Israel, You David's royal Son,
   Who in the Lord's Name comes, the King and blessed One.

   To You, before Your passion they sang their hymns of praise;
   To You, now high exalted, our melody we raise:
   You did accept their praises; accept the praise we bring,
   Who in all good delights, you good and gracious King.

Theodulph of Orleans

The Refrain for the Vespers Lessons

The LORD is my light and my salvation: Whom then shall I fear?* The LORD is the strength of my life; of whom then shall I be afraid?

Psalm 27:1

The Vespers Psalm   *I Cannot Count Your Mighty Acts*

But I shall always wait in patience,* and shall praise you more and more.

My mouth shall recount your mighty acts and saving deeds all day long;* though I cannot know the number of them.

I will begin with the mighty works of the Lord GOD;* I will recall your righteousness, yours alone.

Psalm 71:14–16

The Refrain

The LORD is my light and my salvation: Whom then shall I fear?* The LORD is the strength of my life; of whom then shall I be afraid?

The Cry of the Church

O Lamb of God, that takes away the sins of the world, have mercy upon me.

O Lamb of God, that takes away the sins of the world, have mercy upon me.

O Lamb of God, that takes away the sins of the world, grant me your peace.

The Lord's Prayer

The Prayer Appointed for the Week

Almighty and everlasting God, in Christ you have revealed your glory among the nations: Preserve the works of your mercy, that your Church throughout the world may persevere with steadfast faith in the confession of your Name; through Jesus Christ our Lord, who lives and reigns with you and the Holy Spirit, one God, for ever and ever. *Amen.*†

The Concluding Prayer of the Church

Protect me, Lord, as I stay awake; watch over me as I sleep, that awake I may watch with Christ, and asleep, rest in his peace. *Amen.*†

The Morning Office   **To Be Observed on the Hour or Half Hour**
Between 6 and 9 a.m.

The Call to Prayer

Proclaim the greatness of the LORD our God and worship him upon his holy hill;* for the LORD our God is the Holy One.

Psalm 99:9

The Request for Presence

Be pleased, O LORD, to deliver me;* O LORD make haste to help me.

Psalm 40:14

The Greeting

But you, O LORD my God, oh, deal with me according to your Name;* for your tender mercy's sake, deliver me.

For I am poor and needy,* and my heart is wounded within me.

Psalm 109:20–21

The Refrain for the Morning Lessons

The LORD is full of compassion and mercy,* slow to anger and of great kindness.

Psalm 103:8

A Reading

Of Jesus, it is written: "In the morning, long before dawn, he got up and left the
house and went off to a lonely place and prayed there."

Mark 1:35

The Refrain

The LORD is full of compassion and mercy,* slow to anger and of great kindness.

The Morning Psalm   *The LORD Preserves All Those Who Love Him*

The LORD is near to those who call upon him,* to all who call upon him faithfully.

He fulfills the desire of those who fear him;* he hears their cry and helps them.

The LORD preserves all those who love him,* but he destroys all the wicked.

Psalm 145:19–21

The Refrain

The LORD is full of compassion and mercy,* slow to anger and of great kindness.

The Cry of the Church

In the evening, in the morning, and at noonday, I will complain and lament,* and
he will hear my voice.

Psalm 55:18

The Lord's Prayer

The Prayer Appointed for the Week

Almighty and everlasting God, in Christ you have revealed your glory among the
nations: Preserve the works of your mercy, that your Church throughout the
world may persevere with steadfast faith in the confession of your Name;
through Jesus Christ our Lord, who lives and reigns with you and the Holy
Spirit, one God, for ever and ever. *Amen.*†

The Concluding Prayer of the Church

Lord God, almighty and everlasting Father, you have brought me in safety to this
new day: Preserve me with your mighty power, that I may not fall into sin, nor
be overcome by adversity; and in all I do direct me to the fulfilling of your purpose; through Jesus Christ my Lord. *Amen.*†

The Midday Office   To Be Observed on the Hour or Half Hour
                                     Between 11 a.m. and 2 p.m.

The Call to Prayer
Come now and look upon the works of the LORD,* what awesome things he has
   done on earth.

Psalm 46:9

The Request for Presence
O LORD, I call to you; come to me quickly;* hear my voice when I cry to you.

Psalm 141:1

The Greeting
When I was in trouble, I called to the LORD;* I called to the LORD, and he answered
   me.

The Refrain for the Midday Lessons
Let them be put to shame and thrown back,* all those who are enemies of Zion.

Psalm 129:5

A Reading
You must keep to what you have been taught and know to be true; remember who
   your teachers were, and how, ever since you were a child, you have known the
   holy scriptures—from these you can learn the wisdom that leads to salvation
   through faith in Christ Jesus. All scripture is inspired by God and useful for
   refuting error, for guiding people's lives and teaching them to be upright. This
   is how someone who is dedicated to God becomes fully equipped and ready
   for any good work.

2 Timothy 3:14–17

The Refrain
Let them be put to shame and thrown back,* all those who are enemies of Zion.

The Midday Psalm   *Your Word Is a Light Upon My Path*
Your word is a lantern to my feet* and a light upon my path.
I have sworn and am determined* to keep your righteous judgments.
I am deeply troubled;* preserve my life, O LORD, according to your word.
Accept, O LORD, the willing tribute of my lips,* and teach me your judgments.
My life is always in my hand,* yet I do not forget your law.
The wicked have set a trap for me,* but I have not strayed from your
   commandments.
Your decrees are my inheritance for ever;* truly, they are the joy of my heart.
I have applied my heart to fulfill your statutes* for ever and to the end.

Psalm 119:105–112

The Refrain
Let them be put to shame and thrown back,* all those who are enemies of Zion.

The Small Verse
From my secret sins cleanse me, Lord. And from all strange evils deliver me.

The Lord's Prayer

The Prayer Appointed for the Week
Almighty and everlasting God, in Christ you have revealed your glory among the
    nations: Preserve the works of your mercy, that your Church throughout the
    world may persevere with steadfast faith in the confession of your Name;
    through Jesus Christ our Lord, who lives and reigns with you and the Holy
    Spirit, one God, for ever and ever. *Amen.*†

The Concluding Prayer of the Church
Lord Jesus Christ, by your death you took away the sting of death: Grant me to so
    follow in faith where you have led the way, that I may at length fall asleep
    peacefully in you and wake in your likeness; for your tender mercies' sake.
    Amen.†

The Vespers Office To Be Observed on the Hour or Half Hour
Between 5 and 8 p.m.

The Call to Prayer
Praise the LORD, all you nations;* laud him, all you peoples.
For his loving-kindness toward us is great,* and the faithfulness of the LORD
    endures for ever.

Psalm 117:1–2

The Request for Presence
Help us, O God our Savior, for the glory of your Name;* deliver us and forgive us
    our sins, for your Name's sake.

Psalm 79:9

The Greeting
You are to be praised, O God, in Zion . . .
To you that hear prayer shall all flesh come,* because of their transgressions.

Psalm 65:1–2

The Hymn *The Canticle of Simeon*
    Lord, you now have set your servant free
    To go in peace as you have promised;
    For these eyes of mine have seen the Savior,
    Whom you have prepared for all the world to see:
    A Light to enlighten the nations,
    And the glory of your people Israel.

    Glory to the Father, and to the Son, and to the Holy Spirit:
    As it was in the beginning, is now, and will be for ever.

The Refrain for the Vespers Lessons
Your love, O LORD, reaches to the heavens,* and your faithfulness to the clouds.

Psalm 36:5

The Vespers Psalm   *The LORD Shall Preserve You*
I lift up my eyes to the hills;* from where is my help to come?
My help comes from the LORD,* the maker of heaven and earth.
He will not let your foot be moved* and he who watches over you will not fall
    asleep.
Behold, he who keeps watch over Israel* shall neither slumber nor sleep;
The LORD himself watches over you;* the LORD is your shade at your right hand,
So that the sun shall not strike you by day,* nor the moon by night.
The LORD shall preserve you from all evil;* it is he who shall keep you safe.
The LORD shall watch over your going out and your coming in,* from this time
    forth for evermore.

Psalm 121

The Refrain
Your love, O LORD, reaches to the heavens,* and your faithfulness to the clouds.

The Small Verse
The people that walked in darkness have seen a great light; on the inhabitants of a
    country in shadow dark as death light has blazed forth.

Isaiah 9:1

The Lord's Prayer

The Prayer Appointed for the Week
Almighty and everlasting God, in Christ you have revealed your glory among the
    nations: Preserve the works of your mercy, that your Church throughout the
    world may persevere with steadfast faith in the confession of your Name;
    through Jesus Christ our Lord, who lives and reigns with you and the Holy
    Spirit, one God, for ever and ever. *Amen.*†

Concluding Prayers of the Church
Lord Jesus Christ, by your death you took away the sting of death: Grant me so to
    follow in faith where you have led the way, that I may at length fall asleep peace-
    fully in you and wake up in your likeness; for your tender mercies' sake. *Amen.*†

May the souls of the faithful departed, through the mercy of God, rest in eternal
    peace. *Amen.*

The Morning Office   To Be Observed on the Hour or Half Hour
                                            Between 6 and 9 a.m.

The Call to Prayer
I will call upon God, and the LORD will deliver me.
In the evening, in the morning, and at the noonday, he will hear my voice.
He will bring me safely back . . . God who is enthroned of old, will hear me.†

The Request for Presence
Show us your mercy, O LORD,* and grant us your salvation.

Psalm 85:7

The Greeting
Happy are those whom you choose and draw to your courts to dwell there!*
    they will be satisfied by the beauty of your house, by the holiness of your
    temple.

Psalm 65:4

The Refrain for the Morning Lessons
Happy are the people whose strength is in you!* whose hearts are set on the
    pilgrims' way.

Psalm 84:4

A Reading
And Jacob was left alone. Then someone wrestled with him until daybreak who,
    seeing that he could not master him, struck him on the hip socket, and Jacob's
    hip was dislocated as he wrestled with him. He said, 'Let me go, for day is
    breaking.' Jacob replied, 'I will not let you go unless you bless me.' The other
    said, 'What is your name?' 'Jacob,' he replied. He said, 'No longer are you to be
    called Jacob, but Israel since you have shown your strength against God and
    men and have prevailed.' Then Jacob asked, 'Please tell me your name.' He
    replied, 'Why do you ask me my name?' With that, he blessed him there. Jacob
    named the place Peniel, 'Because I have seen God face to face,' he said, 'and
    have survived.'

Genesis 32:25–31

The Refrain
Happy are the people whose strength is in you!* whose hearts are set on the
    pilgrims' way.

The Morning Psalm   *To You, O My Strength, Will I Sing*
For my part, I will sing of your strength;* I will celebrate your love in the morning;
For you have become my stronghold,* a refuge in the day of my trouble.
To you, O my Strength, will I sing;* for you, O God, are my stronghold and my
    merciful God.

Psalm 59:18–20

The Refrain
Happy are the people whose strength is in you!* whose hearts are set on the
    pilgrims' way.

The Small Verse
    . . . My soul has a desire and longing for the courts of the LORD; my heart and my
    flesh rejoice in the living God.

Psalm 84:1

The Lord's Prayer

The Prayer Appointed for the Week

Almighty and everlasting God, in Christ you have revealed your glory among the nations: Preserve the works of your mercy, that your Church throughout the world may persevere with steadfast faith in the confession of your Name; through Jesus Christ our Lord, who lives and reigns with you and the Holy Spirit, one God, for ever and ever. *Amen.*†

The Concluding Prayer of the Church

Lord God, almighty and everlasting Father, you have brought me in safety to this new day: Preserve me with your mighty power, that I may not fall into sin, nor be overcome by adversity; and in all I do direct me to the fulfilling of your purpose; through Jesus Christ my Lord. *Amen.*†

The Midday Office   **To Be Observed on the Hour or Half Hour**
Between 11 a.m. and 2 p.m.

The Call to Prayer

Ascribe to the LORD, you families of the peoples;* ascribe to the LORD honor and power.

Ascribe to the LORD the honor due his Name;* bring offerings and come into his courts.

Worship the LORD in the beauty of holiness;* let the whole earth tremble before him.

Tell it out among the nations: "The LORD is King!* he has made the world so firm that it cannot be moved; he will judge the peoples with equity."

Psalm 96:7–10

The Request for Presence

Hear, O Shepherd of Israel, leading Joseph like a flock;* shine forth, you that are enthroned upon the cherubim.

In the presence of Ephraim, Benjamin, and Manasseh,* stir up your strength and come to help us.

Restore us, O God of hosts;* show the light of your countenance, and we shall be saved.

Psalm 80:1–3

The Greeting

Into your hands I commend my spirit,* for you have redeemed me, O LORD, O God of truth.

Psalm 31:5

The Refrain for the Midday Lessons

Happy is the nation whose God is the LORD!* happy the people he has chosen to be his own!

Psalm 33:12

A Reading

Do not absent yourself from your own assemblies, as some do, but encourage each
other; the more so as you see the Day drawing near.

Hebrews 10:25

The Refrain

Happy is the nation whose God is the Lord!* happy the people he has chosen to be
his own!

The Midday Psalm   *May They Prosper Who Love You*

I was glad when they said to me,* "Let us go to the house of the Lord."

Now our feet are standing* within your gates, O Jerusalem.

Jerusalem is built as a city* that is at unity with itself;

To which the tribes go up, the tribes of the Lord,* the assembly of Israel, to praise
the Name of the Lord.

For there are the thrones of judgment,* the thrones of the house of David.

Pray for the peace of Jerusalem:* "May they prosper who love you.

Peace be within your walls* and quietness within your towers.

For my brethren and companions' sake,* I pray for your prosperity.

Because of the house of the Lord our God,* I will seek to do you good."

Psalm 122

The Refrain

Happy is the nation whose God is the Lord!* happy the people he has chosen to be
his own!

The Gloria

The Lord's Prayer

The Prayer Appointed for the Week

Almighty and everlasting God, in Christ you have revealed your glory among the
nations: Preserve the works of your mercy, that your Church throughout the
world may persevere with steadfast faith in the confession of your Name;
through Jesus Christ our Lord, who lives and reigns with you and the Holy
Spirit, one God, for ever and ever. *Amen.*†

The Concluding Prayer of the Church

Almighty God, who after the creation of the world rested from all your works and
sanctified a day of rest for all your creatures: Grant that I, putting away all
earthly anxieties, may be duly prepared for the service of public worship, and
grant as well that my Sabbath upon earth may be a preparation for the eternal
rest promised to your people in heaven; through Jesus Christ our Lord. *Amen.*†

The Vespers Office   To Be Observed on the Hour or Half Hour
    Between 5 and 8 p.m.

The Call to Prayer
Great is the Lord and greatly to be praised;* there is no end to his greatness.

Psalm 145:3

The Request for Presence
"Hide not your face from your servant;* be swift and answer me, . . .
Draw near to me and redeem me; . . ."

Psalm 69:19–20

The Greeting
Blessed is the Lord!* for he has heard the voice of my prayer.

Psalm 28:7

The Hymn   *Shall We Gather at the River*

Shall we gather at the river,
Where bright angel feet have trod,
With its crystal tide forever flowing
By the throne of God?
Yes, we'll gather at the river,
The beautiful, beautiful river;
Gather with the saints at the river
That flows by the throne of God.

On the margin of the river,
Washing up its silver spray,
We will walk and worship ever,
All the happy golden day.
Yes, we'll gather at the river,
The beautiful, beautiful river;
Gather with the saints at the river
That flows by the throne of God.

Ere we reach the shining river,
Lay we every burden down;
Grace our spirits will deliver,
And provide a robe and crown.
Yes, we'll gather at the river,
The beautiful, beautiful river;
Gather with the saints at the river
That flows by the throne of God.

Soon we'll reach the shining river,
Soon our pilgrimage will cease;
Soon our happy hearts will quiver
With the melody of peace.
Yes, we'll gather at the river,
The beautiful, beautiful river;
Gather with the saints at the river
That flows by the throne of God.

Robert Lowry

The Refrain for the Vespers Lessons
Therefore I will praise you upon the lyre for your faithfulness, O my God;* I will
    sing to you with the harp, O Holy One of Israel.

Psalm 71:22

The Vespers Psalm   *That Which We Have Heard and Known*
That which we have heard and known, and what our forefathers have told us,* we
    will not hide from their children.
We will recount to generations to come the praiseworthy deeds and the power of
    the Lord,* and the wonderful works he has done.
He gave his decrees to Jacob and established a law for Israel,* which he
    commanded them to teach their children;

That the generations to come might know, and the children yet unborn;* that they
    in their turn might tell it to their children;
So that they might put their trust in God,* and not forget the deeds of God, but
    keep his commandments;
And not be like their forefathers, a stubborn and rebellious generation,* a generation
    whose heart was not steadfast, and whose spirit was not faithful to God.

Psalm 78:3–8

The Refrain

Therefore I will praise you upon the lyre for your faithfulness, O my God;* I will
    sing to you with the harp, O Holy One of Israel.

The Gloria

The Lord's Prayer

The Prayer Appointed for the Week

Almighty and everlasting God, in Christ you have revealed your glory among the
    nations: Preserve the works of your mercy, that your Church throughout the
    world may persevere with steadfast faith in the confession of your Name;
    through Jesus Christ our Lord, who lives and reigns with you and the Holy
    Spirit, one God, for ever and ever. *Amen.*†

The Concluding Prayer of the Church

O God, the source of eternal light: Shed forth your unending day upon all of us
    who watch for you, that our lips may praise you, our lives may bless you, and
    our worship may give you glory; through Jesus Christ our Lord. *Amen.*†

The Morning Office   **To Be Observed on the Hour or Half Hour
Between 6 and 9 a.m.**

The Call to Prayer

Ascribe to the LORD, you families of the peoples;* ascribe to the LORD honor and
    power.
Ascribe to the LORD the honor due his Name;* bring offerings and come into his
    courts.
Worship the LORD in the beauty of holiness;* let the whole earth tremble before him.

Psalm 96:7ff

The Request for Presence

Send out your light and your truth, that they may lead me,* and bring me to your
    holy hill and to your dwelling;

That I may go to the altar of God, to the God of my joy and gladness;* and on the
   harp I will give thanks to you, O God my God.

Psalm 43:3–4

The Greeting

As the deer longs for the water-brooks,* so longs my soul for you, O God.
My soul is athirst for God, athirst for the living God.

Psalm 42:1–2

The Refrain for the Morning Lessons

For who is God, but the LORD?* who is the Rock except our God?

Psalm 18:32

A Reading

Moses made this song before all the people of Israel: "Listen, heavens, while I
   speak; hear, earth, the words that I shall say! May my teaching fall like rain,
   may my word drop down like the dew, like showers on the grass, like light rain
   on the turf! For I shall proclaim the name of YAHWEH. Oh, I tell the greatness of
   our God! He is the Rock, his work is perfect, for all his ways are equitable. A
   trustworthy God who does no wrong, he is the Honest, the Upright One!"

Deuteronomy 32:1–4

The Refrain

For who is God, but the LORD?* who is the Rock except our God?

The Morning Psalm   *I Will Offer the Sacrifice of Thanksgiving*

O LORD, I am your servant;* I am your servant and the child of your handmaid;
   you have freed me from my bonds.
I will offer you the sacrifice of thanksgiving* and call upon the Name of the LORD.
I will fulfill my vows to the LORD* in the presence of all his people,
In the courts of the LORD's house,* in the midst of you, O Jerusalem. Hallelujah!

Psalm 116:14–17

The Refrain

For who is God, but the LORD?* who is the Rock except our God?

The Cry of the Church

Lord, have mercy on us. Christ, have mercy on us. Lord, have mercy on us.

The Lord's Prayer

The Prayer Appointed for the Week

Almighty and everlasting God, increase in me the gifts of faith, hope, and charity;
   and, that I may obtain what you promise, make me love what you command;
   through Jesus Christ our Lord, who lives and reigns with you and the Holy
   Spirit, one God, for ever and ever. *Amen.*†

The Concluding Prayer of the Church

Lord God, almighty and everlasting Father, you have brought me in safety to this
   new day: Preserve me with your mighty power, that I may not fall into sin, nor

be overcome by adversity; and in all I do direct me to the fulfilling of your purpose; through Jesus Christ my Lord. *Amen.*†

The Midday Office   To Be Observed on the Hour or Half Hour
                                 Between 11 a.m. and 2 p.m.

The Call to Prayer
The Lord is King; let the earth rejoice;* let the multitude of the isles be glad.
                                                                    Psalm 97:1

The Request for Presence
Hear, O Shepherd of Israel, leading Joseph like a flock;* shine forth, you that are
    enthroned upon the cherubim.

                                                                    Psalm 80:1

The Greeting
Yours is the day, yours also is the night;* you established the moon and the sun.
You fixed all the boundaries of the earth;* you made both summer and winter.
                                                                Psalm 74:15–16

The Refrain for the Midday Lessons
The earth, O Lord, is full of your love;* instruct me in your statutes.
                                                                Psalm 119:64

A Reading
On each of us God's favor has been bestowed in whatever way Christ allotted
    it . . . And to some, his 'gift' was that they should be apostles; to some,
    prophets; to some, evangelists; to some, pastors and teachers; to knit God's
    holy people together for the work of service to build up the Body of Christ,
    until we all reach a unity in faith and knowledge of the Son of God and form
    the perfect Man, fully mature with the fullness of Christ himself.

                                                            Ephesians 4:7, 11–13

The Refrain
The earth, O Lord, is full of your love;* instruct me in your statutes.

The Midday Psalm   *The Righteous Shall Flourish Like a Palm Tree*
The righteous shall flourish like a palm tree,* and shall spread abroad like a cedar
    of Lebanon.
Those who are planted in the house of the Lord* shall flourish in the courts of our
    God;
They shall still bear fruit in old age;* they shall be green and succulent;
That they may show how upright the Lord is,* my Rock, in whom there is no
    fault.

                                                            Psalm 92:11–14

The Refrain
The earth, O Lord, is full of your love;* instruct me in your statutes.

The Gloria

The Lord's Prayer

The Prayer Appointed for the Week
Almighty and everlasting God, increase in me the gifts of faith, hope, and charity; and, that I may obtain what you promise, make me love what you command; through Jesus Christ our Lord, who lives and reigns with you and the Holy Spirit, one God, for ever and ever. *Amen.*†

The Concluding Prayer of the Church
O God, you make me glad with the weekly remembrance of the glorious resurrection of your Son my Lord: Give me this day such blessing through my worship of you, that the week to come may be spent in your favor; through Jesus Christ our Lord. *Amen.*†

The Vespers Office   **To Be Observed on the Hour or Half Hour**
                                          Between 5 and 8 p.m.

The Call to Prayer
Bless the Lord, you angels of his, you mighty ones who do his bidding,* and hearken to the voice of his word.
Bless the Lord, all you his hosts,* you ministers of his who do his will.
Bless the Lord, all you works of his, in all places of his dominion;* bless the Lord, O my soul.

Psalm 103:20–22

The Request for Presence
Hear, O Shepherd of Israel, leading Joseph like a flock;* shine forth, you that are enthroned upon the cherubim.

Psalm 80:1

The Greeting
Praise God from whom all blessings flow;
Praise Him all creatures here below;
Praise Him above, you heavenly hosts;
Praise Father, Son, and Holy Ghost.
Doxology

The Hymn   *Come, Let Us Join Our Friends Above*
   Come, let us join our friends above who have obtained the prize,
   And on the eagle wings of love to joys celestial rise.
   Let saints on earth unite to sing with those to glory gone,
   For all the servants of our King in earth and heaven are one.

One family we dwell in him, our church above, beneath,
Though now divided by the stream, the narrow stream of death;
One army of the living God, to his command we bow;
Part of his host have crossed the flood, and part are crossing now.

Ten thousand to their endless home this solemn moment fly,
And though we are to the margin come, and we expect to die,
Even now by faith we join our hands with those that went before,
And greet the blood-besprinkled bands on the eternal shore.

Charles Wesley

The Refrain for the Vespers Lessons
I will be joyful in the LORD;* I will glory in his victory.

Psalm 35:9

The Vespers Psalm   *Lift Up Your Heads, O Gates*
Lift up your heads, O gates; lift them high, O everlasting doors;* and the King of
    glory shall come in.
"Who is this King of glory?"* "The LORD, strong and mighty, the LORD, mighty in
    battle."
Lift up your heads, O gates; lift them high, O everlasting doors;* and the King of
    glory shall come in.
"Who is he, this King of glory?"* "The LORD of hosts, he is the King of glory."

Psalm 24:7–10

The Refrain
I will be joyful in the LORD;* I will glory in his victory.

The Gloria

The Lord's Prayer

The Prayer Appointed for the Week
Almighty and everlasting God, increase in me the gifts of faith, hope, and charity;
    and, that I may obtain what you promise, make me love what you command;
    through Jesus Christ our Lord, who lives and reigns with you and the Holy
    Spirit, one God, for ever and ever. *Amen.*†

Concluding Prayers of the Church
O God, you have brought us near to an innumerable company of angels, and to
    the spirits of just men made perfect: Grant me during my earthly pilgrimage to
    abide in their fellowship, and in your heavenly country to become partakers of
    their joy; through Jesus Christ our Lord, who lives and reigns with you and the
    Holy Spirit, one God, now and for ever. *Amen.*†

Lord God, whose Son our Savior Jesus Christ, triumphed over the powers of death
    and prepared for us our place in the new Jerusalem: Grant that I, who have this
    day given thanks for his resurrection, may praise you in the City of which he is
    the light, and where he lives and reigns for ever and ever. *Amen.*†

The Morning Office   To Be Observed on the Hour or Half Hour
                                        Between 6 and 9 a.m.

The Call to Prayer
Be strong and let your heart take courage,* all you who wait for the LORD.
Psalm 31:24

The Request for Presence
O LORD, watch over us* and save us from this generation for ever.
Psalm 12:7

The Greeting
Restore us, O God of hosts;* show the light of your countenance, and we shall be
   saved.

Psalm 80:3

The Refrain for the Morning Lessons
You strengthen me more and more;* you enfold and comfort me.
Psalm 71:21

A Reading   *October 28 celebrates the lives of St. Simon and St. Jude. The two*
                   apostles, tradition says, went as missionaries to Persia. Little
                   more is known of St. Jude except for the one book attributed to
                   him. Of St. Simon, we know only that the gospels refer to him as
                   Simon, the Zealot.

Jesus said: "I shall not leave you orphans; I shall come to you. In a short time the
   world will no longer see me; but you will see that I live and you also will live.
   On that day you will know that I am in the Father and you in me and I in you.
   Whoever holds my commandments and keeps them is the one who loves me;
   and whoever loves me will be loved by my Father, and I shall love him and
   reveal myself to him."
Judas—not Judas Iscariot—said to him, "Lord, what has happened, that you
   intend to show yourself to us and not to the world?"
Jesus replied: "Anyone who loves me will keep my word, and my Father will love
   him, and we shall come to him and make a home in him. Anyone who does not
   love me does not keep my words. And the word that you hear is not my own: it
   is the word of the Father who sent me. I have said these things to you while still
   with you; but the Paraclete, the Holy Spirit, whom the Father will send in my
   name will teach you everything and remind you of all I have said to you."

John 14:18–26

The Refrain
You strengthen me more and more;* you enfold and comfort me.

The Morning Psalm   *He Holds Our Souls in Life*
Bless our God, you peoples;* make the voice of his praise to be heard;
Who holds our souls in life,* and will not allow our feet to slip.

For you, O God, have proved us;* you have tried us just as silver is tried.
You brought us into the snare;* you laid heavy burdens upon our backs.
You let enemies ride over our heads; we went through fire and water;* but you
brought us out into a place of refreshment.
I will enter your house with burnt-offerings and will pay you my vows,* which I
promised with my lips and spoke with my mouth when I was in trouble.
If I had found evil in my heart,* the Lord would not have heard me;
But in truth God has heard me;* he has attended to the voice of my prayer.

Psalm 66:7–12, 16–17

The Refrain
You strengthen me more and more;* you enfold and comfort me.

The Gloria

The Lord's Prayer

The Prayer Appointed for the Week
Almighty and everlasting God, increase in me the gifts of faith, hope, and charity;
and, that I may obtain what you promise, make me love what you command;
through Jesus Christ our Lord, who lives and reigns with you and the Holy
Spirit, one God, for ever and ever. *Amen.*†

The Concluding Prayer of the Church
O God, I thank you for the glorious company of the apostles, and especially on
this day for Simon and Jude; and I pray that, as they were faithful and zealous
in their mission, so I may with ardent devotion make known the love and
mercy of our Lord and Savior Jesus Christ; who lives and reigns with you and
the Holy Spirit, one God, for ever and ever. *Amen.*†

The Midday Office   **To Be Observed on the Hour or Half Hour**
                                     Between 11 a.m. and 2 p.m.

The Call to Prayer
Sing to God, O kingdoms of the earth;* sing praises to the Lord.
He rides in the heavens, the ancient heavens;* he sends forth his voice, his mighty
voice.

Psalm 68:33–34

The Request for Presence
May the glory of the Lord endure for ever;* may the Lord rejoice in all his works.

Psalm 104:32

The Greeting
Let the words of my mouth and the meditation of my heart be acceptable in your
sight,* O Lord, my strength and my redeemer.

Psalm 19:14

The Refrain for the Midday Lessons
My tongue will proclaim your righteousness all day long.

Psalm 71:24

A Reading
From Jude, servant of Jesus Christ and brother of James; to those who are called, to those who are dear to God the Father and kept safe for Jesus Christ, mercy, peace, and love be yours in abundance . . .
. . . you, my dear friends, must build yourselves up on the foundation of your most holy faith, praying in the Holy Spirit; keep yourselves within the love of God and wait for the mercy of our Lord Jesus Christ to give you eternal life. To some you must be compassionate because they are wavering; others you must save by snatching them from the fire; to others again you must be compassionate but wary, hating even the tunic stained by their bodies.

Jude:1–2, 20–23

The Refrain
My tongue will proclaim your righteousness all day long.

The Midday Psalm   *By Your Commandments You Give Me Life*
O LORD, your word is everlasting;* it stands firm in the heavens.
Your faithfulness remains from one generation to another;* you established the earth, and it abides.
By your decree these continue to this day,* for all things are your servants.
If my delight had not been in your law,* I should have perished in my affliction.
I will never forget your commandments,* because by them you give me life.
I am yours; oh, that you would save me!* for I study your commandments.
Though the wicked lie in wait for me to destroy me,* I will apply my mind to your decrees.
I see that all things come to an end,* but your commandment has no bounds.

Psalm 119:89–96

The Refrain
My tongue will proclaim your righteousness all day long.

The Gloria

The Lord's Prayer

The Prayer Appointed for the Week
Almighty and everlasting God, increase in me the gifts of faith, hope, and charity; and, that I may obtain what you promise, make me love what you command; through Jesus Christ our Lord, who lives and reigns with you and the Holy Spirit, one God, for ever and ever. *Amen.*†

The Concluding Prayer of the Church
O God, who through Your blessed Apostles Simon and Jude have brought me to the knowledge of Your Name, grant me both to celebrate their eternal glory by

making progress in virtues and by celebrating their glory, to advance in virtue. Through our Lord. *Amen.*

adapted from The Short Breviary

The Vespers Office   To Be Observed on the Hour or Half Hour
                                                        Between 5 and 8 p.m.

The Call to Prayer

It is a good thing to give thanks to the Lord* and to sing praises to your Name, O Most High;

To tell of your loving-kindness early in the morning* and of your faithfulness in the night season.

Psalm 92:1–2

The Request for Presence

Hear my prayer, O God;* give ear to the words of my mouth.

Psalm 54:2

The Greeting

I will thank you, O Lord my God, with all my heart,* and glorify your Name for evermore.

Psalm 86:12

The Hymn

Give us the wings of faith to rise within the veil,
and see the saints above,
how great their joys,
how bright their glories be.

We ask them whence their victory came;
they, with united breath,
ascribe their conquest to the Lamb,
their triumph to his death.

They marked the footsteps that he trod,
his zeal inspired their quest,
and following their incarnate God,
they reached the promised rest.

Our glorious Leader claims our praise
for his own pattern given;
while the long cloud of witnesses
show the same path to heaven.

Isaac Watts

The Refrain for the Vespers Lessons

I will bless the Lord who gives me counsel;* my heart teaches me, night after night.

Psalm 16:7

The Vespers Psalm   *Show Me the Road That I Must Walk*

My spirit faints within me;* my heart within me is desolate.

I remember the time past; I muse upon all your deeds;* I consider the works of
     your hands.

I spread out my hands to you;* my soul gasps to you like a thirsty land.

O LORD, make haste to answer me; my spirit fails me;* do not hide your face from
     me or I shall be like those who go down to the Pit.

Let me hear of your loving-kindness in the morning, for I put my trust in you;*
     show me the road that I must walk, for I lift up my soul to you.

Psalm 143:4–8

The Refrain

I will bless the LORD who gives me counsel;* my heart teaches me, night after night.

The Small Verse

Happy are the people whose strength is in you!* whose hearts are set on the pil-
     grims' way,

For one day in your courts is better than a thousand in my own room,* and to
     stand at the threshold of the house of my God than to dwell in the tents of the
     wicked.

Psalm 84:4, 9

The Lord's Prayer

The Prayer Appointed for the Week

Almighty and everlasting God, increase in me the gifts of faith, hope, and charity;
     and, that I may obtain what you promise, make me love what you command;
     through Jesus Christ our Lord, who lives and reigns with you and the Holy
     Spirit, one God, for ever and ever. *Amen.*†

Concluding Prayers of the Church

Almighty God, by your Holy Spirit you have made us one with your saints in
     heaven and on earth: grant that in my earthly pilgrimage I may always be sup-
     ported by this fellowship of love and prayer, and know myself to be sur-
     rounded by their witness to your power and mercy. I ask this for the sake of
     Jesus Christ, in whom all my intercessions are acceptable through the Spirit,
     and who lives and reigns for ever and ever. *Amen.*†

Save me, O Lord, while I am awake, and keep me while I sleep. That I may wake
     in Christ and rest in peace.

adapted from THE SHORT BREVIARY

The Morning Office   **To Be Observed on the Hour or Half Hour**
                                          Between 6 and 9 a.m.

The Call to Prayer

God has gone up with a shout,* the LORD with the sound of the ram's horn.

Sing praises to God, sing praises;* sing praises to our King, sing praises.

For God is king of all the earth;* sing praises with all your skill.
God reigns over the nations;* God sits upon his holy throne.

Psalm 47:5–8

The Request for Presence
Early in the morning I cry out to you,* for in your word is my trust.

Psalm 119:147

The Greeting
Not to us, O Lord, not to us, but to your Name give glory;* because of your love
  and because of your faithfulness.

Psalm 115:1

The Refrain for the Morning Lessons
Those who are planted in the house of the Lord* shall flourish in the courts of our
  God.

Psalm 92:12

A Reading
Jesus taught us, saying: "The Father loves the Son and has entrusted everything to
  his hands.
Anyone who believes in the Son has eternal life, but anyone who refuses to believe
  in the Son will never see life: God's retribution hangs over him."

John 3:35–36

The Refrain
Those who are planted in the house of the Lord* shall flourish in the courts of our
  God.

The Morning Psalm   *He Remembers That We Are but Dust*
He has not dealt with us according to our sins,* nor rewarded us according to our
  wickedness.
For as the heavens are high above the earth,* so is his mercy great upon those who
  fear him.
As far as the east is from the west,* so far has he removed our sins from us.
As a father cares for his children,* so does the Lord care for those who fear him.
For he himself knows whereof we are made;* he remembers that we are but dust.

Psalm 103:10–14

The Refrain
Those who are planted in the house of the Lord* shall flourish in the courts of our
  God.

The Short Verse
'I am the Alpha and the Omega,' says the Lord God, who is, who was, and who is
  to come, the Almighty.

Revelation 1:8

The Lord's Prayer

The Prayer Appointed for the Week
Almighty and everlasting God, increase in me the gifts of faith, hope, and charity; and, that I may obtain what you promise, make me love what you command; through Jesus Christ our Lord, who lives and reigns with you and the Holy Spirit, one God, for ever and ever. *Amen.*†

The Concluding Prayer of the Church
Lord God, almighty and everlasting Father, you have brought me in safety to this new day: Preserve me with your mighty power, that I may not fall into sin, nor be overcome by adversity; and in all I do direct me to the fulfilling of your purpose; through Jesus Christ my Lord. *Amen.*†

The Midday Office   To Be Observed on the Hour or Half Hour
Between 11 a.m. and 2 p.m.

The Call to Prayer
Sing to the LORD and bless his Name;* proclaim the good news of his salvation from day to day.
Declare his glory among the nations* and his wonders among all peoples.
For great is the LORD and greatly to be praised;* he is more to be feared than all gods.

Psalm 96:2–4

The Request for Presence
I have gone astray like a sheep that is lost;* search for your servant, for I do not forget your commandments.

Psalm 119:176

The Greeting
When your word goes forth it gives light;* it gives understanding to the simple.

Psalm 119:130

The Refrain for the Midday Lessons
He will not let your foot be moved* and he who watches over you will not fall asleep.

Psalm 121:3

A Reading
And as well as this, the Spirit too comes to help us in our weakness, for, when we do not know how to pray properly, then the Spirit personally makes our petitions for us in groans that cannot be put into words; and he who can see into all hearts knows what the Spirit means because the prayers that the Spirit makes for God's holy people are always in accordance with the mind of God.

Romans 8:26–27

The Refrain
He will not let your foot be moved* and he who watches over you will not fall asleep.

The Midday Psalm   *The LORD Will Not Abandon His People*

He that planted the ear, does he not hear?* he that formed the eye, does he not see?

He who admonishes the nations, will he not punish?* he who teaches all the
world, has he no knowledge?

The LORD knows our human thoughts;* how like a puff of wind they are.

Happy are they whom you instruct, O Lord!* whom you teach out of your law;

To give them rest in evil days,* until a pit is dug for the wicked.

For the LORD will not abandon his people,* nor will he forsake his own.

For judgment will again be just,* and all the true of heart will follow it.

Psalm 94:9–15

The Refrain

He will not let your foot be moved* and he who watches over you will not fall
asleep.

The Gloria

The Lord's Prayer

The Prayer Appointed for the Week

Almighty and everlasting God, increase in me the gifts of faith, hope, and charity;
and, that I may obtain what you promise, make me love what you command;
through Jesus Christ our Lord, who lives and reigns with you and the Holy
Spirit, one God, for ever and ever. *Amen.*†

The Concluding Prayer of the Church

God of mystery, God of love, send your Spirit into our hearts with gifts of wisdom
and peace, fortitude and charity. We long to love and serve you. Faithful God,
make us faithful. This we ask through the intercession of all your saints. *Amen.*

THE NEW COMPANION TO THE BREVIARY

The Vespers Office   **To Be Observed on the Hour or Half Hour**
Between 5 and 8 p.m.

The Call to Prayer

Let Israel rejoice in his Maker;* let the children of Zion be joyful in their King.

Let them praise his Name in the dance;* let them sing praise to him with timbrel
and harp.

For the LORD takes pleasure in his people* and adorns the poor with victory.

Let the faithful rejoice in triumph;* let them be joyful on their beds.

Psalm 149:2–5

The Request for Presence

Show us your mercy, O LORD,* and grant us your salvation.

Psalm 85:7

The Greeting

Zion hears and is glad, and the cities of Judah rejoice,* because of your judgments,
O LORD.

The Hymn   *More Love to Thee*

More love to Thee,
O Christ, more love to Thee!
Hear Thou the Prayer I make on bended knee;
this is my earnest plea,
more love to Thee,
O Christ, more love to Thee.

Once earthly joy I craved,
sought peace and rest;
now Thee alone I seek; give me what is best:
this all my prayer shall be,
more love to Thee,
O Christ, more love to Thee.

Then shall my latest breath
whisper Thy praise;
this be the parting cry my heart shall raise;
this still my prayer shall be,
more love to Thee,
O Christ, more love to Thee.

Elizabeth Prentiss

The Refrain for the Vespers Lessons

For one day in your courts is better than a thousand in my own room,* and to
stand at the threshold of the house of my God than to dwell in the tents of the
wicked.

Psalm 84:9

The Vespers Psalm   *My Boundaries Enclose a Pleasant Land*

O Lord, you are my portion and my cup;* it is you who uphold my lot.

My boundaries enclose a pleasant land;* indeed, I have a goodly heritage.

I will bless the Lord who gives me counsel;* my heart teaches me, night after
night.

I have set the Lord always before me;* because he is at my right hand I shall not
fall.

My heart, therefore, is glad, and my spirit rejoices;* my body also shall rest in
hope.

For you will not abandon me to the grave,* nor let your holy one see the Pit.

You will show me the path of life;* in your presence there is fullness of joy, and in
your right hand are pleasures for evermore.

Psalm 16:5–11

The Refrain

For one day in your courts is better than a thousand in my own room,* and to
stand at the threshold of the house of my God than to dwell in the tents of the
wicked.

The Gloria

The Lord's Prayer

The Prayer Appointed for the Week

Almighty and everlasting God, increase in me the gifts of faith, hope, and charity;
   and, that I may obtain what you promise, make me love what you command;
   through Jesus Christ our Lord, who lives and reigns with you and the Holy
   Spirit, one God, for ever and ever. *Amen.*†

The Concluding Prayer of the Church

Father, all-powerful and ever-living God,
we do well always and everywhere to give you thanks.
All things are of your making,
all times and seasons obey your laws,
but you chose to create us in your own image,
setting us over the whole world in all its wonder.
You made us the steward of creation,
to praise you day by day for the marvels of your wisdom and power.

THE ROMAN MISSAL

The Morning Office   To Be Observed on the Hour or Half Hour
                                        Between 6 and 9 a.m.

The Call to Prayer

Love the LORD, all you who worship him;* the LORD protects the faithful, but
   repays to the full those who act haughtily.

Psalm 31:23

The Request for Presence

O LORD, I call to you; my Rock, do not be deaf to my cry;* lest, if you do not hear
   me, I become like those who go down to the Pit.

Psalm 28:1

The Greeting

Your way, O God, is holy;* who is as great as our God?

Psalm 77:13

The Refrain for the Morning Lessons

Protect my life and deliver me;* let me not be put to shame, for I have trusted in you.

Psalm 25:19

A Reading

Asked by the Pharisees when the kingdom of God was to come, he gave them this
   answer, 'The coming of the kingdom of God does not admit of observation and
   there will be no one to say, "Look, it is here! Look, it is there!" For look, the
   kingdom of God is among you.'

Luke 17:20–21

The Refrain

Protect my life and deliver me;* let me not be put to shame, for I have trusted in you.

The Morning Psalm   *In the Shadow of Your Wings Will I Take Refuge*

Be merciful to me, O God, be merciful, for I have taken refuge in you;* in the
   shadow of your wings will I take refuge until this time of trouble has gone by.
I will call upon the Most High God,* the God who maintains my cause.
He will send from heaven and save me; he will confound those who trample upon
   me;* God will send forth his love and his faithfulness.

Psalm 57:1–3

The Refrain

Protect my life and deliver me;* let me not be put to shame, for I have trusted in
   you.

The Cry of the Church

In the evening, in the morning, and at noonday, I will complain and lament,* and
   he will hear my voice.

Psalm 55:18

The Lord's Prayer

The Prayer Appointed for the Week

Almighty and everlasting God, increase in me the gifts of faith, hope, and charity;
   and, that I may obtain what you promise, make me love what you command;
   through Jesus Christ our Lord, who lives and reigns with you and the Holy
   Spirit, one God, for ever and ever. *Amen.*†

The Concluding Prayer of the Church

Lord God, almighty and everlasting Father, you have brought me in safety to this
   new day: Preserve me with your mighty power, that I may not fall into sin, nor
   be overcome by adversity; and in all I do direct me to the fulfilling of your purpose; through Jesus Christ my Lord. *Amen.*†

The Midday Office   To Be Observed on the Hour or Half Hour
                                              Between 11 a.m. and 2 p.m.

The Call to Prayer

Hallelujah! Sing to the Lord a new song;* sing his praise in the congregation of the
   faithful.

Psalm 149:1

The Request for Presence

You are good and you bring forth good;* instruct me in your statutes.

Psalm 119:68

The Greeting

Be exalted, O Lord, in your might;* we will sing and praise your power.

Psalm 21:14

The Refrain for the Midday Lessons

It is better to rely on the LORD* than to put any trust in flesh.
It is better to rely on the LORD* than to put any trust in rulers.

Psalm 118:8–9

A Reading

Of Wisdom, the scribe wrote: "But the One who knows all discovers her, he has
grasped her with his own intellect, he has set the earth firm for evermore and
filled it with four-footed beasts, he sends the light—and it goes, he recalls it—
and trembling it obeys; the stars shine joyfully at their posts; when he calls
them, they answer, 'Here we are'; they shine to delight their Creator. It is he
who is our God, no other can compare with him. He has uncovered the whole
way of knowledge and shown it to his servant Jacob, to Israel his well-beloved;
only then did she appear on earth and live among human beings.

Baruch 3:32–38

The Refrain

It is better to rely on the LORD* than to put any trust in flesh.
It is better to rely on the LORD* than to put any trust in rulers.

The Midday Psalm   *The Judgments of the LORD Are Sweeter Far Than Honey*

The law of the LORD is perfect and revives the soul;* the testimony of the LORD is
sure and gives wisdom to the innocent.
The statutes of the LORD are just and rejoice the heart;* the commandment of the
LORD is clear and gives light to the eyes.
The fear of the LORD is clean and endures for ever;* the judgments of the LORD are
true and righteous altogether.
More to be desired are they than gold, more than much fine gold,* sweeter far than
honey, than honey in the comb.
By them also is your servant enlightened,* and in keeping them there is great
reward.

Psalm 19:7–11

The Refrain

It is better to rely on the LORD* than to put any trust in flesh.
It is better to rely on the LORD* than to put any trust in rulers.

The Gloria

The Lord's Prayer

The Prayer Appointed for the Week

Almighty and everlasting God, increase in me the gifts of faith, hope, and charity;
and, that I may obtain what you promise, make me love what you command;
through Jesus Christ our Lord, who lives and reigns with you and the Holy
Spirit, one God, for ever and ever. *Amen.*†

The Concluding Prayer of the Church

God of justice, God of mercy, bless all those who are surprised with pain this day
from suffering caused by their own weakness or that of others. Let what we
suffer teach us to be merciful; let our sins teach us to forgive. This I ask through
the intercession of Jesus and all who died forgiving those who oppressed them.
Amen.†

The Vespers Office   **To Be Observed on the Hour or Half Hour**
                                                    Between 5 and 8 p.m.

The Call to Prayer

Come now and see the works of God,* how wonderful he is in his doing toward
all people.

Psalm 66:4

The Request for Presence

Let your countenance shine upon your servant* and teach me your statutes.

Psalm 119:135

The Greeting

I will praise you upon the lyre for your faithfulness, O my God;* I will sing to you
with the harp, O Holy One of Israel.

based on Psalm 71:22

The Hymn   *The Call of Christ*

Sing them over again to me,
Wonderful words of Life;
Let me more of their beauty see,
Wonderful words of Life.
Words of life and beauty, teach me faith and duty:
Beautiful words, wonderful words,
Wonderful words of Life,
Beautiful words, wonderful words,
Wonderful words of Life.

Christ, the blessed One, gives to all,
Wonderful words of Life.
Sinner, list to the loving call,
Wonderful words of Life.
All so freely given, wooing us to heaven:
Beautiful words, wonderful words,
Wonderful words of Life,
Beautiful words, wonderful words,
Wonderful words of Life.

Sweetly echo the gospels' call,
Wonderful words of Life.
Offer pardon and peace to all,
Wonderful words of Life.
Jesus, only Savior, sanctify for ever:
Beautiful words, wonderful words,
Wonderful words of Life,
Beautiful words, wonderful words,
Wonderful words of Life.

Philip P. Bliss

The Refrain for the Vespers Lessons

The LORD, the God of gods, has spoken;* he has called the earth from the rising of
the sun to its setting.

Psalm 50:1

The Vespers Psalm   God Has Gone Up with a Shout

Clap your hands, all you peoples;* shout to God with a cry of joy.

God has gone up with a shout,* the LORD with the sound of the ram's-horn.

Sing praises to God, sing praises;* sing praises to our King, sing praises.

For God is King of all the earth;* sing praises with all your skill.

God reigns over the nations;* God sits upon his holy throne.

The nobles of the peoples have gathered together* with the people of the God of
Abraham.

The rulers of the earth belong to God,* and he is highly exalted.

Psalm 47:1, 5–10

The Refrain

The LORD, the God of gods, has spoken;* he has called the earth from the rising of
the sun to its setting.

The Small Verse

Create in me a clean heart, O God,* and renew a right spirit within me.

Psalm 51:11

The Lord's Prayer

The Prayer Appointed for the Week

Almighty and everlasting God, increase in me the gifts of faith, hope, and charity;
and, that I may obtain what you promise, make me love what you command;
through Jesus Christ our Lord, who lives and reigns with you and the Holy
Spirit, one God, for ever and ever. *Amen.*†

The Concluding Prayer of the Church

Protect us, Lord, as we stay awake; watch over us as we sleep, that awake we may
watch with Christ, and asleep, rest in his peace. *Amen.*

The Morning Office

To Be Observed on the Hour or Half Hour
Between 6 and 9 a.m.

The Call to Prayer

The Lord is King; let the people tremble;* he is enthroned upon the cherubim; let
the earth shake.

Psalm 99:1

The Request for Presence

Be seated on your lofty throne, O Most High;* O Lord, judge the nations.

Psalm 7:8

The Greeting

Save us, O Lord our God, and gather us from among the nations,* that we may
give thanks to your holy Name and glory in your praise.

Psalm 106:47

The Refrain for the Morning Lessons

Let all the earth fear the Lord;* let all who dwell in the world stand in awe of him.

Psalm 33:8

A Reading

He had gone into the Temple and was teaching, when the chief priests and the
elders of the people came to him and said, 'What authority have you for acting
like this? And who gave you this authority?' In reply Jesus said to them, 'And I
will ask you a question, just one; if you tell me the answer to it, then I will tell
you my authority for acting like this. John's baptism: what was its origin, heavenly or human?' And they argued this way among themselves, 'If we say heavenly, he will retort to us, "Then why did you refuse to believe in him?"; but if
we say human, we have the people to fear, for they all hold that John was a
prophet.' So their reply to Jesus was, 'We do not know.' And he retorted to
them, 'Nor will I tell you my authority for acting like this.'

Matthew 21:23–27

The Refrain

Let all the earth fear the Lord;* let all who dwell in the world stand in awe of him.

The Morning Psalm   *The Just Shall Not Put Their Hands to Evil*

Those who trust in the Lord are like Mount Zion,* which cannot be moved, but
stands fast for ever.
The hills stand about Jerusalem;* so does the Lord stand round about his people,
from this time forth for evermore.
The scepter of the wicked shall not hold sway over the land allotted to the just,* so
that the just shall not put their hands to evil.

Psalm 125:1–3

The Refrain

Let all the earth fear the Lord;* let all who dwell in the world stand in awe of him.

The Small Verse

'I am the Alpha and the Omega,' says the Lord God, who is, who was, and who is
to come, the Almighty.

Revelation 1:8

The Lord's Prayer

The Prayer Appointed for the Week

Almighty and everlasting God, increase in me the gifts of faith, hope, and charity;
and, that I may obtain what you promise, make me love what you command;
through Jesus Christ our Lord, who lives and reigns with you and the Holy
Spirit, one God, for ever and ever. *Amen.*†

Concluding Prayers of the Church

Lord God, almighty and everlasting Father, you have brought me in safety to this
new day: Preserve me with your mighty power, that I may not fall into sin, nor
be overcome by adversity; and in all I do direct me to the fulfilling of your purpose; through Jesus Christ my Lord. *Amen.*†

Lord God Almighty, you have made all the peoples of the earth for your glory, to
serve you in freedom and in peace: Give to the people of our country a zeal for
justice and the strength of forbearance, that we may use our liberty in accordance with your gracious will; through Jesus Christ our Lord, who lives and
reigns with you and the Holy Spirit, one God, for ever and ever. *Amen.*†

The Midday Office   To Be Observed on the Hour or Half Hour
                                        Between 11 a.m. and 2 p.m.

The Call to Prayer

I will offer you a freewill sacrifice* and praise your Name, O LORD, for it is good.

Psalm 54:6

The Request for Presence

Look well whether there be any wickedness in me* and lead me in the way that is
everlasting.

Psalm 139:23

The Greeting

O God, you know my foolishness,* and my faults are not hidden from you.

Psalm 69:6

The Refrain for the Midday Lessons

So teach us to number our days* that we may apply our hearts to wisdom.

Psalm 90:12

A Reading

Wisdom has built herself a house, she has hewn her seven pillars, she has slaugh-
tered her beasts, drawn her wine, she has laid her table. She has dispatched her

maidservants and proclaimed from the height above the city, 'Who is simple? Let him come this way.' To the fool she says, 'Come and eat my bread, drink the wine which I have drawn! Leave foolishness behind you and you will live, go forwards in the ways of perception.' The first principle of wisdom is the fear of YAHWEH.

What God's holy ones know—this is understanding. For by me your days will be multiplied, and your years of life increased.

Proverbs 9:1–6, 10–11

The Refrain

So teach us to number our days* that we may apply our hearts to wisdom.

The Midday Psalm   *How Deep I Find Your Thoughts, O God!*

For you yourself created my inmost parts;* you knit me together in my mother's womb.

I will thank you because I am marvelously made;* your works are wonderful, and I know it well.

My body was not hidden from you,* while I was being made in secret and woven in the depths of the earth.

Your eyes beheld my limbs, yet unfinished in the womb; all of them were written in your book;* they were fashioned day by day, when as yet there was none of them.

How deep I find your thoughts, O God!* how great is the sum of them!

If I were to count them, they would be more in number than the sand;* to count them all, my life span would need to be like yours.

Psalm 139:13–17

The Refrain

So teach us to number our days* that we may apply our hearts to wisdom.

The Cry of the Church

Lord, have mercy on us. Christ, have mercy on us. Lord, have mercy on us.

The Lord's Prayer

The Prayer Appointed for the Week

Almighty and everlasting God, increase in me the gifts of faith, hope, and charity; and, that I may obtain what you promise, make me love what you command; through Jesus Christ our Lord, who lives and reigns with you and the Holy Spirit, one God, for ever and ever. *Amen.*†

The Concluding Prayer of the Church

Almighty and eternal God, ruler of all things in heaven and earth: Mercifully accept the prayers of your people everywhere, and strengthen each of us to do your will; through Jesus Christ our Lord. *Amen.*†

The Vespers Office   To Be Observed on the Hour or Half Hour
                                              Between 5 and 8 p.m.

The Call to Prayer

Come, let us sing to the LORD;* let us shout for joy to the Rock of our salvation.
Let us come before his presence with thanksgiving* and raise a loud shout to him
     with psalms.
For the LORD is a great God,* and a great King above all gods.
In his hands are the caverns of the earth,* and the heights of the hills are his also.
The sea is his, for he made it,* and his hands have molded the dry land.

Psalm 95:1–5

The Request for Presence

To you I lift up my eyes,* to you enthroned in the heavens.

Psalm 123:1

The Greeting

I put my trust in your mercy;* my heart is joyful because of your saving help.

Psalm 13:5

The Hymn

O God of love, O King of peace,   Whom shall we trust but you, O Lord?
Make wars throughout the world to cease;   Where rest but on Your faithful word?
The wrath of sinful man restrain: None ever called on you in vain:
Give peace, O God, give peace again!   Give peace, O God, give peace again!

Remember, Lord, your works of old,   Where saints and angels dwell above,
The wonders that our fathers told;   All hearts are knit in holy love;
Remember not our sin's dark stain: O bind us in that heavenly chain:
Give peace, O God, give peace again!   Give peace, O God, give peace again!

Sir Henry W. Baker

The Refrain for the Vespers Lessons

For we are your people and the sheep of your pasture;* we will give you thanks
     for ever and show forth your praise from age to age.

Psalm 79:13

The Vespers Psalm   *Those Who Sowed with Tears Will Reap with Songs of Joy*

When the LORD restored the fortunes of Zion,* then were we like those who
     dream.
Then was our mouth filled with laughter,* and our tongue with shouts of joy.
Then they said among the nations,* "The LORD has done great things for them."
The LORD has done great things for us,* and we are glad indeed.
Restore our fortunes, O LORD,* like the watercourses of the Negev.
Those who sowed with tears* will reap with songs of joy.
Those who go out weeping, carrying the seed,* will come again with joy,
     shouldering their sheaves.

Psalm 126:1–7

The Refrain
For we are your people and the sheep of your pasture;* we will give you thanks
for ever and show forth your praise from age to age.

The Cry of the Church
O God, come to my assistance! O Lord, make haste to help me!

The Lord's Prayer

The Prayer Appointed for the Week
Almighty and everlasting God, increase in me the gifts of faith, hope, and charity;
and, that I may obtain what you promise, make me love what you command;
through Jesus Christ our Lord, who lives and reigns with you and the Holy
Spirit, one God, for ever and ever. *Amen.*†

The Concluding Prayer of the Church
May God, the Lord, bless us with heavenly benediction, and make us pure and
holy in his sight.
May the riches of his glory abound in us.
May He instruct us with the word of truth, inform us with the Gospel of salvation,
and enrich us with his love, Through Jesus Christ, our Lord.

Gelasian Sacramentary

The Morning Office   To Be Observed on the Hour or Half Hour
                                                Between 6 and 9 a.m.

The Call to Prayer
I will call upon God,* and the Lord will deliver me.
God, who is enthroned of old, will hear me.

Psalm 55:17, 20

The Request for Presence
Our God will come and will not keep silence;* before him there is a consuming
flame, and round about him a raging storm.

Psalm 50:3

The Greeting
For your Name's sake, O Lord,* forgive my sin, for it is great.

Psalm 25:10

The Refrain for the Morning Lessons
Help me, O Lord my God;* save me for your mercy's sake.

Psalm 109:25

A Reading
Jesus said: "For God sent his Son into the world not to judge the world, but so that
through him the world might be saved. No one who believes in him will be

judged; but whoever does not believe in him is judged already, because that person does not believe in the Name of God's only Son."

John 3:17–19

The Refrain
Help me, O Lord my God;* save me for your mercy's sake.

The Morning Psalm   *Let Them Offer a Sacrifice of Thanksgiving*
He sent forth his word and healed them* and saved them from the grave.
Let them give thanks to the Lord for his mercy* and the wonders he does for his children.
Let them offer a sacrifice of thanksgiving* and tell of his acts with shouts of joy.

Psalm 107:20–22

The Refrain
Help me, O Lord my God;* save me for your mercy's sake.

The Cry of the Church
O God, come to my assistance! O Lord, make haste to help me!

The Lord's Prayer

The Prayer Appointed for the Week
Almighty and everlasting God, increase in me the gifts of faith, hope, and charity; and, that I may obtain what you promise, make me love what you command; through Jesus Christ our Lord, who lives and reigns with you and the Holy Spirit, one God, for ever and ever. *Amen.*†

The Concluding Prayer of the Church
Lord God, almighty and everlasting Father, you have brought me in safety to this new day: Preserve me with your mighty power, that I may not fall into sin, nor be overcome by adversity; and in all I do direct me to the fulfilling of your purpose; through Jesus Christ my Lord. *Amen.*†

The Midday Office   To Be Observed on the Hour or Half Hour
                                     Between 11 a.m. and 2 p.m.

The Call to Prayer
Come, let us bow down, and bend the knee,* and kneel before the Lord, our Maker.
For he is our God, and we are the people of his pasture and the sheep of his hand.

Psalm 95:6–7

The Request for Presence
Hear my prayer, O God;* do not hide yourself from my petition.
Listen to me and answer me.

Psalm 55:1–2

The Greeting
"God, you know my foolishness,* and my faults are not hidden from you.
Answer me, O Lord, for your love is kind;* in your great compassion, turn to me."

Psalm 69:6ff

The Refrain for the Midday Lessons
Our sins are stronger than we are,* but you will blot them out.

Psalm 65:3

A Reading
This is the gospel concerning his Son who, in terms of human nature was born a
descendant of David and who, in terms of the Spirit and of holiness was desig-
nated Son of God in power by resurrection from the dead . . .

Romans 1:3–4

The Refrain
Our sins are stronger than we are,* but you will blot them out.

The Midday Psalm   *The Lord Is a Friend to Those Who Fear Him*
Who are they who fear the Lord?* he will teach them the way that they should
choose.
They shall dwell in prosperity,* and their offspring shall inherit the land.
The Lord is a friend to those who fear him* and will show them his covenant.

Psalm 25:11–13

The Refrain
Our sins are stronger than we are,* but you will blot them out.

The Cry of the Church
Even so, come, Lord Jesus!

The Lord's Prayer

The Prayer Appointed for the Week
Almighty and everlasting God, increase in me the gifts of faith, hope, and charity;
and, that I may obtain what you promise, make me love what you command;
through Jesus Christ our Lord, who lives and reigns with you and the Holy
Spirit, one God, for ever and ever. *Amen.†*

The Concluding Prayer of the Church
Almighty God, whose most dear Son went not up to joy before he first suffered
pain, and did not enter into glory before he was crucified: Mercifully grant that
I, walking in the way of the cross, may find it to be none other than the way of
life and peace; through Jesus Christ your Son my Lord. *Amen.†*

The Vespers Office   To Be Observed on the Hour or Half Hour
                                                    Between 5 and 8 p.m.

The Call to Prayer
Glory in his holy Name;* let the hearts of those who seek the LORD rejoice.
Psalm 105:3

The Request for Presence
For God alone my soul in silence waits;* truly, my hope is in him.
Psalm 62:6

The Greeting
Out of Zion, perfect in its beauty,* God reveals himself in glory.
Psalm 50:2

The Hymn   *O Zion, Haste*
O Zion, haste, your mission high fulfilling,
To tell to all the world that God is Light;
That He who made all nations is not willing
One soul should perish, lost in shades of night.
Publish glad tidings, tidings of peace,
Tidings of Jesus, redemption and release.

Proclaim to every people, tongue, and nation
That God, in whom they live and move, is Love:
Tell how He stooped to save His lost creation,
And died on earth that man might live above.
Publish glad tidings, tidings of peace,
Tidings of Jesus, redemption and release.

Give of your sons to bear the message glorious;
Give of your wealth to speed them on their way;
Pour out your soul for them in prayer victorious;
And all you spend dear Jesus will repay.
Publish glad tidings, tidings of peace,
Tidings of Jesus, redemption and release.
Mary Thomson

The Refrain for the Vespers Lessons
Let my mouth be full of your praise* and your glory all the day long.
Psalm 71:8

The Vespers Psalm   *The Heavens Declare the Glory of God*
The heavens declare the glory of God,* and the firmament shows his handiwork.
One day tells its tale to another,* and one night imparts knowledge to another.
Although they have no words or language,* and their voices are not heard,
Their sound has gone out into all lands,* and their message to the ends of the
    world.

In the deep has he set a pavilion for the sun;* it comes forth like a bridegroom out
   of his chamber; it rejoices like a champion to run its course.
It goes forth from the uttermost edge of the heavens and runs about to the end of it
   again;* nothing is hidden from its burning heat.

Psalm 19:1–6

The Refrain
Let my mouth be full of your praise* and your glory all the day long.

The Cry of the Church
Lord, have mercy upon us. Christ, have mercy upon us. Lord, have mercy upon us.

The Lord's Prayer

The Prayer Appointed for the Week
Almighty and everlasting God, increase in me the gifts of faith, hope, and charity;
   and, that I may obtain what you promise, make me love what you command;
   through Jesus Christ our Lord, who lives and reigns with you and the Holy
   Spirit, one God, for ever and ever. *Amen.*†

Concluding Prayers of the Church
Almighty God, who has promised to hear the petitions of those who ask in your
   Son's Name: I beseech you mercifully to incline your ear to me who have made
   my prayers and supplications to you; and grant that those things which I have
   faithfully asked according to your will, may effectually be obtained, to the
   relief of my necessity, and to setting forth of your glory; through Jesus Christ
   my Lord. *Amen.*†

May the souls of the faithful departed, through the mercy of God, rest in eternal
   peace. *Amen.*

The Morning Office   To Be Observed on the Hour or Half Hour
                                      Between 6 and 9 a.m.

The Call to Prayer
Bless the LORD, you angels of his, you mighty ones who do his bidding,* and hear-
   ken to the voice of his word.
Bless the LORD, all you hosts,* you ministers of his who do his will.
Bless the LORD, all you works of his, in all places of his dominion;* bless the LORD,
   O my soul.

Psalm 103:20–22

The Request for Presence
Give ear to my words, O LORD;* consider my meditation.
Hearken to my cry for help, my King and my God,* for I make my prayer to you.
In the morning, LORD, you hear my voice;* early in the morning I make my appeal
   and watch for you.

Psalm 5:1–3

The Greeting

O God, you will keep in perfect peace those whose minds are fixed on you; for in returning and rest we shall be saved; in quietness and trust shall be our strength.

adapted from Isaiah 26:3, 30:15

The Refrain for the Morning Lessons

The Lord's will stands fast for ever,* and the designs of his heart from age to age.

Psalm 33:11

A Reading   *At the end of October, and during the first two days of November, the Church honors the lives and witness of all its saints and commemorates the souls of the faithful departed.*

After that I saw a huge number, impossible for anyone to count, of people from every nation, race, tribe and language; they were standing in front of the throne and in front of the Lamb, dressed in white robes and holding palms in their hands. They shouted in a loud voice, 'Salvation to our God, who sits on the throne, and to the Lamb!' And all the angels who were standing in a circle round the throne, surrounding the elders and the four living creatures, prostrated themselves before the throne, and touched the ground with their foreheads, worshipping God with these words:

Amen. Praise and glory and wisdom,

thanksgiving and honor and power and strength

to our God for ever and ever. Amen.

One of the elders then spoke and asked me, 'Who are these people, dressed in white robes, and where have they come from?' I answered him, 'You can tell me, sir.' Then he said, 'These are the people who have been through the great trial; they have washed their robes white again in the blood of the Lamb. That is why they are standing in front of God's throne and serving him day and night in his sanctuary; and the One who sits on the throne will spread his tent over them. *They will never hunger or thirst again; sun and scorching wind will never plague them,* because the Lamb who is at the heart of the throne *will be their shepherd and will guide them to springs of living water;* and God will wipe away all tears from their eyes.

Revelation 7:9–17

The Refrain

The Lord's will stands fast for ever,* and the designs of his heart from age to age.

The Morning Psalm   *Who May Abide Upon Your Holy Hill*

Lord, who may dwell in your tabernacle?* who may abide upon your holy hill?

Whoever leads a blameless life and does what is right,* who speaks the truth from his heart.

There is no guile upon his tongue; he does no evil to his friend;* he does not heap contempt upon his neighbor.

In his sight the wicked is rejected,* but he honors those who fear the Lord.

He has sworn to do no wrong* and does not take back his word.

He does not give his money in hope of gain,* nor does he take a bribe against the
innocent.

Whoever does these things* shall never be overthrown.

Psalm 15

The Refrain
The LORD's will stands fast for ever,* and the designs of his heart from age to age.

The Small Verse
The people that walked in darkness have seen a great light; on those who have
lived in a land of deep shadow a light has shown.

Isaiah 9:1

The Lord's Prayer

The Prayer Appointed for the Week
Almighty and everlasting God, increase in me the gifts of faith, hope, and charity;
and, that I may obtain what you promise, make me love what you command;
through Jesus Christ our Lord, who lives and reigns with you and the Holy
Spirit, one God, for ever and ever. *Amen.*†

Concluding Prayers of the Church
Lord God, almighty and everlasting Father, you have brought me in safety to this
new day: Preserve me with your mighty power, that I may not fall into sin, nor
be overcome by adversity; and in all I do direct me to the fulfilling of your purpose; through Jesus Christ my Lord. *Amen.*†

May the souls of the faithful departed, through the mercy of God, rest in peace.
Amen.

The Midday Office   To Be Observed on the Hour or Half Hour
                                              Between 11 a.m. and 2 p.m.

The Call to Prayer
Hallelujah! How good it is to sing praises to our God!* how pleasant it is to honor
him with praise!

Psalm 147:1

The Request for Presence
Remember me, O LORD, with the favor you have for your people,* and visit me
with your saving help;

That I may see the prosperity of your elect and be glad with the gladness of your
people,* that I may glory with your inheritance.

Psalm 106:4–5

The Greeting
In you, O LORD, have I taken refuge;* let me never be ashamed.

Psalm 71:1

The Refrain for the Midday Lessons
Your statutes have been like songs to me* wherever I have lived like a stranger.

Psalm 119:54

A Reading
But what you have come to is Mount Zion and the city of the living God, the heavenly Jerusalem where the millions of angels have gathered for the festival, with the whole Church of first-born sons, enrolled as citizens of heaven. You have come to God himself, the supreme Judge, and to the spirits of the upright who have been made perfect.

Hebrews 12:22–24

The Refrain
Your statutes have been like songs to me* wherever I have lived like a stranger.

The Midday Psalm
The Lord loveth His foundation upon the holy mountains,* the gates of Sion more than all the tents of Jacob.
Glorious things are said of thee,* O city of God!
I will number Rahab and Babylon* among those avowing Me;
Behold the Philistines and Tyre and the people of Ethiopia* are gathered there.
Shall it not be said on Sion: "This man and that is born therein,* and the Most High Himself hath founded her?"
In His book the Lord recordeth nations and princes* who hail from there.
This is the joyous cry of all: "My dwelling is in thee!"

Psalm 86, THE SHORT BREVIARY

The Refrain
Your statutes have been like songs to me* wherever I have lived like a stranger.

The Cry of the Church
Lord, have mercy on us. Christ, have mercy on us. Lord, have mercy on us.

The Lord's Prayer

The Prayer Appointed for the Week
Almighty and everlasting God, increase in me the gifts of faith, hope, and charity; and, that I may obtain what you promise, make me love what you command; through Jesus Christ our Lord, who lives and reigns with you and the Holy Spirit, one God, for ever and ever. *Amen.*†

Concluding Prayers of the Church
Almighty God, you have knit together your elect in one communion and fellowship in the mystical body of your Son Christ our Lord: Give me grace so to follow your blessed saints in all virtuous and godly living, that I may come to those ineffable joys that you have prepared for those who truly love you; through Jesus Christ our Lord, who with you and the Holy Spirit lives and reigns, one God, in glory everlasting. *Amen.*†

Almighty God, who after the creation of the world rested from all your works and sanctified a day of rest for all your creatures: Grant that I, putting away all earthly anxieties, may be duly prepared for the service of public worship, and grant as well that my Sabbath upon earth may be a preparation for the eternal rest promised to your people in heaven; through Jesus Christ our Lord. *Amen.*†

The Vespers Office   To Be Observed on the Hour or Half Hour
                                                                   Between 5 and 8 p.m.

The Call to Prayer
Sing with joy to God our strength* and raise a loud shout to the God of Jacob.
Raise a song and sound the timbrel,* the merry harp and the lyre.
Blow the ram's-horn at the new moon,* and at the full moon, the day of our feast.
                                                                        Psalm 81:1–3

The Request for Presence
O God, do not be silent;* do not keep still nor hold your peace, O God.
                                                                        Psalm 83:1

The Greeting
I will sing of mercy and justice;* to you, O LORD, will I sing praises.
                                                                        Psalm 101:1

The Hymn   *Faith of Our Fathers*
     Faith of our fathers, living still,
     in spite of dungeon, fire and sword;
     O how our hearts beat high with joy
     whenever we hear that glorious word!
     Faith of our fathers, holy faith!
     We will be true to thee till death.

     Faith of our fathers, we will strive
     to win all nations unto thee;
     and through the truth that comes from God,
     we shall all then be truly free.
     Faith of our fathers, holy faith!
     We will be true to thee till death.

     Faith of our fathers, we will love,
     both friend and foe in all our strife;
     and preach you, too, as love knows how
     by kindly words and virtuous life.
     Faith of our fathers, holy faith!
     We will be true to thee till death.
                                    Fredrick Faber

The Refrain for the Vespers Lessons

I am like a green olive tree in the house of God;* I trust in the mercy of God for
ever and ever.

Psalm 52:8

The Vespers Psalm   *This Is Glory for All His Faithful People*

Let them praise his Name in the dance;* let them sing praise to him with timbrel
and harp.

For the LORD takes pleasure in his people* and adorns the poor with victory.

Let the praises of God be in their throat* . . . this is glory for all his faithful people.
Hallelujah!

Psalm 149:4–6a, 9b

The Refrain

I am like a green olive tree in the house of God;* I trust in the mercy of God for
ever and ever.

The Small Verse

The Lord is my shepherd and nothing is wanting to me. In green pastures He hath
settled me.

THE SHORT BREVIARY

The Lord's Prayer

The Prayer Appointed for the Week

Almighty and everlasting God, increase in me the gifts of faith, hope, and charity;
and, that I may obtain what you promise, make me love what you command;
through Jesus Christ our Lord, who lives and reigns with you and the Holy
Spirit, one God, for ever and ever. *Amen.*†

Concluding Prayers of the Church

Almighty and everlasting God, who has given us in one feast to venerate the merits of all Your saints, we beseech You through the multitude of intercessors, to
grant us the desired abundance of Your mercy. Through our Lord.

THE SHORT BREVIARY

Almighty God, who after the creation of the world rested from all your works and
sanctified a day of rest for all your creatures: Grant that I, putting away all
earthly anxieties, may be duly prepared for the service of public worship, and
grant as well that my Sabbath upon earth may be a preparation for the eternal
rest promised to your people in heaven; through Jesus Christ our Lord. *Amen.*†

May the souls of the faithful departed, through the mercy of God, rest in peace.
Amen.

October Compline

Sunday
The Night Office   To Be Observed Before Retiring

The Call to Prayer
May the Lord Almighty grant me and those I love a peaceful night and a perfect
    end. *Amen.*†

The Request for Presence
Our help is in the Name of the Lord; the maker of heaven and earth.

The Greeting
Almighty God, my heavenly Father: I have sinned against you, through my own
    fault, in thought, and word, and deed, and in what I have done and what I
    have left undone. For the sake of your Son our Lord Jesus Christ, forgive me all
    my offenses; and grant that I may serve you in newness of life, to the glory of
    your Name. *Amen.*†

The Reading   *from* DIVINA COMMEDIA
Oft have I seen at some cathedral door
A laborer, pausing in the dust and heat,
Lay down his burden, and with reverent feet
Enter, and cross himself, and on the floor
Kneel to repeat his paternoster o'er;
Far off noises of the world retreat;
The loud vociferations of the street
Become an indistinguishable roar.
So, as I enter here from day to day,
And leave my burden by this minster gate,
Kneeling in prayer, and not ashamed to pray,
The tumult of the time disconsolate
To inarticulate murmurs dies away,
While the eternal ages watch and wait.
                    Henry Wadsworth Longfellow

The Gloria

The Psalm   *The LORD Heard My Voice*
The breakers of death rolled over me,* and the torrents of oblivion made me afraid.
The cords of hell entangled me,* and the snares of death were set for me.
I called upon the LORD in my distress* and cried out to my God for help.
He heard my voice from his heavenly dwelling;* my cry of anguish came to his ears.
                                                    Psalm 18:4–7

The Gloria

The Small Verse
Into your hands, O Lord, I commend my spirit; for you have redeemed me, O
    Lord, O God of truth. Keep me, O Lord, as the apple of your eye; hide me
    under the shadow of your wings.†

The Lord's Prayer

The Petition

Watch, O Lord, with those who wake, or watch, or weep tonight, and give Your
angels and saints charge over those who sleep. Tend Your sick ones, O Lord
Christ. Rest Your weary ones. Bless Your dying ones. Soothe Your suffering
ones. Shield Your joyous ones, and all for Your love's sake. *Amen*.§

The Final Thanksgiving

Lord, you now have set your servant free to go in peace as you have promised; for
these eyes of mine have seen the Savior, whom you have prepared for all the
world to see: a Light to enlighten the nations, and the glory of your people
Israel. Glory to the Father, and to the Son, and to the Holy Spirit: as it was in the
beginning, is now, and will be for ever. *Amen.*

Monday
The Night Office   To Be Observed Before Retiring

The Call to Prayer

May the Lord Almighty grant me and those I love a peaceful night and a perfect
end. *Amen.*†

The Request for Presence

Our help is in the Name of the Lord; the maker of heaven and earth.

The Greeting

Almighty God, my heavenly Father: I have sinned against you, through my own
fault, in thought, and word, and deed, and in what I have done and what I
have left undone. For the sake of your Son our Lord Jesus Christ, forgive me all
my offenses; and grant that I may serve you in newness of life, to the glory of
your Name. *Amen.*†

The Reading

When we read the lives of the saints, we are struck by a certain large leisure which
went hand in hand with remarkable effectiveness. They were never hurried;
they did comparatively few things, and these not necessarily striking or impor-
tant; and they troubled very little about their influence. Yet they always
seemed to hit the mark; their simplest actions had a distinction, an exquisite-
ness that suggest the artist. The reason is not so far to seek. Their sainthood lay
in their habit of referring the smallest actions to God. They lived in God; they
acted from a pure motive of love towards God. They were free from self-regard
as from slavery to the good opinion of others. God saw and God rewarded:

what else did they need? They possessed God and possessed themselves in God. Hence the inalienable dignity of the meek, quiet figures that seem to produce such marvelous effects with such humble materials.

from CREATIVE PRAYER

The Gloria

The Psalm   *The LORD Shall Reign For Ever*

Happy are they who have the God of Jacob for their help!* whose hope is in the
    LORD their God;

Who made heaven and earth, the seas, and all that is in them;* who keeps his
    promise for ever;

Who gives justice to those who are oppressed,* and food to those who hunger.

The LORD sets the prisoners free; the LORD opens the eyes of the blind;* the LORD
    lifts up those who are bowed down;

The LORD loves the righteous; the LORD cares for the stranger;* he sustains the
    orphan and widow, but frustrates the way of the wicked.

The LORD shall reign for ever,* your God, O Zion, throughout all generations.
    Hallelujah!

Psalm 146:4–9

The Gloria

The Small Verse

Into your hands, O Lord, I commend my spirit; for you have redeemed me,
    O Lord, O God of truth. Keep me, O Lord, as the apple of your eye; hide me
    under the shadow of your wings.†

The Lord's Prayer

The Petition

Watch, O Lord, with those who wake, or watch, or weep tonight, and give Your
    angels and saints charge over those who sleep. Tend Your sick ones, O Lord
    Christ. Rest Your weary ones. Bless Your dying ones. Soothe Your suffering
    ones. Shield Your joyous ones, and all for Your love's sake. *Amen.*§

The Final Thanksgiving

Lord, you now have set your servant free to go in peace as you have promised; for
    these eyes of mine have seen the Savior, whom you have prepared for all the
    world to see: a Light to enlighten the nations, and the glory of your people
    Israel. Glory to the Father, and to the Son, and to the Holy Spirit: as it was in the
    beginning, is now, and will be for ever. *Amen.*

Tuesday
The Night Office   To Be Observed Before Retiring

The Call to Prayer
May the Lord Almighty grant me and those I love a peaceful night and a perfect
    end. *Amen.*✝

The Request for Presence
Our help is in the Name of the Lord; the maker of heaven and earth.

The Greeting
Almighty God, my heavenly Father: I have sinned against you, through my own
    fault, in thought, and word, and deed, and in what I have done and what I
    have left undone. For the sake of your Son our Lord Jesus Christ, forgive me all
    my offenses; and grant that I may serve you in newness of life, to the glory of
    your Name. *Amen.*✝

The Reading
Moses called all Israel together and said to them, 'Listen, Israel, to the laws and
    customs that I proclaim to you today. Learn them and take care to observe them.
'YAHWEH our God has made a covenant with us at Horeb. YAHWEH made this
    covenant not with our ancestors, but with us, with all of us alive here today. On
    the mountain, from the heart of the fire, YAHWEH spoke to you face to face, while
    I stood between you and YAHWEH to let you know what YAHWEH was saying,
    since you were afraid of the fire and had not gone up the mountain. He said:
' "I am YAHWEH your God who brought you out of Egypt, out of the place of slave-
    labor.
' "You will have no gods other than me.
' "You must not make yourselves any image or any likeness of anything in heaven
    above or on earth beneath or in the waters under the earth; you must not bow
    down to these gods or serve them. For I, YAHWEH your God, am a jealous God
    and I punish the parents' fault in the children, the grandchildren and the great-
    grandchildren, among those who hate me; but I show faithful love to thou-
    sands, to those who love me and keep my commandments.
' "You must not misuse the name of YAHWEH your God, for YAHWEH will not leave
    unpunished anyone who uses his name for what is false.
' "Observe the Sabbath day and keep it holy, as YAHWEH your God has com-
    manded you. Labor for six days, doing all your work, but the seventh day is a
    Sabbath for YAHWEH your God. You must not do any work that day, neither
    you, nor your son, nor your daughter, nor your servants—male or female—nor
    your ox, nor your donkey, nor any of your animals, nor the foreigner who has
    made a home with you; so that your servants male and female, may rest, as
    you do. Remember that you were once a slave in Egypt, and that YAHWEH your
    God brought you out of there with a mighty hand and outstretched arm; this is
    why YAHWEH your God has commanded you to keep the Sabbath day.

' "Honor your father and your mother, as YAHWEH your God has commanded you, so that you may have long life and may prosper in the country which YAHWEH your God is giving you.

' "You must not kill.

' "You must not commit adultery.

' "You must not steal.

' "You must not give false witness against your fellow.

' "You must not set your heart on your neighbor's spouse, you must not set your heart on your neighbor's house or field, or servant—man or woman—or ox, or donkey or any of your neighbor's possessions."

'These were the words YAHWEH spoke to you when you were all assembled on the mountain. Thunderously, he spoke to you from the heart of the fire, in cloud and thick darkness. He added nothing, but wrote them on two tablets of stone which he gave to me.'

Deuteronomy 5:1–22

The Gloria

The Psalm   *You Have Set My Heart at Liberty*

My soul cleaves to the dust;* give me life according to your word.

I have confessed my ways, and you answered me;* instruct me in your statutes.

Make me understand the way of your commandments,* that I may meditate on your marvelous works.

My soul melts away for sorrow;* strengthen me according to your word.

Take from me the way of lying;* let me find grace through your law.

I have chosen the way of faithfulness;* I have set your judgments before me.

I hold fast to your decrees;* O LORD, let me not be put to shame.

I will run the way of your commandments,* for you have set my heart at liberty.

Psalm 119:25–32

The Gloria

The Small Verse

Into your hands, O Lord, I commend my spirit; for you have redeemed me, O Lord, O God of truth. Keep me, O Lord, as the apple of your eye; hide me under the shadow of your wings.†

The Lord's Prayer

The Petition

Watch, O Lord, with those who wake, or watch, or weep tonight, and give Your angels and saints charge over those who sleep. Tend Your sick ones, O Lord Christ. Rest Your weary ones. Bless Your dying ones. Soothe Your suffering ones. Shield Your joyous ones, and all for Your love's sake. *Amen.*§

The Final Thanksgiving

Lord, you now have set your servant free to go in peace as you have promised; for these eyes of mine have seen the Savior, whom you have prepared for all the world to see: a Light to enlighten the nations, and the glory of your people Israel. Glory to the Father, and to the Son, and to the Holy Spirit: as it was in the beginning, is now, and will be for ever. *Amen.*

❧

Wednesday
The Night Office   To Be Observed Before Retiring

The Call to Prayer

May the Lord Almighty grant me and those I love a peaceful night and a perfect end. *Amen.*†

The Request for Presence

Our help is in the Name of the Lord; the maker of heaven and earth.

The Greeting

Almighty God, my heavenly Father: I have sinned against you, through my own fault, in thought, and word, and deed, and in what I have done and what I have left undone. For the sake of your Son our Lord Jesus Christ, forgive me all my offenses; and grant that I may serve you in newness of life, to the glory of your Name. *Amen.*†

The Reading

Though I speak with the tongues of men and of angels, and have not charity, I am become as sounding brass, or a tinkling cymbal. And though I have the gift of prophecy, and understand all mysteries, and all knowledge; and though I have all faith, so that I could remove mountains, and give my body to be burned, and have not charity, it profits me nothing. Charity suffers long, and is kind; charity envies not, charity vaunts not itself, is not puffed up, does not behave itself unseemly, seeks not her own, is not easily provoked, thinks no evil; rejoices not in iniquity, but rejoices in truth; bears all things, believes all things, hopes all things, endures all things. Charity never fails; but whether there be prophecies, they shall fail; whether there be tongues, they shall cease; whether there be knowledge, it shall vanish away. For we know in part, and we prophesy in part. But when that which is perfect is come, then that which is in part shall be done away.

1 Corinthians 13:1–10

The Gloria

The Psalm   *An Evening Song*

O LORD, you are my portion and my cup;* it is you who uphold my lot.
My boundaries enclose a pleasant land;* indeed, I have a goodly heritage.
I will bless the LORD who gives me counsel;* my heart teaches me night after night.

I have set the LORD always before me;* because he is at my right hand I shall not fall.

My heart, therefore, is glad, and my spirit rejoices;* my body also shall rest in hope.

For you will not abandon me to the grave,* nor let your holy one see the Pit.

You will show me the path of life;* in your presence is fullness of joy, and in your
   right hand are pleasures for evermore.

Psalm 16:5–11

The Gloria

The Small Verse

Into your hands, O Lord, I commend my spirit; for you have redeemed me,
   O Lord, O God of truth. Keep me, O Lord, as the apple of your eye; hide me
   under the shadow of your wings.†

The Lord's Prayer

The Petition

Watch, O Lord, with those who wake, or watch, or weep tonight, and give Your
   angels and saints charge over those who sleep. Tend Your sick ones, O Lord
   Christ. Rest Your weary ones. Bless Your dying ones. Soothe Your suffering
   ones. Shield Your joyous ones, and all for Your love's sake. *Amen.*§

The Final Thanksgiving

Lord, you now have set your servant free to go in peace as you have promised; for
   these eyes of mine have seen the Savior, whom you have prepared for all the
   world to see: a Light to enlighten the nations, and the glory of your people
   Israel. Glory to the Father, and to the Son, and to the Holy Spirit: as it was in the
   beginning, is now, and will be for ever. *Amen.*

Thursday
The Night Office   To Be Observed Before Retiring

The Call to Prayer

May the Lord Almighty grant me and those I love a peaceful night and a perfect
   end. *Amen.*†

The Request for Presence

Our help is in the Name of the Lord; the maker of heaven and earth.

The Greeting

Almighty God, my heavenly Father: I have sinned against you, through my own
   fault, in thought, and word, and deed, and in what I have done and what I

have left undone. For the sake of your Son our Lord Jesus Christ, forgive me all my offenses; and grant that I may serve you in newness of life, to the glory of your Name. *Amen.*†

The Reading   *The Rising*

Let us go forth,
In the goodness of our merciful Father,
In the gentleness of our brother Jesus,
In the radiance of his Holy Spirit,
In the faith of the apostles,
In the joyful praise of the angels,
In the holiness of the saints,
In the courage of the martyrs.

Let us go forth,
In the wisdom of our all-seeing Father,
In the patience of our all-loving brother,
In the truth of the all-knowing Spirit,
In the learning of the apostles,
In the gracious guidance of the angels,
In the patience of the saints,
In the self-control of the martyrs.

Such is the path of all servants of Christ,
The path from death to eternal life.

from CELTIC PRAYERS

The Gloria

The Psalm   *Your Loving-kindness Is Greater Than the Heavens*

Be merciful to me, O God, be merciful, for I have taken refuge in you;* in the
    shadow of your wings will I take refuge until this time of trouble has gone by.
My heart is firmly fixed, O God, my heart is fixed;* I will sing and make melody.
Wake up, my spirit; awake, lute and harp;* I myself will waken the dawn.
I will confess you among the peoples, O LORD;* I will sing praise to you among the
    nations.
For your loving-kindness is greater than the heavens,* and your faithfulness
    reaches to the clouds.
Exalt yourself above the heavens, O God,* and your glory over all the earth.

Psalm 57:1, 7–11

The Gloria

The Small Verse

Into your hands, O Lord, I commend my spirit; for you have redeemed me,
    O Lord, O God of truth. Keep me, O Lord, as the apple of your eye; hide me
    under the shadow of your wings.†

The Lord's Prayer

The Petition
Watch, O Lord, with those who wake, or watch, or weep tonight, and give Your angels and saints charge over those who sleep. Tend Your sick ones, O Lord Christ. Rest Your weary ones. Bless Your dying ones. Soothe Your suffering ones. Shield Your joyous ones, and all for Your love's sake. *Amen.*§

The Final Thanksgiving
Lord, you now have set your servant free to go in peace as you have promised; for these eyes of mine have seen the Savior, whom you have prepared for all the world to see: a Light to enlighten the nations, and the glory of your people Israel. Glory to the Father, and to the Son, and to the Holy Spirit: as it was in the beginning, is now, and will be for ever. *Amen.*

꙳

Friday
The Night Office   To Be Observed Before Retiring

The Call to Prayer
May the Lord Almighty grant me and those I love a peaceful night and a perfect end. *Amen.*†

The Request for Presence
Our help is in the Name of the Lord; the maker of heaven and earth.

The Greeting
Almighty God, my heavenly Father: I have sinned against you, through my own fault, in thought, and word, and deed, and in what I have done and what I have left undone. For the sake of your Son our Lord Jesus Christ, forgive me all my offenses; and grant that I may serve you in newness of life, to the glory of your Name. *Amen.*†

The Reading   *Litany of Penitence*
Most holy and merciful Father:
I confess to you and to the whole communion of saints in heaven and on earth.
I have not loved you with my whole heart, and mind, and strength. I have not loved my neighbors as myself. I have not forgiven others, as I have been forgiven.
Have mercy on me, Lord.
I have been deaf to your call to serve, as Christ served us. I have not been true to the mind of Christ. I have grieved your Holy Spirit.

Have mercy on me, Lord.

I confess to you, Lord, all my past unfaithfulness: the pride, hypocrisy, and impatience of my life,

I confess to you, Lord.

My self-indulgent appetites and ways, and my exploitation of other people,

I confess to you, Lord.

My anger at my own frustration, and my envy of those more fortunate than I,

I confess to you, Lord.

My intemperate love of worldly goods and comforts, and my dishonesty in daily life and work,

I confess to you, Lord.

My negligence in prayer and worship, and my failure to commend the faith that is in me,

I confess to you, Lord.

Accept my repentance, Lord, for the wrongs I have done: for my blindness to human need and suffering, and my indifference to injustice and cruelty,

Accept my repentance, Lord.

For all false judgments, for uncharitable thoughts toward my neighbors, and for my prejudice and contempt toward those who differ from me,

Accept my repentance, Lord.

For my waste and pollution of your creation, and my lack of concern for those who come after us,

Accept my repentance, Lord.

Restore me, good Lord, and let your anger depart from me,

Favorably hear me for your mercy is great.

Accomplish in me and all of your church the work of your salvation,

That I may show forth your glory in the world.

By the cross and passion of your Son our Lord,

Bring me with all your saints to the joy of his resurrection.†

The Gloria

The Psalm   *Have Pity on Me, LORD, For I Am Weak*

LORD, do not rebuke me in your anger;* do not punish me in your wrath.

Have pity on me, LORD, for I am weak;* heal me, LORD, for my bones are racked.

My spirit shakes with terror;* how long, O LORD, how long?

Turn, O LORD, and deliver me;* save me for your mercy's sake.

For in death no one remembers you;* and who will give you thanks in the grave?

I grow weary because of my groaning;* every night I drench my bed and flood my couch with tears.

My eyes are wasted with grief* and worn away because of all my enemies.

Depart from me, all evildoers,* for the LORD has heard the sound of my weeping.

The LORD has heard my supplication;* the LORD accepts my prayer.

Psalm 6:1–9

The Gloria

The Small Verse

Into your hands, O Lord, I commend my spirit; for you have redeemed me, O
Lord, O God of truth. Keep me, O Lord, as the apple of your eye; hide me
under the shadow of your wings.†

The Lord's Prayer

The Petition

Watch, O Lord, with those who wake, or watch, or weep tonight, and give Your
angels and saints charge over those who sleep. Tend Your sick ones, O Lord
Christ. Rest Your weary ones. Bless Your dying ones. Soothe Your suffering
ones. Shield Your joyous ones, and all for Your love's sake. *Amen.*§

The Final Thanksgiving

Lord, you now have set your servant free to go in peace as you have promised; for
these eyes of mine have seen the Savior, whom you have prepared for all the
world to see: a Light to enlighten the nations, and the glory of your people
Israel. Glory to the Father, and to the Son, and to the Holy Spirit: as it was in the
beginning, is now, and will be for ever. *Amen.*

Saturday
The Night Office   To Be Observed Before Retiring

The Call to Prayer

May the Lord Almighty grant me and those I love a peaceful night and a perfect
end. *Amen.*†

The Request for Presence

Our help is in the Name of the Lord; the maker of heaven and earth.

The Greeting

Almighty God, my heavenly Father: I have sinned against you, through my own
fault, in thought, and word, and deed, and in what I have done and what I
have left undone. For the sake of your Son our Lord Jesus Christ, forgive me all
my offenses; and grant that I may serve you in newness of life, to the glory of
your Name. *Amen.*†

The Reading   *The Angels Will Deliver Us*

When anyone prays, the angels that minister to God and watch over mankind
gather round about him and join him in his prayer. Nor is that all. Every
Christian—each of the "little ones" who are in the Church—has an angel of his
own, who "Always beholds the face of our Father which is in heaven"
(Matthew 18:10), and who looks upon the Godhead of the Creator. This angel

prays with us and works with us, as far as he can, to obtain the things for which we ask.

"The angel of the Lord," so it is written, "encamps beside those who fear the Lord and delivers them" (Psalm 33:8), while Jacob speaks of "the angel who delivers me from all evils" (Genesis 48:16): and what he says is true not of himself only but of all those who set their trust in God. It would seem, then, that when a number of faithful meet together genuinely for the glory of Christ, since they all fear the Lord, each of them will have, encamped beside him, his own angel whom God has appointed to guard him and care for him. So, when the saints are assembled, there will be a double Church, one of men and one of angels.

Origen of Alexandria

The Gloria

The Psalm   *He Shall Give His Angels Charge Over You*

Your eyes have only to behold* to see the reward of the wicked.

Because you have made the LORD your refuge,* and the Most High your habitation,

There shall no evil happen to you,* neither shall any plague come near your dwelling.

For he shall give his angels charge over you,* to keep you in all your ways.

They shall bear you in their hands,* lest you dash your foot against a stone.

You shall tread upon the lion and adder;* you shall trample the young lion and the serpent under your feet.

Psalm 91:8–13

The Gloria

The Small Verse

Into your hands, O Lord, I commend my spirit; for you have redeemed me, O Lord, O God of truth. Keep me, O Lord, as the apple of your eye; hide me under the shadow of your wings.†

The Lord's Prayer

The Petition

Watch, O Lord, with those who wake, or watch, or weep tonight, and give Your angels and saints charge over those who sleep. Tend Your sick ones, O Lord Christ. Rest Your weary ones. Bless Your dying ones. Soothe Your suffering ones. Shield Your joyous ones, and all for Your love's sake. *Amen.*§

The Final Thanksgiving

Lord, you now have set your servant free to go in peace as you have promised; for these eyes of mine have seen the Savior, whom you have prepared for all the world to see: a Light to enlighten the nations, and the glory of your people Israel. Glory to the Father, and to the Son, and to the Holy Spirit: as it was in the beginning, is now, and will be for ever. *Amen.*

The Gloria

Glory be to God the Father, God the Son, and God the Holy Spirit. As it was in the beginning, so it is now and so it shall ever be, world without end. Alleluia. *Amen.*

The Lord's Prayer

Our Father, who art in heaven, hallowed be your Name.
May your kingdom come, and your will be done, on earth as in heaven.
Give us today our daily bread.
Forgive us our sins as we forgive those who sin against us.
Lead us not into temptation, but deliver us from evil;
for yours are the kingdom and the power and the glory
forever and ever. *Amen.*

Compline Prayers for November Are Located on Page 275.

The Following Holy Days Occur in November:
The Feast of All Saints: *November 1*
The Feast of All Souls: *November 2*
The Feast of St. Andrew the Apostle: *November 30*
(The season of Advent, a time of preparation for the coming into human flesh of God among us, commences on the Sunday nearest to the Feast of St. Andrew the Apostle, November 30. The first Sunday of Advent is the first day of the Church's liturgical year.)

November

The Morning Office   To Be Observed on the Hour or Half Hour
                                      Between 6 and 9 a.m.

The Call to Prayer
Enter his gates with thanksgiving; go into his courts with praise;* give thanks to
    him and call upon his Name.

                                                                Psalm 100:3

The Request for Presence
Satisfy us by your loving-kindness in the morning* so shall we rejoice and be glad
    all the days of our life.

                                                                Psalm 90:14

The Greeting
I will give thanks to you, O Lord, with my whole heart;* I will tell of all your mar-
    velous works.
I will be glad and rejoice in you;* I will sing your Name, O Most High.

                                                                Psalm 9:1–2

The Refrain for the Morning Lessons
In God the Lord, whose word I praise, in God I trust and will not be afraid,* for
    what can mortals do to me?

                                                                Psalm 56:10

A Reading   *Although popular thinking tends to honor only the canonized,*
                        scripture names all Christians as "saints." To further empha-
                        size this truth, the Church on November 1 and 2 holds the
                        twin feasts of All Saints and All Souls in recognition of the
                        lives of all those who have kept the faith.

Jesus taught us, saying: "Do not store up treasures for yourselves on earth, where
    moth and woodworm destroy them and thieves can break in and steal. But
    store up treasures for yourselves in heaven, where neither moth nor wood-
    worm destroys them and thieves cannot break in and steal. For wherever your
    treasure is, there will your heart be too."

                                                                Matthew 6:19–21

The Refrain
In God the Lord, whose word I praise, in God I trust and will not be afraid,* for
    what can mortals do to me?

The Morning Psalm   *Bless the Lord, O My Soul*
Bless the Lord, you angels of his, you mighty ones who do his bidding,* and
    hearken to the voice of his word.
Bless the Lord, all you his hosts,* you ministers of his who do his will.
Bless the Lord, all you works of his, in all places of his dominion;* bless the Lord,
    O my soul.

                                                                Psalm 103:20–22

The Refrain

In God the LORD, whose word I praise, in God I trust and will not be afraid,* for
 what can mortals do to me?

The Gloria

The Lord's Prayer

The Prayer Appointed for the Week

Almighty and merciful God, it is only by your gift that your faithful people offer
 you true and laudable service: Grant that I may run without stumbling to
 obtain your heavenly promises; through Jesus Christ our Lord, who lives and
 reigns with you and the Holy Spirit, one God, now and for ever. *Amen.*†

Concluding Prayers of the Church

Almighty God, you have knit together your elect in one communion and fellowship in the mystical body of your Son Christ our Lord: Give me grace so to follow your blessed saints in all virtuous and godly living, that I may come to
 those ineffable joys that you have prepared for those who truly love you;
 through Jesus Christ our Lord. Who with you and the Holy Spirit lives and
 reigns, one God, in glory everlasting. *Amen.*†

Lord God, almighty and everlasting Father, you have brought me in safety to this
 new day: Preserve me with your mighty power, that I may not fall into sin, nor
 be overcome by adversity; and in all I do direct me to the fulfilling of your purpose; through Jesus Christ my Lord. *Amen.*†

May the souls of the faithful departed through the mercy of God rest in peace. *Amen.*

The Midday Office   To Be Observed on the Hour or Half Hour
                                             Between 11 a.m. and 2 p.m.

The Call to Prayer

Open my lips, O Lord,* and my mouth shall proclaim your praise.
Had you desired it, I would have offered sacrifice,* but you take no delight in
 burnt offerings.
The sacrifice of God is a troubled spirit;* and a broken and contrite heart, O God,
 you will not despise.

Psalm 51:16–18

The Request for Presence

Show us the light of your countenance, O God,* and come to us.

based on Psalm 67:1

The Greeting

You, O LORD, are my lamp;* my God, you make my darkness bright.
With you I will break down an enclosure;* with the help of my God I will scale any
 wall.

Psalm 18:29–30

The Refrain for the Midday Lessons

Happy are those who trust in the Lord!* they do not resort to evil spirits or turn to
false gods.

Psalm 40:4

A Reading

The saints in each generation are joined to those who have gone before, and are
filled like them with light to become a golden chain in which each saint is a
separate link, united to the next by faith, works and love. So in the one God
they form a single chain which cannot quickly be broken.

Simeon the New Theologian

The Refrain

Happy are those who trust in the Lord!* they do not resort to evil spirits or turn to
false gods.

The Midday Psalm   *Come and Listen*

Come and listen, all you who fear God,* and I will tell you what he has done for me.
I called out to him with my mouth,* and his praise was on my tongue.
If I had found evil in my heart,* the Lord would not have heard me;
But in truth God has heard me;* he has attended to the voice of my prayer.
Blessed be God, who has not rejected my prayer,* nor withheld his love from me.

Psalm 66:14–18

The Refrain

Happy are those who trust in the Lord!* they do not resort to evil spirits or turn to
false gods.

The Cry of the Church

Even so, come, Lord Jesus!

The Lord's Prayer

The Prayer Appointed for the Week

Almighty and merciful God, it is only by your gift that your faithful people offer
you true and laudable service: Grant that I may run without stumbling to
obtain your heavenly promises; through Jesus Christ our Lord, who lives and
reigns with you and the Holy Spirit, one God, now and for ever. *Amen.*†

Concluding Prayers of the Church

Almighty God, you have knit together your elect in one communion and fellowship in the mystical body of your Son Christ our Lord: Give me grace so to follow your blessed saints in all virtuous and godly living, that I may come to
those ineffable joys that you have prepared for those who truly love you;
through Jesus Christ our Lord. Who with you and the Holy Spirit lives and
reigns, one God, in glory everlasting. *Amen.*†

O God, you make me glad with the weekly remembrance of the glorious resurrection of your Son my Lord: Give me this day such blessing through my worship

of you, that the week to come may be spent in your favor; through Jesus Christ our Lord. *Amen.*†

May the souls of the faithful departed through the mercy of God rest in peace. *Amen.*

The Vespers Office   To Be Observed on the Hour or Half Hour
                                                    Between 5 and 8 p.m.

The Call to Prayer
Come let us bow down, and bend the knee* and kneel before the LORD our Maker.
For he is our God* and we are the people of his pasture and the sheep of his hand.

Psalm 95:6–7

The Request for Presence
I call upon you, O God, for you will answer me;* incline your ear to me, and hear my words.

Psalm 17:6

The Greeting
You are God: I praise you; you are the Lord: I acclaim you;
You are the eternal Father: all creation worships you.
Throughout the world the holy Church acclaims you: Father, of majesty unbounded, your true and only Son, worthy of all worship, and the Holy Spirit, advocate and guide.
As these have been from the beginning, so they are now and evermore shall be. Alleluia.

based on the Te Deum and Gloria

The Hymn

Let saints on earth in concert sing
With those whose work is done;
For all the servants of our King
In heaven and earth are one.

Jesus, be our constant guide;
Then, when the word is given,
Bid Jordan's narrow stream divide,
And bring us safe to heaven.

Charles Wesley

Even now by faith we join our hands
With those that went before,
And greet the ever living bands
On the eternal shore.

The Refrain for the Vespers Lessons
O, LORD, you are my portion and my cup;* it is you who uphold my lot.

Psalm 16:5

The Vespers Psalm   *When I Awake, I Shall Be Satisfied, Beholding Your Likeness*
My footsteps hold fast to the ways of your law;* in your paths my feet shall not stumble.

I call upon you, O God, for you will answer me;* incline your ear to me and hear
my words.
Show me your marvelous loving-kindness,* O Savior of those who take refuge at
your right hand from those who rise up against them.
Keep me as the apple of your eye;* hide me under the shadow of your wings,
Deliver me, O Lord, by your hand* from those whose portion in life is this world;
Whose bellies you fill with your treasure,* who are well supplied with children
and leave their wealth to their little ones.
But at my vindication I shall see your face;* when I awake, I shall be satisfied,
beholding your likeness.

Psalm 17:5–8, 14–16

The Refrain
O, Lord, you are my portion and my cup;* it is you who uphold my lot.

The Lord's Prayer

The Prayer Appointed for the Week
Almighty and merciful God, it is only by your gift that your faithful people offer
you true and laudable service: Grant that I may run without stumbling to
obtain your heavenly promises; through Jesus Christ our Lord, who lives and
reigns with you and the Holy Spirit, one God, now and for ever. *Amen.*†

Concluding Prayers of the Church
Almighty God, you have knit together your elect in one communion and fellowship in the mystical body of your Son Christ our Lord: Give me grace so to follow your blessed saints in all virtuous and godly living, that I may come to
those ineffable joys that you have prepared for those who truly love you;
through Jesus Christ our Lord. Who with you and the Holy Spirit lives and
reigns, one God, in glory everlasting. *Amen.*†

Lord Jesus, stay with me, for evening is at hand and the day is past; be my companion in the way, kindle my heart, and awaken hope, that I may know you as
you are revealed in Scripture and in the breaking of bread. Grant this for the
sake of your love toward me. *Amen.*†

May the souls of the faithful departed through the mercy of God rest in peace.
Amen.

The Morning Office   To Be Observed on the Hour or Half Hour
                                             Between 6 and 9 a.m.

The Call to Prayer
Worship the Lord in the beauty of holiness;* let the whole earth tremble before
him.

Psalm 96:9

The Request for Presence *New Day*

This new day you give to me
From your great eternity
This new day now enfold
Me in your loving hold

You are the star of the morn
You are the day newly born
You are the light of our night
You are the Savior by your might

God be in me this day
God ever with me stay
God be in the night
Keep us by thy light
God be in my heart
God abide, never depart.
David Adam

The Greeting

The LORD lives! Blessed is my Rock!* Exalted is the God of my salvation!
Psalm 18:46

The Refrain for the Morning Lessons

The fool has said in his heart, "There is no God."
Psalm 14:1

A Reading

Although popular thinking tends to honor only the canonized, scripture names all Christians as "saints." To further emphasize this truth, the Church on November 1 and 2 holds the twin feasts of All Saints and All Souls in recognition of the lives of all those who have kept the faith.

Jesus taught us, saying: "Everyone whom the Father gives me will come to me; I will certainly not reject anyone who comes to me, because I have come from heaven, not to do my will, but to do the will of him who sent me. Now the will of him who sent me is that I should lose nothing of all that he has given to me, but that I should raise it up on the last day. It is my Father's will that whoever sees the Son and believes in him should have eternal life, and that I should raise that person on the last day."

John 6:37–40

The Refrain

The fool has said in his heart, "There is no God."

The Morning Psalm *This Is My Prayer to You*

But as for me, this is my prayer to you,* at the time you have set, O LORD:
"In your great mercy, O God,* answer me with your unfailing help.
Save me from the mire; do not let me sink;* let me be rescued from those who hate
    me and out of the deep waters.
Let not the torrent of waters wash over me, neither let the deep swallow me up;*
    do not let the Pit shut its mouth upon me.
Answer me, O LORD, for your love is kind;* in your great compassion, turn to me."
Psalm 69:14–18

The Refrain
The fool has said in his heart, "There is no God."

The Cry of the Church
O God, come to my assistance! O Lord, make haste to help me!

The Lord's Prayer

The Prayer Appointed for the Week
Almighty and merciful God, it is only by your gift that your faithful people offer
you true and laudable service: Grant that I may run without stumbling to
obtain your heavenly promises; through Jesus Christ our Lord, who lives and
reigns with you and the Holy Spirit, one God, now and for ever. *Amen.*†

Concluding Prayers of the Church
Almighty God, with whom still live the spirits of those who die in the Lord, and
with whom the souls of the faithful are in joy and felicity: I give you heartfelt
thanks for the good examples of all your servants, who, having finished their
course in faith, now find rest and refreshment. May I, with all who have died in
the true faith of your Holy Name, have perfect fulfillment and bliss in your
eternal and everlasting glory; through Jesus Christ my Lord. *Amen.*†

Lord God, almighty and everlasting Father, you have brought me in safety to this
new day: Preserve me with your mighty power, that I may not fall into sin, nor
be overcome by adversity; and in all I do direct me to the fulfilling of your purpose; through Jesus Christ my Lord. *Amen.*†

May the souls of the faithful departed through the mercy of God rest in peace.
Amen.

The Midday Office To Be Observed on the Hour or Half Hour
Between 11 a.m. and 2 p.m.

The Call to Prayer
Hallelujah! Sing to the LORD a new song;* sing his praise in the congregation of the
faithful.
Let Israel rejoice in his Maker;* let the children of Zion be joyful in their King.
Let them praise his Name in the dance;* let them sing praise to him with timbrel
and harp.
For the LORD takes pleasure in his people* and adorns the poor with victory.

Psalm 149:1–4

The Request for Presence
Restore us, O God of hosts;* show the light of your countenance, and we shall be
saved.

Psalm 80:7

The Greeting

Not to us, O LORD, not to us, but to your Name give glory;* because of your love
and because of your faithfulness.

Psalm 115:1

The Refrain for the Midday Lessons

Righteousness and justice are the foundations of your throne;* love and truth go
before your face.

Psalm 89:14

A Reading

What I am saying, brothers, is that mere human nature cannot inherit the kingdom
of God: what is perishable cannot inherit what is imperishable. Now I am
going to tell you a mystery: we are not all going to fall asleep, but we are all
going to be changed, instantly, in the twinkling of an eye, when the last trumpet sounds. The trumpet is going to sound, and then the dead will be raised
imperishable, and we shall be changed, because this perishable nature of ours
must put on imperishability, this mortal nature must put on immortality.

1 Corinthians 15:50–53

The Refrain

Righteousness and justice are the foundations of your throne;* love and truth go
before your face.

The Midday Psalm   *He Redeems Your Life from the Grave*

Bless the LORD, O my soul,* and all that is within me, bless his holy Name.
Bless the LORD, O my soul,* and forget not all his benefits.
He forgives all your sins* and heals all your infirmities;
He redeems your life from the grave* and crowns you with mercy and loving-
kindness;
He satisfies you with good things,* and your youth is renewed like an eagle's.

Psalm 103:1–5

The Refrain

Righteousness and justice are the foundations of your throne;* love and truth go
before your face.

The Gloria

The Lord's Prayer

The Prayer Appointed for the Week

Almighty and merciful God, it is only by your gift that your faithful people offer
you true and laudable service: Grant that I may run without stumbling to
obtain your heavenly promises; through Jesus Christ our Lord, who lives and
reigns with you and the Holy Spirit, one God, now and for ever. *Amen.*†

Concluding Prayers of the Church

Almighty God, with whom still live the spirits of those who die in the Lord, and
with whom the souls of the faithful are in joy and felicity: I give you heartfelt

thanks for the good examples of all your servants, who, having finished their course in faith, now find rest and refreshment. May I, with all who have died in the true faith of your Holy Name, have perfect fulfillment and bliss in your eternal and everlasting glory; through Jesus Christ my Lord. *Amen.*†

God, you have prepared in peace the path I must follow today. Help me to walk straight on that path. If I speak, remove lies from my lips. If I am hungry, take away from me all complaint. If I have plenty, destroy pride in me. May I go through the day calling on you, you, O Lord, who know no other Lord.

Ethiopian

May the souls of the faithful departed through the mercy of God rest in peace. *Amen.*

The Vespers Office   To Be Observed on the Hour or Half Hour
                                                  Between 5 and 8 p.m.

The Call to Prayer
The righteous will be glad . . .
And they will say, "Surely, there is a reward for the righteous;* surely, there is a God who rules in the earth."

Psalm 58:10–11

The Request for Presence
Make me understand the way of your commandments,* that I may meditate on your marvelous works.

Psalm 119:27

The Greeting
You have made me glad by your acts, O LORD;* and I shout for joy because of the works of your hands.

Psalm 92:4

The Hymn   *The Church's One Foundation*
The Church's one foundation is Jesus Christ her Lord;
She is his new creation by water and the word;
From heaven he came and sought her to be his holy bride;
With his own blood he bought her, and for her life he died.

Elect from every nation, yet one o'er all the earth,
Her charter of salvation: one Lord, one faith, one birth;
One holy name she blesses, partakes one holy food.
And to one hope she presses, with every grace endued.

Though with a scornful wonder this world sees her oppressed,
By schisms rent asunder, by heresies distressed,
Yet saints their watch are keeping; Their cry goes up: "How long?"
And soon the night of weeping shall be the morn of song.

Mid toil and tribulation, and tumult of her war,
She waits the consummation of peace forevermore;
Till with the vision glorious her longing eyes are blest,
And the great church victorious shall be a church at rest.

Yet she on earth has union with God the Three in One,
And mystic sweet communion with those whose rest is won:
O happy ones and holy! Lord, give us grace that we,
Like them, the meek and lowly, may live eternally.

Samuel J. Stone

The Refrain for the Vespers Lessons
My mouth shall speak of wisdom,* and my heart shall meditate on understanding.

Psalm 49:2

The Vespers Psalm   *Your Wonders Are More Than I Can Count*
Great things are they that you have done, O LORD my God! how great your
    wonders and your plans for us!* there is none who can be compared with you.
Oh, that I could make them known and tell them!* but they are more than I can
    count.

Psalm 40:5–6

The Refrain
My mouth shall speak of wisdom,* and my heart shall meditate on understanding.

The Gloria

The Lord's Prayer

The Prayer Appointed for the Week
Almighty and merciful God, it is only by your gift that your faithful people offer
    you true and laudable service: Grant that I may run without stumbling to
    obtain your heavenly promises; through Jesus Christ our Lord, who lives and
    reigns with you and the Holy Spirit, one God, now and for ever. *Amen.*†

Concluding Prayers of the Church
Almighty God, with whom still live the spirits of those who die in the Lord, and
    with whom the souls of the faithful are in joy and felicity: I give you heartfelt
    thanks for the good examples of all your servants, who, having finished their
    course in faith, now find rest and refreshment. May I, with all who have died in
    the true faith of your Holy Name, have perfect fulfillment and bliss in your
    eternal and everlasting glory; through Jesus Christ my Lord. *Amen.*†

O God, the King eternal, whose light divides the day from the night and turns the
    shadow of death into the morning: Drive far from me all wrong desires, incline
    my heart to keep your law, and guide my feet into the way of peace; that, hav-
    ing done your will with cheerfulness during the day, I may, when night comes,
    rejoice to give you thanks; through Jesus Christ my Lord. *Amen.*†

May the souls of the faithful departed through the mercy of God rest in peace. *Amen.*

The Morning Office

To Be Observed on the Hour or Half Hour
Between 6 and 9 a.m.

The Call to Prayer
Be glad, you righteous, and rejoice in the LORD;* shout for joy, all who are true of
heart.

Psalm 32:12

The Request for Presence
Open my eyes, that I may see* the wonders of your law.
Psalm 119:18

The Greeting
With my whole heart I seek you;* let me not stray from your commandments.
Psalm 119:10

The Refrain for the Morning Lessons
I hate those who have a divided heart,* but your law do I love.
Psalm 119:113

A Reading
Jesus taught us, saying: "Be on your guard, stay awake, because you never know
when the time will come. It is like a man travelling abroad: he has gone from
his home, and left his servants in charge, each with his own work to do; and he
has told the doorkeeper to stay awake. So stay awake, because you do not
know when the master of the house is coming, evening, midnight, cockcrow of
dawn; if he comes unexpectedly, he must not find you asleep. And what I am
saying to you I say to all: Stay awake!"

Mark 13:33–37

The Refrain
I hate those who have a divided heart,* but your law do I love.

The Morning Psalm   *He Brought Them to the Harbor They Were Bound For*
Some went down to the sea in ships* and plied their trade in deep waters;
They behold the works of the LORD* and his wonder in the deep.
Then he spoke, and a stormy wind arose,* which tossed high the waves of the sea.
They mounted up to the heavens and fell back to the depths;* their hearts melted
because of their peril.
They reeled and staggered like drunkards* and were at their wits' end.
Then they cried to the LORD in their trouble,* and he delivered them from their
distress.
He stilled the storm to a whisper* and quieted the waves of the sea.
Then they were glad because of the calm,* and he brought them to the harbor they
were bound for.
Let them give thanks to the LORD for his mercy* and the wonders he does for his
children.

Let them exalt him in the congregation of the people* and praise him in the council of the elders.

Psalm 107:23–32

The Refrain
I hate those who have a divided heart,* but your law do I love.

The Small Verse
The Lord is my shepherd and nothing is wanting to me. In green pastures He has settled me.

THE SHORT BREVIARY

The Lord's Prayer

The Prayer Appointed for the Week
Almighty and merciful God, it is only by your gift that your faithful people offer you true and laudable service: Grant that I may run without stumbling to obtain your heavenly promises; through Jesus Christ our Lord, who lives and reigns with you and the Holy Spirit, one God, now and for ever. *Amen.*†

The Concluding Prayer of the Church
Lord God, almighty and everlasting Father, you have brought me in safety to this new day: Preserve me with your mighty power, that I may not fall into sin, nor be overcome by adversity; and in all I do direct me to the fulfilling of your purpose; through Jesus Christ my Lord. *Amen.*†

The Midday Office

To Be Observed on the Hour or Half Hour
Between 11 a.m. and 2 p.m.

The Call to Prayer
Sing to him, sing praise to him,* and speak of all his marvelous works.

Psalm 105:2

The Request for Presence
Let your countenance shine upon your servant* and teach me your statutes.

Psalm 119:135

The Greeting
Let all who seek you rejoice and be glad in you;* let those who love your salvation say for ever, "Great is the LORD!"

Psalm 70:4

The Refrain for the Midday Lessons
Happy are those who act with justice* and always do right!

Psalm 106:3

A Reading
'Come, let us talk this over,' says YAHWEH. 'Though your sins are like scarlet, they shall be white as snow; though they are red as crimson, they shall be like wool.

If you are willing to obey, you shall eat the good things of the earth. But if you refuse and rebel, the sword shall eat you instead—for Yahweh's mouth has spoken.'

Isaiah 1:18–20

The Refrain
Happy are those who act with justice* and always do right!

The Midday Psalm   *You Are My Refuge and My Stronghold*
He who dwells in the shelter of the Most High,* abides under the shadow of the
   Almighty.
He shall say to the Lord, "You are my refuge and my stronghold,* my God in
   whom I put my trust."
He shall deliver you from the snare of the hunter* and from the deadly pestilence.
He shall cover you with his pinions, and you shall find refuge under his wings;*
   his faithfulness shall be a shield and buckler.
You shall not be afraid of any terror by night,* nor of the arrow that flies by day;
Of the plague that stalks in the darkness,* nor of the sickness that lays waste at
   mid-day.

Psalm 91:1–6

The Refrain
Happy are those who act with justice* and always do right!

The Gloria

The Lord's Prayer

The Prayer Appointed for the Week
Almighty and merciful God, it is only by your gift that your faithful people offer
   you true and laudable service: Grant that I may run without stumbling to
   obtain your heavenly promises; through Jesus Christ our Lord, who lives and
   reigns with you and the Holy Spirit, one God, now and for ever. *Amen.*†

The Concluding Prayer of the Church
God of mercy,
this midday moment of rest
is your welcome gift.
Bless the work we have begun,
make good its defects
and let us finish it in a way that pleases you.
Grant this through Christ our Lord. *Amen.*

The Liturgy of the Hours, vol. I

The Vespers Office   To Be Observed on the Hour or Half Hour
                                   Between 5 and 8 p.m.

The Call to Prayer
I will bless the Lord at all times;* his praise shall ever be in my mouth.

Psalm 34:1

The Request for Presence
Your word is a lantern to my feet* and a light upon my path.
Accept, O Lord, the willing tribute of my lips,* and teach me your judgments.

Psalm 119:105ff

The Greeting
You, O Lord, are my lamp;* my God, you make my darkness bright.

Psalm 18:29

The Hymn

Giver of life, eternal Lord,	To God the Father, God the Son
Your own redeemed defend.	And God the Spirit, three in one,
Mother of grace, your children save	Praise, honor, might and glory be
And help them to the end.	From age to age eternally.

adapted from The Short Breviary

All you who high above the stars
In heavenly glory reign!
May we through your prevailing prayers
Unto your joys attain.

The Refrain for the Vespers Lessons
Your love, O Lord, for ever will I sing;* from age to age my mouth will proclaim
   your faithfulness.

Psalm 89:1

The Vespers Psalm   *A Broken and Contrite Heart, O God, You Will Not Despise*
Open my lips, O Lord,* and my mouth shall proclaim your praise.
Had you desired it, I would have offered sacrifice,* but you take no delight in
   burnt-offerings.
The sacrifice of God is a troubled spirit;* a broken and contrite heart, O God, you
   will not despise.

Psalm 51:16–18

The Refrain
Your love, O Lord, for ever will I sing;* from age to age my mouth will proclaim
   your faithfulness.

The Gloria

The Lord's Prayer

The Prayer Appointed for the Week

Almighty and merciful God, it is only by your gift that your faithful people offer
you true and laudable service: Grant that I may run without stumbling to
obtain your heavenly promises; through Jesus Christ our Lord, who lives and
reigns with you and the Holy Spirit, one God, now and for ever. *Amen.*†

The Concluding Prayer of the Church

Protect me, Lord, as I stay awake; watch over me as I sleep, that awake I may
watch with Christ, and asleep, rest in his peace. *Amen.*

The Morning Office   To Be Observed on the Hour or Half Hour
                                            Between 6 and 9 a.m.

The Call to Prayer

Sing to the LORD with the harp,* with the harp and the voice of song.
With trumpets and the sound of the horn* shout with joy before the King, the
LORD.

Psalm 98:6–7

The Request for Presence

Our soul waits for the LORD;* he is our help and our shield.
Indeed, our heart rejoices in him,* for in his holy Name we put our trust.
Let your loving-kindness, O LORD, be upon us,* as we have put our trust in you.

Psalm 33:20–22

The Greeting

How deep I find your thoughts, O God!* how great is the sum of them!
If I were to count them, they would be more in number than the sand;* to count
them all, my life span would need to be like yours.

Psalm 139:16–17

The Refrain for the Morning Lessons

The LORD has sworn an oath to David;* in truth, he will not break it:
"A son, the fruit of your body* will I set upon your throne."

Psalm 132:11–12

A Reading

Concerning the commandments, Jesus taught us, saying: "This is the first: *Listen,
Israel, the Lord our God is the One, only Lord, and you must love the Lord your God
with all your heart, with all your soul,* with all your mind, *and with all your
strength.* The second is this: *You must love your neighbor as yourself.* There is no
commandment greater than these."

Mark 12:29–31

The Refrain

The LORD has sworn an oath to David;* in truth, he will not break it:
"A son, the fruit of your body* will I set upon your throne."

The Morning Psalm   *I Will Walk with Sincerity of Heart*

I will sing of mercy and justice;* to you, O LORD, will I sing praises.

I will strive to follow a blameless course; oh, when will you come to me?* I will
   walk with sincerity of heart within my house.

I will set no worthless thing before my eyes;* I hate the doers of evil deeds; they
   shall not remain with me.

A crooked heart shall be far from me;* I will not know evil.

Those who in secret slander their neighbors I will destroy;* those who have a
   haughty look and a proud heart I cannot abide.

Psalm 101:1–5

The Refrain

The LORD has sworn an oath to David;* in truth, he will not break it:
"A son, the fruit of your body* will I set upon your throne."

The Gloria

The Lord's Prayer

The Prayer Appointed for the Week

Almighty and merciful God, it is only by your gift that your faithful people offer
   you true and laudable service: Grant that I may run without stumbling to
   obtain your heavenly promises; through Jesus Christ our Lord, who lives and
   reigns with you and the Holy Spirit, one God, now and for ever. *Amen.*†

The Concluding Prayer of the Church

Lord God, almighty and everlasting Father, you have brought me in safety to this
   new day: Preserve me with your mighty power, that I may not fall into sin, nor
   be overcome by adversity; and in all I do direct me to the fulfilling of your purpose; through Jesus Christ my Lord. *Amen.*†

The Midday Office   To Be Observed on the Hour or Half Hour
                                       Between 11 a.m. and 2 p.m.

The Call to Prayer

Sing to the LORD with thanksgiving;* make music to our God upon the harp.

Psalm 147:7

The Request for Presence

Hear the voice of my prayer when I cry out to you,* when I lift up my hands to
   your holy of holies.

Psalm 28:2

The Greeting

You are the LORD, most high over all the earth;* you are exalted far above all gods.

Psalm 97:9

The Refrain for the Midday Lessons

Tell it out among all the nations: "The Lord is King!* he has made the world so firm that it cannot be moved; he will judge all the peoples with equity."

Psalm 96:10

A Reading

The brother of our Lord wrote, saying: "Remember this, my dear brothers: everyone should be quick to listen but slow to speak and slow to human anger; God's saving justice is never served by human anger; so do away with all impurities and remnants of evil. Humbly welcome the Word which has been planted in you and can save your souls."

James 1:19–21

The Refrain

Tell it out among all the nations: "The Lord is King!* he has made the world so firm that it cannot be moved; he will judge all the peoples with equity."

The Midday Psalm   *Righteousness and Justice Are the Foundations of His Throne*

The Lord is King; let the earth rejoice;* let the multitude of the isles be glad.

Clouds and darkness are round about him,* righteousness and justice are the foundations of his throne.

A fire goes before him* and burns up his enemies on every side.

His lightnings light up the world;* the earth sees it and is afraid.

The mountains melt like wax at the presence of the Lord,* at the presence of the Lord of the whole earth.

The heavens declare his righteousness,* and all the peoples see his glory.

Psalm 97:1–6

The Refrain

Tell it out among all the nations: "The Lord is King!* he has made the world so firm that it cannot be moved; he will judge all the peoples with equity."

The Small Verse

Happy are the people whose strength is in you!* whose hearts are set on the pilgrims' way,

For one day in your courts is better than a thousand in my own room,* and to stand at the threshold of the house of my God than to dwell in the tents of the wicked.

Psalm 84:4, 9

The Lord's Prayer

The Prayer Appointed for the Week

Almighty and merciful God, it is only by your gift that your faithful people offer you true and laudable service: Grant that I may run without stumbling to obtain your heavenly promises; through Jesus Christ our Lord, who lives and reigns with you and the Holy Spirit, one God, now and for ever. *Amen.*†

The Concluding Prayer of the Church

Let us bless the Lord God living and true! Let us always render him praise, glory, honor, blessing, and all good things! Amen. Amen. So be it! So be it!

St. Francis of Assisi

The Vespers Office   To Be Observed on the Hour or Half Hour
                                       Between 5 and 8 p.m.

The Call to Prayer

Be glad, you righteous, and rejoice in the LORD;* shout for joy, all who are true of heart.

Psalm 32:12

The Request for Presence

Exalt yourself above the heavens, O God,* and your glory over all the earth.

Psalm 57:11

The Greeting

May God give us his blessing,* and may all the ends of the earth stand in awe of him.

Psalm 67:7

The Hymn   *Come Holy Dove*

When I feel alone   When I am sad
Your presence is ever with me.   Your joy will make me glad.
Come Holy Dove   Come Holy Dove
Cover with love   Cover with love

When I am in the dark   When I am sick and ill
Your light is all around me.   Your health will heal me still.
Come Holy Dove   Come Holy Dove
Cover with love   Cover with love

When I am in the cold   Spirit be about my head
Your warmth will enfold me.   Spirit peace around me shed
Come Holy Dove   Spirit light about my way
Cover with love   Spirit guardian night and day

When I feel weak   Come Holy Dove
Your strength will seek me.   Cover with love
Come Holy Dove
Cover with love   *David Adam*

The Refrain for the Vespers Lessons

Let your ways be known upon earth,* your saving health among all nations.

Psalm 67:2

The Vespers Psalm

Hear my plea of innocence, O LORD; give heed to my cry;* listen to my prayer, which does not come from lying lips.

Let my vindication come forth from your presence;* let your eyes be fixed on justice.

Weigh my heart, summon me by night,* melt me down; you will find no impurity in me.

I give no offense with my mouth as others do;* I have heeded the words of your lips.

Psalm 17:1–5

The Refrain

Let your ways be known upon earth,* your saving health among all nations.

The Cry of the Church

In the evening, in the morning, and at noonday, I will complain and lament,* and he will hear my voice.

Psalm 55:18

The Lord's Prayer

The Prayer Appointed for the Week

Almighty and merciful God, it is only by your gift that your faithful people offer you true and laudable service: Grant that I may run without stumbling to obtain your heavenly promises; through Jesus Christ our Lord, who lives and reigns with you and the Holy Spirit, one God, now and for ever. *Amen.*†

The Concluding Prayer of the Church

Almighty and eternal God, rulers of all things in heaven and earth: Mercifully accept the prayers of your people everywhere, and strengthen each of us to do your will; through Jesus Christ my Lord. *Amen.*†

The Morning Office   **To Be Observed on the Hour or Half Hour**
                                       Between 6 and 9 a.m.

The Call to Prayer

Wake up, my spirit; awake lute and harp;* I myself will waken the dawn.

Psalm 57:8

The Request for Presence

You are the LORD; do not withhold your compassion from me;* let your love and your faithfulness keep me safe forever,

Psalm 40:12

The Greeting

My heart is firmly fixed, O God, my heart is fixed;* I will sing and make melody.

Psalm 57:7

The Refrain for the Morning Lessons

Cast your burden upon the LORD, and he will sustain you;* he will never let the righteous stumble.

Psalm 55:24

A Reading

Jesus went on to say, 'What is the kingdom of God like? What shall I compare it with? It is like a mustard seed which a man took and threw into his garden: it grew and became a tree, and the birds of the air sheltered in its branches.'

Luke 13:18–19

The Refrain

Cast your burden upon the LORD, and he will sustain you;* he will never let the righteous stumble.

The Morning Psalm   *May the LORD Strengthen You Out of Zion*

May the LORD answer you in the day of trouble,* the Name of the God of Jacob defend you;

Send you help from his holy place* and strengthen you out of Zion;

Remember all your offerings* and accept your burnt sacrifice;

Grant you your heart's desire* and prosper all your plans.

We will shout for joy at your victory and triumph in the Name of our God;* may the LORD grant all your requests.

Psalm 20:1–5

The Refrain

Cast your burden upon the LORD, and he will sustain you;* he will never let the righteous stumble.

The Small Verse

My soul thirsts for the strong, living God and all that is within me cries out to him.

The Lord's Prayer

The Prayer Appointed for the Week

Almighty and merciful God, it is only by your gift that your faithful people offer you true and laudable service: Grant that I may run without stumbling to obtain your heavenly promises; through Jesus Christ our Lord, who lives and reigns with you and the Holy Spirit, one God, now and for ever. *Amen.*†

The Concluding Prayer of the Church

Lord God, almighty and everlasting Father, you have brought me in safety to this new day: Preserve me with your mighty power, that I may not fall into sin, nor be overcome by adversity; and in all I do direct me to the fulfilling of your purpose; through Jesus Christ my Lord. *Amen.*†

The Midday Office   To Be Observed on the Hour or Half Hour
                                     Between 11 a.m. and 2 p.m.

The Call to Prayer
Be strong and let your heart take courage,* all you who wait for the LORD.
                                                    Psalm 31:24

The Request for Presence
Hear my cry, O God,* and listen to my prayer.
I call upon you from the ends of the earth.
                              Psalm 61:1–2

The Greeting
I love you, O LORD of my strength,* O LORD my stronghold, my crag, and my
    haven.
                                                    Psalm 18:1

The Refrain for the Midday Lessons
Though my father and my mother forsake me,* the LORD will sustain me.
                                                    Psalm 27:14

A Reading
The prayer of the Apostle: "May the God of peace make you perfect and holy; and
    may your spirit, life and body be kept blameless for the coming of our Lord
    Jesus Christ."
                                                    1 Thessalonians 5:23

The Refrain
Though my father and my mother forsake me,* the LORD will sustain me.

The Midday Psalm   *The Righteous Will Be Kept in Everlasting Remembrance*
Light shines in the darkness for the upright;* the righteous are merciful and full of
    compassion.
It is good for them to be generous in lending* and to manage their affairs with justice.
For they will never be shaken;* the righteous will be kept in everlasting
    remembrance.
They will not be afraid of any evil rumors;* their heart is right; they put their trust
    in the Lord.
Their heart is established and will not shrink,* until they see their desire upon
    their enemies.
They have given freely to the poor,* and their righteousness stands fast for ever;
    they will hold up their head with honor.
The wicked will see it and be angry; they will gnash their teeth and pine away;*
    the desires of the wicked will perish.
                                                    Psalm 112:4–10

The Refrain
Though my father and my mother forsake me,* the LORD will sustain me.

The Cry of the Church

In the evening, in the morning, and at noonday, I will complain and lament,* and
  he will hear my voice.

Psalm 55:18

The Lord's Prayer

The Prayer Appointed for the Week

Almighty and merciful God, it is only by your gift that your faithful people offer
  you true and laudable service: Grant that I may run without stumbling to
  obtain your heavenly promises; through Jesus Christ our Lord, who lives and
  reigns with you and the Holy Spirit, one God, now and for ever. *Amen.*†

The Concluding Prayer of the Church

Blessed be the God, and Father of my Lord Jesus Christ, who has not rejected my
  prayer, nor withheld his love from me.

The Vespers Office   To Be Observed on the Hour or Half Hour
                                                    Between 5 and 8 p.m.

The Call to Prayer

Come let us sing to the LORD;* let us shout for joy to the Rock of our salvation.
Let us come before his presence with thanksgiving* and raise a loud shout to him
  with psalms.
For the LORD is a great God,* and a great King above all gods.
In his hands are the caverns of the earth,* and the heights of the hills are his also.
The sea is his, for he made it,* and his hands have molded the dry land.

Psalm 95:1–5

The Request for Presence

Accept, O LORD, the willing tribute of my lips,* and teach me your judgments.

Psalm 119:108

The Greeting

O LORD of hosts,* happy are they who put their trust in you!

Psalm 84:12

The Hymn   *He Leadeth Me: O Blessed Thought*

He leadeth me: O blessed thought!
O words with heavenly comfort fraught!
Whatever I do, wherever I be,
It is God's hand that leadeth me.
He leadeth me, he leadeth me;
By his own hand he leadeth me;
His faithful follower I would be,
For by his hand he leadeth me.

Sometimes amid scenes of deepest gloom,
Sometimes where Eden's bowers bloom,
By waters still, o'er troubled sea,
Still it is his hand that leadeth me.
He leadeth me, he leadeth me;
By his own hand he leadeth me;
His faithful follower I would be,
For by his hand he leadeth me.

And when my task on earth is done,
When by your grace the victory's won,
Even death's cold wave I will not flee,
Since God through Jordan leadeth me.
He leadeth me, he leadeth me;
By his own hand he leadeth me;
His faithful follower I would be,
For by his hand he leadeth me.

Joseph Gilmore

The Refrain for the Vespers Lessons

You have been gracious to your land, O LORD,* you have restored the good fortune
of Jacob.

Psalm 85:1

The Vespers Psalm   *I Will Listen to What the LORD God Is Saying*

Show us your mercy, O LORD,* and grant us your salvation.

I will listen to what the LORD God is saying,* for he is speaking peace to his faithful
people and to those who turn their hearts to him.

Truly, his salvation is very near to those who fear him,* that his glory may dwell in
our land.

Mercy and truth have met together;* righteousness and peace have kissed each other.

Truth shall spring up from the earth,* and righteousness shall look down from
heaven.

The LORD will indeed grant prosperity,* and our land will yield its increase.

Righteousness shall go before him,* and peace shall be a pathway for his feet.

Psalm 85:7–13

The Refrain

You have been gracious to your land, O LORD,* you have restored the good fortune
of Jacob.

The Gloria

The Lord's Prayer

The Prayer Appointed for the Week

Almighty and merciful God, it is only by your gift that your faithful people offer
you true and laudable service: Grant that I may run without stumbling to

obtain your heavenly promises; through Jesus Christ our Lord, who lives and reigns with you and the Holy Spirit, one God, now and for ever. *Amen.*†

The Concluding Prayer of the Church
O holy God, as evening falls remain with us. Remember our good deeds and forgive our failings. Help us to reflect upon and live according to your covenant of love. Be with our lonely and elderly sisters and brothers in the evening of their lives. May all who long to see you face to face know the comfort of your presence. This we ask in union with all who have gone before us blessing and proclaiming you by the fidelity of their lives. *Amen.*

THE NEW COMPANION TO THE BREVIARY

The Morning Office   **To Be Observed on the Hour or Half Hour Between 6 and 9 a.m.**

The Call to Prayer
Bless our God, you peoples;* make the voice of his praise to be heard;
Who holds our souls in life,* and will not allow our feet to slip.

Psalm 66:7–8

The Request for Presence
I call with my whole heart;* answer me, O LORD, that I may keep your statutes.
Hear my voice, O LORD, according to your loving-kindness;* according to your judgments, give me life.

Psalm 119:145ff

The Greeting
I am bound by the vow I made to you, O God;* I will present to you thank-offerings;
For you have rescued my soul from death and my feet from stumbling,* that I may walk before God in the light of the living.

Psalm 56:11–12

The Refrain for the Morning Lessons
Keep watch over my life, for I am faithful;* save your servant whose trust is in you.

adapted from Psalm 86:2

A Reading
He called the people and his disciples to him and said, 'If anyone wants to be a follower of mine, let him renounce himself and take up his cross and follow me. Anyone who wants to save his life will lose it; but anyone who loses his life for my sake, and for the sake of the gospel, will save it. What gain, then, is it for anyone to win the whole world and forfeit his life? And indeed what can anyone offer in exchange for his life? For if anyone in this sinful and adulterous generation is ashamed of me and of my words, the Son of man will also be ashamed of him when he comes in the glory of his Father with the holy angels.'

Mark 8:34–38

The Refrain
Keep watch over my life, for I am faithful;* save your servant whose trust is in you.

The Morning Psalm   *Happy Are the People Whose Strength Is in You*
Happy are they who dwell in your house!* they will always be praising you.
Happy are the people whose strength is in you!* whose hearts are set on the
    pilgrims' way.
Those who go through the desolate valley will find it a place of springs,* for the
    early rains have covered it with pools of water.
They will climb from height to height,* and the God of gods will reveal himself in
    Zion.
Lord God of hosts, hear my prayer;* hearken, O God of Jacob.
Behold our defender, O God;* and look upon the face of your Anointed.
For one day in your courts is better than a thousand in my own room,* and to
    stand at the threshold of the house of my God than to dwell in the tents of the
    wicked.

Psalm 84:3–9

The Refrain
Keep watch over my life, for I am faithful;* save your servant whose trust is in you.

The Cry of the Church
Lord, have mercy on us. Christ, have mercy on us. Lord, have mercy on us.

The Lord's Prayer

The Prayer Appointed for the Week
Almighty and merciful God, it is only by your gift that your faithful people offer
    you true and laudable service: Grant that I may run without stumbling to
    obtain your heavenly promises; through Jesus Christ our Lord, who lives and
    reigns with you and the Holy Spirit, one God, now and for ever. *Amen.*†

The Concluding Prayer of the Church
Lord God, almighty and everlasting Father, you have brought me in safety to this
    new day: Preserve me with your mighty power, that I may not fall into sin, nor
    be overcome by adversity; and in all I do direct me to the fulfilling of your pur-
    pose; through Jesus Christ my Lord. *Amen.*†

The Midday Office   To Be Observed on the Hour or Half Hour
                                                      Between 11 a.m. and 2 p.m.

The Call to Prayer
Worship the Lord in the beauty of holiness;* let the whole earth tremble before him.
Psalm 96:9

The Request for Presence
Remember not our past sins; let your compassion be swift to meet us.
Psalm 79:8

The Greeting

There is forgiveness with you;* therefore you shall be feared.

Psalm 130:3

The Refrain for the Midday Lessons

The LORD has pleasure in those who fear him,* in those who await his gracious favor.

Psalm 147:12

A Reading

The Apostle wrote, saying: "But when the kindness and love of God our Savior for humanity were revealed it was not because of any upright actions we had done ourselves; it was for no reason except his own faithful love that he saved us, by means of the cleansing water of rebirth and renewal in the Holy Spirit which he has so generously poured over us through Jesus Christ our Savior; so that, justified by his grace, we should become heirs in hope of eternal life. This is doctrine that you can rely on."

Titus 3:4–8

The Refrain

The LORD has pleasure in those who fear him,* in those who await his gracious favor.

The Midday Psalm　　　　　　　　　　　*Into Your Hands I Commend My Spirit*

In you, O LORD, have I taken refuge; let me never be put to shame;* deliver me in your righteousness.

Incline your ear to me;* make haste to deliver me.

Be my strong rock, a castle to keep me safe, for you are my crag and my stronghold;* for the sake of your Name, lead me and guide me.

Into your hands I commend my spirit,* for you have redeemed me, O LORD, O God of truth.

Psalm 31:1–3, 5

The Refrain

The LORD has pleasure in those who fear him,* in those who await his gracious favor.

The Small Verse

Create in me a clean heart, O God,* and renew a right spirit within me.

Cast me not away from your presence* and take not your holy Spirit from me.

Give me the joy of your saving help again* and sustain me with your bountiful spirit.

Psalm 51:11–13

The Lord's Prayer

The Prayer Appointed for the Week

Almighty and merciful God, it is only by your gift that your faithful people offer you true and laudable service: Grant that I may run without stumbling to obtain your heavenly promises; through Jesus Christ our Lord, who lives and reigns with you and the Holy Spirit, one God, now and for ever. *Amen.*†

The Concluding Prayer of the Church

Lord Jesus Christ, by your death you took away the sting of death: Grant me to so follow in faith where you have led the way, that I may at length fall asleep peacefully in you and wake in your likeness; for your tender mercies' sake. *Amen.*†

The Vespers Office   To Be Observed on the Hour or Half Hour
Between 5 and 8 p.m.

The Call to Prayer

O tarry and await the LORD's pleasure; be strong, and he shall comfort your heart;* wait patiently for the LORD.

Psalm 27:18

The Request for Presence

I have said to the LORD, "You are my God;* listen, O LORD, to my supplication."

Psalm 140:6

The Greeting

I am bound by the vow I made to you, O God;* I will present to you thank-offerings;

For you have rescued my soul from death and my feet from stumbling,* that I may walk before God in the light of the living.

Psalm 56:11–12

The Hymn   *Take Time to Be Holy*

Take time to be holy, speak oft with your Lord;
Abide in Him always, and feed on His Word:
Make friends of God's children, help those who are weak;
Forgetting in nothing His blessing to seek.

Take time to be holy, The world rushes on;
Spend much time in secret with Jesus alone:
By looking to Jesus like Him you shall be;
Your friend in your conduct His likeness shall see.

Take time to be holy, be calm in your soul;
Each thought and each motive beneath His control;
Thus led by His Spirit to fountains of love,
You soon shall be fitted for service above.

William Longstaff

The Refrain for the Vespers Lessons

Purge me from my sin, and I shall be pure;* wash me, and I shall be clean indeed.

Psalm 51:8

The Vespers Psalm   *God Reveals Himself in Glory*

The LORD, the God of gods, has spoken;* he has called the earth from the rising of
  the sun to its setting.

Out of Zion, perfect in its beauty,* God reveals himself in glory.

Our God will come and will not keep silence;* before him there is a consuming
  flame, and round about him a raging storm.

He calls the heavens and the earth from above* to witness the judgment of his
  people.

"Gather before me my loyal followers,* those who have made a covenant with
  me* and sealed it with sacrifice."

Let the heavens declare the rightness of his cause;* for God himself is judge.

Psalm 50:1–6

The Refrain

Purge me from my sin, and I shall be pure;* wash me, and I shall be clean indeed.

The Cry of the Church

Lord, have mercy on us. Christ, have mercy on us. Lord, have mercy on us.

The Lord's Prayer

The Prayer Appointed for the Week

Almighty and merciful God, it is only by your gift that your faithful people offer
  you true and laudable service: Grant that I may run without stumbling to
  obtain your heavenly promises; through Jesus Christ our Lord, who lives and
  reigns with you and the Holy Spirit, one God, now and for ever. *Amen.*†

Concluding Prayers of the Church

Almighty God, who has promised to hear the petitions of those who ask in your
  Son's Name: I beseech you mercifully to incline your ear to me who have made
  my prayers and supplications to you; and grant that those things which I have
  faithfully asked according to your will, may effectually be obtained, to the
  relief of my necessity, and to the setting forth of your glory; through Jesus
  Christ my Lord. *Amen.*†

May the souls of the faithful departed, through the mercy of God, rest in eternal
  peace. *Amen.*

The Morning Office   To Be Observed on the Hour or Half Hour
                                                      Between 6 and 9 a.m.

The Call to Prayer

Hallelujah! Praise the Name of the LORD;* give praise, you servants of the LORD.

Psalm 135:1

The Request for Presence

In your righteousness, deliver and set me free;* incline your ear to me and save me.

Psalm 71:2

The Greeting
O LORD, I am your servant;* I am your servant and the child of your handmaid;
   you have freed me from my bonds.

Psalm 116:14

The Refrain for the Morning Lessons
This is the LORD's doing,* and it is marvelous in our eyes.

Psalm 118:23

A Reading
In the course of their journey he came to a village, and a woman named Martha
   welcomed him into her house. She had a sister called Mary, who sat down at
   the Lord's feet and listened to him speaking. Now Martha, who was distracted
   with serving, came to him and said, 'Lord, do you not care that my sister is
   leaving me to do all the serving by myself? Please tell her to help me.' But the
   Lord answered, 'Martha, Martha,' he said, 'you worry and fret about so many
   things, and yet few are needed, indeed only one. It is Mary who has chosen the
   better part, and it is not to be taken from her.'

Luke 10:38–42

The Refrain
This is the LORD's doing,* and it is marvelous in our eyes.

The Morning Psalm   *How Shall I Repay the LORD?*
How shall I repay the LORD* for all the good things he has done for me?
I will lift up the cup of salvation* and call upon the Name of the LORD.
I will fulfill my vows to the LORD* in the presence of all his people.

Psalm 116:10–12

The Refrain
This is the LORD's doing,* and it is marvelous in our eyes.

The Gloria

The Lord's Prayer

The Prayer Appointed for the Week
Almighty and merciful God, it is only by your gift that your faithful people offer
   you true and laudable service: Grant that I may run without stumbling to
   obtain your heavenly promises; through Jesus Christ our Lord, who lives and
   reigns with you and the Holy Spirit, one God, now and for ever. *Amen.*†

The Concluding Prayer of the Church
Lord God, almighty and everlasting Father, you have brought me in safety to this
   new day: Preserve me with your mighty power, that I may not fall into sin, nor
   be overcome by adversity; and in all I do direct me to the fulfilling of your purpose; through Jesus Christ my Lord. *Amen.*†

The Midday Office   To Be Observed on the Hour or Half Hour
                                     Between 11 a.m. and 2 p.m.

The Call to Prayer
Hallelujah! Praise God in his holy temple;* praise him in the firmament of his
     power.
Praise him for his mighty acts;* praise him for his excellent greatness.
Praise him with the blast of the ram's-horn;* praise him with lyre and harp.
Praise him with timbrel and dance;* praise him with strings and pipe.
Praise him with resounding cymbals;* praise him with loud-clanging cymbals.
Let everything that has breath* praise the LORD. Hallelujah!

Psalm 150:1–6

The Request for Presence
LORD, hear my prayer, and in your faithfulness heed my supplications;* answer
     me in your righteousness.

Psalm 143:1

The Greeting
My eyes are fixed on you, O my Strength;* for you, O God, are my stronghold.

Psalm 59:10

The Refrain for the Midday Lessons
Blessed be the LORD God of Israel,* from age to age. Amen. Amen.

Psalm 41:13

A Reading
I, the prisoner in the Lord, urge you therefore to lead a life worthy of the vocation
     to which you were called. With all humility and gentleness, and with patience,
     support each other in love. Take every care to preserve the unity of the Spirit by
     the peace that binds you together.

Ephesians 4:1–3

The Refrain
Blessed be the LORD God of Israel,* from age to age. Amen. Amen.

The Midday Psalm   *Let the Hills Ring Out with Joy Before the LORD*
Let the sea make a noise and all that is in it,* the lands and those who dwell
     therein.
Let the rivers clap their hands,* and let the hills ring out with joy before the LORD,
     when he comes to judge the earth.
In righteousness shall he judge the world* and the peoples with equity.

Psalm 98:8–10

The Refrain
Blessed be the LORD God of Israel,* from age to age. Amen. Amen.

The Gloria

The Lord's Prayer

The Prayer Appointed for the Week

Almighty and merciful God, it is only by your gift that your faithful people offer
you true and laudable service: Grant that I may run without stumbling to
obtain your heavenly promises; through Jesus Christ our Lord, who lives and
reigns with you and the Holy Spirit, one God, now and for ever. *Amen.*†

The Concluding Prayer of the Church

O God, the source of light: Shed forth your unending day upon all of us who
watch for you, that our lips may praise you, our lives may bless you, and our
worship may give you glory; through Jesus Christ our Lord. *Amen.*†

The Vespers Office **To Be Observed on the Hour or Half Hour**
Between 5 and 8 p.m.

The Call to Prayer

Let the Name of the LORD be blessed,* from this time forth for evermore.
From the rising of the sun to its going down* let the Name of the LORD be praised.

Psalm 113:2–3

The Request for Presence

Let my cry come before you, O LORD;* give me understanding, according to your
word.
Let my supplication come before you;* deliver me, according to your promise.

Psalm 119:169–170

The Greeting

The Lord is in his holy temple; Let all the earth keep silence before him. *Amen.*

The Hymn *The Day You Gave Us, Lord, Is Ended*

The day you gave us, Lord, is ended;
The darkness falls at your behest;
To you our morning hymns ascended;
Your praise shall hallow now our rest.

We thank you that your church, unsleeping
While earth rolls onward into light,
Through all the world her watch is keeping,
And rests not now by day or night.

As over each continent and island
The dawn leads on another day,
The voice of prayer is never silent,
Nor die the strains of praise away.

So be it, Lord; your throne shall never,
Like earth's proud empires pass away.
Your kingdom stands, and grows forever,
Till all your creatures own your sway.

John Ellerton

The Refrain for the Vespers Lessons
Turn again to your rest, O my soul,* for the Lord has treated you well.

Psalm 116:6

The Vespers Psalm   *You Will Arise and Have Compassion on Zion*
You will arise and have compassion on Zion, for it is time to have mercy upon
    her;* indeed, the appointed time has come.
For your servants love her very rubble,* and are moved to pity even for her dust.
The nations shall fear your Name, O Lord,* and all the kings of the earth your glory.
For the Lord will build up Zion,* and his glory will appear.
He will look with favor on the prayer of the homeless;* he will not despise their plea.

Psalm 102:13–17

The Refrain
Turn again to your rest, O my soul,* for the Lord has treated you well.

The Small Verse
Blessed be the Lord God of Israel for he has visited and delivered us. Alleluia,
    alleluia, alleluia.

The Lord's Prayer

The Prayer Appointed for the Week
Almighty and merciful God, it is only by your gift that your faithful people offer
    you true and laudable service: Grant that I may run without stumbling to
    obtain your heavenly promises; through Jesus Christ our Lord, who lives and
    reigns with you and the Holy Spirit, one God, now and for ever. *Amen.*†

The Concluding Prayer of the Church
Almighty God, who after the creation of the world rested from all your works and
    sanctified a day of rest for all your creatures: Grant that I, putting away all
    earthly anxieties, may be duly prepared for the service of public worship, and
    grant as well that my Sabbath upon the earth may be a preparation for the eternal
    rest promised to your people in heaven; through Jesus Christ our Lord. *Amen.*†

The Morning Office   **To Be Observed on the Hour or Half Hour**
                                          Between 6 and 9 a.m.

The Call to Prayer
Come, let us sing to the Lord;* let us rejoice this day in the strength of our salvation.
Let us come into His presence with thanksgiving,* and raise a loud shout to Him
    with psalms.

adapted from Psalm 95:1–2

The Request for Presence

Hear, O Shepherd of Israel, leading Joseph like a flock;* shine forth, you that are
    enthroned upon the cherubim.
In the presence of Ephraim, Benjamin, and Manasseh,* stir up your strength and
    come to help us,
Restore us, O God of hosts;* show the light of your countenance, and we shall be
    saved.

Psalm 80:1–3

The Greeting

It is a good thing to give thanks to the LORD,* and to sing praises to your Name,
    O Most High;
To tell of your loving-kindness early in the morning* and of your faithfulness in
    the night season;
For as it was in the beginning, it is now and it evermore shall be. Alleluia.

Psalm 92:1–2, Gloria

The Refrain for the Morning Lessons

Incline my heart, O God, to your ways.* Turn my eyes from longing after vanities.

based on Psalm 119:36–37

A Reading

Jesus taught us, saying: "Sell your possessions and give to those in need. Get your-
    selves purses that do not wear out, treasure that will not fail you, in heaven
    where no thief can reach it and no moth destroy it. For wherever your treasure
    is, that is where your heart will be too."

Luke 12:33–34

The Refrain

Incline my heart, O God, to your ways.* Turn my eyes from longing after vanities.

The Morning Psalm   *I Walk Before God in the Light of the Living*

In God the LORD, whose word I praise, in God I trust and will not be afraid,* for
    what can mortals do to me?
I am bound by the vow I made to you, O God;* I will present to you thank-
    offerings;
For you have rescued my soul from death and my feet from stumbling,* that I may
    walk before God in the light of the living.

Psalm 56:10–12

The Refrain

Incline my heart, O God, to your ways.* Turn my eyes from longing after vanities.

The Gloria

The Lord's Prayer

The Prayer Appointed for the Week

O God, whose blessed Son came into the world that he might destroy the works of
    the devil and make us children of God and heirs of eternal life: Grant that, hav-

ing this hope, I may purify myself as he is pure; that, when he comes again with power and great glory, I may be made like him in his eternal and glorious kingdom; where he lives and reigns with you and the Holy Spirit, one God, for ever and ever. *Amen.*†

The Concluding Prayer of the Church

Lord God, almighty and everlasting Father, you have brought me in safety to this new day: Preserve me with your mighty power, that I may not fall into sin, nor be overcome by adversity; and in all I do direct me to the fulfilling of your purpose; through Jesus Christ my Lord. *Amen.*†

The Midday Office To Be Observed on the Hour or Half Hour
Between 11 a.m. and 2 p.m.

The Call to Prayer

Come, let us sing to the LORD;* let us shout for joy to the Rock of our salvation.
Let us come before his presence with thanksgiving* and raise a loud shout to him with psalms.
For the LORD is a great God,* and a great King above all gods.
In his hands are the caverns of the earth,* and the heights of the hills are his also.
The sea is his, for he made it,* and his hands have molded the dry land.

Psalm 95:1–5

The Request for Presence

May God give us his blessing,* and may all the ends of the earth stand in awe of him.

Psalm 67:7

The Greeting

You, O LORD, are a shield about me;* you are my glory, the one who lifts up my head.
I call aloud upon the LORD,* and he answers me from his holy hill;
I lie down and go to sleep;* I wake again, because the LORD sustains me.

Psalm 3:3–5

The Refrain for the Midday Lessons

May the glory of the LORD endure for ever;* may the LORD rejoice in all his works.

Psalm 104:32

A Reading

Job said: "I know that I have a living defender and that he will rise up last, on the dust of the earth. After my awakening, he will set me close to him. And from my flesh I shall look on God. He whom I shall see will take my part: my eyes will be gazing on no stranger."

Job 19:25–27

The Refrain

May the glory of the LORD endure for ever;* may the LORD rejoice in all his works.

The Midday Psalm   *Having You I Desire Nothing Upon Earth*

Whom have I in heaven but you?* and having you I desire nothing upon earth.

Though my flesh and my heart should waste away,* God is the strength of my
    heart and my portion for ever.

Truly, those who forsake you will perish;* you destroy all who are unfaithful.

But it is good for me to be near God;* I have made the Lord GOD my refuge.

Psalm 73:25–28

The Refrain

May the glory of the LORD endure for ever;* may the LORD rejoice in all his works.

The Cry of the Church

O God, come to my assistance! O Lord, make haste to help me!

The Lord's Prayer

The Prayer Appointed for the Week

O God, whose blessed Son came into the world that he might destroy the works of
    the devil and make us children of God and heirs of eternal life: Grant that, hav-
    ing this hope, I may purify myself as he is pure; that, when he comes again
    with power and great glory, I may be made like him in his eternal and glorious
    kingdom; where he lives and reigns with you and the Holy Spirit, one God, for
    ever and ever. *Amen.*†

The Concluding Prayer of the Church

O God, on this first day of the week, I join all creation and people of all ages in
    praising you. Your kindness and forgiveness flow like a river through the cen-
    turies refreshing our faith, our hope and our love. May you be forever praised
    throughout all the ages. *Amen.*

The Vespers Office   **To Be Observed on the Hour or Half Hour**
                                          Between 5 and 8 p.m.

The Call to Prayer

Hallelujah! Praise the Name of the LORD;* give praise, you servants of the LORD,

You who stand in the house of the LORD,* in the courts of the house of our God.

Praise the LORD, for the LORD is good;* sing praises to his Name, for it is lovely.

Psalm 135:1–3

The Request for Presence

Incline your ear to me;* make haste to deliver me.

Psalm 31:2

The Greeting

The Lord is in his holy temple; Let all the earth keep silence before him. *Amen.*

Traditional

The Hymn

Glory be to God on high, and peace, good will to all.
We praise you, we bless you, we worship you,
We give thanks to you for thy great glory:
O Lord God, heavenly King, God the Father Almighty.
O Lord, the only begotten Son, Jesus Christ;
O Lord God, Lamb of God, Son of the Father
That takes away the sins of the world, have mercy on us.
You that take away the sins of the world, receive our prayer.
You that sit at the right of God the Father, have mercy upon us.
For you only are holy; you only are the Lord;
You only, O Christ, with the Holy Ghost,
Are most high in the glory of God the Father.

Doxology

The Refrain for the Vespers Lessons
Give thanks to the LORD, for he is good,* and his mercy endures for ever.

Psalm 107:1

The Vespers Psalm   *My Soul Is Athirst for the Living God*
As the deer longs for the water-brooks,* so longs my soul for you, O God.
My soul is athirst for God, athirst for the living God;* when shall I come to appear
before the presence of God?
My tears have been my food day and night, while all day long they say to me,*
"Where now is your God?"
I pour out my soul when I think on these things:* how I went with the multitude
and led them into the house of God,
With the voice of praise and thanksgiving,* among those who keep holy-day.
Why are you so full of heaviness, O my soul?* and why are you so disquieted
within me?
Put your trust in God;* for I will yet give thanks to him, who is the help of my
countenance, and my God.

Psalm 42:1–7

The Refrain
Give thanks to the LORD, for he is good,* and his mercy endures for ever.

The Gloria

The Lord's Prayer

The Prayer Appointed for the Week
O God, whose blessed Son came into the world that he might destroy the works of
the devil and make us children of God and heirs of eternal life: Grant that, having this hope, I may purify myself as he is pure; that, when he comes again
with power and great glory, I may be made like him in his eternal and glorious
kingdom; where he lives and reigns with you and the Holy Spirit, one God, for
ever and ever. *Amen.*†

The Concluding Prayer of the Church

Lord God, whose Son our Savior Jesus Christ, triumphed over the powers of death and prepared for us our place in the new Jerusalem: Grant that I, who have this day given thanks for the resurrection, may praise you in the City of which he is the light, and where he lives and reigns for ever and ever. *Amen.*†

The Morning Office	To Be Observed on the Hour or Half Hour
	Between 6 and 9 a.m.

The Call to Prayer

"Come now, let us reason together," says the LORD.

Isaiah 1:18 (KJV)

The Request for Presence

Be my strong rock, a castle to keep me safe;* you are my crag and my stronghold.

Psalm 71:3

The Greeting

The words of the LORD are pure words,* like silver refined from ore and purified seven times in the fire.

Psalm 12:6

The Refrain for the Morning Lessons

"Because the needy are oppressed, and the poor cry out in misery,* I will rise up," says the LORD, "And give them the help they long for."

Psalm 12:5

A Reading

Jesus said: "Anyone who is not with me is against me, and anyone who does not gather in with me throws away. And I tell you, every human sin and blasphemy will be forgiven, but blasphemy against the Spirit will not be forgiven. And anyone who says a word against the Son of man will be forgiven; but no one who speaks against the Holy Spirit will be forgiven either in this world or the next."

Matthew 12:30–32

The Refrain

"Because the needy are oppressed, and the poor cry out in misery,* I will rise up," says the LORD, "And give them the help they long for."

The Morning Psalm   *He Has Shown His People the Power of His Works*

Great are the deeds of the LORD!* they are studied by all who delight in them.

His work is full of majesty and splendor,* and his righteousness endures for ever.

He makes his marvelous works to be remembered;* the LORD is gracious and full of compassion.

He gives food to those who fear him;* he is ever mindful of his covenant.

He has shown his people the power of his works* in giving them the lands of the nations.

The works of his hands are faithfulness and justice;* all his commandments are
sure.
They stand fast for ever and ever,* because they are done in truth and equity.
He sent redemption to his people; he commanded his covenant for ever;* holy and
awesome is his Name.

Psalm 111:2–9

The Refrain
"Because the needy are oppressed, and the poor cry out in misery,* I will rise up,"
says the LORD, "And give them the help they long for."

The Cry of the Church
Even so, come, Lord Jesus!

The Lord's Prayer

The Prayer Appointed for the Week
O God, whose blessed Son came into the world that he might destroy the works of
the devil and make us children of God and heirs of eternal life: Grant that, having this hope, I may purify myself as he is pure; that, when he comes again
with power and great glory, I may be made like him in his eternal and glorious
kingdom; where he lives and reigns with you and the Holy Spirit, one God, for
ever and ever. *Amen.*†

The Concluding Prayer of the Church
Lord God, almighty and everlasting Father, you have brought me in safety to this
new day: Preserve me with your mighty power, that I may not fall into sin, nor
be overcome by adversity; and in all I do direct me to the fulfilling of your purpose; through Jesus Christ my Lord. *Amen.*†

The Midday Office   To Be Observed on the Hour or Half Hour
                                     Between 11 a.m. and 2 p.m.

The Call to Prayer
Hallelujah! Praise the LORD, O my soul!* I will praise the LORD as long as I live; I
will sing praises to God while I have my being.

Psalm 146:1

The Request for Presence
Bow your heavens, O LORD, and come down;* touch the mountains, and they shall
smoke.
Hurl the lightning and scatter them;* shoot out your arrows and rout them.
Stretch out your hand from on high;* rescue me and deliver me from the great
waters, from the hand of foreign peoples,
Whose mouths speak deceitfully* and whose right hand is raised in falsehood.

Psalm 144:5–8

The Greeting

To you I lift up my eyes,* to you enthroned in the heavens.

As the eyes of the servants look to the hand of their masters,* and the eyes of a
maid to the hand of her mistress,

So our eyes look to the LORD our God,* until he shows us his mercy.

Psalm 123:1–3

The Refrain for the Midday Lessons

Blessed be the LORD!* for he has shown me the wonders of his love in a besieged city.

Psalm 31:21

A Reading

Let us keep firm in the hope we profess, because the one who made the promise is
trustworthy.

Hebrews 10:23

The Refrain

Blessed be the LORD!* for he has shown me the wonders of his love in a besieged city.

The Midday Psalm   *I Will Walk in the Presence of the LORD*

Gracious is the LORD and righteous;* our God is full of compassion.

The LORD watches over the innocent;* I was brought very low, and he helped me.

Turn again to your rest, O my soul,* for the LORD has treated you well.

For you have rescued my life from death,* my eyes from tears, and my feet from
stumbling.

I will walk in the presence of the LORD* in the land of the living.

Psalm 116:4–8

The Refrain

Blessed be the LORD!* for he has shown me the wonders of his love in a besieged
city.

The Cry of the Church

Lord, have mercy on us. Christ, have mercy on us. Lord, have mercy on us.

The Lord's Prayer

The Prayer Appointed for the Week

O God, whose blessed Son came into the world that he might destroy the works of
the devil and make us children of God and heirs of eternal life: Grant that, having this hope, I may purify myself as he is pure; that, when he comes again
with power and great glory, I may be made like him in his eternal and glorious
kingdom; where he lives and reigns with you and the Holy Spirit, one God, for
ever and ever. *Amen.*†

The Concluding Prayer of the Church

Almighty and eternal God, ruler of all things in heaven and earth: Mercifully
accept my prayers, and strengthen me to do your will; through Jesus Christ our
Lord. *Amen.*†

The Vespers Office   To Be Observed on the Hour or Half Hour
                                         Between 5 and 8 p.m.

The Call to Prayer
Love the LORD, all you who worship him;* the LORD protects the faithful, but
    repays to the full those who act haughtily.

Psalm 31:23

The Request for Presence
Teach me your way, O LORD, and I will walk in your truth;* knit my heart to you
    that I may fear your Name.

Psalm 86:11

The Greeting
Whom have I in heaven but you?* and having you I desire nothing upon earth.

Psalm 73:25

The Hymn   *I've Found a Friend*
    I've found a friend, O such a friend! He loved me ere I knew Him;
    He drew me with the cords of love, and thus He bound me to Him;
    And round my heart still closely twine those which nought can sever,
    For I am His and He is mine, forever and forever.

    I've found a friend, O such a friend! He bled, He died to save me;
    And not alone the gift of life, but His own self He gave me.
    Nought that I have, mine own I call, I hold it for the Giver,
    My heart, my strength, my life, my all, are His and His forever.

    I've found a friend, O such a friend! So kind and true and tender!
    So wise a Counselor and Guide, so mighty a Defender!
    From Him who loves me now so well, what power my soul can sever?
    Shall life or death, or earth or hell? No, I am His forever.

James Small

The Refrain for the Vespers Lessons
Let the faithful rejoice in triumph;* let them be joyful on their beds.

Psalm 149:5

The Vespers Psalm   *You Yourself Created My Inmost Parts*
If I say, "Surely the darkness will cover me,* and the light around me turn to
    night,"
Darkness is not dark to you; the night is as bright as the day;* darkness and light
    to you are both alike.
For you yourself created my inmost parts;* you knit me together in my mother's
    womb.

Psalm 139:10–12

The Refrain
Let the faithful rejoice in triumph;* let them be joyful on their beds.

The Gloria

The Lord's Prayer

The Prayer Appointed for the Week
O God, whose blessed Son came into the world that he might destroy the works of
the devil and make us children of God and heirs of eternal life: Grant that, having this hope, I may purify myself as he is pure; that, when he comes again
with power and great glory, I may be made like him in his eternal and glorious
kingdom; where he lives and reigns with you and the Holy Spirit, one God, for
ever and ever. *Amen.*†

The Concluding Prayer of the Church
God be in my head
and in my understanding.
God be in my mouth
and in my speaking.
God be in my heart
and in my thinking.
God be at mine end
and my departing.
       Sarum Primer, 1527

The Morning Office   To Be Observed on the Hour or Half Hour
                                                  Between 6 and 9 a.m.

The Call to Prayer
Hallelujah! Praise the Name of the LORD;* give praise, you servants of the LORD,
Praise the LORD, for the LORD is good;* sing praises to his Name, for it is lovely.
For I know that the LORD is great,* and that our Lord is above all gods.

                                                 Psalm 135:1ff

The Request for Presence
Satisfy us by your loving-kindness in the morning;* so shall we rejoice and be glad
all the days of our life.

                                                Psalm 90:14

The Greeting
Out of Zion, perfect in its beauty,* God reveals himself in glory.
Let the heavens declare the rightness of his cause;* for God himself is judge.

                                               Psalm 50:2, 6

The Refrain for the Morning Lessons
Wake up, my spirit; awake, lute and harp;* I myself will waken the dawn.

                                               Psalm 108:2

A Reading

Jesus taught us, saying: "Remain in me, as I in you. As a branch cannot bear fruit all by itself, unless it remains part of the vine, neither can you unless you remain in me. I am the vine, you are the branches."

John 15:4–5

The Refrain

Wake up, my spirit; awake, lute and harp;* I myself will waken the dawn.

The Morning Psalm　　　　　　　　　*May All the Nations Bless Themselves in Him and Call Him Blessed*

Long may he live! and may there be given to him gold from Arabia;* may prayer be made for him always, and may they bless him all the day long.

May there be abundance of grain on the earth, growing thick even on the hilltops;* may its fruit flourish like Lebanon, and its grain like grass upon the earth.

May his Name remain for ever and be established as long as the sun endures;* may all the nations bless themselves in him and call him blessed.

Psalm 72:15–17

The Refrain

Wake up, my spirit; awake, lute and harp;* I myself will waken the dawn.

The Gloria

The Lord's Prayer

The Prayer Appointed for the Week

O God, whose blessed Son came into the world that he might destroy the works of the devil and make us children of God and heirs of eternal life: Grant that, having this hope, I may purify myself as he is pure; that, when he comes again with power and great glory, I may be made like him in his eternal and glorious kingdom; where he lives and reigns with you and the Holy Spirit, one God, for ever and ever. *Amen.*†

The Concluding Prayer of the Church

Lord God, almighty and everlasting Father, you have brought me in safety to this new day: Preserve me with your mighty power, that I may not fall into sin, nor be overcome by adversity; and in all I do direct me to the fulfilling of your purpose; through Jesus Christ my Lord. *Amen.*†

The Midday Office　　　　　　　　To Be Observed on the Hour or Half Hour
Between 11 a.m. and 2 p.m.

The Call to Prayer

Let the words of my mouth and the meditation of my heart be acceptable in your sight,* O LORD, my strength and my redeemer.

Psalm 19:14

The Request for Presence
Open my eyes, that I may see* the wonders of your law.

Psalm 119:18

The Greeting
My God, my rock in whom I put my trust,* my shield, the horn of my salvation, and my refuge; you are worthy of praise. ·

Psalm 18:2

The Refrain for the Midday Lessons
When I called, you answered me;* you increased my strength within me.

Psalm 138:4

A Reading
Finally, grow strong in the Lord, with the strength of his power. So stand your ground, with *truth a belt round your waist,* and *uprightness a breastplate,* wearing for shoes on your feet *the eagerness to spread the gospel of peace* and always carrying the shield of faith so that you can use it to quench the burning arrows of the Evil One. And then you must *take salvation as your helmet* and the sword of the Spirit, that is, the word of God.

Ephesians 6:10, 14–17

The Refrain
When I called, you answered me;* you increased my strength within me.

The Midday Psalm   *Give Me Life in Your Ways*
Teach me, O Lord, the way of your statutes,* and I shall keep it to the end.
Give me understanding, and I shall keep your law;* I shall keep it with all my heart.
Make me go in the path of your commandments,* for that is my desire.
Incline my heart to your decrees* and not to unjust gain.
Turn my eyes from watching what is worthless;* give me life in your ways.

Psalm 119:33–37

The Refrain
When I called, you answered me;* you increased my strength within me.

The Gloria

The Lord's Prayer

The Prayer Appointed for the Week
O God, whose blessed Son came into the world that he might destroy the works of the devil and make us children of God and heirs of eternal life: Grant that, having this hope, I may purify myself as he is pure; that, when he comes again with power and great glory, I may be made like him in his eternal and glorious kingdom; where he lives and reigns with you and the Holy Spirit, one God, for ever and ever. *Amen.*†

The Concluding Prayer of the Church

Heavenly Father, in you I live and move and have my being: I humbly pray you so
to guide and govern me by your Holy Spirit, that in all cares and occupations
of my life I may not forget you, but may remember that I am ever walking in
your sight; through Jesus Christ my Lord. *Amen.*†

The Vespers Office   **To Be Observed on the Hour or Half Hour**
                                Between 5 and 8 p.m.

The Call to Prayer

Blessed be the LORD, the God of Israel, from everlasting and to everlasting;* and
let all people say, "Amen!" Hallelujah!

Psalm 106:48

The Request for Presence

Be my strong rock, a castle to keep me safe;* you are my crag and my stronghold.

Psalm 71:3

The Greeting

Your way, O God, is holy;* who is as great as our God?

Psalm 77:13

The Hymn   *We Are Climbing Jacob's Ladder*

We are climbing Jacob's ladder;   If you love him, why not serve him?
We are climbing Jacob's ladder,   If you love him, why not serve him?
We are climbing Jacob's ladder;   If you love him, why not serve him?
Soldiers of the cross.   Soldiers of the cross.

Every round goes higher, higher;   We are climbing higher, higher,
Every round goes higher, higher,   We are climbing higher, higher,
Every round goes higher, higher,   We are climbing higher, higher,
Soldiers of the cross.   Soldiers of the cross.

African-American Spiritual

Sinner, do you love my Jesus?
Sinner, do you love my Jesus?
Sinner, do you love my Jesus?
Soldiers of the cross.

The Refrain for the Vespers Lessons

Truth shall spring up from the earth,* and righteousness shall look down from
heaven.

Psalm 85:11

The Vespers Psalm   *This Is the LORD's Doing*

Open for me the gates of righteousness;* I will enter them; I will offer thanks to the
LORD.
"This is the gate of the LORD;* he who is righteous may enter."

I will give thanks to you, for you answered me* and have become my salvation.
The same stone which the builders rejected* has become the chief cornerstone.
This is the LORD's doing,* and it is marvelous in our eyes.
On this day the LORD has acted;* we will rejoice and be glad in it.

Psalm 118:19–24

The Refrain

Truth shall spring up from the earth,* and righteousness shall look down from
heaven.

The Cry of the Church

In the evening, in the morning, and at noonday, I will complain and lament,* and
he will hear my voice.

Psalm 55:18

The Lord's Prayer

The Prayer Appointed for the Week

O God, whose blessed Son came into the world that he might destroy the works of
the devil and make us children of God and heirs of eternal life: Grant that, having this hope, I may purify myself as he is pure; that, when he comes again
with power and great glory, I may be made like him in his eternal and glorious
kingdom; where he lives and reigns with you and the Holy Spirit, one God, for
ever and ever. *Amen.*†

The Concluding Prayer of the Church

Lord Jesus, stay with me, for evening is at hand and the day is past; be my companion in the way, kindle my heart, and awaken hope, that I may know you as
you are revealed in Scripture and in the breaking of bread. Grant this for the
sake of your love toward me. *Amen.*†

The Morning Office
 To Be Observed on the Hour or Half Hour
Between 6 and 9 a.m.

The Call to Prayer

Wake up, my spirit; awake lute and harp;* I myself will waken the dawn.

Psalm 57:8

The Request for Presence

O God of hosts,* show the light of your countenance, and we shall be saved.

Psalm 80:7

The Greeting

My lips will sing with joy when I play to you,* and so will my soul, which you
have redeemed.

Psalm 71:23

The Refrain for the Morning Lessons
Send forth your strength, O God;* establish, O God, what you have wrought for us.

Psalm 68:28

A Reading
Jesus taught the people, saying: "Good people draw what is good from the store of goodness in their hearts; bad people draw what is bad from the store of badness. For the words of the mouth flow out of what fills the heart."

Luke 6:45

The Refrain
Send forth your strength, O God;* establish, O God, what you have wrought for us.

The Morning Psalm   *Happy Are the People of Whom This Is So*
Rescue me from the hurtful sword* and deliver me from the hand of foreign peoples,
Whose mouths speak deceitfully* and whose right hand is raised in falsehood.
May our sons be like plants well nurtured from their youth,* and our daughters like sculptured corners of a palace.
May our barns be filled to overflowing with all manner of crops;* may the flocks in our pastures increase by thousands and tens of thousands; may our cattle be fat and sleek.
May there be no breaching of the walls, no going into exile,* no wailing in the public squares.
Happy are the people of whom this is so!* happy are the people whose God is the LORD!

Psalm 144:11–16

The Refrain
Send forth your strength, O God;* establish, O God, what you have wrought for us.

The Gloria

The Lord's Prayer

The Prayer Appointed for the Week
O God, whose blessed Son came into the world that he might destroy the works of the devil and make us children of God and heirs of eternal life: Grant that, having this hope, I may purify myself as he is pure; that, when he comes again with power and great glory, I may be made like him in his eternal and glorious kingdom; where he lives and reigns with you and the Holy Spirit, one God, for ever and ever. *Amen.*†

The Concluding Prayer of the Church
Lord God, almighty and everlasting Father, you have brought me in safety to this new day: Preserve me with your mighty power, that I may not fall into sin, nor be overcome by adversity; and in all I do direct me to the fulfilling of your purpose; through Jesus Christ my Lord. *Amen.*†

The Midday Office

To Be Observed on the Hour or Half Hour
Between 11 a.m. and 2 p.m.

The Call to Prayer
Praise the LORD, for the LORD is good;* sing praises to his Name, for it is lovely.

Psalm 135:3

The Request for Presence
Hear the voice of my prayer when I cry out to you,* when I lift up my hands to
    your holy of holies.

Psalm 28:2

The Greeting
You are God: we praise you;
You are the Lord: we acclaim you;
You are the eternal Father:
All creation worships you.
To you all angels, all the powers of heaven,
Cherubim and Seraphim, sing in endless praise:
    Holy, holy, holy Lord, God of power and might,
    heaven and earth are full of your glory.

Te Deum

The Refrain for the Midday Lessons
But it is good for me to be near God;* I have made the Lord GOD my refuge.

Psalm 73:28

A Reading
Blessed be the God and Father of our Lord Jesus Christ, the merciful Father and
    the God who gives us every possible encouragement; he supports us in every
    hardship, so that we are able to come to the support of others, in every hard-
    ship of theirs because of the encouragement we ourselves receive from God.

2 Corinthians 1:3–4

The Refrain
But it is good for me to be near God;* I have made the Lord GOD my refuge.

The Midday Psalm   *I Will Thank You with an Unfeigned Heart*
Happy are they whose way is blameless,* who walk in the law of the LORD!
Happy are they who observe his decrees* and seek him with all their hearts!
Who never do any wrong,* but always walk in his ways.
You laid down your commandments,* that we should fully keep them.
Oh, that my ways were made so direct* that I might keep your statutes!
Then I should not be put to shame,* when I regard all your commandments.
I will thank you with an unfeigned heart,* when I have learned your righteous
    judgments.
I will keep your statutes;* do not utterly forsake me.

Psalm 119:1–8

The Refrain

But it is good for me to be near God;* I have made the Lord GOD my refuge.

The Gloria

The Lord's Prayer

The Prayer Appointed for the Week

O God, whose blessed Son came into the world that he might destroy the works of
the devil and make us children of God and heirs of eternal life: Grant that, having this hope, I may purify myself as he is pure; that, when he comes again
with power and great glory, I may be made like him in his eternal and glorious
kingdom; where he lives and reigns with you and the Holy Spirit, one God, for
ever and ever. *Amen.*†

The Concluding Prayer of the Church

Almighty and eternal God, ruler of all things in heaven and earth: Mercifully
accept my prayers, and strengthen me to do your will; through Jesus Christ our
Lord. *Amen.*†

The Vespers Office   **To Be Observed on the Hour or Half Hour**
                                                        Between 5 and 8 p.m.

The Call to Prayer

Sing to God, O kingdoms of the earth;* sing praises to the LORD.
He rides in the heavens, the ancient heavens;* he sends forth his voice, his mighty
voice.

Psalm 68:33–34

The Request for Presence

Protect me, O God, for I take refuge in you;* I have said to the LORD, "You are my
LORD, my good above all other."

Psalm 16:1

The Greeting

Praise God from whom all blessings flow; Praise Him all creatures here below;
Praise Him above, you heavenly hosts; Praise Father, Son, and Holy Ghost.

Doxology

The Hymn

Creator of the circling sky,   At his command let every fear
Who made all things by power most high,   Of hostile foemen disappear;
Your Providence will never cease   Let civil strife give way to peace,
To rule Your works in might and peace.   And pestilence and famine cease.

O now send Your Angel earthward,   To God the Father glory be;
Assigned by You to be our guard,   For those the Savior has set free,
That now his presence may begin   Anointed by the Holy Ghost,
To keep us from all stain of sin.   Are guarded by the Angel host.

adapted from THE SHORT BREVIARY

The Refrain for the Vespers Lessons
I will bear witness that the LORD is righteous;* I will praise the Name of the LORD
Most High.

Psalm 7:18

The Vespers Psalm   *Turn Again to Your Rest, O My Soul*
The LORD watches over the innocent;* I was brought very low, and he helped me.
Turn again to your rest, O my soul,* for the LORD has treated you well.
For you have rescued my life from death,* my eyes from tears, and my feet from
stumbling.
I will walk in the presence of the LORD* in the land of the living.

Psalm 116:5–8

The Refrain
I will bear witness that the LORD is righteous;* I will praise the Name of the LORD
Most High.

The Cry of the Church
Even so, come, Lord Jesus!

The Lord's Prayer

The Prayer Appointed for the Week
O God, whose blessed Son came into the world that he might destroy the works of
the devil and make us children of God and heirs of eternal life: Grant that, having this hope, I may purify myself as he is pure; that, when he comes again
with power and great glory, I may be made like him in his eternal and glorious
kingdom; where he lives and reigns with you and the Holy Spirit, one God, for
ever and ever. *Amen.*†

The Concluding Prayer of the Church
Spirit of God, promise of Jesus, come to our help at the close of this day. Come
with forgiveness and healing love. Come with life and hope. Come with all
that we need to continue in the way of your truth. So may we praise you in the
Trinity forever. *Amen.*

THE NEW COMPANION TO THE BREVIARY

The Morning Office   To Be Observed on the Hour or Half Hour

Between 6 and 9 a.m.

The Call to Prayer
Hallelujah! Give thanks to the LORD for he is good,* for his mercy endures for ever.

Psalm 106:1

The Request for Presence
I call with my whole heart;* answer me, O LORD, that I may keep your statutes.

Psalm 119:145

The Greeting

To you, O Lord, I lift up my soul; my God, I put my trust in you;* let me not be
humiliated, nor let my enemies triumph over me.
Let none who look to you be put to shame.

Psalm 25:1–2

The Refrain for the Morning Lessons

No good things will the Lord withhold* from those who walk with integrity.

Psalm 84:11

A Reading

Jesus said: "The servant who knows what his master wants, but has got nothing
ready and done nothing in accord with those wishes, will be given a great
many strokes of the lash. The one who did not know, but has acted in such a
way that he deserves a beating will be given fewer strokes. When someone is
given a great deal, a great deal will be demanded of that person; when someone is entrusted with a great deal, of that person even more will be expected."

Luke 12:47–48

The Refrain

No good things will the Lord withhold* from those who walk with integrity.

The Morning Psalm   *Lead Me, O Lord, and Make Your Way Straight Before Me*

Give ear to my words, O Lord;* consider my meditation.
Hearken to my cry for help, my King and my God,* for I make my prayer to you.
In the morning, Lord, you hear my voice;* early in the morning I make my appeal
and watch for you.
For you are not a God who takes pleasure in wickedness,* and evil cannot dwell
with you.
Braggarts cannot stand in your sight;* you hate all those who work wickedness.
You destroy those who speak lies;* the bloodthirsty and deceitful, O Lord, you
abhor.
But as for me, through the greatness of your mercy I go into your house;* I will
bow down toward your holy temple in awe of you.
Lead me, O Lord, in your righteousness, because of those who lie in wait for me;*
make your way straight before me.

Psalm 5:1–8

The Refrain

No good things will the Lord withhold* from those who walk with integrity.

The Cry of the Church

Lord, have mercy on us. Christ, have mercy on us. Lord, have mercy on us.

The Lord's Prayer

The Prayer Appointed for the Week

O God, whose blessed Son came into the world that he might destroy the works of
the devil and make us children of God and heirs of eternal life: Grant that, hav-

ing this hope, I may purify myself as he is pure; that, when he comes again with power and great glory, I may be made like him in his eternal and glorious kingdom; where he lives and reigns with you and the Holy Spirit, one God, for ever and ever. *Amen.*†

The Concluding Prayer of the Church

Lord God, almighty and everlasting Father, you have brought me in safety to this new day: Preserve me with your mighty power, that I may not fall into sin, nor be overcome by adversity; and in all I do direct me to the fulfilling of your purpose; through Jesus Christ my Lord. *Amen.*†

The Midday Office

To Be Observed on the Hour or Half Hour Between 11 a.m. and 2 p.m.

The Call to Prayer

"Come now, let us reason together," says the LORD.

Isaiah 1:18 (KJV)

The Request for Presence

Awake, O my God, decree justice;* let the assembly of peoples gather around you.
Let the malice of the wicked come to an end, but establish the righteous;* for you test the mind and heart, O righteous God.

Psalm 7:7, 10

The Greeting

Deliver me, O LORD, by your hand* from those whose portion in life is this world . . .

Psalm 17:14

The Refrain for the Midday Lessons

Righteousness shall go before him,* and peace shall be a pathway for his feet.

Psalm 85:13

A Reading

In the year of King Uzziah's death I saw the Lord seated on a high and lofty throne; his train filled the sanctuary. Above him stood seraphs, each one with six wings: two to cover its face, two to cover its feet and two for flying; and they were shouting these words to each other: "Holy, holy, holy is YAHWEH Sabaoth. His glory fills the whole earth." The door-posts shook at the sound of their shouting, and the Temple was full of smoke. Then I said: "Woe is me! I am lost, for I am a man of unclean lips and I live among a people of unclean lips, and my eyes have seen the King, YAHWEH Sabaoth." Then one of the seraphs flew to me, holding in its hand a live coal which it had taken from the altar with a pair of tongs. With this it touched my mouth and said: "Look, this has touched your lips, your guilt has been removed and your sin forgiven."

Isaiah 6:1–8

The Refrain
Righteousness shall go before him,* and peace shall be a pathway for his feet.

The Midday Psalm   *You Lengthen My Stride Beneath Me*
It is God who girds me about with strength* and makes my way secure.
He makes me sure-footed like a deer* and lets me stand firm on the heights.
He trains my hands for battle* and my arms for bending even a bow of bronze.
You have given me your shield of victory;* your right hand also sustains me; your
    loving care makes me great.
You lengthen my stride beneath me,* and my ankles do not give way.

Psalm 18:33–37

The Refrain
Righteousness shall go before him,* and peace shall be a pathway for his feet.

The Cry of the Church
Lord, have mercy on us. Christ, have mercy on us. Lord, have mercy on us.

The Lord's Prayer

The Prayer Appointed for the Week
O God, whose blessed Son came into the world that he might destroy the works of
    the devil and make us children of God and heirs of eternal life: Grant that, hav-
    ing this hope, I may purify myself as he is pure; that, when he comes again
    with power and great glory, I may be made like him in his eternal and glorious
    kingdom; where he lives and reigns with you and the Holy Spirit, one God, for
    ever and ever. *Amen.*†

The Concluding Prayer of the Church
Renew in my heart, O God, the gift of your Holy Spirit, so that I may love you
    fully in all that I do and love all others as Christ loves me. May all that I do pro-
    claim the good news that you are God with us. *Amen.*†

The Vespers Office   To Be Observed on the Hour or Half Hour
                                                    Between 5 and 8 p.m.

The Call to Prayer
Rejoice in the LORD, you righteous,* and give thanks to his holy Name.

Psalm 97:12

The Request for Presence
Send forth your strength, O God;* establish, O God, what you have wrought for us.

Psalm 68:28

The Greeting
One generation shall praise your works to another* and shall declare your power.

Psalm 145:4

The Hymn   *As the Bridegroom to His Chosen*

As the bridegroom to his chosen,   As the ruby in the setting,
As the king unto his realm,   As the honey in the comb,
As the keep unto his castle,   As the light within the lantern,
As the pilot to the helm,   As the father in the home,
So, Lord, are you to me.   So, Lord, are you to me.

As the fountain in the garden,   As the sunshine in the heavens,
As the candle in the dark,   As the image in the glass,
As the treasure in the coffer,   As the fruit unto the fig tree,
As the manna in the ark,   As the dew upon the grass,
So, Lord, are you to me.   So, Lord, are you to me.

John Tauler

As the music at the banquet,
As the stamp unto the seal,
As the medicine to the fainting,
As the winecup at the meal,
So, Lord, are you to me.

The Refrain for the Vespers Lessons
The hills stand about Jerusalem;* so does the LORD stand round about his people,
from this time forth for evermore.

Psalm 125:2

The Vespers Psalm   *Your Love Is Before My Eyes*
Test me, O LORD, and try me;* examine my heart and my mind.
For your love is before my eyes;* I have walked faithfully with you.
I have not sat with the worthless,* nor do I consort with the deceitful.
I have hated the company of evildoers;* I will not sit down with the wicked.
I will wash my hands in innocence, O LORD,* that I may go in procession round
your altar,
Singing aloud a song of thanksgiving* and recounting all your wonderful deeds.

Psalm 26:2–7

The Refrain
The hills stand about Jerusalem;* so does the LORD stand round about his people,
from this time forth for evermore.

The Small Verse
But if you will not serve the Lord, choose today whom you wish to serve . . . As
for me and my House, we will serve YAHWEH.

Joshua 24:15

The Lord's Prayer

The Prayer Appointed for the Week
O God, whose blessed Son came into the world that he might destroy the works of
the devil and make us children of God and heirs of eternal life: Grant that, hav-

ing this hope, I may purify myself as he is pure; that, when he comes again with power and great glory, I may be made like him in his eternal and glorious kingdom; where he lives and reigns with you and the Holy Spirit, one God, for ever and ever. *Amen.*†

The Concluding Prayer of the Church

Lord God Almighty, you have made all the peoples of the earth for your glory, to serve you in freedom and in peace: Give to the people of our country a zeal for justice and the strength of forbearance, that we may use our liberty in accordance with your gracious will; through Jesus Christ our Lord, who lives and reigns with you and the Holy Spirit, one God, for ever and ever. *Amen.*†

The Morning Office   To Be Observed on the Hour or Half Hour
                                                        Between 6 and 9 a.m.

The Call to Prayer

Come now and see the works of God,* how wonderful he is in his doing toward all people.

Psalm 66:4

The Request for Presence

Satisfy us by your loving-kindness in the morning;* so shall we rejoice and be glad all the days of our life.

Psalm 90:14

The Greeting

Save us, O LORD our God, and gather us from among the nations,* that we may give thanks to your holy Name and glory in your praise.

Psalm 106:47

The Refrain for the Morning Lessons

Mercy and truth have met together;* righteousness and peace have kissed each other.

Psalm 85:10

A Reading

Jesus taught us, saying: "Be compassionate just as your Father is compassionate. Do not judge, and you will not be judged; do not condemn, and you will not be condemned; forgive, and you will be forgiven. Give, and there will be gifts for you: a full measure, pressed down, shaken together, and overflowing, will be poured into your lap; because the standard you use will be the standard used for you."

Luke 6:36–38

The Refrain

Mercy and truth have met together;* righteousness and peace have kissed each other.

The Morning Psalm   *We Walk, O LORD, in the Light of Your Presence*

Righteousness and justice are the foundations of your throne;* love and truth go
    before your face.
Happy are the people who know the festal shout!* they walk, O LORD, in the light
    of your presence.
They rejoice daily in your Name;* they are jubilant in your righteousness.
For you are the glory of their strength,* and by your favor our might is exalted.
Truly, the LORD is our ruler;* the Holy One of Israel is our King.

Psalm 89:14–18

The Refrain

Mercy and truth have met together;* righteousness and peace have kissed each
    other.

The Cry of the Church

Lord, have mercy on us. Christ, have mercy on us. Lord, have mercy on us.

The Lord's Prayer

The Prayer Appointed for the Week

O God, whose blessed Son came into the world that he might destroy the works of
    the devil and make us children of God and heirs of eternal life: Grant that, hav-
    ing this hope, I may purify myself as he is pure; that, when he comes again
    with power and great glory, I may be made like him in his eternal and glorious
    kingdom; where he lives and reigns with you and the Holy Spirit, one God, for
    ever and ever. *Amen.*†

The Concluding Prayer of the Church

Lord God, almighty and everlasting Father, you have brought me in safety to this
    new day: Preserve me with your mighty power, that I may not fall into sin, nor
    be overcome by adversity; and in all I do direct me to the fulfilling of your pur-
    pose; through Jesus Christ my Lord. *Amen.*†

The Midday Office   **To Be Observed on the Hour or Half Hour**
Between 11 a.m. and 2 p.m.

The Call to Prayer

"Come now, let us reason together," says the LORD.

Isaiah 1:18 (KJV)

The Request for Presence

O God, be not far from me;* come quickly to help me, O my God.

Psalm 71:12

The Greeting

"You are my God, and I will thank you;* you are my God and I will exalt you."

Psalm 118:28

The Refrain for the Midday Lessons

The same stone that the builders rejected* has become the chief cornerstone.
This is the LORD'S doing,* and it is marvelous in our eyes.

Psalm 118:22–23

A Reading

St. Paul said: ". . . I am alive; yet it is no longer I, but Christ living in me. The life
that I am now living, subject to the limitation of human nature, I am living in
faith, faith in the Son of God who loved me and gave himself for me."

Galatians 2:20

The Refrain

The same stone that the builders rejected* has become the chief cornerstone.
This is the LORD'S doing,* and it is marvelous in our eyes.

The Midday Psalm   *We Are His*

Be joyful in the LORD, all you lands;* serve the LORD with gladness and come
before his presence with a song.
Know this: The LORD himself is God;* he himself has made us, and we are his; we
are his people and the sheep of his pasture.
Enter his gates with thanksgiving; go into his courts with praise;* give thanks to
him and call upon his Name.
For the LORD is good; his mercy is everlasting;* and his faithfulness endures from
age to age.

Psalm 100:1–4

The Refrain

The same stone that the builders rejected* has become the chief cornerstone.
This is the LORD'S doing,* and it is marvelous in our eyes.

The Cry of the Church

Lord, have mercy on us. Christ, have mercy on us. Lord, have mercy on us.

The Lord's Prayer

The Prayer Appointed for the Week

O God, whose blessed Son came into the world that he might destroy the works of
the devil and make us children of God and heirs of eternal life: Grant that, having this hope, I may purify myself as he is pure; that, when he comes again
with power and great glory, I may be made like him in his eternal and glorious
kingdom; where he lives and reigns with you and the Holy Spirit, one God, for
ever and ever. *Amen.*†

The Concluding Prayer of the Church

Lord Jesus Christ, by your death you took away the sting of death: Grant me to so
follow in faith where you have led the way, that I may at length fall asleep
peacefully in you and wake in your likeness; for your tender mercies' sake.
Amen.†

The Vespers Office
To Be Observed on the Hour or Half Hour
Between 5 and 8 p.m.

The Call to Prayer
I will call upon God,* and the LORD will deliver me.
In the evening, in the morning, and at the noonday, I will complain and lament,*
    and he will hear my voice.
He will bring me safely back . . . God, who is enthroned of old, will hear me.

Psalm 55:17ff

The Request for Presence
Teach me your way, O LORD, and I will walk in your truth;* knit my heart to you
    that I may fear your Name.

Psalm 86:11

The Greeting
To you, O LORD, I lift up my soul;* my God I put my trust in you . . .

Psalm 25:1

The Hymn   *How Can We Sinners Know*

How can we sinners know   The meek and lowly heart
Our sins on earth forgiven?   That in our Savior was,
How can my gracious Savior show   To us that Spirit does impart
My name inscribed in heaven?   And signs us with his cross.

We by his Spirit prove   Our nature's turned, our mind
And know the things of God,   Transformed in all its powers,
The things which freely of his love And both the witnesses are joined
He has on us bestowed.   The Spirit of God with ours.

Charles Wesley

The Refrain for the Vespers Lessons
As far as the east is from the west,* so far has he removed our sins from us.

Psalm 103:12

The Vespers Psalm   *You Are the Holy One, Enthroned Upon the Praises of Israel*
My God, my God, why have you forsaken me?* and are so far from my cry and
    from the words of my distress?
O my God, I cry in the daytime, but you do not answer;* by night as well, but I
    find no rest.
Yet you are the Holy One,* enthroned upon the praises of Israel.
Our forefathers put their trust in you;* they trusted, and you delivered them.
They cried out to you and were delivered;* they trusted in you and were not put to
    shame.

Psalm 22:1-5

The Refrain
As far as the east is from the west,* so far has he removed our sins from us.

The Cry of the Church
O God, come to my assistance! O Lord, make haste to help me!

The Lord's Prayer

The Prayer Appointed for the Week
O God, whose blessed Son came into the world that he might destroy the works of
the devil and make us children of God and heirs of eternal life: Grant that, having this hope, I may purify myself as he is pure; that, when he comes again
with power and great glory, I may be made like him in his eternal and glorious
kingdom; where he lives and reigns with you and the Holy Spirit, one God, for
ever and ever. *Amen.*†

Concluding Prayers of the Church
Almighty God, who has promised to hear the petitions of those who ask in your
Son's Name: I beseech you mercifully to incline your ear to me who have made
my prayers and supplications to you; and grant that those things which I have
faithfully asked according to your will, may effectually be obtained, to the
relief of my necessity, and to the setting forth of your glory; through Jesus
Christ my Lord. *Amen.*†

May the souls of the faithful departed, through the mercy of God, rest in eternal
peace. *Amen.*

The Morning Office   To Be Observed on the Hour or Half Hour
                                         Between 6 and 9 a.m.

The Call to Prayer
Ascribe to the LORD the glory due his Name;* worship the LORD in the beauty of
holiness.

Psalm 29:2

The Request for Presence
O God, you are my God; eagerly I seek you;* my soul thirsts for you, my flesh
faints for you, as in barren and dry land where there is no water.

Psalm 63:1

The Greeting
We have heard with our ears, O God, our forefathers have told us,* the deeds you
did in their days, in the days of old.

Psalm 44:1

The Refrain for the Morning Lessons
They do not know, neither do they understand; they go about in darkness . . .

Psalm 82:5

A Reading

Jesus said: "I am the bread of life. No one who comes to me will ever hunger; no
one who believes in me will ever thirst."

John 6:35

The Refrain

They do not know, neither do they understand; they go about in darkness . . .

The Morning Psalm   *Whoever Is Wise Will Ponder These Things*

The LORD changed rivers into deserts,* and water-springs into thirsty ground,
A fruitful land into salt flats,* because of the wickedness of those who dwell there.
He changed deserts into pools of water* and dry land into water-springs.
He settled the hungry there,* and they founded a city to dwell in.
They sowed fields, and planted vineyards,* and brought in a fruitful harvest.
He blessed them, so that they increased greatly;* he did not let their herds
    decrease.
Yet when they were diminished and brought low,* through stress of adversity and
    sorrow,
(He pours contempt on princes* and makes them wander in trackless wastes)
He lifted up the poor out of misery* and multiplied their families like flocks of
    sheep.
The upright will see this and rejoice,* but all wickedness will shut its mouth.
Whoever is wise will ponder these things,* and consider well the mercies of the
    LORD.

Psalm 107:33–43

The Refrain

They do not know, neither do they understand; they go about in darkness . . .

The Gloria

The Lord's Prayer

The Prayer Appointed for the Week

O God, whose blessed Son came into the world that he might destroy the works of
    the devil and make us children of God and heirs of eternal life: Grant that, hav-
    ing this hope, I may purify myself as he is pure; that, when he comes again
    with power and great glory, I may be made like him in his eternal and glorious
    kingdom; where he lives and reigns with you and the Holy Spirit, one God, for
    ever and ever. *Amen.*†

The Concluding Prayer of the Church

Lord God, almighty and everlasting Father, you have brought me in safety to this
    new day: Preserve me with your mighty power, that I may not fall into sin, nor
    be overcome by adversity; and in all I do direct me to the fulfilling of your pur-
    pose; through Jesus Christ my Lord. *Amen.*†

The Midday Office   To Be Observed on the Hour or Half Hour
                                              Between 11 a.m. and 2 p.m.

The Call to Prayer
Ascribe to the LORD the honor due his Name;* bring offerings and come into his
    courts.

Psalm 96:8

The Request for Presence
Accept, O LORD, the willing tribute of my lips,* and teach me your judgments.
Psalm 119:108

The Greeting
I give you thanks, O God, I give you thanks,* calling upon your Name and declar-
    ing all your wonderful deeds.

based on Psalm 75:1

The Refrain for the Midday Lessons
My tongue will proclaim your righteousness all day long.
Psalm 71:24

A Reading
Moses then said to God, "Look, if I go to the Israelites and say to them, 'The God
    of your ancestors has sent me to you,' and they say to me, 'What is his name?'
    what am I to tell them?" God said to Moses, "I am he who is." And he said,
    "This is what you are to say to the Israelites, 'I am has sent me to you.' " God
    further said to Moses, "You are to tell the Israelites, 'YAHWEH, the God of your
    ancestors, the God of Abraham, the God of Isaac and the God of Jacob, has sent
    me to you.' This is my name for all time, and thus I am to be invoked for all
    generations to come."

Exodus 3:13–15

The Refrain
My tongue will proclaim your righteousness all day long.

The Midday Psalm   *I Will Declare the Mysteries of Ancient Times*
Hear my teaching, O my people;* incline your ears to the words of my mouth.
I will open my mouth in a parable;* I will declare the mysteries of ancient times.
That which we have heard and known, and what our forefathers have told us,* we
    will not hide from their children.
We will recount to generations to come the praiseworthy deeds and the power of
    the LORD,* and the wonderful works he has done.
He gave his decrees to Jacob and established a law for Israel,* which he
    commanded them to teach their children;
That the generations to come might know, and the children yet unborn;* that they
    in their turn might tell it to their children;
So that they might put their trust in God,* and not forget the deeds of God, but
    keep his commandments.

Psalm 78:1–7

The Refrain
My tongue will proclaim your righteousness all day long.

The Gloria

The Lord's Prayer

The Prayer Appointed for the Week
O God, whose blessed Son came into the world that he might destroy the works of
    the devil and make us children of God and heirs of eternal life: Grant that, hav-
    ing this hope, I may purify myself as he is pure; that, when he comes again
    with power and great glory, I may be made like him in his eternal and glorious
    kingdom; where he lives and reigns with you and the Holy Spirit, one God, for
    ever and ever. *Amen.*†

The Concluding Prayer of the Church
O God, the source of eternal light: Shed forth your unending day upon all of us
    who watch for you, that our lips may praise you, our lives may bless you, and
    our worship may give you glory; through Jesus Christ our Lord. *Amen.*†

The Vespers Office   **To Be Observed on the Hour or Half Hour
Between 5 and 8 p.m.**

The Call to Prayer
We will bless the LORD,* from this time forth for evermore. Hallelujah!
Psalm 115:18

The Request for Presence
Answer me when I call, O God, defender of my cause;* you set me free when I am
    hard-pressed; have mercy on me and hear my prayer.
Psalm 4:1

The Greeting
Be exalted, O LORD, in your might;* we will sing and praise your power.
Psalm 21:14

The Hymn   *Lord Jesus, Think on Me*

Lord Jesus, think on me,   Lord Jesus, think on me,
And purge away my sin;   Nor let me go astray;
From earth-born passions set me free,   Through darkness and perplexity
And make me pure within.   You point the heavenly way.

Lord Jesus, think on me,   Lord Jesus, think on me,
With care and woe oppressed;   That, when the flood is past,
Let your loving servant be,   I may the eternal brightness see,
And taste your promised rest.   And share your joy at last.

Synesius of Cyrene

The Refrain for the Vespers Lessons
. . . I call upon you all the day long.

Psalm 86:3

The Vespers Psalm   *My Days Drift Away Like Smoke*

LORD, hear my prayer, and let my cry come before you;* hide not your face from
　　me in the day of my trouble.
Incline your ear to me;* when I call, make haste to answer me,
For my days drift away like smoke,* and my bones are hot as burning coals.
My heart is smitten like grass and withered,* so that I forget to eat my bread.
Because of the voice of my groaning* I am but skin and bones.
I have become like a vulture in the wilderness,* like an owl among the ruins.
I lie awake and groan;* I am like a sparrow, lonely on a house-top.

Psalm 102:1–7

The Refrain
. . . I call upon you all the day long.

The Gloria

The Lord's Prayer

The Prayer Appointed for the Week

O God, whose blessed Son came into the world that he might destroy the works of
　　the devil and make us children of God and heirs of eternal life: Grant that, hav-
　　ing this hope, I may purify myself as he is pure; that, when he comes again
　　with power and great glory, I may be made like him in his eternal and glorious
　　kingdom; where he lives and reigns with you and the Holy Spirit, one God, for
　　ever and ever. *Amen.*✝

The Concluding Prayer of the Church

For an angel of peace, faithful guardian and guide of our souls and our bodies, we
　　beseech thee, O Lord.

Orthodox

❧

The Morning Office   To Be Observed on the Hour or Half Hour

Between 6 and 9 a.m.

The Call to Prayer
Sing to the LORD and bless his Name;* proclaim the good news of his salvation
　　from day to day.

Declare his glory among the nations* and his wonders among all peoples.
For great is the LORD and greatly to be praised;* he is more to be feared than all
gods.

Psalm 96:2–4

The Request for Presence
Satisfy us by your loving-kindness in the morning;* so shall we rejoice and be glad
all the days of our life.

Psalm 90:14

The Greeting
Awesome things will you show us in your righteousness, O God of our salvation,*
O Hope of all the ends of the earth and of the seas that are far away.

Psalm 65:5

The Refrain for the Morning Lessons
For he shall give his angels charge over you,* to keep you in all your ways.

Psalm 91:11

A Reading
From the sermon of St. Paul in Antioch: "My brothers, I want you to realize that it
is through him that forgiveness of sins is being proclaimed to you. Through
him justification from all sins from which the Law of Moses was unable to jus-
tify is being offered to every believer. So be careful—or what the prophets say
will happen to you. *Cast your eyes around you, mockers; be amazed, and perish! For
I am doing something in your own days that you would never believe if you were told
of it."*

Acts 13:38–41

The Refrain
For he shall give his angels charge over you,* to keep you in all your ways.

The Morning Psalm   *There Are the Thrones of the House of David*
I was glad when they said to me,* "Let us go to the house of the LORD."
Now our feet are standing* within your gates, O Jerusalem.
Jerusalem is built as a city* that is at unity with itself;
To which the tribes go up, the tribes of the LORD,* the assembly of Israel, to praise
the Name of the LORD.
For there are the thrones of judgment,* the thrones of the house of David.

Psalm 122:1–5

The Refrain
For he shall give his angels charge over you,* to keep you in all your ways.

The Cry of the Church
O Lord, hear my prayer and let my cry come unto you. Thanks be to God.

THE SHORT BREVIARY

The Lord's Prayer

The Prayer Appointed for the Week

Blessed Lord, who caused all holy Scriptures to be written for our learning: Grant me so to hear them, read, mark, learn, and inwardly digest them, that I may embrace and ever hold fast the blessed hope of everlasting life, which you have given us in our Savior Jesus Christ; who lives and reigns with you and the Holy Spirit, one God, for ever and ever. *Amen.*†

The Concluding Prayer of the Church

Lord God, almighty and everlasting Father, you have brought me in safety to this new day: Preserve me with your mighty power, that I may not fall into sin, nor be overcome by adversity; and in all I do direct me to the fulfilling of your purpose; through Jesus Christ my Lord. *Amen.*†

The Midday Office   **To Be Observed on the Hour or Half Hour**
                                         Between 11 a.m. and 2 p.m.

The Call to Prayer

God has gone up with a shout,* the LORD with the sound of the ram's-horn.
Sing praises to God, sing praises;* sing praises to our King, sing praises.
For God is King of all the earth;* sing praises with all your skill.
God reigns over the nations;* God sits upon his holy throne.

Psalm 47:5–8

The Request for Presence

Let the peoples praise you, O God;* let all the peoples praise you.

Psalm 67:3

The Greeting

For you alone are the Holy One, you alone are the Lord, you alone are the Most High, Jesus Christ, with the Holy Spirit, in the glory of God the Father.

The Refrain for the Midday Lessons

Tell it out among the nations: "The LORD is King!* he has made the world so firm that it cannot be moved; he will judge the peoples with equity."

Psalm 96:10

A Reading

Rejoice heart and soul, daughter of Zion! Shout for joy, daughter of Jerusalem! Look your king is approaching, he is vindicated and victorious, humble and riding on a donkey, on a colt, the foal of the donkey. He will banish chariots from Ephraim and horses from Jerusalem; the bow of war will be banished. He will proclaim peace to the nations, his empire will stretch from sea to sea, from the River to the limits of the earth.

Zechariah 9:9–10

The Refrain

Tell it out among the nations: "The LORD is King!* he has made the world so firm that it cannot be moved; he will judge the peoples with equity."

The Midday Psalm   *Your Throne, O God, Endures For Ever and Ever*

My heart is stirring with a noble song; let me recite what I have fashioned for the
king;* my tongue shall be the pen of a skilled writer.

You are the fairest of men;* grace flows from your lips, because God has blessed
you for ever.

Strap your sword upon your thigh, O mighty warrior,* in your pride and in your
majesty.

Ride out and conquer in the cause of truth* and for the sake of justice.

Your right hand will show you marvelous things;* your arrows are very sharp, O
mighty warrior.

The peoples are falling at your feet,* and the king's enemies are losing heart.

Your throne, O God, endures for ever and ever,* a scepter of righteousness is the
scepter of your kingdom; you love righteousness and hate iniquity.

Therefore God, your God, has anointed you* with the oil of gladness above your
fellows.

All your garments are fragrant with myrrh, aloes, and cassia,* and the music of
strings from ivory palaces makes you glad.

Kings' daughters stand among the ladies of the court;* on your right hand is the
queen, adorned with the gold of Ophir.

Psalm 45:1–10

The Refrain

Tell it out among the nations: "The LORD is King!* he has made the world so firm
that it cannot be moved; he will judge the peoples with equity."

The Gloria

The Lord's Prayer

The Prayer Appointed for the Week

Blessed Lord, who caused all holy Scriptures to be written for our learning: Grant
me so to hear them, read, mark, learn, and inwardly digest them, that I may
embrace and ever hold fast the blessed hope of everlasting life, which you have
given us in our Savior Jesus Christ; who lives and reigns with you and the
Holy Spirit, one God, for ever and ever. *Amen.*†

The Concluding Prayer of the Church

O God, you make me glad with the weekly remembrance of the glorious resurrection of your Son my Lord: Give me this day such blessing through my worship
of you, that the week to come may be spent in your favor; through Jesus Christ
our Lord. *Amen.*†

The Vespers Office   **To Be Observed on the Hour or Half Hour**
                                        Between 5 and 8 p.m.

The Call to Prayer

Open my lips, O LORD,* and my mouth shall proclaim your praise.

Psalm 51:16

The Request for Presence
Hear, O LORD, and have mercy upon me;* O LORD, be my helper.
Psalm 30:11

The Greeting
Blessed be the Lord GOD, the God of Israel,* who alone does wondrous deeds!
And blessed be his glorious Name for ever!* and may all the earth be filled with
his glory. Amen. Amen.
Psalm 72:18–19

The Hymn   *God Will Take Care of You*

Be not dismayed whatever betide,
God will take care of you;
Beneath his wings of love abide,
God will take care of you.

Through days of toil when heart does fail,
God will take care of you;
When dangers fierce your path assail,
God will take care of you.

All you may need He will provide,
God will take care of you;
Nothing you ask will be denied,
God will take care of you.

No matter what may be the test,
God will take care of you;
Lean, weary one, upon his breast,
God will take care of you.

God will take care of you,
Through every day,
Over all the way;
He will take care of you,
God will take care of you.
Civilla Martin

The Refrain for the Vespers Lessons
It is better to rely on the LORD* than to put any trust in flesh.
It is better to rely on the LORD* than to put any trust in rulers.
Psalm 118:8–9

The Vespers Psalm   *He Does Not Forsake His Faithful Ones*
Our steps are directed by the LORD;* he strengthens those in whose way he
delights.
If they stumble, they shall not fall headlong,* for the LORD holds them by the hand.
I have been young and now I am old,* but never have I seen the righteous
forsaken, or their children begging bread.
The righteous are always generous in their lending,* and their children shall be a
blessing.
Turn from evil, and do good,* and dwell in the land for ever.
For the LORD loves justice;* he does not forsake his faithful ones.
They shall be kept safe for ever,* but the offspring of the wicked shall be
destroyed.
The righteous shall possess the land* and dwell in it for ever.
The mouth of the righteous utters wisdom,* and their tongue speaks what is right.
The law of their God is in their heart,* and their footsteps shall not falter.
Psalm 37:24–33

The Refrain
It is better to rely on the LORD* than to put any trust in flesh.
It is better to rely on the LORD* than to put any trust in rulers.

The Small Verse
Their sound goes forth to all the earth and their speech to the end of the world.
adapted from THE SHORT BREVIARY

The Lord's Prayer

The Prayer Appointed for the Week
Blessed Lord, who caused all holy Scriptures to be written for our learning: Grant
me so to hear them, read, mark, learn, and inwardly digest them, that I may
embrace and ever hold fast the blessed hope of everlasting life, which you have
given us in our Savior Jesus Christ; who lives and reigns with you and the
Holy Spirit, one God, for ever and ever. *Amen.*†

The Concluding Prayer of the Church
Lord God, whose Son our Savior Jesus Christ, triumphed over the powers of death
and prepared for us our place in the new Jerusalem: Grant that I, who have this
day given thanks for his resurrection, may praise you in the City of which he is
the light, and where he lives and reigns for ever and ever. *Amen.*†

The Morning Office   To Be Observed on the Hour or Half Hour
Between 6 and 9 a.m.

The Call to Prayer
Love the LORD, all you who worship him;* the LORD protects the faithful, but
repays to the full those who act haughtily.
Be strong and let your heart take courage,* all you who wait for the LORD.
Psalm 31:23–24

The Request for Presence
Be my strong rock, a castle to keep me safe, for you are my crag and my strong-
hold;* for the sake of your Name, lead me and guide me.
Psalm 31:3

The Greeting
How great is your goodness, O LORD!* which you have laid up for those who fear
you; which you have done in the sight of all.
Psalm 31:19

The Refrain for the Morning Lessons
Blessed be the LORD!* for he has shown me the wonders of his love in a besieged city.
Psalm 31:21

A Reading
Jesus taught us, saying: "It is easier for heaven and earth to disappear than for one
little stroke to drop out of the Law."
Luke 16:17

The Refrain
Blessed be the LORD!* for he has shown me the wonders of his love in a besieged city.

The Morning Psalm   *He Asked You for Life, and You Gave It to Him*
The king rejoices in your strength, O LORD;* how greatly he exults in your victory!
You have given him his heart's desire;* you have not denied him the request of his
    lips.
For you meet him with blessings of prosperity,* and set a crown of fine gold upon
    his head.
He asked you for life, and you gave it to him:* length of days, for ever and ever.
His honor is great, because of your victory;* splendor and majesty have you
    bestowed upon him.
For you will give him everlasting felicity* and will make him glad with the joy of
    your presence.
For the king puts his trust in the LORD;* because of the loving-kindness of the Most
    High, he will not fall.

Psalm 21:1–7

The Refrain
Blessed be the LORD!* for he has shown me the wonders of his love in a besieged city.

The Cry of the Church
In the evening, in the morning, and at noonday, I will complain and lament,* and
    he will hear my voice.

Psalm 55:18

The Lord's Prayer

The Prayer Appointed for the Week
Blessed Lord, who caused all holy Scriptures to be written for our learning: Grant
    me so to hear them, read, mark, learn, and inwardly digest them, that I may
    embrace and ever hold fast the blessed hope of everlasting life, which you have
    given us in our Savior Jesus Christ; who lives and reigns with you and the
    Holy Spirit, one God, for ever and ever. *Amen.*†

The Concluding Prayer of the Church
Lord God, almighty and everlasting Father, you have brought me in safety to this
    new day: Preserve me with your mighty power, that I may not fall into sin, nor
    be overcome by adversity; and in all I do direct me to the fulfilling of your pur-
    pose; through Jesus Christ my Lord. *Amen.*†

The Midday Office   To Be Observed on the Hour or Half Hour
                                          Between 11 a.m. and 2 p.m.

The Call to Prayer
Sing to the LORD with the harp,* with the harp and the voice of song.
With trumpets and the sound of the horn* shout with joy before the King, the LORD.

Psalm 98:6–7

The Request for Presence
Show us the light of your countenance, O God,* and come to us.

based on Psalm 67:1

The Greeting
O Lord, what are we that you should care for us?* mere mortals that you should
think of us?
We are like a puff of wind;* our days are like a passing shadow.

Psalm 144:3–4

The Refrain for the Midday Lessons
Shout with joy to the Lord, all you lands;* lift up your voice, rejoice, and sing.

Psalm 98:5

A Reading
And let us never slacken in doing good; for if we do not give up, we shall have our
harvest in due time. So then, as long as we have the opportunity let all our
actions be for the good of everybody, and especially of those who belong to the
household of faith.

Galatians 6:9–10

The Refrain
Shout with joy to the Lord, all you lands;* lift up your voice, rejoice, and sing.

The Midday Psalm   *He That Planted the Ear, Does He Not Hear?*
O Lord God of vengeance,* O God of vengeance, show yourself.
Rise up, O Judge of the world;* give the arrogant their just deserts.
How long shall the wicked, O Lord,* how long shall the wicked triumph?
They bluster in their insolence;* all evildoers are full of boasting.
They crush your people, O Lord,* and afflict your chosen nation.
They murder the widow and the stranger* and put the orphans to death.
Yet they say, "The Lord does not see,* the God of Jacob takes no notice."
Consider well, you dullards among the people;* when will you fools understand?
He that planted the ear, does he not hear?* he that formed the eye, does he not see?
He who admonishes the nations, will he not punish?* he who teaches all the
world, has he no knowledge?
The Lord knows our human thoughts;* how like a puff of wind they are.
Happy are they whom you instruct, O Lord!* whom you teach out of your law;
To give them rest in evil days,* until a pit is dug for the wicked.
For the Lord will not abandon his people,* nor will he forsake his own.
For judgment will again be just,* and all the true of heart will follow it.

Psalm 94:1–15

The Refrain
Shout with joy to the Lord, all you lands;* lift up your voice, rejoice, and sing.

The Gloria

The Lord's Prayer

The Prayer Appointed for the Week

Blessed Lord, who caused all holy Scriptures to be written for our learning: Grant me so to hear them, read, mark, learn, and inwardly digest them, that I may embrace and ever hold fast the blessed hope of everlasting life, which you have given us in our Savior Jesus Christ; who lives and reigns with you and the Holy Spirit, one God, for ever and ever. *Amen.*†

The Concluding Prayer of the Church

Almighty and everlasting God, who willed that our Savior should take upon Him our flesh and suffer death upon the Cross, that all mankind should follow the example of His great humility, mercifully grant that we may both follow the example of His patience and also be made partakers of His resurrection. Through the same Jesus Christ. *Amen.*

adapted from The Short Breviary

The Vespers Office   To Be Observed on the Hour or Half Hour
                                                        Between 5 and 8 p.m.

The Call to Prayer

Be joyful in God, all you lands;* sing the glory of his Name; sing the glory of his praise.
Say to God, "How awesome are your deeds! . . .
All the earth bows down before you,* sings to you, sings out your Name."

Psalm 66:1–3

The Request for Presence

Let your loving-kindness, O Lord, be upon us,* as we have put our trust in you.

Psalm 33:22

The Greeting

Blessed is the Lord!* for he has heard the voice of my prayer.

Psalm 28:7

The Hymn   *What Wondrous Love Is This*

What wondrous Love is this, O my soul, O my soul,
What wondrous Love is this, O my soul!
What wondrous Love is this that caused the Lord of bliss
To bear the dreadful curse for my soul, for my soul,
To bear the dreadful curse for my soul!

When I was sinking down, sinking down, sinking down,
When I was sinking down, sinking down,
When I was sinking down beneath God's righteous frown,
Christ laid aside his crown for my soul, for my soul,
Christ laid aside his crown for my soul.

To God and to the Lamb I will sing, I will sing,
To God and to the Lamb I will sing;
To God and to the Lamb who is the great I Am,
While millions join the theme, I will sing, I will sing;
While millions join the theme, I will sing!

And when from death I'm free, I'll sing on, I'll sing on,
And when from death I'm free, I'll sing on;
And when from death I'm free, I'll sing and joyful be,
And through eternity, I'll sing on, I'll sing on,
And through eternity, I'll sing on!

American Folk Song

The Refrain for the Vespers Lessons
Turn again to your rest, O my soul,* for the LORD has treated you well.
For you have rescued my life from death,* my eyes from tears, and my feet from
stumbling.

Psalm 116:6–7

The Vespers Psalm   *You Are with Me*
The LORD is my shepherd;* I shall not be in want.
He makes me lie down in green pastures* and leads me beside still waters.
He revives my soul* and guides me along right pathways for his Name's sake.
Though I walk through the valley of the shadow of death, I shall fear no evil;* for
you are with me; your rod and your staff, they comfort me.
You spread a table before me in the presence of those who trouble me;* you have
anointed my head with oil, and my cup is running over.
Surely your goodness and mercy shall follow me all the days of my life,* and I will
dwell in the house of the LORD for ever.

Psalm 23

The Refrain
Turn again to your rest, O my soul,* for the LORD has treated you well.
For you have rescued my life from death,* my eyes from tears, and my feet from
stumbling.

The Cry of the Church
O Lord, hear my prayer and let my cry come unto you. Thanks be to God.

THE SHORT BREVIARY

The Lord's Prayer

The Prayer Appointed for the Week
Blessed Lord, who caused all holy Scriptures to be written for our learning: Grant
me so to hear them, read, mark, learn, and inwardly digest them, that I may
embrace and ever hold fast the blessed hope of everlasting life, which you have
given us in our Savior Jesus Christ; who lives and reigns with you and the
Holy Spirit, one God, for ever and ever. *Amen*.†

The Concluding Prayer of the Church

Grant me and all of your people the gift of your Spirit, that we may know Christ and make him known; and through him, at all times and in all places, may give thanks to you in all things. *Amen.*†

The Morning Office   **To Be Observed on the Hour or Half Hour**
                             Between 6 and 9 a.m.

The Call to Prayer

Come and listen, all you who fear God,* and I will tell you what he has done for me.
                                                    Psalm 66:14

The Request for Presence

May God be merciful to us and bless us,* show us the light of his countenance and come to us.
Let your ways be known upon earth,* your saving health among all nations.
                                                    Psalm 67:1–2

The Greeting

Your statutes have been like songs to me* wherever I have lived as a stranger.
                                                    Psalm 119:54

The Refrain for the Morning Lessons

Purge me from my sin, and I shall be pure; wash me, and I shall be clean indeed.
                                                    Psalm 51:8

A Reading

Jesus declared publicly: "Whoever believes in me believes not in me but in the one who sent me, and whoever sees me, sees the one who sent me. I have come into the world as light, to prevent anyone who believes in me from staying in the dark anymore. If anyone hears my words and does not keep them faithfully, it is not I who shall judge such a person, since I have come not to judge the world, but to save the world: anyone who rejects and refuses my words has his judge already: the word itself that I have spoken will be his judge on the last day."
                                                    John 12:44–48

The Refrain

Purge me from my sin, and I shall be pure;* wash me, and I shall be clean indeed.

The Morning Psalm   *Show Me the Road I Must Walk*

LORD, hear my prayer, and in your faithfulness heed my supplications;* answer me in your righteousness.
My spirit faints within me;* my heart within me is desolate.
I remember the time past; I muse upon all your deeds;* I consider the works of your hands.
I spread out my hands to you;* my soul gasps to you like a thirsty land.
O LORD, make haste to answer me; my spirit fails me;* do not hide your face from me or I shall be like those who go down to the Pit.

Let me hear of your loving-kindness in the morning, for I put my trust in you;*
show me the road that I must walk, for I lift up my soul to you.

Psalm 143:1, 4–8

The Refrain
Purge me from my sin, and I shall be pure;* wash me, and I shall be clean indeed.

The Cry of the Church
Even so, come, Lord Jesus!

The Lord's Prayer

The Prayer Appointed for the Week
Blessed Lord, who caused all holy Scriptures to be written for our learning: Grant
me so to hear them, read, mark, learn, and inwardly digest them, that I may
embrace and ever hold fast the blessed hope of everlasting life, which you have
given us in our Savior Jesus Christ; who lives and reigns with you and the
Holy Spirit, one God, for ever and ever. *Amen.*†

The Concluding Prayer of the Church
Lord God, almighty and everlasting Father, you have brought me in safety to this
new day: Preserve me with your mighty power, that I may not fall into sin, nor
be overcome by adversity; and in all I do direct me to the fulfilling of your purpose; through Jesus Christ my Lord. *Amen.*†

The Midday Office   To Be Observed on the Hour or Half Hour
Between 11 a.m. and 2 p.m.

The Call to Prayer
Praise Him, from whom all blessings flow; praise Him all creatures here below;
praise Him, you heavenly hosts; praise Father, Son and Holy Ghost.

Traditional

The Request for Presence
Be my strong rock, a castle to keep me safe, for you are my crag and my stronghold;* for the sake of your Name, lead me and guide me.

Psalm 31:3

The Greeting
To you, O LORD, I lift up my soul;* my God, I put my trust in you . . .

Psalm 25:1

The Refrain for the Midday Lessons
Happy are they all who fear the LORD,* and who follow in his ways!

Psalm 28:1

A Reading
YAHWEH spoke to Moses and said, "Speak to Aaron and his sons and say: 'This is
how you must bless the Israelites. You will say: *May YAHWEH bless you and keep*

you. May YAHWEH let his face shine on you and be gracious to you. May YAHWEH show his face and bring you peace.' This is how they must call down my name on the Israelites, and then I shall bless them."

Numbers 6:22–27

The Refrain
Happy are they all who fear the LORD,* and who follow in his ways!

The Midday Psalm   *Our Help Is in the Name of the LORD*
If the LORD had not been on our side,* let Israel now say.
If the LORD had not been on our side,* when enemies rose up against us;
Then would they have swallowed us up alive* in their fierce anger toward us;
Then would the waters have overwhelmed us* and the torrent gone over us;
Then would the raging waters* have gone right over us.
Blessed be the LORD!* he has not given us over to be a prey for their teeth.
We have escaped like a bird from the snare of the fowler;* the snare is broken, and
    we have escaped.
Our help is in the Name of the LORD,* the maker of heaven and earth.

Psalm 124

The Refrain
Happy are they all who fear the LORD,* and who follow in his ways!

The Small Verse
The Lord is king. He has put on glorious apparel. Let all the nations praise him.
    Let those of every tongue bow before him. Alleluia, alleluia, alleluia.

Traditional

The Lord's Prayer

The Prayer Appointed for the Week
Blessed Lord, who caused all holy Scriptures to be written for our learning: Grant
    me so to hear them, read, mark, learn, and inwardly digest them, that I may
    embrace and ever hold fast the blessed hope of everlasting life, which you have
    given us in our Savior Jesus Christ; who lives and reigns with you and the
    Holy Spirit, one God, for ever and ever. *Amen.*†

The Concluding Prayer of the Church
Come forth, O Christ, and help me. For your name's sake deliver me.

Traditional

The Vespers Office   To Be Observed on the Hour or Half Hour
                                      Between 5 and 8 p.m.

The Call to Prayer
Praise God, from whom all blessings flow; praise him, all creatures here below;
    praise him above, you heavenly hosts; praise Father, Son and Holy Ghost.

Doxology

The Request for Presence
Show your goodness, O Lord, to those who are good* and to those who are true of
heart.

Psalm 125:4

The Greeting
Out of the mouths of infants and children* your majesty is praised above the
heavens.

Psalm 8:2

The Hymn   *We Believe in One True God*
We believe in one true God, Father, Son, and Holy Ghost,
An ever present help in need, praised by all the heavenly host;
By whose mighty power alone, all is made and wrought and done.

We believe in Jesus Christ, Son of God and Mary's Son,
Who descended from his throne and thus our salvation won;
By whose cross and death are we lifted from sin's misery.

We confess the Holy Ghost, who from both forever proceeds;
Who upholds and comforts us in our trials, fears, and needs.
Blest and Holy Trinity, praise for ever be to Thee!

Tobias Clausnitzer

The Refrain for the Vespers Lessons
We have heard with our ears, O God, our forefathers have told us,* the deeds you
did in their days, in the days of old.

Psalm 44:1

The Vespers Psalm   *God Is My King from Ancient Times*
Yet God is my King from ancient times,* victorious in the midst of the earth.
You divided the sea by your might* and shattered the heads of the dragons upon
the waters;
You crushed the heads of Leviathan* and gave him to the people of the desert for
food.
You split open spring and torrent;* you dried up ever-flowing rivers.
Yours is the day, yours also the night;* you established the moon and the sun.
You fixed all the boundaries of the earth;* you made both summer and winter.

Psalm 74:11–16

The Refrain
We have heard with our ears, O God, our forefathers have told us,* the deeds you
did in their days, in the days of old.

The Gloria

The Lord's Prayer

The Prayer Appointed for the Week

Blessed Lord, who caused all holy Scriptures to be written for our learning: Grant me so to hear them, read, mark, learn, and inwardly digest them, that I may embrace and ever hold fast the blessed hope of everlasting life, which you have given us in our Savior Jesus Christ; who lives and reigns with you and the Holy Spirit, one God, for ever and ever. *Amen.*†

The Concluding Prayer of the Church

Almighty and eternal God, ruler of all things in heaven and earth: Mercifully accept my prayer, and strengthen me to do your will; through Jesus Christ our Lord. *Amen.*†

The Morning Office   **To Be Observed on the Hour or Half Hour**
Between 6 and 9 a.m.

The Call to Prayer

Praise God from whom all blessings flow; praise him, all creatures here below; praise him above, you heavenly hosts; praise Father, Son and Holy Ghost.

Doxology

The Request for Presence

Send out your light and your truth, that they may lead me,* and bring me to your holy hill and to your dwelling;

That I may go to the altar of God, to the God of my joy and gladness;* and on the harp I will give thanks to you, O God my God.

Psalm 43:3–4

The Greeting

Splendor and honor and kingly power are yours by right, O Lord our God,

For you created everything that is, and by your will they were created and have their being.

A Song to the Lamb

The Refrain for the Morning Lessons

And yet my people did not hear my voice,* and Israel would not obey me.

Psalm 84:11

A Reading

Then Jesus said to his disciples, 'In truth I tell you, it is hard for someone rich to enter the kingdom of Heaven. Yes, I tell you again, it is easier for a camel to pass through the eye of a needle than for someone rich to enter the kingdom of Heaven.' When the disciples heard this they were astonished. 'Who can be saved, then?' they said. Jesus gazed at them. 'By human resources,' he told them, 'this is impossible; for God everything is possible.'

Matthew 19:23–26

The Refrain

And yet my people did not hear my voice,* and Israel would not obey me.

The Morning Psalm   *Proclaim the Greatness of Our God*

Proclaim the greatness of the LORD our God and fall down before his footstool;* he
    is the Holy One.

Moses and Aaron among his priests, and Samuel among those who call upon his
    Name,* they called upon the LORD, and he answered them.

He spoke to them out of the pillar of cloud;* they kept his testimonies and the
    decree that he gave them.

O LORD our God, you answered them indeed;* you were a God who forgave them,
    yet punished them for their evil deeds.

Proclaim the greatness of the LORD our God and worship him upon his holy hill;*
    for the LORD our God is the Holy One.

Psalm 99:5–9

The Refrain

And yet my people did not hear my voice,* and Israel would not obey me.

The Small Verse

The people that walked in darkness have seen a great light; on those who live in a
    land of deep shadow a light has shone.

Isaiah 9:1

The Lord's Prayer

The Prayer Appointed for the Week

Blessed Lord, who caused all holy Scriptures to be written for our learning: Grant
    me so to hear them, read, mark, learn, and inwardly digest them, that I may
    embrace and ever hold fast the blessed hope of everlasting life, which you have
    given us in our Savior Jesus Christ; who lives and reigns with you and the
    Holy Spirit, one God, for ever and ever. *Amen.†*

The Concluding Prayer of the Church

Lord God, almighty and everlasting Father, you have brought me in safety to this
    new day: Preserve me with your mighty power, that I may not fall into sin, nor
    be overcome by adversity; and in all I do direct me to the fulfilling of your pur-
    pose; through Jesus Christ my Lord. *Amen.†*

The Midday Office   To Be Observed on the Hour or Half Hour
                                     Between 11 a.m. and 2 p.m.

The Call to Prayer

Hallelujah! Praise the LORD, O my soul!* I will praise the LORD as long as I live; I
    will sing praises to my God while I have my being.

Psalm 146:1

The Request for Presence

Remember me, O LORD, with the favor you have for your people,* and visit me
    with your saving help;

That I may see the prosperity of your elect and be glad with the gladness of your
people,* that I may glory with your inheritance.

Psalm 106:4–5

The Greeting
You are to be praised, O God, in Zion . . .
To you that hear prayer shall all flesh come,* because of their transgressions.

Psalm 65:1–2

The Refrain for the Midday Lessons
Your statutes have been like songs to me* wherever I have lived like a stranger.

Psalm 119:54

A Reading
But you are *a chosen race, a kingdom of priests, a holy nation, a people to be a personal
possession* to sing the praises of God who called you out of the darkness into his
wonderful light. Once you were *a non-people* and now you are the People of
God; once you were *outside his pity;* now you *have received pity.*

1 Peter 2:9–10

The Refrain
Your statutes have been like songs to me* wherever I have lived like a stranger.

The Midday Psalm   *In His Holy Name We Put Our Trust*
Behold, the eye of the Lord is upon those who fear him,* on those who wait upon
his love,
To pluck their lives from death,* and to feed them in time of famine.
Our soul waits for the Lord;* he is our help and our shield.
Indeed, our heart rejoices in him,* for in his holy Name we put our trust.
Let your loving-kindness, O Lord, be upon us,* as we have put our trust in you.

Psalm 33:18–22

The Refrain
Your statutes have been like songs to me* wherever I have lived like a stranger.

The Small Verse
Keep me, Lord, as the apple of your eye and carry me under the shadow of your
wings.

Traditional

The Lord's Prayer

The Prayer Appointed for the Week
Blessed Lord, who caused all holy Scriptures to be written for our learning: Grant
me so to hear them, read, mark, learn, and inwardly digest them, that I may
embrace and ever hold fast the blessed hope of everlasting life, which you have
given us in our Savior Jesus Christ; who lives and reigns with you and the
Holy Spirit, one God, for ever and ever. *Amen.*†

The Concluding Prayer of the Church

May God himself order my days and make them acceptable in his sight. Blessed
be the Lord always, my strength and my redeemer.

Traditional

The Vespers Office   **To Be Observed on the Hour or Half Hour**
                                       Between 5 and 8 p.m.

The Call to Prayer

But I will call upon God,* and the LORD will deliver me.
In the evening, in the morning, and at noonday, I will complain and lament,* and
he will hear my voice.
He will bring me safely back . . .
God, who is enthroned of old, will hear me.

Psalm 55:17ff

The Request for Presence

I cry out to you, O LORD;* I say, "You are my refuge, my portion in the land of the
living."

Psalm 142:5

The Greeting

I will confess you among the peoples, O LORD;* I will sing praises to you among
the nations.

Psalm 108:3

The Hymn   *Have Your Own Way, Lord*

Have Your own way, Lord! Have Your own way!
You are the potter, I am the clay.
Mold me and make me after your will,
While I am waiting, yielded and still.

Have Your own way, Lord! Have Your own way!
Search me and try me, Savior today!
Wash me just now, Lord, wash me just now,
As in Your presence humbly I bow.

Have Your own way, Lord! Have Your own way!
Wounded and weary, help me I pray!
Power, all power, surely is Thine!
Touch me and heal me, Savior divine!

Have Your own way, Lord! Have Your own way!
Hold over my being absolute sway.
Fill with your Spirit till all shall see
Christ only, always, living in me!

Adelaide Pollard

The Refrain for the Vespers Lessons

The LORD will hear the desire of the humble;* you will strengthen their heart and
your ears shall hear.

Psalm 10:18

The Vespers Psalm   *He Has Heard the Voice of My Prayer*

Blessed is the LORD!* for he has heard the voice of my prayer.

The LORD is my strength and my shield;* my heart trusts in him, and I have been
helped;

Therefore my heart dances for joy,* and in my song will I praise him.

The LORD is the strength of his people,* a safe refuge for his anointed.

Save your people and bless your inheritance;* shepherd them and carry them for
ever.

Psalm 28:7–11

The Refrain

The LORD will hear the desire of the humble;* you will strengthen their heart and
your ears shall hear.

The Small Verse

The Lord is my shepherd and nothing is wanting to me. In green pastures He hath
settled me.

THE SHORT BREVIARY

The Lord's Prayer

The Prayer Appointed for the Week

Blessed Lord, who caused all holy Scriptures to be written for our learning: Grant
me so to hear them, read, mark, learn, and inwardly digest them, that I may
embrace and ever hold fast the blessed hope of everlasting life, which you have
given us in our Savior Jesus Christ; who lives and reigns with you and the
Holy Spirit, one God, for ever and ever. *Amen.*†

The Concluding Prayer of the Church

Lead me not into temptation. Deliver me from evil. Yours are the kingdom and the
glory.

The Morning Office   **To Be Observed on the Hour or Half Hour**
Between 6 and 9 a.m.

The Call to Prayer

Come, let us bow down, and bend the knee,* and kneel before the LORD our
Maker.

For he is our God,* and we are the people of his pasture and the sheep of his
hand . . .

Psalm 95:6–7

The Request for Presence
So teach us to number our days* that we may apply our hearts to wisdom.

Psalm 90:12

The Greeting
My God, my rock in whom I put my trust,* my shield, the horn of my salvation, and my refuge; you are worthy of praise.

Psalm 18:2

The Refrain for the Morning Lessons
My eyes are upon the faithful in the land, that they may dwell with me . . .

Psalm 101:6

A Reading
Then the angel showed me the river of life, rising from the throne of God and of the Lamb and flowing crystal-clear. Down the middle of the city street, on either bank of the river were the trees of life, which bear twelve crops of fruit in a year, one in each month, and the leaves of which are cure for the nations. The curse of destruction will be abolished. The throne of God and of the Lamb will be in the city; his servants will worship him, they will see him face to face, and his name will be written on their foreheads. And night will be abolished; they will not need lamplight or sunlight, because the Lord God will be shining on them. They will reign for ever and ever.

Revelation 22:1–5

The Refrain
My eyes are upon the faithful in the land, that they may dwell with me . . .

The Morning Psalm   *Be Seated on Your Lofty Throne, O Most High*
Awake, O my God, decree justice;* let the assembly of the peoples gather round you.
Be seated on your lofty throne, O Most High;* O LORD, judge the nations.
Let the malice of the wicked come to an end, but establish the righteous;* for you test the mind and heart, O righteous God.
God is my shield and defense;* he is the savior of the true in heart.
God is a righteous judge;* God sits in judgment every day.

Psalm 7:7–8, 10–12

The Refrain
My eyes are upon the faithful in the land, that they may dwell with me . . .

The Cry of the Church
O God, come to my assistance! O Lord, make haste to help me!

The Lord's Prayer

The Prayer Appointed for the Week
Blessed Lord, who caused all holy Scriptures to be written for our learning: Grant me so to hear them, read, mark, learn, and inwardly digest them, that I may

embrace and ever hold fast the blessed hope of everlasting life, which you have given us in our Savior Jesus Christ; who lives and reigns with you and the Holy Spirit, one God, for ever and ever. *Amen*.†

The Concluding Prayer of the Church
Lord God, almighty and everlasting Father, you have brought me in safety to this new day: Preserve me with your mighty power, that I may not fall into sin, nor be overcome by adversity; and in all I do direct me to the fulfilling of your purpose; through Jesus Christ my Lord. *Amen*.†

The Midday Office   To Be Observed on the Hour or Half Hour
                                     Between 11 a.m. and 2 p.m.

The Call to Prayer
Search for the Lord and his strength;* continually seek his face.
Psalm 105:4

The Request for Presence
You are good and you bring forth good;* instruct me in your statutes.
Psalm 119:68

The Greeting
When your word goes forth it gives light;* it gives understanding to the simple.
Psalm 119:130

The Refrain for the Midday Lessons
You strengthen me more and more;* you enfold and comfort me.
Psalm 71:21

A Reading
Well now, you who say, 'Today or tomorrow, we are off to this or that town; we are going to spend a year there, trading, and make some money.' You never know what will happen tomorrow: you are no more than a mist that appears for a little while and then disappears. Instead of this, you should say, 'If it is the Lord's will, we shall still be alive to do this or that.'

James 4:13–15

The Refrain
You strengthen me more and more;* you enfold and comfort me.

The Midday Psalm   *The Lord Chose David His Servant*
Then the Lord woke as though from sleep,* like a warrior refreshed with wine.
He struck his enemies on the backside* and put them to perpetual shame.
He rejected the tent of Joseph* and did not choose the tribe of Ephraim;
He chose instead the tribe of Judah* and Mount Zion, which he loved.
He built his sanctuary like the heights of heaven,* like the earth which he founded for ever.
He chose David his servant,* and took him away from the sheepfolds.

He brought him from following the ewes,* to be a shepherd over Jacob his people
  and over Israel his inheritance.
So he shepherded them with a faithful and true heart* and guided them with the
  skillfulness of his hands.

Psalm 78:65–72

The Refrain
You strengthen me more and more;* you enfold and comfort me.

The Gloria

The Lord's Prayer

The Prayer Appointed for the Week
Blessed Lord, who caused all holy Scriptures to be written for our learning: Grant
  me so to hear them, read, mark, learn, and inwardly digest them, that I may
  embrace and ever hold fast the blessed hope of everlasting life, which you have
  given us in our Savior Jesus Christ; who lives and reigns with you and the
  Holy Spirit, one God, for ever and ever. *Amen.*†

The Concluding Prayer of the Church
Lord, make me according to thy heart.
Brother Lawrence

The Vespers Office   **To Be Observed on the Hour or Half Hour**
                                              Between 5 and 8 p.m.

The Call to Prayer
Behold now, bless the LORD, all you servants of the LORD,* you that stand by night
  in the house of our LORD.

Psalm 134:1

The Request for Presence
For God alone my soul in silence waits;* from him comes my salvation.

Psalm 62:1

The Greeting
Yours is the day, yours also the night;* you established the moon and the sun.
You fixed all the boundaries of the earth;* you made both summer and winter.

Psalm 74:15–16

The Hymn   *Open My Eyes, That I May See*
        Open my eyes, that I may see
        Glimpses of the truth you have for me;
        Place in my hands the wonderful key
        That will unclasp and set me free.
        Silently now I wait for thee,
        Ready, my God, your will to see.
        Open my eyes, illumine me, Spirit divine!

Open my ears, that I may hear
Voices of truth you send me clear;
And while the wave notes fall on my ear,
Everything false will disappear.
Silently now I wait for thee,
Ready, my God, your will to see.
Open my ears, illumine me, Spirit divine!

Open my mouth and let me bear
Gladly the warm truth everywhere;
Open my heart and let me prepare
Love with your children thus to share.
Silently now I wait for thee,
Ready, my God, your will to see.
Open my heart, illumine me, Spirit divine!

Clara Scott

The Refrain for the Vespers Lessons

. . . Surely, there is a reward for the righteous; surely, there is a God who rules in the earth.

Psalm 58:11b

The Vespers Psalm   *The LORD's Will Stands Forever*

By the word of the LORD were the heavens made,* by the breath of his mouth all the heavenly hosts.

He gathers up the waters of the ocean as in a water-skin* and stores up the depths of the sea.

Let all the earth fear the LORD;* let all who dwell in the world stand in awe of him.

For he spoke, and it came to pass;* he commanded, and it stood fast.

The LORD brings the will of the nations to naught;* he thwarts the designs of the peoples.

But the LORD's will stands fast for ever,* and the designs of his heart from age to age.

Psalm 33:6–11

The Refrain

Surely, there is a reward for the righteous; surely, there is a God who rules in the earth.

The Gloria

The Lord's Prayer

The Prayer Appointed for the Week

Blessed Lord, who caused all holy Scriptures to be written for our learning: Grant me so to hear them, read, mark, learn, and inwardly digest them, that I may embrace and ever hold fast the blessed hope of everlasting life, which you have given us in our Savior Jesus Christ; who lives and reigns with you and the Holy Spirit, one God, for ever and ever. *Amen.*†

The Concluding Prayer of the Church
May Almighty God grant me a peaceful night and a perfect end. *Amen.*

The Morning Office   To Be Observed on the Hour or Half Hour
                                      Between 6 and 9 a.m.

The Call to Prayer
Hallelujah! Praise the Name of the LORD,* give praise, you servants of the LORD,
You who stand in the house of the LORD,* in the courts of the house of our God.
Praise the LORD, for the LORD is good;* sing praises to his Name, for it is lovely.
Psalm 136:1–3

The Request for Presence
I have said to the LORD, "You are my God;* listen, O LORD, to my supplication."
Psalm 140:6

The Greeting
You are the LORD, most high over all the earth;* you are exalted far above all gods.
Psalm 97:9

The Refrain for the Morning Lessons
The human mind and heart are a mystery; but God will loose an arrow at them,*
    and suddenly they will be wounded.

Psalm 64:7

A Reading
Jesus said: "Everything has been entrusted to me by my Father; and no one knows
    who the Son is except the Father, and who the Father is except the Son and
    those to whom the Son chooses to reveal him."

Luke 10:22

The Refrain
The human mind and heart are a mystery; but God will loose an arrow at them,*
    and suddenly they will be wounded.

The Morning Psalm   *My Heart Shall Meditate on Understanding*
Hear this, all you peoples; hearken, all you who dwell in the world,* you of high
    degree and low, rich and poor together.
My mouth shall speak of wisdom,* and my heart shall meditate on
    understanding.
I will incline my ear to a proverb* and set forth my riddle upon the harp.
Why should I be afraid in evil days,* when the wickedness of those at my heels
    surrounds me,
The wickedness of those who put their trust in their goods,* and boast of their
    great riches?
We can never ransom ourselves,* or deliver to God the price of our life;
For the ransom of our life is so great,* that we should never have enough to pay it,
In order to live for ever and ever,* and never see the grave.

For we see that the wise die also; like the dull and stupid they perish* and leave
   their wealth to those who come after them.
Their graves shall be their homes for ever, their dwelling places from generation to
   generation,* though they call the lands after their own names.
Even though honored, they cannot live for ever;* they are like the beasts that perish.

Psalm 49:1–14

The Refrain
The human mind and heart are a mystery; but God will loose an arrow at them,*
   and suddenly they will be wounded.

The Cry of the Church
O God, come to my assistance! O Lord, make haste to help me!

The Lord's Prayer

The Prayer Appointed for the Week
Blessed Lord, who caused all holy Scriptures to be written for our learning: Grant
   me so to hear them, read, mark, learn, and inwardly digest them, that I may
   embrace and ever hold fast the blessed hope of everlasting life, which you have
   given us in our Savior Jesus Christ; who lives and reigns with you and the
   Holy Spirit, one God, for ever and ever. *Amen.*†

The Concluding Prayer of the Church
Lord God, almighty and everlasting Father, you have brought me in safety to this
   new day: Preserve me with your mighty power, that I may not fall into sin, nor
   be overcome by adversity; and in all I do direct me to the fulfilling of your purpose; through Jesus Christ my Lord. *Amen.*†

The Midday Office
**To Be Observed on the Hour or Half Hour
Between 11 a.m. and 2 p.m.**

The Call to Prayer
Bless God in the congregation;* bless the LORD, you that are of the fountain of
   Israel.

Psalm 68:26

The Request for Presence
Accept, O LORD, the willing tribute of my lips,* and teach me your judgments.

Psalm 119:108

The Greeting
Let the words of my mouth and the meditation of my heart be acceptable in your
   sight,* O LORD, my strength and my redeemer.

Psalm 19:14

The Refrain for the Midday Lessons
Hallelujah! Happy are they who fear the Lord* and have great delight in his commandments.

Psalm 112:1

A Reading
So be very careful about the sort of lives you lead, like intelligent and not like
   senseless people. Make the best of the present time, for it is a wicked age.

Ephesians 5:15–16

The Refrain
Hallelujah! Happy are they who fear the Lord* and have great delight in his commandments.

The Midday Psalm   *The Lord Is My Light and My Salvation*
The Lord is my light and my salvation; whom then shall I fear?* the Lord is the
   strength of my life; of whom then shall I be afraid?
When evildoers came upon me to eat up my flesh,* it was they, my foes and my
   adversaries, who stumbled and fell.
Though an army should encamp against me,* yet my heart shall not be afraid;
And though war should rise up against me,* yet will I put my trust in him.
One thing have I asked of the Lord; one thing I seek;* that I may dwell in the
   house of the Lord all the days of my life;
To behold the fair beauty of the Lord* and to seek him in his temple.

Psalm 27:1–6

The Refrain
Hallelujah! Happy are they who fear the Lord* and have great delight in his commandments.

The Cry of the Church
O Lord, hear my prayer and let my cry come unto you. Thanks be to God.

The Short Breviary

The Lord's Prayer

The Prayer Appointed for the Week
Blessed Lord, who caused all holy Scriptures to be written for our learning: Grant
   me so to hear them, read, mark, learn, and inwardly digest them, that I may
   embrace and ever hold fast the blessed hope of everlasting life, which you have
   given us in our Savior Jesus Christ; who lives and reigns with you and the
   Holy Spirit, one God, for ever and ever. *Amen.*†

The Concluding Prayer of the Church
Lord Jesus Christ, by your death you took away the sting of death: Grant me to so
   follow in faith where you have led the way, that I may at length fall asleep
   peacefully in you and wake in your likeness; for your tender mercies' sake.
   Amen.†

The Vespers Office

To Be Observed on the Hour or Half Hour
Between 5 and 8 p.m.

The Call to Prayer

The LORD is my strength and my shield;* my heart trusts in him, and I have been
helped;
Therefore my heart dances for joy,* and in my song will I praise him.

Psalm 28:8–9

The Request for Presence

I have gone astray like a sheep that is lost;* search for your servant, for I do not
forget your commandments.

Psalm 119:176

The Greeting

How great is your goodness, O LORD! which you have laid up for those who fear
you;* which you have done in the sight of all for those who put their trust in
you.

Psalm 31:19

The Hymn   *Lord, I Want to Be a Christian*

Lord, I want to be a Christian in my heart, in my heart;
Lord, I want to be a Christian in my heart, in my heart;
Lord, I want to be a Christian in my heart, in my heart.

Lord, I want to be more loving in my heart, in my heart;
Lord, I want to be more loving in my heart, in my heart;
Lord, I want to be more loving in my heart, in my heart.

Lord, I want to be more holy in my heart, in my heart;
Lord, I want to be more holy in my heart, in my heart;
Lord, I want to be more holy in my heart, in my heart.

Lord, I want to be like Jesus in my heart, in my heart;
Lord, I want to be like Jesus in my heart, in my heart;
Lord, I want to be like Jesus in my heart, in my heart.

African-American Spiritual

The Refrain for the Vespers Lessons

Mercy and truth have met together;* righteousness and peace have kissed each
other.

Psalm 85:10

The Vespers Psalm   *Bring Me to Your Holy Hill*

Send out your light and your truth, that they may lead me,* and bring me to your
holy hill and to your dwelling;
That I may go to the altar of God, to the God of my joy and gladness;* and on the
harp I will give thanks to you, O God my God.

Why are you so full of heaviness, O my soul?* and why are you so disquieted within me?

Put your trust in God;* for I will yet give thanks to him, who is the help of my countenance, and my God.

Psalm 43:3–6

The Refrain

Mercy and truth have met together;* righteousness and peace have kissed each other.

The Small Verse

My help is in the Name of the Lord who made heaven and earth and all that is in them. Thanks be to God.

Traditional

The Lord's Prayer

The Prayer Appointed for the Week

Blessed Lord, who caused all holy Scriptures to be written for our learning: Grant me so to hear them, read, mark, learn, and inwardly digest them, that I may embrace and ever hold fast the blessed hope of everlasting life, which you have given us in our Savior Jesus Christ; who lives and reigns with you and the Holy Spirit, one God, for ever and ever. *Amen.*†

Concluding Prayers of the Church

Almighty God, who has promised to hear the petitions of those who ask in your Son's Name: I beseech you mercifully to incline your ear to me who have made my prayers and supplications to you; and grant that those things which I have faithfully asked according to your will, I may effectually obtain, to the relief of my necessity, and to the setting forth of your glory; through Jesus Christ my Lord. *Amen.*†

May the souls of the faithful departed, through the mercy of God, rest in eternal peace. *Amen.*

The Morning Office	To Be Observed on the Hour or Half Hour
	Between 6 and 9 a.m.

The Call to Prayer

Wake up, my spirit; awake, lute and harp;* I myself will waken the dawn.

Psalm 57:8

The Request for Presence

O Lamb of God, that takes away the sins of the world, have mercy upon me.
O Lamb of God, that takes away the sins of the world, have mercy upon me.
O Lamb of God, that takes away the sins of the world, grant me your peace.

Agnus Dei

The Greeting

For you alone are the Holy One, you alone are the Lord, you alone are the Most
High, Jesus Christ, with the Holy Spirit, in the Glory of God the Father.

The Refrain for the Morning Lessons

Into your hands I commend my spirit,* for you have redeemed me, O LORD,
O God of truth.

Psalm 31:5

A Reading

Jesus taught us, saying: "In truth I tell you, if two of you on earth agree to ask anything at all, it will be granted to you by my Father in heaven. For where two or
three meet in my name, I am there among them."

Matthew 18:19–20

The Refrain

Into your hands I commend my spirit,* for you have redeemed me, O LORD,
O God of truth.

The Morning Psalm   *You Are My Confidence, O LORD, Since I Was Young*

In you, O LORD, have I taken refuge;* let me never be ashamed.

In your righteousness, deliver me and set me free;* incline your ear to me and save
me.

Be my strong rock, a castle to keep me safe;* you are my crag and my stronghold.

Deliver me, my God, from the hand of the wicked,* from the clutches of the evildoer and the oppressor.

For you are my hope, O Lord GOD,* my confidence since I was young.

I have been sustained by you ever since I was born; from my mother's womb you
have been my strength;* my praise shall be always of you.

I have become a portent to many;* but you are my refuge and my strength.

Let my mouth be full of your praise* and your glory all the day long.

Do not cast me off in my old age;* forsake me not when my strength fails.

Psalm 71:1–9

The Refrain

Into your hands I commend my spirit,* for you have redeemed me, O LORD,
O God of truth.

The Cry of the Church

Even so, come, Lord Jesus!

The Lord's Prayer

The Prayer Appointed for the Week

Blessed Lord, who caused all holy Scriptures to be written for our learning: Grant
me so to hear them, read, mark, learn, and inwardly digest them, that I may
embrace and ever hold fast the blessed hope of everlasting life, which you have
given us in our Savior Jesus Christ; who lives and reigns with you and the
Holy Spirit, one God, for ever and ever. *Amen.*†

The Concluding Prayer of the Church

Lord God, almighty and everlasting Father, you have brought me in safety to this new day: Preserve me with your mighty power, that I may not fall into sin, nor be overcome by adversity; and in all I do direct me to the fulfilling of your purpose; through Jesus Christ my Lord. *Amen.*†

The Midday Office   **To Be Observed on the Hour or Half Hour**
                                     Between 11 a.m. and 2 p.m.

The Call to Prayer

Ascribe to the LORD, you families of the peoples;* ascribe to the LORD honor and power.
Ascribe to the LORD the honor due his Name;* bring offerings and come into his courts.
Worship the LORD in the beauty of holiness; . . .

Psalm 96:7–9

The Request for Presence

For God alone my soul in silence waits;* truly, my hope is in him.

Psalm 62:6

The Greeting

Happy are the people whose strength is in you!* whose hearts are set on the pilgrims' way.

Psalm 84:4

The Refrain for the Midday Lessons

I will bless the LORD who gives me counsel.

Psalm 16:7

A Reading

So if in Christ there is anything that will move you, any incentive in love, any fellowship in the Spirit, any warmth or sympathy—I appeal to you, make my joy complete by being of a single mind, one in love, one in heart and one in mind.

Phillippians 2:1–2

The Refrain

I will bless the LORD who gives me counsel.

The Midday Psalm   *I Will Sing Praises to the God of Jacob*

We give you thanks, O God, we give you thanks,* calling upon your Name and declaring all your wonderful deeds.
"I will appoint a time," says God;* "I will judge with equity.
Though the earth and all its inhabitants are quaking,* I will make its pillars fast.
I will say to the boasters, 'Boast no more,'* and to the wicked, 'Do not toss your horns;

Do not toss your horns so high,* nor speak with a proud neck.' "

For judgment is neither from the east nor from the west,* nor yet from the wilderness or the mountains.

It is God who judges;* he puts down one and lifts up another.

For in the Lord's hand there is a cup, full of spiced and foaming wine, which he pours out,* and all the wicked of the earth shall drink and drain the dregs.

But I will rejoice for ever; I will sing praises to the God of Jacob.* He shall break off all the horns of the wicked; but the horns of the righteous shall be exalted.

Psalm 75

The Refrain

I will bless the Lord who gives me counsel.

The Small Verse

Lead me not into temptation. Deliver me from evil. Yours are the kingdom and the glory.

Traditional

The Lord's Prayer

The Prayer Appointed for the Week

Blessed Lord, who caused all holy Scriptures to be written for our learning: Grant me so to hear them, read, mark, learn, and inwardly digest them, that I may embrace and ever hold fast the blessed hope of everlasting life, which you have given us in our Savior Jesus Christ; who lives and reigns with you and the Holy Spirit, one God, for ever and ever. *Amen.*†

The Concluding Prayer of the Church

O God, the source of eternal light: Shed forth your unending day upon all of us who watch for you, that our lips may praise you, our lives may bless you, and our worship may give you glory; through Jesus Christ our Lord. *Amen.*†

The Vespers Office   To Be Observed on the Hour or Half Hour
                                               Between 5 and 8 p.m.

The Call to Prayer

Give thanks to the Lord, for he is good,* and his mercy endures for ever.

Psalm 107:1

The Request for Presence

So teach us to number our days* that we may apply our hearts to wisdom.

Psalm 90:12

The Greeting

Remember not the sins of my youth and my transgressions;* remember me according to your love and for the sake of your goodness, O Lord.

Psalm 25:6

The Hymn   *Near to the Heart of God*

There is a place of quiet rest,
Near to the heart of God;
A place where sin cannot molest,
Near to the heart of God.
O Jesus, blest Redeemer,
Sent from the heart of God,
Hold us who wait before you
Near to the heart of God.

There is a place of full release,
Near to the heart of God;
A place where all is joy and peace,
Near to the heart of God.
O Jesus, blest Redeemer,
Sent from the heart of God,
Hold us who wait before you
Near to the heart of God.

Cleland McAfee

There is a place of comfort sweet,
Near to the heart of God;
A place where we and the Savior meet,
Near to the heart of God.
O Jesus, blest Redeemer,
Sent from the heart of God,
Hold us who wait before you
Near to the heart of God.

The Refrain for the Vespers Lessons
Behold, God is my helper;* it is the Lord who sustains my life.

Psalm 54:4

The Vespers Psalm   *The LORD Says, "You Are Children of the Most High"*
God takes his stand in the council of heaven;* he gives judgment in the midst of
    the gods:
"How long will you judge unjustly,* and show favor to the wicked?
Save the weak and the orphan;* defend the humble and needy;
Rescue the weak and the poor;* deliver them from the power of the wicked.
They do not know, neither do they understand;* they go about in darkness; all the
    foundations of the earth are shaken.
Now I say to you, 'You are gods,* and all of you children of the Most High;
Nevertheless, you shall die like mortals,* and fall like any prince.' "
Arise, O God, and rule the earth,* for you shall take all nations for your own.

Psalm 82

The Refrain
Behold, God is my helper;* it is the Lord who sustains my life.

The Small Verse
The Lord is my shepherd and nothing is wanting to me. In green pastures He hath
    settled me.

THE SHORT BREVIARY

The Lord's Prayer

The Prayer Appointed for the Week

Blessed Lord, who caused all holy Scriptures to be written for our learning: Grant me so to hear them, read, mark, learn, and inwardly digest them, that I may embrace and ever hold fast the blessed hope of everlasting life, which you have given us in our Savior Jesus Christ; who lives and reigns with you and the Holy Spirit, one God, for ever and ever. *Amen.*†

The Concluding Prayer of the Church

Almighty God, who after the creation of the world rested from all your works and sanctified a day of rest for all your creatures: Grant that I, putting away all earthly anxieties, may be duly prepared for the service of public worship, and grant as well that my Sabbath upon earth may be a preparation for the eternal rest promised to your people in heaven; through Jesus Christ our Lord. *Amen.*†

The Morning Office | To Be Observed on the Hour or Half Hour Between 6 and 9 a.m.

The Call to Prayer

Be glad, you righteous, and rejoice in the Lord;* shout for joy, all who are true of heart.

Psalm 32:12

The Request for Presence

May God be merciful to us and bless us,* show us the light of his countenance and come to us.

Psalm 67:1

The Greeting

Out of Zion, perfect in its beauty,* God reveals himself in glory.

Psalm 50:2

The Refrain for the Morning Lessons

Their sound has gone out into all the lands,* and their message to the ends of the world.

Psalm 19:4

A Reading

As he was walking by the Lake of Galilee he saw two brothers, Simon, who was called Peter, and his brother Andrew; they were making a cast into the lake with their net, for they were fishermen. And he said to them, 'Come after me and I will make you fishers of people.' And at once they left their nets and followed him.

Matthew 4:18–20

The Refrain
Their sound has gone out into all the lands,* and their message to the ends of the
world.

The Morning Psalm   *Happy Are All Who Take Refuge in Him*
Why are the nations in an uproar?* Why do the peoples mutter empty threats?
Why do the kings of the earth rise up in revolt, and the princes plot together,*
against the LORD and against his Anointed?
"Let us break their yoke," they say;* "let us cast off their bonds from us."
He whose throne is in heaven is laughing;* the LORD has them in derision.
Then he speaks to them in his wrath,* and his rage fills them with terror.
"I myself have set my king* upon my holy hill of Zion."
Let me announce the decree of the LORD;* he said to me, "You are my Son; this day
have I begotten you.
Ask of me, and I will give you the nations for your inheritance* and the ends of the
earth for your possession.
You shall crush them with an iron rod* and shatter them like a piece of pottery."
And now, you kings, be wise;* be warned, you rulers of the earth.
Submit to the LORD with fear,* and with trembling bow before him;
Lest he be angry and you perish;* for his wrath is quickly kindled.
Happy are they all* who take refuge in him!

Psalm 2

The Refrain
Their sound has gone out into all the lands,* and their message to the ends of the
world.

The Small Verse
Blessed be the Lord God of Israel for he has visited and delivered us. Alleluia,
alleluia, alleluia.

Traditional

The Lord's Prayer

The Prayer Appointed for the Week
Almighty and everlasting God, whose will it is to restore all things in your well-
beloved Son, the King of kings and Lord of lords: Mercifully grant that the peoples of the earth, divided and enslaved by sin, may be freed and brought
together under his most gracious rule; who lives and reigns with you and the
Holy Spirit, one God, now and for ever. *Amen.*†

The Concluding Prayer of the Church
Lord God, almighty and everlasting Father, you have brought me in safety to this
new day: Preserve me with your mighty power, that I may not fall into sin, nor
be overcome by adversity; and in all I do direct me to the fulfilling of your purpose; through Jesus Christ my Lord. *Amen.*†

The Midday Office   To Be Observed on the Hour or Half Hour
                                      Between 11 a.m. and 2 p.m.

The Call to Prayer
In the temple of the Lord* all are crying, "Glory!"
                                      Psalm 29:9

The Request for Presence
Fight those who fight me, O Lord;* attack those who are attacking me.
. . . say to my soul, "I am your salvation."
                                      Psalm 35:1, 3

The Greeting
Blessed be the Lord God, the God of Israel,* who alone does wondrous deeds!
And blessed be his glorious Name for ever!* and may all the earth be filled with
   his glory. Amen. Amen.
                                      Psalm 72:18–19

The Refrain for the Midday Lessons
Blessed be the Lord God of Israel,* from age to age. Amen. Amen.
                                      Psalm 41:13

A Reading
Coasts and islands, listen to me, pay attention distant peoples. Yahweh called me
   when I was in the womb, before my birth he had pronounced my name. He
   made my mouth like a sharp sword, he hid me in the shadow of his hand. He
   made me into a sharpened arrow and concealed me in his quiver. He said to
   me, 'Israel, you are my servant, through whom I shall manifest my glory.' But I
   said, 'My toil has been futile, I have exhausted myself for nothing, to no purpose.' Yet all the while my cause was with Yahweh and my reward with God.
   And now Yahweh has spoken, who formed me in the womb to be his servant,
   to bring Jacob back to him and reunite Israel to him;—I shall be honored in
   Yahweh's eyes, and my God has been my strength.—He said, 'It is not enough
   for you to be my servant, to restore the tribes of Jacob and bring back the survivors of Israel; I shall make you a light to the nations so that my salvation may
   reach the remotest parts of the earth.'
                                      Isaiah 49:1–6

The Refrain
Blessed be the Lord God of Israel,* from age to age. Amen. Amen.

The Midday Psalm   *My Soul Has a Desire for the Court of the Lord*
How dear to me is your dwelling, O Lord of hosts!* My soul has a desire and
   longing for the courts of the Lord; my heart and my flesh rejoice in the living God.
The sparrow has found her a house and the swallow a nest where she may lay her
   young;* by the side of your altars, O Lord of hosts, my King and my God.
Happy are they who dwell in your house!* they will always be praising you.

Happy are the people whose strength is in you!* whose hearts are set on the
   pilgrims' way.
Those who go through the desolate valley will find it a place of springs,* for the
   early rains have covered it with pools of water.

Psalm 84:1–5

The Refrain

Blessed be the LORD God of Israel,* from age to age. Amen. Amen.

The Cry of the Church

Lord, have mercy on us. Christ, have mercy on us. Lord, have mercy on us.

The Lord's Prayer

The Prayer Appointed for the Week

Almighty and everlasting God, whose will it is to restore all things in your well-
   beloved Son, the King of kings and Lord of lords: Mercifully grant that the peoples of the earth, divided and enslaved by sin, may be freed and brought
   together under his most gracious rule; who lives and reigns with you and the
   Holy Spirit, one God, now and for ever. *Amen.*†

The Concluding Prayer of the Church

O God, you make me glad with the weekly remembrance of the glorious resurrection of your Son my Lord: Give me this day such blessing through my worship
   of you, that the week to come may be spent in your favor; through Jesus Christ
   our Lord. *Amen.*†

The Vespers Office   **To Be Observed on the Hour or Half Hour**
                                                    Between 5 and 8 p.m.

The Call to Prayer

Let my mouth be full of your praise* and your glory all the day long.
Do not cast me off in my old age;* forsake me not when my strength fails.

Psalm 71:8–9

The Request for Presence

Let your loving-kindness, O LORD, be upon us,* as we have put our trust in you.

Psalm 33:22

The Greeting

To you I lift up my eyes,* to you enthroned in the heavens.
As the eyes of servants look to the hand of their masters,* and the eyes of a maid to
   the hand of her mistress,
So my eyes look to the LORD my God,* until he shows me his mercy.

based on Psalm 123:1–3

The Hymn 　　　　　　　　*Lead On, O King Eternal*

Lead On, O King eternal, the day of march has come;
Henceforth in fields of conquest your tents will be our home.
Through days of preparation your grace has made us strong;
And now, O King eternal, we lift our battle song.

Lead on, O King eternal, till sin's fierce war shall cease,
And holiness shall whisper the sweet amen of peace.
For not with swords loud clashing, nor roll of stirring drums;
With deeds of love and mercy the heavenly kingdom comes.

Lead on, O King eternal, we follow not with fears,
For gladness breaks like morning wherever your face appears.
Your cross is lifted over us, we journey in its light;
The crown awaits the conquest; lead on, O God of might.

Ernest Shurtleff

The Refrain for the Vespers Lessons
In truth God has heard me;* he has attended to the voice of my prayer.

Psalm 66:17

The Vespers Psalm 　　　　　　*The LORD Does Wonders for His Faithful*

Know that the LORD does wonders for the faithful;* when I call upon the LORD, he
will hear me.
Tremble, then, and do not sin;* speak to your heart in silence upon your bed.
Offer the appointed sacrifices* and put your trust in the LORD.
Many are saying, "Oh, that we might see better times!"* Lift up the light of your
countenance upon us, O LORD.
You have put gladness in my heart,* more than when grain and wine and oil
increase.
I lie down in peace; at once I fall asleep;* for only you, LORD, make me dwell in
safety.

Psalm 4:3–8

The Refrain
In truth God has heard me;* he has attended to the voice of my prayer.

The Cry of the Church
O Lord, hear my prayer and let my cry come unto you. Thanks be to God.

THE SHORT BREVIARY

The Lord's Prayer

The Prayer Appointed for the Week
Almighty and everlasting God, whose will it is to restore all things in your well-
beloved Son, the King of kings and Lord of lords: Mercifully grant that the peoples of the earth, divided and enslaved by sin, may be freed and brought
together under his most gracious rule; who lives and reigns with you and the
Holy Spirit, one God, now and for ever. *Amen.†*

Concluding Prayers of the Church

We humbly beseech Your majesty, O Lord, that as blessed Andrew the Apostle was both a preacher and a ruler of Your Church, so he may unceasingly intercede for us with You. Through our Lord. *Amen.*

adapted from THE SHORT BREVIEARY

Lord God, whose Son our Savior Jesus Christ, triumphed over the powers of death and prepared for us our place in the new Jerusalem: Grant that I, who have this day given thanks for his resurrection, may praise you in the City of which he is the light, and where he lives and reigns for ever and ever. *Amen.*†

The Morning Office   **To Be Observed on the Hour or Half Hour Between 6 and 9 a.m.**

The Call to Prayer

Bless the LORD, O my soul,* and all that is within me, bless his holy Name.
Bless the LORD, O my soul,* and forget not all his benefits.

Psalm 103:1–2

The Request for Presence

Protect me, O God, for I take refuge in you;* I have said to the LORD, "You are my Lord, my good above all other."

Psalm 16:1

The Greeting

I love you, O LORD my strength,* O LORD my stronghold, my crag, and my haven.

Psalm 18:1

The Refrain for the Morning Lessons

Purge me from my sin, and I shall be pure;* wash me, and I shall be clean indeed.

Psalm 51:8

A Reading   *On November 30, the Church celebrates the Feast of St. Andrew the Apostle, the brother of St. Peter and the Church's most revered missionary to the pagans. The patron saint of both Russia and Scotland, he suffered martyrdom on the x-shaped cross that has become his symbol.*

The next day as John [the Baptizer] stood there again with two of his disciples, Jesus went past, and John looked towards him and said, 'Look, there is the lamb of God.' And the disciples heard what he said and followed Jesus. Jesus turned round, saw them following and said, 'What do you want?' They answered, 'Rabbi'—which means Teacher—'where do you live?' He replied, 'Come and see'; so they went and saw where he lived, and stayed with him that day. It was about the tenth hour. One of these two who became followers of Jesus after hearing what John had said was Andrew, the brother of Simon Peter. The first thing Andrew did was to find his brother and say to him, 'We have found the Messiah'—which means the Christ—and he took Simon to

Jesus. Jesus looked at him and said, 'You are Simon son of John; you are to be called Cephas'—which means Rock.

John 1:35–42

The Refrain
Purge me from my sin, and I shall be pure;* wash me, and I shall be clean indeed.

The Morning Psalm   *The Commandment of the* LORD *Is Clear*
The law of the LORD is perfect and revives the soul;* the testimony of the LORD is
   sure and gives wisdom to the innocent.
The statutes of the LORD are just and rejoice the heart;* the commandment of the
   LORD is clear and gives light to the eyes.
The fear of the LORD is clean and endures for ever;* the judgments of the LORD are
   true and righteous altogether.
More to be desired are they than gold, more than much fine gold,* sweeter far than
   honey, than honey in the comb.
By them also is your servant enlightened,* and in keeping them there is great
   reward.

Psalm 19:7–11

The Refrain
Purge me from my sin, and I shall be pure;* wash me, and I shall be clean indeed.

The Cry of the Church
O Lamb of God, that takes away the sins of the world, have mercy upon me.
O Lamb of God, that takes away the sins of the world, have mercy upon me.
O Lamb of God, that takes away the sins of the world, grant me your peace.

The Lord's Prayer

The Prayer Appointed for the Week
Almighty and everlasting God, whose will it is to restore all things in your well-
   beloved Son, the King of kings and Lord of lords: Mercifully grant that the peoples of the earth, divided and enslaved by sin, may be freed and brought
   together under his most gracious rule; who lives and reigns with you and the
   Holy Spirit, one God, now and for ever. *Amen.*†

Concluding Prayers of the Church
Almighty God, who gave such grace to your Apostle Andrew that he readily
   obeyed the call of your Son Jesus Christ, and brought his brother with him:
   Give us, who are called by your holy Word, grace to follow him without delay,
   and to bring those near to us into his gracious presence; who lives and reigns
   with you and the Holy Spirit, one God, now and for ever. *Amen.*†

Lord God, almighty and everlasting Father, you have brought me in safety to this
   new day: Preserve me with your mighty power, that I may not fall into sin, nor
   be overcome by adversity; and in all I do direct me to the fulfilling of your purpose; through Jesus Christ my Lord. *Amen.*†

The Midday Office   To Be Observed on the Hour or Half Hour
                                     Between 11 a.m. and 2 p.m.

The Call to Prayer
Sing to the LORD a new song,* for he has done marvelous things.

Psalm 98:1

The Request for Presence
Remember me, O LORD, with the favor you have for your people,* and visit me
   with your saving help;
That I may see the prosperity of your elect* and be glad with the gladness of your
   people, that I may glory with your inheritance.

Psalm 106:4–5

The Greeting
Your righteousness, O God, reaches to the heavens;* you have done great things;
   who is like you, O God?

Psalm 71:19

The Refrain for the Midday Lessons
I will sing to the LORD as long as I live;* I will praise my God while I have my
   being.

Psalm 104:34

A Reading
The word is very near to you; it is in your mouth and in your heart, that is, the word of
   faith, the faith which we preach, that if you declare with your mouth that Jesus
   is Lord, and if you believe with your heart that God raised him from the dead,
   then you will be saved. It is by believing with the heart that you are justified,
   and by making the declaration with your lips that you are saved.

Romans 10:8b–11

The Refrain
I will sing to the LORD as long as I live;* I will praise my God while I have my
   being.

The Midday Psalm   *Such Is the Generation of Those Who Seek Him*
The earth is the LORD's and all that is in it,* the world and all who dwell therein.
For it is he who founded it upon the seas* and made it firm upon the rivers of the
   deep.
"Who can ascend the hill of the LORD?* and who can stand in his holy place?"
"Those who have clean hands and a pure heart,* who have not pledged them-
   selves to falsehood, nor sworn by what is a fraud.
They shall receive a blessing from the LORD* and a just reward from the God of
   their salvation."
Such is the generation of those who seek him,* of those who seek your face, O God
   of Jacob.

Psalm 24:1–6

The Refrain
I will sing to the LORD as long as I live;* I will praise my God while I have my
being.

The Cry of the Church
Be, Lord, my helper and forsake me not. Do not despise me, O God, my savior.
THE SHORT BREVIARY

The Lord's Prayer

The Prayer Appointed for the Week
Almighty and everlasting God, whose will it is to restore all things in your well-
beloved Son, the King of kings and Lord of lords: Mercifully grant that the peoples of the earth, divided and enslaved by sin, may be freed and brought
together under his most gracious rule; who lives and reigns with you and the
Holy Spirit, one God, now and for ever. *Amen.*†

Concluding Prayers of the Church
Almighty and everlasting God, who kindled the flame of love in the heart of your
holy martyr Andrew: Grant to me your humble servant, a faith and power of
love, that I who rejoice in his triumph may profit by his example; through Jesus
Christ our Lord, who lives and reigns with you and the Holy Spirit, one God,
for ever and ever. *Amen.*†

Direct me, O Lord, in all my doings with your most gracious favor, and further me
with your continual help; that in all my work begun, continued, and ended in
you, I may glorify your holy name, and finally, by your mercy, obtain everlasting life; through Jesus Christ my Lord. *Amen.*†

The Vespers Office To Be Observed on the Hour or Half Hour
Between 5 and 8 p.m.

The Call to Prayer
Tell it out among the nations: "The LORD is King!* he has made the world so firm
that it cannot be moved; he will judge the peoples with equity."
Psalm 96:10

The Request for Presence
Restore our fortunes, O LORD,* like the watercourses of the Negev.
Psalm 126:5

The Greeting
Whom have I in heaven but you?* and having you I desire nothing upon earth.
Psalm 73:25

The Hymn
Hearken to the anthem glorious
Of the martyrs robed in white;
They, like Christ, in death victorious
Dwell forever in the light.

Living, they proclaimed salvation,
Heaven endowed with grace and power;
And they died in imitation
Of their Savior's final hour.

Christ, for cruel traitors pleading,
Triumphed in his parting breath
Over all miracles preceding
His inestimable death.

Take from him what you will give him,
Of his fullness grace for grace;
Strive to think him, speak him, live him,
Till you find him face to face.

Christopher Smart

The Refrain for the Vespers Lessons
Those who sowed with tears* will reap with songs of joy.
Those who go out weeping, carrying the seed,* will come again with joy, shouldering their sheaves.

Psalm 126:6–7

The Vespers Psalm　　　　　　　*You Have Set a Banner for Those Who Fear You*
O God, you have cast us off and broken us;* you have been angry; oh, take us back to you again.
You have shaken the earth and split it open;* repair the cracks in it, for it totters.
You have made your people know hardship;* you have given us wine that makes us stagger.
You have set up a banner for those who fear you,* to be a refuge from the power of the bow.
Save us by your right hand and answer us,* that those who are dear to you may be delivered.

Psalm 60:1–5

The Refrain
Those who sowed with tears* will reap with songs of joy.
Those who go out weeping, carrying the seed,* will come again with joy, shouldering their sheaves.

The Cry of the Church
Even so, come, Lord Jesus!

The Lord's Prayer

The Prayer Appointed for the Week
Almighty and everlasting God, whose will it is to restore all things in your well-beloved Son, the King of kings and Lord of lords: Mercifully grant that the peoples of the earth, divided and enslaved by sin, may be freed and brought

together under his most gracious rule; who lives and reigns with you and the Holy Spirit, one God, now and for ever. *Amen.*†

Concluding Prayers of the Church

Almighty God, who gave to your servant Andrew boldness to confess the Name of our Savior Jesus Christ before the rulers of this world, and courage to die for this faith: Grant that I may always be ready to give a reason for the hope that is in me, and to suffer gladly for the sake of my Lord Jesus Christ; who lives and reigns with you and the Holy Spirit, one God, for ever and ever. *Amen.*†

Almighty God, you have surrounded me with a great cloud of witnesses: Grant that I, encouraged by the good example of your servant Andrew; may persevere in running the race that is set before me, until at last I may with him attain to your eternal joy; through Jesus Christ, the pioneer and perfecter of our faith, who lives and reigns with you and the Holy Spirit, one God, for ever and ever. *Amen.*†

The Morning Office   To Be Observed on the Hour or Half Hour
                                      Between 6 and 9 a.m.

The Call to Prayer

God has gone up with a shout,* the LORD with the sound of the ram's-horn.
Sing praises to God, sing praises;* sing praises to our King, sing praises.
For God is King of all the earth;* sing praises with all your skill.
God reigns over the nations;* God sits upon his holy throne.

Psalm 47:5–8

The Request for Presence

Let all who seek you rejoice and be glad in you;* let those who love your salvation say for ever, "Great is the LORD!"

Psalm 70:4

The Greeting

Out of Zion, perfect in its beauty,* God reveals himself in glory.

Psalm 50:2

The Refrain for the Morning Lessons

The fool has said in his heart, "There is no God." . . .

Psalm 14:1

A Reading

The apostles said to the Lord, 'Increase our faith.' The Lord replied, 'If you had faith like a mustard seed you could say to this mulberry tree, "Be uprooted and planted in the sea," and it would obey you.'

Luke 17:5–6

The Refrain

The fool has said in his heart, "There is no God." . . .

The Morning Psalm   *The LORD Will Root Out the Remembrance of the Evil*

The eyes of the LORD are upon the righteous,* and his ears are open to their cry.

The face of the LORD is against those who do evil,* to root out the remembrance of them from the earth.

The righteous cry, and the LORD hears them* and delivers them from all their troubles.

The LORD is near to the brokenhearted* and will save those whose spirits are crushed.

Many are the troubles of the righteous,* but the LORD will deliver him out of them all.

He will keep safe all his bones;* not one of them shall be broken.

              Psalm 34:15–20

The Refrain

The fool has said in his heart, "There is no God." . . .

The Gloria

The Lord's Prayer

The Prayer Appointed for the Week

Almighty and everlasting God, whose will it is to restore all things in your well-beloved Son, the King of kings and Lord of lords: Mercifully grant that the peoples of the earth, divided and enslaved by sin, may be freed and brought together under his most gracious rule; who lives and reigns with you and the Holy Spirit, one God, now and for ever. *Amen.*†

The Concluding Prayer of the Church

Lord God, almighty and everlasting Father, you have brought me in safety to this new day: Preserve me with your mighty power, that I may not fall into sin, nor be overcome by adversity; and in all I do direct me to the fulfilling of your purpose; through Jesus Christ my Lord. *Amen.*†

The Midday Office   To Be Observed on the Hour or Half Hour

Between 11 a.m. and 2 p.m.

The Call to Prayer

Hallelujah! Sing to the LORD a new song;* sing his praise in the congregation of the faithful.

              Psalm 149:1

The Request for Presence

Hear, O Shepherd of Israel, leading Joseph like a flock;* shine forth, you that are enthroned upon the cherubim.

              Psalm 80:1

The Greeting

The LORD is in his holy temple; let all the earth keep silence before him. *Amen.*

              Traditional

The Refrain for the Midday Lessons

The LORD shall watch over your going out and your coming in* from this time
forth for evermore.

Psalm 121:8

A Reading

Oh, come to the water all you who are thirsty; though you have no money, come!
Buy and eat; come, buy milk and wine without money, free! Why spend money
on what cannot nourish and your wages on what fails to satisfy? Listen carefully to me, and you will have good things to eat and rich food to enjoy. Pay
attention, come to me; listen, and you will live. I shall make an everlasting
covenant with you in fulfillment of the favors promised to David.

Isaiah 55:1–3

The Refrain

The LORD shall watch over your going out and your coming in,* from this time
forth for evermore.

The Midday Psalm   *The LORD Has Cut the Cords of the Wicked*

"Greatly have they oppressed me since my youth,"* let Israel now say;
"Greatly have they oppressed me since my youth,* but they have not prevailed
against me."
The plowmen plowed upon my back* and made their furrows long.
The LORD, the Righteous One,* has cut the cords of the wicked.
Let them be put to shame and thrown back,* all those who are enemies of Zion.
Let them be like grass upon the housetops,* which withers before it can be
plucked;
Which does not fill the hand of the reaper,* nor the bosom of him who binds the
sheaves;
So that those who go by say not so much as, "The LORD prosper you.* We wish you
well in the Name of the LORD."

Psalm 129

The Refrain

The LORD shall watch over your going out and your coming in,* from this time
forth for evermore.

The Gloria

The Lord's Prayer

The Prayer Appointed for the Week

Almighty and everlasting God, whose will it is to restore all things in your well-
beloved Son, the King of kings and Lord of lords: Mercifully grant that the peoples of the earth, divided and enslaved by sin, may be freed and brought
together under his most gracious rule; who lives and reigns with you and the
Holy Spirit, one God, now and for ever. *Amen.*†

The Concluding Prayer of the Church
Let us bless the Lord God living and true! Let us always render him praise, glory, honor, blessing, and all good things! Amen. Amen. So be it! So be it!

St. Francis of Assisi

The Vespers Office   To Be Observed on the Hour or Half Hour
                                             Between 5 and 8 p.m.

The Call to Prayer
Give thanks to the LORD, for he is good;* his mercy endures for ever.
Let Israel now proclaim,* "His mercy endures for ever."
Let the house of Aaron now proclaim,* "His mercy endures for ever."
Let those who fear the LORD now proclaim,* "His mercy endures for ever."

Psalm 118:1–4

The Request for Presence
Show me the light of your countenance, O God,* and come to me.

based on Psalm 67:1

The Greeting
But you, O LORD, are gracious and full of compassion,* slow to anger, and full of kindness and truth.

Psalm 86:15

The Hymn   *Jesus Shall Reign*
  Jesus shall reign wherever the sun
  Does its successive journeys run;
  His kingdom spread from shore to shore,
  Till moons shall wax and wane no more.

  To Jesus endless prayer be made,
  And endless praises crown his head;
  His name like sweet perfume shall rise
  With every morning sacrifice.

  People and realms of every tongue
  Dwell on his love with sweetest song;
  And infant voices shall proclaim
  Their early blessings on his name.

  Blessings abound wherever he reigns;
  All prisoners leap and loose their chains;
  The weary find eternal rest,
  And all who suffer want are blessed.

Let every creature rise and bring
Honors peculiar to our King;
Angels descend with songs again,
And earth repeat the loud amen!

Isaac Watts

The Refrain for the Vespers Lessons

Remember me, O Lord, with the favor you have for your people,* and visit me
with your saving help.

Psalm 106:4

The Vespers Psalm   *He Will Judge the People with His Truth*

Ascribe to the Lord, you families of the peoples;* ascribe to the Lord honor and
power.

Ascribe to the Lord the honor due his Name;* bring offerings and come into his
courts.

Worship the Lord in the beauty of holiness;* let the whole earth tremble before
him.

Tell it out among the nations: "The Lord is King!* he has made the world so firm
that it cannot be moved; he will judge the peoples with equity."

Let the heavens rejoice, and let the earth be glad; let the sea thunder and all that is
in it;* let the field be joyful and all that is therein.

Then shall all the trees of the wood shout for joy before the Lord when he comes,*
when he comes to judge the earth.

He will judge the world with righteousness* and the peoples with his truth.

Psalm 96:7–13

The Refrain

Remember me, O Lord, with the favor you have for your people,* and visit me
with your saving help.

The Small Verse

The Lord is my shepherd and nothing is wanting to me. In green pastures He hath
settled me.

The Short Breviary

The Lord's Prayer

The Prayer Appointed for the Week

Almighty and everlasting God, whose will it is to restore all things in your well-
beloved Son, the King of kings and Lord of lords: Mercifully grant that the peoples of the earth, divided and enslaved by sin, may be freed and brought
together under his most gracious rule; who lives and reigns with you and the
Holy Spirit, one God, now and for ever. *Amen.*†

The Concluding Prayer of the Church

O Lord my God, I am not worthy to have you come under my roof; yet you have
called me to stand in this house, and to serve at this work. To you and to your

service I devote myself, body, soul, and spirit. Fill my memory with the record of your mighty works; enlighten my understanding with the light of your Holy Spirit; and may all the desires of my heart and will center in what you would have me do. Make me an instrument of your salvation for the people entrusted to my care, and grant that by my life and teaching I may set forth your true and living Word. Be always with me in carrying out the duties of my faith. In prayer, quicken my devotion; in praises, heighten my love and gratitude; in conversation, give me readiness of thought and expression; and grant that, by the clearness and brightness of your holy Word, all the world may be drawn into your blessed kingdom. All this I ask for the sake of your Son our Savior Jesus Christ. *Amen.*†

The Morning Office   To Be Observed on the Hour or Half Hour
Between 6 and 9 a.m.

The Call to Prayer
Taste and see that the LORD is good;* happy are they who trust in him!
Psalm 34:8

The Request for Presence
Gladden the soul of your servant,* for to you, O LORD, I lift up my soul.
Psalm 86:4

The Greeting
With my whole heart I seek you;* let me not stray from your commandments.
Psalm 119:10

The Refrain for the Morning Lessons
I will bear witness that the LORD is righteous;* I will praise the Name of the LORD Most High.
Psalm 7:18

A Reading
When the people saw that neither Jesus nor his disciples were there, they got into those boats and crossed to Capernaum to look for Jesus. When they found him on the other side, they said to him, 'Rabbi, when did you come here?' Jesus answered: 'In truth I tell you, you are looking for me not because you have seen the signs but because you had all the bread you wanted to eat. Do not work for food that goes bad, but work for food that endures for eternal life, which the Son of man will give you, for on him the Father, God himself, has set his seal.'
John 6:24–27

The Refrain
I will bear witness that the LORD is righteous;* I will praise the Name of the LORD Most High.

The Morning Psalm   *I Will Exalt You, O LORD*

I will exalt you, O LORD, because you have lifted me up* and have not let my
    enemies triumph over me.

O LORD my God, I cried out to you,* and you restored me to health.

You brought me up, O LORD, from the dead;* you restored my life as I was going
    down to the grave.

Sing to the LORD, you servants of his;* give thanks for the remembrance of his
    holiness.

For his wrath endures but the twinkling of an eye,* his favor for a lifetime.

Psalm 30:1–5

The Refrain

I will bear witness that the LORD is righteous;* I will praise the Name of the LORD
    Most High.

The Small Verse

Let me seek the Lord while he may still be found. I will call upon his name while
    he is near.

Traditional

The Lord's Prayer

The Prayer Appointed for the Week

Almighty and everlasting God, whose will it is to restore all things in your well-
    beloved Son, the King of kings and Lord of lords: Mercifully grant that the peo-
    ples of the earth, divided and enslaved by sin, may be freed and brought
    together under his most gracious rule; who lives and reigns with you and the
    Holy Spirit, one God, now and for ever. *Amen.*†

The Concluding Prayer of the Church

Lord God, almighty and everlasting Father, you have brought me in safety to this
    new day: Preserve me with your mighty power, that I may not fall into sin, nor
    be overcome by adversity; and in all I do direct me to the fulfilling of your pur-
    pose; through Jesus Christ my Lord. *Amen.*†

The Midday Office   To Be Observed on the Hour or Half Hour
Between 11 a.m. and 2 p.m.

The Call to Prayer

Let Israel rejoice in his Maker;* let the children of Zion be joyful in their King.

Psalm 149:2

The Request for Presence

Make me understand the way of your commandments,* that I may meditate on
    your marvelous works.

Psalm 119:27

The Greeting
How deep I find your thoughts, O God!* how great is the sum of them!
Psalm 139:16

The Refrain for the Midday Lessons
I will thank you, O Lord my God, with all my heart* and glorify your Name for evermore.
Psalm 86:12

A Reading
Moses taught the people, saying: 'When you have entered the country which Yahweh your God is giving you as heritage, when you have taken possession of it and are living in it, you must set aside the first-fruits of all produce of the soil raised by you in your country, given you by Yahweh your God. You must put these in a basket and go to the place where Yahweh your God chooses to give his name a home. You will go to the priest then in office and say to him, "Today I declare to Yahweh my God that I have reached the country which Yahweh swore to our ancestors that he would give us." . . . You must then rejoice in all the good things that Yahweh your God has bestowed on you and your family—you, the Levite and the foreigner living with you.'
Deuteronomy 26:1–3, 11

The Refrain
I will thank you, O Lord my God, with all my heart* and glorify your Name for evermore.

The Midday Psalm   *Enter into His Courts with Praise*
Be joyful in the Lord, all you lands;* serve the Lord with gladness and come before his presence with a song.
Know this: The Lord himself is God;* he himself has made us, and we are his; we are his people and the sheep of his pasture.
Enter his gates with thanksgiving; go into his courts with praise;* give thanks to him and call upon his Name.
For the Lord is good; his mercy is everlasting;* and his faithfulness endures from age to age.
Psalm 100:1–4

The Refrain
I will thank you, O Lord my God, with all my heart* and glorify your Name for evermore.

The Cry of the Church
Lord, have mercy on us. Christ, have mercy on us. Lord, have mercy on us.

The Lord's Prayer

The Prayer Appointed for the Week
Almighty and everlasting God, whose will it is to restore all things in your well-beloved Son, the King of kings and Lord of lords: Mercifully grant that the peo-

ples of the earth, divided and enslaved by sin, may be freed and brought together under his most gracious rule; who lives and reigns with you and the Holy Spirit, one God, now and for ever. *Amen.*†

The Concluding Prayer of the Church

Lord Jesus Christ, you said to your apostles, "Peace I give to you; my own peace I leave with you": Regard not my sins but my faith, and give to me and all your church the peace and unity of that heavenly City, where with the Father and the Holy Spirit you live and reign, now and for ever. *Amen.*†

The Vespers Office   **To Be Observed on the Hour or Half Hour**
Between 5 and 8 p.m.

The Call to Prayer

Sing to the LORD, you servants of his;* give thanks for the remembrance of his holiness.
For his wrath endures but the twinkling of an eye,* his favor for a lifetime.

Psalm 30:4–5

The Request for Presence

Show us the light of your countenance, O God,* and come to us.

based on Psalm 67:1

The Greeting

Your statutes have been like songs to me* wherever I have lived as a stranger.
I remember your Name in the night, O LORD,* and dwell upon your law.
This is how it has been with me,* because I have kept your commandments.

Psalm 119:54–56

The Hymn

We plow the fields and scatter the good seed on the land,
But it is fed and watered by God's almighty hand;
He sends the snow in winter, the warmth to swell the grain,
The breezes and the sunshine, and soft refreshing rain.

He only is the Maker of all things near and far;
He paints the wayside flower, He lights the evening star;
The winds and waves obey Him, by Him the birds are fed;
Much more to us, His children, He gives our daily bread.

We thank You, then, O Father, for all things bright and good,
The seed-time and the harvest, our life, our health, our food;
Accept the gifts we offer for all Your love imparts,
And what You most desire, our humble, thankful hearts.

Mathias Claudius

The Refrain for the Vespers Lessons

Righteousness shall go before him,* and peace shall be a pathway for his feet.

Psalm 85:13

The Vespers Psalm   *Let All the Earth Shout for Joy and Sing*

Awesome things will you show us in your righteousness, O God of our salvation,*
   O Hope of all the ends of the earth and of the seas that are far away.
You make fast the mountains by your power;* they are girded about with might.
You still the roaring of the seas,* the roaring of their waves, and the clamor of the
   peoples.
Those who dwell at the ends of the earth will tremble at your marvelous signs;*
   you make the dawn and the dusk to sing for joy.
You visit the earth and water it abundantly; you make it very plenteous;* the river
   of God is full of water.
You prepare the grain,* for so you provide for the earth.
You drench the furrows and smooth out the ridges;* with heavy rain you soften
   the ground and bless its increase.
You crown the year with your goodness,* and your paths overflow with plenty.
May the fields of the wilderness be rich for grazing,* and the hills be clothed with
   joy.
May the meadows cover themselves with flocks, and the valleys cloak themselves
   with grain;* let them shout for joy and sing.

Psalm 65:5–14

The Refrain

Righteousness shall go before him,* and peace shall be a pathway for his feet.

The Cry of the Church

Even so, come, Lord Jesus!

The Lord's Prayer

The Prayer Appointed for the Week

Almighty and everlasting God, whose will it is to restore all things in your well-
   beloved Son, the King of kings and Lord of lords: Mercifully grant that the peoples of the earth, divided and enslaved by sin, may be freed and brought
   together under his most gracious rule; who lives and reigns with you and the
   Holy Spirit, one God, now and for ever. *Amen.*†

The Concluding Prayer of the Church

May Almighty God grant me a peaceful night and a perfect end. *Amen.*

The Morning Office   To Be Observed on the Hour or Half Hour
                                      Between 6 and 9 a.m.

The Call to Prayer

Sing with joy to God our strength* and raise a loud shout to the God of Jacob.
Raise a song and sound the timbrel,* the merry harp, and the lyre.
Blow the ram's-horn at the new moon,* and at the full moon, the day of our feast.
For this is a statute for Israel,* a law of the God of Jacob.

Psalm 81:1–4

The Request for Presence

Teach me your way, O Lord,* and I will walk in your truth; knit my heart to you
that I may fear your Name.

Psalm 86:11

The Greeting

My mouth shall recount your mighty acts and saving deeds all day long;* though I
cannot know the number of them.

Psalm 71:15

The Refrain for the Morning Lessons

Sing to the Lord with thanksgiving;* make music to our God upon the harp.

Psalm 147:7

A Reading

Jesus taught us, saying: "I am telling you not to worry about your life and what
you are to eat, nor about your body and what you are to wear. Surely life is
more than food, and the body more than clothing! Look at the birds in the sky.
They do not sow or reap or gather into barns; yet our heavenly Father feeds
them. Are you not worth much more than they are? Can any of you, however
much you worry, add one single cubit to your span of life? And why worry
about clothing? Think of the flowers growing in the fields; they never have to
work or spin; yet I assure you that not even Solomon in all his royal robes was
clothed like one of these. Now if that is how God clothes the wild flowers
growing in the field which are there today and thrown into the furnace tomorrow, will he not much more look after you, you who have so little faith?"

Matthew 6:25–30

The Refrain

Sing to the Lord with thanksgiving;* make music to our God upon the harp.

The Morning Psalm   *You Crown the Year with Your Goodness*

You visit the earth and water it abundantly; you make it very plenteous;* the river
of God is full of water.
You prepare the grain,* for so you provide for the earth.
You drench the furrows and smooth out the ridges;* with heavy rain you soften
the ground and bless its increase.
You crown the year with your goodness,* and your paths overflow with plenty.
May the fields of the wilderness be rich for grazing,* and the hills be clothed with
joy.
May the meadows cover themselves with flocks, and the valleys cloak themselves
with grain;* let them shout for joy and sing.

Psalm 65:9–14

The Refrain

Sing to the Lord with thanksgiving;* make music to our God upon the harp.

The Gloria

The Lord's Prayer

The Prayer Appointed for the Week

Almighty and everlasting God, whose will it is to restore all things in your well-beloved Son, the King of kings and Lord of lords: Mercifully grant that the peoples of the earth, divided and enslaved by sin, may be freed and brought together under his most gracious rule; who lives and reigns with you and the Holy Spirit, one God, now and for ever. *Amen.*†

Concluding Prayers of the Church

Almighty and gracious Father, I give you thanks for the fruits of the earth in their season and for the labors of those who harvest them. Make me, I pray, a faithful steward of your great bounty, for the provision of our necessities and the relief of all who are in need, to the glory of your Name; through Jesus Christ our Lord, who lives and reigns with you and the Holy Spirit, one God now and for ever. *Amen.*†

Lord God, almighty and everlasting Father, you have brought me in safety to this new day: Preserve me with your mighty power, that I may not fall into sin, nor be overcome by adversity; and in all I do direct me to the fulfilling of your purpose; through Jesus Christ my Lord. *Amen.*†

The Midday Office   To Be Observed on the Hour or Half Hour
                                             Between 11 a.m. and 2 p.m.

The Call to Prayer
Come, let us sing to the LORD;* let us shout for joy to the Rock of our salvation.
Let us come before his presence with thanksgiving* and raise a loud shout to him with psalms.
For the LORD is a great God,* and a great King above all gods.

Psalm 95:1–3

The Request for Presence
Let the peoples praise you, O God;* let all the peoples praise you.

Psalm 67:3

The Greeting
You have made me glad by your acts, O LORD;* and I shout for joy because of the works of your hands.

Psalm 92:4

The Refrain for the Midday Lessons
Yours are the heavens; the earth also is yours;* you laid the foundations of the world and all that is in it.

Psalm 89:11

A Reading
Make no mistake about this, my dear brothers: all that is good, all that is perfect, is given us from above; it comes down from the Father of all light; with him there

is no such thing as alteration, no shadow caused by change. By his own choice he gave birth to us by the message of the truth so that we should be a sort of firstfruits of all his creation.

James 1:16–18

The Refrain

Yours are the heavens; the earth also is yours;* you laid the foundations of the world and all that is in it.

The Midday Psalm

His Mercy Endures For Ever

Give thanks to the Lord of lords,* for his mercy endures for ever.
Who by wisdom made the heavens,* for his mercy endures for ever;
Who spread out the earth upon the waters,* for his mercy endures for ever;
Who created great lights,* for his mercy endures for ever;
The sun to rule the day,* for his mercy endures for ever;
The moon and the stars to govern the night,* for his mercy endures for ever.

Psalm 136:3, 5–9

The Refrain

Yours are the heavens; the earth also is yours;* you laid the foundations of the world and all that is in it.

The Gloria

The Lord's Prayer

The Prayer Appointed for the Week

Almighty and everlasting God, whose will it is to restore all things in your well-beloved Son, the King of kings and Lord of lords: Mercifully grant that the peoples of the earth, divided and enslaved by sin, may be freed and brought together under his most gracious rule; who lives and reigns with you and the Holy Spirit, one God, now and for ever. *Amen.*†

The Concluding Prayer of the Church

Grant me and all your people the gift of your Spirit, that we may know Christ and all make him known; and through him, at all times and in all places, may give thanks to you in all things. *Amen.*†

The Vespers Office

To Be Observed on the Hour or Half Hour
Between 5 and 8 p.m.

The Call to Prayer

Blessed be the Lord, the God of Israel, from everlasting and to everlasting;* and let all the people say, "Amen!" Hallelujah!

Psalm 106:48

The Request for Presence

Send forth your strength, O God;* establish, O God, what you have wrought for us.

Psalm 68:28

The Greeting
My heart is firmly fixed, O God, my heart is fixed;* I will sing and make melody.

Psalm 57:7

The Hymn
> Come, you thankful people, come, raise the song of harvest home:
> All is safely gathered in, ere the winter storms begin;
> God, our Maker, does provide for our wants to be supplied;
> Come to God's own temple, come, raise the song of harvest home.
>
> All the world is God's own field, fruit unto his praise to yield;
> Wheat and tares together sown, unto joy or sorrow grown:
> First the blade, and then the ear, then the full corn shall appear:
> Grant, O harvest Lord, that we wholesome grain and pure may be.
>
> Even so, Lord quickly come to your final harvest home;
> Gather you your people in, free from sorrow, free from sin;
> There, for ever purified, in your presence to abide;
> Come, with all your angels come, raise the glorious harvest home.

Henry Alford

The Refrain for the Vespers Lessons
I trust in the mercy of God for ever and ever.

Psalm 52:8b

The Vespers Psalm   *Let My Prayer Be as the Evening Sacrifice*
O LORD, I call to you; come to me quickly;* hear my voice when I cry to you.
Let my prayer be set forth in your sight as incense,* the lifting up of my hands as
    the evening sacrifice.
Set a watch before my mouth, O LORD, and guard the door of my lips;* let not my
    heart incline to any evil thing.
Let me not be occupied in wickedness with evildoers,* nor eat of their choice foods.
Let the righteous smite me in friendly rebuke;* let not the oil of the unrighteous
    anoint my head; for my prayer is continually against their wicked deeds.
Let their rulers be overthrown in stony places,* that they may know my words are
    true.

Psalm 141:1–6

The Refrain
I trust in the mercy of God for ever and ever.

The Cry of the Church
Even so, come, Lord Jesus!

The Lord's Prayer

The Prayer Appointed for the Week
Almighty and everlasting God, whose will it is to restore all things in your well-
    beloved Son, the King of kings and Lord of lords: Mercifully grant that the peo-

ples of the earth, divided and enslaved by sin, may be freed and brought together under his most gracious rule; who lives and reigns with you and the Holy Spirit, one God, now and for ever. *Amen.*†

Concluding Prayers of the Church

Accept, O Lord, my thanks and praise for all that you have done for me. I thank you for the splendor of the whole creation, for the beauty of this world, for the wonder of life, and for the mystery of love. Above all, I thank you for your Son Jesus Christ; for the truth of His Word and the example of his life; for his steadfast obedience, by which he overcame death; and for his rising to life again, in which we are raised to the life of your kingdom. *Amen.*†

Almighty God, whose loving hand has given me all that I possess: Grant me grace that I may honor you with my substance, and, remembering the account which I must one day give, may be a faithful steward of your bounty, through Jesus Christ our Lord. *Amen.*†

The Morning Office   To Be Observed on the Hour or Half Hour
                                      Between 6 and 9 a.m.

The Call to Prayer
Search for the LORD and his strength;* continually seek his face.

Psalm 105:4

The Request for Presence
O Lamb of God, that takes away the sins of the world, have mercy upon me.
O Lamb of God, that takes away the sins of the world, have mercy upon me.
O Lamb of God, that takes away the sins of the world, grant me your peace.

The Greeting
O God, you know my foolishness,* and my faults are not hidden from you.

Psalm 69:6

The Refrain for the Morning Lessons
Our sins are stronger than we are,* but you will blot them out.

Psalm 65:3

A Reading
He put another parable before them, 'The kingdom of Heaven may be compared to a man who sowed good seed in his field. While everybody was asleep, his enemy came, sowed darnel all among the wheat, and made off. When the new wheat sprouted and ripened, then the darnel appeared as well. The owner's laborers went to him and said, "Sir, was it not good seed that you sowed in your field? If so, where does this darnel come from?" He said to them, "Some enemy has done this." And the laborers said, "Do you want us to go and weed it out?" But he said, "No, because, when you weed out the darnel you might pull up the wheat with it. Let them both grow till harvest; and at harvest time I

shall say to the reapers: First collect the darnel and tie it in bundles to be burnt, then gather the wheat into my barn." '

Matthew 13:24–30

The Refrain

Our sins are stronger than we are,* but you will blot them out.

The Morning Psalm　　　　　　　　　　　　　　*Teach Us to Number Our Days*

Our iniquities you have set before you,* and our secret sins in the light of your countenance.

When you are angry, all our days are gone;* we bring our years to an end like a sigh.

The span of our life is seventy years, perhaps in strength even eighty;* yet the sum of them is but labor and sorrow, for they pass away quickly and we are gone.

Who regards the power of your wrath?* who rightly fears your indignation?

So teach us to number our days* that we may apply our hearts to wisdom.

Psalm 90:8–12

The Refrain

Our sins are stronger than we are,* but you will blot them out.

The Cry of the Church

O God, come to my assistance! O Lord, make haste to help me!

The Lord's Prayer

The Prayer Appointed for the Week

Almighty and everlasting God, whose will it is to restore all things in your well-beloved Son, the King of kings and Lord of lords: Mercifully grant that the peoples of the earth, divided and enslaved by sin, may be freed and brought together under his most gracious rule; who lives and reigns with you and the Holy Spirit, one God, now and for ever. *Amen.*†

The Concluding Prayer of the Church

Lord God, almighty and everlasting Father, you have brought me in safety to this new day: Preserve me with your mighty power, that I may not fall into sin, nor be overcome by adversity; and in all I do direct me to the fulfilling of your purpose; through Jesus Christ my Lord. *Amen.*†

The Midday Office　　　　　　　　　　To Be Observed on the Hour or Half Hour
　　　　　　　　　　　　　　　　　　　　Between 11 a.m. and 2 p.m.

The Call to Prayer

Ascribe to the LORD the honor due his Name;* bring offerings and come into his courts.

Psalm 96:8

The Request for Presence

Let your countenance shine upon your servant* and teach me your statutes.

Psalm 119:135

The Greeting

I will give thanks to you, O LORD, with my whole heart;* I will tell of all your marvelous works.

Psalm 9:1

The Refrain for the Midday Lessons

Among the gods there is none like you, O LORD,* nor anything like your works.

Psalm 86:8

A Reading

The end of all things is near, so keep your minds calm and sober for prayer. Above all preserve an intense love for each other, since *love covers over many a sin.*

1 Peter 4:7–8

The Refrain

Among the gods there is none like you, O LORD,* nor anything like your works.

The Midday Psalm   *You Have Declared Your Power Among the Peoples*

I will remember the works of the LORD,* and call to mind your wonders of old time.

I will meditate on all your acts* and ponder your mighty deeds.

Your way, O God, is holy;* who is so great a god as our God?

You are the God who works wonders* and have declared your power among the peoples.

Psalm 77:11–14

The Refrain

Among the gods there is none like you, O LORD,* nor anything like your works.

The Cry of the Church

Even so, come, Lord Jesus!

The Lord's Prayer

The Prayer Appointed for the Week

Almighty and everlasting God, whose will it is to restore all things in your well-beloved Son, the King of kings and Lord of lords: Mercifully grant that the peoples of the earth, divided and enslaved by sin, may be freed and brought together under his most gracious rule; who lives and reigns with you and the Holy Spirit, one God, now and for ever. *Amen.*†

The Concluding Prayer of the Church

Lord Jesus Christ, by your death you took away the sting of death: Grant me to so follow in faith where you have led the way, that I may at length fall asleep peacefully in you and wake in your likeness; for your tender mercies' sake. *Amen.*†

The Vespers Office   To Be Observed on the Hour or Half Hour
Between 5 and 8 p.m.

The Call to Prayer
I will call upon God,* and the LORD will deliver me.
In the evening, in the morning, and at noonday, I will complain and lament,* and
    he will hear my voice.
He will bring me safely back . . .* God, who is enthroned of old, will hear me.
Psalm 55:17ff

The Request for Presence
You are the LORD; do not withhold your compassion from me;* let your love and
    your faithfulness keep me safe for ever.
Psalm 40:12

The Greeting
I remember your Name in the night, O LORD,* and dwell upon your law.
Psalm 119:55

The Hymn
Let us give thanks to God our Father for all his gifts
so freely bestowed upon us.
For the beauty and wonder of your creation, in earth and sky and sea,
I thank you, Lord.
For all that is gracious in the lives of men and women,
revealing the image of Christ,
I thank you, Lord.
For my daily food and drink, my home and family, and friends,
I thank you, Lord.
For a mind to think, and a heart to love, and hands to serve,
I thank you, Lord.
For health and strength to work, and leisure to rest and play,
I thank you, Lord.
For the brave and courageous,
who are patient in suffering and faithful in adversity,
I thank you, Lord.
For all valiant seekers after truth, liberty, and justice,
I thank you, Lord.
For the communion of saints, in all times and places,
I thank you, Lord.

Above all, I give you thanks for the great mercies and promises given to us in
Christ Jesus our Lord; to him be praise and glory, with you, O Father, and the
Holy Spirit, now and for ever. *Amen.*†

The Refrain for the Vespers Lessons
Unless the LORD watches over the city,* in vain the watchman keeps his vigil.
Psalm 127:2

The Vespers Psalm   *Proclaim the Things That He Has Done*

But the LORD is enthroned for ever;* he has set up his throne for judgment.

It is he who rules the world with righteousness;* he judges the peoples with
equity.

The LORD will be a refuge for the oppressed,* a refuge in time of trouble.

Those who know your Name will put their trust in you,* for you never forsake
those who seek you, O LORD.

Sing praise to the LORD who dwells in Zion;* proclaim to the peoples the things he
has done.

Psalm 9:7–11

The Refrain

Unless the LORD watches over the city,* in vain the watchman keeps his vigil.

The Small Verse

Open, Lord, my eyes that I may see. Open, Lord, my ears that I may hear. Open,
Lord, my heart and my mind that I may understand. So shall I turn to you and
be healed.

Traditional

The Lord's Prayer

The Prayer Appointed for the Week

Almighty and everlasting God, whose will it is to restore all things in your well-
beloved Son, the King of kings and Lord of lords: Mercifully grant that the peoples of the earth, divided and enslaved by sin, may be freed and brought
together under his most gracious rule; who lives and reigns with you and the
Holy Spirit, one God, now and for ever. *Amen.*†

Concluding Prayers of the Church

Almighty God, who has promised to hear the petitions of those who ask in your
Son's Name: I beseech you mercifully to incline your ear to me who have made
my prayers and supplications to you; and grant that those things which I have
faithfully asked according to your will, I may effectually obtain, to the relief of
my necessity, and to the setting forth of your glory; through Jesus Christ my
Lord. *Amen.*†

May the souls of the faithful departed, through the mercy of God, rest in eternal
peace. *Amen.*

The Morning Office   **To Be Observed on the Hour or Half Hour
Between 6 and 9 a.m.**

The Call to Prayer

Let us bless the LORD,* from this time forth for evermore. Hallelujah!

based on Psalm 115:18

The Request for Presence
I cry out to you, O LORD,* I say, "You are my refuge, my portion in the land of the
  living."
Psalm 142:5

The Greeting
I will confess you among the peoples, O LORD;* I will sing praises to you among
  the nations.
For your loving-kindness is greater than the heavens,* and your faithfulness
  reaches to the clouds.
Psalm 108:3–4

The Refrain for the Morning Lessons
For the LORD God is both sun and shield;* he will give grace and glory.
Psalm 84:10

A Reading
Jesus queried us, saying: "How can people maintain that the Christ is son of
  David? Why, David himself says in the Book of Psalms:
  The Lord declared to my Lord,
  take your seat at my right hand,
  till I have made your enemies
  your footstool.
David here calls him Lord; how then can he be his son?"
Luke 20:41–44

The Refrain
For the LORD God is both sun and shield;* he will give grace and glory.

The Morning Psalm   *Sound the Timbrel, the Merry Harp, and the Lyre*
Sing with joy to God our strength* and raise a loud shout to the God of Jacob.
Raise a song and sound the timbrel,* the merry harp, and the lyre.
Blow the ram's-horn at the new moon,* and at the full moon, the day of our feast.
For this is a statute for Israel,* a law of the God of Jacob.
Psalm 81:1–4

The Refrain
For the LORD God is both sun and shield;* he will give grace and glory.

The Gloria

The Lord's Prayer

The Prayer Appointed for the Week
Almighty and everlasting God, whose will it is to restore all things in your well-
  beloved Son, the King of kings and Lord of lords: Mercifully grant that the peoples of the earth, divided and enslaved by sin, may be freed and brought
  together under his most gracious rule; who lives and reigns with you and the
  Holy Spirit, one God, now and for ever. *Amen.*†

The Concluding Prayer of the Church

Lord God, almighty and everlasting Father, you have brought me in safety to this new day: Preserve me with your mighty power, that I may not fall into sin, nor be overcome by adversity; and in all I do direct me to the fulfilling of your purpose; through Jesus Christ my Lord. *Amen.*†

The Midday Office
To Be Observed on the Hour or Half Hour
Between 11 a.m. and 2 p.m.

The Call to Prayer

Open my lips, O LORD,* and my mouth shall proclaim your praise.

Psalm 51:16

The Request for Presence

Look well whether there be any wickedness in me* and lead me in the way that is everlasting.

Psalm 139:23

The Greeting

O LORD, I am your servant;* I am your servant and the child of your handmaid; you have freed me from my bonds.

Psalm 116:14

The Refrain for the Midday Lessons

Unless the LORD builds the house,* their labor is in vain who build it.

Psalm 127:1

A Reading

A prayer of the prophet Habakkuk; tone as for dirges: YAHWEH, I have heard of your renown; your work, YAHWEH, inspires me with dread. Make it live again in our time, make it known in our time; in wrath remember mercy.

Habakkuk 3:1–2

The Refrain

Unless the LORD builds the house,* their labor is in vain who build it.

The Midday Psalm
Light Has Sprung Up for the Righteous

Zion hears and is glad, and the cities of Judah rejoice,* because of your judgments, O LORD.

For you are the LORD, most high over all the earth;* you are exalted far above all gods.

The LORD loves those who hate evil;* he preserves the lives of his saints and delivers them from the hand of the wicked.

Light has sprung up for the righteous,* and joyful gladness for those who are truehearted.

Psalm 97:8–12

The Refrain
Unless the LORD builds the house,* their labor is in vain who build it.

The Cry of the Church
Even so, come, Lord Jesus!

The Lord's Prayer

The Prayer Appointed for the Week
Almighty and everlasting God, whose will it is to restore all things in your well-beloved Son, the King of kings and Lord of lords: Mercifully grant that the peoples of the earth, divided and enslaved by sin, may be freed and brought together under his most gracious rule; who lives and reigns with you and the Holy Spirit, one God, now and for ever. *Amen.*†

The Concluding Prayer of the Church
O God, the source of eternal light: Shed forth your unending day upon all of us who watch for you, that our lips may praise you, our lives may bless you, and our worship may give you glory; through Jesus Christ our Lord. *Amen.*†

The Vespers Office   **To Be Observed on the Hour or Half Hour**
                                          Between 5 and 8 p.m.

The Call to Prayer
Let everything that has breath* praise the LORD. Hallelujah!
Psalm 150:6

The Request for Presence
O God, you are my God; eagerly I seek you;* my soul thirsts for you, my flesh faints for you, as in a barren and dry land where there is no water.
Therefore I have gazed upon you in your holy place,* that I might behold your power and your glory.
Psalm 63:1–2

The Greeting
Your loving-kindness is better than life itself;* my lips shall give you praise.
So will I bless you as long as I live* and lift up my hands in your Name.
Psalm 63:3–4

The Hymn   *We Gather Together*
We gather together to ask the Lord's blessing;
He chastens and hastens his will to make known;
The wicked oppressing now cease from distressing:
Sing praises to his Name; he forgets not his own.

Beside us to guide us, our God with us joining,
Ordaining, maintaining his kingdom divine;
So from the beginning the fight we were winning:
You, Lord, were at our side: all glory be thine!

We all do extol You, You leader triumphant,
And pray that you still our defender will be.
Let your congregation escape tribulation:
Your Name be ever praised! O Lord, make us free!

Anonymous

The Refrain for the Vespers Lessons
The Lord is my light and my salvation; whom then shall I fear?* the Lord is the strength of my life; of whom then shall I be afraid?

Psalm 27:1

The Vespers Psalm   *Glory in His Holy Name*
Give thanks to the Lord and call upon his Name;* make known his deeds among the peoples.
Sing to him, sing praises to him,* and speak of all his marvelous works.
Glory in his holy Name;* let the hearts of those who seek the Lord rejoice.
Search for the Lord and his strength;* continually seek his face.
Remember the marvels he has done,* his wonders and the judgments of his mouth,
He is the Lord our God;* his judgments prevail in all the world.

Psalm 105:1–5, 7

The Refrain
The Lord is my light and my salvation; whom then shall I fear?* the Lord is the strength of my life; of whom then shall I be afraid?

The Cry of the Church
O Lamb of God, that takes away the sins of the world, have mercy upon me.
O Lamb of God, that takes away the sins of the world, have mercy upon me.
O Lamb of God, that takes away the sins of the world, grant me your peace.

The Lord's Prayer

The Prayer Appointed for the Week
Almighty and everlasting God, whose will it is to restore all things in your well-beloved Son, the King of kings and Lord of lords: Mercifully grant that the peoples of the earth, divided and enslaved by sin, may be freed and brought together under his most gracious rule; who lives and reigns with you and the Holy Spirit, one God, now and for ever. *Amen.*†

The Concluding Prayer of the Church
Almighty God, who after the creation of the world rested from all your works and sanctified a day of rest for all your creatures: Grant that I, putting away all earthly anxieties, may be duly prepared for the service of public worship, and grant as well that my Sabbath upon earth may be a preparation for the eternal rest promised to your people in heaven; through Jesus Christ our Lord. *Amen.*†

November Compline

Sunday
The Night Office   To Be Observed Before Retiring

The Call to Prayer
May the Lord Almighty grant me and those I love a peaceful night and a perfect
    end. *Amen.*†

The Request for Presence
Our help is in the Name of the Lord; the maker of heaven and earth.

The Greeting
Almighty God, my heavenly Father: I have sinned against you, through my own
    fault, in thought, and word, and deed, in what I have done and what I have left
    undone. For the sake of your Son our Lord Jesus Christ, forgive me all my
    offenses; and grant that I may serve you in newness of life, to the glory of your
    Name. *Amen.*†

The Reading
You are the future,
the red sky before sunrise
over the fields of time.

You are the cock's crow when night is done,
you are the dew and the bells of matins,
maiden, stranger, mother, death.

You create yourself in ever-changing shapes
that rise from the stuff of our days—
unsung, unmourned, undescribed,
like a forest we never knew.

You are the deep innerness of all things,
the last word that can never be spoken.
To each of us you reveal yourself differently:
to the ship as coastline, to the shore as a ship.
                                        Rainer Maria Rilke

The Gloria

The Psalm   *I Will Ponder Your Mighty Deeds*
I think of God, I am restless,* I ponder, and my spirit faints.
I consider the days of old;* I remember the years long past;
I commune with my heart in the night;* I ponder and search my mind.
I will remember the works of the LORD,* and call to mind your wonders of old
    time.
I will meditate on all your acts* and ponder your mighty deeds.
Your way, O God, is holy;* who is so great a god as our God?
                                        Psalm 3:5–6, 11–13

The Gloria

The Small Verse

Into your hands, O Lord, I commend my spirit; for you have redeemed me, O
   Lord, O God of truth. Keep me, O Lord, as the apple of your eye; hide me
   under the shadow of your wings.†

The Lord's Prayer

The Petition

Watch, O Lord, with those who wake, or watch, or weep tonight, and give Your
   angels and saints charge over those who sleep. Tend Your sick ones, O Lord
   Christ. Rest Your weary ones. Bless Your dying ones. Soothe Your suffering
   ones. Shield Your joyous ones, and all for Your love's sake. *Amen.*§

The Final Thanksgiving

Lord, you now have set your servant free to go in peace as you have promised; for
   these eyes of mine have seen the Savior, whom you have prepared for all the
   world to see: a Light to enlighten the nations, and the glory of your people
   Israel. Glory to the Father, and to the Son, and to the Holy Spirit: as it was in the
   beginning, is now, and will be for ever. *Amen.*

Monday
The Night Office   To Be Observed Before Retiring

The Call to Prayer

May the Lord Almighty grant me and those I love a peaceful night and a perfect
   end. *Amen.*†

The Request for Presence

Our help is in the Name of the Lord; the maker of heaven and earth.

The Greeting

Almighty God, my heavenly Father: I have sinned against you, through my own
   fault, in thought, and word, and deed, in what I have done and what I have left
   undone. For the sake of your Son our Lord Jesus Christ, forgive me all my
   offenses; and grant that I may serve you in newness of life, to the glory of your
   Name. *Amen.*†

The Reading   *The Lord Is My Chosen Portion*

The Lord is my chosen portion;
he is my strength and my might.
I will bless the Lord at all times;
his praise shall be in my mouth.

Though the fig tree does not blossom
and no fruit is on the vines,
yet I will give thanks to the Lord,
I will sing praises to him.

Though the produce of the olive fails
and the fields yield no food,
yet I will praise the name of God,
I will magnify him with thanksgiving.

Though the flock is cut off from the fold
and there is no herd in the stalls,
yet I will rejoice in the Lord,
I will exult in the God of my salvation.❖

The Gloria

The Psalm   *Happy Are They Who Have the God of Jacob for Their Help*

Happy are they who have the God of Jacob for their help!* whose hope is in the
    LORD their God;
Who made heaven and earth, the seas, and all that is in them;* who keeps his
    promise for ever;
Who gives justice to those who are oppressed,* and food to those who hunger.
The LORD sets the prisoners free; the LORD opens the eyes of the blind;* the LORD
    lifts up those who are bowed down;
The LORD loves the righteous; the LORD cares for the stranger;* he sustains the
    orphan and widow, but frustrates the way of the wicked.
The LORD shall reign for ever,* your God, O Zion, throughout all generations.
    Hallelujah!

Psalm 146:4–9

The Gloria

The Small Verse

Into your hands, O Lord, I commend my spirit; for you have redeemed me, O
    Lord, O God of truth. Keep me, O Lord, as the apple of your eye; hide me
    under the shadow of your wings.†

The Lord's Prayer

The Petition

Watch, O Lord, with those who wake, or watch, or weep tonight, and give Your
    angels and saints charge over those who sleep. Tend Your sick ones, O Lord
    Christ. Rest Your weary ones. Bless Your dying ones. Soothe Your suffering
    ones. Shield Your joyous ones, and all for Your love's sake. *Amen.*§

The Final Thanksgiving

Lord, you now have set your servant free to go in peace as you have promised; for
    these eyes of mine have seen the Savior, whom you have prepared for all the

world to see: a Light to enlighten the nations, and the glory of your people Israel. Glory to the Father, and to the Son, and to the Holy Spirit: as it was in the beginning, is now, and will be for ever. *Amen.*

༄

Tuesday
The Night Office   To Be Observed Before Retiring

The Call to Prayer
May the Lord Almighty grant me and those I love a peaceful night and a perfect
  end. *Amen.*†

The Request for Presence
Our help is in the Name of the Lord; the maker of heaven and earth.

The Greeting
Almighty God, my heavenly Father: I have sinned against you, through my own
  fault, in thought, and word, and deed, in what I have done and what I have left
  undone. For the sake of your Son our Lord Jesus Christ, forgive me all my
  offenses; and grant that I may serve you in newness of life, to the glory of your
  Name. *Amen.*†

The Reading
Great and holy is the Lord,
  the holiest of holy ones for every generation.
Majesty precedes him,
  and following him is the rush of many waters.
Grace and truth surround his presence;
  truth and justice and righteousness are the foundations of his throne.
Separating light from deep darkness,
  by the knowledge of his mind he has established the dawn.
When all his angels had witnessed it they sang aloud;
  for he showed them what they had not known
Crowning the hills with fruit,
  good food for every living being.
Blessed be he who makes the earth by his power
  establishing the world in his wisdom.
In his understanding he stretched out the heavens,
  and brought forth wind from his storehouses.
He made lightning for the rain,
  and caused mists to rise from the end of the earth.

                                                              Dead Sea Scrolls

The Gloria

The Psalm   *May the* LORD *Strengthen You Out of Zion*

May the LORD answer you in the day of trouble,* the Name of the God of Jacob
    defend you;

Send you help from his holy place* and strengthen you out of Zion;

Remember all your offerings* and accept your burnt sacrifice;

Grant you your heart's desire* and prosper all your plans.

We will shout for joy at your victory and triumph in the Name of our God;* may
    the LORD grant all your requests.

Now I know that the LORD gives victory to his anointed;* he will answer him out
    of his holy heaven, with the victorious strength of his right hand.

Some put their trust in chariots and some in horses,* but we will call upon the
    Name of the LORD our God.

They collapse and fall down,* but we will arise and stand upright.

O LORD, give victory to the king* and answer us when we call.

Psalm 20

The Gloria

The Small Verse

Into your hands, O Lord, I commend my spirit; for you have redeemed me,
    O Lord, O God of truth. Keep me, O Lord, as the apple of your eye; hide me
    under the shadow of your wings.†

The Lord's Prayer

The Petition

Watch, O Lord, with those who wake, or watch, or weep tonight, and give Your
    angels and saints charge over those who sleep. Tend Your sick ones, O Lord
    Christ. Rest Your weary ones. Bless Your dying ones. Soothe Your suffering
    ones. Shield Your joyous ones, and all for Your love's sake. *Amen.*§

The Final Thanksgiving

Lord, you now have set your servant free to go in peace as you have promised; for
    these eyes of mine have seen the Savior, whom you have prepared for all the
    world to see: a Light to enlighten the nations, and the glory of your people
    Israel. Glory to the Father, and to the Son, and to the Holy Spirit: as it was in the
    beginning, is now, and will be for ever. *Amen.*

Wednesday
The Night Office   To Be Observed Before Retiring

The Call to Prayer
May the Lord Almighty grant me and those I love a peaceful night and a perfect
    end. *Amen.*†

The Request for Presence
Our help is in the Name of the Lord; the maker of heaven and earth.

The Greeting
Almighty God, my heavenly Father: I have sinned against you, through my own
    fault, in thought, and word, and deed, in what I have done and what I have left
    undone. For the sake of your Son our Lord Jesus Christ, forgive me all my
    offenses; and grant that I may serve you in newness of life, to the glory of your
    Name. *Amen.*†

The Reading   *A Mind to Know You*
Grant me, O Lord my God,
a mind to know you,
a heart to seek you,
wisdom to find you,
conduct pleasing to you,
faithful perseverance in waiting for you,
and a hope of finally embracing you.
                    St. Thomas Aquinas

The Gloria

The Psalm   *I Lie Down in Peace*
Answer me when I call, O God, defender of my cause;* you set me free when I am
    hard-pressed; have mercy on me and hear my prayer.
"You mortals, how long will you dishonor my glory;* how long will you worship
    dumb idols and run after false gods?"
Know that the LORD does wonders for the faithful;* when I call upon the LORD, he
    will hear me.
Tremble, then, and do not sin;* speak to your heart in silence upon your bed.
Offer the appointed sacrifices* and put your trust in the LORD.
Many are saying, "Oh, that we might see better times!"* Lift up the light of your
    countenance upon us, O LORD.
You have put gladness in my heart,* more than when grain and wine and oil
    increase.
I lie down in peace; at once I fall asleep;* for only you, LORD, make me dwell in
    safety.
                                                        Psalm 4

The Gloria

The Small Verse

Into your hands, O Lord, I commend my spirit; for you have redeemed me, O
Lord, O God of truth. Keep me, O Lord, as the apple of your eye; hide me
under the shadow of your wings.†

The Lord's Prayer

The Petition

Watch, O Lord, with those who wake, or watch, or weep tonight, and give Your
angels and saints charge over those who sleep. Tend Your sick ones, O Lord
Christ. Rest Your weary ones. Bless Your dying ones. Soothe Your suffering
ones. Shield Your joyous ones, and all for Your love's sake. *Amen.*§

The Final Thanksgiving

Lord, you now have set your servant free to go in peace as you have promised; for
these eyes of mine have seen the Savior, whom you have prepared for all the
world to see: a Light to enlighten the nations, and the glory of your people
Israel. Glory to the Father, and to the Son, and to the Holy Spirit: as it was in the
beginning, is now, and will be for ever. *Amen.*

⚜

Thursday
The Night Office   To Be Observed Before Retiring

The Call to Prayer

May the Lord Almighty grant me and those I love a peaceful night and a perfect
end. *Amen.*†

The Request for Presence

Our help is in the Name of the Lord; the maker of heaven and earth.

The Greeting

Almighty God, my heavenly Father: I have sinned against you, through my own
fault, in thought, and word, and deed, in what I have done and what I have left
undone. For the sake of your Son our Lord Jesus Christ, forgive me all my
offenses; and grant that I may serve you in newness of life, to the glory of your
Name. *Amen.*†

The Reading   *Late Have I Loved Thee*

Late have I loved thee, O beauty so ancient and so new; late have I loved thee: for
behold you were within me, and I outside; and I sought you outside and in my
unloveliness fell upon those things, yet had they not been in you, they would
not have been at all. You called and cried to me to break open my deafness: and

you did send forth your beams and shine upon me and chase away my blindness: you breathed fragrance upon me, and I drew in my breath and I do now
pant for you: I tasted you, and now hunger and thirst for you: you touched me,
and I have burned for your peace.

St. Augustine

The Gloria

The Psalm   *Keep Me as the Apple of Your Eye*
I call upon you, O God, for you will answer me;* incline your ear to me and hear
my words.
Show me your marvelous loving-kindness,* O Savior of those who take refuge at
your right hand from those who rise up against them.
Keep me as the apple of your eye;* hide me under the shadow of your wings,
From the wicked who assault me,* from my deadly enemies who surround me.

Psalm 17:6–9

The Gloria

The Small Verse
Into your hands, O Lord, I commend my spirit; for you have redeemed me,
O Lord, O God of truth. Keep me, O Lord, as the apple of your eye; hide me
under the shadow of your wings.†

The Lord's Prayer

The Petition
Watch, O Lord, with those who wake, or watch, or weep tonight, and give Your
angels and saints charge over those who sleep. Tend Your sick ones, O Lord
Christ. Rest Your weary ones. Bless Your dying ones. Soothe Your suffering
ones. Shield Your joyous ones, and all for Your love's sake. *Amen.*§

The Final Thanksgiving
Lord, you now have set your servant free to go in peace as you have promised; for
these eyes of mine have seen the Savior, whom you have prepared for all the
world to see: a Light to enlighten the nations, and the glory of your people
Israel. Glory to the Father, and to the Son, and to the Holy Spirit: as it was in the
beginning, is now, and will be for ever. *Amen.*

Friday
The Night Office   To Be Observed Before Retiring

The Call to Prayer
May the Lord Almighty grant me and those I love a peaceful night and a perfect
    end. *Amen.*†

The Request for Presence
Our help is in the Name of the Lord; the maker of heaven and earth.

The Greeting
Almighty God, my heavenly Father: I have sinned against you, through my own
    fault, in thought, and word, and deed, in what I have done and what I have left
    undone. For the sake of your Son our Lord Jesus Christ, forgive me all my
    offenses; and grant that I may serve you in newness of life, to the glory of your
    Name. *Amen.*†

The Reading   *Litany of Penitence*
Most holy and merciful Father:
I confess to you and to the whole communion of saints in heaven and on earth.
I have not loved you with my whole heart, and mind, and strength. I have not loved
    my neighbors as myself. I have not forgiven others, as I have been forgiven.
Have mercy on me, Lord.
I have been deaf to your call to serve, as Christ served us. I have not been true to
    the mind of Christ. I have grieved your Holy Spirit.
Have mercy on me, Lord.
I confess to you, Lord, all my past unfaithfulness: the pride, hypocrisy, and impa-
    tience of my life,
I confess to you, Lord.
My self-indulgent appetites and ways, and my exploitation of other people,
I confess to you, Lord.
My anger at my own frustration, and my envy of those more fortunate than I,
I confess to you, Lord.
My intemperate love of worldly goods and comforts, and my dishonesty in daily
    life and work,
I confess to you, Lord.
My negligence in prayer and worship, and my failure to commend the faith that is
    in me,
I confess to you, Lord.
Accept my repentance, Lord, for the wrongs I have done: for my blindness to
    human need and suffering, and my indifference to injustice and cruelty,
Accept my repentance, Lord.
For all false judgments, for uncharitable thoughts toward my neighbors, and for
    my prejudice and contempt toward those who differ from me,
Accept my repentance, Lord.
For my waste and pollution of your creation, and my lack of concern for those
    who come after us,

Accept my repentance, Lord.
Restore me, good Lord, and let your anger depart from me,
Favorably hear me for your mercy is great.
Accomplish in me and all of your church the work of your salvation,
That I may show forth your glory in the world.
By the cross and passion of your Son our Lord,
Bring me with all your saints to the joy of his resurrection.†

The Gloria

The Psalm   *Have Pity on Me, LORD, for I Am Weak*

LORD, do not rebuke me in your anger;* do not punish me in your wrath.
Have pity on me, LORD, for I am weak;* heal me, LORD, for my bones are racked.
My spirit shakes with terror;* how long, O LORD, how long?
Turn, O LORD, and deliver me;* save me for your mercy's sake.
For in death no one remembers you;* and who will give you thanks in the grave?
I grow weary because of my groaning;* every night I drench my bed and flood my
     couch with tears.
My eyes are wasted with grief* and worn away because of all my enemies.
Depart from me, all evildoers,* for the LORD has heard the sound of my weeping.
The LORD has heard my supplication;* the LORD accepts my prayer.

Psalm 6:1–9

The Gloria

The Small Verse

Into your hands, O Lord, I commend my spirit; for you have redeemed me,
     O Lord, O God of truth. Keep me, O Lord, as the apple of your eye; hide me
     under the shadow of your wings.†

The Lord's Prayer

The Petition

Watch, O Lord, with those who wake, or watch, or weep tonight, and give Your
     angels and saints charge over those who sleep. Tend Your sick ones, O Lord
     Christ. Rest Your weary ones. Bless Your dying ones. Soothe Your suffering
     ones. Shield Your joyous ones, and all for Your love's sake. *Amen.*§

The Final Thanksgiving

Lord, you now have set your servant free to go in peace as you have promised; for
     these eyes of mine have seen the Savior, whom you have prepared for all the
     world to see: a Light to enlighten the nations, and the glory of your people
     Israel. Glory to the Father, and to the Son, and to the Holy Spirit: as it was in the
     beginning, is now, and will be for ever. *Amen.*

Saturday
The Night Office   To Be Observed Before Retiring

The Call to Prayer

May the Lord Almighty grant me and those I love a peaceful night and a perfect
end. *Amen.*†

The Request for Presence

Our help is in the Name of the Lord; the maker of heaven and earth.

The Greeting

Almighty God, my heavenly Father: I have sinned against you, through my own
fault, in thought, and word, and deed, in what I have done and what I have left
undone. For the sake of your Son our Lord Jesus Christ, forgive me all my
offenses; and grant that I may serve you in newness of life, to the glory of your
Name. *Amen.*†

The Reading

Then I saw a *new heaven and a new earth;* the first heaven and the first earth had dis-
appeared now, and there was no longer any sea. I saw the holy city, the new
Jerusalem, coming down out of heaven from God, prepared as a bride dressed
for her husband. Then I heard a loud voice call from the throne, 'Look, here
God lives among human beings. He will make *his home among them, they will be
his people,* and he will be their God, *God-with-them. He will wipe away all tears
from their eyes;* there will be no more death, and no more mourning or sadness
or pain. The world of the past has gone.'

Then the One sitting on the throne spoke, 'Look I am making the whole of creation
new. Write this, "What I am saying is trustworthy and will come true." ' Then
he said to me, 'It has already happened. I am the Alpha and the Omega, the
Beginning and the End. I will give water from the well of life free to anybody
who is thirsty; anyone who proves victorious will inherit these things; and *I
will be his God and he will be my son.* But the legacy for cowards, for those who
break their word, or worship obscenities, for murderers and the sexually
immoral, and for sorcerers, worshippers of false gods or any other sort of liars,
is the second death in the burning lake of sulfur.'

Revelation 21:1–8

The Gloria

The Psalm   *The God of Gods Will Reveal Himself in Zion*

How dear to me is your dwelling, O LORD of hosts!* My soul has a desire and
longing for the courts of the LORD; my heart and my flesh rejoice in the living
God.

The sparrow has found her a house and the swallow a nest where she may lay her
young;* by the side of your altars, O LORD of hosts, my King and my God.

Happy are they who dwell in your house!* they will always be praising you.

Happy are the people whose strength is in you!* whose hearts are set on the
pilgrims' way.

Those who go through the desolate valley will find it a place of springs,* for the
early rains have covered it with pools of water.

They will climb from height to height,* and the God of gods will reveal himself in
Zion.

LORD God of hosts, hear my prayer;* hearken, O God of Jacob.

Behold our defender, O God;* and look upon the face of your Anointed.

Psalm 84:1–8

The Gloria

The Small Verse

Into your hands, O Lord, I commend my spirit; for you have redeemed me,
O Lord, O God of truth. Keep me, O Lord, as the apple of your eye; hide me
under the shadow of your wings.†

The Lord's Prayer

The Petition

Watch, O Lord, with those who wake, or watch, or weep tonight, and give Your
angels and saints charge over those who sleep. Tend Your sick ones, O Lord
Christ. Rest Your weary ones. Bless Your dying ones. Soothe Your suffering
ones. Shield Your joyous ones, and all for Your love's sake. *Amen*.§

The Final Thanksgiving

Lord, you now have set your servant free to go in peace as you have promised; for
these eyes of mine have seen the Savior, whom you have prepared for all the
world to see: a Light to enlighten the nations, and the glory of your people
Israel. Glory to the Father, and to the Son, and to the Holy Spirit: as it was in the
beginning, is now, and will be for ever. *Amen*.

The season of Advent, which contains four Sundays, begins, in the Western church, on the Sunday nearest to November 30. The first Sunday of Advent is also the first day of the new liturgical, or church, year.

The Lord's Prayer

Our Father, who art in heaven, hallowed be your Name.
May your kingdom come, and your will be done, on earth as in heaven.
Give us today our daily bread.
Forgive us our sins as we forgive those who sin against us.
Lead us not into temptation, but deliver us from evil;
for yours are the kingdom and the power and the glory
forever and ever. *Amen.*

Compline Prayers for Advent Are Located on Page 415.

The Following Holy Days Occur in Advent:
The Feast of St. Thomas, the Apostle: *December 21*

Advent

The Morning Office   To Be Observed on the Hour or Half Hour
                                              Between 6 and 9 a.m.

The Call to Prayer
Hallelujah! I will give thanks to the LORD with my whole heart,* in the assembly of
    the upright, in the congregation.

Psalm 111:1

The Request for Presence
Let them know that you, whose Name is YAHWEH,* you alone are the Most High
    over all the earth.

Psalm 83:18

The Greeting
I shall always wait in patience,* and shall praise you more and more.

Psalm 71:14

The Refrain for the Morning Lessons
The same stone which the builders rejected* has become the chief cornerstone.

Psalm 118:22

A Reading   *During Advent the Church celebrates the messianic works of the
                     Hebrew prophets, especially that of the prophet Isaiah. Advent
                     emphasizes as well the promise of the second coming of the
                     Messiah in kingly triumph.*

Jesus taught us, saying: "As it was in Noah's day, so will it be when the Son of
    man comes. For in those days before the Flood people were eating, drinking,
    taking wives, taking husbands, right up to the day Noah went into the ark, and
    they suspected nothing till the Flood came and swept them away. This is what
    it will be like when the Son of man comes."

Matthew 24:37–39

The Refrain
The same stone which the builders rejected* has become the chief cornerstone.

The Morning Psalm   *In His Time Shall the Righteous Flourish*
Give the King your justice, O God,* and your righteousness to the King's Son;
That he may rule your people righteously* and the poor with justice;
That the mountains may bring prosperity to the people,* and the little hills bring
    righteousness.
He shall defend the needy among the people;* he shall rescue the poor and crush
    the oppressor.
He shall live as long as the sun and moon endure,* from one generation to another.
He shall come down like rain upon the mown field,* like showers that water the
    earth.

In his time shall the righteous flourish;* there shall be abundance of peace till the moon shall be no more.

He shall rule from sea to sea,* and from the River to the ends of the earth.

Psalm 72:1–8

The Refrain

The same stone which the builders rejected* has become the chief cornerstone.

The Cry of the Church

Even so, come, Lord Jesus.

The Lord's Prayer

The Prayer Appointed for the Week

Almighty God, give all of us grace to cast away the works of darkness, and put on the armor of light, now in the time of this mortal life in which your Son Jesus Christ came to visit us in great humility; that in the last day, when he shall come again in his glorious majesty to judge both the living and the dead, we may rise to the life immortal; through him who lives and reigns with you and the Holy Spirit, one God, now and for ever. *Amen.*†

The Concluding Prayer of the Church

Lord God, almighty and everlasting Father, you have brought me in safety to this new day: Preserve me with your mighty power, that I may not fall into sin, nor be overcome by adversity; and in all I do direct me to the fulfilling of your purpose; through Jesus Christ my Lord. *Amen.*†

The Midday Office **To Be Observed on the Hour or Half Hour Between 11 a.m. and 2 p.m.**

The Call to Prayer

God is the Lord; he has shined upon us;* form a procession with branches up to the horns of the altar.

Psalm 118:27

The Request for Presence

Open my lips, O Lord* and my mouth shall proclaim your praise.

Psalm 51:16

The Greeting

Let all who seek you rejoice and be glad in you;* let those who love your salvation say for ever, "Great is the Lord!"

Psalm 70:4

The Refrain for the Midday Lessons

The words of the Lord are tried in the fire;* he is a shield to all who trust in him.

Psalm 18:31

A Reading

The vision of Isaiah son of Amoz, concerning Judah and Jerusalem: It will happen in the final days that the mountain of Yahweh's house will rise higher than the mountains and tower above the heights. Then all the nations will stream to it, many peoples will come to it and say, 'Come, let us go up to the mountain of Yahweh, to the house of the God of Jacob that he may teach us his ways so that we may walk in his paths.' For the Law will issue from Zion and the word of Yahweh from Jerusalem. Then he will judge between the nations and arbitrate between many peoples. They will hammer their swords into plowshares and their spears into sickles. Nation will not lift sword against nation, no longer will they learn to make war. House of Jacob, come, let us walk in Yahweh's light.

Isaiah 2:1–5

The Refrain

The words of the Lord are tried in the fire;* he is a shield to all who trust in him.

The Midday Psalm   *There Are the Thrones of the House of David*

I was glad when they said to me,* "Let us go to the house of the Lord."
Now our feet are standing* within your gates, O Jerusalem.
Jerusalem is built as a city* that is at unity with itself;
To which the tribes go up, the tribes of the Lord,* the assembly of Israel, to praise the Name of the Lord.
For there are the thrones of judgment,* the thrones of the house of David.
Pray for the peace of Jerusalem:* "May they prosper who love you.
Peace be within your walls* and quietness within your towers.
For my brethren and companions' sake,* I pray for your prosperity.
Because of the house of the Lord our God,* I will seek to do you good."

Psalm 122

The Refrain

The words of the Lord are tried in the fire;* he is a shield to all who trust in him.

The Small Verse

Blessed be the Lord God of Israel for he has visited and delivered us. Alleluia, alleluia, alleluia.

Traditional

The Lord's Prayer

The Prayer Appointed for the Week

Almighty God, give all of us grace to cast away the works of darkness, and put on the armor of light, now in the time of this mortal life in which your Son Jesus Christ came to visit us in great humility; that in the last day, when he shall come again in his glorious majesty to judge both the living and the dead, we may rise to the life immortal; through him who lives and reigns with you and the Holy Spirit, one God, now and for ever. *Amen.*†

The Concluding Prayer of the Church

O God, you make me glad with the weekly remembrance of the glorious resurrection of your Son my Lord: Give me this day such blessing through my worship of you, that the week to come may be spent in your favor; through Jesus Christ our Lord. *Amen.*†

The Vespers Office   To Be Observed on the Hour or Half Hour
                                               Between 5 and 8 p.m.

The Call to Prayer

Enter his gates with thanksgiving; go into his courts with praise;* give thanks to him and call upon his Name.

Psalm 100:3

The Request for Presence

May God give us his blessing,* and may all the ends of the earth stand in awe of him.

Psalm 67:7

The Greeting

We give you thanks, O God, we give you thanks,* calling upon your Name and declaring all your wonderful deeds.

Psalm 75:1

The Hymn   *Come, Thou Long Expected Jesus*

Come, thou long expected Jesus,   Born your people to deliver,
Born to set your people free;   Born a child, and yet a king,
From our fears and sins release us, Born to reign in us for ever,
Let us find our rest in thee.   Now your gracious kingdom bring.

Israel's strength and consolation,   By your own eternal spirit
Hope of all the earth thou art: Rule in all our hearts alone;
Dear desire of every nation,   By your all sufficient merit
Joy of every longing heart.   Raise us to your glorious throne.

Charles Wesley

The Refrain for the Vespers Lessons

I will fulfill my vows to the Lord* in the presence of all his people.

Psalm 116:16

The Vespers Psalm   *Restore Us, O God of Hosts*

Hear, O Shepherd of Israel, leading Joseph like a flock;* shine forth, you that are enthroned upon the cherubim.

In the presence of Ephraim, Benjamin, and Manasseh,* stir up your strength and come to help us.

Restore us, O God of hosts;* show the light of your countenance, and we shall be saved.

O LORD God of hosts,* how long will you be angered despite the prayers of your
    people?
You have fed them with the bread of tears;* you have given them bowls of tears to
    drink.
You have made us the derision of our neighbors,* and our enemies laugh us to
    scorn.
Restore us, O God of hosts;* show the light of your countenance, and we shall be
    saved.

Psalm 80:1–7

The Refrain
I will fulfill my vows to the LORD* in the presence of all his people.

The Cry of the Church
Even so, come, Lord Jesus!

The Lord's Prayer

The Prayer Appointed for the Week
Almighty God, give all of us grace to cast away the works of darkness, and put on
    the armor of light, now in the time of this mortal life in which your Son Jesus
    Christ came to visit us in great humility; that in the last day, when he shall
    come again in his glorious majesty to judge both the living and the dead, we
    may rise to the life immortal; through him who lives and reigns with you and
    the Holy Spirit, one God, now and for ever. *Amen.*†

The Concluding Prayer of the Church
Lord God, whose Son our Savior Jesus Christ, triumphed over the powers of death
    and prepared for us our place in the new Jerusalem: Grant that I, who have this
    day given thanks for his resurrection, may praise you in the City of which he is
    the light, and where he lives and reigns for ever and ever. *Amen.*†

The Morning Office   To Be Observed on the Hour or Half Hour
                                                    Between 6 and 9 a.m.

The Call to Prayer
Let my mouth be full of your praise* and your glory all the day long.

Psalm 71:8

The Request for Presence
Your word is a lantern to my feet* and a light upon my path.

Psalm 119:105

The Greeting
O God, you have taught me since I was young,* and to this day I tell of your won-
    derful works.

Psalm 71:17

The Refrain for the Morning Lessons
This is the LORD's doing,* and it is marvelous in our eyes.

Psalm 118:23

A Reading
And he went on to tell his parable, 'A man planted a vineyard and leased it to tenants and went abroad for a long while. When the right time came, he sent a servant to the tenant to get his share of the produce of the vineyard. But the
tenants thrashed him, and sent him away empty-handed. But he went on to
send a second servant; they thrashed him too and treated him shamefully and
sent him away empty-handed. He still went on to send a third; they wounded
this one too, and threw him out. Then the owner of the vineyard thought,
"What am I to do? I will send them my own beloved son. Perhaps they will
respect him." But when the tenants saw him they put their heads together saying, "This is the heir, let us kill him so that the inheritance will be ours." So they
threw him out of the vineyard and killed him.
'Now what will the owner of the vineyard do to them? He will come and make an
end of these tenants and give the vineyard to others.' Hearing this they said,
'God forbid!' But he looked hard at them and said, 'Then what does this text in
scripture mean: *The stone which the builders rejected has become the chief cornerstone?* Anyone who falls on that stone will be dashed to pieces; anyone it falls
on will be crushed.'

Luke 20:9–18

The Refrain
This is the LORD's doing,* and it is marvelous in our eyes.

The Morning Psalm   *Early in the Morning I Make My Appeal*
Give ear to my words, O LORD;* consider my meditation.
Hearken to my cry for help, my King and my God,* for I make my prayer to you.
In the morning, LORD, you hear my voice;* early in the morning I make my appeal
and watch for you.
For you are not a God who takes pleasure in wickedness,* and evil cannot dwell
with you.
Braggarts cannot stand in your sight;* you hate all those who work wickedness.
You destroy those who speak lies;* the bloodthirsty and deceitful, O LORD, you
abhor.
But as for me, through the greatness of your mercy I go into your house;* I will
bow down toward your holy temple in awe of you.

Psalm 5:1–7

The Refrain
This is the LORD's doing,* and it is marvelous in our eyes.

The Cry of the Church
Even so, come, Lord Jesus!

The Lord's Prayer

The Prayer Appointed for the Week

Almighty God, give all of us grace to cast away the works of darkness, and put on
the armor of light, now in the time of this mortal life in which your Son Jesus
Christ came to visit us in great humility; that in the last day, when he shall
come again in his glorious majesty to judge both the living and the dead, we
may rise to the life immortal; through him who lives and reigns with you and
the Holy Spirit, one God, now and for ever. *Amen.*†

The Concluding Prayer of the Church

Lord God, almighty and everlasting Father, you have brought me in safety to this
new day: Preserve me with your mighty power, that I may not fall into sin, nor
be overcome by adversity; and in all I do direct me to the fulfilling of your purpose; through Jesus Christ my Lord. *Amen.*†

The Midday Office   To Be Observed on the Hour or Half Hour
                                      Between 11 a.m. and 2 p.m.

The Call to Prayer

Blessed be the LORD, the God of Israel, from everlasting and to everlasting;* and
let all the people say, "Amen!" Hallelujah!

Psalm 106:48

The Request for Presence

Turn to me and have mercy upon me;* give your strength to your servant; and
save the child of your handmaid.

Psalm 86:16

The Greeting

O LORD, your love endures for ever;* do not abandon the works of your hands.

Psalm 138:9

The Refrain for the Midday Lessons

The fear of the LORD is the beginning of wisdom;* those who act accordingly have
a good understanding; his praise endures for ever.

Psalm 111:10

A Reading

Listen now, House of David: are you not satisfied with trying human patience that
you should try God's patience too? The Lord will give you a sign in any case: It
is this: the young woman is with child and will give birth to a son whom she
will call Immanuel. On curds and honey will he feed until he knows how to
refuse the bad and choose the good.

Isaiah 7:13–15

The Refrain

The fear of the LORD is the beginning of wisdom;* those who act accordingly have
a good understanding; his praise endures for ever.

The Midday Psalm   *The LORD Has Pleasure in Those Who Fear Him*

Hallelujah! How good it is to sing praises to our God!* how pleasant it is to honor
   him with praise!

The LORD rebuilds Jerusalem;* he gathers the exiles of Israel.

He heals the brokenhearted* and binds up their wounds.

He counts the number of the stars* and calls them all by their names.

Great is our LORD and mighty in power;* there is no limit to his wisdom.

The LORD lifts up the lowly,* but casts the wicked to the ground.

Sing to the LORD with thanksgiving;* make music to our God upon the harp.

He is not impressed by the might of a horse;* he has no pleasure in the strength of
   a man;

But the LORD has pleasure in those who fear him,* in those who await his gracious
   favor.

Psalm 147:1–7, 11–12

The Refrain

The fear of the LORD is the beginning of wisdom;* those who act accordingly have
   a good understanding; his praise endures for ever.

The Small Verse

The Lord is my shepherd and nothing is wanting to me. In green pastures He hath
   settled me.

THE SHORT BREVIARY

The Lord's Prayer

The Prayer Appointed for the Week

Almighty God, give all of us grace to cast away the works of darkness, and put on
   the armor of light, now in the time of this mortal life in which your Son Jesus
   Christ came to visit us in great humility; that in the last day, when he shall
   come again in his glorious majesty to judge both the living and the dead, we
   may rise to the life immortal; through him who lives and reigns with you and
   the Holy Spirit, one God, now and for ever. *Amen.*†

The Concluding Prayer of the Church

Heavenly Father, you have promised to hear what we ask in the Name of your
   Son: Accept and fulfill my petitions, I pray, not as I ask in my ignorance, nor as
   I deserve in my sinfulness, but as you know and love me in your Son Jesus
   Christ our Lord. *Amen.*†

The Vespers Office   To Be Observed on the Hour or Half Hour
                                        Between 5 and 8 p.m.

The Call to Prayer

Sing to the LORD a new song;* sing to the LORD, all the whole earth.

For great is the LORD and greatly to be praised;* he is more to be feared than all
   gods.

Psalm 96:1, 4

The Request for Presence
Give ear, O LORD, to my prayer,* and attend to the voice of my supplications.
Psalm 86:6

The Greeting
Your way, O God, is holy;* who is so great a god as our God?
Psalm 77:13

The Hymn   *Rejoice, Rejoice, Believers!*
    Rejoice! Rejoice, believers, and let your lights appear!
    The evening is advancing, and darker night is near.
    The Bridegroom is arising, and soon he will draw nigh;
    Up, watch in expectation! At midnight comes the cry.

    See that your lamps are burning, replenish them with oil;
    Look now for your salvation, the end of sin and toil.
    The marriage feast is waiting, the gates wide open stand;
    Rise up, you heirs of glory, the Bridegroom is at hand!

    Our hope and expectation, O Jesus, now appear;
    Arise, you Sun so longed for, above this darkened sphere!
    With hearts and hands uplifted, we plead, O Lord, to see
    The day of earth's redemption, and ever be with thee!
Laurentis Laurenti

The Refrain for the Vespers Lessons
He will judge the world with righteousness* and the peoples with his truth.
Psalm 96:13

The Vespers Psalm   *Light Shines in Darkness for the Upright*
Light shines in the darkness for the upright;* the righteous are merciful and full of
    compassion.
It is good for them to be generous in lending* and to manage their affairs with
    justice.
For they will never be shaken;* the righteous will be kept in everlasting
    remembrance.
They will not be afraid of any evil rumors;* their heart is right; they put their trust
    in the Lord.
Their heart is established and will not shrink,* until they see their desire upon
    their enemies.
They have given freely to the poor,* and their righteousness stands fast for ever;
    they will hold up their head with honor.
The wicked will see it and be angry; they will gnash their teeth and pine away;*
    the desires of the wicked will perish.
Psalm 112:4–10

The Refrain
He will judge the world with righteousness* and the peoples with his truth.

The Small Verse
Come forth, O Christ, and help me. For your name's sake deliver me.

The Lord's Prayer

The Prayer Appointed for the Week
Almighty God, give all of us grace to cast away the works of darkness, and put on
the armor of light, now in the time of this mortal life in which your Son Jesus
Christ came to visit us in great humility; that in the last day, when he shall
come again in his glorious majesty to judge both the living and the dead, we
may rise to the life immortal; through him who lives and reigns with you and
the Holy Spirit, one God, now and for ever. *Amen.*†

The Concluding Prayer of the Church
O God of unchangeable power and eternal light: Look favorably on your whole
Church, that wonderful and sacred mystery; by the effectual working of your
providence, carry out in tranquility the plan of salvation; let the whole world
see and know that things which are cast down are being raised up, and things
which had grown old are being made new, and that all things are being
brought to their perfection by him though whom all things were made, your
Son Jesus Christ our Lord; who lives and reigns with you, in the unity of the
Holy Spirit, one God, for ever and ever. *Amen.*†

The Morning Office   To Be Observed on the Hour or Half Hour
Between 6 and 9 a.m.

The Call to Prayer
Come, let us sing to the LORD;* let us shout for joy to the Rock of our salvation.
Let us come before his presence with thanksgiving* and raise a loud shout to him
with psalms.

Psalm 95:1–2

The Request for Presence
Show us the light of your countenance, O God,* and come to us.
based on Psalm 67:1

The Greeting
To you I lift up my eyes,* to you enthroned in the heavens.
As the eyes of servants look to the hand of their masters,* and the eyes of a maid to
the hand of her mistress,
So our eyes look to the LORD our God,* until he shows us his mercy.

Psalm 123:1–3

The Refrain for the Morning Lessons
I will bear witness that the LORD is righteous;* I will praise the Name of the LORD
Most High.

Psalm 7:18

A Reading

Jesus said: "For this is how God loved the world: he gave his only Son, so that
everyone who believes in him may not perish but may have eternal life. For
God sent his Son into the world not to judge the world, but so that through him
the world might be saved. No one who believes in him will be judged; but
whoever does not believe is judged already, because that person does not
believe in the Name of God's only Son."

John 3:16–18

The Refrain

I will bear witness that the LORD is righteous;* I will praise the Name of the LORD
Most High.

The Morning Psalm   *The LORD Is a Shield About Me*

LORD, how many adversaries I have!* how many there are who rise up against me!

How many there are who say of me,* "There is no help for him in his God."

But you, O LORD, are a shield about me;* you are my glory, the one who lifts up my
head.

I call aloud upon the LORD,* and he answers me from his holy hill;

I lie down and go to sleep;* I wake again, because the LORD sustains me.

Psalm 3:1–5

The Refrain

I will bear witness that the LORD is righteous;* I will praise the Name of the LORD
Most High.

The Small Verse

Keep me, Lord, as the apple of your eye and carry me under the shadow of your
wings.

Traditional

The Lord's Prayer

The Prayer Appointed for the Week

Almighty God, give all of us grace to cast away the works of darkness, and put on
the armor of light, now in the time of this mortal life in which your Son Jesus
Christ came to visit us in great humility; that in the last day, when he shall
come again in his glorious majesty to judge both the living and the dead, we
may rise to the life immortal; through him who lives and reigns with you and
the Holy Spirit, one God, now and for ever. *Amen.*†

The Concluding Prayer of the Church

Lord God, almighty and everlasting Father, you have brought me in safety to this
new day: Preserve me with your mighty power, that I may not fall into sin, nor
be overcome by adversity; and in all I do direct me to the fulfilling of your purpose; through Jesus Christ my Lord. *Amen.*†

The Midday Office   To Be Observed on the Hour or Half Hour
                                     Between 11 a.m. and 2 p.m.

The Call to Prayer
Open my lips, O Lord,* and my mouth shall proclaim your praise.
                                                    Psalm 51:16

The Request for Presence
You are my helper and my deliverer;* do not tarry, O my God.
                                                    Psalm 40:19

The Greeting
Hosanna, LORD, hosanna!* LORD, send us now success.
Blessed is he who comes in the name of the Lord;* we bless you from the house of
    the LORD.
                                                    Psalm 118:25–26

The Refrain for the Midday Lessons
Whom have I in heaven but you?* and having you I desire nothing upon earth.
                                                    Psalm 73:25

A Reading
The days are coming—declares YAHWEH—when the plowman will tread on the
    heels of the reaper and the treader of grapes on the heels of the sower of seed,
    and the mountains will run with new wine and the hills all flow with it. I shall
    restore the fortunes of my people Israel; they will rebuild the ruined cities and
    live in them, they will plant vineyards and drink their wine, they will lay out
    gardens and eat their produce. And I shall plant them in their own soil and
    they will never be uprooted again from the country which I have given them,
    declares YAHWEH, your God.
                                                    Amos 9:13–15

The Refrain
Whom have I in heaven but you?* and having you I desire nothing upon earth.

The Midday Psalm   *Give Praise You Servants of the LORD*
Hallelujah! Give praise, you servants of the LORD;* praise the Name of the LORD.
Let the Name of the LORD be blessed,* from this time forth for evermore.
From the rising of the sun to its going down* let the Name of the LORD be praised.
The LORD is high above all nations,* and his glory above the heavens.
                                                    Psalm 113:1–4

The Refrain
Whom have I in heaven but you?* and having you I desire nothing upon earth.

The Small Verse
My help is in the Name of the Lord who made the heavens and the earth. What
    then shall I fear, of what shall I be afraid?
                                                    Traditional

The Lord's Prayer

The Prayer Appointed for the Week

Almighty God, give all of us grace to cast away the works of darkness, and put on
the armor of light, now in the time of this mortal life in which your Son Jesus
Christ came to visit us in great humility; that in the last day, when he shall
come again in his glorious majesty to judge both the living and the dead, we
may rise to the life immortal; through him who lives and reigns with you and
the Holy Spirit, one God, now and for ever. *Amen.*†

The Concluding Prayer of the Church

Direct me, O Lord, in all my doings with your most gracious favor, and further me
with your continual help; that in all my work begun, continued, and ended in
you, I may glorify your holy name, and finally, by your mercy, obtain everlasting life; through Jesus Christ my Lord. *Amen.*

The Vespers Office   To Be Observed on the Hour or Half Hour
                                             Between 5 and 8 p.m.

The Call to Prayer

Open my lips, O Lord,* and my mouth shall proclaim your praise.
Had you desired it, I would have offered sacrifice,* but you take no delight in
burnt-offerings.
The sacrifice of God is a troubled spirit;* a broken and contrite heart, O God, you
will not despise.

Psalm 51:16–18

The Request for Presence

Out of the depths have I called to you, O LORD; LORD, hear my voice;* let your ears
consider well the voice of my supplication.

Psalm 130:1

The Greeting

You have put gladness in my heart,* more than when grain and wine and oil
increase.
I lie down in peace; at once I fall asleep;* for only you, LORD, make me dwell in
safety.

Psalm 4:7–8

The Hymn

O God, creation's secret force,   Grant this, O Father ever one
Yourself unmoved, yet motion's source,   With Jesus Christ Your only Son
Who from the morn till evening's ray   And Holy Ghost, whom all adore,
Through every change does guide the day: Reigning and blessed forevermore.
                                       adapted from THE SHORT BREVIARY

Grant us, when this short life is past,
The glorious evening that will last;
That, by a holy death attained
Eternal glory may be gained.

The Refrain for the Vespers Lessons

The LORD has sworn an oath to David;* in truth, he will not break it:
"A son, the fruit of your body* will I set upon your throne."

Psalm 132:11–12

The Vespers Psalm   *My Heart, Therefore, Is Glad*

O LORD, you are my portion and my cup;* it is you who uphold my lot.
My boundaries enclose a pleasant land;* indeed, I have a goodly heritage.
I will bless the LORD who gives me counsel;* my heart teaches me, night after night.
I have set the LORD always before me;* because he is at my right hand I shall not fall.
My heart, therefore, is glad, and my spirit rejoices;* my body also shall rest in
    hope.
For you will not abandon me to the grave,* nor let your holy one see the Pit.
You will show me the path of life;* in your presence there is fullness of joy, and in
    your right hand are pleasures for evermore.

Psalm 16:5–11

The Refrain

The LORD has sworn an oath to David;* in truth, he will not break it:
"A son, the fruit of your body* will I set upon your throne."

The Cry of the Church

Even so, come, Lord Jesus!

The Lord's Prayer

The Prayer Appointed for the Week

Almighty God, give all of us grace to cast away the works of darkness, and put on
    the armor of light, now in the time of this mortal life in which your Son Jesus
    Christ came to visit us in great humility; that in the last day, when he shall
    come again in his glorious majesty to judge both the living and the dead, we
    may rise to the life immortal; through him who lives and reigns with you and
    the Holy Spirit, one God, now and for ever. *Amen.*†

The Concluding Prayer of the Church

Stir up Your power, we beseech You, O Lord, and come, that by Your protection
    we may deserve to be rescued from the threatening dangers of our sins and
    saved by Your deliverance. Who lives and reigns with God the Father in the
    unity of the Holy Ghost, God, world without end. *Amen.*

adapted from THE SHORT BREVIARY

The Morning Office   To Be Observed on the Hour or Half Hour
                                      Between 6 and 9 a.m.

The Call to Prayer

Let us make a vow to the LORD our God and keep it;* let all around him bring gifts
    to him who is worthy to be feared.

Psalm 76:11

The Request for Presence

Let my cry come before you, O LORD;* give me understanding, according to your word.

Let my supplication come before you;* deliver me, according to your promise.

Psalm 119:169–170

The Greeting

I will offer you a freewill sacrifice* and praise your Name, O LORD, for it is good.

Psalm 54:6

The Refrain for the Morning Lessons

With my whole heart I seek you;* let me not stray from your commandments.

Psalm 119:10

A Reading

Jesus taught us, saying: "In truth I tell you, all human sins will be forgiven, and all the blasphemies ever uttered; but anyone who blasphemes against the Holy Spirit will never be forgiven, but is guilty of an eternal sin."

Mark 3:28–29

The Refrain

With my whole heart I seek you;* let me not stray from your commandments.

The Morning Psalm   *Only You, LORD, Make Me Dwell in Safety*

Answer me when I call, O God, defender of my cause;* you set me free when I am hard-pressed; have mercy on me and hear my prayer.

"You mortals, how long will you dishonor my glory;* how long will you worship dumb idols and run after false gods?"

Know that the LORD does wonders for the faithful;* when I call upon the LORD, he will hear me.

Tremble, then, and do not sin;* speak to your heart in silence upon your bed.

Offer the appointed sacrifices* and put your trust in the LORD.

Many are saying, "Oh, that we might see better times!"* Lift up the light of your countenance upon us, O LORD.

You have put gladness in my heart,* more than when grain and wine and oil increase.

I lie down in peace; at once I fall asleep;* for only you, LORD, make me dwell in safety.

Psalm 4

The Refrain

With my whole heart I seek you;* let me not stray from your commandments.

The Cry of the Church

O God, come to my assistance! O Lord, make haste to help me!

The Lord's Prayer

The Prayer Appointed for the Week

Almighty God, give all of us grace to cast away the works of darkness, and put on the armor of light, now in the time of this mortal life in which your Son Jesus

Christ came to visit us in great humility; that in the last day, when he shall come again in his glorious majesty to judge both the living and the dead, we may rise to the life immortal; through him who lives and reigns with you and the Holy Spirit, one God, now and for ever. *Amen.*†

The Concluding Prayer of the Church
Lord God, almighty and everlasting Father, you have brought me in safety to this new day: Preserve me with your mighty power, that I may not fall into sin, nor be overcome by adversity; and in all I do direct me to the fulfilling of your purpose; through Jesus Christ my Lord. *Amen.*†

The Midday Office   To Be Observed on the Hour or Half Hour
                                            Between 11 a.m. and 2 p.m.

The Call to Prayer
"Come now, let us reason together," says the Lord.
                                            Isaiah 1:18 (KJV)

The Request for Presence
O LORD, I call to you; come to me quickly;* hear my voice when I cry to you.
                                            Psalm 141:1

The Greeting
In you, O LORD, have I taken refuge;* let me never be ashamed.
                                            Psalm 71:1

The Refrain for the Midday Lessons
Happy are they all who fear the LORD,* and who follow in his ways!
                                            Psalm 128:1

A Reading
"What are your endless sacrifices to me?" says YAHWEH. "I am sick of burnt offerings of rams and the fat of calves. I take no pleasure in the blood of bulls and lambs and goats. When you come and present yourselves before me, who asked you to trample through my courts? Bring no more futile cereal offerings, the smoke from them fills me with disgust. Take your wrong-doing out of my sight. Cease doing evil. Learn to do good, search for justice, discipline the violent, be just to the orphan, plead for the widow."
                                            Isaiah 1:11–13a, 16b–17

The Refrain
Happy are they all who fear the LORD,* and who follow in his ways!

The Midday Psalm   *Happy Are They Who Delight in the LORD*
Happy are they who have not walked in the counsel of the wicked,* nor lingered in the way of sinners, nor sat in the seats of the scornful!
Their delight is in the law of the LORD,* and they meditate on his law day and night.

They are like trees planted by streams of water, bearing fruit in due season, with leaves that do not wither;* everything they do shall prosper.

It is not so with the wicked;* they are like chaff which the wind blows away.

Therefore the wicked shall not stand upright when judgment comes,* nor the sinner in the council of the righteous.

For the LORD knows the way of the righteous,* but the way of the wicked is doomed.

Psalm 1

The Refrain

Happy are they all who fear the LORD,* and who follow in his ways!

The Cry of the Church

Be, Lord, my helper and forsake me not. Do not despise me, O God, my savior.

THE SHORT BREVIARY

The Lord's Prayer

The Prayer Appointed for the Week

Almighty God, give all of us grace to cast away the works of darkness, and put on the armor of light, now in the time of this mortal life in which your Son Jesus Christ came to visit us in great humility; that in the last day, when he shall come again in his glorious majesty to judge both the living and the dead, we may rise to the life immortal; through him who lives and reigns with you and the Holy Spirit, one God, now and for ever. *Amen.*†

The Concluding Prayer of the Church

Direct me, O Lord, in all my doings with your most gracious favor, and further me with your continual help; that in all my work begun, continued, and ended in you, I may glorify your holy name, and finally, by your mercy, obtain everlasting life; through Jesus Christ our Lord. *Amen.*†

The Vespers Office
To Be Observed on the Hour or Half Hour
Between 5 and 8 p.m.

The Call to Prayer

Come, let us sing to the LORD;* let us shout for joy to the Rock of our salvation.

Let us come before his presence with thanksgiving* and raise a loud shout to him with psalms.

For the LORD is a great God,* and a great King above all gods.

In his hand are the caverns of the earth,* and the heights of the hills are his also.

The sea is his, for he made it,* and his hands have molded the dry land.

Psalm 95:1–5

The Request for Presence

May God be merciful to us and bless us,* show us the light of his countenance and come to us.

Psalm 67:1

The Greeting
Exalt yourself above the heavens, O God,* and your glory over all the earth.

Psalm 57:6

The Hymn
    Comfort, comfort you my people, speak you peace, so says our God;
    Comfort those who sit in darkness mourning beneath their sorrow's load.
    Speak you to Jerusalem of the peace that waits for them;
    Tell her that her sins I cover, and her warfare now is over.

    Hark, the voice of one that cries out in the desert far and near,
    Calling us to new repentance since the kingdom now is here.
    Oh, the warning cry obey! Now prepare for God a way;
    Let the valleys rise to meet him and the hills bow down to greet him.

    Make you straight what long was crooked, make the rougher places plain;
    Let your hearts be true and humble, as befits his holy reign.
    For the glory of the Lord now over earth is shed abroad;
    And the flesh will see the token that his word is never broken.

Johann Olearius

The Refrain for the Vespers Lessons
Those who trust in the Lord are like Mount Zion,* which cannot be moved, but
    stands fast for ever.

Psalm 125:1

The Vespers Psalm   *The Words of the LORD Are Pure Words*
"Because the needy are oppressed, and the poor cry out in misery,* I will rise up,"
    says the LORD, "and give them the help they long for."
The words of the LORD are pure words,* like silver refined from ore and purified
    seven times in the fire.
O LORD, watch over us* and save us from this generation for ever.
The wicked prowl on every side,* and that which is worthless is highly prized by
    everyone.

Psalm 12:5–8

The Refrain
Those who trust in the Lord are like Mount Zion,* which cannot be moved, but
    stands fast for ever.

The Cry of the Church
Even so, come, Lord Jesus!

The Lord's Prayer

The Prayer Appointed for the Week
Almighty God, give all of us grace to cast away the works of darkness, and put on
    the armor of light, now in the time of this mortal life in which your Son Jesus

Christ came to visit us in great humility; that in the last day, when he shall
come again in his glorious majesty to judge both the living and the dead, we
may rise to the life immortal; through him who lives and reigns with you and
the Holy Spirit, one God, now and for ever. *Amen.*†

The Concluding Prayer of the Church
Protect us, Lord, as we stay awake; watch over us as we sleep, that awake we may
watch with Christ, and asleep, rest in peace. *Amen.*

The Morning Office   To Be Observed on the Hour or Half Hour
Between 6 and 9 a.m.

The Call to Prayer
Know this: The LORD himself is God;* he himself has made us, and we are his; we
are his people and the sheep of his pasture.

Psalm 100:2

The Request for Presence
For God alone my soul in silence waits;* truly, my hope is in him.

Psalm 62:6

The Greeting
Your testimonies are very sure,* and holiness adorns your house, O LORD, for ever
and for evermore.

Psalm 93:6

The Refrain for the Morning Lessons
Blessed is he who comes in the name of the Lord;* we bless you from the house of
the LORD.

Psalm 118:26

A Reading
In the sixth month the angel Gabriel was sent by God to a town in Galilee called
Nazareth, to a virgin betrothed to a man called Joseph, of the House of David;
and the virgin's name was Mary. He went in and said to her, 'Rejoice, you who
enjoy God's favor! The Lord is with you.' She was deeply disturbed by these
words and asked herself what this greeting could mean, but the angel said to
her, 'Mary, do not be afraid; you have won God's favor.'

Luke 1:26–31

The Refrain
Blessed is he who comes in the name of the Lord;* we bless you from the house of
the LORD.

The Morning Psalm   *Your Garments Are Fragrant with Myrrh, Aloes, and Cassia*
My heart is stirring with a noble song; let me recite what I have fashioned for the
king;* my tongue shall be the pen of a skilled writer.

You are the fairest of men;* grace flows from your lips, because God has blessed
you for ever.

Strap your sword upon your thigh, O mighty warrior,* in your pride and in your
majesty.

Ride out and conquer in the cause of truth* and for the sake of justice.

Your right hand will show you marvelous things;* your arrows are very sharp,
O mighty warrior.

The peoples are falling at your feet,* and the king's enemies are losing heart.

Your throne, O God, endures for ever and ever,* a scepter of righteousness is the
scepter of your kingdom; you love righteousness and hate iniquity.

Therefore God, your God, has anointed you* with the oil of gladness above your
fellows.

All your garments are fragrant with myrrh, aloes, and cassia,* and the music of
strings from ivory palaces makes you glad.

Kings' daughters stand among the ladies of the court;* on your right hand is the
queen, adorned with the gold of Ophir.

"Hear, O daughter; consider and listen closely;* forget your people and your
father's house.

The king will have pleasure in your beauty;* he is your master; therefore do him
honor."

Psalm 45:1–12

The Refrain

Blessed is he who comes in the name of the Lord;* we bless you from the house of
the Lord.

The Cry of the Church

O God, come to my assistance! O Lord, make haste to help me!

The Lord's Prayer

The Prayer Appointed for the Week

Almighty God, give all of us grace to cast away the works of darkness, and put on
the armor of light, now in the time of this mortal life in which your Son Jesus
Christ came to visit us in great humility; that in the last day, when he shall
come again in his glorious majesty to judge both the living and the dead, we
may rise to the life immortal; through him who lives and reigns with you and
the Holy Spirit, one God, now and for ever. *Amen.†*

The Concluding Prayer of the Church

Lord God, almighty and everlasting Father, you have brought me in safety to this
new day: Preserve me with your mighty power, that I may not fall into sin, nor
be overcome by adversity; and in all I do direct me to the fulfilling of your purpose; through Jesus Christ my Lord. *Amen.†*

The Midday Office   To Be Observed on the Hour or Half Hour
                                       Between 11 a.m. and 2 p.m.

The Call to Prayer
Praise God from whom all blessings flow; praise him, all creatures here below;
    praise him, you heavenly hosts; praise Father, Son and Holy Ghost.

                                                              Traditional

The Request for Presence
Hear my prayer, O LORD,* and give ear to my cry; . . .
For I am but a sojourner with you,* a wayfarer, as all my forebears were.

                                                        Psalm 39:13–14

The Greeting
With my whole heart I seek you;* let me not stray from your commandments.

                                                         Psalm 119:10

The Refrain for the Midday Lessons
The LORD loves those who hate evil; he preserves the lives of his saints* and deliv-
    ers them from the hand of the wicked.

                                                          Psalm 97:10

A Reading
First of all, do not forget that in the final days there will come sarcastic scoffers
    whose life is ruled by their passions. 'What has happened to the promise of his
    coming?' they will say, 'Since our Fathers died everything has gone on just as it
    has since the beginning of creation!' They deliberately ignore the fact that long
    ago there were the heavens and the earth, formed out of water and through
    water by the Word of God, and that it was through these same factors that the
    world of those days was destroyed by floodwaters. . . . But there is one thing,
    my dear friends, that you must never forget: . . . The Day of the Lord will come
    like a thief, and then with a roar the sky will vanish, the elements will catch fire
    and melt away, the earth and all that it contains will be burned up.

                                                         2 Peter 3:3ff

The Refrain
The LORD loves those who hate evil; he preserves the lives of his saints* and deliv-
    ers them from the hand of the wicked.

The Midday Psalm   *The Fool Has Said in His Heart, "There Is No God."*
The fool has said in his heart, "There is no God."* All are corrupt and commit
    abominable acts; there is none who does any good.
The LORD looks down from heaven upon us all,* to see if there is any who is wise,
    if there is one who seeks after God.
Every one has proved faithless; all alike have turned bad;* there is none who does
    good; no, not one.
Have they no knowledge, all those evildoers* who eat up my people like bread
    and do not call upon the LORD?

See how they tremble with fear,* because God is in the company of the righteous.
Their aim is to confound the plans of the afflicted,* but the Lord is their refuge.
Oh, that Israel's deliverance would come out of Zion!* when the Lord restores the
   fortunes of his people, Jacob will rejoice and Israel be glad.

Psalm 14

The Refrain
The Lord loves those who hate evil; he preserves the lives of his saints* and delivers them from the hand of the wicked.

The Cry of the Church
O God, come to my assistance! O Lord, make haste to help me!

The Lord's Prayer

The Prayer Appointed for the Week
Almighty God, give all of us grace to cast away the works of darkness, and put on
   the armor of light, now in the time of this mortal life in which your Son Jesus
   Christ came to visit us in great humility; that in the last day, when he shall
   come again in his glorious majesty to judge both the living and the dead, we
   may rise to the life immortal; through him who lives and reigns with you and
   the Holy Spirit, one God, now and for ever. *Amen.*†

The Concluding Prayer of the Church
Almighty and everlasting God, by whose Spirit the whole body of your faithful is
   governed and sanctified: Receive my supplications and prayers which I offer
   before you for all members of your holy Church, that in our vocation and ministry we all may truly serve you through our Lord and Savior Jesus Christ.
   Amen.†

The Vespers Office   To Be Observed on the Hour or Half Hour
                                           Between 5 and 8 p.m.

The Call to Prayer
Come now and see the works of God,* how wonderful he is in his doing toward
   all people.
In his might he rules for ever; his eyes keep watch over the nations;* let no rebel
   rise up against him.

Psalm 66:4, 6

The Request for Presence
Show us your mercy, O Lord,* and grant us your salvation.

Psalm 85:7

The Greeting
Praise God from whom all blessings flow; praise Him all creatures here below;
   praise Him above, you heavenly hosts; praise Father, Son, and Holy Ghost.

Traditional Doxology

The Hymn

Let all mortal flesh keep silence, and with fear and trembling stand;
Ponder nothing earthly minded, for with blessing in his hand
Christ our God to earth descended, our full homage to demand.

Rank on rank the host of heaven spreads its vanguard on the way,
As the light of light descending from the realm of endless day,
That the powers of hell may vanish as the darkness clears away.

At his feet the six-winged seraph; cherubim with sleepless eye,
Veil their faces to the Presence, as with ceaseless voice they cry,
"Alleluia, Alleluia! Alleluia, Lord Most High!"

Liturgy of St. James

The Refrain for the Vespers Lessons
Our sins are stronger than we are,* but you will blot them out.

Psalm 65:3

The Vespers Psalm   *Be Seated on Your Lofty Throne, O Most High*
Awake, O my God, decree justice;* let the assembly of the peoples gather round
     you.
Be seated on your lofty throne, O Most High;* O LORD, judge the nations.
Let the malice of the wicked come to an end, but establish the righteous;* for you
     test the mind and heart, O righteous God.
God is my shield and defense;* he is the savior of the true in heart.
God is a righteous judge;* God sits in judgment every day.

Psalm 7:7–8, 10–12

The Refrain
Our sins are stronger than we are,* but you will blot them out.

The Small Verse
The Lord is my shepherd and nothing is wanting to me. In green pastures He hath
     settled me.

THE SHORT BREVIARY

The Lord's Prayer

The Prayer Appointed for the Week
Almighty God, give all of us grace to cast away the works of darkness, and put on
     the armor of light, now in the time of this mortal life in which your Son Jesus
     Christ came to visit us in great humility; that in the last day, when he shall
     come again in his glorious majesty to judge both the living and the dead, we
     may rise to the life immortal; through him who lives and reigns with you and
     the Holy Spirit, one God, now and for ever. *Amen.*†

The Concluding Prayer of the Church

Help each one of us, gracious Father, to live in such magnanimity and restraint
that the Head of the Church may never have cause to say to any one of us, This
is my body, broken by you.

Prayer from China

The Morning Office

To Be Observed on the Hour or Half Hour
Between 6 and 9 a.m.

The Call to Prayer

Come now and see the works of God,* how wonderful he is in his doing toward
all people.

Psalm 66:4

The Request for Presence

Show me your marvelous loving-kindness,* O Savior of those who take refuge at
your right hand from those who rise up against them.
Keep me as the apple of your eye;* hide me under the shadow of your wings.

Psalm 17:7–8

The Greeting

Hosanna, LORD, hosanna! . . . Blessed is he who comes in the name of the LORD;*
we bless you from the house of the LORD.

Psalm 118:25–26

The Refrain for the Morning Lessons

For God, who commanded the light to shine out of darkness, hath shined in our
hearts, to give the light of the knowledge of the glory of God in the face of
Jesus Christ.

2 Corinthians 4:6 (KJV)

A Reading

Jesus taught the people, saying: "The children of this world take wives and hus-
bands, but those who are judged worthy of a place in the other world and in
the resurrection from the dead do not marry because they can no longer die, for
they are the same as the angels, and being children of the resurrection they are
children of God. And Moses himself implies that the dead rise again, in the
passage about the bush where he calls the Lord *the God of Abraham, the God of
Isaac and the God of Jacob*. Now he is God, not of the dead, but of the living; for to
him everyone is alive."

Luke 20:35–38

The Refrain

For God, who commanded the light to shine out of darkness, hath shined in our
hearts, to give the light of the knowledge of the glory of God in the face of
Jesus Christ.

The Morning Psalm   *What Is Man That You Should Be Mindful of Him?*

O LORD our Governor,* how exalted is your Name in all the world!

Out of the mouths of infants and children* your majesty is praised above the
     heavens.

When I consider your heavens, the work of your fingers,* the moon and the stars
     you have set in their courses,

What is man that you should be mindful of him?* the son of man that you should
     seek him out?

You have made him but little lower than the angels;* you adorn him with glory
     and honor;

You give him mastery over the works of your hands;* you put all things under his
     feet:

All sheep and oxen,* even the wild beasts of the field,

The birds of the air, the fish of the sea,* and whatsoever walks in the paths of the sea.

O LORD our Governor,* how exalted is your Name in all the world!

Psalm 8:1–2, 4–10

The Refrain

For God, who commanded the light to shine out of darkness, hath shined in our
     hearts, to give the light of the knowledge of the glory of God in the face of
     Jesus Christ.

The Cry of the Church

Even so, come, Lord Jesus!

The Lord's Prayer

The Prayer Appointed for the Week

Almighty God, give all of us grace to cast away the works of darkness, and put on
     the armor of light, now in the time of this mortal life in which your Son Jesus
     Christ came to visit us in great humility; that in the last day, when he shall
     come again in his glorious majesty to judge both the living and the dead, we
     may rise to the life immortal; through him who lives and reigns with you and
     the Holy Spirit, one God, now and for ever. *Amen.*†

The Concluding Prayer of the Church

Lord God, almighty and everlasting Father, you have brought me in safety to this
     new day: Preserve me with your mighty power, that I may not fall into sin, nor
     be overcome by adversity; and in all I do direct me to the fulfilling of your pur-
     pose; through Jesus Christ my Lord. *Amen.*†

The Midday Office   **To Be Observed on the Hour or Half Hour**
                                     Between 11 a.m. and 2 p.m.

The Call to Prayer

Give thanks to the LORD, for he is good;* his mercy endures for ever.

Psalm 118:29

The Request for Presence
You are the LORD; do not withhold your compassion from me;* let your love and
　　your faithfulness keep me safe for ever.

Psalm 40:12

The Greeting
There is forgiveness with you;* therefore you shall be feared.

Psalm 130:3

The Refrain for the Midday Lessons
For you, O LORD, are good and forgiving,* and great is your love toward all who
　　call upon you.

Psalm 86:5

A Reading
And, that day, you will say: 'I praise you, YAHWEH, you have been angry with me
　　but your anger is now appeased and you have comforted me. Look, he is the
　　God of my salvation: I shall have faith and not be afraid, for YAHWEH is my
　　strength and my song, he has been my salvation.' Joyfully you will draw water
　　from the springs of salvation and, that day, you will say, 'Praise YAHWEH,
　　invoke his name. Proclaim his deeds to the people, declare his name sublime.'

Isaiah 12:1–4

The Refrain
For you, O LORD, are good and forgiving,* and great is your love toward all who
　　call upon you.

The Midday Psalm　　　　　　　*We Will Call Upon the Name of the LORD Our God*
May the LORD answer you in the day of trouble,* the Name of the God of Jacob
　　defend you;
Send you help from his holy place* and strengthen you out of Zion;
Remember all your offerings* and accept your burnt sacrifice;
Grant you your heart's desire* and prosper all your plans.
We will shout for joy at your victory and triumph in the Name of our God;* may
　　the LORD grant all your requests.
Now I know that the LORD gives victory to his anointed;* he will answer him out
　　of his holy heaven, with the victorious strength of his right hand.
Some put their trust in chariots and some in horses,* but we will call upon the
　　Name of the LORD our God.
They collapse and fall down,* but we will arise and stand upright.
O LORD, give victory to the king* and answer us when we call.

Psalm 20

The Refrain
For you, O LORD, are good and forgiving,* and great is your love toward all who
　　call upon you.

The Cry of the Church

In the evening, in the morning, and at noonday, I will complain and lament,* and
he will hear my voice.

Psalm 55:18

The Lord's Prayer

The Prayer Appointed for the Week

Almighty God, give all of us grace to cast away the works of darkness, and put on
the armor of light, now in the time of this mortal life in which your Son Jesus
Christ came to visit us in great humility; that in the last day, when he shall
come again in his glorious majesty to judge both the living and the dead, we
may rise to the life immortal; through him who lives and reigns with you and
the Holy Spirit, one God, now and for ever. *Amen.*†

The Concluding Prayer of the Church

Lord Jesus Christ, by your death you took away the sting of death: Grant me to so
follow in faith where you have led the way, that I may at length fall asleep
peacefully in you and wake in your likeness; for your tender mercies' sake.
Amen.†

The Vespers Office   To Be Observed on the Hour or Half Hour
                                       Between 5 and 8 p.m.

The Call to Prayer

Behold now, bless the LORD, all you servants of the LORD,* you that stand by night
in the house of the LORD.
Lift up your hands in the holy place and bless the LORD;* the LORD who made
heaven and earth bless you out of Zion.

Psalm 134

The Request for Presence

Look upon me and answer me, O LORD my God;* give light to my eyes, lest I sleep
in death.

Psalm 13:3

The Greeting

O LORD, I am not proud;* I have no haughty looks.
I do not occupy myself with great matters,* or with things that are too hard for me.
But I still my soul and make it quiet, like a child upon its mother's breast;* my soul
is quieted within me.

Psalm 131:1–3

The Hymn

Lo, how a rose e'er blooming
From tender stem has sprung!
Of Jesse's lineage coming,
As those of old have sung.
It came a floweret bright,
Amid the cold of winter,
When half spent was the night.

Isaiah 'twas foretold it,
The Rose I have in mind;
With Mary we behold it,
The Virgin Mother kind.
To show God's love aright,
She bore to us a Savior,
When half spent was the night.

German, 15th Century

The Refrain for the Vespers Lessons

Those who are planted in the house of the LORD* shall flourish in the courts of our
God.

Psalm 92:12

The Vespers Psalm   *Let Me Announce the Decree of the LORD*

Why are the nations in an uproar?* Why do the peoples mutter empty threats?
Why do the kings of the earth rise up in revolt, and the princes plot together,*
against the LORD and against his Anointed?
"Let us break their yoke," they say;* "let us cast off their bonds from us."
He whose throne is in heaven is laughing;* the Lord has them in derision.
Then he speaks to them in his wrath,* and his rage fills them with terror.
"I myself have set my king* upon my holy hill of Zion."
Let me announce the decree of the LORD:* he said to me, "You are my Son; this day
have I begotten you.
Ask of me, and I will give you the nations for your inheritance* and the ends of the
earth for your possession.
You shall crush them with an iron rod* and shatter them like a piece of pottery."
And now, you kings, be wise;* be warned, you rulers of the earth.
Submit to the LORD with fear,* and with trembling bow before him;
Lest he be angry and you perish;* for his wrath is quickly kindled.
Happy are they all* who take refuge in him!

Psalm 2

The Refrain

Those who are planted in the house of the LORD* shall flourish in the courts of our
God.

The Cry of the Church
Even so, come, Lord Jesus!

The Lord's Prayer

The Prayer Appointed for the Week
Almighty God, give all of us grace to cast away the works of darkness, and put on
the armor of light, now in the time of this mortal life in which your Son Jesus

Christ came to visit us in great humility; that in the last day, when he shall
come again in his glorious majesty to judge both the living and the dead, we
may rise to the life immortal; through him who lives and reigns with you and
the Holy Spirit, one God, now and for ever. *Amen.*†

Concluding Prayers of the Church

Almighty God, who has promised to hear the petitions of those who ask in your
Son's Name: I beseech you mercifully to incline your ear to me who have made
my prayers and supplications to you; and grant that those things which I have
faithfully asked according to your will, I may effectually obtain, to the relief of
my necessity, and to the setting forth of your glory; through Jesus Christ my
Lord. *Amen.*†

May the souls of the faithful departed, through the mercy of God, rest in eternal
peace. *Amen.*

The Morning Office   To Be Observed on the Hour or Half Hour
                               Between 6 and 9 a.m.

The Call to Prayer

Come now and look upon the works of the LORD,* what awesome things he has
done on earth.

Psalm 46:9

The Request for Presence

O LORD . . . answer us when we call.

Psalm 20:9

The Greeting

My eyes are fixed on you, O my Strength;* for you, O God, are my stronghold.

Psalm 59:10

The Refrain for the Morning Lessons

As a father cares for his children,* so does the LORD care for those who fear him.

Psalm 103:13

A Reading

The gospeler wrote, saying: "Now all this took place to fulfill what the Lord had
spoken through the prophet: *Look! The virgin is with child and will give birth to a
son whom they will call Immanuel,* a name which means 'God-is-with-us.' "

Matthew 1:22–23

The Refrain

As a father cares for his children,* so does the LORD care for those who fear him.

The Morning Psalm   *Who May Abide on Your Holy Hill*

LORD, who may dwell in your tabernacle?* who may abide upon your holy hill?
Whoever leads a blameless life and does what is right,* who speaks the truth from
his heart.

There is no guile upon his tongue; he does no evil to his friend;* he does not heap
    contempt upon his neighbor.
In his sight the wicked is rejected,* but he honors those who fear the LORD.
He has sworn to do no wrong* and does not take back his word.
He does not give his money in hope of gain,* nor does he take a bribe against the
    innocent.
Whoever does these things* shall never be overthrown.

Psalm 15

The Refrain
As a father cares for his children,* so does the LORD care for those who fear him.

The Cry of the Church
Lord, have mercy on us. Christ, have mercy on us. Lord, have mercy on us.

The Lord's Prayer

The Prayer Appointed for the Week
Almighty God, give all of us grace to cast away the works of darkness, and put on
    the armor of light, now in the time of this mortal life in which your Son Jesus
    Christ came to visit us in great humility; that in the last day, when he shall
    come again in his glorious majesty to judge both the living and the dead, we
    may rise to the life immortal; through him who lives and reigns with you and
    the Holy Spirit, one God, now and for ever. *Amen.*†

The Concluding Prayer of the Church
Lord God, almighty and everlasting Father, you have brought me in safety to this
    new day: Preserve me with your mighty power, that I may not fall into sin, nor
    be overcome by adversity; and in all I do direct me to the fulfilling of your pur-
    pose; through Jesus Christ my Lord. *Amen.*†

The Midday Office　　　　　　　**To Be Observed on the Hour or Half Hour**
　　　　　　　　　　　　　　　　　　　　　Between 11 a.m. and 2 p.m.

The Call to Prayer
Be strong and let your heart take courage,* all you who wait for the LORD.

Psalm 31:24

The Request for Presence
Give ear to my words, O LORD;* consider my meditation.
Hearken to my cry for help, my King and my God,* for I make my prayer to you.

Psalm 5:1–2

The Greeting
You are God; we praise you;
You are the Lord: we acclaim you;
You are the eternal Father:
All creation worships you.

To you all angels, all powers of heaven,
Cherubim and Seraphim, sing in endless praise:
> Holy, holy, holy Lord, God of power and might,
> heaven and earth are full of your glory.

Te Deum

The Refrain for the Midday Lessons

Great peace have they who love your law;* for them there is no stumbling block.

Psalm 119:165

A Reading

Yes, I know what plans I have in mind for you, YAHWEH declares, plans for peace, not for disaster, to give you a future and a hope. When you call to me and come and pray to me, I shall listen to you. When you search for me, you will find me; when you search wholeheartedly for me, I shall let you find me . . .

Jeremiah 29:11–14a

The Refrain

Great peace have they who love your law;* for them there is no stumbling block.

The Midday Psalm   *We Will Sing Out Our Joy For Ever*

But all who take refuge in you will be glad;* they will sing out their joy for ever.
You will shelter them,* so that those who love your Name may exult in you.
For you, O LORD, will bless the righteous;* you will defend them with your favor
as with a shield.

Psalm 5:13–15

TÏhe Refrain

Great peace have they who love your law;* for them there is no stumbling block.

The Cry of the Church

O Lord, hear my prayer and let my cry come unto you. Thanks be to God.

THE SHORT BREVIARY

The Lord's Prayer

The Prayer Appointed for the Week

Almighty God, give all of us grace to cast away the works of darkness, and put on the armor of light, now in the time of this mortal life in which your Son Jesus Christ came to visit us in great humility; that in the last day, when he shall come again in his glorious majesty to judge both the living and the dead, we may rise to the life immortal; through him who lives and reigns with you and the Holy Spirit, one God, now and for ever. *Amen.*†

The Concluding Prayer of the Church

O God, the source of eternal light: Shed forth your unending day upon all of us who watch for you, that our lips may praise you, our lives may bless you, and our worship may give you glory; through Jesus Christ our Lord. *Amen.*†

The Vespers Office

To Be Observed on the Hour or Half Hour Between 5 and 8 p.m.

The Call to Prayer
Bless our God, you peoples;* make the voice of his praise to be heard;
Who holds our souls in life,* and will not allow our feet to slip.

Psalm 66:7–8

The Request for Presence
O God of hosts;* show us the light of your countenance, and we shall be saved.

Psalm 80:7

The Greeting
As the eyes of servants look to the hand of their masters,* and the eyes of a maid to
the hand of her mistress,
So my eyes look to you, O LORD my God.

based on Psalm 123:2–3

The Hymn

I sing the mighty power of God,
That made the mountains rise;
That spread the flowing seas abroad,
And built the lofty skies.
I sing the wisdom that ordained
The sun to rule the day;
The moon shines full at his command,
And all the stars obey.

I sing the goodness of the Lord,
That filled the earth with food;
He formed the creatures with his word,
And then pronounced them good.
Lord, how your wonders are displayed,
Wherever I turn my eye:
If I survey the ground I tread,
Or gaze upon the sky!

There's not a plant or flower below,
But makes your glories known;
And clouds arise, and tempests blow,
By order of your throne;
While all that borrows life from you
Is ever in your care,
And everywhere that man can be,
You, God, are present there.

Isaac Watts

The Refrain for the Vespers Lessons
And now, what is my hope?* O Lord, my hope is in you.

Psalm 39:8

The Vespers Psalm   *Proclaim to the Peoples the Things He Has Done*
I will give thanks to you, O LORD, with my whole heart;* I will tell of all your
marvelous works.
I will be glad and rejoice in you;* I will sing to your Name, O Most High.
But the LORD is enthroned for ever;* he has set up his throne for judgment.
It is he who rules the world with righteousness;* he judges the peoples with
equity.

The LORD will be a refuge for the oppressed,* a refuge in time of trouble.

Those who know your Name will put their trust in you,* for you never forsake those who seek you, O LORD.

Sing praise to the LORD who dwells in Zion;* proclaim to the peoples the things he has done.

Psalm 9:1–2, 7–11

The Refrain
And now, what is my hope?* O Lord, my hope is in you.

The Cry of the Church
Even so, come, Lord Jesus!

The Lord's Prayer

The Prayer Appointed for the Week
Almighty God, give all of us grace to cast away the works of darkness, and put on the armor of light, now in the time of this mortal life in which your Son Jesus Christ came to visit us in great humility; that in the last day, when he shall come again in his glorious majesty to judge both the living and the dead, we may rise to the life immortal; through him who lives and reigns with you and the Holy Spirit, one God, now and for ever. *Amen.*†

The Concluding Prayer of the Church
Almighty God, who after the creation of the world rested from all your works and sanctified a day of rest for all your creatures: Grant that I, putting away all earthly anxieties, may be duly prepared for the service of public worship, and grant as well that my Sabbath upon earth may be a preparation for the eternal rest promised to your people in heaven; through Jesus Christ our Lord. *Amen.*†

The Morning Office   To Be Observed on the Hour or Half Hour
Between 6 and 9 a.m.

The Call to Prayer
I will sing of mercy and justice;* to you, O LORD, will I sing praises.

Psalm 101:1

The Request for Presence
But as for me, O LORD, I cry to you for help;* in the morning my prayer comes before you.

Psalm 88:14

The Greeting

Your testimonies are very sure,* and holiness adorns your house, O LORD, for ever
and for evermore.

Psalm 93:6

The Refrain for the Morning Lessons

This is the LORD's doing,* and it is marvelous in our eyes.

Psalm 118:23

A Reading   *During Advent, the Church remembers with thanksgiving the life
and ministry of John the Baptizer, cousin of Our Lord and the
promised messenger of His first coming.*

Jesus began to talk to the people about John: "What did you go into the desert to
see? A reed swaying in the breeze? No! Then what did you go out to see? A
man dressed in fine clothes? Look, those who go in magnificent clothes and
live luxuriously are to be found at royal courts! Then what did you go to see? A
prophet? Yes, I tell you, and much more than a prophet: he is the one of whom
scripture says: *Look I am going to send my messenger in front of you to prepare your
way before you.* I tell you, of all the children born to women, there is no one
greater than John; yet the least in the kingdom of God is greater than he."

Luke 7:25–28

The Refrain

This is the LORD's doing,* and it is marvelous in our eyes.

The Morning Psalm   *Sing to the LORD a New Song*

Hallelujah! Sing to the LORD a new song;* sing his praise in the congregation of the
faithful.

Let Israel rejoice in his Maker;* let the children of Zion be joyful in their King.

Let them praise his Name in the dance;* let them sing praise to him with timbrel
and harp.

For the LORD takes pleasure in his people* and adorns the poor with victory.

Let the faithful rejoice in triumph;* let them be joyful on their beds.

Let the praises of God be in their throat* and a two-edged sword in their hand;

To wreak vengeance on the nations* and punishment on the peoples;

To bind their kings in chains* and their nobles with links of iron;

To inflict on them the judgment decreed;* this is glory for all his faithful people.
Hallelujah!

Psalm 149

The Refrain

This is the LORD's doing,* and it is marvelous in our eyes.

The Cry of the Church

Even so, come, Lord Jesus!

The Lord's Prayer

The Prayer Appointed for the Week

Merciful God, who sent your messengers the prophets to preach repentance and prepare the way for our salvation: Grant us grace to heed their warnings and forsake our sins, that we may greet with joy the coming of Jesus Christ our Redeemer; who lives and reigns with you and the Holy Spirit, one God, now and for ever. *Amen.*†

The Concluding Prayer of the Church

Lord God, almighty and everlasting Father, you have brought me in safety to this new day: Preserve me with your mighty power, that I may not fall into sin, nor be overcome by adversity; and in all I do direct me to the fulfilling of your purpose; through Jesus Christ my Lord. *Amen.*†

The Midday Office — To Be Observed on the Hour or Half Hour Between 11 a.m. and 2 p.m.

The Call to Prayer

Hallelujah! Praise the Name of the Lord;* give praise, you servants of the Lord,
You who stand in the house of the Lord,* in the courts of the house of our God.
Praise the Lord, for the Lord is good;* sing praises to his Name, for it is lovely.

Psalm 135:1–3

The Request for Presence

Let them know that you, whose Name is Yahweh,* you alone are the Most High over all the earth.

Psalm 83:18

The Greeting

. . . My heart sings to you without ceasing;* O Lord my God, I will give you thanks for ever.

Psalm 30:13

The Refrain for the Midday Lessons

When I called, you answered me;* you increased my strength within me.

Psalm 138:4

A Reading

A shoot will spring from the stock of Jesse, a new shoot will grow from his roots. On him will rest the spirit of Yahweh, the spirit of wisdom and insight, the spirit of counsel and power, the spirit of knowledge and fear of Yahweh: his inspiration will lie in fearing Yahweh. His judgment will not be by appearances, his verdict not given on hearsay. He will judge the weak with integrity and give fair sentence for the humblest in the land. He will strike the country with the rod of his mouth and with the breath of his lips bring death to the wicked. Uprightness will be a belt around his waist, and constancy the belt about his hips.

Isaiah 11:1–5

The Refrain
When I called, you answered me;* you increased my strength within me.

The Midday Psalm   *My Foot Stands on Level Ground*
Give judgment for me, O Lord, for I have lived with integrity;* I have trusted in
    the Lord and have not faltered.
Test me, O Lord, and try me;* examine my heart and my mind.
For your love is before my eyes;* I have walked faithfully with you.
I have not sat with the worthless,* nor do I consort with the deceitful.
I have hated the company of evildoers;* I will not sit down with the wicked.
I will wash my hands in innocence, O Lord,* that I may go in procession round
    your altar,
Singing aloud a song of thanksgiving* and recounting all your wonderful deeds.
Lord, I love the house in which you dwell* and the place where your glory abides.
Do not sweep me away with sinners,* nor my life with those who thirst for blood,
Whose hands are full of evil plots,* and their right hand full of bribes.
As for me, I will live with integrity;* redeem me, O Lord, and have pity on me.
My foot stands on level ground;* in the full assembly I will bless the Lord.

Psalm 26

The Refrain
When I called, you answered me;* you increased my strength within me.

The Cry of the Church
Even so, come, Lord Jesus!

The Lord's Prayer

The Prayer Appointed for the Week
Merciful God, who sent your messengers the prophets to preach repentance and
    prepare the way for our salvation: Grant us grace to heed their warnings and
    forsake our sins, that we may greet with joy the coming of Jesus Christ our
    Redeemer; who lives and reigns with you and the Holy Spirit, one God, now
    and for ever. *Amen.*†

The Concluding Prayer of the Church
O God, you make me glad with the weekly remembrance of the glorious resurrec-
    tion of your Son my Lord: Give me this day such blessing through my worship
    of you, that the week to come may be spent in your favor; through Jesus Christ
    our Lord. *Amen.*†

The Vespers Office   **To Be Observed on the Hour or Half Hour**
                                                            Between 5 and 8 p.m.

The Call to Prayer
Open my lips, O Lord,* and my mouth shall proclaim your praise.

Psalm 51:16

The Request for Presence

Be my strong rock, a castle to keep me safe,* for you are my crag and my stronghold; for the sake of your Name, lead me and guide me.

Psalm 31:3

The Greeting

O gracious Light, pure brightness of the everlasting Father in heaven, O Jesus
Christ, holy and blessed! Now as we come to the setting of the sun, and our
eyes behold the vesper light, we sing your praises O God: Father, Son and Holy
Spirit. You are worthy at all times to be praised by happy voices, O Son of God,
O giver of life, and to be glorified through all the worlds.

Phos Hilaron

The Hymn   *Lift Up Your Heads, You Mighty Gates*

Lift up your heads, you mighty gates;   Redeemer, come, with us abide;
Behold, the King of glory waits;   Our hearts to you we open wide;
The King of kings is drawing near;   Let us your inner presence feel;
The Savior of the world is here!   Your grace and love in us reveal.

Fling wide the portals of your heart;   Your Holy Spirit lead us on
Make it a temple, set apart   Until our glorious goal is won;
From earthly use for heaven's employ,   Eternal praise, eternal fame
Adorned with prayer and love and joy.   Be offered, Savior, to your name!

George Weissel

The Refrain for the Vespers Lessons

For you have rescued my soul from death and my feet from stumbling,* that I may
walk before God in the light of the living.

Psalm 56:12

The Vespers Psalm   *Tremble at the Presence of the Lord*

Hallelujah! When Israel came out of Egypt,* the house of Jacob from a people of
strange speech,
Judah became God's sanctuary* and Israel his dominion.
The sea beheld it and fled;* Jordan turned and went back.
The mountains skipped like rams,* and the little hills like young sheep.
What ailed you, O sea, that you fled?* O Jordan, that you turned back?
You mountains, that you skipped like rams?* you little hills like young sheep?
Tremble, O earth, at the presence of the Lord,* at the presence of the God of Jacob,
Who turned the hard rock into a pool of water* and flint-stone into a flowing
spring.

Psalm 114

The Refrain

For you have rescued my soul from death and my feet from stumbling,* that I may
walk before God in the light of the living.

The Small Verse

Into your hands I commend my spirit for you have redeemed me, O God of my
life. Glory be to the Father, and to the Son and to the comforting Spirit.

Traditional

The Lord's Prayer

The Prayer Appointed for the Week

Merciful God, who sent your messengers the prophets to preach repentance and
prepare the way for our salvation: Grant us grace to heed their warnings and
forsake our sins, that we may greet with joy the coming of Jesus Christ our
Redeemer; who lives and reigns with you and the Holy Spirit, one God, now
and for ever. *Amen.*†

The Concluding Prayer of the Church

O God, you have brought me near to an innumerable company of angels, and to
the spirits of just men made perfect: Grant me during my earthly pilgrimage to
abide in their fellowship, and in your heavenly country to become partakers of
their joy; through Jesus Christ our Lord, who lives and reigns with you and the
Holy Spirit, one God, now and for ever. *Amen.*†

The Morning Office   To Be Observed on the Hour or Half Hour
                                    Between 6 and 9 a.m.

The Call to Prayer

Open my lips, O LORD,* and my mouth shall proclaim your praise.

Psalm 51:16

The Request for Presence

Open my eyes, that I may see* the wonders of your law.

Psalm 119:18

The Greeting

I will thank you, O LORD my God, with all my heart,* and glorify your Name for
evermore.

Psalm 86:12

The Refrain for the Morning Lessons

For who is God, but the LORD?* who is the Rock, except our God?

Psalm 18:32

A Reading

As he was returning to the city in the early morning, he felt hungry. Seeing a fig tree
by the road, he went up to it and found nothing on it but leaves. And he said to
it 'May you never bear fruit again,' and instantly the fig tree withered. The disciples were amazed when they saw it and said, 'How is it that the fig tree withered instantly?' Jesus answered, 'In truth I tell you, if you have faith and do not
doubt at all, not only will you do what I have done to the fig tree, but even if

you say to this mountain, "Be pulled up and thrown into the sea," it will be done. And if you have faith, everything you ask for in prayer, you will receive.'

Matthew 21:18–22

The Refrain
For who is God, but the Lord?* who is the Rock, except our God?

The Morning Psalm   *He Sends Redemption to His People*
Great are the deeds of the Lord!* they are studied by all who delight in them.
His work is full of majesty and splendor,* and his righteousness endures for ever.
He makes his marvelous works to be remembered;* the Lord is gracious and full of compassion.
He gives food to those who fear him;* he is ever mindful of his covenant.
He has shown his people the power of his works* in giving them the lands of the nations.
The works of his hands are faithfulness and justice;* all his commandments are sure.
They stand fast for ever and ever,* because they are done in truth and equity.
He sent redemption to his people; he commanded his covenant for ever;* holy and awesome is his Name.

Psalm 111:2–9

The Refrain
For who is God, but the Lord?* who is the Rock, except our God?

The Cry of the Church
Even so, come, Lord Jesus!

The Lord's Prayer

The Prayer Appointed for the Week
Merciful God, who sent your messengers the prophets to preach repentance and prepare the way for our salvation: Grant us grace to heed their warnings and forsake our sins, that we may greet with joy the coming of Jesus Christ our Redeemer; who lives and reigns with you and the Holy Spirit, one God, now and for ever. *Amen.*†

The Concluding Prayer of the Church
Lord God, almighty and everlasting Father, you have brought me in safety to this new day: Preserve me with your mighty power, that I may not fall into sin, nor be overcome by adversity; and in all I do direct me to the fulfilling of your purpose; through Jesus Christ my Lord. *Amen.*†

The Midday Office   To Be Observed on the Hour or Half Hour
                                     Between 11 a.m. and 2 p.m.

The Call to Prayer
Be glad, you righteous, and rejoice in the Lord;* shout for joy, all who are true of heart.

Psalm 32:12

The Request for Presence

LORD, hear my prayer, and let my cry come before you;* hide not your face from
me in the day of my trouble.

Psalm 102:1

The Greeting

Into your hands I commend my spirit,* for you have redeemed me, O LORD,
O God of truth.

Psalm 31:5

The Refrain for the Midday Lessons

My help comes from the LORD,* the maker of heaven and earth.

Psalm 121:2

A Reading

Listen and you will live. I shall make an everlasting covenant with you in fulfillment of the favors promised to David. Look, I have made him a witness to the
peoples, a leader and lawgiver to the peoples. Look, you will summon a nation
unknown to you, a nation unknown to you will hurry to you for the sake of
YAHWEH your God, because the Holy One of Israel has glorified you.

Isaiah 55:3b–5

The Refrain

My help comes from the LORD,* the maker of heaven and earth.

The Midday Psalm   *Let Everything That Has Breath Praise the LORD*

Hallelujah! Praise God in his holy temple;* praise him in the firmament of his
power.
Praise him for his mighty acts;* praise him for his excellent greatness.
Praise him with the blast of the ram's-horn;* praise him with lyre and harp.
Praise him with timbrel and dance;* praise him with strings and pipe.
Praise him with resounding cymbals;* praise him with loud-clanging cymbals.
Let everything that has breath* praise the LORD. Hallelujah!

Psalm 150

The Refrain

My help comes from the LORD,* the maker of heaven and earth.

The Cry of the Church

O God, come to my assistance! O Lord, make haste to help me!

The Lord's Prayer

The Prayer Appointed for the Week

Merciful God, who sent your messengers the prophets to preach repentance and
prepare the way for our salvation: Grant us grace to heed their warnings and
forsake our sins, that we may greet with joy the coming of Jesus Christ our
Redeemer; who lives and reigns with you and the Holy Spirit, one God, now
and for ever. *Amen.*†

The Concluding Prayer of the Church

O God, the King eternal, whose light divides the day and the night and turns the shadow of death into the morning: Drive far from me all wrong desires, incline my heart to keep your law, and guide my feet into the way of peace; that, having done your will with cheerfulness during the day, I may, when night comes, rejoice to give you thanks; through Jesus Christ my Lord. *Amen.*†

The Vespers Office   **To Be Observed on the Hour or Half Hour Between 5 and 8 p.m.**

The Call to Prayer

Come now and look upon the works of the LORD,* what awesome things he has done on earth.

Psalm 46:9

The Request for Presence

May God be merciful to us and bless us,* show us the light of his countenance and come to us.

Let your ways be known upon earth,* your saving health among all nations.

Psalm 67:1–2

The Greeting

O LORD of hosts,* happy are they who put their trust in you!

Psalm 84:12

The Hymn

> Once he came in blessing, all our ills redressing;
> Came in likeness lowly, Son of God most holy;
> Bore the cross to save us, hope and freedom gave us.
>
> Still he comes within us, still his voice would win us
> From the sins that hurt us, would to Truth convert us:
> Not in torment hold us, but in love enfold us.
>
> Thus, if you can but name him, not ashamed to claim him,
> But will trust him boldly not to love him coldly,
> He will then receive you, heal you, and forgive you.
>
> One who can endure, a bright reward secures.
> Come, then, O Lord Jesus, from our sins release us;
> Let us here confess you till in heaven we bless you.

Jan Roh

The Refrain for the Vespers Lessons

Bless the LORD, you angels of his, you mighty ones who do his bidding,* and hearken to the voice of his word.

Psalm 103:20

The Vespers Psalm   *Praise the Lord from the Heavens*

Hallelujah! Praise the Lord from the heavens;* praise him in the heights.

Praise him, all you angels of his;* praise him, all his host.

Praise him, sun and moon;* praise him, all you shining stars.

Praise him, heaven of heavens,* and you waters above the heavens.

Let them praise the Name of the Lord;* for he commanded, and they were created.

He made them stand fast for ever and ever;* he gave them a law which shall not pass away.

Psalm 148:1–6

The Refrain

Bless the Lord, you angels of his, you mighty ones who do his bidding,* and hearken to the voice of his word.

The Small Verse

In the sight of the Angels I praise You. I adore at Your holy temple and give praise to Your Name.

adapted from The Short Breviary

The Lord's Prayer

The Prayer Appointed for the Week

Merciful God, who sent your messengers the prophets to preach repentance and prepare the way for our salvation: Grant us grace to heed their warnings and forsake our sins, that we may greet with joy the coming of Jesus Christ our Redeemer; who lives and reigns with you and the Holy Spirit, one God, now and for ever. *Amen.*†

The Concluding Prayer of the Church

O God, who in Your ineffable providence has deigned to send Your holy Angels to watch over us, grant to Your suppliants always to find safety in their protection and in eternity to share their happiness. Through our Lord.

The Short Breviary

The Morning Office   To Be Observed on the Hour or Half Hour
Between 6 and 9 a.m.

The Call to Prayer

Bless God in the congregation;* bless the Lord, you that are of the fountain of Israel.

Psalm 68:26

The Request for Presence

Look upon your covenant;* the dark places of the earth are haunts of violence.

Psalm 74:19

The Greeting
Deliver me, O LORD, by your hand* from those whose portion in life is this world.
Psalm 17:14

The Refrain for the Morning Lessons
. . . when God restores the fortunes of his people Jacob will rejoice and Israel be glad.
Psalm 53:6b

A Reading
Concerning the birth of John the Baptizer, scripture says: "The time came for Elizabeth to have her child, and she gave birth to a son; and when her neighbors and relations heard that the Lord had lavished on her his faithful love, they shared her joy. Now it happened that on the eighth day they came to circumcise the child; they were going to call him Zechariah after his father, but his mother spoke up. 'No,' she said, 'he is to be called John.' They said to her, 'But no one in your family has that name,' and made signs to his father to find out what he wanted him called. The father asked for a writing tablet and wrote, 'His name is John.' And they were all astonished. At that instant his power of speech returned and he spoke and praised God. All their neighbors were filled with awe and the whole affair was talked about throughout the hill country of Judaea. All those who heard of it treasured it in their hearts. 'What will this child turn out to be?' they wondered. And indeed the hand of the Lord was with him. . . . Meanwhile the child grew up and his spirit grew strong. And he lived in the desert until the day he appeared openly to Israel."
Luke 1:57–66, 80

The Refrain
. . . when God restores the fortunes of his people Jacob will rejoice and Israel be glad.

The Morning Psalm   *Joy Comes in the Morning*
I will exalt you, O LORD, because you have lifted me up* and have not let my enemies triumph over me.
O LORD my God, I cried out to you,* and you restored me to health.
You brought me up, O LORD, from the dead;* you restored my life as I was going down to the grave.
Sing to the LORD, you servants of his;* give thanks for the remembrance of his holiness.
For his wrath endures but the twinkling of an eye,* his favor for a lifetime.
Weeping may spend the night,* but joy comes in the morning.
Psalm 30:1–6

The Refrain
. . . when God restores the fortunes of his people Jacob will rejoice and Israel be glad.

The Small Verse

Keep me, Lord, as the apple of your eye and carry me under the shadow of your wings.

Traditional

The Lord's Prayer

The Prayer Appointed for the Week

Merciful God, who sent your messengers the prophets to preach repentance and prepare the way for our salvation: Grant us grace to heed their warnings and forsake our sins, that we may greet with joy the coming of Jesus Christ our Redeemer; who lives and reigns with you and the Holy Spirit, one God, now and for ever. *Amen.*†

The Concluding Prayer of the Church

Lord God, almighty and everlasting Father, you have brought me in safety to this new day: Preserve me with your mighty power, that I may not fall into sin, nor be overcome by adversity; and in all I do direct me to the fulfilling of your purpose; through Jesus Christ my Lord. *Amen.*†

The Midday Office   To Be Observed on the Hour or Half Hour Between 11 a.m. and 2 p.m.

The Call to Prayer

Open my lips, O Lord,* and my mouth shall proclaim your praise.

Psalm 51:16

The Request for Presence

Let my cry come before you, O Lord;* give me understanding, according to your word.

Let my supplication come before you;* deliver me, according to your promise.

Psalm 119:169–170

The Greeting

How priceless is your love, O God!* your people take refuge under the shadow of your wings.

They feast upon the abundance of your house;* you give them drink from the river of your delights.

For with you is the well of life,* and in your light we see light.

Psalm 36:7–9

The Refrain for the Midday Lessons

Mercy and truth have met together;* righteousness and peace have kissed each other.

Psalm 85:10

A Reading

. . . do not judge anything before the due time, until the Lord comes; he will bring to light everything that is hidden in darkness and reveal the designs of all hearts. Then everyone will receive from God the appropriate commendation.

1 Corinthians 4:5

The Refrain

Mercy and truth have met together;* righteousness and peace have kissed each other.

The Midday Psalm   *All the Paths of the Lord Are Love and Faithfulness*

Gracious and upright is the Lord;* therefore he teaches sinners in his way.
He guides the humble in doing right* and teaches his way to the lowly.
All the paths of the Lord are love and faithfulness* to those who keep his covenant and his testimonies.
Who are they who fear the Lord?* he will teach them the way that they should choose.
They shall dwell in prosperity,* and their offspring shall inherit the land.
The Lord is a friend to those who fear him* and will show them his covenant.
My eyes are ever looking to the Lord,* for he shall pluck my feet out of the net.

Psalm 25:7–9, 11–14

The Refrain

Mercy and truth have met together;* righteousness and peace have kissed each other.

The Small Verse

Lord, be merciful to me, a sinner. Christ, be merciful to me, a sinner. Father, be merciful to me, a sinner. Spirit, be merciful to me, a sinner. Lord, be merciful to me, a sinner.

Traditional

The Lord's Prayer

The Prayer Appointed for the Week

Merciful God, who sent your messengers the prophets to preach repentance and prepare the way for our salvation: Grant us grace to heed their warnings and forsake our sins, that we may greet with joy the coming of Jesus Christ our Redeemer; who lives and reigns with you and the Holy Spirit, one God, now and for ever. *Amen.*†

The Concluding Prayer of the Church

Let us bless the Lord God living and true! Let us always render him praise, glory, honor, blessing, and all good things! Amen. Amen. So be it! So be it!

St. Francis of Assisi

The Vespers Office

To Be Observed on the Hour or Half Hour
Between 5 and 8 p.m.

The Call to Prayer
Sing to the LORD with thanksgiving;* make music to our God upon the harp.

Psalm 147:7

The Request for Presence
Let your countenance shine upon your servant* and teach me your statutes.

Psalm 119:135

The Greeting
How glorious you are!* more splendid than the everlasting mountains!

Psalm 76:4

The Hymn

Hark! The glad sound! The Savior comes,
the Savior promised long:
let every heart prepare a throne,
and every voice a song.

He comes, the broken heart to bind,
the bleeding soul to cure;
and with the treasures of his grace
to enrich the humble poor.

He comes, the prisoners to release
in Satan's bondage held;
the gates of brass before him burst,
the iron fetters yield.

Our glad hosannas, Prince of Peace,
your welcome shall proclaim;
and heaven's eternal arches ring
with your beloved Name.

Phillip Doddridge

The Refrain for the Vespers Lessons
Your love, O LORD, for ever will I sing;* from age to age my mouth will proclaim
your faithfulness.

Psalm 89:1

The Vespers Psalm　　　　　　　　　　　*Send Out Your Light and Your Truth*
Send out your light and your truth, that they may lead me,* and bring me to your
holy hill and to your dwelling;
That I may go to the altar of God, to the God of my joy and gladness;* and on the
harp I will give thanks to you, O God my God.
Why are you so full of heaviness, O my soul?* and why are you so disquieted
within me?
Put your trust in God;* for I will yet give thanks to him, who is the help of my
countenance, and my God.

Psalm 43:3–6

The Refrain
Your love, O LORD, for ever will I sing;* from age to age my mouth will proclaim
your faithfulness.

The Cry of the Church
Even so, come, Lord Jesus!

The Lord's Prayer

The Prayer Appointed for the Week
Merciful God, who sent your messengers the prophets to preach repentance and
    prepare the way for our salvation: Grant us grace to heed their warnings and
    forsake our sins, that we may greet with joy the coming of Jesus Christ our
    Redeemer; who lives and reigns with you and the Holy Spirit, one God, now
    and for ever. *Amen.*✝

The Concluding Prayer of the Church
Lord Jesus Christ, you have prepared a quiet place for us in your Father's eternal
    home. Watch over our welfare on this perilous journey, shade us from the
    burning heat of day, and keep our lives free of evil until the end. *Amen.*

THE LITURGY OF THE HOURS, VOL. III

The Morning Office   To Be Observed on the Hour or Half Hour
                                              Between 6 and 9 a.m.

The Call to Prayer
Rejoice in the LORD, you righteous,* and give thanks to his holy Name.
Psalm 97:12

The Request for Presence
Bow down your ear, O LORD, and answer me,* for I am poor and in misery.
Keep watch over my life, for I am faithful;* save your servant who puts his trust in
    you.
Psalm 86:1–2

The Greeting
Blessed is the LORD!* for he has heard the voice of my prayer.
Psalm 28:7

The Refrain for the Morning Lessons
Blessed are they which do hunger and thirst after righteousness: for they shall be
    filled.
Matthew 5:6 (KJV)

A Reading
In due course John the Baptist appeared; he proclaimed this message in the desert
    of Judaea, 'Repent, for the kingdom of Heaven is close at hand.' This was the
    man spoken of by the prophet Isaiah when he said: *A voice of one that cries in the
    desert, 'Prepare a way for the Lord, make his paths straight.'* This man John wore a
    garment made of camel-hair with a leather loin-cloth round his waist, and his
    food was locusts and wild honey. Then Jerusalem and all Judaea and the whole
    Jordan district made their way to him, and as they were baptized by him in the
    river Jordan they confessed their sins.
Matthew 3:1–6

The Refrain

Blessed are they which do hunger and thirst after righteousness: for they shall be filled.

The Morning Psalm   *My Soul Longs for You*

As the deer longs for the water-brooks,* so longs my soul for you, O God.

My soul is athirst for God, athirst for the living God;* when shall I come to appear before the presence of God?

My tears have been my food day and night, while all day long they say to me,* "Where now is your God?"

I pour out my soul when I think on these things:* how I went with the multitude and led them into the house of God,

With the voice of praise and thanksgiving,* among those who keep holy-day.

Why are you so full of heaviness, O my soul?* and why are you so disquieted within me?

Put your trust in God;* for I will yet give thanks to him, who is the help of my countenance, and my God.

Psalm 42:1–7

The Refrain

Blessed are they which do hunger and thirst after righteousness: for they shall be filled.

The Small Verse

My soul thirsts for the strong, living God and all that is within me cries out to him.

Traditional

The Lord's Prayer

The Prayer Appointed for the Week

Merciful God, who sent your messengers the prophets to preach repentance and prepare the way for our salvation: Grant us grace to heed their warnings and forsake our sins, that we may greet with joy the coming of Jesus Christ our Redeemer; who lives and reigns with you and the Holy Spirit, one God, now and for ever. *Amen.*†

The Concluding Prayer of the Church

Lord God, almighty and everlasting Father, you have brought me in safety to this new day: Preserve me with your mighty power, that I may not fall into sin, nor be overcome by adversity; and in all I do direct me to the fulfilling of your purpose; through Jesus Christ my Lord. *Amen.*†

The Midday Office   **To Be Observed on the Hour or Half Hour**
                                                      Between 11 a.m. and 2 p.m.

The Call to Prayer

Come, let us sing to the Lord;* let us shout for joy to the Rock of our salvation.

Let us come before his presence with thanksgiving* and raise a loud shout to him with psalms.

For the LORD is a great God,* and a great King above all gods.
In his hand are the caverns of the earth,* and the heights of the hills are his also.
The sea is his, for he made it,* and his hands have molded the dry land.

Psalm 95:1–5

The Request for Presence
Remember not our past sins;* let your compassion be swift to meet us.

Psalm 79:8

The Greeting
Zion hears and is glad, and the cities of Judah rejoice,* because of your judgments,
O LORD.

Psalm 97:8

The Refrain for the Midday Lessons
I will listen to what the LORD God is saying,* for he is speaking peace to his faithful
people and to those who turn their hearts to him.

Psalm 85:8

A Reading
"Look, the days are coming, YAHWEH declares, when I shall fulfill the promise of
happiness I made to the House of Israel and the House of Judah: In those days
and at that time, I shall make an upright Branch grow for David, who will do
what is just and upright in the country. In those days Judah will triumph and
Israel live in safety. And this is the name the city will be called: Yahweh-is-our-
Saving-Justice."

Jeremiah 33:14–16

The Refrain
I will listen to what the LORD God is saying,* for he is speaking peace to his faithful
people and to those who turn their hearts to him.

The Midday Psalm   *Let Your Heart Take Courage*
How great is your goodness, O LORD! which you have laid up for those who fear
you;* which you have done in the sight of all for those who put their trust in
you.
You hide them in the covert of your presence from those who slander them;* you
keep them in your shelter from the strife of tongues.
Blessed be the LORD!* for he has shown me the wonders of his love in a besieged
city.
Love the LORD, all you who worship him;* the LORD protects the faithful, but
repays to the full those who act haughtily.
Be strong and let your heart take courage,* all you who wait for the LORD.

Psalm 31:19–21, 23–24

The Refrain
I will listen to what the LORD God is saying,* for he is speaking peace to his faithful
people and to those who turn their hearts to him.

The Cry of the Church
Even so, come, Lord Jesus!

The Lord's Prayer

The Prayer Appointed for the Week
Merciful God, who sent your messengers the prophets to preach repentance and
 prepare the way for our salvation: Grant us grace to heed their warnings and
 forsake our sins, that we may greet with joy the coming of Jesus Christ our
 Redeemer; who lives and reigns with you and the Holy Spirit, one God, now
 and for ever. *Amen.*†

The Concluding Prayer of the Church
Direct me, O Lord, on all my doings with your most gracious favor, and further
 me with your continual help; that in all my work begun, continued, and ended
 in you, I may glorify your holy name, and finally, by your mercy, obtain everlasting life; through Jesus Christ my Lord. *Amen.*†

The Vespers Office   To Be Observed on the Hour or Half Hour
                                                          Between 5 and 8 p.m.

The Call to Prayer
Come, let us sing to the LORD;* let us shout for joy to the Rock of our salvation.
                                                                        Psalm 95:1

The Request for Presence
May the glory of the LORD endure for ever;* may the LORD rejoice in all his works.
                                                                        Psalm 104:32

The Greeting
How great is your goodness, O LORD! which you have laid up for those who fear
 you;* which you have done in the sight of all for those who put their trust in you.
                                                                        Psalm 31:19

The Hymn
The setting sun now dies away,   To God the Father, God the Son,
And darkness comes at close of day;   And Holy Spirit, Three in One,
Your brightest beams, dear Lord impart,   Trinity blessed whom we adore,
And let them shine within our heart.   Be praise and glory evermore.

                                                          Geoffrey Laylock
We praise your name with joy this night;
Please watch and guide us till the light;
Joining the music of the blessed,
O Lord, we sing ourselves to rest.

The Refrain for the Vespers Lessons
I am small and of little account,* yet I do not forget your commandments.
                                                                        Psalm 119:141

The Vespers Psalm   *How Priceless Is Your Love, O God*

Your love, O LORD, reaches to the heavens,* and your faithfulness to the clouds.

Your righteousness is like the strong mountains, your justice like the great deep;* you save both man and beast, O LORD.

How priceless is your love, O God!* your people take refuge under the shadow of your wings.

They feast upon the abundance of your house;* you give them drink from the river of your delights.

For with you is the well of life,* and in your light we see light.

Continue your loving-kindness to those who know you,* and your favor to those who are true of heart.

Psalm 36:5–10

The Refrain

I am small and of little account,* yet I do not forget your commandments.

The Small Verse

Those who sowed with tears* will reap with songs of joy.

Those who go out weeping, carrying the seed,* will come again with joy, shouldering their sheaves.

Psalm 126:6–7

The Lord's Prayer

The Prayer Appointed for the Week

Merciful God, who sent your messengers the prophets to preach repentance and prepare the way for our salvation: Grant us grace to heed their warnings and forsake our sins, that we may greet with joy the coming of Jesus Christ our Redeemer; who lives and reigns with you and the Holy Spirit, one God, now and for ever. *Amen.*†

The Concluding Prayer of the Church

Almighty God, to whom our needs are known before we even ask, Help me to ask only what accords with your will; and those good things which I dare not, or in my blindness I cannot ask, grant for the sake of your Son Jesus Christ our Lord. *Amen.*†

The Morning Office   **To Be Observed on the Hour or Half Hour**
Between 6 and 9 a.m.

The Call to Prayer

Worship the LORD in the beauty of holiness;* let the whole earth tremble before him.

Psalm 96:9

The Request for Presence

Show us the light of your countenance, O God,* and come to us.

based on Psalm 67:1

The Greeting

Seven times a day do I praise you,* because of your righteous judgments.

Psalm 119:164

The Refrain for the Morning Lessons

Let integrity and uprightness preserve me,* for my hope has been in you.

Psalm 25:20

A Reading

Now it happened that one day while he was teaching the people in the Temple and proclaiming the good news, the chief priests and the scribes came up, together with the elders, and spoke to him. 'Tell us,' they said, 'what authority have you for acting like this? Or who gives you this authority?' In reply he said to them, 'And I will ask you a question, just one. Tell me: John's baptism: what was its origin, heavenly or human?' And they debated this way among themselves, 'If we say heavenly, he will retort, "why did you refuse to believe him?"; and if we say human, the whole people will stone us, for they are convinced that John was a prophet.' So their reply was that they did not know where it came from. And Jesus said to them, 'Nor will I tell you my authority for acting like this.'

Luke 20:1–8

The Refrain

Let integrity and uprightness preserve me,* for my hope has been in you.

The Morning Psalm   *Take Delight in the* Lord

Do not fret yourself because of evildoers;* do not be jealous of those who do wrong.

For they shall soon wither like the grass,* and like the green grass fade away.

Put your trust in the Lord and do good;* dwell in the land and feed on its riches.

Take delight in the Lord,* and he shall give you your heart's desire.

Commit your way to the Lord and put your trust in him,* and he will bring it to pass.

He will make your righteousness as clear as the light* and your just dealing as the noonday.

Be still before the Lord* and wait patiently for him.

Psalm 37:1–7

The Refrain

Let integrity and uprightness preserve me,* for my hope has been in you.

The Cry of the Church

O Lamb of God, that takes away the sins of the world, have mercy upon me.

O Lamb of God, that takes away the sins of the world, have mercy upon me.

O Lamb of God, that takes away the sins of the world, grant me your peace.

The Lord's Prayer

The Prayer Appointed for the Week

Merciful God, who sent your messengers the prophets to preach repentance and prepare the way for our salvation: Grant us grace to heed their warnings and forsake our sins, that we may greet with joy the coming of Jesus Christ our Redeemer; who lives and reigns with you and the Holy Spirit, one God, now and for ever. *Amen.*†

The Concluding Prayer of the Church

Lord God, almighty and everlasting Father, you have brought me in safety to this new day: Preserve me with your mighty power, that I may not fall into sin, nor be overcome by adversity; and in all I do direct me to the fulfilling of your purpose; through Jesus Christ my Lord. *Amen.*†

The Midday Office   To Be Observed on the Hour or Half Hour
                                     Between 11 a.m. and 2 p.m.

The Call to Prayer

Glory in his holy Name;* let the hearts of those who seek the LORD rejoice.

Psalm 105:3

The Request for Presence

Let your compassion come to me, that I may live,* for your law is my delight.

Psalm 119:77

The Greeting

Your righteousness, O God, reaches to the heavens;* you have done great things; who is like you, O God?

Psalm 71:19

The Refrain for the Midday Lessons

"I will instruct you and teach you in the way that you should go;* I will guide you with my eye.
Do not be like horse or mule, which have no understanding;* who must be fitted with bit and bridle, or else they will not stay near you."

Psalm 32:9–10

A Reading

Once the oppression is past, and the devastation has stopped and those now trampling on the country have gone away, the throne will be made secure in faithful love, and on it will sit in constancy within the tent of David a judge seeking fair judgment and pursuing uprightness.

Isaiah 16:4b–5

The Refrain

"I will instruct you and teach you in the way that you should go;* I will guide you with my eye.
Do not be like horse or mule, which have no understanding;* who must be fitted with bit and bridle, or else they will not stay near you."

The Midday Psalm   *Never Have I Seen the Righteous Forsaken*
Our steps are directed by the LORD;* he strengthens those in whose way he
    delights.
If they stumble, they shall not fall headlong,* for the LORD holds them by the hand.
I have been young and now I am old,* but never have I seen the righteous
    forsaken, . . .

Psalm 37:24–26

The Refrain
"I will instruct you and teach you in the way that you should go;* I will guide you
    with my eye.
Do not be like horse or mule, which have no understanding;* who must be fitted
    with bit and bridle, or else they will not stay near you."

The Cry of the Church
Lord, have mercy on us. Christ, have mercy on us. Lord, have mercy on us.

The Lord's Prayer

The Prayer Appointed for the Week
Merciful God, who sent your messengers the prophets to preach repentance and
    prepare the way for our salvation: Grant us grace to heed their warnings and
    forsake our sins, that we may greet with joy the coming of Jesus Christ our
    Redeemer; who lives and reigns with you and the Holy Spirit, one God, now
    and for ever. *Amen.*†

The Concluding Prayer of the Church
Open, Lord, my eyes that I may see.
Open, Lord, my ears that I may hear.
Open, Lord, my heart and my mind that I may understand.
So shall I turn to you and be healed.

Traditional

The Vespers Office   To Be Observed on the Hour or Half Hour
                                                 Between 5 and 8 p.m.

The Call to Prayer
God is the LORD; he has shined upon us;* form a procession with branches up to
    the horns of the altar.

Psalm 118:27

The Request for Presence
Hear the voice of my prayer when I cry out to you,* when I lift up my hands to
    your holy of holies.

Psalm 28:2

The Greeting

All your works praise you, O LORD,* and your faithful servants bless you.
They make known the glory of your kingdom and speak of your power . . . * and
    the glorious splendor of your kingdom.

Psalm 145:10–12

The Hymn

> Of the Father's love begotten, ere the winds began to be,
> He is Alpha and Omega, he the source, the ending he
> Of the things that are, that have been and that future years shall see.
>
> O you heights of heaven adore him; angel hosts, his praises sing;
> Powers, dominions, bow before him, and extol our God and King;
> Let no tongue on earth be silent, every voice in concert ring.
>
> Christ, to you with God the Father, and O Holy Ghost, to thee,
> Hymn and chant and high thanksgiving, and unwearied praises be:
> Honor, glory and dominion, and eternal victory.

Aurelius Clemens Prudentius

The Refrain for the Vespers Lessons

Those who trust in the LORD are like Mount Zion,* which cannot be moved, but
    stands fast for ever.

Psalm 125:1

The Vespers Psalm　　　　　　　　　　　*Let Your Ways Be Known Upon Earth*

May God be merciful to us and bless us,* show us the light of his countenance and
    come to us.
Let your ways be known upon earth,* your saving health among all nations.
Let the peoples praise you, O God;* let all the peoples praise you.
Let the nations be glad and sing for joy,* for you judge the peoples with equity and
    guide all the nations upon earth.
Let the peoples praise you, O God;* let all the peoples praise you.

Psalm 67:1–5

The Refrain

Those who trust in the LORD are like Mount Zion,* which cannot be moved, but
    stands fast for ever.

The Small Verse

The earth is the Lord's and all the fullness thereof, the world and we who dwell
    within. Thanks be to God.

Traditional

The Lord's Prayer

The Prayer Appointed for the Week

Merciful God, who sent your messengers the prophets to preach repentance and
    prepare the way for our salvation: Grant us grace to heed their warnings and

forsake our sins, that we may greet with joy the coming of Jesus Christ our Redeemer; who lives and reigns with you and the Holy Spirit, one God, now and for ever. *Amen.*†

The Concluding Prayer of the Church

May God himself order my days and make them acceptable in his sight. Blessed is the Lord always, my strength and my redeemer.

Traditional

The Morning Office

To Be Observed on the Hour or Half Hour Between 6 and 9 a.m.

The Call to Prayer

Know this: The LORD himself is God;* he himself has made us, and we are his; we are his people and the sheep of his pasture.

Psalm 100:2

The Request for Presence

Lead me, O LORD, in your righteousness, . . . * make your way straight before me.

Psalm 5:8

The Greeting

Hosannah, LORD, hosannah!* LORD, send us now success.

Blessed is he who comes in the name of the Lord;* we bless you from the house of the LORD.

God is the LORD; he has shined upon us;* form a procession with branches up to the horns of the altar.

Psalm 118:25–27

The Refrain for the Morning Lessons

Let not those who hope in you be put to shame through me, Lord GOD of hosts;* let not those who seek you be disgraced because of me, O God of Israel.

Psalm 69:7

A Reading

Of the Baptizer, scripture says: "A feeling of expectancy had grown among the people, who were beginning to wonder whether John might be the Christ, so John declared before them all, 'I baptize you with water, but someone is coming, someone who is more powerful than me, and I am not fit to undo the strap of his sandals; he will baptize you with the Holy Spirit and fire. His winnowing-fan is in his hand, to clear his threshing floor and to gather the wheat into his barn; but the chaff he will burn in a fire that will never go out.' And he proclaimed the good news to the people with many other exhortations too."

Luke 3:15–18

The Refrain

Let not those who hope in you be put to shame through me, Lord GOD of hosts;* let not those who seek you be disgraced because of me, O God of Israel.

The Morning Psalm   *Shepherd Your Inheritance, O LORD*

Blessed is the LORD!* for he has heard the voice of my prayer.

The LORD is my strength and my shield;* my heart trusts in him, and I have been
    helped;

Therefore my heart dances for joy,* and in my song will I praise him.

The LORD is the strength of his people,* a safe refuge for his anointed.

Save your people and bless your inheritance;* shepherd them and carry them for
    ever.

Psalm 28:7–11

The Refrain

Let not those who hope in you be put to shame through me, Lord GOD of hosts;*
    let not those who seek you be disgraced because of me, O God of Israel.

The Cry of the Church

O God, come to my assistance! O Lord, make haste to help me!

The Lord's Prayer

The Prayer Appointed for the Week

Merciful God, who sent your messengers the prophets to preach repentance and
    prepare the way for our salvation: Grant us grace to heed their warnings and
    forsake our sins, that we may greet with joy the coming of Jesus Christ our
    Redeemer; who lives and reigns with you and the Holy Spirit, one God, now
    and for ever. *Amen.*†

The Concluding Prayer of the Church

Lord God, almighty and everlasting Father, you have brought me in safety to this
    new day: Preserve me with your mighty power, that I may not fall into sin, nor
    be overcome by adversity; and in all I do direct me to the fulfilling of your pur-
    pose; through Jesus Christ my Lord. *Amen.*†

The Midday Office   To Be Observed on the Hour or Half Hour
                                          Between 11 a.m. and 2 p.m.

The Call to Prayer

Bless God in the congregation;* bless the LORD, you that are of the fountain of
    Israel.

Psalm 68:26

The Request for Presence

Be my strong rock, a castle to keep me safe;* you are my crag and my stronghold.

Psalm 71:3

The Greeting

Your way, O God, is holy;* who is so great a god as our God?

Psalm 77:13

The Refrain for the Midday Lessons

He who dwells in the shelter of the Most High,* abides under the shadow of the Almighty.

Psalm 91:1

A Reading

For YAHWEH Sabaoth says this: A little while now, and I shall shake the heavens and the earth, the sea and the dry land. I shall shake all the nations, and the treasure of all the nations will flow in, and I shall fill this Temple with glory, says YAHWEH Sabaoth . . . The glory of this new Temple will surpass that of the old, says YAHWEH Sabaoth, and in this place I shall give peace—YAHWEH Sabaoth declares.

Haggai 2:6–7, 9

The Refrain

He who dwells in the shelter of the Most High,* abides under the shadow of the Almighty.

The Midday Psalm　　　　　　　　　　　　　　*O Israel, Trust in the LORD*

O Israel, trust in the LORD;* he is their help and their shield.

O house of Aaron, trust in the LORD;* he is their help and their shield.

You who fear the LORD, trust in the LORD;* he is their help and their shield.

The LORD has been mindful of us, and he will bless us;* he will bless the house of Israel; he will bless the house of Aaron;

He will bless those who fear the LORD,* both small and great together.

May the LORD increase you more and more,* you and your children after you.

May you be blessed by the LORD,* the maker of heaven and earth.

The heaven of heavens is the LORD's,* but he entrusted the earth to its peoples.

But we will bless the LORD,* from this time forth for evermore. Hallelujah!

Psalm 115:9–16, 18

The Refrain

He who dwells in the shelter of the Most High,* abides under the shadow of the Almighty.

Cry of the Church

O Lamb of God, that takes away the sins of the world, have mercy upon me.

O Lamb of God, that takes away the sins of the world, have mercy upon me.

O Lamb of God, that takes away the sins of the world, grant me your peace.

The Lord's Prayer

The Prayer Appointed for the Week

Merciful God, who sent your messengers the prophets to preach repentance and prepare the way for our salvation: Grant us grace to heed their warnings and forsake our sins, that we may greet with joy the coming of Jesus Christ our Redeemer; who lives and reigns with you and the Holy Spirit, one God, now and for ever. *Amen.*†

The Concluding Prayer of the Church

Lord Jesus Christ, by your death you took away the sting of death: Grant me to so
follow in faith where you have led the way, that I may at length fall asleep
peacefully in you and wake in your likeness; for your tender mercies' sake.
Amen.†

The Vespers Office   To Be Observed on the Hour or Half Hour
                                                           Between 5 and 8 p.m.

The Call to Prayer

Taste and see that the Lord is good;* happy are they who trust in him!

Psalm 34:8

The Request for Presence

Turn to me and have pity on me . . .
The sorrows of my heart have increased . . .
Look upon my adversity and misery* and forgive me all my sin.

Psalm 25:15–17

The Greeting

It is a good thing to give thanks to the Lord,* and to sing praises to your Name,
O Most High;
To tell of your loving-kindness early in the morning* and of your faithfulness in
the night season.

Psalm 92:1–2

The Hymn

The King shall come when morning dawns and light triumphant breaks;
When beauty gilds the eastern hills and life to joy awakes.
Not, as of old, a little child, to bear, and fight, and die,
But crowned with glory like the sun that lights the morning sky.
The King shall come when morning dawns and earth's dark night is past;
O haste the rising of that morn, the day that shall ever last;
And let the endless bliss begin, by weary saints foretold,
When right shall triumph over wrong, and truth shall be extolled.
The King shall come when morning dawns and light and beauty brings:
Hail, Christ the Lord! Your people pray, come quickly, King of Kings.

Greek

The Refrain for the Vespers Lessons

When I was in trouble, I called to the Lord;* I called to the Lord, and he answered
me.

Psalm 120:1

The Vespers Psalm   *In You, O Lord, Have I Taken Refuge*

In you, O Lord, have I taken refuge; let me never be put to shame;* deliver me in
your righteousness.

Incline your ear to me;* make haste to deliver me.

Be my strong rock, a castle to keep me safe, for you are my crag and my
stronghold;* for the sake of your Name, lead me and guide me.

Take me out of the net that they have secretly set for me,* for you are my tower of
strength.

Into your hands I commend my spirit,* for you have redeemed me, O Lord, O
God of truth.

Psalm 31:1–5

The Refrain

When I was in trouble, I called to the Lord;* I called to the Lord, and he answered
me.

The Cry of the Church

Be, Lord, my helper and forsake me not. Do not despise me, O God, my savior.

THE SHORT BREVIARY

The Lord's Prayer

The Prayer Appointed for the Week

Merciful God, who sent your messengers the prophets to preach repentance and
prepare the way for our salvation: Grant us grace to heed their warnings and
forsake our sins, that we may greet with joy the coming of Jesus Christ our
Redeemer; who lives and reigns with you and the Holy Spirit, one God, now
and for ever. *Amen.*†

Concluding Prayers of the Church

Almighty God, who has promised to hear the petitions of those who ask in your
Son's Name: I beseech you mercifully to incline your ear to me who have made
my prayers and supplications to you; and grant that those things which I have
faithfully asked according to your will, I may effectually obtain, to the relief of
my necessity, and to the setting forth of your glory; through Jesus Christ my
Lord. *Amen.*†

May the souls of the faithful departed, through the mercy of God, rest in eternal
peace. *Amen.*

The Morning Office   To Be Observed on the Hour or Half Hour
Between 6 and 9 a.m.

The Call to Prayer

Bless the Lord, you angels of his, you mighty ones who do his bidding,* and hearken to the voice of his word.

Bless the Lord, all you his hosts,* you ministers of his who do his will.

Bless the Lord, all you works of his, in all places of his dominion;* bless the Lord,
O my soul.

Psalm 103:20–22

The Request for Presence
Show me the light of your countenance, O God,* and come to me.
based on Psalm 67:1

The Greeting
As the deer longs for the water-brooks,* so longs my soul for you, O God.
Psalm 42:1

The Refrain for the Morning Lessons
The same stone which the builders rejected* has become the chief cornerstone.
This is the LORD's doing,* and it is marvelous in our eyes.
Psalm 118:22–23

A Reading
Then Jesus appeared: he came from Galilee to the Jordan to be baptized by John.
John tried to dissuade him, with the words, 'It is I who need baptism from you,
and yet you come to me!' But Jesus replied, 'Leave it like this for the time
being; it is fitting that we should, in this way, do all that uprightness demands.'
Then John gave in to him. And when Jesus had been baptized he at once came
up from the water, and suddenly the heavens opened and he saw the Spirit of
God descending like a dove and coming down on him. And suddenly there
was a voice from heaven, 'This is my Son, the Beloved; my favor rests on him.'
Matthew 3:13–17

The Refrain
The same stone which the builders rejected* has become the chief cornerstone.
This is the LORD's doing,* and it is marvelous in our eyes.

The Morning Psalm   *In a Little While the Wicked Shall Be No More*
In a little while the wicked shall be no more;* you shall search out their place, but
they will not be there.
But the lowly shall possess the land;* they will delight in abundance of peace.
The wicked plot against the righteous* and gnash at them with their teeth.
The LORD laughs at the wicked,* because he sees that their day will come.
The wicked draw their sword and bend their bow to strike down the poor and
needy,* to slaughter those who are upright in their ways.
Their sword shall go through their own heart,* and their bow shall be broken.
The little that the righteous has* is better than great riches of the wicked.
For the power of the wicked shall be broken,* but the LORD upholds the righteous.
Psalm 37:11–18

The Refrain
The same stone which the builders rejected* has become the chief cornerstone.
This is the LORD's doing,* and it is marvelous in our eyes.

The Cry of the Church
Even so, come, Lord Jesus!

The Lord's Prayer

The Prayer Appointed for the Week

Merciful God, who sent your messengers the prophets to preach repentance and prepare the way for our salvation: Grant us grace to heed their warnings and forsake our sins, that we may greet with joy the coming of Jesus Christ our Redeemer; who lives and reigns with you and the Holy Spirit, one God, now and for ever. *Amen.*✝

The Concluding Prayer of the Church

Lord God, almighty and everlasting Father, you have brought me in safety to this new day: Preserve me with your mighty power, that I may not fall into sin, nor be overcome by adversity; and in all I do direct me to the fulfilling of your purpose; through Jesus Christ my Lord. *Amen.*✝

The Midday Office   To Be Observed on the Hour or Half Hour
                                     Between 11 a.m. and 2 p.m.

The Call to Prayer

May these words of mine please him;* I will rejoice in the LORD.

Psalm 104:35

The Request for Presence

Set a watch before my mouth, O LORD, and guard the door of my lips;* let not my heart incline to any evil thing.

Let me not be occupied in wickedness with evildoers,* nor eat of their choice foods.

Let the righteous smite me in friendly rebuke;* let not the oil of the unrighteous anoint my head.

Psalm 141:3–5

The Greeting

I long for your salvation, O LORD,* and your law is my delight.

Let me live, and I will praise you,* and let your judgments help me.

Psalm 119:174–175

The Refrain for the Midday Lessons

O God, you have taught me since I was young,* and to this day I tell of your wonderful works.

Psalm 71:17

A Reading

"For the Lord YAHWEH says this: Look, I myself shall take care of my flock and look after it . . . I myself shall pasture my sheep, I myself shall give them rest—declares the Lord YAHWEH. I shall look for the lost one, bring back the stray, bandage the injured and make the sick strong. I shall watch over the fat and healthy. I shall be a true shepherd to them."

Ezekiel 34:11, 15–16

The Refrain

O God, you have taught me since I was young,* and to this day I tell of your wonderful works.

The Midday Psalm   *The LORD Does Not Forsake His Faithful Ones*

Our steps are directed by the LORD;* he strengthens those in whose way he
delights.

If they stumble, they shall not fall headlong,* for the LORD holds them by the hand.

For the LORD loves justice;* he does not forsake his faithful ones.

They shall be kept safe for ever,* but the offspring of the wicked shall be
destroyed.

The righteous shall possess the land* and dwell in it for ever.

The mouth of the righteous utters wisdom,* and their tongue speaks what is right.

The law of their God is in their heart,* and their footsteps shall not falter.

Psalm 37:24–25, 29–33

The Refrain

O God, you have taught me since I was young,* and to this day I tell of your wonderful works.

The Small Verse

Into your hands I commend my spirit for you have redeemed me, O God of my
life. Glory be to the Father, and to the Son and to the comforting Spirit.

Traditional

The Lord's Prayer

The Prayer Appointed for the Week

Merciful God, who sent your messengers the prophets to preach repentance and
prepare the way for our salvation: Grant us grace to heed their warnings and
forsake our sins, that we may greet with joy the coming of Jesus Christ our
Redeemer; who lives and reigns with you and the Holy Spirit, one God, now
and for ever. *Amen.*†

The Concluding Prayer of the Church

O God, the source of eternal light: Shed forth your unending day upon all of us
who watch for you, that our lips may praise you, our lives may bless you, and
our worship may give you glory; through Jesus Christ our Lord. *Amen.*†

The Vespers Office   To Be Observed on the Hour or Half Hour
Between 5 and 8 p.m.

The Call to Prayer

Come, let us sing to the LORD;* let us shout for joy to the Rock of our salvation.

Let us come before his presence with thanksgiving* and raise a loud shout to him
with psalms.

For the LORD is a great God,* and a great king above all gods.

Psalm 95:1–3

The Request for Presence

Send out your light and your truth, that they may lead me,* and bring me to your
   holy hill and to your dwelling.

Psalm 43:3

The Greeting

You, O LORD, are my lamp;* my God, you make my darkness bright.

Psalm 18:29

The Hymn

Holy, holy, holy! Lord God the Almighty!
Early in the morning our song shall rise to Thee;
Holy, holy, holy, merciful and mighty!
God in three Persons, blessed Trinity!

Holy, holy, holy! All the saints adore Thee,
Casting down their golden crowns around the glassy sea;
Cherubim and seraphim falling down before Thee,
Who were, and are, and evermore shall be.

Holy, holy, holy! Though the darkness hides Thee,
Though the eye of sinful man Your glory may not see;
Only You are holy; there is none beside Thee,
Perfect in power, in love, and purity.

Holy, holy, holy! Lord God Almighty!
All Your works shall praise Your name, in earth, and sky, and sea;
Holy, holy, holy; merciful and mighty!
God in three Persons, blessed Trinity!

Reginald Heber

The Refrain for the Vespers Lessons

Seven times a day do I praise you,* because of your righteous judgments.
Great peace have they who love your law;* for them there is no stumbling block.

Psalm 119:164–165

The Vespers Psalm   *You Are My Hiding Place*

You are my hiding-place; you preserve me from trouble;* you surround me with
   shouts of deliverance.
"I will instruct you and teach you in the way that you should go;* I will guide you
   with my eye.
Do not be like horse or mule, which have no understanding;* who must be fitted
   with bit and bridle, or else they will not stay near you."
Great are the tribulations of the wicked;* but mercy embraces those who trust in
   the LORD.
Be glad, you righteous, and rejoice in the LORD;* shout for joy, all who are true of
   heart.

Psalm 32:8–12

The Refrain
Seven times a day do I praise you,* because of your righteous judgments.
Great peace have they who love your law;* for them there is no stumbling block.

The Cry of the Church
Even so, come, Lord Jesus!

The Lord's Prayer

The Prayer Appointed for the Week
Merciful God, who sent your messengers the prophets to preach repentance and
    prepare the way for our salvation: Grant us grace to heed their warnings and
    forsake our sins, that we may greet with joy the coming of Jesus Christ our
    Redeemer; who lives and reigns with you and the Holy Spirit, one God, now
    and for ever. *Amen.*†

The Concluding Prayer of the Church
Almighty God, who after the creation of the world rested from all your works and
    sanctified a day of rest for all your creatures: Grant that I, putting away all
    earthly anxieties, may be duly prepared for the service of public worship, and
    grant as well that my Sabbath upon earth may be a preparation for the eternal
    rest promised to your people in heaven; through Jesus Christ our Lord. *Amen.*†

The Morning Office   To Be Observed on the Hour or Half Hour
                                              Between 6 and 9 a.m.

The Call to Prayer
Hallelujah! Praise the LORD, O my soul!* I will praise the LORD as long as I live; I
    will sing praises to my God while I have my being.

Psalm 146:1

The Request for Presence
Set a watch before my mouth, O LORD, and guard the door of my lips;* let not my
    heart incline to any evil thing.
Let me not be occupied in wickedness with evildoers,* nor eat of their choice
    foods.
Let the righteous smite me in friendly rebuke;* let not the oil of the unrighteous
    anoint my head.

Psalm 141:3–5

The Greeting

Not to us, O LORD, not to us, but to your Name give glory;* because of your love and because of your faithfulness.

Psalm 115:1

The Refrain for the Morning Lessons

Let the words of my mouth and the meditation of my heart be acceptable in your sight,* O LORD, my strength and my redeemer.

Psalm 19:14

A Reading   *Traditionally the Church has used the third week of Advent as a time for giving particular attention and adoration to the Virgin and her role as bearer and mother of our Lord.*

As the child's father and mother were wondering at the things that were being said about him, Simeon blessed them and said to Mary his mother, 'Look, he is destined for the fall and for the rise of many in Israel, destined to be a sign that is opposed—and a sword will pierce your soul too—so that the secret thoughts of many may be laid bare.'

Luke 2:33–35

The Refrain

Let the words of my mouth and the meditation of my heart be acceptable in your sight,* O LORD, my strength and my redeemer.

The Morning Psalm   *How Long Will You Hide Your Face from Me?*

How long, O LORD? will you forget me for ever?* how long will you hide your face from me?

How long shall I have perplexity in my mind, and grief in my heart, day after day?* how long shall my enemy triumph over me?

Look upon me and answer me, O LORD my God;* give light to my eyes, lest I sleep in death;

Lest my enemy say, "I have prevailed over him,"* and my foes rejoice that I have fallen.

But I put my trust in your mercy;* my heart is joyful because of your saving help.

I will sing to the LORD, for he has dealt with me richly;* I will praise the Name of the LORD Most High.

Psalm 13

The Refrain

Let the words of my mouth and the meditation of my heart be acceptable in your sight,* O LORD, my strength and my redeemer.

The Cry of the Church

O God, come to my assistance! O Lord, make haste to help me!

The Lord's Prayer

The Prayer Appointed for the Week

Stir up your power, O Lord, and with great might come among us; and, because we are sorely hindered by our sins, let your bountiful grace and mercy speedily help and deliver us; through Jesus Christ our Lord, to whom, with you and the Holy Spirit, be honor and glory now and for ever. *Amen.*†

The Concluding Prayer of the Church

Lord God, almighty and everlasting Father, you have brought me in safety to this new day: Preserve me with your mighty power, that I may not fall into sin, nor be overcome by adversity; and in all I do direct me to the fulfilling of your purpose; through Jesus Christ my Lord. *Amen.*†

The Midday Office   To Be Observed on the Hour or Half Hour
                                     Between 11 a.m. and 2 p.m.

The Call to Prayer

Come and listen, all you who fear God,* and I will tell you what he has done for me.

Psalm 66:14

The Request for Presence

I call upon you, O God, for you will answer me;* incline your ear to me and hear my words.

Psalm 17:6

The Greeting

The Lord is in his holy temple; let all the earth keep silence before him. Amen.

Traditional

The Refrain for the Midday Lessons

The Lord is my strength and my song,* and he has become my salvation.

Psalm 118:14

A Reading

What you have come to is nothing known to the senses: not a *blazing fire*, or *gloom* or *total darkness*, or a *storm*; or *trumpet blast* or the *sound of a voice speaking* . . . But what you have come to is Mount Zion and the city of the living God, the heavenly Jerusalem where the millions of angels have gathered for the festival, with the whole Church of first-born sons, enrolled as citizens of heaven. You have come to God himself, the supreme Judge, and to the spirits of the upright who have been made perfect; and to Jesus, the mediator of a new covenant, and to purifying blood which pleads more insistently than Abel's.

Hebrews 12:18ff

The Refrain

The Lord is my strength and my song,* and he has become my salvation.

The Midday Psalm   *God Has Gone Up with a Shout*

Clap your hands, all you peoples;* shout to God with a cry of joy.
For the LORD Most High is to be feared;* he is the great King over all the earth.
He subdues the peoples under us,* and the nations under our feet.
He chooses our inheritance for us,* the pride of Jacob whom he loves.
God has gone up with a shout,* the LORD with the sound of the ram's-horn.
Sing praises to God, sing praises;* sing praises to our King, sing praises.
For God is King of all the earth;* sing praises with all your skill.
God reigns over the nations;* God sits upon his holy throne.
The nobles of the peoples have gathered together* with the people of the God of
     Abraham.
The rulers of the earth belong to God,* and he is highly exalted.

Psalm 47

The Refrain
The LORD is my strength and my song,* and he has become my salvation.

The Cry of the Church
Even so, come, Lord Jesus!

The Lord's Prayer

The Prayer Appointed for the Week
Stir up your power, O Lord, and with great might come among us; and, because
     we are sorely hindered by our sins, let your bountiful grace and mercy speed-
     ily help and deliver us; through Jesus Christ our Lord, to whom, with you and
     the Holy Spirit, be honor and glory now and for ever. *Amen.*†

The Concluding Prayer of the Church
O God, you make me glad with the weekly remembrance of the glorious resurrec-
     tion of your Son my Lord: Give me this day such blessing through my worship
     of you, that the week to come may be spent in your favor; through Jesus Christ
     our Lord. *Amen.*†

The Vespers Office   To Be Observed on the Hour or Half Hour
                                                  Between 5 and 8 p.m.

The Call to Prayer
Hallelujah! Praise the LORD from the heavens;* praise him in the heights.

Psalm 148:1

The Request for Presence
You are my helper and my deliverer;* O LORD, do not tarry.

Psalm 70:6

The Greeting
O LORD, I am your servant;* I am your servant and the child of your handmaid;
     you have freed me from my bonds.

Psalm 116:14

The Hymn

When peace, like a river, attends to my way,
When sorrows like sea billows roll;
Whatever my lot, You have taught me to say,
It is well, it is well with my soul.
It is well with my soul,
It is well, it is well with my soul.

And, Lord, haste the day when faith will be sight,
The clouds be rolled back as a scroll,
The trump shall resound and the Lord shall descend,
"Even so," it is well with my soul.
It is well with my soul,
It is well, it is well with my soul.

Horatio Spafford

The Refrain for the Vespers Lessons
Turn again to your rest, O my soul,* for the LORD has treated you well.

Psalm 116:6

The Vespers Psalm   *My Soul Is Content*
O God, you are my God; eagerly I seek you;* my soul thirsts for you, my flesh
    faints for you, as in a barren and dry land where there is no water.
Therefore I have gazed upon you in your holy place,* that I might behold your
    power and your glory.
For your loving-kindness is better than life itself;* my lips shall give you praise.
So will I bless you as long as I live* and lift up my hands in your Name.
My soul is content, as with marrow and fatness,* and my mouth praises you with
    joyful lips,
When I remember you upon my bed,* and meditate on you in the night watches.
For you have been my helper,* and under the shadow of your wings I will rejoice.

Psalm 63:1–7

The Refrain
Turn again to your rest, O my soul,* for the LORD has treated you well.

The Cry of the Church
Even so, come, Lord Jesus!

The Lord's Prayer

The Prayer Appointed for the Week
Stir up your power, O Lord, and with great might come among us; and, because
    we are sorely hindered by our sins, let your bountiful grace and mercy speed-
    ily help and deliver us; through Jesus Christ our Lord, to whom, with you and
    the Holy Spirit, be honor and glory now and for ever. *Amen.*†

The Concluding Prayer of the Church

Lord God, whose Son our Savior Jesus Christ, triumphed over the powers of death and prepared for us our place in the new Jerusalem: Grant that I, who have this day given thanks for his resurrection, may praise you in the City of which he is the light, and where he lives and reigns for ever and ever. *Amen.*†

The Morning Office　　　　　　　To Be Observed on the Hour or Half Hour
　　　　　　　　　　　　　　　　　　　　　　　Between 6 and 9 a.m.

The Call to Prayer

Bless the LORD, you angels of his, you mighty ones who do his bidding,* and hearken to the voice of his word.
Bless the LORD, all you his hosts,* you ministers of his who do his will.
Bless the LORD, all you works of his,* in all places of his dominion . . .

Psalm 103:20–22

The Request for Presence

Be seated on your lofty throne, O Most High;* O LORD, judge the nations.

Psalm 7:8

The Greeting

Not to us, O LORD, not to us, but to your Name give glory;* because of your love and because of your faithfulness.

Psalm 115:1

The Refrain for the Morning Lessons

On this day the LORD has acted;* we will rejoice and be glad in it.

Psalm 118:24

A Reading

Mary set out at that time and went as quickly as she could into the hill country to a town in Judah. She went into Zechariah's house and greeted Elizabeth. Now it happened that as soon as Elizabeth heard Mary's greeting, the child leapt in her womb and Elizabeth was filled with the Holy Spirit. She gave a loud cry and said, 'Of all women you are the most blessed, and blessed is the fruit of your womb. Why should I be honored with a visit from the mother of my Lord? Look, the moment your greeting reached my ears, the child in my womb leapt for joy. Yes, blessed is she who believed that the promise made her by the Lord would be fulfilled.'

Luke 1:39–45

The Refrain

On this day the LORD has acted;* we will rejoice and be glad in it.

The Morning Psalm　　　　　　　　　　　*O LORD, I Am Your Servant*

O LORD, I am your servant;* I am your servant and the child of your handmaid; you have freed me from my bonds.
I will offer you the sacrifice of thanksgiving* and call upon the Name of the LORD.

I will fulfill my vows to the LORD* in the presence of all his people,
In the courts of the LORD's house,* in the midst of you, O Jerusalem. Hallelujah!

Psalm 116:14–17

The Refrain
On this day the LORD has acted;* we will rejoice and be glad in it.

The Cry of the Church
Let us praise the Lord, whom the Angels are praising, whom the Cherubim and
Seraphim proclaim: Holy, holy, holy!

THE SHORT BREVIARY

The Lord's Prayer

The Prayer Appointed for the Week
Stir up your power, O Lord, and with great might come among us; and, because
we are sorely hindered by our sins, let your bountiful grace and mercy speedily help and deliver us; through Jesus Christ our Lord, to whom, with you and
the Holy Spirit, be honor and glory now and for ever. *Amen.*†

The Concluding Prayer of the Church
Lord God, almighty and everlasting Father, you have brought me in safety to this
new day: Preserve me with your mighty power, that I may not fall into sin, nor
be overcome by adversity; and in all I do direct me to the fulfilling of your purpose; through Jesus Christ my Lord. *Amen.*†

The Midday Office   To Be Observed on the Hour or Half Hour
                                  Between 11 a.m. and 2 p.m.

The Call to Prayer
Bless the LORD, you angels of his, you mighty ones who do his bidding,* and hear-
ken to the voice of his word.
Bless the LORD, all you his hosts,* you ministers of his who do his will.
Bless the LORD, all you works of his, in all places of his dominion;* bless the LORD,
O my soul.

Psalm 103:20–22

The Request for Presence
I am a stranger here on earth;* do not hide your commandments from me.

Psalm 119:19

The Greeting
I am bound by the vow I made to you, O God;* I will present to you thank-
offerings;
For you have rescued my soul from death and my feet from stumbling,* that I may
walk before God in the light of the living.

Psalm 56:11–12

The Refrain for the Midday Lessons

Glory be to him whose power, working in us, can do infinitely more than we can ask or imagine; glory be to him from generation to generation in the Church and in Christ Jesus for ever and ever. Amen.

Ephesians 3:20–21

A Reading

Good faith has vanished; anyone abstaining from evil is victimized. YAHWEH saw this and was displeased that there was no fair judgement. He saw there was no one and wondered there was no one to intervene. So he made his own arm his mainstay, his own saving justice his support. He put on saving justice like a breastplate, on his head the helmet of salvation. He put on the clothes of vengeance like a tunic and wrapped himself in jealousy like a cloak. To each he repays his due, retribution to his enemies, reprisals on his foes, to the coasts and islands he will repay their due. From the west, YAHWEH's name will be feared, and from the east his glory, for he will come like a pent-up stream impelled by the breath of YAHWEH. Then for Zion will come a redeemer, for those who stop rebelling in Jacob, declares YAHWEH.

Isaiah 59:15–20

The Refrain

Glory be to him whose power, working in us, can do infinitely more than we can ask or imagine; glory be to him from generation to generation in the Church and in Christ Jesus for ever and ever. Amen.

The Midday Psalm   *He Has Made the Whole World So Sure It Cannot Be Moved*

The LORD is King; he has put on splendid apparel;* the LORD has put on his apparel and girded himself with strength.

He has made the whole world so sure* that it cannot be moved;

Ever since the world began, your throne has been established;* you are from everlasting.

The waters have lifted up, O LORD, the waters have lifted up their voice;* the waters have lifted up their pounding waves.

Mightier than the sound of many waters, mightier than the breakers of the sea,* mightier is the LORD who dwells on high.

Your testimonies are very sure,* and holiness adorns your house, O LORD, for ever and for evermore.

Psalm 93

The Refrain

Glory be to him whose power, working in us, can do infinitely more than we can ask or imagine; glory be to him from generation to generation in the Church and in Christ Jesus for ever and ever. Amen.

The Cry of the Church

Even so, come, Lord Jesus!

The Lord's Prayer

The Prayer Appointed for the Week
Stir up your power, O Lord, and with great might come among us; and, because
we are sorely hindered by our sins, let your bountiful grace and mercy speedily help and deliver us; through Jesus Christ our Lord, to whom, with you and
the Holy Spirit, be honor and glory now and for ever. *Amen.*†

The Concluding Prayer of the Church
O God, the King eternal, whose light divides the day from the night and turns the
shadow of death into the morning: Drive from me all wrong desires, incline my
heart to keep your law, and guide my feet into the way of peace; that, having
done your will with cheerfulness during the day, I may, when night comes,
rejoice to give you thanks; through Jesus Christ my Lord. *Amen.*†

The Vespers Office   **To Be Observed on the Hour or Half Hour**
                                          Between 5 and 8 p.m.

The Call to Prayer
Let the Name of the LORD be blessed,* from this time forth for evermore.
From the rising of the sun to its going down* let the Name of the LORD be praised.
Psalm 113:2–3

The Request for Presence
Hear my prayer, O God;* do not hide yourself from my petition.
Listen to me and answer me . . .
Psalm 55:1–2

The Greeting
The Lord is in his holy temple; let all the earth keep silence before him.
Traditional

The Hymn
At the name of Jesus every knee will bow,
Every tongue confess him King of glory now
'Tis the Father's pleasure, we should call him Lord,
Who from the beginning was the mighty Word.

In your hearts enthrone him; there, let him subdue
All that is not holy, all that is not true;
May your voice entreat him in temptation's hour;
Let his will enfold you in its light and power.

Brothers, this Lord Jesus shall return again,
With his Father's glory, o'er the earth to reign;
He is God the Savior; He is Christ the Lord,
Ever to be worshipped, always blessed, adored.
C. Noel

The Refrain for the Vespers Lessons

Put your trust in God;* for I will yet give thanks to him, who is the help of my
    countenance, and my God.

Psalm 42:7

The Vespers Psalm   *We Will Praise Your Name For Ever*

We have heard with our ears, O God, our forefathers have told us,* the deeds you
    did in their days, in the days of old.

How with your hand you drove the peoples out and planted our forefathers in the
    land;* how you destroyed nations and made your people flourish.

For they did not take the land by their sword, nor did their arm win the victory for
    them;* but your right hand, your arm, and the light of your countenance,
    because you favored them.

You are my King and my God;* you command victories for Jacob.

Through you we pushed back our adversaries;* through your Name we trampled
    on those who rose up against us.

For I do not rely on my bow,* and my sword does not give me the victory.

Surely, you gave us victory over our adversaries* and put those who hate us to
    shame.

Every day we gloried in God,* and we will praise your Name for ever.

Psalm 44:1–8

The Refrain

Put your trust in God;* for I will yet give thanks to him, who is the help of my
    countenance, and my God.

The Cry of the Church

O God, come to my assistance! O Lord, make haste to help me!

The Lord's Prayer

The Prayer Appointed for the Week

Stir up your power, O Lord, and with great might come among us; and, because
    we are sorely hindered by our sins, let your bountiful grace and mercy speed-
    ily help and deliver us; through Jesus Christ our Lord, to whom, with you and
    the Holy Spirit, be honor and glory now and for ever. *Amen.*†

The Concluding Prayer of the Church

Save me, Lord, while I am awake and keep me while I sleep, that I may wake with
    Christ and rest in peace. *Amen.*

The Morning Office   **To Be Observed on the Hour or Half Hour
                                      Between 6 and 9 a.m.**

The Call to Prayer

Come, let us sing to the LORD;* let us shout for joy to the Rock of our salvation.

Psalm 95:1

The Request for Presence
Bow your heavens, O LORD, and come down;* touch the mountains, and they shall
    smoke.

Psalm 144:5

The Greeting
My lips will sing with joy when I play to you,* and so will my soul, which you
    have redeemed.

Psalm 71:23

The Refrain for the Morning Lessons
Your love, O LORD, for ever will I sing;* from age to age my mouth will proclaim
    your faithfulness.

Psalm 89:1

A Reading
Because you have kept my commandment to persevere, I will keep you safe in the
    time of trial which is coming for the whole world, to put the people of the
    world to the test. I am coming soon: hold firmly to what you already have, and
    let no one take your victor's crown away from you. Anyone who proves victo-
    rious I will make into a pillar in the sanctuary of my God, and it will stay there
    for ever; I will inscribe on it the name of my God and the name of the city of my
    God, the new Jerusalem which is coming down from my God in heaven, and
    my own new name as well. Let anyone who can hear, listen to what the Spirit is
    saying to the churches.

Revelation 3:10–13

The Refrain
Your love, O LORD, for ever will I sing;* from age to age my mouth will proclaim
    your faithfulness.

The Morning Psalm   *His Mercy Is Great*
He has not dealt with us according to our sins,* nor rewarded us according to our
    wickedness.
For as the heavens are high above the earth,* so is his mercy great upon those who
    fear him.
As far as the east is from the west,* so far has he removed our sins from us.
As a father cares for his children,* so does the LORD care for those who fear him.
For he himself knows whereof we are made;* he remembers that we are but dust.

Psalm 103:10–13

The Refrain
Your love, O LORD, for ever will I sing;* from age to age my mouth will proclaim
    your faithfulness.

The Cry of the Church
Even so, come, Lord Jesus!

The Lord's Prayer

The Prayer Appointed for the Week

Stir up your power, O Lord, and with great might come among us; and, because
we are sorely hindered by our sins, let your bountiful grace and mercy speedily help and deliver us; through Jesus Christ our Lord, to whom, with you and
the Holy Spirit, be honor and glory now and for ever. *Amen.*†

The Concluding Prayer of the Church

Lord God, almighty and everlasting Father, you have brought me in safety to this
new day: Preserve me with your mighty power, that I may not fall into sin, nor
be overcome by adversity; and in all I do direct me to the fulfilling of your purpose; through Jesus Christ my Lord. *Amen.*†

The Midday Office   To Be Observed on the Hour or Half Hour
                                          Between 11 a.m. and 2 p.m.

The Call to Prayer

Praise God from whom all blessings flow; praise him, all creatures here below;
praise him above, you heavenly hosts; praise Father, Son and Holy Ghost.

Doxology

The Request for Presence

May the glory of the Lord endure for ever;* may the Lord rejoice in all his works.

Psalm 104:32

The Greeting

Hosanna, Lord, hosanna!* Lord, send us now success.
Blessed is he who comes in the name of the Lord; . . .
God is the Lord; he has shined upon us;* form a procession with branches up to
the horns of the altar.

Psalm 118:25–27

The Refrain for the Midday Lessons

I will walk in the presence of the Lord* in the land of the living.

Psalm 116:8

A Reading

Listen, my God, listen to us; open your eyes and look at our plight and at the city
that bears your name. Relying not on your upright deeds but on your great
mercy, we pour out our plea to you. Listen, Lord! Forgive, Lord! Hear, Lord,
and act! For your own sake, my God do not delay—since your city and your
people alike bear your name.

Daniel 9:18–19

The Refrain

I will walk in the presence of the Lord* in the land of the living.

The Midday Psalm   *The Works of the LORD Are Sure*

Rejoice in the LORD, you righteous;* it is good for the just to sing praises.
Praise the LORD with the harp;* play to him upon the psaltery and lyre.
Sing for him a new song;* sound a fanfare with all your skill upon the trumpet.
For the word of the LORD is right,* and all his works are sure.
He loves righteousness and justice;* the loving-kindness of the LORD fills the
     whole earth.

Psalm 33:1–5

The Refrain

I will walk in the presence of the LORD* in the land of the living.

The Cry of the Church

Even so, come, Lord Jesus!

The Lord's Prayer

The Prayer Appointed for the Week

Stir up your power, O Lord, and with great might come among us; and, because
     we are sorely hindered by our sins, let your bountiful grace and mercy speed-
     ily help and deliver us; through Jesus Christ our Lord, to whom, with you and
     the Holy Spirit, be honor and glory now and for ever. *Amen.*†

The Concluding Prayer of the Church

Almighty and eternal God, ruler of all things in heaven and earth: Mercifully
     accept the prayers of your people everywhere, and strengthen each of us to do
     your will; through Jesus Christ my Lord. *Amen.*†

The Vespers Office   **To Be Observed on the Hour or Half Hour**
                                                    Between 5 and 8 p.m.

The Call to Prayer

Praise the LORD, all you nations;* laud him, all you peoples.
For his loving-kindness toward us is great,* and the faithfulness of the LORD
     endures for ever. . . .

Psalm 117:1–2

The Request for Presence

O LORD, do not forsake me;* be not far from me, O my God.
Make haste to help me,* O Lord of my salvation.

Psalm 38:21–22

The Greeting

You are my refuge and shield;* my hope is in your word.

Psalm 119:114

The Hymn

> There's a song in the air! There's a star in the sky!
> There's a mother's deep prayer and a baby's low cry!
> And the star rains its fire while the beautiful sing,
> For the manger of Bethlehem cradles a King!

> There's a tumult of joy over the wonderful birth,
> For the Virgin's sweet boy is the Lord of the earth.
> Ay! The star rains its fire while the beautiful sing,
> For the manger of Bethlehem cradles a King!

> In the light of that star lie the ages impearled;
> And that song from afar has swept over the world.
> Every hearth is aflame, and the beautiful sing
> And we greet in His cradle our Savior and king!

Josiah Holland

The Refrain for the Vespers Lessons

. . . it is good for me to be near God;* I have made the Lord GOD my refuge.

Psalm 73:28

The Vespers Psalm   *Great Things Have You Done, O LORD My God*

I waited patiently upon the LORD;* he stooped to me and heard my cry.

He lifted me out of the desolate pit, out of the mire and clay;* he set my feet upon a high cliff and made my footing sure.

He put a new song in my mouth, a song of praise to our God;* many shall see, and stand in awe, and put their trust in the LORD.

Happy are they who trust in the LORD!* they do not resort to evil spirits or turn to false gods.

Great things are they that you have done, O LORD my God! how great your wonders and your plans for us!* there is none who can be compared with you.

Oh, that I could make them known and tell them!* but they are more than I can count.

Psalm 40:1–6

The Refrain

. . . it is good for me to be near God;* I have made the Lord GOD my refuge.

The Cry of the Church

Lord, have mercy on us. Christ, have mercy on us. Lord, have mercy on us.

The Lord's Prayer

The Prayer Appointed for the Week

Stir up your power, O Lord, and with great might come among us; and, because we are sorely hindered by our sins, let your bountiful grace and mercy speedily help and deliver us; through Jesus Christ our Lord, to whom, with you and the Holy Spirit, be honor and glory now and for ever. *Amen.*✝

The Concluding Prayer of the Church

Save me, O Lord, while I am awake and keep me while I sleep, that I may wake in
Christ and rest in peace.

adapted from The Short Breviary

The Morning Office   To Be Observed on the Hour or Half Hour
                                        Between 6 and 9 a.m.

The Call to Prayer

My mouth shall speak the praise of the Lord;* let all flesh bless his holy Name for
ever and ever.

Psalm 145:22

The Request for Presence

O Lamb of God, that takes away the sins of the world, have mercy on me.
O Lamb of God, that takes away the sins of the world, have mercy on me.
O Lamb of God, that takes away the sins of the world, grant me your peace.

Agnus Dei

The Greeting

Your love, O Lord, reaches to the heavens,* and your faithfulness to the clouds.

Psalm 36:5

The Refrain for the Morning Lessons

I will exalt you, O God my King,* and bless your Name for ever and ever.

Psalm 145:1

A Reading

Near the cross of Jesus stood his mother and his mother's sister, Mary the wife of
Clopas, and Mary of Magdela. Seeing his mother and the disciple whom he
loved standing near her, Jesus said to his mother, 'Woman, this is your son.'
Then to the disciple he said, 'This is your mother.' And from that hour the disciple took her into his home.

John 19:25–27

The Refrain

I will exalt you, O God my King,* and bless your Name for ever and ever.

The Morning Psalm   *The Lord Will Make Good His Purposes*

I will give thanks to you, O Lord, with my whole heart;* before the gods I will sing
your praise.
I will bow down toward your holy temple and praise your Name,* because of
your love and faithfulness;
For you have glorified your Name* and your word above all things.
When I called, you answered me;* you increased my strength within me.
All the kings of the earth will praise you, O Lord,* when they have heard the
words of your mouth.
They will sing of the ways of the Lord,* that great is the glory of the Lord.

Though the LORD be high, he cares for the lowly;* he perceives the haughty from afar.
Though I walk in the midst of trouble, you keep me safe;* you stretch forth your
hand against the fury of my enemies; your right hand shall save me.
The LORD will make good his purpose for me;* O LORD, your love endures for
ever; do not abandon the works of your hands.

Psalm 138

The Refrain
I will exalt you, O God my King,* and bless your Name for ever and ever.

The Cry of the Church
O God, come to my assistance! O Lord, make haste to help me!

The Lord's Prayer

The Prayer Appointed for the Week
Stir up your power, O Lord, and with great might come among us; and, because
we are sorely hindered by our sins, let your bountiful grace and mercy speedily help and deliver us; through Jesus Christ our Lord, to whom, with you and
the Holy Spirit, be honor and glory now and for ever. *Amen.*†

The Concluding Prayer of the Church
Lord God, almighty and everlasting Father, you have brought me in safety to this
new day: Preserve me with your mighty power, that I may not fall into sin, nor
be overcome by adversity; and in all I do direct me to the fulfilling of your purpose; through Jesus Christ my Lord. *Amen.*†

The Midday Office
To Be Observed on the Hour or Half Hour
Between 11 a.m. and 2 p.m.

The Call to Prayer
Bless the LORD, O my soul,* and all that is within me, bless his holy Name.

Psalm 103:1

The Request for Presence
Hearken to my voice, O LORD, when I call;* have mercy on me and answer me.
You speak in my heart and say, "Seek my face."* Your face, LORD, will I seek.
Hide not your face from me,* nor turn away your servant in displeasure.

Psalm 27:10–12

The Greeting
I restrain my feet from every evil way,* that I may keep your word.

Psalm 119:101

The Refrain for the Midday Lessons
For one day in your courts is better than a thousand in my own room,* and to stand
at the threshold of the house of my God than to dwell in the tents of the wicked.

Psalm 84:9

A Reading

As there were false prophets in the past history of our people, so you too will have your false teachers, who will insinuate their own disruptive views and, by disowning the Lord who brought them freedom, will bring upon themselves a speedy destruction. Many will copy their debauched behavior and the Way of Truth will be brought into disrepute on their account.

2 Peter 2:1–2

The Refrain

For one day in your courts is better than a thousand in my own room,* and to stand at the threshold of the house of my God than to dwell in the tents of the wicked.

The Midday Psalm   *Ascribe to the LORD the Glory Due His Name*

Ascribe to the LORD, you gods,* ascribe to the LORD glory and strength.

Ascribe to the LORD the glory due his Name;* worship the LORD in the beauty of holiness.

The voice of the LORD is upon the waters; the God of glory thunders;* the LORD is upon the mighty waters.

The voice of the LORD is a powerful voice;* the voice of the LORD is a voice of splendor.

The voice of the LORD breaks the cedar trees;* the LORD breaks the cedars of Lebanon;

He makes Lebanon skip like a calf,* and Mount Hermon like a young wild ox.

The voice of the LORD splits the flames of fire; the voice of the LORD shakes the wilderness;* the LORD shakes the wilderness of Kadesh.

The voice of the LORD makes the oak trees writhe* and strips the forests bare.

And in the temple of the LORD* all are crying, "Glory!"

Psalm 29:1–9

The Refrain

For one day in your courts is better than a thousand in my own room,* and to stand at the threshold of the house of my God than to dwell in the tents of the wicked.

The Cry of the Church

O Lamb of God, that takes away the sins of the world, have mercy upon me.
O Lamb of God, that takes away the sins of the world, have mercy upon me.
O Lamb of God, that takes away the sins of the world, grant me your peace.

The Lord's Prayer

The Prayer Appointed for the Week

Stir up your power, O Lord, and with great might come among us; and, because we are sorely hindered by our sins, let your bountiful grace and mercy speedily help and deliver us; through Jesus Christ our Lord, to whom, with you and the Holy Spirit, be honor and glory now and for ever. *Amen.*†

The Concluding Prayer of the Church

God of justice, God of mercy, bless all those who are surprised with pain this day
from suffering caused by their own weakness or that of others. Let what we
suffer teach us to be merciful; let our sins teach us to forgive. This we ask
through the intercession of Jesus and all who died forgiving those who
oppressed them. *Amen.*

THE NEW COMPANION TO THE BREVIARY

The Vespers Office   To Be Observed on the Hour or Half Hour
Between 5 and 8 p.m.

The Call to Prayer

Praise the LORD, all you nations;* laud him, all you peoples.
For his loving-kindness toward us is great,* and the faithfulness of the LORD
endures for ever. Hallelujah!

Psalm 117

The Request for Presence

Gladden the soul of your servant,* for to you, O LORD, I lift up my soul.

Psalm 86:4

The Greeting

One generation shall praise your works to another* and shall declare your power.

Psalm 145:4

The Hymn

Sing praise to God who reigns above, the God of all creation,
The God of power, the God of love, the God of our salvation;
With healing balm my soul he fills, And every faithless murmur stills:
To God all praise and glory.

What God's almighty power has made, his gracious mercy keeps;
By morning glow or evening shade his watchful eye ne'er sleeps;
Within the kingdom of his might, Lo! All is just and all is right:
To God all praise and glory.

Then all my gladsome way along, I sing aloud your praises,
That men may hear the grateful song my voice unwearied raises;
Be joyful in the Lord, my heart, both soul and body, bear your part:
To God all praise and glory.

O you who name Christ's holy name, give God all praise and glory;
All you who own his power, proclaim aloud the wondrous story!
Cast each false idol from his throne. The Lord is God and he alone:
To God all praise and glory.

Johann Schultz

The Refrain for the Vespers Lessons
Happy are they all who fear the LORD,* and who follow in his ways!

Psalm 128:1

The Vespers Psalm   *The LORD of Hosts Is the King of Glory*
Lift up your heads, O gates; lift them high, O everlasting doors;* and the King of
    glory shall come in.
"Who is this King of glory?"* "The LORD, strong and mighty, the LORD, mighty in
    battle."
Lift up your heads, O gates; lift them high, O everlasting doors;* and the King of
    glory shall come in.
"Who is he, this King of glory?"* "The LORD of hosts, he is the King of glory."

Psalm 24:7–10

The Refrain
Happy are they all who fear the LORD,* and who follow in his ways!

The Cry of the Church
Even so, come, Lord Jesus!

The Lord's Prayer

The Prayer Appointed for the Week
Stir up your power, O Lord, and with great might come among us; and, because
    we are sorely hindered by our sins, let your bountiful grace and mercy speed-
    ily help and deliver us; through Jesus Christ our Lord, to whom, with you and
    the Holy Spirit, be honor and glory now and for ever. *Amen.*†

The Concluding Prayer of the Church
May Almighty God grant me a peaceful night and a perfect end. *Amen.*

The Morning Office   **To Be Observed on the Hour or Half Hour**
                                      Between 6 and 9 a.m.

The Call to Prayer
Open my lips, O LORD,* and my mouth shall proclaim your praise.

Psalm 51:16

The Request for Presence
Bow down your ear, O LORD, and answer me . . .
Keep watch over my life, for I am faithful.

Psalm 86:1–2

The Greeting
Lord, you have been our refuge* from one generation to another.
Before the mountains were brought forth, or the land and the earth were born,*
    from age to age you are God.

Psalm 90:1–2

The Refrain for the Morning Lessons

Truly, his salvation is very near to those who fear him,* that his glory may dwell in our land.

Psalm 85:9

A Reading

The beginning of the gospel about Jesus Christ, the Son of God. It is written in the prophet of Isaiah: *Look, I am going to send my messenger in front of you to prepare your way before you. A voice of one that cries in the desert: Prepare a way for the Lord, make his paths straight.* John the Baptist was in the desert, proclaiming a baptism of repentance for the forgiveness of sins.

Mark 1:1–4

The Refrain

Truly, his salvation is very near to those who fear him,* that his glory may dwell in our land.

The Morning Psalm   *Bless Our God, You People*

Come now and see the works of God,* how wonderful he is in his doing toward all people.

In his might he rules for ever; his eyes keep watch over the nations;* let no rebel rise up against him.

Bless our God, you peoples;* make the voice of his praise to be heard;

Who holds our souls in life,* and will not allow our feet to slip.

Psalm 66:4, 6–8

The Refrain

Truly, his salvation is very near to those who fear him,* that his glory may dwell in our land.

The Cry of the Church

Be, Lord, my helper and forsake me not. Do not despise me, O God, my savior.

THE SHORT BREVIARY

The Lord's Prayer

The Prayer Appointed for the Week

Stir up your power, O Lord, and with great might come among us; and, because we are sorely hindered by our sins, let your bountiful grace and mercy speedily help and deliver us; through Jesus Christ our Lord, to whom, with you and the Holy Spirit, be honor and glory now and for ever. *Amen.*†

The Concluding Prayer of the Church

Lord God, almighty and everlasting Father, you have brought me in safety to this new day: Preserve me with your mighty power, that I may not fall into sin, nor be overcome by adversity; and in all I do direct me to the fulfilling of your purpose; through Jesus Christ my Lord. *Amen.*†

The Midday Office   To Be Observed on the Hour or Half Hour
Between 11 a.m. and 2 p.m.

The Call to Prayer
Sing to God, O kingdoms of the earth;* sing praises to the Lord.
He rides in the heavens, the ancient heavens;* he sends forth his voice, his mighty
voice.

Psalm 68:33–34

The Request for Presence
For God alone my soul in silence waits;* from him comes my salvation.

Psalm 62:1

The Greeting
Awesome things will you show us in your righteousness,* O God of our salvation,
O Hope of all the ends of the earth . . .

Psalm 65:5

The Refrain for the Midday Lessons
Happy are they who trust in the LORD!

Psalm 40:4

A Reading
Go up on a high mountain, messenger of Zion. Shout as loud as you can, messenger of Jerusalem! Shout fearlessly, say to the towns of Judah, 'Here is your
God.' Here is Lord YAHWEH coming with power, his arm maintains his authority, his reward is with him and his prize precedes him. He is like a shepherd
feeding his flock, gathering lambs in his arms, holding them against his breast
and leading to their rest the mother ewes.

Isaiah 40:9–11

The Refrain
Happy are they who trust in the LORD!

The Midday Psalm   *Light Shines in the Darkness for the Upright*
Hallelujah! Happy are they who fear the Lord* and have great delight in his
commandments!
Their descendants will be mighty in the land;* the generation of the upright will
be blessed.
Wealth and riches will be in their house,* and their righteousness will last for ever.
Light shines in the darkness for the upright;* the righteous are merciful and full of
compassion.
It is good for them to be generous in lending* and to manage their affairs with
justice.
For they will never be shaken;* the righteous will be kept in everlasting
remembrance.
They will not be afraid of any evil rumors;* their heart is right; they put their trust
in the Lord.

Their heart is established and will not shrink,* until they see their desire upon
their enemies.
They have given freely to the poor,* and their righteousness stands fast for ever;
they will hold up their head with honor.
The wicked will see it and be angry; they will gnash their teeth and pine away;*
the desires of the wicked will perish.

Psalm 112

The Refrain
Happy are they who trust in the LORD!

The Cry of the Church
Be, Lord, my helper and forsake me not. Do not despise me, O God, my savior.

THE SHORT BREVIARY

The Lord's Prayer

The Prayer Appointed for the Week
Stir up your power, O Lord, and with great might come among us; and, because
we are sorely hindered by our sins, let your bountiful grace and mercy speedily help and deliver us; through Jesus Christ our Lord, to whom, with you and
the Holy Spirit, be honor and glory now and for ever. *Amen.*†

The Concluding Prayer of the Church
May God have mercy on me, forgive me my sins and bring me to life everlasting.
In Jesus' name. *Amen.*

The Vespers Office   To Be Observed on the Hour or Half Hour
                                      Between 5 and 8 p.m.

The Call to Prayer
Let us come before his presence with thanksgiving* and raise a loud shout to him
with psalms.

Psalm 95:2

The Request for Presence
Remember not our past sins; let your compassion be swift to meet us;* for we have
been brought very low.
Help us, O God our Savior, for the glory of your Name;* deliver us and forgive us
our sins, for your Name's sake.

Psalm 79:8–9

The Greeting
Exalt yourself above the heavens, O God,* and your glory over all the earth.

Psalm 57:11

The Hymn

Celestial Word, proceeding from
The Eternal Father's breast,
And in the wend of ages come
To aid a world distressed:

Enlighten, Lord, and set on fire
Our Spirits with Your love,
That dead to earth they may aspire
And live to joys above.

To God the Father, God the Son
And Holy Ghost to Thee
As heretofore, when time is done
Unending glory be.

adapted from The Short Breviary

The Refrain for the Vespers Lessons
. . . when the Lord restores the fortunes of his people, Jacob will rejoice and Israel be glad.

Psalm 14:7b

The Vespers Psalm   *The Eyes of All Wait Upon You, O Lord*
The Lord is faithful in all his words* and merciful in all his deeds.
The Lord upholds all those who fall;* he lifts up those who are bowed down.
The eyes of all wait upon you, O Lord,* and you give them their food in due season.
You open wide your hand* and satisfy the needs of every living creature.
The Lord is righteous in all his ways* and loving in all his works.

Psalm 145:14–18

The Refrain
. . . when the Lord restores the fortunes of his people, Jacob will rejoice and Israel be glad.

The Cry of the Church
Even so, come, Lord Jesus!

The Lord's Prayer

The Prayer Appointed for the Week
Stir up your power, O Lord, and with great might come among us; and, because we are sorely hindered by our sins, let your bountiful grace and mercy speedily help and deliver us; through Jesus Christ our Lord, to whom, with you and the Holy Spirit, be honor and glory now and for ever. *Amen.†*

The Concluding Prayer of the Church
Blessed be the Lord God of Israel for he has visited and delivered us. Alleluia, alleluia, alleluia.

Traditional

The Morning Office

To Be Observed on the Hour or Half Hour
Between 6 and 9 a.m.

The Call to Prayer
I will call upon God,* and the Lord will deliver me.
In the evening, in the morning, and at noonday, I will complain and lament,* and
    he will hear my voice.
He will bring me safely back . . . * God, who is enthroned of old, will hear me.
Psalm 55:17ff

The Request for Presence
Be pleased, O God, to deliver me;* O Lord, make haste to help me.
Psalm 70:1

The Greeting
Happy are they whom you choose and draw to your courts to dwell there!* they
    will be satisfied by the beauty of your house, by the holiness of your temple.
Psalm 65:4

The Refrain for the Morning Lessons
Our soul waits for the Lord;* he is our help and our shield.
Psalm 33:20

A Reading
Now his mother and his brothers arrived, and standing outside, sent in a message
    asking for him. A crowd was sitting round him at the time the message was
    passed to him, 'Look, your mother and brothers and sisters are outside asking
    for you.' He replied, 'Who are my mother and my brothers? Anyone who does
    the will of God, that person is my brother and sister and mother.'
Mark 3:31–35

The Refrain
Our soul waits for the Lord;* he is our help and our shield.

The Morning Psalm   *For God Alone My Soul in Silence Waits*
For God alone my soul in silence waits;* truly, my hope is in him.
He alone is my rock and my salvation,* my stronghold, so that I shall not be
    shaken.
In God is my safety and my honor;* God is my strong rock and my refuge.
Put your trust in him always, O people,* pour out your hearts before him, for God
    is our refuge.
Those of high degree are but a fleeting breath,* even those of low estate cannot be
    trusted.
On the scales they are lighter than a breath,* all of them together.
Put no trust in extortion; in robbery take no empty pride;* though wealth increase,
    set not your heart upon it.

God has spoken once, twice have I heard it,* that power belongs to God.
Steadfast love is yours, O Lord,* for you repay everyone according to his deeds.

Psalm 62:6–14

The Refrain
Our soul waits for the LORD;* he is our help and our shield.

The Cry of the Church
O God, come to my assistance! O Lord, make haste to help me!

The Lord's Prayer

The Prayer Appointed for the Week
Stir up your power, O Lord, and with great might come among us; and, because
we are sorely hindered by our sins, let your bountiful grace and mercy speedily help and deliver us; through Jesus Christ our Lord, to whom, with you and
the Holy Spirit, be honor and glory now and for ever. *Amen.*†

The Concluding Prayer of the Church
Lord God, almighty and everlasting Father, you have brought me in safety to this
new day: Preserve me with your mighty power, that I may not fall into sin, nor
be overcome by adversity; and in all I do direct me to the fulfilling of your purpose; through Jesus Christ my Lord. *Amen.*†

The Midday Office   To Be Observed on the Hour or Half Hour
                                         Between 11 a.m. and 2 p.m.

The Call to Prayer
Sing to the LORD with thanksgiving;* make music to our God upon the harp.

Psalm 147:7

The Request for Presence
Hear, O Shepherd of Israel, leading Joseph like a flock;* shine forth, you that are
enthroned upon the cherubim.

Psalm 80:1

The Greeting
Exalt yourself above the heavens, O God,* and your glory over all the earth.

Psalm 57:6

The Refrain for the Midday Lessons
The LORD has sworn and he will not recant:* "You are a priest for ever after the
order of Melchizedek."

Psalm 110:4

A Reading
Whoever believes that Jesus is the Christ is a child of God, and whoever loves the
father loves the son. In this way we know that we love God's children, when
we love God and keep his commandments. This is what the love of God is:

keeping his commandments. Nor are his commandments burdensome, because every child of God overcomes the world. And this is the victory that has overcome the world—our faith.

1 John 5:1–4

The Refrain
The LORD has sworn and he will not recant:* "You are a priest for ever after the order of Melchizedek."

The Midday Psalm   *All Kings Shall Bow Down Before Him*
All kings shall bow down before him,* and all the nations do him service.
For he shall deliver the poor who cries out in distress,* and the oppressed who has no helper.
He shall have pity on the lowly and poor;* he shall preserve the lives of the needy.
He shall redeem their lives from oppression and violence,* and dear shall their blood be in his sight.
Long may he live! and may there be given to him gold from Arabia;* may prayer be made for him always, and may they bless him all the day long.
May there be abundance of grain on the earth, growing thick even on the hilltops;* may its fruit flourish like Lebanon, and its grain like grass upon the earth.
May his Name remain for ever and be established as long as the sun endures;* may all the nations bless themselves in him and call him blessed.
Blessed be the Lord GOD, the God of Israel,* who alone does wondrous deeds!
And blessed be his glorious Name for ever!* and may all the earth be filled with his glory. Amen. Amen.

Psalm 72:11–19

The Refrain
The LORD has sworn and he will not recant:* "You are a priest for ever after the order of Melchizedek."

The Cry of the Church
Even so, come, Lord Jesus!

The Lord's Prayer

The Prayer Appointed for the Week
Stir up your power, O Lord, and with great might come among us; and, because we are sorely hindered by our sins, let your bountiful grace and mercy speedily help and deliver us; through Jesus Christ our Lord, to whom, with you and the Holy Spirit, be honor and glory now and for ever. *Amen.*†

The Concluding Prayer of the Church
Lord Jesus Christ, by your death you took away the sting of death: Grant me to so follow in faith where you have led the way, that I may at length fall asleep peacefully in you and wake in your likeness; for your tender mercies' sake. *Amen.*†

The Vespers Office   To Be Observed on the Hour or Half Hour
                                              Between 5 and 8 p.m.

The Call to Prayer
I will call upon the Lord,* and so shall I be saved from my enemies.

> *Psalm 18:3*

The Request for Presence
I have said to the Lord, "You are my God;* Listen, O Lord, to my supplication."

> *Psalm 140:6*

The Greeting
But you, O Lord my God, oh, deal with me according to your Name;* for your ten-
der mercy's sake, deliver me.
For I am poor and needy,* and my heart is wounded within me.

> *Psalm 109:20–21*

The Hymn

Hail to the Lord's Anointed, great David's greater Son!
Hail in the time appointed, his reign on earth begun!
He comes to break oppression, to set the captive free;
To take away transgression, and rule in equity.

He comes with succor speedy to those who suffer wrong;
To help the poor and needy, and bid the weak be strong;
To give them songs for sighing, their darkness turn to light,
Whose souls condemned and dying, are precious in his sight.

He shall come down like showers upon the fruitful earth;
Love, joy, and hope like flowers, spring in his path to birth.
Before him, on the mountains, shall peace, the herald, go,
And righteousness, in fountains, from hill and valley flow.

To him shall prayer unceasing and daily vows ascend;
His kingdom still increasing, a kingdom without end.
The tide of time shall never his covenant remove;
His name shall stand forever; that name to us is love.

> *James Montgomery*

The Refrain for the Vespers Lessons
For the Lord has heard the sound of my weeping.
The Lord has heard my supplication;* the Lord accepts my prayer.

> *Psalm 6:8–9*

The Vespers Psalm   *The God of Gods Will Reveal Himself in Zion*
How dear to me is your dwelling, O Lord of hosts!* My soul has a desire and
longing for the courts of the Lord; my heart and my flesh rejoice in the living God.
The sparrow has found her a house and the swallow a nest where she may lay her
young;* by the side of your altars, O Lord of hosts, my King and my God.

Happy are they who dwell in your house!* they will always be praising you.
Happy are the people whose strength is in you!* whose hearts are set on the
pilgrims' way.
Those who go through the desolate valley will find it a place of springs,* for the
early rains have covered it with pools of water.
They will climb from height to height,* and the God of gods will reveal himself in
Zion.

Psalm 84:1–6

The Refrain
For the Lord has heard the sound of my weeping.
The Lord has heard my supplication;* the Lord accepts my prayer.

The Cry of the Church
Be, Lord, my helper and forsake me not. Do not despise me, O God, my savior.
THE SHORT BREVIARY

The Lord's Prayer

The Prayer Appointed for the Week
Stir up your power, O Lord, and with great might come among us; and, because
we are sorely hindered by our sins, let your bountiful grace and mercy speedily help and deliver us; through Jesus Christ our Lord, to whom, with you and
the Holy Spirit, be honor and glory now and for ever. *Amen.†*

Concluding Prayers of the Church
Almighty God, who has promised to hear the petitions of those who ask in your
Son's Name: I beseech you mercifully to incline your ear to me who have made
my prayers and supplications to you; and grant that those things which I have
faithfully asked according to your will, I may effectually obtain, to the relief of
my necessity, and to the setting forth of your glory; through Jesus Christ my
Lord. *Amen.†*

May the souls of the faithful departed, through the mercy of God, rest in eternal
peace. *Amen.*

The Morning Office   **To Be Observed on the Hour or Half Hour
Between 6 and 9 a.m.**

The Call to Prayer
Proclaim with me the greatness of the Lord;* let us exalt his Name together.

Psalm 34:3

The Request for Presence
Open my eyes, that I may see* the wonders of your law.

Psalm 119:18

The Greeting
I will confess you among the peoples, O Lord;* I will sing praise to you among the
nations.

For your loving-kindness is greater than the heavens,* and your faithfulness
    reaches to the clouds.

Psalm 57:9–10

The Refrain for the Morning Lessons
Let the sorrowful sighing of the prisoners come before you,* and by your great
    might spare those who are condemned to die.

Psalm 79:11

A Reading
Zechariah, the father of John the Baptizer, being filled with the Holy Spirit, spoke
    this prophecy about his son, saying: "And you, little child, you shall be called
    Prophet of the Most High, for you will go before *the Lord to prepare a way for him*,
    to give his people knowledge of salvation through forgiveness of their sins,
    because of the faithful love of our God in which the rising Sun has come from
    on high to visit us, to give light to *those who live in darkness and the shadow dark as
    death*, and to guide our feet into *the way of peace*."

Luke 1:76–79

The Refrain
Let the sorrowful sighing of the prisoners come before you,* and by your great
    might spare those who are condemned to die.

The Morning Psalm   *Arise, O God, and Rule the Earth*
God takes his stand in the council of heaven;* he gives judgment in the midst of
    the gods:
"How long will you judge unjustly,* and show favor to the wicked?
Save the weak and the orphan;* defend the humble and needy;
Rescue the weak and the poor;* deliver them from the power of the wicked.
They do not know, neither do they understand;* they go about in darkness; all the
    foundations of the earth are shaken.
Now I say to you, 'You are gods,* and all of you children of the Most High;
Nevertheless, you shall die like mortals,* and fall like any prince.' "
Arise, O God, and rule the earth,* for you shall take all nations for your own.

Psalm 82

The Refrain
Let the sorrowful sighing of the prisoners come before you,* and by your great
    might spare those who are condemned to die.

The Cry of the Church
Even so, come, Lord Jesus!

The Lord's Prayer

The Prayer Appointed for the Week
Stir up your power, O Lord, and with great might come among us; and, because
    we are sorely hindered by our sins, let your bountiful grace and mercy speed-

ily help and deliver us; through Jesus Christ our Lord, to whom, with you and
the Holy Spirit, be honor and glory now and for ever. *Amen*.†

The Concluding Prayer of the Church
Lord God, almighty and everlasting Father, you have brought me in safety to this
new day: Preserve me with your mighty power, that I may not fall into sin, nor
be overcome by adversity; and in all I do direct me to the fulfilling of your purpose; through Jesus Christ my Lord. *Amen*.†

The Midday Office   To Be Observed on the Hour or Half Hour
                                              Between 11 a.m. and 2 p.m.

The Call to Prayer
'Come, we will go up to YAHWEH's mountain, to the Temple of the God of Jacob so
that he may teach us his ways and we may walk in his paths.'

Micah 4:2

The Request for Presence
Hear, O Shepherd of Israel, leading Joseph like a flock;* shine forth, you that are
enthroned upon the cherubim.

Psalm 80:1

The Greeting
The LORD lives! Blessed is my Rock!* Exalted is the God of my salvation!

Psalm 18:46

The Refrain for the Midday Lessons
"I will appoint a time," says God;* "I will judge with equity. . . ."

Psalm 75:2

A Reading
But you (Bethlehem) Ephrathah, the least of the clans of Judah, from you will
come for me a future ruler of Israel whose origins go back to the distant past, to
the days of old. Hence YAHWEH will abandon them only until she who is in
labor gives birth, and then those who survive of his race will be reunited to the
Israelites. He will take his stand and he will shepherd them with the power of
YAHWEH, with the majesty of the name of his God, and they will be secure, for
his greatness will extend henceforth to the most distant parts of the country.

Micah 5:1–3

The Refrain
"I will appoint a time," says God;* "I will judge with equity. . . ."

The Midday Psalm   *Your Dominion Endures Throughout the Ages*
I will exalt you, O God my King,* and bless your Name for ever and ever.
Every day will I bless you* and praise your Name for ever and ever.
Great is the LORD and greatly to be praised;* there is no end to his greatness.
One generation shall praise your works to another* and shall declare your power.

I will ponder the glorious splendor of your majesty* and all your marvelous works.

They shall speak of the might of your wondrous acts,* and I will tell of your greatness.

They shall publish the remembrance of your great goodness;* they shall sing of your righteous deeds.

The LORD is gracious and full of compassion,* slow to anger and of great kindness.

The LORD is loving to everyone* and his compassion is over all his works.

All your works praise you, O LORD,* and your faithful servants bless you.

They make known the glory of your kingdom* and speak of your power;

That the peoples may know of your power* and the glorious splendor of your kingdom.

Your kingdom is an everlasting kingdom;* your dominion endures throughout all ages.

Psalm 145:1–13

The Refrain
"I will appoint a time," says God;* "I will judge with equity. . . ."

The Cry of the Church
Even so, come, Lord Jesus!

The Lord's Prayer

The Prayer Appointed for the Week
Stir up your power, O Lord, and with great might come among us; and, because we are sorely hindered by our sins, let your bountiful grace and mercy speedily help and deliver us; through Jesus Christ our Lord, to whom, with you and the Holy Spirit, be honor and glory now and for ever. *Amen.*†

The Concluding Prayer of the Church
O God, the source of eternal light: Shed forth your unending day upon all of us who watch for you, that our lips may praise you, our lives may bless you, and our worship may give you glory; through Jesus Christ our Lord. *Amen.*†

The Vespers Office   To Be Observed on the Hour or Half Hour
Between 5 and 8 p.m.

The Call to Prayer
Come now and look upon the works of the LORD,* what awesome things he has done on earth.

Psalm 46:9

The Request for Presence
Hear my cry, O God,* and listen to my prayer.
I call upon you from the ends of the earth . . .

Psalm 61:1–2

The Greeting

O ruler of the universe, Lord God, great deeds are they that you have done, surpassing human understanding.

Your ways are ways of righteousness and truth, O King of all the ages.

Traditional

The Hymn

When morning gilds the skies, my heart awaking cries,
May Jesus Christ be praised!
Alike at work and prayer, to Jesus I repair;
May Jesus Christ be praised.

Whenever the church bell peals over hill and dell,
May Jesus Christ be praised!
O hark to what it sings, as joyously it rings,
May Jesus Christ be praised.

The night becomes as day, when from the heart we say,
May Jesus Christ be praised!
The powers of darkness fear, when this sweet chant they hear,
May Jesus Christ be praised.

In heaven's eternal bliss the loveliest strain is this,
May Jesus Christ be praised!
Let earth, and sea, and sky, from depth to height reply,
May Jesus Christ be praised.

German

The Refrain for the Vespers Lessons

Happy are those who act with justice* and always do what is right!

Psalm 106:3

The Vespers Psalm *The LORD Comes in Holiness*

The Lord gave the word;* great was the company of women who bore the tidings:

"Kings with their armies are fleeing away;* the women at home are dividing the spoils."

Though you lingered among the sheepfolds,* you shall be like a dove whose wings are covered with silver, whose feathers are like green gold.

When the Almighty scattered kings,* it was like snow falling in Zalmon.

O mighty mountain, O hill of Bashan!* O rugged mountain, O hill of Bashan!

Why do you look with envy, O rugged mountain, at the hill which God chose for his resting place?* truly, the LORD will dwell there for ever.

The chariots of God are twenty thousand, even thousands of thousands;* the Lord comes in holiness from Sinai.

You have gone up on high and led captivity captive; you have received gifts even from your enemies,* that the LORD God might dwell among them.

Blessed be the Lord day by day,* the God of our salvation, who bears our burdens.

He is our God, the God of our salvation;* God is the LORD, by whom we escape
    death.

Psalm 68:11–20

The Refrain
Happy are those who act with justice* and always do what is right!

The Cry of the Church
Even so, come, Lord Jesus!

The Lord's Prayer

The Prayer Appointed for the Week
Stir up your power, O Lord, and with great might come among us; and, because
    we are sorely hindered by our sins, let your bountiful grace and mercy speed-
    ily help and deliver us; through Jesus Christ our Lord, to whom, with you and
    the Holy Spirit, be honor and glory now and for ever. *Amen.*†

The Concluding Prayer of the Church
Almighty God, who after the creation of the world rested from all your works and
    sanctified a day of rest for all your creatures: Grant that I, putting away all
    earthly anxieties, may be duly prepared for the service of public worship, and
    grant as well that my Sabbath upon earth may be a preparation for the eternal
    rest promised to your people in heaven; through Jesus Christ our Lord. *Amen.*†

∼⁂∽

The Morning Office   To Be Observed on the Hour or Half Hour
                                                      Between 6 and 9 a.m.

The Call to Prayer
Sing to the LORD and bless his Name;* proclaim the good news of his salvation
    from day to day.
Declare his glory among the nations* and his wonders among all peoples.
For great is the LORD and greatly to be praised;* he is more to be feared than all
    gods.

Psalm 96:2–4

The Request for Presence
Satisfy us by your loving-kindness in the morning;* so shall we rejoice and be glad
    all the days of our life.

Psalm 90:14

The Greeting
Awesome things will you show us in your righteousness, O God of our salvation,*
  O Hope of all the ends of the earth and of the seas that are far away.

Psalm 65:5

The Refrain for the Morning Lessons
You shall not be afraid of any terror by night,* nor of the arrow that flies by day.

Psalm 91:5

A Reading   *During the fourth and final week of Advent, the Church is mindful*
                  in particular of the life and role of St. Joseph, husband of the
                  Virgin and earthly father to our Lord.

This is how Jesus Christ came to be born. His mother Mary was betrothed to
  Joseph; but before they came to live together she was found to be with child
  through the Holy Spirit. Her husband Joseph, being an upright man and wanting to spare her disgrace, decided to divorce her informally. He had made up
  his mind to do this when suddenly the angel of the Lord appeared to him in a
  dream and said, 'Joseph son of David, do not be afraid to take Mary home as
  your wife, because she has conceived what is in her by the Holy Spirit. She will
  give birth to a son and you must name him Jesus, because he is the one who is
  to save his people from their sins.' Now all this took place to fulfill what the
  Lord had spoken through the prophet: *Look! The virgin is with child and will give
  birth to a son whom they will call Immanuel,* a name which means 'God-is-with-
  us.' When Joseph woke up he did what the angel of the Lord had told him to
  do: he took his wife to his home; he had not had intercourse with her when she
  gave birth to a son; and he named him Jesus.

Matthew 1:18–25

The Refrain
You shall not be afraid of any terror by night,* nor of the arrow that flies by day.

The Morning Psalm   *Let the Name of the LORD Be Blessed*
Hallelujah! Give praise, you servants of the LORD;* praise the Name of the LORD.
Let the Name of the LORD be blessed,* from this time forth for evermore.
From the rising of the sun to its going down* let the Name of the LORD be praised.
The LORD is high above all nations,* and his glory above the heavens.
Who is like the LORD our God, who sits enthroned on high* but stoops to behold
  the heavens and the earth?
He takes up the weak out of the dust* and lifts up the poor from the ashes.
He sets them with the princes,* with the princes of his people.
He makes the woman of a childless house* to be a joyful mother of children.

Psalm 113

The Refrain
You shall not be afraid of any terror by night,* nor of the arrow that flies by day.

The Cry of the Church
O Lord, hear my prayer and let my cry come unto you. Thanks be to God.
THE SHORT BREVIARY

The Lord's Prayer

The Prayer Appointed for the Week
Purify my conscience, Almighty God, by your daily visitation, that your Son Jesus
Christ, at his coming, may find in me a mansion prepared for himself; who
lives and reigns with you and the Holy Spirit, one God, now and for ever.
Amen.†

The Concluding Prayer of the Church
Lord God, almighty and everlasting Father, you have brought me in safety to this
new day: Preserve me with your mighty power, that I may not fall into sin, nor
be overcome by adversity; and in all I do direct me to the fulfilling of your purpose; through Jesus Christ my Lord. *Amen.*†

The Midday Office   To Be Observed on the Hour or Half Hour
                           Between 11 a.m. and 2 p.m.

The Call to Prayer
God has gone up with a shout,* the LORD with the sound of the ram's-horn.
Sing praises to God, sing praises;* sing praises to our King, sing praises.
For God is King of all the earth;* sing praises with all your skill.
God reigns over the nations;* God sits upon his holy throne.
Psalm 47:5–8

The Request for Presence
Let the peoples praise you, O God;* let all the peoples praise you.
Psalm 67:3

The Greeting
For you alone are the Holy One, you alone are the Lord, you alone are the Most
High, Jesus Christ, with the Holy Spirit, in the glory of God the Father.

The Refrain for the Midday Lessons
Tell it out among the nations: "The LORD is King!"
Psalm 96:10

A Reading
Look, the days are coming, YAHWEH declares, when I shall raise an upright Branch
of David; he will reign as king and be wise, doing what is just and upright in
the country. In his days Judah will triumph and Israel live in safety. And this is
the name he will be called, 'Yahweh-is-our-Saving-Justice.'
Jeremiah 23:5–6

The Refrain
Tell it out among the nations: "The LORD is King!"

The Midday Psalm   *Great Are the Deeds of the* Lord

Hallelujah! I will give thanks to the Lord with my whole heart,* in the assembly of
the upright, in the congregation.

Great are the deeds of the Lord!* they are studied by all who delight in them.

His work is full of majesty and splendor,* and his righteousness endures for ever.

He makes his marvelous works to be remembered;* the Lord is gracious and full
of compassion.

He gives food to those who fear him;* he is ever mindful of his covenant.

He has shown his people the power of his works* in giving them the lands of the
nations.

The works of his hands are faithfulness and justice;* all his commandments are sure.

They stand fast for ever and ever,* because they are done in truth and equity.

He sent redemption to his people; he commanded his covenant for ever;* holy and
awesome is his Name.

The fear of the Lord is the beginning of wisdom;* those who act accordingly have
a good understanding; his praise endures for ever.

Psalm 111

The Refrain
Tell it out among the nations: "The Lord is King!"

The Cry of the Church
Even so, come, Lord Jesus!

The Lord's Prayer

The Prayer Appointed for the Week
Purify my conscience, Almighty God, by your daily visitation, that your Son Jesus
Christ, at his coming, may find in me a mansion prepared for himself; who lives
and reigns with you and the Holy Spirit, one God, now and for ever. *Amen.*†

The Concluding Prayer of the Church
O God, you make me glad with the weekly remembrance of the glorious resurrection of your Son my Lord: Give me this day such blessing through my worship
of you, that the week to come may be spent in your favor; through Jesus Christ
our Lord. *Amen.*†

The Vespers Office   To Be Observed on the Hour or Half Hour
                                                    Between 5 and 8 p.m.

The Call to Prayer
Open my lips, O Lord,* and my mouth shall proclaim your praise.

Psalm 51:16

The Request for Presence
"Hear, O Lord, and have mercy upon me;* O Lord, be my helper."

Psalm 30:11

The Greeting
Blessed be the Lord GOD, the God of Israel,* who alone does wondrous deeds!
And blessed be his glorious Name for ever!* and may all the earth be filled with
 his glory. Amen. Amen.

Psalm 72:18–19

The Hymn

Savior of the nations, come;
Virgin's Son, here make your home!
Marvel now, O heaven and earth,
That the Lord chose such a birth.

Not by human flesh and blood;
By the Spirit of our God
Was the word of God made flesh,
Woman's offspring, pure and fresh.

Martin Luther

The Refrain for the Vespers Lessons
It is better to rely on the LORD* than to put any trust in flesh.
It is better to rely on the LORD* than to put any trust in rulers.

Psalm 118:8–9

The Vespers Psalm   *This God Is Our God For Ever*
Your praise, like your Name, O God, reaches to the world's end;* your right hand
 is full of justice.
Let Mount Zion be glad and the cities of Judah rejoice,* because of your
 judgments.
Make the circuit of Zion; walk round about her;* count the number of her towers.
Consider well her bulwarks; examine her strongholds;* that you may tell those
 who come after.
This God is our God for ever and ever;* he shall be our guide for evermore.

Psalm 48:9–13

The Refrain
It is better to rely on the LORD* than to put any trust in flesh.
It is better to rely on the LORD* than to put any trust in rulers.

The Small Verse
Their sound goes forth to all the earth and their speech to the end of the world.

adapted from THE SHORT BREVIARY

The Lord's Prayer

The Prayer Appointed for the Week
Purify my conscience, Almighty God, by your daily visitation, that your Son Jesus
 Christ, at his coming, may find in me a mansion prepared for himself; who
 lives and reigns with you and the Holy Spirit, one God, now and for ever.
 Amen.✝

Concluding Prayers of the Church
Almighty God, by whose grace and power your disciple Thomas triumphed over
 doubt and was faithful: Grant me, who now remember him in thanksgiving,
 to also come to be so faithful in my witness to you in this world, that I may

receive with him the crown of life; through Jesus Christ our Lord, who lives and reigns with you and the Holy Spirit, one God for ever and ever. *Amen.*†

Lord God, whose Son our Savior Jesus Christ, triumphed over the powers of death and prepared for us our place in the new Jerusalem: Grant that I, who have this day given thanks for his resurrection, may praise you in the City of which he is the light, and where he lives and reigns for ever and ever. *Amen.*†

The Morning Office   **To Be Observed on the Hour or Half Hour Between 6 and 9 a.m.**

The Call to Prayer

Love the Lord, all you who worship him;* the Lord protects the faithful, but repays to the full those who act haughtily.
Be strong and let your heart take courage,* all you who wait for the Lord.

Psalm 31:23–24

The Request for Presence

Be my strong rock, a castle to keep me safe, for you are my crag and my strong-hold;* for the sake of your Name, lead me and guide me.

Psalm 31:3

The Greeting

How great is your goodness, O Lord!* which you have laid up for those who fear you; which you have done in the sight of all.

Psalm 31:19

The Refrain for the Morning Lessons

Be strong and let your heart take courage,* all you who wait for the Lord.

Psalm 31:24

A Reading   *On December 21, the Church recalls and gives thanks for St. Thomas, the Apostle known as "Thomas the Doubter" for his questioning of Christ's resurrection. Thomas was also the first to proclaim Christ's divinity after the resurrection.*

Thomas, called the Twin, who was one of the Twelve, was not with them when Jesus came. So the other disciples said to him, 'We have seen the Lord,' but he answered, 'Unless I can see the holes that the nails made in his hands and can put my finger into the holes they made, and unless I can put my hand into his side, I refuse to believe.' Eight days later the disciples were in the house again and Thomas was with them. The doors were closed, but Jesus came in and stood among them. 'Peace be with you,' he said. Then he spoke to Thomas, 'Put your finger here; look here are my hands. Give me your hand; put it into my side. Do not be unbelieving any more but believe.' Thomas replied, 'My Lord and my God!' Jesus said to him: 'You believe because you can see me. Blessed are those who have not seen and yet believe.'

John 20:24–29

The Refrain
Be strong and let your heart take courage,* all you who wait for the LORD.

The Morning Psalm   *Those Who Sowed with Tears Will Reap with Songs of Joy*
When the LORD restored the fortunes of Zion,* then were we like those who
    dream.
Then was our mouth filled with laughter,* and our tongue with shouts of joy.
Then they said among the nations,* "The LORD has done great things for them."
The LORD has done great things for us,* and we are glad indeed.
Restore our fortunes, O LORD,* like the watercourses of the Negev.
Those who sowed with tears* will reap with songs of joy.
Those who go out weeping, carrying the seed,* will come again with joy,
    shouldering their sheaves.

Psalm 126

The Refrain
Be strong and let your heart take courage,* all you who wait for the LORD.

The Cry of the Church
In the evening, in the morning, and at noonday, I will complain and lament,* and
    he will hear my voice.

Psalm 55:18

The Lord's Prayer

The Prayer Appointed for the Week
Purify my conscience, Almighty God, by your daily visitation, that your Son Jesus
    Christ, at his coming, may find in me a mansion prepared for himself; who
    lives and reigns with you and the Holy Spirit, one God, now and for ever.
    Amen.†

Concluding Prayers of the Church
Everliving God, who strengthened your apostle Thomas with firm and certain
    faith in your Son's resurrection: Grant me so perfectly and without doubt to
    believe in Jesus Christ, our Lord and our God, that my faith may never be
    found wanting in your sight; through him who lives and reigns with you and
    the Holy Spirit, one God, now and for ever. Amen.†

Lord God, almighty and everlasting Father, you have brought me in safety to this
    new day: Preserve me with your mighty power, that I may not fall into sin, nor
    be overcome by adversity; and in all I do direct me to the fulfilling of your pur-
    pose; through Jesus Christ my Lord. Amen.†

The Midday Office   To Be Observed on the Hour or Half Hour
                                        Between 11 a.m. and 2 p.m.

The Call to Prayer
Sing to the LORD with the harp,* with the harp and the voice of song.

With trumpets and the sound of the horn* shout with joy before the King, the
LORD.

Psalm 98:6–7

The Request for Presence

Show us the light of your countenance, O God,* and come to us.

based on Psalm 67:1

The Greeting

O LORD, what are we that you should care for us?* mere mortals that you should
think of us?
We are like a puff of wind;* our days are like a passing shadow.

Psalm 144:3–4

The Refrain for the Midday Lessons

Shout with joy to the LORD, all you lands;* lift up your voice, rejoice, and sing.

Psalm 98:5

A Reading

Do not lose your fearlessness now, then, since the reward is so great. You will need
perseverance if you are to do God's will and gain what he has promised. Only *a
little while now, a very little while, for come he certainly will before too long. My
upright person will live through faith but if he draws back, my soul will take no pleasure
in him.* We are not the sort of people who *draw back,* and are lost by it; we are the
sort who keep faith until our souls are saved. Only faith can guarantee the blessings that we hope for, or prove the existence of realities that are unseen.

Hebrews 10:35–11:1

The Refrain

Shout with joy to the LORD, all you lands;* lift up your voice, rejoice, and sing.

The Midday Psalm   *The Faithfulness of the LORD Endures*

Praise the LORD, all you nations;* laud him, all you peoples.
For his loving-kindness toward us is great,* and the faithfulness of the LORD
endures for ever. Hallelujah!

Psalm 117

The Refrain

Shout with joy to the LORD, all you lands;* lift up your voice, rejoice, and sing.

The Cry of the Church

Even so, come, Lord Jesus!

The Lord's Prayer

The Prayer Appointed for the Week

Purify my conscience, Almighty God, by your daily visitation, that your Son Jesus
Christ, at his coming, may find in me a mansion prepared for himself; who
lives and reigns with you and the Holy Spirit, one God, now and for ever.
Amen.†

Concluding Prayers of the Church

Almighty God, by your Holy Spirit you have made us one with your saints in heaven and on earth: Grant that in my earthly pilgrimage I may always be supported by this fellowship of love and prayer, and know myself to be surrounded by their witness to your power and mercy. I ask this for the sake of Jesus Christ, in whom all my intercessions are acceptable through the Spirit, and who lives and reigns for ever and ever. *Amen.*†

Almighty and everlasting God, who willed that our Savior should take upon Him our flesh and suffer death upon the Cross, that all mankind should follow the example of His great humility, mercifully grant that we may both follow the example of His patience and also be made partakers of His resurrection. Through the same Jesus Christ. *Amen.*

adapted from THE SHORT BREVIARY

The Vespers Office   **To Be Observed on the Hour or Half Hour**
                                      Between 5 and 8 p.m.

The Call to Prayer

Be joyful in God, all you lands;* sing the glory of his Name; sing the glory of his praise.
Say to God, "How awesome are your deeds! . . .
All the earth bows down before you,* sings to you, sings out your Name."

Psalm 66:1–3

The Request for Presence

Let your loving-kindness, O LORD, be upon us,* as we have put our trust in you.

Psalm 33:22

The Greeting

Blessed is the LORD!* for he has heard the voice of my prayer.

Psalm 28:7

The Hymn

How often, Lord, your face has shone
On doubting souls whose wills were true!
You Christ of Peter and of John
You are the Christ of Thomas too.

He loved you well, and firmly said,
"Come, let us go, and die with him";
Yet when your Easter news was spread,
Mid all its light his faith was dim.

His brethren's word he would not take,
But craved to touch those hands of thine;
When you did your appearance make,
He saw, and hailed his Lord Divine.

He saw you risen; at once he rose
To full belief's unclouded height;
And still through his confession flows
To Christian souls your life and light.

O Savior, make your presence known
To all who doubt your Word and thee;
And teach us in that Word alone
To find the truth that sets us free.

adapted from William Bright

The Refrain for the Vespers Lessons

Turn again to your rest, O my soul,* for the Lord has treated you well.

For you have rescued my life from death,* my eyes from tears, and my feet from stumbling.

Psalm 116:6–7

The Vespers Psalm　　　　　　　　　*I Will Declare Your Name to My Brethren*

I am poured out like water,* all my bones are out of joint; my heart within my breast is melting wax.

My mouth is dried out like a pot-shard; my tongue sticks to the roof of my mouth;* and you have laid me in the dust of the grave.

Packs of dogs close me in, and gangs of evildoers circle around me;* they pierce my hands and my feet; I can count all my bones.

They stare and gloat over me;* they divide my garments among them; they cast lots for my clothing.

Be not far away, O Lord;* you are my strength; hasten to help me.

Save me from the sword,* my life from the power of the dog.

Save me from the lion's mouth,* my wretched body from the horns of wild bulls.

I will declare your Name to my brethren;* in the midst of the congregation I will praise you.

Psalm 22:14–21

The Refrain

Turn again to your rest, O my soul,* for the Lord has treated you well.

For you have rescued my life from death,* my eyes from tears, and my feet from stumbling.

The Cry of the Church

O Lord, hear my prayer and let my cry come unto you. Thanks be to God.

The Short Breviary

The Lord's Prayer

The Prayer Appointed for the Week

Purify my conscience, Almighty God, by your daily visitation, that your Son Jesus Christ, at his coming, may find in me a mansion prepared for himself; who lives and reigns with you and the Holy Spirit, one God, now and for ever. *Amen.*†

Concluding Prayers of the Church

Almighty God, you have surrounded me with a great cloud of witnesses: Grant that I, encouraged by the good example of your servant Thomas, may persevere in running the race that is set before me, until at last I may with him attain to your eternal joy; through Jesus Christ, the pioneer and perfecter of our faith, who lives and reigns with you and the Holy Spirit, one God, for ever and ever. *Amen.*†

Grant me and all of your people the gift of your Spirit, that we may know Christ and make him known; and through him, at all times and in all places, may give thanks to you in all things. *Amen.*†

The Morning Office   To Be Observed on the Hour or Half Hour
Between 6 and 9 a.m.

The Call to Prayer
Come and listen, all you who fear God,* and I will tell you what he has done for me.
Psalm 66:14

The Request for Presence
May God be merciful to us and bless us,* show us the light of his countenance and
come to us.
Let your ways be known upon earth,* your saving health among all nations.
Psalm 67:1–2

The Greeting
Your statutes have been like songs to me* wherever I have lived as a stranger.
Psalm 119:54

The Refrain for the Morning Lessons
Create in me a clean heart, O God,* and renew a right spirit within me.
Psalm 51:11

A Reading
Jesus taught us, saying: "But the hour is coming—indeed is already here—when
true worshippers will worship the Father in spirit and truth: that is the kind of
worshipper the Father seeks. God is spirit, and those who worship must worship in spirit and truth."
John 4:23–24

The Refrain
Create in me a clean heart, O God,* and renew a right spirit within me.

The Morning Psalm   *You, O God, Have Heard My Vows*
Hear my cry, O God,* and listen to my prayer.
I call upon you from the ends of the earth* with heaviness in my heart; set me
upon the rock that is higher than I.
For you have been my refuge,* a strong tower against the enemy.
I will dwell in your house for ever;* I will take refuge under the cover of your
wings.
For you, O God, have heard my vows;* you have granted me the heritage of those
who fear your Name.
Psalm 61:1–5

The Refrain
Create in me a clean heart, O God,* and renew a right spirit within me.

The Cry of the Church
Even so, come, Lord Jesus!

The Lord's Prayer

The Prayer Appointed for the Week

Purify my conscience, Almighty God, by your daily visitation, that your Son Jesus Christ, at his coming, may find in me a mansion prepared for himself; who lives and reigns with you and the Holy Spirit, one God, now and for ever. *Amen.*†

The Concluding Prayer of the Church

Lord God, almighty and everlasting Father, you have brought me in safety to this new day: Preserve me with your mighty power, that I may not fall into sin, nor be overcome by adversity; and in all I do direct me to the fulfilling of your purpose; through Jesus Christ my Lord. *Amen.*†

The Midday Office   **To Be Observed on the Hour or Half Hour**
                                     Between 11 a.m. and 2 p.m.

The Call to Prayer

Praise Him from whom all blessings flow; praise Him all creatures here below; praise Him you heavenly hosts; praise Father, Son and Holy Ghost.

Traditional

The Request for Presence

Be my strong rock, a castle to keep me safe, for you are my crag and my stronghold;* for the sake of your Name, lead me and guide me.

Psalm 31:3

The Greeting

To you, O LORD, I lift up my soul;* my God, I put my trust in you . . .

Psalm 25:1

The Refrain for the Midday Lessons

Happy are they all who fear the LORD,* and who follow in his ways!

Psalm 28:1

A Reading

Joyfully you will draw water from the springs of salvation and, that day, you will say, 'Praise YAHWEH, invoke his name. Proclaim his deeds to the people, declare his name sublime. Sing of YAHWEH, for his works are majestic, make them known throughout the world. Cry and shout for joy, you who live in Zion, For the Holy One of Israel is among you in his greatness.'

Isaiah 12:3–6

The Refrain

Happy are they all who fear the LORD,* and who follow in his ways!

The Midday Psalm   *The LORD Will Bless Both Small and Great Who Trust Him*

Not to us, O LORD, not to us, but to your Name give glory;* because of your love and because of your faithfulness.

Why should the heathen say,* "Where then is their God?"

Our God is in heaven;* whatever he wills to do he does.

Their idols are silver and gold,* the work of human hands.

They have mouths, but they cannot speak;* eyes have they, but they cannot see;

They have ears, but they cannot hear;* noses, but they cannot smell;

They have hands, but they cannot feel; feet, but they cannot walk;* they make no
    sound with their throat.

Those who make them are like them,* and so are all who put their trust in them.

O Israel, trust in the LORD;* he is their help and their shield.

O house of Aaron, trust in the LORD;* he is their help and their shield.

You who fear the LORD, trust in the LORD;* he is their help and their shield.

The LORD has been mindful of us, and he will bless us;* he will bless the house of
    Israel; he will bless the house of Aaron;

He will bless those who fear the LORD,* both small and great together.

Psalm 115:1–13

The Refrain

Happy are they all who fear the LORD,* and who follow in his ways!

The Small Verse

The Lord is king. He has put on glorious apparel. Let all the nations praise him.
    Let those of every tongue bow before him. Alleluia, alleluia, alleluia.

Traditional

The Lord's Prayer

The Prayer Appointed for the Week

Purify my conscience, Almighty God, by your daily visitation, that your Son Jesus
    Christ, at his coming, may find in me a mansion prepared for himself; who
    lives and reigns with you and the Holy Spirit, one God, now and for ever.
    Amen.†

The Concluding Prayer of the Church

Come forth, O Christ, and help me. For your name's sake deliver me.

Traditional

The Vespers Office   To Be Observed on the Hour or Half Hour
                                     Between 5 and 8 p.m.

The Call to Prayer

Praise God, from whom all blessings flow; praise him, all creatures here below;
    praise him above, you heavenly hosts; praise Father, Son and Holy Ghost.

Doxology

The Request for Presence

Show your goodness, O LORD, to those who are good* and to those who are true of
    heart.

Psalm 125:4

The Greeting

Out of the mouths of infants and children* your majesty is praised above the
heavens.

Psalm 8:2

The Hymn

Lord Jesus Christ, be present now,
And let your Holy Spirit bow
All hearts in love and truth today
To hear your word and keep your way.

May your glad tidings always bring
Good news to men, that they may sing
Of how you came to save all men.
Instruct us till you come again.

To God the Father and the Son
And Holy Spirit, three in one;
To you, O blessed Trinity,
Be praise throughout eternity.

*Anonymous, translated
by Catherine Winkworth*

The Refrain for the Vespers Lessons

We have heard with our ears, O God, our forefathers have told us,* the deeds you
did in their days, in the days of old.

Psalm 44:1

The Vespers Psalm   *Let the Nations Be Glad and Sing for Joy*

May God be merciful to us and bless us,* show us the light of his countenance and
come to us.

Let your ways be known upon earth,* your saving health among all nations.

Let the peoples praise you, O God;* let all the peoples praise you.

Let the nations be glad and sing for joy,* for you judge the peoples with equity and
guide all the nations upon earth.

Let the peoples praise you, O God;* let all the peoples praise you.

The earth has brought forth her increase;* may God, our own God, give us his
blessing.

May God give us his blessing,* and may all the ends of the earth stand in awe of
him.

Psalm 67

The Refrain

We have heard with our ears, O God, our forefathers have told us,* the deeds you
did in their days, in the days of old.

The Call to Prayer

Even so, come, Lord Jesus!

The Lord's Prayer

The Prayer Appointed for the Week

Purify my conscience, Almighty God, by your daily visitation, that your Son Jesus
Christ, at his coming, may find in me a mansion prepared for himself; who
lives and reigns with you and the Holy Spirit, one God, now and for ever.
Amen.†

The Concluding Prayer of the Church

Almighty and eternal God, ruler of all things in heaven and earth: Mercifully accept my prayer, and strengthen me to do your will; through Jesus Christ our Lord. *Amen.*†

The Morning Office   To Be Observed on the Hour or Half Hour
                                       Between 6 and 9 a.m.

The Call to Prayer

Praise God from whom all blessings flow; praise him, all creatures here below; praise him above, you heavenly hosts; praise Father, Son and Holy Ghost.

Doxology

The Request for Presence

Send out your light and your truth, that they may lead me,* and bring me to your holy hill and to your dwelling;

That I may go to the altar of God, to the God of my joy and gladness;* and on the harp I will give thanks to you, O God my god.

Psalm 43:3–4

The Greeting

Splendor and honor and kingly power are yours by right, O Lord our God,

For you created everything that is, and by your will they were created and have their being.

A Song to the Lamb

The Refrain for the Morning Lessons

For one day in your courts is better than a thousand in my own room,* and to stand at the threshold of the house of my God than to dwell in the tents of the wicked.

Psalm 84:9

A Reading

. . . the angel said to her, 'Mary, do not be afraid; you have won God's favor. Look! You are to conceive in your womb and bear a son, and you must name him Jesus. He will be great and will be called Son of the Most High. The Lord God will give him the throne of his ancestor David; he will rule over the House of Jacob for ever and his reign will have no end.' Mary said to the angel, 'But how can this come about, since I have no knowledge of man?' The angel answered, 'The Holy Spirit will come upon you, and the power of the Most High will cover you with its shadow. And so the child will be holy and will be called Son of God. And I tell you this too: your cousin Elizabeth also, in her old age, has conceived a son, and she whom people called barren is now in her sixth month, *for nothing is impossible to God.*' Mary said, 'You see before you the Lord's servant, let it happen to me as you have said.' And the angel left her.

Luke 1:30–38

The Refrain

For one day in your courts is better than a thousand in my own room,* and to stand
at the threshold of the house of my God than to dwell in the tents of the wicked.

The Morning Psalm   *Who Can Stand in His Holy Place*

The earth is the LORD's and all that is in it,* the world and all who dwell therein.

For it is he who founded it upon the seas* and made it firm upon the rivers of the
deep.

"Who can ascend the hill of the LORD?* and who can stand in his holy place?"

"Those who have clean hands and a pure heart,* who have not pledged
themselves to falsehood, nor sworn by what is a fraud.

They shall receive a blessing from the LORD* and a just reward from the God of
their salvation."

Such is the generation of those who seek him,* of those who seek your face, O God
of Jacob.

Psalm 24:1–6

The Refrain

For one day in your courts is better than a thousand in my own room,* and to
stand at the threshold of the house of my God than to dwell in the tents of the
wicked.

The Small Verse

The people that walked in darkness have seen a great light; on those who live in a
land of deep shadow a light has shone.

Isaiah 9:1

The Lord's Prayer

The Prayer Appointed for the Week

Purify my conscience, Almighty God, by your daily visitation, that your Son Jesus
Christ, at his coming, may find in me a mansion prepared for himself; who lives
and reigns with you and the Holy Spirit, one God, now and for ever. *Amen.*†

The Concluding Prayer of the Church

Lord God, almighty and everlasting Father, you have brought me in safety to this
new day: Preserve me with your mighty power, that I may not fall into sin, nor
be overcome by adversity; and in all I do direct me to the fulfilling of your purpose; through Jesus Christ my Lord. *Amen.*†

The Midday Office   To Be Observed on the Hour or Half Hour
Between 11 a.m. and 2 p.m.

The Call to Prayer

Hallelujah! Praise the LORD, O my soul!* I will praise the LORD as long as I live, I
will sing praises to my God while I have my being.

Psalm 146:1

The Request for Presence

Remember me, O LORD, with the favor you have for your people,* and visit me
    with your saving help;

That I may see the prosperity of your elect and be glad with the gladness of your
    people,* that I may glory with your inheritance.

Psalm 106:4–5

The Greeting

You are to be praised, O God, in Zion . . .

To you that hear prayer shall all flesh come,* because of their transgressions.

Psalm 65:1–2

The Refrain for the Midday Lessons

Your statutes have been like songs to me* wherever I have lived like a stranger.

Psalm 119:54

A Reading

Besides, you know the time has come; the moment is here for you to stop sleeping
    and wake up, because by now our salvation is nearer than when we first began
    to believe. The night is nearly over, daylight is on the way; so let us throw off
    everything that belongs to darkness and equip ourselves for the light.

Romans 13:11–12

The Refrain

Your statutes have been like songs to me* wherever I have lived like a stranger.

The Midday Psalm   *Such Knowledge Is Too Wonderful for Me*

LORD, you have searched me out and known me;* you know my sitting down and
    my rising up; you discern my thoughts from afar.

You trace my journeys and my resting-places* and are acquainted with all my
    ways.

Indeed, there is not a word on my lips,* but you, O LORD, know it altogether.

You press upon me behind and before* and lay your hand upon me.

Such knowledge is too wonderful for me;* it is so high that I cannot attain to it.

Where can I go then from your Spirit?* where can I flee from your presence?

If I climb up to heaven, you are there;* if I make the grave my bed, you are there
    also.

If I take the wings of the morning* and dwell in the uttermost parts of the sea,

Even there your hand will lead me* and your right hand hold me fast.

Psalm 139:1–9

The Refrain

Your statutes have been like songs to me* wherever I have lived like a stranger.

The Small Verse

Keep me, Lord, as the apple of your eye and carry me under the shadow of your
    wings.

Traditional

The Lord's Prayer

The Prayer Appointed for the Week

Purify my conscience, Almighty God, by your daily visitation, that your Son Jesus
  Christ, at his coming, may find in me a mansion prepared for himself; who lives
  and reigns with you and the Holy Spirit, one God, now and for ever. *Amen.*†

The Concluding Prayer of the Church

May God himself order my days and make them acceptable in his sight. Blessed
  be the Lord always, my strength and my redeemer.

Traditional

The Vespers Office   To Be Observed on the Hour or Half Hour
                                                     Between 5 and 8 p.m.

The Call to Prayer

But I will call upon God,* and the LORD will deliver me.
In the evening, in the morning, and at noonday, I will complain and lament,* and
  he will hear my voice.
He will bring me safely back . . .
God, who is enthroned of old, will hear me.

Psalm 55:17ff

The Request for Presence

I cry out to you, O LORD;* I say, "You are my refuge, my portion in the land of the
  living."

Psalm 142:5

The Greeting

I will confess you among the peoples, O LORD;* I will sing praises to you among
  the nations.

Psalm 108:3

The Hymn

  Love divine, all loves excelling, joy of heaven, to earth come down;
  Fix us in your humble dwelling; all your faithful mercies crown!
  Jesus, you are all compassion, pure, unbounded love you art;
  Visit us with your salvation; enter every trembling heart.

  Breathe, O breathe your loving Spirit into every troubled breast!
  Let us all in you inherit; let us find that second rest.
  Take away our bent to sinning; Alpha and Omega be;
  End of faith, as its beginning, set our hearts at liberty.

  Come, Almighty to deliver, let us all your life receive;
  Suddenly return and never, nevermore your temples leave.
  You we would be always blessing, serve you as your hosts above,
  Pray and praise you without ceasing, glory in your perfect love.

Finish, then, your new creation; pure and spotless let us be.
Let us see your great salvation perfectly restored in thee;
Changed from glory into glory, till in heaven we take our place,
Till we cast our crowns before thee, lost in wonder, love, and praise.

Charles Wesley

The Refrain for the Vespers Lessons
The LORD will hear the desire of the humble;* you will strengthen their heart and
your ears shall hear.

Psalm 10:18

The Vespers Psalm   *Let All Who Seek You Rejoice*
You are the LORD; do not withhold your compassion from me;* let your love and
your faithfulness keep me safe for ever,
For innumerable troubles have crowded upon me; my sins have overtaken me,
and I cannot see;* they are more in number than the hairs of my head, and my
heart fails me.
Be pleased, O LORD, to deliver me;* O LORD, make haste to help me.
Let them be ashamed and altogether dismayed who seek after my life to destroy
it;* let them draw back and be disgraced who take pleasure in my misfortune.
Let those who say "Aha!" and gloat over me be confounded* because they are
ashamed.
Let all who seek you rejoice in you and be glad;* let those who love your salvation
continually say, "Great is the LORD!"
Though I am poor and afflicted,* the Lord will have regard for me.
You are my helper and my deliverer,* do not tarry, O my God.

Psalm 40:12–19

The Refrain
The LORD will hear the desire of the humble;* you will strengthen their heart and
your ears shall hear.

The Small Verse
The Lord is my shepherd and nothing is wanting to me. In green pastures He hath
settled me.

THE SHORT BREVIARY

The Lord's Prayer

The Prayer Appointed for the Week
Purify my conscience, Almighty God, by your daily visitation, that your Son Jesus
Christ, at his coming, may find in me a mansion prepared for himself; who
lives and reigns with you and the Holy Spirit, one God, now and for ever.
Amen.†

The Concluding Prayer of the Church
Lead me not into temptation. Deliver me from evil. Yours are the kingdom and the
glory.

The Morning Office To Be Observed on the Hour or Half Hour
Between 6 and 9 a.m.

The Call to Prayer

Come, let us bow down, and bend the knee,* and kneel before the LORD our
Maker.
For he is our God,* and we are the people of his pasture and the sheep of his
hand . . .

Psalm 95:6–7

The Request for Presence

So teach us to number our days* that we may apply our hearts to wisdom.

Psalm 90:12

The Greeting

My God, my rock in whom I put my trust,* my shield, the horn of my salvation,
and my refuge; you are worthy of praise.

Psalm 18:2

The Refrain for the Morning Lessons

My eyes are upon the faithful in the land, that they may dwell with me . . .

Psalm 101:6

A Reading

Jesus taught the people saying: "Were I to testify on my own behalf, my testimony
would not be true; but there is another witness who speaks on my behalf, and I
know that his testimony is true. You sent messengers to John, and he gave his
testimony to the truth—not that I depend on human testimony; no, it is for
your salvation that I mention it. John was a lamp lit and shining and for a time
you were content to enjoy the light that he gave. But my testimony is greater
than John's: the deeds my Father has given me to perform, these same deeds of
mine testify that the Father has sent me."

John 5:31–36

The Refrain

My eyes are upon the faithful in the land, that they may dwell with me . . .

The Morning Psalm   *The Eye of the LORD Is Upon Those Who Fear Him*

The LORD looks down from heaven,* and beholds all the people in the world.
From where he sits enthroned he turns his gaze* on all who dwell on the earth.
He fashions all the hearts of them* and understands all their works.
There is no king that can be saved by a mighty army;* a strong man is not
delivered by his great strength.
The horse is a vain hope for deliverance;* for all its strength it cannot save.
Behold, the eye of the LORD is upon those who fear him,* on those who wait upon
his love,
To pluck their lives from death,* and to feed them in time of famine.
Our soul waits for the LORD;* he is our help and our shield.

Indeed, our heart rejoices in him,* for in his holy Name we put our trust.
Let your loving-kindness, O LORD, be upon us,* as we have put our trust in you.

Psalm 33:13–22

The Refrain
My eyes are upon the faithful in the land, that they may dwell with me . . .

The Cry of the Church
O God, come to my assistance! O Lord, make haste to help me!

The Lord's Prayer

The Prayer Appointed for the Week
Purify my conscience, Almighty God, by your daily visitation, that your Son Jesus
Christ, at his coming, may find in me a mansion prepared for himself; who lives
and reigns with you and the Holy Spirit, one God, now and for ever. *Amen.*†

The Concluding Prayer of the Church
Lord God, almighty and everlasting Father, you have brought me in safety to this
new day: Preserve me with your mighty power, that I may not fall into sin, nor
be overcome by adversity; and in all I do direct me to the fulfilling of your purpose; through Jesus Christ my Lord. *Amen.*†

The Midday Office   To Be Observed on the Hour or Half Hour
                                          Between 11 a.m. and 2 p.m.

The Call to Prayer
Search for the LORD and his strength;* continually seek his face.

Psalm 105:4

The Request for Presence
You are good and you bring forth good;* instruct me in your statutes.

Psalm 119:68

The Greeting
When your word goes forth it gives light;* it gives understanding to the simple.

Psalm 119:130

The Refrain for the Midday Lessons
You strengthen me more and more; you enfold and comfort me.

Psalm 71:21

A Reading
YAHWEH, God of the House of Jacob, Abraham's redeemer, says this, 'No longer
shall Jacob be disappointed, no more shall his face grow pale, for when he sees
his children, my creatures, home again with him, he will acknowledge my
name as holy, he will acknowledge the Holy One of Jacob to be holy and will
hold the God of Israel in awe. Erring spirits will learn to understand and mur-
murers accept instruction.'

Isaiah 29:22–24

The Refrain

You strengthen me more and more;* you enfold and comfort me.

The Midday Psalm   *Hear, O Shepherd of Israel, Leading Joseph Like a Flock*

Hear, O Shepherd of Israel, leading Joseph like a flock;* shine forth, you that are
    enthroned upon the cherubim.

In the presence of Ephraim, Benjamin, and Manasseh,* stir up your strength and
    come to help us.

Restore us, O God of hosts;* show the light of your countenance, and we shall be
    saved.

Let your hand be upon the man of your right hand,* the son of man you have
    made so strong for yourself.

And so will we never turn away from you;* give us life, that we may call upon
    your Name.

Restore us, O Lord God of hosts;* show the light of your countenance, and we
    shall be saved.

Psalm 80:1–3, 16–18

The Refrain

You strengthen me more and more;* you enfold and comfort me.

The Cry of the Church

Even so, come, Lord Jesus!

The Lord's Prayer

The Prayer Appointed for the Week

Purify my conscience, Almighty God, by your daily visitation, that your Son Jesus
    Christ, at his coming, may find in me a mansion prepared for himself; who lives
    and reigns with you and the Holy Spirit, one God, now and for ever. *Amen.*†

The Concluding Prayer of the Church

O God, author of peace and lover of concord, to know you is eternal life and to
    serve you is perfect freedom: Defend me, your humble servant, in all assaults
    of my enemies; that I, surely trusting in your defense, may not fear the power
    of any adversary; through the might of Jesus Christ my Lord. *Amen.*†

The Vespers Office   **To Be Observed on the Hour or Half Hour**
                                          Between 5 and 8 p.m.

The Call to Prayer

Behold now, bless the Lord, all you servants of the Lord,* you that stand by night
    in the house of our Lord.

Psalm 134:1

The Request for Presence

For God alone my soul in silence waits;* from him comes my salvation.

Psalm 62:1

The Greeting
Yours is the day, yours also the night;* you established the moon and the sun.
You fixed all the boundaries of the earth;* you made both summer and winter.

Psalm 74:15–16

The Hymn
>Praise to the Lord, Almighty, the King of creation:
>O my soul, praise him, for he is your health and salvation.
>All you who hear,
>Now to his altar draw near,
>Joining in glad adoration.
>
>Praise to the Lord who does prosper your work and defend you;
>Surely his goodness and mercy shall daily attend you.
>Ponder anew
>What the Almighty can do,
>Who with his love does befriend you.
>
>Praise to the Lord, O let all that is in me adore him!
>All that has life and breath come now in praises before him!
>Let the Amen
>Sound from his people again:
>Now as we worship before him.

J. Neander

The Refrain for the Vespers Lessons
The LORD's will stands fast for ever,* and the designs of his heart from age to age.

Psalm 33:11

The Vespers Psalm   *The LORD Shall Reign For Ever*
Hallelujah! Praise the LORD, O my soul!* I will praise the LORD as long as I live; I
    will sing praises to my God while I have my being.
Put not your trust in rulers, nor in any child of earth,* for there is no help in them.
When they breathe their last, they return to earth,* and in that day their thoughts
    perish.
Happy are they who have the God of Jacob for their help!* whose hope is in the
    LORD their God;
Who made heaven and earth, the seas, and all that is in them;* who keeps his
    promise for ever;
Who gives justice to those who are oppressed,* and food to those who hunger.
The LORD sets the prisoners free; the LORD opens the eyes of the blind;* the LORD
    lifts up those who are bowed down;
The LORD loves the righteous; the LORD cares for the stranger;* he sustains the
    orphan and widow, but frustrates the way of the wicked.
The LORD shall reign for ever,* your God, O Zion, throughout all generations.
    Hallelujah!

Psalm 146

The Refrain
The LORD's will stands fast for ever,* and the designs of his heart from age to age.

The Cry of the Church
Even so, come, Lord Jesus!

The Lord's Prayer

The Prayer Appointed for the Week
Purify my conscience, Almighty God, by your daily visitation, that your Son Jesus
   Christ, at his coming, may find in me a mansion prepared for himself; who
   lives and reigns with you and the Holy Spirit, one God, now and for ever.
   Amen.†

The Concluding Prayer of the Church
May Almighty God grant me a peaceful night and a perfect end. *Amen.*

The Morning Office   To Be Observed on the Hour or Half Hour
                                                        Between 6 and 9 a.m.

The Call to Prayer
Hallelujah! Praise the Name of the LORD;* give praise, you servants of the LORD,
You who stand in the house of the LORD,* in the courts of the house of our God.
Praise the LORD, for the LORD is good;* sing praises to his Name, for it is lovely.

Psalm 136:1–3

The Request for Presence
I have said to the LORD, "You are my God;* listen, O LORD, to my supplication."

Psalm 140:6

The Greeting
You are the LORD, most high over all the earth;* you are exalted far above all gods.

Psalm 97:9

The Refrain for the Morning Lessons
Everyone will stand in awe and declare God's deeds;* they will recognize his
   works.

Psalm 64:9

A Reading
Now a great sign appeared in heaven: a woman, robed with the sun, standing on
   the moon, and on her head a crown of twelve stars. She was pregnant, and in
   labor, crying aloud in the pangs of childbirth. Then a second sign appeared in
   the sky: there was a huge red dragon with seven heads and ten horns, and each
   of the seven heads crowned with a coronet. Its tail swept a third of the *stars
   from the sky and hurled them to the ground,* and the dragon stopped in front of the
   woman as she was at the point of giving birth, so that he could eat the child as
   soon as it was born. The woman *was delivered of a boy,* the son who was *to rule*

the nations with an iron scepter, and the child was taken straight up to God and to his throne, while the woman escaped into the desert, where God has prepared a place for her to be looked after for twelve hundred and sixty days.

Revelation 12:1–6

The Refrain
Everyone will stand in awe and declare God's deeds;* they will recognize his works.

The Morning Psalm

The LORD Has Pleasure in Those Who Await His Gracious Favor

Hallelujah! How good it is to sing praises to our God!* how pleasant it is to honor him with praise!

The LORD rebuilds Jerusalem;* he gathers the exiles of Israel.

He heals the brokenhearted* and binds up their wounds.

He counts the number of the stars* and calls them all by their names.

Great is our LORD and mighty in power;* there is no limit to his wisdom.

The LORD lifts up the lowly,* but casts the wicked to the ground.

Sing to the LORD with thanksgiving;* make music to our God upon the harp.

He covers the heavens with clouds* and prepares rain for the earth;

He makes grass to grow upon the mountains* and green plants to serve mankind.

He provides food for flocks and herds* and for the young ravens when they cry.

He is not impressed by the might of a horse;* he has no pleasure in the strength of a man;

But the LORD has pleasure in those who fear him,* in those who await his gracious favor.

Psalm 147:1–12

The Refrain
Everyone will stand in awe and declare God's deeds;* they will recognize his works.

The Cry of the Church
O God, come to my assistance! O Lord, make haste to help me!

The Lord's Prayer

The Prayer Appointed for the Week
Purify my conscience, Almighty God, by your daily visitation, that your Son Jesus Christ, at his coming, may find in me a mansion prepared for himself; who lives and reigns with you and the Holy Spirit, one God, now and for ever. *Amen.*†

The Concluding Prayer of the Church
Lord God, almighty and everlasting Father, you have brought me in safety to this new day: Preserve me with your mighty power, that I may not fall into sin, nor be overcome by adversity; and in all I do direct me to the fulfilling of your purpose; through Jesus Christ my Lord. *Amen.*†

The Midday Office   To Be Observed on the Hour or Half Hour
                                     Between 11 a.m. and 2 p.m.

The Call to Prayer
Bless God in the congregation;* bless the LORD, you that are of the fountain of
  Israel.

Psalm 68:26

The Request for Presence
Accept, O LORD, the willing tribute of my lips,* and teach me your judgments.
Psalm 119:108

The Greeting
Let the words of my mouth and the meditation of my heart be acceptable in your
  sight,* O LORD, my strength and my redeemer.

Psalm 19:14

The Refrain for the Midday Lessons
Hallelujah! Happy are they who fear the Lord* and have great delight in his commandments.

Psalm 112:1

A Reading
Jerusalem, turn your eyes to the east, see the joy that is coming to you from God.
  Look, the children you watched go away are on their way home; reassembled
  from east and west, they are on their way home at the Holy One's command,
  rejoicing in God's glory.

Baruch 4:36–37

The Refrain
Hallelujah! Happy are they who fear the Lord* and have great delight in his commandments.

The Midday Psalm   *He Has Raised Up Strength for His People*
Praise the LORD from the earth,* you sea-monsters and all deeps;
Fire and hail, snow and fog,* tempestuous wind, doing his will;
Mountains and all hills,* fruit trees and all cedars;
Wild beasts and all cattle,* creeping things and winged birds;
Kings of the earth and all peoples,* princes and all rulers of the world;
Young men and maidens,* old and young together.
Let them praise the Name of the LORD,* for his Name only is exalted, his splendor
  is over earth and heaven.
He has raised up strength for his people and praise for all his loyal servants,* the
  children of Israel, a people who are near him. Hallelujah!

Psalm 148:7–14

The Refrain
Hallelujah! Happy are they who fear the Lord* and have great delight in his commandments.

The Cry of the Church
O Lord, hear my prayer and let my cry come unto you. Thanks be to God.

THE SHORT BREVIARY

The Lord's Prayer

The Prayer Appointed for the Week
Purify my conscience, Almighty God, by your daily visitation, that your Son Jesus
    Christ, at his coming, may find in me a mansion prepared for himself; who lives
    and reigns with you and the Holy Spirit, one God, now and for ever. *Amen.†*

The Concluding Prayer of the Church
Lord Jesus Christ, by your death you took away the sting of death: Grant me to so
    follow in faith where you have led the way, that I may at length fall asleep peace-
    fully in you and wake in your likeness; for your tender mercies' sake. *Amen.†*

The Vespers Office   **To Be Observed on the Hour or Half Hour**
                                           Between 5 and 8 p.m.

The Call to Prayer
The LORD is my strength and my shield;* my heart trusts in him, and I have been
    helped;
Therefore my heart dances for joy,* and in my song will I praise him.

Psalm 28:8–9

The Request for Presence
I have gone astray like a sheep that is lost;* search for your servant, for I do not
    forget your commandments.

Psalm 119:176

The Greeting
How great is your goodness, O LORD! which you have laid up for those who fear
    you;* which you have done in the sight of all for those who put their trust in
    you.

Psalm 31:19

The Hymn
All praise to you, O God, this night   Enlighten us, O blessed Light,
For all the blessings of the light;   And give us rest throughout this night.
Keep us, we pray, O king of kings,   O strengthen us, that for your sake,
Beneath your own almighty wings.   We all may serve you when we wake.

                                                            Thomas Ken

Forgive us, Lord, through Christ your Son,
Whatever wrong this day we've done;
Your peace give to the world, O Lord,
That men might live in one accord.

The Refrain for the Vespers Lessons

Mercy and truth have met together;* righteousness and peace have kissed each other.

Psalm 85:10

The Vespers Psalm   *He Redeems Our Life*

Bless the LORD, O my soul,* and all that is within me, bless his holy Name.

Bless the LORD, O my soul,* and forget not all his benefits.

He forgives all your sins* and heals all your infirmities;

He redeems your life from the grave* and crowns you with mercy and loving-kindness;

He satisfies you with good things,* and your youth is renewed like an eagle's.

The LORD executes righteousness* and judgment for all who are oppressed.

He made his ways known to Moses* and his works to the children of Israel.

The LORD is full of compassion and mercy,* slow to anger and of great kindness.

He will not always accuse us,* nor will he keep his anger for ever.

He has not dealt with us according to our sins,* nor rewarded us according to our wickedness.

For as the heavens are high above the earth,* so is his mercy great upon those who fear him.

As far as the east is from the west,* so far has he removed our sins from us.

As a father cares for his children,* so does the LORD care for those who fear him.

For he himself knows whereof we are made;* he remembers that we are but dust.

Psalm 103:1–14

The Refrain

Mercy and truth have met together;* righteousness and peace have kissed each other.

The Small Verse

My help is in the Name of the Lord who made heaven and earth and all that is in them. Thanks be to God.

Traditional

The Lord's Prayer

The Prayer Appointed for the Week

Purify my conscience, Almighty God, by your daily visitation, that your Son Jesus Christ, at his coming, may find in me a mansion prepared for himself; who lives and reigns with you and the Holy Spirit, one God, now and for ever. *Amen.*†

Concluding Prayers of the Church

Almighty God, who has promised to hear the petitions of those who ask in your Son's Name: I beseech you mercifully to incline your ear to me who have made my prayers and supplications to you; and grant that those things which I have faithfully asked according to your will, I may effectually obtain, to the relief of my necessity, and to the setting forth of your glory; through Jesus Christ my Lord. *Amen.*†

May the souls of the faithful departed, through the mercy of God, rest in eternal peace. *Amen.*

Advent Compline

Sunday
The Night Office   To Be Observed Before Retiring

The Call to Prayer
May the Lord Almighty grant me and those I love a peaceful night and a perfect
   end. *Amen.*†

The Request for Presence
Our help is in the Name of the Lord; the maker of heaven and earth.

The Greeting
Almighty God, my heavenly Father: I have sinned against you, through my own
   fault, in thought, and word, and deed, in what I have done and what I have left
   undone. For the sake of your Son our Lord Jesus Christ, forgive me all my
   offenses; and grant that I may serve you in newness of life, to the glory of your
   Name. *Amen.*†

The Reading   *The Magnificat*
My soul doth magnify the Lord,
And my spirit hath rejoiced in God my Savior;
For he hath regarded the low estate of his handmaiden:
For, behold, henceforth all generations shall call me blessed,
For he that is mighty hath done to me great things;
And holy is his name,
And his mercy is on them that fear him from generation to generation.
He hath showed strength with his arm;
He hath scattered the proud in the imagination of their hearts.
He hath put down the mighty from their seats, and exalted them of low degree.
He hath filled the hungry with good things; and the rich he hath sent away empty.
He hath holpen his servant Israel, in remembrance of his mercy
As he spake to our fathers, to Abraham, and to his seed for ever.

Luke 1:46–55 (KJV)

The Cry of the Church
Come, thou long expected Jesus!

The Psalm   *I Will Sing and Make Melody*
My heart is firmly fixed, O God, my heart is fixed;* I will sing and make melody.
Wake up, my spirit; awake, lute and harp;* I myself will waken the dawn.
I will confess you among the peoples, O LORD;* I will sing praises to you among
   the nations.
For your loving-kindness is greater than the heavens,* and your faithfulness
   reaches to the clouds.
Exalt yourself above the heavens, O God,* and your glory over all the earth.

Psalm 108:1–5

The Cry of the Church
Even so, come, Lord Jesus!

The Small Verse

Into your hands, O Lord, I commend my spirit; for you have redeemed me, O
Lord, O God of truth. Keep me, O Lord, as the apple of your eye; hide me
under the shadow of your wings.†

The Lord's Prayer

The Petition

Watch, O Lord, with those who wake, or watch, or weep tonight, and give Your
angels and saints charge over those who sleep. Tend Your sick ones, O Lord
Christ. Rest Your weary ones. Bless Your dying ones. Soothe Your suffering
ones. Shield Your joyous ones, and all for Your love's sake. *Amen.*§

The Final Thanksgiving

Lord, you now have set your servant free to go in peace as you have promised; for
these eyes of mine have seen the Savior, whom you have prepared for all the
world to see: a Light to enlighten the nations, and the glory of your people
Israel. Glory to the Father, and to the Son, and to the Holy Spirit: as it was in the
beginning, is now, and will be for ever. *Amen.*

Monday

The Night Office   To Be Observed Before Retiring

The Call to Prayer

May the Lord Almighty grant me and those I love a peaceful night and a perfect
end. *Amen.*†

The Request for Presence

Our help is in the Name of the Lord; the maker of heaven and earth.

The Greeting

Almighty God, my heavenly Father: I have sinned against you, through my own
fault, in thought, and word, and deed, in what I have done and what I have left
undone. For the sake of your Son our Lord Jesus Christ, forgive me all my
offenses; and grant that I may serve you in newness of life, to the glory of your
Name. *Amen.*†

The Reading   *The General Thanksgiving*

Almighty God, Father of all mercies,
We your unworthy servants
Do give you most humble and hearty thanks
For all your goodness and loving-kindness

To us and to all men.
We bless you for our creation, preservation,
And all the blessings of this life;
But above all for your inestimable love
In the redemption of the world by our Lord Jesus Christ,
For the means of grace, and for the hope of glory.
And, we beseech you,
Give us that due sense of all your mercies,
That our hearts may be unfeignedly thankful;
And that we show forth your praise,
Not only with our lips, but in our lives,
By giving up ourselves to your service,
And by walking before you
In holiness and righteousness all our days;
Through Jesus Christ our Lord,
To whom, with you and the Holy Ghost,
Be all honor and glory, world without end. *Amen.*†

The Cry of the Church
Come, thou long expected Jesus!

The Psalm   *May God Come to Us*
May God be merciful to us and bless us,* show us the light of his countenance and
    come to us.
Let your ways be known upon earth,* your saving health among all nations.
Let the peoples praise you, O God;* let all the peoples praise you.
Let the nations be glad and sing for joy,* for you judge the peoples with equity and
    guide all the nations upon earth.
Let the peoples praise you, O God;* let all the peoples praise you.
The earth has brought forth her increase;* may God, our own God, give us his
    blessing.
May God give us his blessing,* and may all the ends of the earth stand in awe of him.
                                                              Psalm 67

The Cry of the Church
Even so, come, Lord Jesus!

The Small Verse
Into your hands, O Lord, I commend my spirit; for you have redeemed me, O
    Lord, O God of truth. Keep me, O Lord, as the apple of your eye; hide me
    under the shadow of your wings.†

The Lord's Prayer

The Petition
Watch, O Lord, with those who wake, or watch, or weep tonight, and give Your
    angels and saints charge over those who sleep. Tend Your sick ones, O Lord

Christ. Rest Your weary ones. Bless Your dying ones. Soothe Your suffering ones. Shield Your joyous ones, and all for Your love's sake. *Amen.*§

The Final Thanksgiving
Lord, you now have set your servant free to go in peace as you have promised; for these eyes of mine have seen the Savior, whom you have prepared for all the world to see: a Light to enlighten the nations, and the glory of your people Israel. Glory to the Father, and to the Son, and to the Holy Spirit: as it was in the beginning, is now, and will be for ever. *Amen.*

Tuesday
The Night Office   To Be Observed Before Retiring

The Call to Prayer
May the Lord Almighty grant me and those I love a peaceful night and a perfect end. *Amen.*†

The Request for Presence
Our help is in the Name of the Lord; the maker of heaven and earth.

The Greeting
Almighty God, my heavenly Father: I have sinned against you, through my own fault, in thought, and word, and deed, in what I have done and what I have left undone. For the sake of your Son our Lord Jesus Christ, forgive me all my offenses; and grant that I may serve you in newness of life, to the glory of your Name. *Amen.*†

The Reading
The people that walked in darkness have seen a great light;
On the inhabitants of a country in shadow dark as death light has blazed forth.
You have enlarged the nation, you have increased its joy;
They rejoice before you as people rejoice at harvest time,
As they exult when they are dividing the spoils.
For the yoke that weighed on it, the bar across its shoulders,
The rod of its oppressor,
These you have broken as on the day of Midian.
For all the footgear clanking over the ground
And all the clothing rolled in blood,
Will be burnt, will be food for the flames.
For a son has been born for us, a son has been given to us,
And dominion has been laid on his shoulders;

And this is the name he has been given,
'Wonder-Counselor, Mighty-God,
Eternal-Father, Prince-of-Peace,'
To extend his dominion in boundless peace,
Over the throne of David and over his kingdom
To make it secure and sustain it
In fair judgment and integrity.
From this time onwards and for ever,
The jealous love of YAHWEH Sabaoth will do this.

Isaiah 9:1–6

The Cry of the Church
Come, thou long expected Jesus!

The Psalm   *Behold, I Come*
Great things are they that you have done, O LORD my God! how great your
    wonders and your plans for us!* there is none who can be compared with
    you.
Oh, that I could make them known and tell them!* but they are more than I can
    count.
In sacrifice and offering you take no pleasure* (you have given me ears to hear you);
Burnt-offering and sin-offering you have not required,* and so I said, "Behold, I
    come.
In the roll of the book it is written concerning me:* 'I love to do your will, O my
    God; your law is deep in my heart.' "

Psalm 40:5–9

The Cry of the Church
Even so, come, Lord Jesus!

The Small Verse
Into your hands, O Lord, I commend my spirit; for you have redeemed me,
    O Lord, O God of truth. Keep me, O Lord, as the apple of your eye; hide me
    under the shadow of your wings.†

The Lord's Prayer

The Petition
Watch, O Lord, with those who wake, or watch, or weep tonight, and give Your
    angels and saints charge over those who sleep. Tend Your sick ones, O Lord
    Christ. Rest Your weary ones. Bless Your dying ones. Soothe Your suffering
    ones. Shield Your joyous ones, and all for Your love's sake. *Amen.*§

The Final Thanksgiving
Lord, you now have set your servant free to go in peace as you have promised; for
    these eyes of mine have seen the Savior, whom you have prepared for all the
    world to see: a Light to enlighten the nations, and the glory of your people
    Israel. Glory to the Father, and to the Son, and to the Holy Spirit: as it was in the
    beginning, is now, and will be for ever. *Amen.*

❧

Wednesday
The Night Office   To Be Observed Before Retiring

The Call to Prayer
May the Lord Almighty grant me and those I love a peaceful night and a perfect
end. *Amen.*†

The Request for Presence
Our help is in the Name of the Lord; the maker of heaven and earth.

The Greeting
Almighty God, my heavenly Father: I have sinned against you, through my own
fault, in thought, and word, and deed, in what I have done and what I have left
undone. For the sake of your Son our Lord Jesus Christ, forgive me all my
offenses; and grant that I may serve you in newness of life, to the glory of your
Name. *Amen.*†

The Hymn   *The Divine Image*

To Mercy, Pity, Peace, and Love   Then every man, of every clime,
All pray in their distress;   That prays in his distress,
And to these virtues of delight   Prays to the human form divine,
Return their thankfulness.   Love, Mercy, Pity, Peace.

For Mercy, Pity, Peace, and Love   And all must love the human form,
Is God, our Father dear,   In heathen, Turk, or Jew:
And Mercy, Pity, Peace, and Love   Where Mercy, Love, and Pity dwell
Is man, His child and care.   There God is dwelling too.

For Mercy has a human heart,   *William Blake*
Pity a human face.
And Love, the human form divine,
And Peace, the human dress.

The Cry of the Church
Come, thou long expected Jesus!

The Psalm   *God, Your God, Has Anointed You*
Your throne, O God, endures for ever and ever,* a scepter of righteousness is the
scepter of your kingdom; you love righteousness and hate iniquity.
Therefore God, your God, has anointed you* with the oil of gladness above your
fellows.
All your garments are fragrant with myrrh, aloes, and cassia,* and the music of
strings from ivory palaces makes you glad.

Kings' daughters stand among the ladies of the court;* on your right hand is the
queen, adorned with the gold of Ophir.

Psalm 45:7–10

The Cry of the Church

Even so, come, Lord Jesus!

The Small Verse

Into your hands, O Lord, I commend my spirit; for you have redeemed me,
O Lord, O God of truth. Keep me, O Lord, as the apple of your eye; hide me
under the shadow of your wings.†

The Lord's Prayer

The Petition

Watch, O Lord, with those who wake, or watch, or weep tonight, and give Your
angels and saints charge over those who sleep. Tend Your sick ones, O Lord
Christ. Rest Your weary ones. Bless Your dying ones. Soothe Your suffering
ones. Shield Your joyous ones, and all for Your love's sake. *Amen.*§

The Final Thanksgiving

Lord, you now have set your servant free to go in peace as you have promised; for
these eyes of mine have seen the Savior, whom you have prepared for all the
world to see: a Light to enlighten the nations, and the glory of your people
Israel. Glory to the Father, and to the Son, and to the Holy Spirit: as it was in the
beginning, is now, and will be for ever. *Amen.*

Thursday
The Night Office   To Be Observed Before Retiring

The Call to Prayer

May the Lord Almighty grant me and those I love a peaceful night and a perfect
end. *Amen.*†

The Request for Presence

Our help is in the Name of the Lord; the maker of heaven and earth.

The Greeting

Almighty God, my heavenly Father: I have sinned against you, through my own
fault, in thought, and word, and deed, in what I have done and what I have left
undone. For the sake of your Son our Lord Jesus Christ, forgive me all my
offenses; and grant that I may serve you in newness of life, to the glory of your
Name. *Amen.*†

The Reading

Here is my servant whom I uphold,
My chosen one in whom my soul delights.
I have sent my spirit upon him,
He will bring fair judgment to the nations.
He does not cry out or raise his voice,
His voice is not heard in the street;
He does not break the crushed reed
Or snuff the faltering wick.
Faithfully he presents his fair judgment;
He will not grow faint, he will not be crushed
Until he has established fair judgment on earth,
And the coasts and islands are waiting for his instruction.

Isaiah 42:1–4

The Cry of the Church

Come, thou long expected Jesus!

The Psalm   *The LORD Will Show Us His Covenant*

Gracious and upright is the LORD;* therefore he teaches sinners in his way.
He guides the humble in doing right* and teaches his way to the lowly.
All the paths of the LORD are love and faithfulness* to those who keep his
    covenant and his testimonies.
For your Name's sake, O LORD,* forgive my sin, for it is great.
Who are they who fear the LORD?* he will teach them the way that they should choose.
The LORD is a friend to those who fear him* and will show them his covenant.

Psalm 25:7–11, 13

The Cry of the Church

Even so, come, Lord Jesus!

The Small Verse

Into your hands, O Lord, I commend my spirit; for you have redeemed me,
    O Lord, O God of truth. Keep me, O Lord, as the apple of your eye; hide me
    under the shadow of your wings.†

The Lord's Prayer

The Petition

Watch, O Lord, with those who wake, or watch, or weep tonight, and give Your
    angels and saints charge over those who sleep. Tend Your sick ones, O Lord
    Christ. Rest Your weary ones. Bless Your dying ones. Soothe Your suffering
    ones. Shield Your joyous ones, and all for Your love's sake. *Amen.*§

The Final Thanksgiving

Lord, you now have set your servant free to go in peace as you have promised; for
    these eyes of mine have seen the Savior, whom you have prepared for all the
    world to see: a Light to enlighten the nations, and the glory of your people
    Israel. Glory to the Father, and to the Son, and to the Holy Spirit: as it was in the
    beginning, is now, and will be for ever. *Amen.*

⚜

Friday
The Night Office   To Be Observed Before Retiring

The Call to Prayer
May the Lord Almighty grant me and those I love a peaceful night and a perfect
 end. *Amen.*†

The Request for Presence
Our help is in the Name of the Lord; the maker of heaven and earth.

The Greeting
Almighty God, my heavenly Father: I have sinned against you, through my own
 fault, in thought, and word, and deed, in what I have done and what I have left
 undone. For the sake of your Son our Lord Jesus Christ, forgive me all my
 offenses; and grant that I may serve you in newness of life, to the glory of your
 Name. *Amen.*†

The Reading   *Catherine of Siena on the Virgin*
If I consider your own great counsel, eternal Trinity, I see that in your light you
 saw the dignity and nobility of the human race. So, just as love compelled you
 to draw us out of yourself, so that same love compelled you to buy us back
 when we were lost. In fact, you showed that you loved us before we existed,
 when you chose to draw us out of yourself only for love. But you have shown
 us greater love still by giving us yourself, shutting yourself up today in the
 pouch of humanity. And what more could you have given us than to give your
 very self? So you can truly ask us, "What should I or could I have done for you
 that I have not done?" I see, then, that whatever your wisdom saw, in that great
 council of yours, as best for our salvation, is what your mercy willed, and what
 your power has today accomplished. So in that council your power, your wisdom, and your mercy agreed to our salvation, O eternal Trinity. In that council
 your great mercy chose to be merciful to your creature, and you, O eternal
 Trinity, chose to fulfill your truth in us by giving us eternal life. For this you
 had created us, that we might share and be glad in you. But your justice dis-
 agreed with us, protesting in the great council that justice, which lasts for ever,
 is just as much your hallmark as is mercy. Therefore, since your justice leaves
 no evil unpunished nor any good unrewarded, we could not be saved because
 we could not make satisfaction to you for our sin.
So what do you do? What way did your eternal unfathomable Wisdom find to fulfill
 your truth and be merciful, and to satisfy your justice as well? What remedy did
 you give us? O see what a fitting remedy! You arranged to give us the Word, your
 only-begotten Son. He would take on the clay of our flesh which had offended
 you so that when he suffered in that humanity your justice would be satisfied—
 not by humanity's power, but by the power of divinity united with that humanity. And so your truth was fulfilled, and both justice and mercy were satisfied.

O Mary, I see this Word given to you, living in you yet not separated from the Father—just as the word one has in one's mind does not leave one's heart or become separated from it even though the word is externalized and communicated to others. In these things our human dignity is revealed—that God should have done such and so great things for us.

And even more: in you, O Mary, our human strength and freedom are today revealed, for after the deliberation of such and so great a council, the angel was sent to you to announce to you the mystery of divine counsel and to seek to know your will, and God's son did not come down to your womb until you had given your will's consent. He waited at the door for you to open to him; for he wanted to come into you, but he would never have entered unless you had opened to him, saying, "Here I am, God's servant; let it be done to me as you have said."

The strength and freedom of the will is clearly revealed, then, for no good nor any evil can be done without that will. Nor is there any devil or other creature that can drive it to the guilt of deadly sin without its consent. Nor, on the other hand, can it be driven to do anything good unless it so chooses. The eternal Godhead, O Mary, was knocking at your door, but unless you had opened that door of your will, God would not have taken flesh in you. Blush, my soul, when you see that today God has become your relative in Mary. Today you have been shown that even though you were made without your help, you will not be saved without your help, for today God is knocking at the door of Mary's will and waiting for her to open to Him.

O Mary, my tenderest love! In you is written the Word from whom we have the teaching of life. You are the tablet that sets this teaching before us. I see that this Word, once written in you, was never without the cross of holy desire. Even as He was conceived within you, desire to die for the salvation of humankind was engrafted and bound into Him. This is why He had been made flesh. So it was a great cross for Him to carry for such a long time that desire, when He would have liked to see it realized at once. In fact, the Godhead was united even with Christ's body in the tomb and with His soul in limbo, and afterwards with both his soul and body. The relationship was so entered into and sealed that it will never be dissolved, any more than it has been broken up to now.

Catherine of Siena

The Cry of the Church
Come, thou long expected Jesus!

The Psalm   *For God Alone My Soul in Silence Waits*
For God alone my soul in silence waits;* truly, my hope is in him.
He alone is my rock and my salvation,* my stronghold, so that I shall not be shaken.
In God is my safety and my honor;* God is my strong rock and my refuge.
Put your trust in him always, O people,* pour out your hearts before him, for God is our refuge.
God has spoken once, twice have I heard it,* that power belongs to God.

Psalm 62:6–9, 13

The Cry of the Church

Even so, come, Lord Jesus!

The Small Verse

Into your hands, O Lord, I commend my spirit; for you have redeemed me,
   O Lord, O God of truth. Keep me, O Lord, as the apple of your eye; hide me
   under the shadow of your wings.†

The Lord's Prayer

The Petition

Watch, O Lord, with those who wake, or watch, or weep tonight, and give Your
   angels and saints charge over those who sleep. Tend Your sick ones, O Lord
   Christ. Rest Your weary ones. Bless Your dying ones. Soothe Your suffering
   ones. Shield Your joyous ones, and all for Your love's sake. *Amen*.§

The Final Thanksgiving

Lord, you now have set your servant free to go in peace as you have promised; for
   these eyes of mine have seen the Savior, whom you have prepared for all the
   world to see: a Light to enlighten the nations, and the glory of your people
   Israel. Glory to the Father, and to the Son, and to the Holy Spirit: as it was in the
   beginning, is now, and will be for ever. *Amen.*

Saturday
The Night Office   To Be Observed Before Retiring

The Call to Prayer

May the Lord Almighty grant me and those I love a peaceful night and a perfect
   end. *Amen.*†

The Request for Presence

Our help is in the Name of the Lord; the maker of heaven and earth.

The Greeting

Almighty God, my heavenly Father: I have sinned against you, through my own
   fault, in thought, and word, and deed, in what I have done and what I have left
   undone. For the sake of your Son our Lord Jesus Christ, forgive me all my
   offenses; and grant that I may serve you in newness of life, to the glory of your
   Name. *Amen.*†

The Reading

". . . for my thoughts are not your thoughts and your ways are not my ways,"
   declares YAHWEH. "For the heavens are as high above the earth as my ways are

above your ways, my thoughts above your thoughts. For, as the rain and the snow come down from the sky and do not return before having watered the earth, fertilizing it and making it germinate to provide seed for the sower and food to eat, so it is with the word that goes from my mouth: it will not return to me unfulfilled or before having carried out my good pleasure and having achieved what it was sent to do."

Isaiah 55:8–11

The Cry of the Church
Come, thou long expected Jesus!

The Psalm   *Out of Zion, Perfect in Its Beauty*
The LORD, the God of gods, has spoken;* he has called the earth from the rising of the sun to its setting.
Out of Zion, perfect in its beauty,* God reveals himself in glory.
Our God will come and will not keep silence;* before him there is a consuming flame, and round about him a raging storm.
He calls the heavens and the earth from above* to witness the judgment of his people.
"Gather before me my loyal followers,* those who have made a covenant with me and sealed it with sacrifice."
Let the heavens declare the rightness of his cause;* for God himself is judge.

Psalm 50:1–6

The Cry of the Church
Even so, come, Lord Jesus!

The Small Verse
Into your hands, O Lord, I commend my spirit; for you have redeemed me, O Lord, O God of truth. Keep me, O Lord, as the apple of your eye; hide me under the shadow of your wings.†

The Lord's Prayer

The Petition
Watch, O Lord, with those who wake, or watch, or weep tonight, and give Your angels and saints charge over those who sleep. Tend Your sick ones, O Lord Christ. Rest Your weary ones. Bless Your dying ones. Soothe Your suffering ones. Shield Your joyous ones, and all for Your love's sake. *Amen.*§

The Final Thanksgiving
Lord, you now have set your servant free to go in peace as you have promised; for these eyes of mine have seen the Savior, whom you have prepared for all the world to see: a Light to enlighten the nations, and the glory of your people Israel. Glory to the Father, and to the Son, and to the Holy Spirit: as it was in the beginning, is now, and will be for ever. *Amen.*

The Gloria

Glory be to God the Father, God the Son, and God the Holy Spirit. As it was
in the beginning, so it is now and so it shall ever be, world without end.
Alleluia. *Amen.*

The Lord's Prayer

Our Father, who art in heaven, hallowed be your Name.
May your kingdom come, and your will be done, on earth as in heaven.
Give us today our daily bread.
Forgive us our sins as we forgive those who sin against us.
Lead us not into temptation, but deliver us from evil;
for yours are the kingdom and the power and the glory
forever and ever. *Amen.*

Compline Prayers for the First Week of Christmas Are Located on Page 471.

The Following Holy Days Occur within the first week of Christmas:
The Eve of the Nativity of Our Lord: *December 24*
The Feast of The Nativity of Our Lord: Christmas Day: *December 25*
The Feast of St. Stephen: *December 26*
The Feast of St. John: *December 27*
The Commemoration of the Holy Innocents: *December 28*
The Fifth Day of the Octave of Christmas: *December 29*
The Feast of the Holy Family: *December 30*
The Eve of the Feast of the Holy Name: *December 31*

The First Week
of Christmas

The Morning Office

To Be Observed on the Hour or Half Hour
Between 6 and 9 a.m.

The Call to Prayer
Wake up, my spirit; awake, lute and harp;* I myself will waken the dawn.

Psalm 57:8

The Request for Presence
O Lamb of God, that takes away the sins of the world, have mercy upon me.
O Lamb of God, that takes away the sins of the world, have mercy upon me.
O Lamb of God, that takes away the sins of the world, grant me your peace.

Agnus Dei

The Greeting
For you alone are the Holy One, you alone are the Lord, you alone are the Most
   High, Jesus Christ, with the Holy Spirit, in the Glory of God the Father.

The Refrain for the Morning Lessons
Be strong and let your heart take courage,* all you who wait for the LORD.

Psalm 31:24

A Reading   *The Prophecy of the Priest Zechariah, Father of John the Baptizer*
Zechariah was filled with the Holy Spirit and spoke this prophecy: "*Blessed be the*
   Lord, the God of Israel, for he has visited his people, he has *set them free,* and he
   has established for us a saving power in the House of his servant David, just as
   he proclaimed, by the mouth of his holy prophets from ancient times, that he
   would save us from our *enemies and from the hands of all those who hate us,* and
   show *faithful love to our ancestors, and so keep in mind his holy covenant.* This was
   the oath he swore to our father Abraham, that he would grant us, free from
   fear, to be delivered from the hands of our enemies, to serve him in holiness
   and uprightness in his presence, all our days."

Luke 1:67–75

The Refrain
Be strong and let your heart take courage,* all you who wait for the LORD.

The Morning Psalm   *In the Roll of the Book It Is Written Concerning Me*
In sacrifice and offering you take no pleasure* (you have given me ears to hear you);
Burnt-offering and sin-offering you have not required,* and so I said, "Behold, I
   come.
In the roll of the book it is written concerning me:* 'I love to do your will, O my
   God; your law is deep in my heart.' "

Psalm 40:7–9

The Refrain
Be strong and let your heart take courage,* all you who wait for the LORD.

The Cry of the Church
Even so, come, Lord Jesus!

The Lord's Prayer

The Prayer Appointed for the Week

Purify my conscience, Almighty God, by your daily visitation, that your Son Jesus Christ, at his coming, may find in me a mansion prepared for himself; who lives and reigns with you and the Holy Spirit, one God, now and for ever. Amen.✝

The Concluding Prayer of the Church

Lord God, almighty and everlasting Father, you have brought me in safety to this new day: Preserve me with your mighty power, that I may not fall into sin, nor be overcome by adversity; and in all I do direct me to the fulfilling of your purpose; through Jesus Christ my Lord. Amen.✝

The Midday Office

To Be Observed on the Hour or Half Hour Between 11 a.m. and 2 p.m.

The Call to Prayer

Ascribe to the LORD, you families of the peoples;* ascribe to the LORD honor and power.
Ascribe to the LORD the honor due his Name;* bring offerings and come into his courts.
Worship the LORD in the beauty of holiness . . .

Psalm 96:7–9

The Request for Presence

For God alone my soul in silence waits;* truly, my hope is in him.

Psalm 62:6

The Greeting

Happy are the people whose strength is in you!* whose hearts are set on the pilgrims' way.

Psalm 84:4

The Refrain for the Midday Lessons

My heart, therefore, is glad, and my spirit rejoices;* my body also shall rest in hope.

Psalm 16:9

A Reading

YAHWEH declares, "Because of this, my people will know my name, because of this they will know when the day comes, that it is I saying, 'Here I am!' How beautiful on the mountains, are the feet of the messenger announcing peace, of the messenger of good news, who proclaims salvation and says to Zion, 'Your God is king!' The voices of your watchmen! Now they raise their voices, shouting for joy together, for with their own eyes they have seen YAHWEH returning to Zion. Break into shouts together, shouts for joy, you ruins of Jerusalem; for YAHWEH has consoled his people, he has redeemed Jerusalem. YAHWEH has bared his holy arm for all the nations to see, and all the ends of the earth have seen the salvation of our God."

Isaiah 52:6–10

The Refrain
My heart, therefore, is glad, and my spirit rejoices;* my body also shall rest in hope.

The Midday Psalm   The Lord of Hosts Is with Us
There is a river whose streams make glad the city of God,* the holy habitation of the Most High.

God is in the midst of her; she shall not be overthrown;* God shall help her at the break of day.

The nations make much ado, and the kingdoms are shaken;* God has spoken, and the earth shall melt away.

The Lord of hosts is with us;* the God of Jacob is our stronghold.

Psalm 46:5–8

The Refrain
My heart, therefore, is glad, and my spirit rejoices;* my body also shall rest in hope.

The Small Verse
'I am the Alpha and the Omega,' says the Lord God, who is, who was, and who is to come, the Almighty.

Revelation 1:8

The Lord's Prayer

The Prayer Appointed for the Week
Purify my conscience, Almighty God, by your daily visitation, that your Son Jesus Christ, at his coming, may find in me a mansion prepared for himself; who lives and reigns with you and the Holy Spirit, one God, now and for ever. *Amen.*†

The Concluding Prayer of the Church
O God, the source of eternal light: Shed forth your unending day upon all of us who watch for you, that our lips may praise you, our lives may bless you, and our worship may give you glory; through Jesus Christ our Lord. *Amen.*†

The Vespers Office   To Be Observed on the Hour or Half Hour
Between 5 and 8 p.m.

The Call to Prayer
Give thanks to the Lord, for he is good,* and his mercy endures for ever.

Psalm 107:1

The Request for Presence
So teach us to number our days* that we may apply our hearts to wisdom.

Psalm 90:12

The Greeting

Remember not the sins of my youth and my transgressions;* remember me
according to your love and for the sake of your goodness, O LORD.

Psalm 25:6

The Hymn   *Silent Night*

Silent night, Holy night,   Silent night, Holy night,
All is calm, all is bright.   Son of God, love's pure light
Round yon virgin mother and child.   Radiant beams from thy holy face,
Holy infant, so tender and mild,   With the dawn of redeeming grace,
Sleep in heavenly peace.   Jesus, Lord, at thy birth.
Sleep in heavenly peace.   Jesus, Lord, at thy birth.

Silent night, Holy night,   *Joseph Mohr*
Shepherds quake at the sight,
Glories stream from heaven afar,
Heavenly hosts sing alleluia;
Christ the Savior is born!
Christ the Savior is born!

The Refrain for the Vespers Lessons

Behold, God is my helper;* it is the LORD who sustains my life.

Psalm 54:4

The Vespers Psalm   *Come Now and Look Upon the Works of the LORD*

Come now and look upon the works of the LORD,* what awesome things he has
done on earth.
"Be still, then, and know that I am God;* I will be exalted among the nations; I will
be exalted in the earth."
The LORD of hosts is with us;* the God of Jacob is our stronghold.

Psalm 46:9, 11–12

The Refrain

Behold, God is my helper;* it is the LORD who sustains my life.

The Small Verse

The Lord is my shepherd and nothing is wanting to me. In green pastures He hath
settled me.

THE SHORT BREVIARY

The Lord's Prayer

The Prayer Appointed for the Week

Purify my conscience, Almighty God, by your daily visitation, that your Son Jesus
Christ, at his coming, may find in me a mansion prepared for himself; who
lives and reigns with you and the Holy Spirit, one God, now and for ever.
Amen.✝

The Concluding Prayer of the Church

O God, you make us glad by the yearly festival of the birth of your only Son Jesus Christ: Grant that I, who joyfully receive him as my Redeemer, may with sure confidence behold him when he comes to be our Judge; who lives and reigns with you and the Holy Spirit, one God, now and for ever. *Amen.*†

❧

The Morning Office   To Be Observed on the Hour or Half Hour
Between 6 and 9 a.m.

The Call to Prayer

Be glad, you righteous, and rejoice in the Lord;* shout for joy, all who are true of heart.

Psalm 32:12

The Request for Presence

Let the peoples praise you, O God;* let all the peoples praise you.

Let the nations be glad and sing for joy,* for you judge the peoples with equity and guide all the nations upon earth.

Let the peoples praise you, O God;* let all the peoples praise you.

Psalm 67:3–5

The Greeting

. . . O Lord my God, I will give you thanks for ever.

Psalm 30:13

The Refrain for the Morning Lessons

In the roll of the book it is written concerning me . . .

Psalm 40:9

A Reading

Now it happened that at this time Caesar Augustus issued a decree that a census should be made of the whole inhabited world. This census—the first—took place while Quirinius was governor of Syria, and everyone went to be registered, each to his own town. So Joseph set out from the town of Nazareth in Galilee for Judaea, to David's town called Bethlehem, since he was of David's House and line, in order to be registered together with Mary, his betrothed, who was with child. Now it happened that, while they were there, the time came for her to have her child, and she gave birth to a son, her first-born. She wrapped him in swaddling clothes and laid him in a manger because there was no room for them in the living-space. In the countryside close by there were shepherds out in the fields keeping guard over their sheep during the watches of the night. An angel of the Lord stood over them and the glory of the Lord shone around them. They were terrified, but the angel said, 'Do not be afraid. Look, I bring you news of great joy, a joy to be shared by the whole people. Today in the town of David, a Savior has been born to you; he is Christ the Lord. And here is a sign for you: you will find a baby wrapped in swaddling clothes and lying in a manger.' And all at once with the angel there was a great throng of the hosts of heaven, praising God with the words: Glory to God in the highest heaven, and on earth peace for those he favors. Now it happened that when the angels had gone from them into heaven, the shepherds said to one another, 'Let us go to Bethlehem and see this event which the Lord has made known to us.' So they hurried away and found Mary and Joseph, and the baby lying in the manger. When they saw the child they repeated what they had been told about him, and everyone who heard it was astonished at what the shepherds said to them. As for Mary, she treasured all these things and pondered them in her heart. And the shepherds went back glorifying and praising God for all they had heard and seen, just as they had been told.

Luke 2:1–20

The Refrain
In the roll of the book it is written concerning me . . .

The Morning Psalm
Shout with Joy to the LORD

Sing to the LORD a new song,* for he has done marvelous things.
With his right hand and his holy arm* has he won for himself the victory.
The LORD has made known his victory;* his righteousness has he openly shown in the sight of the nations.
He remembers his mercy and faithfulness to the house of Israel,* and all the ends of the earth have seen the victory of our God.
Shout with joy to the LORD, all you lands;* lift up your voice, rejoice, and sing.
Sing to the LORD with the harp,* with the harp and the voice of song.
With trumpets and the sound of the horn* shout with joy before the King, the LORD.
Let the sea make a noise and all that is in it,* the lands and those who dwell therein.
Let the rivers clap their hands,* and let the hills ring out with joy before the LORD, when he comes to judge the earth.
In righteousness shall he judge the world* and the peoples with equity.

Psalm 98

The Refrain
In the roll of the book it is written concerning me . . .

The Gloria

The Lord's Prayer

The Prayer Appointed for the Week
Almighty God, you have given your only-begotten Son to take our nature upon him, and to be born this day of a pure virgin: Grant that I, who have been born

again and made your child by adoption and grace, may daily be renewed by your Holy Spirit; through my Lord Jesus Christ, to whom with you and the same Spirit be honor and glory, now and for ever. *Amen.*†

The Concluding Prayer of the Church

O God, you have caused the holy night to shine with the brightness of the true Light: Grant that I, who have known the mystery of that Light on earth, may also enjoy him perfectly in heaven; where with you and the Holy Spirit he lives and reigns, one God, in glory everlasting. *Amen.*†

The Midday Office	To Be Observed on the Hour or Half Hour
	Between 11 a.m. and 2 p.m.

The Call to Prayer

Come, let us bow down, and bend the knee,* and kneel before the Lord our Maker.

For he is our God, and we are the people of his pasture and the sheep of his hand.*
Oh, that today you would hearken to his voice!

Psalm 95:6–7

The Request for Presence

My merciful God comes to meet me . . .

Psalm 59:11

The Greeting

I will give you thanks for what you have done* and declare the goodness of your Name in the presence of the godly.

Psalm 52:9

The Refrain for the Midday Lessons

Let me announce the decree of the Lord:* he said to me, "You are my Son; this day have I begotten you."

Psalm 2:7

A Reading

My dear friends, let us love each other, since love is from God and everyone who loves is a child of God and knows God. Whoever fails to love does not know God, because God is love. This is the revelation of God's love for us, that God sent his only Son into the world that we might have life through him. Love consists in this: it is not we who loved God, but God loved us and sent his Son to expiate our sins.

1 John 4:7–10

The Refrain

Let me announce the decree of the Lord:* he said to me, "You are my Son; this day have I begotten you."

The Midday Psalm   *Righteousness and Peace Have Kissed Each Other*

I will listen to what the Lord God is saying,* for he is speaking peace to his faithful
 people and to those who turn their hearts to him.

Truly, his salvation is very near to those who fear him,* that his glory may dwell in
 our land.

Mercy and truth have met together;* righteousness and peace have kissed each
 other.

Truth shall spring up from the earth,* and righteousness shall look down from
 heaven.

The Lord will indeed grant prosperity,* and our land will yield its increase.

Righteousness shall go before him,* and peace shall be a pathway for his feet.

Psalm 85:8–13

The Refrain

Let me announce the decree of the Lord:* he said to me, "You are my Son; this day
 have I begotten you."

The Gloria

The Lord's Prayer

The Prayer Appointed for the Week

Almighty God, you have given your only-begotten Son to take our nature upon
 him, and to be born this day of a pure virgin: Grant that I, who have been born
 again and made your child by adoption and grace, may daily be renewed by
 your Holy Spirit; through my Lord Jesus Christ, to whom with you and the
 same Spirit be honor and glory, now and for ever. *Amen.†*

The Concluding Prayer of the Church

O God, you have caused the holy night to shine with the brightness of the true
 Light: Grant that I, who have known the mystery of that Light on earth, may
 also enjoy him perfectly in heaven; where with you and the Holy Spirit he lives
 and reigns, one God, in glory everlasting. *Amen.†*

The Vespers Office   To Be Observed on the Hour or Half Hour
Between 5 and 8 p.m.

The Call to Prayer

Sing to the Lord a new song;* sing to the Lord, all the whole earth.

Sing to the Lord and bless his Name;* proclaim the good news of his salvation
 from day to day.

Declare his glory among the nations* and his wonders among all peoples.

Psalm 96:1–3

The Request for Presence

Exalt yourself above the heavens, O God,* and your glory over all the earth.

Psalm 57:6

The Greeting
I will offer you a freewill sacrifice* and praise your Name, O Lord, for it is good.
For you have rescued me from every trouble . . .

Psalm 54:6–7

The Hymn   *Joy to the World*

Joy to the world! The Lord is come:
Let earth receive her King;
Let every heart prepare him room,
And heaven and nature sing,
And heaven and nature sing,
And heaven and nature sing.

Joy to the world! The Savior reigns;
Let us our songs employ,
While fields and floods, rocks, hills, and plains,
Repeat the sounding joy,
Repeat the sounding joy,
Repeat the sounding joy.

No more let sins or sorrows grow,
Nor thorns infest the ground;
He comes to make his blessings flow
Far as the curse is found,
Far as the curse is found,
Far as the curse is found.

He rules the world with truth and grace,
And makes the nations prove
The glories of his righteousness,
And wonders of his love,
And wonders of his love,
And wonders of his love.

Isaac Watts

The Refrain for the Vespers Lessons
I lie down and go to sleep;* I wake again, because the Lord sustains me.

Psalm 3:5

The Vespers Psalm   *My Heart Is Glad, My Spirit Rejoices,*
                                        My Body Shall Rest in Peace

O Lord, you are my portion and my cup;* it is you who uphold my lot.
My boundaries enclose a pleasant land;* indeed, I have a goodly heritage.
I will bless the Lord who gives me counsel;* my heart teaches me, night after
   night.
I have set the Lord always before me;* because he is at my right hand I shall not
   fall.
My heart, therefore, is glad, and my spirit rejoices;* my body also shall rest in hope.

For you will not abandon me to the grave,* nor let your holy one see the Pit.
You will show me the path of life;* in your presence there is fullness of joy, and in
    your right hand are pleasures for evermore.

Psalm 16:5–11

The Refrain
I lie down and go to sleep;* I wake again, because the LORD sustains me.

The Gloria

The Lord's Prayer

The Prayer Appointed for the Week
Almighty God, you have given your only-begotten Son to take our nature upon
    him, and to be born this day of a pure virgin: Grant that I, who have been born
    again and made your child by adoption and grace, may daily be renewed by
    your Holy Spirit; through my Lord Jesus Christ, to whom with you and the
    same Spirit be honor and glory, now and for ever. *Amen.*†

The Concluding Prayer of the Church
O God, you have caused the holy night to shine with the brightness of the true
    Light: Grant that I, who have known the mystery of that Light on earth, may
    also enjoy him perfectly in heaven; where with you and the Holy Spirit he lives
    and reigns, one God, in glory everlasting. *Amen.*†

The Morning Office   **To Be Observed on the Hour or Half Hour**
Between 6 and 9 a.m.

The Call to Prayer
Hallelujah! Praise the LORD, O my soul!* I will praise the LORD as long as I live; I
    will sing praises to my God while I have my being.

Psalm 146:1

The Request for Presence
Set a watch before my mouth, O LORD, and guard the door of my lips;* let not my
    heart incline to any evil thing.
Let me not be occupied in wickedness with evildoers,* nor eat of their choice
    foods.
Let the righteous smite me in friendly rebuke;* let not the oil of the unrighteous
    anoint my head.

Psalm 141:3–5

The Greeting

Not to us, O Lord, not to us, but to your Name give glory;* because of your love
   and because of your faithfulness.

Psalm 115:1

The Refrain for the Morning Lessons

. . . the testimony of the Lord is sure and gives wisdom to the innocent.

Psalm 19:7b

A Reading   *St. Stephen, who was one of the first class of seven deacons appointed
         by the Apostles in Jerusalem, was also the first Christian martyr.
         Because of his testimony as the first to die for the faith of Christ, the
         Church observes his feast day immediately after that which cele-
         brates the birth of Stephen's Lord.*

Jesus said to the people: "This is why—look—I am sending you prophets and wise
   men and scribes; some you will slaughter and crucify, some you will scourge in
   the synagogues and hunt from town to town; and so you will draw down on
   yourselves the blood of every upright person that has been shed on the earth,
   from the blood of Abel to the holy blood of Zechariah son of Barachiah whom
   you murdered between the sanctuary and the altar. In truth I tell you, it will all
   recoil on this generation."

Matthew 23:34–36

The Refrain

. . . the testimony of the Lord is sure and gives wisdom to the innocent.

The Morning Psalm   *Into Your Hands I Commend My Spirit*

In you, O Lord, have I taken refuge; let me never be put to shame;* deliver me in
   your righteousness.
Incline your ear to me;* make haste to deliver me.
Be my strong rock, a castle to keep me safe, for you are my crag and my
   stronghold;* for the sake of your Name, lead me and guide me.
Take me out of the net that they have secretly set for me,* for you are my tower of
   strength.
Into your hands I commend my spirit,* for you have redeemed me, O Lord, O
   God of truth.

Psalm 31:1–5

The Refrain

. . . the testimony of the Lord is sure and gives wisdom to the innocent.

The Cry of the Church

O God, come to my assistance! O Lord, make haste to help me!

The Lord's Prayer

The Prayer Appointed for the Week

Almighty God, you have given your only-begotten Son to take our nature upon
him, and to be born of a pure virgin: Grant that I, who have been born again
and made your child by adoption and grace, may daily be renewed by your
Holy Spirit; through my Lord Jesus Christ, to whom with you and the same
Spirit be honor and glory, now and for ever. *Amen.*†

Concluding Prayers of the Church

I give you thanks, O Lord of Glory, for the example of the first martyr Stephen,
who looked up to heaven and prayed for his persecutors to your Son Jesus
Christ, who stands at your right hand; where he lives and reigns with you and
the Holy Spirit, one God, in glory everlasting. *Amen.*†

Lord God, almighty and everlasting Father, you have brought me in safety to this
new day: Preserve me with your mighty power, that I may not fall into sin, nor
be overcome by adversity; and in all I do direct me to the fulfilling of your purpose; through Jesus Christ my Lord. *Amen.*†

The Midday Office   **To Be Observed on the Hour or Half Hour**
Between 11 a.m. and 2 p.m.

The Call to Prayer

Come and listen, all you who fear God,* and I will tell you what he has done for me.
Psalm 66:14

The Request for Presence

I call upon you, O God, for you will answer me;* incline your ear to me and hear
my words.
Psalm 17:6

The Greeting

The Lord is in his holy temple; let all the earth keep silence before him. Amen.
Traditional

The Refrain for the Midday Lessons

The LORD is my strength and my song,* and he has become my salvation.
Psalm 118:14

A Reading

Stephen was filled with grace and power and began to work miracles and great
signs among the people. Then certain people came forward to debate with
Stephen, some from Cyrene and Alexandria who were members of the synagogue called the Synagogue of Freedmen, and others from Cilicia and Asia.
They found they could not stand up against him because of his wisdom, and
the Spirit that prompted what he said. So they procured some men to say, 'We
heard him using blasphemous language against Moses and against God.'
Having turned people against him as well as the elders and scribes, they took
Stephen by surprise, and arrested him and brought him before the Sanhedrin.

There they put up false witnesses to say, 'This man is always making speeches against this holy place and the Law. We have heard him say that Jesus, the Nazarene, is going to destroy this Place and alter the traditions that Moses handed down to us.' The members of the Sanhedrin all looked intently at Stephen, and his face appeared to them like the face of an angel . . . They were infuriated . . . and ground their teeth at him. But Stephen, filled with the Holy Spirit, gazed into heaven and saw the glory of God, and Jesus standing at God's right hand. 'Look! I can see heaven thrown open,' he said, 'and the Son of man standing at the right hand of God.' All the members of the council shouted out and stopped their ears with their hands; then they made a concerted rush at him, thrust him out of the city and stoned him. The witnesses put down their clothes at the feet of a young man called Saul. As they were stoning him, Stephen said in invocation, 'Lord Jesus, receive my spirit.' Then he knelt down and said aloud, 'Lord, do not hold this sin against them.' And with these words he fell asleep.

Acts 6:8–15, 7:54–60

The Refrain
The Lord is my strength and my song,* and he has become my salvation.

The Midday Psalm   *My Times Are in Your Hands*
I have become a reproach to all my enemies and even to my neighbors,* a dismay
    to those of my acquaintance; when they see me in the street they avoid me.
I am forgotten like a dead man, out of mind;* I am as useless as a broken pot.
For I have heard the whispering of the crowd; fear is all around;* they put their
    heads together against me; they plot to take my life.
But as for me, I have trusted in you, O Lord.* I have said, "You are my God.
My times are in your hand;* rescue me from the hand of my enemies, and from
    those who persecute me.
Make your face to shine upon your servant.*"

Psalm 31:11–16

The Refrain
The Lord is my strength and my song,* and he has become my salvation.

The Gloria

The Lord's Prayer

The Prayer Appointed for the Week
Almighty God, you have given your only-begotten Son to take our nature upon
him, and to be born of a pure virgin: Grant that I, who have been born again
and made your child by adoption and grace, may daily be renewed by your
Holy Spirit; through my Lord Jesus Christ, to whom with you and the same
Spirit be honor and glory, now and for ever. *Amen.*†

Concluding Prayers of the Church

Almighty God, who gave to your servant Stephen boldness to confess the Name of our Savior Jesus Christ before the rulers of this world, and courage to die for this faith: Grant that I may always be ready to give a reason for the hope that is in me, and to suffer gladly for the sake of our Lord Jesus Christ; who lives and reigns with you and the Holy Spirit, one God, for ever and ever. *Amen.*†

O God, you make me glad with the weekly remembrance of the glorious resurrection of your Son my Lord: Give me this day such blessing through my worship of you, that the week to come may be spent in your favor; through Jesus Christ our Lord. *Amen.*†

The Vespers Office   To Be Observed on the Hour or Half Hour
                                                              Between 5 and 8 p.m.

The Call to Prayer

Hallelujah! Praise the LORD from the heavens;* praise him in the heights.

Psalm 148:1

The Request for Presence

You are my helper and my deliverer,* O LORD, do not tarry.

Psalm 70:6

The Greeting

O LORD, I am your servant;* I am your servant and the child of your handmaid; you have freed me from my bonds.

Psalm 116:14

The Hymn   *Good King Wenceslaus*

Good King Wenceslaus looked out on the feast of Stephen.
When the snow lay round about, deep and crisp and even.
Brightly shone the moon that night, though the frost was cruel,
When a poor man came in sight gathering winter fuel.

"Hither, page, and stand by me if you know it telling.
Yonder peasant, who is he, where and what his dwelling?"
"Sire, he lives a good league hence, underneath the mountain
Right against the forest fence, by Saint Agnes' fountain."

"Bring me flesh and bring me wine, bring me pine-logs hither.
You and I will see him dine when we bear them thither."
Page and monarch forth they went, forth they went together.
Through the rude winds' wild lament, and the bitter weather.

"Sire, the night is darker now, and the wind blows stronger.
Fails my heart I know not how, I can go no longer."
"Mark my footsteps, my good page, tread now in them boldly.
You shall find the winter's rage freeze your blood less coldly."

In his master's steps he trod where the snow lay dented.
Heat was in the very sod which the saint had printed.
Therefore, Christian men, be sure, wealth or rank possessing.
You who now will bless the poor, shall yourselves find blessing.

Unknown

The Refrain for the Vespers Lessons

Be strong and let your heart take courage,* all you who wait for the LORD.

Psalm 31:24

The Vespers Psalm   *Come, Children, and Listen to Me*

Fear the LORD, you that are his saints,* for those who fear him lack nothing.

The young lions lack and suffer hunger,* but those who seek the LORD lack
   nothing that is good.

Come, children, and listen to me;* I will teach you the fear of the LORD.

Many are the troubles of the righteous,* but the LORD will deliver him out of them
   all.

The LORD ransoms the life of his servants,* and none will be punished who trust in
   him.

Psalm 34:9–11, 19, 22

The Refrain

Be strong and let your heart take courage,* all you who wait for the LORD.

The Gloria

The Lord's Prayer

The Prayer Appointed for the Week

Almighty God, you have given your only-begotten Son to take our nature upon
   him, and to be born of a pure virgin: Grant that I, who have been born again
   and made your child by adoption and grace, may daily be renewed by your
   Holy Spirit; through my Lord Jesus Christ, to whom with you and the same
   Spirit be honor and glory, now and for ever. *Amen.†*

The Concluding Prayer of the Church

Almighty God, by your Holy Spirit you have made me one with your saints in
   heaven and on earth: Grant that in my earthly pilgrimage I may always be supported by this fellowship of love and prayer, and know myself to be surrounded by their witness to your power and mercy. I ask this for the sake of
   Jesus Christ, in whom all my intercessions are acceptable through the Spirit,
   and who lives and reigns for ever and ever. *Amen.†*

The Morning Office

The Call to Prayer

Bless the LORD, you angels of his, you mighty ones who do his bidding,* and hearken to the voice of his word.

Bless the LORD, all you his hosts,* you ministers of his who do his will.

Bless the LORD, all you works of his,* in all places of his dominion . . .

Psalm 103:20–22

The Request for Presence

Be seated on your lofty throne, O Most High;* O LORD, judge the nations.

Psalm 7:8

The Greeting

Not to us, O LORD, not to us, but to your Name give glory;* because of your love and because of your faithfulness.

Psalm 115:1

The Refrain for the Morning Lessons

The LORD is my strength and my song,* and he has become my salvation.

Psalm 118:14

A Reading

On the second day of Christmas, the Church celebrates the life of St. John, whom Scripture refers to as "the beloved disciple." The only one of the original twelve to not suffer martyrdom, St. John spent all of his long life writing and preaching.

Peter turned and saw the disciple whom Jesus loved following them—the one who had leaned back close to his chest at the supper and had said to him, 'Lord, who is it that will betray you?' Seeing him, Peter said to Jesus, 'What about him, Lord?' Jesus answered, 'If I want him to stay behind until I come, what does it matter to you? You are to follow me.' The rumor then went out among the brothers that this disciple would not die. Yet Jesus had not said to Peter, 'He will not die,' but, 'If I want him to stay behind till I come.' This disciple is the one who vouches for these things and has written them down, and we know that his testimony is true. There was much else that Jesus did; if it were written down in detail. I do not suppose the world itself would hold all the books that would be written.

The Conclusion of the Gospel of St. John (21:20–25)

The Refrain

The LORD is my strength and my song,* and he has become my salvation.

The Morning Psalm

It Is a Good Thing to Tell of Your Loving-kindness in the Morning

It is a good thing to give thanks to the LORD,* and to sing praises to your Name, O Most High;

To tell of your loving-kindness early in the morning* and of your faithfulness in
the night season;
On the psaltery, and on the lyre,* and to the melody of the harp.
For you have made me glad by your acts, O LORD;* and I shout for joy because of
the works of your hands.

Psalm 92:1–4

The Refrain
The LORD is my strength and my song,* and he has become my salvation.

The Cry of the Church
Let us praise the Lord, whom the Angels are praising, whom the Cherubim and
Seraphim proclaim: Holy, holy, holy!

THE SHORT BREVIARY

The Lord's Prayer

The Prayer Appointed for the Week
Almighty God, you have given your only-begotten Son to take our nature upon
him, and to be born of a pure virgin: Grant that I, who have been born again
and made your child by adoption and grace, may daily be renewed by your
Holy Spirit; through my Lord Jesus Christ, to whom with you and the same
Spirit be honor and glory, now and for ever. *Amen.*†

Concluding Prayers of the Church
Shed upon your Church, O Lord, the brightness of your light, that we, being illumined by the teaching of your apostle and evangelist John, may walk in the
light of your truth, that at length we may attain to the fullness of eternal life;
through Jesus Christ our Lord, who lives and reigns with you and the Holy
Spirit, one God, for ever and ever. *Amen.*

Lord God, almighty and everlasting Father, you have brought me in safety to this
new day: Preserve me with your mighty power, that I may not fall into sin, nor
be overcome by adversity; and in all I do direct me to the fulfilling of your purpose; through Jesus Christ my Lord. *Amen.*†

The Midday Office   **To Be Observed on the Hour or Half Hour**
Between 11 a.m. and 2 p.m.

The Call to Prayer
Bless the LORD, you angels of his, you mighty ones who do his bidding,* and hear-
ken to the voice of his word.
Bless the LORD, all you his hosts,* you ministers of his who do his will.
Bless the LORD, all you works of his, in all places of his dominion;* bless the LORD,
O my soul.

Psalm 103:20–22

The Request for Presence

I am a stranger here on earth;* do not hide your commandments from me.

Psalm 119:19

The Greeting

I am bound by the vow I made to you, O God;* I will present to you thank-
offerings;

For you have rescued my soul from death and my feet from stumbling,* that I may
walk before God in the light of the living.

Psalm 56:11–12

The Refrain for the Midday Lessons

Glory be to him whose power, working in us, can do infinitely more than we can
ask or imagine; glory be to him from generation to generation in the Church
and in Christ Jesus for ever and ever. Amen.

Ephesians 3:20–21

A Reading

Something which has existed since the beginning, which we have heard, which
we have seen with our own eyes, which we have watched and touched with
our own hands, the Word of life—this is our theme. That life was made visible;
we saw it and are giving our testimony, declaring to you the eternal life, which
was present to the Father and has been revealed to us. We are declaring to you
what we have seen and heard, so that you too may share our life. Our life is
shared with the Father and with his Son Jesus Christ. We are writing this to you
so that our joy may be complete.

1 John 1:1–4

The Refrain

Glory be to him whose power, working in us, can do infinitely more than we can
ask or imagine; glory be to him from generation to generation in the Church
and in Christ Jesus for ever and ever. Amen.

The Midday Psalm   *The Righteous Shall Spread Abroad Like a Cedar of Lebanon*

The righteous shall flourish like a palm tree,* and shall spread abroad like a cedar
of Lebanon.

Those who are planted in the house of the LORD* shall flourish in the courts of our
God;

They shall still bear fruit in old age;* they shall be green and succulent;

That they may show how upright the LORD is,* my Rock, in whom there is no
fault.

Psalm 92:11–14

The Refrain

Glory be to him whose power, working in us, can do infinitely more than we can
ask or imagine; glory be to him from generation to generation in the Church
and in Christ Jesus for ever and ever. Amen.

The Gloria

The Lord's Prayer

The Prayer Appointed for the Week

Almighty God, you have given your only-begotten Son to take our nature upon
him, and to be born of a pure virgin: Grant that I, who have been born again
and made your child by adoption and grace, may daily be renewed by your
Holy Spirit; through my Lord Jesus Christ, to whom with you and the same
Spirit be honor and glory, now and for ever. *Amen.*†

Concluding Prayers of the Church

I thank you, heavenly Father, for the witness of your apostle and evangelist John
to the Gospel of your Son my Savior; and I pray that after his example, I may
with ready will and heart obey the calling of my Lord, who lives and reigns
with you and the Holy Spirit, one God, now and for ever. *Amen.*†

Almighty God, you have poured upon us the new light of your incarnate Word:
Grant that this light, enkindled in my heart, may shine forth in my life; through
Jesus Christ our Lord, who lives and reigns with you, in the unity of the Holy
Spirit, one God, now and for ever. *Amen.*†

The Vespers Office **To Be Observed on the Hour or Half Hour**
Between 5 and 8 p.m.

The Call to Prayer

Let the Name of the LORD be blessed,* from this time forth for evermore.
From the rising of the sun to its going down* let the Name of the LORD be praised.

Psalm 113:2–3

The Request for Presence

Hear my prayer, O God;* do not hide yourself from my petition.
Listen to me and answer me . . .

Psalm 55:1–2

The Greeting

The Lord is in his holy temple; let all the earth keep silence before him.

Traditional

The Hymn

Come sing, your choirs exultant, those messengers of God,
Through whom the living Gospels came sounding all abroad!
Whose voice proclaimed salvation that poured upon the night,
And drove away the shadows, and filled the world with light.

In one harmonious witness the chosen four combine,
While each his own commission fulfills in every line;
As, in the prophet's vision from out the amber flame
In mystic form and image four living creatures came.

Four-square on this foundation the Church of Christ remains,
A house to stand unshaken by floods or winds or rains.
How blessed this habitation of gospel liberty,
Where with a holy people God dwells in Unity.

Latin, 12th Century

The Refrain for the Vespers Lessons

Why are you so full of heaviness, O my soul?* and why are you so disquieted
within me?

Put your trust in God;* for I will yet give thanks to him, who is the help of my
countenance, and my God.

Psalm 42:6–7

The Vespers Psalm   *He Is Bound to Me in Love*

Because you have made the LORD your refuge,* and the Most High your
habitation,

There shall no evil happen to you,* neither shall any plague come near your
dwelling.

For he shall give his angels charge over you,* to keep you in all your ways.

They shall bear you in their hands,* lest you dash your foot against a stone.

You shall tread upon the lion and adder;* you shall trample the young lion and the
serpent under your feet.

Because he is bound to me in love, therefore will I deliver him;* I will protect him,
because he knows my Name.

He shall call upon me, and I will answer him;* I am with him in trouble; I will
rescue him and bring him to honor.

With long life will I satisfy him,* and show him my salvation.

Psalm 91:9–16

The Refrain

Why are you so full of heaviness, O my soul?* and why are you so disquieted
within me?

Put your trust in God;* for I will yet give thanks to him, who is the help of my
countenance, and my God.

The Cry of the Church

O God, come to my assistance! O Lord, make haste to help me!

The Lord's Prayer

The Prayer Appointed for the Week

Almighty God, you have given your only-begotten Son to take our nature upon
him, and to be born of a pure virgin: Grant that I, who have been born again
and made your child by adoption and grace, may daily be renewed by your
Holy Spirit; through my Lord Jesus Christ, to whom with you and the same
Spirit be honor and glory, now and for ever. *Amen.*†

Concluding Prayers of the Church
Almighty God, whose will it is to be glorified in your saints, and who raised up
    your servant John to be a light in the world: Shine, we pray, in our hearts, that
    we also in our generation may show forth your praise, who called us out of
    darkness into your marvelous light; through Jesus Christ our Lord, who lives
    and reigns with you and the Holy Spirit, one God, now and for ever. *Amen.*†

Save me, Lord, while I am awake and keep me while I sleep, that I may wake with
    Christ and rest in peace. *Amen.*

❧

The Morning Office   To Be Observed on the Hour or Half Hour
                                              Between 6 and 9 a.m.

The Call to Prayer
Come, let us sing to the LORD;* let us shout for joy to the Rock of our salvation.
                                                                    Psalm 95:1

The Request for Presence
Bow your heavens, O LORD, and come down;* touch the mountains, and they shall
    smoke.
                                                                    Psalm 144:5

The Greeting
My lips will sing with joy when I play to you,* and so will my soul, which you
    have redeemed.
                                                                    Psalm 71:23

The Refrain for the Morning Lessons
Remember, LORD, how short life is,* how frail you have made all flesh.
                                                                    Psalm 89:47

A Reading   *On December 28, the Church remembers with sorrow the slaughter
                     of the male infants of Bethlehem. They were indeed the first vic-
                     tims of the persecution of Christians.*

After they had left, suddenly the angel of the Lord appeared to Joseph in a dream
    and said, 'Get up, take the child and his mother with you, and escape into
    Egypt, and stay there until I tell you, because Herod intends to search for the
    child and do away with him.' So Joseph got up and, taking the child and his
    mother with him, left that night for Egypt, where he stayed until Herod was
    dead. This was to fulfill what the Lord had spoken through the prophet: *I called
    my son out of Egypt.* Herod was furious on realizing that he had been fooled by

the wise men, and in Bethlehem and its surrounding district he had all the male children killed who were two years old or less, reckoning by the date he had been careful to ask the wise men. Then were fulfilled the words spoken through the prophet Jeremiah: *A voice is heard in Ramah, lamenting and weeping bitterly: it is Rachel weeping for her children, refusing to be comforted because they are no more.*

Matthew 2:13–18

The Refrain

Remember, LORD, how short life is,* how frail you have made all flesh.

The Morning Psalm   *Show Your Splendor to Our Children*

Return, O LORD; how long will you tarry?* be gracious to your servants.

Satisfy us by your loving-kindness in the morning;* so shall we rejoice and be glad all the days of our life.

Make us glad by the measure of the days that you afflicted us* and the years in which we suffered adversity.

Show your servants your works* and your splendor to their children.

May the graciousness of the LORD our God be upon us;* prosper the work of our hands; prosper our handiwork.

Psalm 90:13–17

The Refrain

Remember, LORD, how short life is,* how frail you have made all flesh.

The Gloria

The Lord's Prayer

The Prayer Appointed for the Week

Almighty God, you have given your only-begotten Son to take our nature upon him, and to be born of a pure virgin: Grant that I, who have been born again and made your child by adoption and grace, may daily be renewed by your Holy Spirit; through my Lord Jesus Christ, to whom with you and the same Spirit be honor and glory, now and for ever. *Amen.*†

Concluding Prayers of the Church

We remember today, O God, the slaughter of the holy innocents of Bethlehem by King Herod. Receive, we pray, into the arms of your mercy all innocent victims; and by your great might frustrate the designs of evil tyrants and establish your rule of justice, love, and peace; through Jesus Christ our Lord, who lives and reigns with you, in the unity of the Holy Spirit, one God, for ever and ever. *Amen.*

Lord God, almighty and everlasting Father, you have brought me in safety to this new day: Preserve me with your mighty power, that I may not fall into sin, nor be overcome by adversity; and in all I do direct me to the fulfilling of your purpose; through Jesus Christ my Lord. *Amen.*†

The Midday Office   To Be Observed on the Hour or Half Hour
                                             Between 11 a.m. and 2 p.m.

The Call to Prayer
Praise God from whom all blessings flow; praise him, all creatures here below;
    praise him above, you heavenly hosts; praise Father, Son and Holy Ghost.
                                                              Doxology

The Request for Presence
May the glory of the LORD endure for ever;* may the LORD rejoice in all his works.
                                                          Psalm 104:32

The Greeting
Hosanna, LORD, hosanna!* LORD, send us now success.
Blessed is he who comes in the name of the Lord . . .
God is the LORD; he has shined upon us;* form a procession with branches up to
    the horns of the altar.
                                                        Psalm 118:25–27

The Refrain for the Midday Lessons
Those who go out weeping, carrying the seed,* will come again in joy, shouldering
    their sheaves.
                                                          Psalm 126:7

A Reading
YAHWEH says this, "A voice is heard in Ramah, lamenting and weeping bitterly: it
    is Rachel weeping for her children, refusing to be comforted for her children,
    because they are no more." YAHWEH says this, "Stop your lamenting, dry your
    eyes, for your labor will have a reward," YAHWEH declares, "and they will
    return from your enemy's country. There is a hope for your future after all,"
    YAHWEH declares, "your children will return to their homeland."
                                                        Jeremiah 31:15–17

The Refrain
Those who go out weeping, carrying the seed,* will come again in joy, shouldering
    their sheaves.

The Midday Psalm   *Our Eyes Look to the LORD Our God*
To you I lift up my eyes,* to you enthroned in the heavens.
As the eyes of servants look to the hand of their masters,* and the eyes of a maid to
    the hand of her mistress,
So our eyes look to the LORD our God,* until he shows us his mercy.
Have mercy upon us, O LORD, have mercy,* for we have had more than enough of
    contempt,
Too much of the scorn of the indolent rich,* and of the derision of the proud.
                                                          Psalm 123

The Refrain
Those who go out weeping, carrying the seed,* will come again in joy, shouldering
   their sheaves.

The Cry of the Church
Lord, have mercy on us; Christ, have mercy on us; Lord, have mercy on us.

The Lord's Prayer

The Prayer Appointed for the Week
Almighty God, you have given your only-begotten Son to take our nature upon
   him, and to be born of a pure virgin: Grant that I, who have been born again
   and made your child by adoption and grace, may daily be renewed by your
   Holy Spirit; through my Lord Jesus Christ, to whom with you and the same
   Spirit be honor and glory, now and for ever. *Amen.*†

Concluding Prayers of the Church
O God, whose beloved Son took children into his arms and blessed them: Give me
   the grace to entrust the holy innocents of Bethlehem to your never-failing care
   and love, and bring me to your heavenly kingdom; through Jesus Christ our
   Lord, who lives and reigns with you and the Holy Spirit, one God, now and for
   ever. *Amen.*†

Almighty and eternal God, ruler of all things in heaven and earth: Mercifully
   accept the prayers of your people everywhere, and strengthen each of us to do
   your will; through Jesus Christ my Lord. *Amen.*†

The Vespers Office   **To Be Observed on the Hour or Half Hour**
                                        Between 5 and 8 p.m.

The Call to Prayer
Praise the LORD, all you nations;* laud him, all you peoples.
For his loving-kindness toward us is great,* and the faithfulness of the LORD
   endures for ever. . . .

Psalm 117:1–2

The Request for Presence
O LORD, do not forsake me;* be not far from me, O my God.
Make haste to help me,* O LORD of my salvation.

Psalm 38:21–22

The Greeting
You are my refuge and shield;* my hope is in your word.

Psalm 119:114

The Hymn

Lully, lullay, you little tiny child,
bye-bye, lully lullay
O sisters, too,
how may we do
for to preserve this day
this poor youngling
for whom we sing
bye-bye, lully, lullay?

Lully, lullay, you little tiny child,
bye-bye, lully lullay
Herod the King,
in his raging charged
he had this day
his men of might,
in his own sight,
all young children to slay.

Lully, lullay, you little tiny child,
bye-bye, lully lullay
That woe is me,
poor child for thee!
And every morn and day,
for thy parting
nor say nor sing
bye-bye, lully lullay.

15th Century

The Refrain for the Vespers Lessons

. . . it is good for me to be near God;* I have made the Lord GOD my refuge.

Psalm 73:28

The Vespers Psalm

But the souls of the upright are in the hands of God,
And no torment can touch them.
To the unenlightened, they appeared to die,
Their departure was regarded as a disaster,
Their leaving us like annihilation;
But they are at peace.
If, as it seemed to us, they suffered punishment,
Their hope was rich with immortality;
Slight was their correction, great will their blessings be.
He has tested them like gold in a furnace,
And accepted them as a perfect burnt offering.
At their time of visitation, they will shine out;
As sparks run through stubble, so will they.
They will judge nations, rule over peoples,
And the Lord will be their king for ever.
Those who trust in him will understand the truth,
Those who are faithful will live with him in love;
For grace and mercy await his holy ones,
And he intervenes on behalf of his chosen.

Wisdom 3:1ff

The Refrain

. . . it is good for me to be near God;* I have made the Lord GOD my refuge.

The Gloria

The Lord's Prayer

The Prayer Appointed for the Week

Almighty God, you have given your only-begotten Son to take our nature upon
him, and to be born of a pure virgin: Grant that I, who have been born again
and made your child by adoption and grace, may daily be renewed by your
Holy Spirit; through my Lord Jesus Christ, to whom with you and the same
Spirit be honor and glory, now and for ever. *Amen.*†

Concluding Prayers of the Church

Give rest, O Christ, to your servants, where sorrow and pain are no more, neither
sighing, but life everlasting. *Amen.*†

Save me, O Lord, while I am awake, and keep me while I sleep that I may wake in
Christ and rest in peace.

adapted from THE SHORT BREVIARY

The Morning Office   To Be Observed on the Hour or Half Hour
                                      Between 6 and 9 a.m.

The Call to Prayer

My mouth shall speak the praise of the LORD;* let all flesh bless his holy Name for
ever and ever.

Psalm 145:22

The Request for Presence

O Lamb of God, that takes away the sins of the world, have mercy on me.
O Lamb of God, that takes away the sins of the world, have mercy on me.
O Lamb of God, that takes away the sins of the world, grant me your peace.

Agnus Dei

The Greeting

Your love, O LORD, reaches to the heavens,* and your faithfulness to the clouds.

Psalm 36:5

The Refrain for the Morning Lessons

I will exalt you, O God my King,* and bless your Name for ever and ever.

Psalm 145:1

A Reading

On the last day, the great day of the festival, Jesus stood and cried out: 'Let anyone who is thirsty come to me! Let anyone who believes in me come and drink! As scripture says, "From his heart shall flow streams of living water." ' He was speaking of the Spirit which those who believe in him were to receive; for there was no Spirit as yet because Jesus had not yet been glorified. Some of the crowd who had been listening said, 'He is indeed the prophet,' and some said, 'He is the Christ,' but others said, 'Would the Christ come from Galilee? Does not scripture say that the Christ must be descended from David and come from Bethlehem, the village where David was?' So the people could not agree about him. Some wanted to arrest him, but no one actually laid a hand on him.

John 7:37–44

The Refrain

I will exalt you, O God my King,* and bless your Name for ever and ever.

The Morning Psalm   *I Love You, O Lord*

I love you, O Lord my strength,* O Lord my stronghold, my crag, and my haven.
My God, my rock in whom I put my trust,* my shield, the horn of my salvation,
    and my refuge; you are worthy of praise.
As for God, his ways are perfect; the words of the Lord are tried in the fire;* he is a
    shield to all who trust in him.
For who is God, but the Lord?* who is the Rock, except our God?

Psalm 18:1–2, 31–32

The Refrain

I will exalt you, O God my King,* and bless your Name for ever and ever.

The Cry of the Church

O God, come to my assistance! O Lord, make haste to help me!

The Lord's Prayer

The Prayer Appointed for the Week

Almighty God, you have given your only-begotten Son to take our nature upon him, and to be born of a pure virgin: Grant that I, who have been born again and made your child by adoption and grace, may daily be renewed by your Holy Spirit; through my Lord Jesus Christ, to whom with you and the same Spirit be honor and glory, now and for ever. *Amen.*†

The Concluding Prayer of the Church

Lord God, almighty and everlasting Father, you have brought me in safety to this new day: Preserve me with your mighty power, that I may not fall into sin, nor be overcome by adversity; and in all I do direct me to the fulfilling of your purpose; through Jesus Christ my Lord. *Amen.*†

The Midday Office

To Be Observed on the Hour or Half Hour Between 11 a.m. and 2 p.m.

The Call to Prayer

Bless the LORD, O my soul,* and all that is within me, bless his holy Name.

Psalm 103:1

The Request for Presence

Hearken to my voice, O LORD, when I call;* have mercy on me and answer me.
You speak in my heart and say, "Seek my face."* Your face, LORD, will I seek.
Hide not your face from me,* nor turn away your servant in displeasure.

Psalm 27:10–12

The Greeting

I restrain my feet from every evil way,* that I may keep your word.

Psalm 119:101

The Refrain for the Midday Lessons

For one day in your courts is better than a thousand in my own room,* and to
stand at the threshold of the house of my God than to dwell in the tents of the
wicked.

Psalm 84:9

A Reading

There are many deceivers at large in the world, refusing to acknowledge Jesus
Christ as coming in human nature. They are the Deceiver; they are the
Antichrist. Watch yourselves, or all our work will be lost and you will forfeit
your full reward. If anybody does not remain in the teaching of Christ but goes
beyond it, he does not have God with him: only those who remain in what he
taught can have the Father and the Son with them. If anyone comes to you
bringing a different doctrine, you must not receive him into your house or even
give him a greeting. Whoever greets him has a share in his wicked activities.

2 John: 7–10

The Refrain

For one day in your courts is better than a thousand in my own room,* and to
stand at the threshold of the house of my God than to dwell in the tents of the
wicked.

The Midday Psalm   *It Is God Who Makes My Way Secure*

It is God who girds me about with strength* and makes my way secure.
He makes me sure-footed like a deer* and lets me stand firm on the heights.
He trains my hands for battle* and my arms for bending even a bow of bronze.
You have given me your shield of victory;* your right hand also sustains me; your
loving care makes me great.
You lengthen my stride beneath me,* and my ankles do not give way.
The LORD lives! Blessed is my Rock!* Exalted is the God of my salvation!

Psalm 18:33–37, 46

The Refrain
For one day in your courts is better than a thousand in my own room,* and to
stand at the threshold of the house of my God than to dwell in the tents of the
wicked.

The Cry of the Church
O Lamb of God, that takes away the sins of the world, have mercy upon me.
O Lamb of God, that takes away the sins of the world, have mercy upon me.
O Lamb of God, that takes away the sins of the world, grant me your peace.

The Lord's Prayer

The Prayer Appointed for the Week
Almighty God, you have given your only-begotten Son to take our nature upon
him, and to be born of a pure virgin: Grant that I, who have been born again
and made your child by adoption and grace, may daily be renewed by your
Holy Spirit; through my Lord Jesus Christ, to whom with you and the same
Spirit be honor and glory, now and for ever. *Amen.*†

The Concluding Prayer of the Church
God of justice, God of mercy, bless all those who are surprised with pain this day
from suffering caused by their own weakness or that of others. Let what we
suffer teach us to be merciful; let our sins teach us to forgive. This we ask
through the intercession of Jesus and all who died forgiving those who
oppressed them. *Amen.*

THE NEW COMPANION TO THE BREVIARY

The Vespers Office   **To Be Observed on the Hour or Half Hour**
Between 5 and 8 p.m.

The Call to Prayer
Praise the LORD, all you nations;* laud him, all you peoples.
For his loving-kindness toward us is great,* and the faithfulness of the LORD
endures for ever. Hallelujah!

Psalm 117

The Request for Presence
Gladden the soul of your servant,* for to you, O LORD, I lift up my soul.

Psalm 86:4

The Greeting
One generation shall praise your works to another* and shall declare your power.

Psalm 145:4

The Hymn

What child is this, who laid to rest,
On Mary's lap is sleeping?
Whom angels greet with anthems sweet,
While shepherds watch are keeping?
This, this is Christ the King,
Whom shepherds guard and angels sing:
Haste, haste to bring him laud,
The babe, the son of Mary.

Why lies he in such mean estate
Where ox and ass are feeding?
Good Christian, fear: for sinners here
The silent Word is pleading.
This, this is Christ the King,
Whom shepherds guard and angels sing:
Haste, haste to bring him laud,
The babe, the son of Mary.

So bring him incense, gold and myrrh,
Come, peasant, king, to own him;
The King of kings salvation brings,
Let loving hearts enthrone him.
This, this is Christ the King,
Whom shepherds guard and angels sing:
Haste, haste to bring him laud,
The babe, the son of Mary.

William Dix

The Refrain for the Vespers Lessons

Happy are they all who fear the LORD,* and who follow in his ways!

Psalm 128:1

The Vespers Psalm   *You Have Put Gladness in My Heart*

Answer me when I call, O God, defender of my cause;* you set me free when I am
  hard-pressed; have mercy on me and hear my prayer.
"You mortals, how long will you dishonor my glory;* how long will you worship
  dumb idols and run after false gods?"
Know that the LORD does wonders for the faithful;* when I call upon the LORD, he
  will hear me.
Tremble, then, and do not sin;* speak to your heart in silence upon your bed.
Offer the appointed sacrifices* and put your trust in the LORD.
Many are saying, "Oh, that we might see better times!"* Lift up the light of your
  countenance upon us, O LORD.
You have put gladness in my heart,* more than when grain and wine and oil
  increase.

I lie down in peace; at once I fall asleep;* for only you, LORD, make me dwell in safety.

Psalm 4

The Refrain
Happy are they all who fear the LORD,* and who follow in his ways!

The Gloria

The Lord's Prayer

The Prayer Appointed for the Week
Almighty God, you have given your only-begotten Son to take our nature upon him, and to be born of a pure virgin: Grant that I, who have been born again and made your child by adoption and grace, may daily be renewed by your Holy Spirit; through my Lord Jesus Christ, to whom with you and the same Spirit be honor and glory, now and for ever. *Amen.*†

The Concluding Prayer of the Church
May Almighty God grant me a peaceful night and a perfect end. *Amen.*

The Morning Office   To Be Observed on the Hour or Half Hour
                                     Between 6 and 9 a.m.

The Call to Prayer
Open my lips, O LORD,* and my mouth shall proclaim your praise.

Psalm 51:16

The Request for Presence
Bow down your ear, O LORD, and answer me . . .
Keep watch over my life, for I am faithful.

Psalm 86:1–2

The Greeting
Lord, you have been our refuge* from one generation to another.
Before the mountains were brought forth, or the land and the earth were born,* from age to age you are God.

Psalm 90:1–2

The Refrain for the Morning Lessons
Truly, his salvation is very near to those who fear him,* that his glory may dwell in our land.

Psalm 85:9

A Reading

When the day came for them to be purified in keeping with the Law of Moses,
they took him [Jesus] up to Jerusalem to present him to the Lord . . . Now in
Jerusalem there was a man named Simeon. He was an upright and devout
man . . . and the Holy Spirit rested on him. It had been revealed to him by the
Holy Spirit that he would not see death until he had set eyes on the Christ of
the Lord. Prompted by the Spirit he came to the Temple; and when the parents
brought in the Child Jesus . . . he took him into his arms and blessed God; and
he said: "Now, Master, you are letting your servant go in peace as you
promised; for my eyes have seen the salvation which you have made ready in
the sight of the nations; a light of revelation for the gentiles and glory for your
people Israel." As the child's father and mother were wondering at these
things that were being said about him, Simeon blessed them and said to Mary
his mother, "Look, he is destined for the fall and for the rise of many in Israel,
destined to be a sign that is opposed—and a sword will pierce your soul too—
so that the secret thoughts of many may be laid bare." There was a prophetess,
too, Anna . . . she had been married seven years before becoming a widow. She
was now eighty-four years old and never left the Temple, serving God night
and day with fasting and prayer. She came up just at that moment and began to
praise God; and she spoke of the child to all who looked forward to the deliverance of Jerusalem.

Luke 2:22–38

The Refrain

Truly, his salvation is very near to those who fear him,* that his glory may dwell in
our land.

The Morning Psalm   *Holiness Adorns Your House For Ever*

The LORD is King; he has put on splendid apparel;* the LORD has put on his
apparel and girded himself with strength.

He has made the whole world so sure* that it cannot be moved;

Ever since the world began, your throne has been established;* you are from
everlasting.

The waters have lifted up, O LORD, the waters have lifted up their voice;* the
waters have lifted up their pounding waves.

Mightier than the sound of many waters, mightier than the breakers of the sea,*
mightier is the LORD who dwells on high.

Your testimonies are very sure,* and holiness adorns your house, O LORD, for ever
and for evermore.

Psalm 93

The Refrain

Truly, his salvation is very near to those who fear him,* that his glory may dwell in
our land.

The Gloria

The Lord's Prayer

The Prayer Appointed for the Week

Almighty God, you have given your only-begotten Son to take our nature upon him, and to be born of a pure virgin: Grant that I, who have been born again and made your child by adoption and grace, may daily be renewed by your Holy Spirit; through my Lord Jesus Christ, to whom with you and the same Spirit be honor and glory, now and for ever. *Amen.*†

The Concluding Prayer of the Church

Lord God, almighty and everlasting Father, you have brought me in safety to this new day: Preserve me with your mighty power, that I may not fall into sin, nor be overcome by adversity; and in all I do direct me to the fulfilling of your purpose; through Jesus Christ my Lord. *Amen.*†

The Midday Office   To Be Observed on the Hour or Half Hour
                                        Between 11 a.m. and 2 p.m.

The Call to Prayer

Sing to God, O kingdoms of the earth;* sing praises to the Lord.
He rides in the heavens, the ancient heavens;* he sends forth his voice, his mighty voice.

Psalm 68:33–34

The Request for Presence

For God alone my soul in silence waits;* from him comes my salvation.

Psalm 62:1

The Greeting

Awesome things will you show us in your righteousness,* O God of our salvation, O Hope of all the ends of the earth . . .

Psalm 65:5

The Refrain for the Midday Lessons

Happy are they who trust in the LORD!* they do not resort to evil spirits or turn to false gods.

Psalm 40:4

A Reading

Every day, as long as this *today* lasts, keep encouraging one another so that none of you is *hardened* by the lure of sin, because we have been granted a share with Christ only if we keep the grasp of our first confidence firm to the end. In this saying: *If only you would listen to him today; do not harden your hearts, as at the Rebellion,* who was it who *listened* and then *rebelled?* Surely all those whom Moses led out of Egypt. And with whom was he *angry for forty years?* Surely with those who sinned and whose *dead bodies fell in the desert.* To whom did he *swear they would never enter his place of rest?* Surely those who would not believe. So we see that it was their refusal to believe which prevented them from entering.

Hebrews 3:13–19

The Refrain
Happy are they who trust in the LORD!* they do not resort to evil spirits or turn to false gods.

The Midday Psalm | The LORD Delivers the Righteous
The eyes of the LORD are upon the righteous,* and his ears are open to their cry.

The face of the LORD is against those who do evil,* to root out the remembrance of them from the earth.

The righteous cry, and the LORD hears them* and delivers them from all their troubles.

The LORD is near to the brokenhearted* and will save those whose spirits are crushed.

Many are the troubles of the righteous,* but the LORD will deliver him out of them all.

Psalm 34:15–19

The Refrain
Happy are they who trust in the LORD!* they do not resort to evil spirits or turn to false gods.

The Cry of the Church
Be, Lord, my helper and forsake me not. Do not despise me, O God, my savior.

THE SHORT BREVIARY

The Lord's Prayer

The Prayer Appointed for the Week
Almighty God, you have given your only-begotten Son to take our nature upon him, and to be born of a pure virgin: Grant that I, who have been born again and made your child by adoption and grace, may daily be renewed by your Holy Spirit; through my Lord Jesus Christ, to whom with you and the same Spirit be honor and glory, now and for ever. *Amen.*†

The Concluding Prayer of the Church
May God have mercy on me, forgive me my sins and bring me to life everlasting. In Jesus' name. *Amen.*

The Vespers Office | To Be Observed on the Hour or Half Hour Between 5 and 8 p.m.

The Call to Prayer
Let us come before his presence with thanksgiving* and raise a loud shout to him with psalms.

Psalm 95:2

The Request for Presence
Remember not our past sins; let your compassion be swift to meet us;* for we have been brought very low.

Help us, O God our Savior, for the glory of your Name;* deliver us and forgive us our sins, for your Name's sake.

Psalm 79:8–9

The Greeting
Exalt yourself above the heavens, O God,* and your glory over all the earth.

Psalm 57:11

The Hymn

Go, tell it on the mountain,
Over the hills and everywhere;
Go, tell it on the mountain,
That Jesus Christ is born.
While shepherds kept their watching
Over silent flocks by night,
Behold throughout the heavens
There shone a holy light.

Go, tell it on the mountain,
Over the hills and everywhere;
Go, tell it on the mountain,
That Jesus Christ is born.
The shepherds feared and trembled,
When lo! Above the earth,
Rang out the angel chorus
That hailed the Savior's birth.

Go, tell it on the mountain,
Over the hills and everywhere;
Go, tell it on the mountain,
That Jesus Christ is born.
Down in a lowly manger
The humble Christ was born,
And God sent us salvation
That blessed Christmas morn.

African-American Spiritual

The Refrain for the Vespers Lessons
When the Lord restores the fortunes of his people, Jacob will rejoice and Israel be glad.

Psalm 14:7b

The Vespers Psalm   *Who May Abide Upon Your Holy Hill?*
Lord, who may dwell in your tabernacle?* who may abide upon your holy hill?
Whoever leads a blameless life and does what is right,* who speaks the truth from his heart.
There is no guile upon his tongue; he does no evil to his friend;* he does not heap contempt upon his neighbor.
In his sight the wicked is rejected,* but he honors those who fear the Lord.
He has sworn to do no wrong* and does not take back his word.
He does not give his money in hope of gain,* nor does he take a bribe against the innocent.
Whoever does these things* shall never be overthrown.

Psalm 15

The Refrain
When the Lord restores the fortunes of his people, Jacob will rejoice and Israel be glad.

The Gloria

The Lord's Prayer

The Prayer Appointed for the Week
Almighty God, you have given your only-begotten Son to take our nature upon
him, and to be born of a pure virgin: Grant that I, who have been born again
and made your child by adoption and grace, may daily be renewed by your
Holy Spirit; through my Lord Jesus Christ, to whom with you and the same
Spirit be honor and glory, now and for ever. *Amen.*†

The Concluding Prayer of the Church
Blessed be the Lord God of Israel for he has visited and delivered us. Alleluia,
alleluia, alleluia.

Traditional

The Morning Office   To Be Observed on the Hour or Half Hour
                                           Between 6 and 9 a.m.

The Call to Prayer
I will call upon God,* and the LORD will deliver me.
In the evening, in the morning, and at noonday, I will complain and lament,* and
he will hear my voice.
He will bring me safely back . . . * God, who is enthroned of old, will hear me.

Psalm 55:17ff

The Request for Presence
Be pleased, O God, to deliver me;* O LORD, make haste to help me.

Psalm 70:1

The Greeting
Happy are they whom you choose and draw to your courts to dwell there!* they
will be satisfied by the beauty of your house, by the holiness of your temple.

Psalm 65:4

The Refrain for the Morning Lessons
Bless the LORD, you angels of his, you mighty ones who do his bidding,* and hearken to the voice of his word.

Psalm 103:20

A Reading
And now I saw heaven open, and a white horse appear; its rider was called
Trustworthy and True; *in uprightness he judges* and makes war. His eyes were

flames of fire, and he was crowned with many coronets; the name written on him was known only to himself, *his cloak was soaked in blood*. He is known by the name, the Word of God. Behind him, dressed in linen of dazzling white, rode the armies of heaven on white horses. From his mouth came a sharp sword with which to strike at unbelievers; he is the one *who will rule them with an iron scepter*, and tread out the wine of the Almighty's fierce retribution. On his cloak and on his thigh a name was written: *King of kings* and *Lord of lords*.

Revelation 19:11–16

The Refrain
Bless the Lord, you angels of his, you mighty ones who do his bidding,* and hearken to the voice of his word.

The Morning Psalm   *Praise the Lord, All Creation, and Bless His Holy Name*
Hallelujah! Praise the Lord from the heavens;* praise him in the heights.
Praise him, all you angels of his;* praise him, all his host.
Praise him, sun and moon;* praise him, all you shining stars.
Praise him, heaven of heavens,* and you waters above the heavens.
Let them praise the Name of the Lord;* for he commanded, and they were created.
He made them stand fast for ever and ever;* he gave them a law which shall not
      pass away.
Praise the Lord from the earth,* you sea-monsters and all deeps;
Fire and hail, snow and fog,* tempestuous wind, doing his will;
Mountains and all hills,* fruit trees and all cedars;
Wild beasts and all cattle,* creeping things and winged birds;
Kings of the earth and all peoples,* princes and all rulers of the world;
Young men and maidens,* old and young together.
Let them praise the Name of the Lord,* for his Name only is exalted, his splendor
      is over earth and heaven.
He has raised up strength for his people and praise for all his loyal servants,* the
      children of Israel, a people who are near him. Hallelujah!

Psalm 148

The Refrain
Bless the Lord, you angels of his, you mighty ones who do his bidding,* and hearken to the voice of his word.

The Cry of the Church
Even so, come, Lord Jesus!

The Lord's Prayer

The Prayer Appointed for the Week
Almighty God, you have given your only-begotten Son to take our nature upon him, and to be born of a pure virgin: Grant that I, who have been born again and made your child by adoption and grace, may daily be renewed by your Holy Spirit; through my Lord Jesus Christ, to whom with you and the same Spirit be honor and glory, now and for ever. *Amen.*†

The Concluding Prayer of the Church

Lord God, almighty and everlasting Father, you have brought me in safety to this new day: Preserve me with your mighty power, that I may not fall into sin, nor be overcome by adversity; and in all I do direct me to the fulfilling of your purpose; through Jesus Christ my Lord. *Amen.*†

The Midday Office   To Be Observed on the Hour or Half Hour
                                       Between 11 a.m. and 2 p.m.

The Call to Prayer

Sing to the LORD with thanksgiving;* make music to our God upon the harp.

Psalm 147:7

The Request for Presence

Hear, O Shepherd of Israel, leading Joseph like a flock;* shine forth, you that are enthroned upon the cherubim.

Psalm 80:1

The Greeting

Exalt yourself above the heavens, O God,* and your glory over all the earth.

Psalm 57:6

The Refrain for the Midday Lessons

The LORD has sworn and he will not recant:* "You are a priest for ever after the order of Melchizedek."

Psalm 110:4

A Reading

For look, I am going to create new heavens and a new earth, and the past will not be remembered and will come no more to mind. Rather be joyful, be glad for ever at what I am creating, for look, I am creating Jerusalem to be 'Joy' and my people to be 'Gladness.' I shall be joyful in Jerusalem and I shall rejoice in my people. No more will the sound of weeping be heard there, nor the sound of a shriek; never again will there be an infant there who lives only a few days, nor an old man who does not run his full course; for the youngest will die at a hundred, and at a hundred the sinner will be accursed. They will build houses and live in them, they will plant vineyards and eat their fruit. They will not build for others to live in, or plant for others to eat; for the days of my people will be like the days of a tree, and my chosen ones will themselves use what they have made. They will not toil in vain, nor bear children destined to disaster, for they are the race of YAHWEH's blessed ones and so are their offspring. Thus, before they call I shall answer, before they stop speaking I shall have heard. The wolf and the lamb will feed together, *the lion will eat hay like the ox,* and dust be the serpent's food. *No hurt, no harm will be done on all my holy mountain,* YAHWEH says.

Isaiah 65:17–25

The Refrain

The LORD has sworn and he will not recant:* "You are a priest for ever after the order of Melchizedek."

The Midday Psalm   *We Will Not Fear*

God is our refuge and strength,* a very present help in trouble.

Therefore we will not fear, though the earth be moved,* and though the mountains be toppled into the depths of the sea;

Though its waters rage and foam,* and though the mountains tremble at its tumult.

The Lord of hosts is with us;* the God of Jacob is our stronghold.

There is a river whose streams make glad the city of God,* the holy habitation of the Most High.

God is in the midst of her; she shall not be overthrown;* God shall help her at the break of day.

The nations make much ado, and the kingdoms are shaken;* God has spoken, and the earth shall melt away.

The Lord of hosts is with us;* the God of Jacob is our stronghold.

Psalm 46:1–8

The Refrain

The LORD has sworn and he will not recant:* "You are a priest for ever after the order of Melchizedek."

The Gloria

The Lord's Prayer

The Prayer Appointed for the Week

Almighty God, you have given your only-begotten Son to take our nature upon him, and to be born of a pure virgin: Grant that I, who have been born again and made your child by adoption and grace, may daily be renewed by your Holy Spirit; through my Lord Jesus Christ, to whom with you and the same Spirit be honor and glory, now and for ever. *Amen.*†

The Concluding Prayer of the Church

Lord Jesus Christ, by your death you took away the sting of death: Grant me to so follow in faith where you have led the way, that I may at length fall asleep peacefully in you and wake in your likeness; for your tender mercies' sake. *Amen.*†

The Vespers Office   To Be Observed on the Hour or Half Hour
Between 5 and 8 p.m.

The Call to Prayer

I will call upon the LORD,* and so shall I be saved from my enemies.

Psalm 18:3

The Request for Presence

I have said to the Lord, "You are my God;* Listen, O Lord, to my supplication."

Psalm 140:6

The Greeting

But you, O Lord my GOD, oh, deal with me according to your Name;* for your
tender mercy's sake, deliver me.

For I am poor and needy,* and my heart is wounded within me.

Psalm 109:20–21

The Hymn

The people who in darkness walked have seen a glorious light;
On them broke forth the heavenly dawn who dwelt in death and night.
To hail your rising, Sun of life, the gathering nations come,
Joyous as when the reapers bear their harvest treasures home.
To us the promised Child is born, to us the Son is given;
Him shall the tribes of earth obey, and all the hosts of heaven.
His name shall be the Prince of Peace for evermore adored,
The Wonderful, the Counsellor. The mighty God and Lord.
His power increasing still shall spread, his reign no end shall know;
Justice shall guard his throne above, and peace abound below.

John Morison

The Refrain for the Vespers Lessons

. . . For the Lord has heard the sound of my weeping
The Lord has heard my supplication;* the Lord accepts my prayer.

Psalm 6:8–9

The Vespers Psalm   *Our God Will Not Keep Silence*

The Lord, the God of gods, has spoken;* he has called the earth from the rising of
the sun to its setting.

Out of Zion, perfect in its beauty,* God reveals himself in glory.

Our God will come and will not keep silence;* before him there is a consuming
flame, and round about him a raging storm.

He calls the heavens and the earth from above* to witness the judgment of his
people.

"Gather before me my loyal followers,* those who have made a covenant with me
and sealed it with sacrifice."

Let the heavens declare the rightness of his cause;* for God himself is judge.

Psalm 50:1–6

The Refrain

. . . For the Lord has heard the sound of my weeping
The Lord has heard my supplication;* the Lord accepts my prayer.

The Cry of the Church

Be, Lord, my helper and forsake me not. Do not despise me, O God, my savior.

The Short Breviary

The Lord's Prayer

The Prayer Appointed for the Week
Almighty God, you have given your only-begotten Son to take our nature upon
him, and to be born of a pure virgin: Grant that I, who have been born again
and made your child by adoption and grace, may daily be renewed by your
Holy Spirit; through my Lord Jesus Christ, to whom with you and the same
Spirit be honor and glory, now and for ever. *Amen.*†

Concluding Prayers of the Church
Eternal Father, you gave to your incarnate Son the holy name of Jesus to be the
sign of our salvation: Plant in every heart, I pray, the love of him who is the
Savior of the world, our Lord Jesus Christ; who lives and reigns with you and
the Holy Spirit, one God, in glory everlasting. *Amen.*†

Almighty God, who has promised to hear the petitions of those who ask in your
Son's Name: I beseech you mercifully to incline your ear to me who have made
my prayers and supplications to you; and grant that those things which I have
faithfully asked according to your will, I may effectually obtain, to the relief of
my necessity, and to the setting forth of your glory; through Jesus Christ my
Lord. *Amen.*†

May the souls of the faithful departed, through the mercy of God, rest in eternal
peace. *Amen.*

Christmas Compline

Sunday
The Night Office

To Be Observed Before Retiring

The Call to Prayer
May the Lord Almighty grant me and those I love a peaceful night and a perfect
end. *Amen.*†

The Request for Presence
Our help is in the Name of the Lord; the maker of heaven and earth.

The Greeting
Almighty God, my heavenly Father: I have sinned against you, through my own
fault, in thought, and word, and deed, in what I have done and what I have left
undone. For the sake of your Son our Lord Jesus Christ, forgive me all my
offenses; and grant that I may serve you in newness of life, to the glory of your
Name. *Amen.*†

The Reading
It is truly just, necessary and beneficent
to give you thanks, holy Lord, all-powerful Father,
Eternal God, through Jesus Christ our Lord.

In celebrating today the octave of your birth,
we celebrate, O Lord, your marvelous deeds,
because she who has given birth is mother and virgin,
and He who was born is infant and God.

For good reason, the heavens have spoken,
the angels have sung, the shepherds were joyful,
the Magi were transformed, the kings seized with fright,
and infants were crowned with the glory of blood.

Nourish, O mother, Him who is your nourishment.
Nourish the bread descended from Heaven
and placed in the manger like the fodder of animals.
The ox saw his Master; the donkey, the crib of his Lord.

He is worthy of circumcision in order to fulfill
all prophecies about Him, our Savior and Lord,
whom Simeon received into the Temple.

Thus let us sing with the angels and the archangels,
with the Thrones and Dominions, with all the choirs
of Heaven, this hymn of glory:

Holy, Holy, Holy, Lord God of Hosts,
Heaven and earth are filled with your glory.
Hosanna in the highest! Blessed is He who comes
in the name of the Lord. Hosanna in the highest!

Galasian Sacramentary

The Gloria

The Psalm   *Who Is the King of Glory?*

Lift up your heads, O gates; lift them high, O everlasting doors;* and the King of
   glory shall come in.

"Who is this King of glory?"* "The LORD, strong and mighty, the LORD, mighty in
   battle."

Lift up your heads, O gates; lift them high, O everlasting doors;* and the King of
   glory shall come in.

"Who is he, this King of glory?"* "The LORD of hosts, he is the King of glory."

Psalm 24:7–10

The Gloria

The Small Verse

Into your hands, O Lord, I commend my spirit; for you have redeemed me, O
   Lord, O God of truth. Keep me, O Lord, as the apple of your eye; hide me
   under the shadow of your wings.†

The Lord's Prayer

The Petition

Watch, O Lord, with those who wake, or watch, or weep tonight, and give Your
   angels and saints charge over those who sleep. Tend Your sick ones, O Lord
   Christ. Rest Your weary ones. Bless Your dying ones. Soothe Your suffering
   ones. Shield Your joyous ones, and all for Your love's sake. *Amen.*§

The Final Thanksgiving

Lord, you now have set your servant free to go in peace as you have promised; for
   these eyes of mine have seen the Savior, whom you have prepared for all the
   world to see: a Light to enlighten the nations, and the glory of your people
   Israel. Glory to the Father, and to the Son, and to the Holy Spirit: as it was in the
   beginning, is now, and will be for ever. *Amen.*

Monday
The Night Office   To Be Observed Before Retiring

The Call to Prayer

May the Lord Almighty grant me and those I love a peaceful night and a perfect
   end. *Amen.*†

The Request for Presence

Our help is in the Name of the Lord; the maker of heaven and earth.

The Greeting

Almighty God, my heavenly Father: I have sinned against you, through my own fault, in thought, and word, and deed, in what I have done and what I have left undone. For the sake of your Son our Lord Jesus Christ, forgive me all my offenses; and grant that I may serve you in newness of life, to the glory of your Name. *Amen.*†

The Reading

How beautiful on the mountains,
Are the feet of the messenger announcing peace,
Of the messenger of good news,
Who proclaims salvation
And says to Zion,
'Your God is king!'
The voices of your watchmen!
Now they raise their voices,
Shouting for joy together,
For with their own eyes they have seen
YAHWEH returning to Zion.
Break into shouts together,
Shouts of joy, you ruins of Jerusalem;
For YAHWEH has consoled his people,
He has redeemed Jerusalem.
YAHWEH has bared his holy arm
For all the nations to see,
And all the ends of the earth
Have seen the salvation of our God.

Isaiah 52:7–10

The Gloria

The Psalm   *May All the Earth Be Filled with His Glory*

All kings shall bow down before him,* and all the nations do him service.
For he shall deliver the poor who cries out in distress,* and the oppressed who has no helper.
He shall have pity on the lowly and poor;* he shall preserve the lives of the needy.
He shall redeem their lives from oppression and violence,* and dear shall their blood be in his sight.
Long may he live! and may there be given to him gold from Arabia;* may prayer be made for him always, and may they bless him all the day long.
May there be abundance of grain on the earth, growing thick even on the hilltops;* may its fruit flourish like Lebanon, and its grain like grass upon the earth.
May his Name remain for ever and be established as long as the sun endures;* may all the nations bless themselves in him and call him blessed.
Blessed be the Lord GOD, the God of Israel,* who alone does wondrous deeds!

And blessed be his glorious Name for ever!* and may all the earth be filled with his glory. Amen. Amen.

Psalm 72:11–19

The Gloria

The Small Verse
Into your hands, O Lord, I commend my spirit; for you have redeemed me, O Lord, O God of truth. Keep me, O Lord, as the apple of your eye; hide me under the shadow of your wings.†

The Lord's Prayer

The Petition
Watch, O Lord, with those who wake, or watch, or weep tonight, and give Your angels and saints charge over those who sleep. Tend Your sick ones, O Lord Christ. Rest Your weary ones. Bless Your dying ones. Soothe Your suffering ones. Shield Your joyous ones, and all for Your love's sake. *Amen.*§

The Final Thanksgiving
Lord, you now have set your servant free to go in peace as you have promised; for these eyes of mine have seen the Savior, whom you have prepared for all the world to see: a Light to enlighten the nations, and the glory of your people Israel. Glory to the Father, and to the Son, and to the Holy Spirit: as it was in the beginning, is now, and will be for ever. *Amen.*

Tuesday
The Night Office   To Be Observed Before Retiring

The Call to Prayer
May the Lord Almighty grant me and those I love a peaceful night and a perfect end. *Amen.*†

The Request for Presence
Our help is in the Name of the Lord; the maker of heaven and earth.

The Greeting
Almighty God, my heavenly Father: I have sinned against you, through my own fault, in thought, and word, and deed, in what I have done and what I have left undone. For the sake of your Son our Lord Jesus Christ, forgive me all my offenses; and grant that I may serve you in newness of life, to the glory of your Name. *Amen.*†

The Reading   *Gloria in Excelsis*

Glory to God in the highest,
and peace to his people on earth.
Lord God, heavenly King,
almighty God and Father,
we worship you, we give you thanks,
we praise you for your glory.
Lord Jesus Christ, only Son of the Father,
Lord God, Lamb of God.
you take away the sins of the world:
have mercy on us;
you are seated at the right hand of the Father:
receive our prayer.
For you alone are the Holy One,
you alone are the Lord,
you alone are the Most High,
Jesus Christ,
with the Holy Spirit,
in the glory of God the Father.

The Gloria

The Psalm   *Let Everything Having Breath Praise the* LORD

Hallelujah! Praise God in his holy temple;* praise him in the firmament of his
    power.
Praise him for his mighty acts;* praise him for his excellent greatness.
Praise him with the blast of the ram's-horn;* praise him with lyre and harp.
Praise him with timbrel and dance;* praise him with strings and pipe.
Praise him with resounding cymbals;* praise him with loud-clanging cymbals.
Let everything that has breath* praise the LORD. Hallelujah!

Psalm 150

The Gloria

The Small Verse

Into your hands, O Lord, I commend my spirit; for you have redeemed me,
    O Lord, O God of truth. Keep me, O Lord, as the apple of your eye; hide me
    under the shadow of your wings.†

The Lord's Prayer

The Petition

Watch, O Lord, with those who wake, or watch, or weep tonight, and give Your
    angels and saints charge over those who sleep. Tend Your sick ones, O Lord
    Christ. Rest Your weary ones. Bless Your dying ones. Soothe Your suffering
    ones. Shield Your joyous ones, and all for Your love's sake. *Amen.*§

The Final Thanksgiving

Lord, you now have set your servant free to go in peace as you have promised; for these eyes of mine have seen the Savior, whom you have prepared for all the world to see: a Light to enlighten the nations, and the glory of your people Israel. Glory to the Father, and to the Son, and to the Holy Spirit: as it was in the beginning, is now, and will be for ever. *Amen.*

❧

Wednesday
The Night Office   To Be Observed Before Retiring

The Call to Prayer

May the Lord Almighty grant me and those I love a peaceful night and a perfect end. *Amen.*✝

The Request for Presence

Our help is in the Name of the Lord; the maker of heaven and earth.

The Greeting

Almighty God, my heavenly Father: I have sinned against you, through my own fault, in thought, and word, and deed, in what I have done and what I have left undone. For the sake of your Son our Lord Jesus Christ, forgive me all my offenses; and grant that I may serve you in newness of life, to the glory of your Name. *Amen.*✝

The Reading

Thus says God, YAHWEH,
Who created the heavens and spread them out,
Who hammered into shape the earth and what comes from it,
Who gave breath to the people on it,
And spirit to those who walk on it:
I, YAHWEH, have called you in saving justice,
I have grasped you by the hand and shaped you;
I have made you a covenant of the people
And light to the nations,
To open the eyes of the blind,
To free the captives from prison,
And those who live in darkness from the dungeon.
I am YAHWEH, that is my name!
I shall not yield my glory to another,
Nor my honor to idols.

See how the former predictions have come true.
Fresh things I now reveal;
Before they appear I tell you of them.

Isaiah 42:5–9

The Gloria

The Psalm   *Come Now and See the Works of the LORD*

Come now and see the works of God,* how wonderful he is in his doing toward
    all people.
He turned the sea into dry land, so that they went through the water on foot,* and
    there we rejoiced in him.
In his might he rules for ever; his eyes keep watch over the nations;* let no rebel
    rise up against him.
Bless our God, you peoples;* make the voice of his praise to be heard;
Who holds our souls in life,* and will not allow our feet to slip.
For you, O God, have proved us;* you have tried us just as silver is tried.
You brought us into the snare;* you laid heavy burdens upon our backs.
You let enemies ride over our heads; we went through fire and water;* but you
    brought us out into a place of refreshment.

Psalm 66:4–11

The Gloria

The Small Verse

Into your hands, O Lord, I commend my spirit; for you have redeemed me,
    O Lord, O God of truth. Keep me, O Lord, as the apple of your eye; hide me
    under the shadow of your wings.†

The Lord's Prayer

The Petition

Watch, O Lord, with those who wake, or watch, or weep tonight, and give Your
    angels and saints charge over those who sleep. Tend Your sick ones, O Lord
    Christ. Rest Your weary ones. Bless Your dying ones. Soothe Your suffering
    ones. Shield Your joyous ones, and all for Your love's sake. *Amen.*§

The Final Thanksgiving

Lord, you now have set your servant free to go in peace as you have promised; for
    these eyes of mine have seen the Savior, whom you have prepared for all the
    world to see: a Light to enlighten the nations, and the glory of your people
    Israel. Glory to the Father, and to the Son, and to the Holy Spirit: as it was in the
    beginning, is now, and will be for ever. *Amen.*

Thursday
The Night Office   To Be Observed Before Retiring

The Call to Prayer
May the Lord Almighty grant me and those I love a peaceful night and a perfect
    end. *Amen.*†

The Request for Presence
Our help is in the Name of the Lord; the maker of heaven and earth.

The Greeting
Almighty God, my heavenly Father: I have sinned against you, through my own
    fault, in thought, and word, and deed, in what I have done and what I have left
    undone. For the sake of your Son our Lord Jesus Christ, forgive me all my
    offenses; and grant that I may serve you in newness of life, to the glory of your
    Name. *Amen.*†

The Reading
He is the image of the unseen God,
The first-born of all creation,
For in him were created all things
In heaven and on earth:
Everything visible and everything invisible,
Thrones, ruling forces, sovereignties, powers—
All things were created through him and for him.
He exists before all things
And in him all things hold together,
And he is the Head of the Body,
That is, the Church.

Colossians 1:15–18

The Gloria

The Psalm   *I Have Found David My Servant*
You spoke once in a vision and said to your faithful people:* "I have set the crown
    upon a warrior and have exalted one chosen out of the people.
I have found David my servant;* with my holy oil have I anointed him.
My hand will hold him fast* and my arm will make him strong.
No enemy shall deceive him,* nor any wicked man bring him down.
I will crush his foes before him* and strike down those who hate him.
My faithfulness and love shall be with him,* and he shall be victorious through
    my Name.
I shall make his dominion extend* from the Great Sea to the River.
He will say to me, 'You are my Father,* my God, and the rock of my salvation.'
I will make him my firstborn* and higher than the kings of the earth.
I will keep my love for him for ever,* and my covenant will stand firm for him."

Psalm 89:19–28

The Gloria

The Small Verse

Into your hands, O Lord, I commend my spirit; for you have redeemed me,
O Lord, O God of truth. Keep me, O Lord, as the apple of your eye; hide me
under the shadow of your wings.†

The Lord's Prayer

The Petition

Watch, O Lord, with those who wake, or watch, or weep tonight, and give Your
angels and saints charge over those who sleep. Tend Your sick ones, O Lord
Christ. Rest Your weary ones. Bless Your dying ones. Soothe Your suffering
ones. Shield Your joyous ones, and all for Your love's sake. *Amen.*§

The Final Thanksgiving

Lord, you now have set your servant free to go in peace as you have promised; for
these eyes of mine have seen the Savior, whom you have prepared for all the
world to see: a Light to enlighten the nations, and the glory of your people
Israel. Glory to the Father, and to the Son, and to the Holy Spirit: as it was in the
beginning, is now, and will be for ever. *Amen.*

Friday
The Night Office   To Be Observed Before Retiring

The Call to Prayer

May the Lord Almighty grant me and those I love a peaceful night and a perfect
end. *Amen.*†

The Request for Presence

Our help is in the Name of the Lord; the maker of heaven and earth.

The Greeting

Almighty God, my heavenly Father: I have sinned against you, through my own
fault, in thought, and word, and deed, in what I have done and what I have left
undone. For the sake of your Son our Lord Jesus Christ, forgive me all my
offenses; and grant that I may serve you in newness of life, to the glory of your
Name. *Amen.*†

The Reading

My mouth will utter the praise of the Lord, of the Lord through whom all things
have been made and who has been made amidst all things; who is the Revealer
of His Father, Creator of His mother; who is the Son of God from His Father

without a mother, the Son of man through His mother without a father. He is as great as the Day of Angels, and as small as a day in the life of men; he is the Word of God before all ages, and the Word made flesh at the destined time. Maker of the sun, He is made beneath the sun. Disposing all the ages from the bosom of the Father, He consecrates this very day in the womb of His mother. In His Father He abides; from His mother He goes forth. Creator of heaven and earth, under the heavens He was born upon earth. Wise beyond all speech, as a speechless child, He is wise. Filling the whole world, He lies in a manger. Ruling the stars, He nurses at His mother's breast. He is great in the form of God and small in the form of a servant, so much so that His greatness is not diminished by His smallness, nor His smallness concealed by His greatness. For when He assumed a human body, He did not forsake divine works. He did not cease to be concerned mightily from one end of the universe to the other, and to order all things delightfully, when, having clothed Himself in the fragility of flesh, He was received into, not confined in, the Virgin's womb. So that, while the food of wisdom was not taken away from the angels, we were to taste how sweet is the Lord.

St. Augustine

The Gloria

The Psalm   *Let Your Saving Health Come to All Nations*

May God be merciful to us and bless us,* show us the light of his countenance and
    come to us.
Let your ways be known upon earth,* your saving health among all nations.
Let the peoples praise you, O God;* let all the peoples praise you.
Let the nations be glad and sing for joy,* for you judge the peoples with equity and
    guide all the nations upon earth.
Let the peoples praise you, O God;* let all the peoples praise you.
The earth has brought forth her increase;* may God, our own God, give us his
    blessing.
May God give us his blessing,* and may all the ends of the earth stand in awe of him.

Psalm 67

The Gloria

The Small Verse

Into your hands, O Lord, I commend my spirit; for you have redeemed me,
    O Lord, O God of truth. Keep me, O Lord, as the apple of your eye; hide me
    under the shadow of your wings.†

The Lord's Prayer

The Petition

Watch, O Lord, with those who wake, or watch, or weep tonight, and give Your
    angels and saints charge over those who sleep. Tend Your sick ones, O Lord
    Christ. Rest Your weary ones. Bless Your dying ones. Soothe Your suffering
    ones. Shield Your joyous ones, and all for Your love's sake. *Amen.*§

The Final Thanksgiving

Lord, you now have set your servant free to go in peace as you have promised; for these eyes of mine have seen the Savior, whom you have prepared for all the world to see: a Light to enlighten the nations, and the glory of your people Israel. Glory to the Father, and to the Son, and to the Holy Spirit: as it was in the beginning, is now, and will be for ever. *Amen.*

❧

Saturday
The Night Office   **To Be Observed Before Retiring**

The Call to Prayer

May the Lord Almighty grant me and those I love a peaceful night and a perfect end. *Amen.*†

The Request for Presence

Our help is in the Name of the Lord; the maker of heaven and earth.

The Greeting

Almighty God, my heavenly Father: I have sinned against you, through my own fault, in thought, and word, and deed, in what I have done and what I have left undone. For the sake of your Son our Lord Jesus Christ, forgive me all my offenses; and grant that I may serve you in newness of life, to the glory of your Name. *Amen.*†

The Reading

There is no rose of such virtue
As is the rose that bore Jesu:
Alleluia.
For in this rose contained was
Heaven and earth in little space:
Ros miranda.
By that rose we may well see
There be one God in Persons Three:
Pares forma.
The angels sang, the shepherds too:
Gloria in excelsis Deo:
Gaudeamus.
Leave we all this world's mirth
And follow we this joyous birth
Transeamus.

Anonymous, c. 1400

The Gloria

The Psalm   *Tell It Out Among the Nations*

Ascribe to the LORD, you families of the peoples;* ascribe to the LORD honor and
    power.

Ascribe to the LORD the honor due his Name;* bring offerings and come into his
    courts.

Worship the LORD in the beauty of holiness;* let the whole earth tremble before
    him.

Tell it out among the nations: "The LORD is King!* he has made the world so firm
    that it cannot be moved; he will judge the peoples with equity."

Psalm 96:7–10

The Gloria

The Small Verse

Into your hands, O Lord, I commend my spirit; for you have redeemed me,
    O Lord, O God of truth. Keep me, O Lord, as the apple of your eye; hide me
    under the shadow of your wings.†

The Lord's Prayer

The Petition

Watch, O Lord, with those who wake, or watch, or weep tonight, and give Your
    angels and saints charge over those who sleep. Tend Your sick ones, O Lord
    Christ. Rest Your weary ones. Bless Your dying ones. Soothe Your suffering
    ones. Shield Your joyous ones, and all for Your love's sake. *Amen.*§

The Final Thanksgiving

Lord, you now have set your servant free to go in peace as you have promised; for
    these eyes of mine have seen the Savior, whom you have prepared for all the
    world to see: a Light to enlighten the nations, and the glory of your people
    Israel. Glory to the Father, and to the Son, and to the Holy Spirit: as it was in the
    beginning, is now, and will be for ever. *Amen.*

The Gloria

Glory be to God the Father, God the Son, and God the Holy Spirit. As it was in the beginning, so it is now and so it shall ever be, world without end. Alleluia. *Amen.*

The Lord's Prayer

Our Father, who art in heaven, hallowed be your Name.
May your kingdom come, and your will be done, on earth as in heaven.
Give us today our daily bread.
Forgive us our sins as we forgive those who sin against us.
Lead us not into temptation, but deliver us from evil;
for yours are the kingdom and the power and the glory
forever and ever. *Amen.*

Compline Prayers for January Are Located on Page 635.

The Following Holy Days Occur in January:
The Holy Name of Our Lord Jesus Christ and/or
The Feast of the Circumcision of Our Lord and/or
The Feast of Mary, Mother of God: *January 1*
The Epiphany of Our Lord Jesus Christ: *January 6*
The Confession of St. Peter, the Apostle: *January 18*
The Confession of St. Paul, the Apostle: *January 25*

January

The Morning Office   To Be Observed on the Hour or Half Hour
                                      Between 6 and 9 a.m.

The Call to Prayer
Sing to the LORD a new song,* for he has done marvelous things.
                                                    Psalm 98:1

The Request for Presence
Create in me a clean heart, O God,* and renew a right spirit within me.
                                                    Psalm 51:11

The Greeting
I am small and of little account,* yet I do not forget your commandments.
                                                    Psalm 119:141

The Refrain for the Morning Lessons
Let my mouth be full of your praise* and your glory all the day long.
                                                    Psalm 71:8

A Reading
In all this Jesus spoke to the crowds in parables; indeed he would never speak to
   them except in parables. This was to fulfill what was spoken by the prophet: *I
   will speak in parables, unfold what has been hidden since the foundation of the
   world.* . . . Jesus asked the people, saying, 'Have you understood all these?'
   They said, 'Yes' And he said to them, 'Well then, every scribe who becomes a
   disciple of the kingdom of Heaven is like a householder who brings out from
   his storeroom new things as well as old.'
                                                    Matthew 13:34–35, 51–52

The Refrain
Let my mouth be full of your praise* and your glory all the day long.

The Morning Psalm   *Sing to the LORD a New Song*
Sing to the LORD a new song,* for he has done marvelous things.
With his right hand and his holy arm* has he won for himself the victory.
The LORD has made known his victory;* his righteousness has he openly shown in
   the sight of the nations.
He remembers his mercy and faithfulness to the house of Israel,* and all the ends
   of the earth have seen the victory of our God.
Shout with joy to the LORD, all you lands;* lift up your voice, rejoice, and sing.
Sing to the LORD with the harp,* with the harp and the voice of song.
With trumpets and the sound of the horn* shout with joy before the King, the LORD.
Let the sea make a noise and all that is in it,* the lands and those who dwell therein.
Let the rivers clap their hands,* and let the hills ring out with joy before the LORD,
   when he comes to judge the earth.
In righteousness shall he judge the world* and the peoples with equity.
                                                    Psalm 98

The Refrain
Let my mouth be full of your praise* and your glory all the day long.

The Cry of the Church

O Lord, hear my prayer and let my cry come unto you. Thanks be to God.

THE SHORT BREVIARY

The Lord's Prayer

The Prayer Appointed for the Week

O God, who wonderfully created, and yet more wonderfully restored, the dignity of human nature: Grant that we may share the divine life of him who humbled himself to share our humanity, your Son Jesus Christ; who lives and reigns with you, in the unity of the Holy Spirit, one God, for ever and ever. *Amen.*

The Concluding Prayer of the Church

Lord God, almighty and everlasting Father, you have brought me in safety to this new day: Preserve me with your mighty power, that I may not fall into sin, nor be overcome by adversity; and in all I do direct me to the fulfilling of your purpose; through Jesus Christ my Lord. *Amen.*†

The Midday Office	To Be Observed on the Hour or Half Hour
	Between 11 a.m. and 2 p.m.

The Call to Prayer

Blessed be the LORD for evermore!* Amen, I say, Amen.

Psalm 89:52

The Request for Presence

May the graciousness of the LORD our God be upon us;* prosper the work of our hands; prosper our handiwork.

Psalm 90:17

The Greeting

Blessed are you, O LORD;* instruct me in your statutes.

Psalm 119:12

The Refrain for the Midday Lessons

"I will instruct you and teach you in the way that you should go;* I will guide you with my eye."

Psalm 32:9

A Reading

'This is the covenant I shall make with the House of Israel when those days have come, YAHWEH declares. Within them I shall plant my Law, writing it on their hearts. Then I shall be their God and they will be my people. There will be no further need for everyone to teach neighbor or brother, saying, "Learn to know YAHWEH!" No, they will all know me, from the least to the greatest, YAHWEH declares, since I shall forgive their guilt and never more call their sin to mind.'

Jeremiah 31:33–34

The Refrain

"I will instruct you and teach you in the way that you should go;* I will guide you with my eye."

The Midday Psalm   *I Will Dwell in the House of the* LORD

The LORD is my shepherd;* I shall not be in want.

He makes me lie down in green pastures* and leads me beside still waters.

He revives my soul* and guides me along right pathways for his Name's sake.

Though I walk through the valley of the shadow of death, I shall fear no evil;* for you are with me; your rod and your staff, they comfort me.

You spread a table before me in the presence of those who trouble me;* you have anointed my head with oil, and my cup is running over.

Surely your goodness and mercy shall follow me all the days of my life,* and I will dwell in the house of the LORD for ever.

Psalm 23

The Refrain

"I will instruct you and teach you in the way that you should go;* I will guide you with my eye."

The Small Verse

My help is in the name of the Lord who made heaven and earth and all that is in them. Thanks be to God.

Traditional

The Lord's Prayer

The Prayer Appointed for the Week

O God, who wonderfully created, and yet more wonderfully restored, the dignity of human nature: Grant that we may share the divine life of him who humbled himself to share our humanity, your Son Jesus Christ; who lives and reigns with you, in the unity of the Holy Spirit, one God, for ever and ever. *Amen.*

The Concluding Prayer of the Church

O God, you make me glad with the weekly remembrance of the glorious resurrection of your Son my Lord: Give me this day such blessing through my worship of you, that the week to come may be spent in your favor; through Jesus Christ our Lord. *Amen.*†

The Vespers Office   **To Be Observed on the Hour or Half Hour**
                                      Between 5 and 8 p.m.

The Call to Prayer

Sing praise to the LORD who dwells in Zion;* proclaim to the peoples the things he has done.

Psalm 9:11

The Request for Presence
To you I lift up my eyes,* to you enthroned in the heavens.

Psalm 123:1

The Greeting
I put my trust in your mercy;* my heart is joyful because of your saving help.

Psalm 13:5

The Hymn
> For all the blessings of the year,
> For all the friends we hold so dear,
> For peace on earth, both far and near,
> We thank You, Lord
>
> For life and health, those common things,
> That every day and hour brings,
> For home, where our affection clings,
> We thank You, Lord
>
> For love of Yours which never tires,
> That all our better thought inspires
> And warms our lives with heavenly fires,
> We thank You, Lord

Albert Hutchinson

The Refrain for the Vespers Lessons
The angel of the Lord encompasses those who fear him,* and he will deliver them.

Psalm 34:7

The Vespers Psalm   *Let All Flesh Bless His Holy Name*
The Lord is near to those who call upon him,* to all who call upon him faithfully.
He fulfills the desire of those who fear him;* he hears their cry and helps them.
The Lord preserves all those who love him,* but he destroys all the wicked.
My mouth shall speak the praise of the Lord;* let all flesh bless his holy Name for
ever and ever.

Psalm 145:19–22

The Refrain
The angel of the Lord encompasses those who fear him,* and he will deliver them.

The Cry of the Church
Lord, have mercy on us. Christ, have mercy on us. Lord, have mercy on us.

The Lord's Prayer

The Prayer Appointed for the Week
O God, who wonderfully created, and yet more wonderfully restored, the dignity
of human nature: Grant that we may share the divine life of him who humbled

himself to share our humanity, your Son Jesus Christ; who lives and reigns
with you, in the unity of the Holy Spirit, one God, for ever and ever. *Amen.*

The Concluding Prayer of the Church
Lord God, whose Son our Savior Jesus Christ, triumphed over the powers of death
and prepared for us our place in the new Jerusalem: Grant that I, who have this
day given thanks for his resurrection, may praise you in the City of which he is
the light, and where he lives and reigns for ever and ever. *Amen.*†

The Morning Office   To Be Observed on the Hour or Half Hour
                                          Between 6 and 9 a.m.

The Call to Prayer
Proclaim with me the greatness of the LORD;* let us exalt his Name together.
                                          Psalm 34:3

The Request for Presence
Open my eyes, that I may see* the wonders of your law.
                                          Psalm 119:18

The Greeting
I will confess you among the peoples, O LORD;* I will sing praise to you among the
nations.
For your loving-kindness is greater than the heavens,* and your faithfulness
reaches to the clouds.
                                          Psalm 57:9–10

The Refrain for the Morning Lessons
Save us, O LORD our God, and gather us from among the nations,* that we may
give thanks to your holy Name and glory in your praise.
                                          Psalm 106:47

A Reading   *In accordance with Jewish law, Jesus was brought by his parents
to be circumcised eight days after his birth (January 1 on our
calendar) and was named by them at that time. Most of the contemporary American church observe these simultaneous events
on January 1 either as the Feast of the Holy Name or the Feast of
the Circumcision or as the Feast of Mary, Mother of God.*

When the eighth day came and the child was to be circumcised, they gave him the
name Jesus, the name the angel had given him before his conception.
                                          Luke 2:21

The Refrain
Save us, O LORD our God, and gather us from among the nations,* that we may
give thanks to your holy Name and glory in your praise.

The Morning Psalm   *Glory in His Holy Name*

Give thanks to the LORD and call upon his Name;* make known his deeds among
  the peoples.

Sing to him, sing praises to him,* and speak of all his marvelous works.

Glory in his holy Name;* let the hearts of those who seek the LORD rejoice.

Search for the LORD and his strength;* continually seek his face.

Remember the marvels he has done,* his wonders and the judgments of his
  mouth,

He has always been mindful of his covenant,* the promise he made for a thousand
  generations:

The covenant he made with Abraham,* the oath that he swore to Isaac,

Which he established as a statute for Jacob,* an everlasting covenant for Israel.

Psalm 105:1–5, 8–10

The Refrain

Save us, O LORD our God, and gather us from among the nations,* that we may
  give thanks to your holy Name and glory in your praise.

The Gloria

The Lord's Prayer

The Prayer Appointed for the Week

O God, who wonderfully created, and yet more wonderfully restored, the dignity
  of human nature: Grant that we may share the divine life of him who humbled
  himself to share our humanity, your Son Jesus Christ; who lives and reigns
  with you, in the unity of the Holy Spirit, one God, for ever and ever. *Amen.*

Concluding Prayers of the Church

Eternal Father, you gave to your incarnate Son the holy name of Jesus to be the
  sign of our salvation: Plant in every heart, I pray, the love of him who is the
  Savior of the world, our Lord Jesus Christ; who lives and reigns with you and
  the Holy Spirit, one God, in glory everlasting. *Amen.*†

Lord God, almighty and everlasting Father, you have brought me in safety to this
  new day: Preserve me with your mighty power, that I may not fall into sin, nor
  be overcome by adversity; and in all I do direct me to the fulfilling of your purpose; through Jesus Christ my Lord. *Amen.*†

The Midday Office   To Be Observed on the Hour or Half Hour
                                               Between 11 a.m. and 2 p.m.

The Call to Prayer

'Come, we will go up to YAHWEH's mountain, to the Temple of the God of Jacob so
  that he may teach us his ways and we may walk in his paths.'

Micah 4:2

The Request for Presence
Hear, O Shepherd of Israel, leading Joseph like a flock;* shine forth, you that are
enthroned upon the cherubim.

Psalm 80:1

The Greeting
The Lord lives! Blessed is my Rock!* Exalted is the God of my salvation!

Psalm 18:46

The Refrain for the Midday Lessons
We give you thanks, O God, we give you thanks,* calling upon your Name and
declaring all your wonderful deeds.

Psalm 75:1

A Reading
Make your own the mind of Christ Jesus: Who, being in the form of God, did not
count equality with God something to be grasped. But he emptied himself, taking the form of a slave, becoming as human beings are; and being in every way
like a human being, he was humbler yet, even to accepting death, death on a
cross. And for this God raised him high, and gave him the name which is above
all other names; so that *all beings* in the heavens, on earth and in the underworld, *should bend the knee* at the name of Jesus.

Philippians 2:5–10

The Refrain
We give you thanks, O God, we give you thanks,* calling upon your Name and
declaring all your wonderful deeds.

The Midday Psalm   *The Righteous Are Like Trees Planted by Streams of Water*
Happy are they who have not walked in the counsel of the wicked,* nor lingered
in the way of sinners, nor sat in the seats of the scornful!
Their delight is in the law of the Lord,* and they meditate on his law day and
night.
They are like trees planted by streams of water, bearing fruit in due season, with
leaves that do not wither;* everything they do shall prosper.
It is not so with the wicked;* they are like chaff which the wind blows away.
Therefore the wicked shall not stand upright when judgment comes,* nor the
sinner in the council of the righteous.
For the Lord knows the way of the righteous,* but the way of the wicked is
doomed.

Psalm 1

The Refrain
We give you thanks, O God, we give you thanks,* calling upon your Name and
declaring all your wonderful deeds.

The Gloria

The Lord's Prayer

The Prayer Appointed for the Week

O God, who wonderfully created, and yet more wonderfully restored, the dignity
of human nature: Grant that we may share the divine life of him who humbled
himself to share our humanity, your Son Jesus Christ; who lives and reigns
with you, in the unity of the Holy Spirit, one God, for ever and ever. *Amen.*

Concluding Prayers of the Church

O God, who appointed Your only-begotten Son to be the Savior of mankind and
bid that He should be called Jesus, mercifully grant that we who venerate His
holy Name on earth, may also enjoy the vision of Him in heaven. Through the
same Jesus Christ. *Amen.*

adapted from The Short Breviary

O God, the source of eternal light: Shed forth your unending day upon all of us
who watch for you, that our lips may praise you, our lives may bless you, and
our worship may give you glory; through Jesus Christ our Lord. *Amen.*†

The Vespers Office   To Be Observed on the Hour or Half Hour
                                      Between 5 and 8 p.m.

The Call to Prayer

Come now and look upon the works of the Lord,* what awesome things he has
done on earth.

Psalm 46:9

The Request for Presence

Hear my cry, O God,* and listen to my prayer.
I call upon you from the ends of the earth . . .

Psalm 61:1–2

The Greeting

Remember your word to your servant,* because you have given me hope.
This is my comfort in my trouble,* that your promise gives me life.

Psalm 119:49–50

The Hymn

Ring out the old, ring in the new,
Ring, happy bells, across the snow:
The year is going, let him go;
Ring out false, ring in the true.

Ring out a slowly dying cause,
And ancient forms of party strife;
Ring in the nobler modes of life,
With sweeter manners, purer laws.

Ring out the shapes of foul disease,
Ring out the narrowing lust of gold;
Ring out the thousand wars of old,
Ring in the thousand years of peace.

Ring in the valiant man and free,
The larger heart, the kindlier hand;
Ring out the darkness of the land,
Ring in the Christ that is to be.

Alfred, Lord Tennyson

The Refrain for the Vespers Lessons

Help us, O God our Savior, for the glory of your Name;* deliver us and forgive us
our sins, for your Name's sake.

Psalm 79:9

The Vespers Psalm   *Take Delight in the LORD*

Do not fret yourself because of evildoers;* do not be jealous of those who do
wrong.
For they shall soon wither like the grass,* and like the green grass fade away.
Put your trust in the LORD and do good;* dwell in the land and feed on its riches.
Take delight in the LORD,* and he shall give you your heart's desire.
Commit your way to the LORD and put your trust in him,* and he will bring it to
pass.
He will make your righteousness as clear as the light* and your just dealing as the
noonday.
Be still before the LORD* and wait patiently for him.

Psalm 37:1–7

The Refrain

Help us, O God our Savior, for the glory of your Name;* deliver us and forgive us
our sins, for your Name's sake.

The Gloria

The Lord's Prayer

The Prayer Appointed for the Week

O God, who wonderfully created, and yet more wonderfully restored, the dignity
of human nature: Grant that we may share the divine life of him who humbled
himself to share our humanity, your Son Jesus Christ; who lives and reigns
with you, in the unity of the Holy Spirit, one God, for ever and ever. *Amen.*

The Concluding Prayer of the Church

Grant, O Father, I pray, that whatever I do in my words, my thoughts, or my work,
I may do all in the Name of the Lord Jesus, giving thanks to you and the Holy
Spirit through Him. *Amen.*

The Morning Office   To Be Observed on the Hour or Half Hour
                                                    Between 6 and 9 a.m.

The Call to Prayer

Love the LORD, all you who worship him;* the LORD protects the faithful, but
repays to the full those who act haughtily.

Psalm 31:23

The Request for Presence

Early in the morning I cry out to you,* for in your word is my trust.

Psalm 119:147

The Greeting

"You are my God, and I will thank you;* you are my God, and I will exalt you."

Psalm 118:28

The Refrain for the Morning Lessons

Our help is in the Name of the LORD,* the maker of heaven and earth.

Psalm 124:8

A Reading

Of John the Baptizer it is written: "When the Jews sent to him priests and Levites from Jerusalem to ask him, 'Who are you?' He declared, he did not deny but declared, 'I am not the Christ . . . I am, as Isaiah prophesied: *A voice of one that cries out in the desert: Prepare a way for the Lord. Make his paths straight.'* Now those who had been sent were Pharisees, and they put this question to him, 'Why are you baptizing if you are not the Christ, and not Elijah, and not the Prophet?' John answered them, 'I baptize with water, but standing among you—unknown to you—is the one who is coming after me; and I am not fit to undo the strap of his sandal.' This happened at Bethany, on the far side of the Jordan, where John was baptizing."

John 1:19–20, 23–28

The Refrain

Our help is in the Name of the LORD,* the maker of heaven and earth.

The Morning Psalm　　　　　*Tremble, O Earth, at the Presence of the LORD*

Hallelujah! When Israel came out of Egypt,* the house of Jacob from a people of strange speech,
Judah became God's sanctuary* and Israel his dominion.
The sea beheld it and fled;* Jordan turned and went back.
The mountains skipped like rams,* and the little hills like young sheep.
What ailed you, O sea, that you fled?* O Jordan, that you turned back?
You mountains, that you skipped like rams?* you little hills like young sheep?
Tremble, O earth, at the presence of the Lord,* at the presence of the God of Jacob,
Who turned the hard rock into a pool of water* and flint-stone into a flowing spring.

Psalm 114

The Refrain

Our help is in the Name of the LORD,* the maker of heaven and earth.

The Cry of the Church

Lord, have mercy on us. Christ, have mercy on us. Lord, have mercy on us.

The Lord's Prayer

The Prayer Appointed for the Week

O God, who wonderfully created, and yet more wonderfully restored, the dignity of human nature: Grant that we may share the divine life of him who humbled

himself to share our humanity, your Son Jesus Christ; who lives and reigns
with you, in the unity of the Holy Spirit, one God, for ever and ever. *Amen.*

The Concluding Prayer of the Church

Lord God, almighty and everlasting Father, you have brought me in safety to this
new day: Preserve me with your mighty power, that I may not fall into sin, nor
be overcome by adversity; and in all I do direct me to the fulfilling of your purpose; through Jesus Christ my Lord. *Amen.*†

The Midday Office	To Be Observed on the Hour or Half Hour
	Between 11 a.m. and 2 p.m.

The Call to Prayer

Hallelujah! Give praise, you servants of the LORD;* praise the Name of the LORD.

Psalm 113:1

The Request for Presence

Hear my voice, O LORD, according to your loving-kindness;* according to your
judgments, give me life.

Psalm 119:149

The Greeting

O LORD of hosts,* happy are they who put their trust in you!

Psalm 84:12

The Refrain for the Midday Lessons

With the faithful you show yourself faithful, O God;* with the forthright you show
yourself forthright.
With the pure you show yourself pure,* but with the crooked you are wily.

Psalm 18:26–27

A Reading

YAHWEH said to Abram, 'Leave your country, your kindred and your father's
house for a country which I shall show you; and I shall make you a great
nation, I shall bless you and make your name famous; you are to be a blessing!
I shall bless those who bless you, and shall curse those who curse you, and all
clans on earth will bless themselves by you.' So Abram went as YAHWEH told
him, and Lot went with him. Abram was seventy-five years old when he left
Haran.

Genesis 12:1–4

The Refrain

With the faithful you show yourself faithful, O God;* with the forthright you show
yourself forthright.
With the pure you show yourself pure,* but with the crooked you are wily.

The Midday Psalm   *May His Name Remain For Ever*

May his Name remain for ever and be established as long as the sun endures;*
    may all the nations bless themselves in him and call him blessed.
Blessed be the Lord GOD, the God of Israel,* who alone does wondrous deeds!
And blessed be his glorious Name for ever!* and may all the earth be filled with
    his glory. Amen. Amen.

Psalm 72:17–19

The Refrain

With the faithful you show yourself faithful, O God;* with the forthright you show
    yourself forthright.
With the pure you show yourself pure,* but with the crooked you are wily.

The Cry of the Church

O God, come to my assistance! O Lord, make haste to help me!

The Lord's Prayer

The Prayer Appointed for the Week

O God, who wonderfully created, and yet more wonderfully restored, the dignity
    of human nature: Grant that we may share the divine life of him who humbled
    himself to share our humanity, your Son Jesus Christ; who lives and reigns
    with you, in the unity of the Holy Spirit, one God, for ever and ever. *Amen.*

The Concluding Prayer of the Church

O Lord, my God, accept the fervent prayers of all of us your people; in the multi-
    tude of your mercies, look with compassion upon all of us who turn to you for
    help; for you are gracious, O lover of souls, and to you we give glory, Father,
    Son, and Holy Spirit, now and forever. *Amen.*†

The Vespers Office   To Be Observed on the Hour or Half Hour
                                                      Between 5 and 8 p.m.

The Call to Prayer

Come, let us bow down, and bend the knee,* and kneel before the LORD our
    Maker.
For he is our God,* and we are the people of his pasture and the sheep of his hand.

Psalm 95:6–7

The Request for Presence

O LORD, watch over us* and save us from this generation for ever.
The wicked prowl on every side,* and that which is worthless is highly prized by
    everyone.

Psalm 12:7–8

The Greeting

How glorious you are!* more splendid than the everlasting mountains!

Psalm 76:4

The Hymn

Blow now the trumpet, blow!
The gladly solemn sound
Let all the nations know,
To earth's remotest bound:
The year of jubilee is come!
The year of jubilee is come!
Return, you ransomed sinners, home.

Jesus, our great high priest,
Has full atonement made;
You weary spirits, rest;
You mournful souls, be glad:
The year of jubilee is come!
The year of jubilee is come!
Return, you ransomed sinners, home.

You who have sold for naught
Your heritage above
Shall have it back unbought,
The gift of Jesus' love:
The year of jubilee is come!
The year of jubilee is come!
Return, you ransomed sinners, home.

The gospel trumpet hear,
The news of heavenly grace;
And saved from earth appear
Before our Savior's face:
The year of jubilee is come!
The year of jubilee is come!
Return to your eternal home.

Charles Wesley

The Refrain for the Vespers Lessons

Tell it out among the nations: "The Lord is King!"

Psalm 96:10

The Vespers Psalm   *God Will Ransom My Life*

Hear this, all you peoples; hearken, all you who dwell in the world,* you of high
   degree and low, rich and poor together.
My mouth shall speak of wisdom,* and my heart shall meditate on
   understanding.
I will incline my ear to a proverb* and set forth my riddle upon the harp.
Why should I be afraid in evil days,* when the wickedness of those at my heels
   surrounds me,
The wickedness of those who put their trust in their goods,* and boast of their
   great riches?
We can never ransom ourselves,* or deliver to God the price of our life;
For the ransom of our life is so great,* that we should never have enough to pay it,
In order to live for ever and ever,* and never see the grave.
But God will ransom my life;* he will snatch me from the grasp of death.

Psalm 49:1–8, 15

The Refrain

Tell it out among the nations: "The Lord is King!"

The Gloria

The Lord's Prayer

The Prayer Appointed for the Week

O God, who wonderfully created, and yet more wonderfully restored, the dignity
   of human nature: Grant that we may share the divine life of him who humbled

himself to share our humanity, your Son Jesus Christ; who lives and reigns with you, in the unity of the Holy Spirit, one God, for ever and ever. *Amen.*

The Concluding Prayer of the Church

Blessed be God, who has not rejected my prayer,* nor withheld his love from me.

Psalm 66:18

The Morning Office

To Be Observed on the Hour or Half Hour
Between 6 and 9 a.m.

The Call to Prayer

But I will call upon God,* and the LORD will deliver me.
In the evening, in the morning, and at noonday,* I will complain and lament,
He will bring me safely back . . . * God, who is enthroned of old, will hear me . . .

Psalm 55:17ff

The Request for Presence

Save me, O God, by your Name;* in your might, defend my cause.
Hear my prayer, O God;* give ear to the words of my mouth.

Psalm 54:1–2

The Greeting

I will offer you the sacrifice of thanksgiving* and call upon the Name of the LORD.

Psalm 116:15

The Refrain for the Morning Lessons

Let all flesh bless his holy Name for ever and ever.

Psalm 145:22

A Reading

Jesus taught the people, saying: "I tell you most solemnly everyone who commits sin is a slave. Now a slave has no permanent standing in the household, but a son belongs to it for ever. So if the Son sets you free, you will indeed be free."

John 8:34–36

The Refrain

Let all flesh bless his holy Name for ever and ever.

The Morning Psalm   *Ascribe to the LORD Glory and Strength*

Ascribe to the LORD, you gods,* ascribe to the LORD glory and strength.
Ascribe to the LORD the glory due his Name;* worship the LORD in the beauty of
   holiness.
The voice of the LORD is upon the waters; the God of glory thunders;* the LORD is
   upon the mighty waters.
The voice of the LORD is a powerful voice;* the voice of the LORD is a voice of
   splendor.
The voice of the LORD breaks the cedar trees;* the LORD breaks the cedars of
   Lebanon;

He makes Lebanon skip like a calf,* and Mount Hermon like a young wild ox.
The voice of the LORD splits the flames of fire; the voice of the LORD shakes the
    wilderness;* the LORD shakes the wilderness of Kadesh.
The voice of the LORD makes the oak trees writhe* and strips the forests bare.
And in the temple of the LORD* all are crying, "Glory!"
The LORD sits enthroned above the flood;* the LORD sits enthroned as King for
    evermore.
The LORD shall give strength to his people;* the LORD shall give his people the
    blessing of peace.

Psalm 29

The Refrain
Let all flesh bless his holy Name for ever and ever.

The Cry of the Church
O Lord, hear my prayer and let my cry come unto you. Thanks be to God.

THE SHORT BREVIARY

The Lord's Prayer

The Prayer Appointed for the Week
O God, who wonderfully created, and yet more wonderfully restored, the dignity
    of human nature: Grant that we may share the divine life of him who humbled
    himself to share our humanity, your Son Jesus Christ; who lives and reigns
    with you, in the unity of the Holy Spirit, one God, for ever and ever. *Amen.*

The Concluding Prayer of the Church
Lord God, almighty and everlasting Father, you have brought me in safety to this
    new day: Preserve me with your mighty power, that I may not fall into sin, nor
    be overcome by adversity; and in all I do direct me to the fulfilling of your pur-
    pose; through Jesus Christ my Lord. *Amen.*†

The Midday Office   To Be Observed on the Hour or Half Hour
                                        Between 11 a.m. and 2 p.m.

The Call to Prayer
Open my lips, O Lord,* and my mouth shall proclaim your praise.
Had you desired it, I would have offered sacrifice,* but you take no delight in
    burnt-offerings.
The sacrifice of God is a troubled spirit;* a broken and contrite heart, O God, you
    will not despise.

Psalm 51:16–18

The Request for Presence
Let your ways be known upon earth,* your saving health among all nations.

Psalm 67:2

The Greeting

I hate those who have a divided heart,* but your law do I love.

Psalm 119:113

The Refrain for the Midday Lessons

I will listen to what the LORD God is saying,* for he is speaking peace to his faithful
people and to those who turn their hearts to him.

Psalm 85:8

A Reading

To sum up the whole matter: fear God and keep his commandments, for that is the
duty of everyone.

Ecclesiates 12:13

The Refrain

I will listen to what the LORD God is saying,* for he is speaking peace to his faithful
people and to those who turn their hearts to him.

The Midday Psalm   *You Who Fear the Lord, Bless the LORD*

O LORD, your Name is everlasting;* your renown, O LORD, endures from age to
age.
For the LORD gives his people justice* and shows compassion to his servants.
The idols of the heathen are silver and gold,* the work of human hands.
They have mouths, but they cannot speak;* eyes have they, but they cannot see.
They have ears, but they cannot hear;* neither is there any breath in their mouth.
Those who make them are like them,* and so are all who put their trust in them.
Bless the LORD, O house of Israel;* O house of Aaron, bless the LORD.
Bless the LORD, O house of Levi;* you who fear the LORD, bless the LORD.
Blessed be the LORD out of Zion,* who dwells in Jerusalem. Hallelujah!

Psalm 135:13–21

The Refrain

I will listen to what the LORD God is saying,* for he is speaking peace to his faithful
people and to those who turn their hearts to him.

The Cry of the Church

Lord, have mercy on us. Christ, have mercy on us. Lord, have mercy on us.

The Lord's Prayer

The Prayer Appointed for the Week

O God, who wonderfully created, and yet more wonderfully restored, the dignity
of human nature: Grant that we may share the divine life of him who humbled
himself to share our humanity, your Son Jesus Christ; who lives and reigns
with you, in the unity of the Holy Spirit, one God, for ever and ever. *Amen.*

The Concluding Prayer of the Church

Heavenly Father, in you I live and move and have my being: I humbly pray you so
to guide and govern me by your Holy Spirit, that in all the cares and occupa-

tions of my life I may not forget you, but may remember that I am ever walking in your sight; through Jesus Christ my Lord. *Amen.*†

The Vespers Office   To Be Observed on the Hour or Half Hour
Between 5 and 8 p.m.

The Call to Prayer
Bless the LORD, you angels of his, you mighty ones who do his bidding,* and hearken to the voice of his word.
Bless the LORD, all you his hosts,* you ministers of his who do his will.
Bless the LORD, all you works of his,* in all places of his dominion;

Psalm 103:20–22

The Request for Presence
LORD God of hosts, hear my prayer;* hearken, O God of Jacob.

Psalm 84:7

The Greeting
Show me your ways, O LORD,* and teach me your paths.
Lead me in your truth and teach me,* for you are the God of my salvation; in you have I trusted all the day long.

Psalm 25:3–4

The Hymn
Songs of thankfulness and praise, Jesus, Lord, to you we raise,
Manifested by the star to the sages from afar;
Branch of royal David's stem in your birth at Bethlehem;
Anthems be to you addressed, God in man made manifest.

Manifest at Jordan's stream, Prophet, Priest, and King supreme;
And at Cana, wedding guest, in your Godhead manifest;
Manifest in power divine, changing water into wine;
Anthems be to you addressed, God in man made manifest.

Manifest in making whole palsied limbs and fainting souls;
Manifest in valiant fight, quelling all the devil's might;
Manifest in gracious will, ever bringing good from ill;
Anthems be to you addressed, God in man made manifest.

Christopher Wordsworth

The Refrain for the Vespers Lessons
But it is good for me to be near God;* I have made the Lord GOD my refuge.

Psalm 73:28

The Vespers Psalm   *O Mighty King, You Have Executed Righteousness in Jacob*
The LORD is King; let the people tremble;* he is enthroned upon the cherubim; let the earth shake.
The LORD is great in Zion;* he is high above all peoples.

Let them confess his Name, which is great and awesome;* he is the Holy One.
"O mighty King, lover of justice, you have established equity;* you have executed
justice and righteousness in Jacob."

Psalm 99:1–4

The Refrain
But it is good for me to be near God;* I have made the Lord GOD my refuge.

The Small Verse
Keep me, Lord, as the apple of your eye and carry me under the shadow of your
wings.

Traditional

The Lord's Prayer

The Prayer Appointed for the Week
O God, who wonderfully created, and yet more wonderfully restored, the dignity
of human nature: Grant that we may share the divine life of him who humbled
himself to share our humanity, your Son Jesus Christ; who lives and reigns
with you, in the unity of the Holy Spirit, one God, for ever and ever. *Amen.*

The Concluding Prayer of the Church
Protect us, Lord, as we stay awake; watch over us as we sleep, that awake we may
watch with Christ, and asleep, rest in his peace. *Amen.*

The Morning Office   To Be Observed on the Hour or Half Hour
                                                      Between 6 and 9 a.m.

The Call to Prayer
Sing to the LORD and bless his Name;* proclaim the good news of his salvation
from day to day.
Declare his glory among the nations* and his wonders among all peoples.
For great is the LORD and greatly to be praised;* he is more to be feared than all
gods.

Psalm 96:2–4

The Request for Presence
Save me, O God,* for the waters have risen up to my neck.

Psalm 69:1

The Greeting
The LORD lives! Blessed is my Rock!* Exalted is the God of my salvation!

Psalm 18:46

The Refrain for the Morning Lessons
He looks at the earth and it trembles;* he touches the mountains and they smoke.

Psalm 104:33

A Reading　　　　　*The Feast of the Epiphany celebrates the manifestation or revealing of our Lord to the gentiles. In the contemporary Church this means an emphasis on the coming of the Magi to Bethlehem with slightly less emphasis on the baptism of Jesus by John and on His first miracle, the wedding at Cana.*

After Jesus had been born at Bethlehem in Judea during the reign of Herod, suddenly some wise men came to Jerusalem from the east asking, 'Where is the infant king of the Jews? We saw his star as it rose and have come to do him homage.' When King Herod heard this he was perturbed, and so was the whole of Jerusalem. He called together all the chief priests and the scribes of the people, and inquired of them where the Christ was to be born. They told him, 'At Bethlehem in Judea, for this is what the prophet wrote: *And you Bethlehem*, in the land of Judah, you are by no means the *least among the leaders of Judah* for *from you will come a leader* who will *shepherd* my people Israel.' Then Herod summoned the wise men to see him privately. He asked them the exact date on which the star had appeared and sent them on to Bethlehem with the words, 'Go and find out all about the child, and when you have found him, let me know, so that I too may do him homage.' Having listened to what the king had to say, they set out. And suddenly the star they had seen rising went forward and halted over the place where the child was. The sight of the star filled them with delight, and going into the house they saw the child with his mother Mary, and falling to their knees they did him homage. Then opening their treasures they offered him gifts of gold and frankincense and myrrh. But they were given warning in a dream not to go back to Herod, and returned to their own country by a different way.

Matthew 2:1–12

The Refrain
He looks at the earth and it trembles;* he touches the mountains and they smoke.

The Morning Psalm　　　　　　　　*The Rulers of the Earth Belong to God*
Clap your hands, all you peoples;* shout to God with a cry of joy.
For the Lord Most High is to be feared;* he is the great King over all the earth.
He subdues the peoples under us,* and the nations under our feet.
He chooses our inheritance for us,* the pride of Jacob whom he loves.
God has gone up with a shout,* the Lord with the sound of the ram's-horn.
Sing praises to God, sing praises;* sing praises to our King, sing praises.
For God is King of all the earth;* sing praises with all your skill.
God reigns over the nations;* God sits upon his holy throne.
The nobles of the peoples have gathered together* with the people of the God of Abraham.
The rulers of the earth belong to God,* and he is highly exalted.

Psalm 47

The Refrain
He looks at the earth and it trembles;* he touches the mountains and they smoke.

The Cry of the Church
O God, come to my assistance! O Lord, make haste to help me!

The Lord's Prayer

The Prayer Appointed for the Week
O God, who wonderfully created, and yet more wonderfully restored, the dignity of human nature: Grant that we may share the divine life of him who humbled himself to share our humanity, your Son Jesus Christ; who lives and reigns with you, in the unity of the Holy Spirit, one God, for ever and ever. *Amen.*

The Concluding Prayer of the Church
Lord God, almighty and everlasting Father, you have brought me in safety to this new day: Preserve me with your mighty power, that I may not fall into sin, nor be overcome by adversity; and in all I do direct me to the fulfilling of your purpose; through Jesus Christ my Lord. *Amen.*†

The Midday Office   To Be Observed on the Hour or Half Hour
                                     Between 11 a.m. and 2 p.m.

The Call to Prayer
God has gone up with a shout,* the LORD with the sound of the ram's-horn.
Sing praises to God, sing praises;* sing praises to our King, sing praises.
For God is King of all the earth;* sing praises with all your skill.
God reigns over the nations;* God sits upon his holy throne.

Psalm 47:5–8

The Request for Presence
Answer me when I call, O God, defender of my cause;* you set me free when I am hard-pressed; have mercy on me and hear my prayer.

Psalm 4:1

The Greeting
Deliver me, my God, from the hand of the wicked,* from the clutches of the evildoer and the oppressor.
For you are my hope, O Lord GOD,* my confidence since I was young.
I have been sustained by you ever since I was born;* from my mother's womb you have been my strength; my praise shall be always of you.

Psalm 71:4–6

The Refrain for the Midday Lessons
Your love, O LORD, for ever will I sing;* from age to age my mouth will proclaim your faithfulness.

Psalm 89:1

A Reading
Arise, shine out, for your light has come, and the glory of YAHWEH has risen on you. Look! Though night still covers the earth and darkness the peoples, on

you YAHWEH is rising and over you his glory can be seen. The nations will come
to your light and kings to your dawning brightness. Lift up your eyes and look
around: all are assembling and coming towards you, your sons coming from
far away and your daughters being carried on the hip. At this sight you will
grow radiant, your heart will throb and dilate, since the riches of the sea will
flow to you, the wealth of the nations will come to you; camels in throngs will
fill your streets, the young camels of Midian and Ephah; everyone in Saba will
come, bringing gold and incense and proclaiming YAHWEH's praises. Why, the
coasts and islands put their hope in me and the vessels of Tarshish take the
lead in bringing your children from far away, and their silver and gold with
them, for the sake of the name of YAHWEH your God, of the holy one of Israel
who has made you glorious.

Isaiah 60:1–6, 9

The Refrain
Your love, O LORD, for ever will I sing;* from age to age my mouth will proclaim
your faithfulness.

The Midday Psalm   *The LORD Has Chosen Israel for His Own*
Hallelujah! Praise the Name of the LORD;* give praise, you servants of the LORD.
You who stand in the house of the LORD,* in the courts of the house of our God.
Praise the LORD, for the LORD is good;* sing praises to his Name, for it is lovely.
For the LORD has chosen Jacob for himself* and Israel for his own possession.
For I know that the LORD is great,* and that our Lord is above all gods.

Psalm 135:1–5

The Refrain
Your love, O LORD, for ever will I sing;* from age to age my mouth will proclaim
your faithfulness.

The Gloria

The Lord's Prayer

The Prayer Appointed for the Week
O God, who wonderfully created, and yet more wonderfully restored, the dignity
of human nature: Grant that we may share the divine life of him who humbled
himself to share our humanity, your Son Jesus Christ; who lives and reigns
with you, in the unity of the Holy Spirit, one God, for ever and ever. *Amen.*

The Concluding Prayer of the Church
In truth God has heard me; he has attended the voice of my prayer. Thanks be to
God. *Amen.*

based on Psalm 66:17

The Vespers Office   To Be Observed on the Hour or Half Hour
Between 5 and 8 p.m.

The Call to Prayer
Bless God in the congregation;* bless the LORD, you that are of the fountain of Israel.

Psalm 68:26

The Request for Presence
O LORD, watch over us* and save us from this generation for ever.
The wicked prowl on every side,* and that which is worthless is highly prized by everyone.

Psalm 12:7–8

The Greeting
One generation shall praise your works to another* and shall declare your power.

Psalm 145:4

The Hymn
We three kings of Orient are, bearing gifts we traverse afar,
Field and fountain, moor and mountain, following yonder star.
O star of wonder, star of night, star with royal beauty bright;
Westward leading still proceeding, guide us to your perfect light.

Born a king on Bethlehem's plain, gold I bring to crown him again
King for ever, ceasing never over us all to reign.
O star of wonder, star of night, star with royal beauty bright;
Westward leading still proceeding, guide us to your perfect light.

Frankincense to offer have I: incense owns a Deity nigh;
Prayer and praising, gladly raising, worship him God Most High.
O star of wonder, star of night, star with royal beauty bright;
Westward leading still proceeding, guide us to your perfect light.

Myrrh is mine; its bitter perfume breathes a life of gathering gloom;
Sorrowing, sighing, bleeding, dying, sealed in the stone cold tomb.
O star of wonder, star of night, star with royal beauty bright;
Westward leading still proceeding, guide us to your perfect light.

Glorious now, behold him arise, King and God and Sacrifice;
Heaven sings alleluia: alleluia the earth replies.
O star of wonder, star of night, star with royal beauty bright;
Westward leading still proceeding, guide us to your perfect light.

John H. Hopkins, Jr.

The Refrain for the Vespers Lessons
The heaven of heavens is the LORD's,* but he entrusted the earth to its peoples.

Psalm 115:16

The Vespers Psalm   *All Kings Shall Bow Down Before Him*

In his time shall the righteous flourish;* there shall be abundance of peace till the moon shall be no more.

He shall rule from sea to sea,* and from the River to the ends of the earth.

His foes shall bow down before him,* and his enemies lick the dust.

The kings of Tarshish and of the isles shall pay tribute,* and the kings of Arabia and Saba offer gifts.

All kings shall bow down before him,* and all the nations do him service.

For he shall deliver the poor who cries out in distress,* and the oppressed who has no helper.

He shall have pity on the lowly and poor;* he shall preserve the lives of the needy.

He shall redeem their lives from oppression and violence,* and dear shall their blood be in his sight.

Long may he live! and may there be given to him gold from Arabia;* may prayer be made for him always, and may they bless him all the day long.

May there be abundance of grain on the earth, growing thick even on the hilltops;* may its fruit flourish like Lebanon, and its grain like grass upon the earth.

Psalm 72:6–15

The Refrain
The heaven of heavens is the LORD's,* but he entrusted the earth to its peoples.

The Cry of the Church
Even so, come, Lord Jesus!

The Lord's Prayer

The Prayer Appointed for the Week
O God, who wonderfully created, and yet more wonderfully restored, the dignity of human nature: Grant that we may share the divine life of him who humbled himself to share our humanity, your Son Jesus Christ; who lives and reigns with you, in the unity of the Holy Spirit, one God, for ever and ever. *Amen.*

The Concluding Prayer of the Church
Grant me, I beseech thee, O merciful God, prudently to study, rightly to understand and perfectly to fulfill that which is pleasing to thee, to the praise and glory of thy name. Amen.

St. Thomas Aquinas

The Morning Office   To Be Observed on the Hour or Half Hour
Between 6 and 9 a.m.

The Call to Prayer
Search for the LORD and his strength;* continually seek his face.

Psalm 105:4

The Request for Presence

Hearken to my voice, O LORD, when I call;* have mercy on me and answer me.
You speak in my heart and say, "Seek my face."* Your face, LORD, will I seek.
Hide not your face from me,* nor turn away your servant in displeasure.

Psalm 27:10–12

The Greeting

What terror you inspire!* who can stand before you when you are angry?

Psalm 76:7

The Refrain for the Morning Lessons

I sought the LORD, and he answered me* and delivered me out of all my terror.

Psalm 34:4

A Reading

Every year his parents used to go to Jerusalem for the feast of Passover. When he was twelve years old, they went up to the feast as usual. When the days of the feast were over and they set off home, the boy Jesus stayed behind in Jerusalem without his parents knowing it. They assumed he was somewhere in the party, and it was only after a day's journey that they went to look for him among their relations and acquaintances. When they failed to find him they went back to Jerusalem looking for him everywhere. It happened that, three days later, they found him at the Temple, sitting among the teachers, listening to them, and asking them questions; and all those who heard him were astounded at his intelligence and his replies. They were overcome when they saw him, and his mother said to him, 'My child, why have you done this to us? See how worried your father and I have been, looking for you.' He replied, 'Why were you looking for me? Did you not know that I must be in my Father's house?' But they did not understand what he meant. He went down with them then and came to Nazareth and lived under their authority. His mother stored up all these things in her heart. And Jesus increased in wisdom, in stature, and in favor with God and with people.

Luke 2:41–52

The Refrain

I sought the LORD, and he answered me* and delivered me out of all my terror.

The Morning Psalm   *They Shall Sing of Your Righteous Deeds*

I will exalt you, O God my King,* and bless your Name for ever and ever.
Every day will I bless you* and praise your Name for ever and ever.
Great is the LORD and greatly to be praised;* there is no end to his greatness.
One generation shall praise your works to another* and shall declare your power.
I will ponder the glorious splendor of your majesty* and all your marvelous works.
They shall speak of the might of your wondrous acts,* and I will tell of your greatness.
They shall publish the remembrance of your great goodness;* they shall sing of
your righteous deeds.

Psalm 145:1–7

The Refrain
I sought the Lord, and he answered me* and delivered me out of all my terror.

The Cry of the Church
Lord, have mercy on us. Christ, have mercy on us. Lord, have mercy on us.

The Lord's Prayer

The Prayer Appointed for the Week
O God, who wonderfully created, and yet more wonderfully restored, the dignity
of human nature: Grant that we may share the divine life of him who humbled
himself to share our humanity, your Son Jesus Christ; who lives and reigns
with you, in the unity of the Holy Spirit, one God, for ever and ever. *Amen.*

The Concluding Prayer of the Church
Lord God, almighty and everlasting Father, you have brought me in safety to this
new day: Preserve me with your mighty power, that I may not fall into sin, nor
be overcome by adversity; and in all I do direct me to the fulfilling of your purpose; through Jesus Christ my Lord. *Amen.*†

The Midday Office   **To Be Observed on the Hour or Half Hour**
Between 11 a.m. and 2 p.m.

The Call to Prayer
Let us bless the Lord, from this time forth for evermore. Hallelujah!
based on Psalm 115:18

The Request for Presence
Send forth your strength, O God;* establish, O God, what you have wrought
for us.
Psalm 68:28

The Greeting
I will thank you, O Lord my God, with all my heart,* and glorify your Name for
evermore.
Psalm 86:12

The Refrain for the Midday Lessons
This is the Lord's doing,* and it is marvelous in our eyes.
Psalm 118:23

A Reading
Let us examine our path, let us ponder it and return to Yahweh. Let us raise our
hearts and hands to God in heaven. We are the ones who have sinned . . .
Lamentations 3:40–42

The Refrain
This is the Lord's doing,* and it is marvelous in our eyes.

The Midday Psalm   *God Has Spoken*

There is a river whose streams make glad the city of God,* the holy habitation of
    the Most High.

God is in the midst of her; she shall not be overthrown;* God shall help her at the
    break of day.

The nations make much ado, and the kingdoms are shaken;* God has spoken, and
    the earth shall melt away.

The LORD of hosts is with us;* the God of Jacob is our stronghold.

Psalm 46:5–8

The Refrain

This is the LORD's doing,* and it is marvelous in our eyes.

The Cry of the Church

O Lord, hear my prayer and let my cry come unto you. Thanks be to God.

THE SHORT BREVIARY

The Lord's Prayer

The Prayer Appointed for the Week

O God, who wonderfully created, and yet more wonderfully restored, the dignity
    of human nature: Grant that we may share the divine life of him who humbled
    himself to share our humanity, your Son Jesus Christ; who lives and reigns
    with you, in the unity of the Holy Spirit, one God, for ever and ever. *Amen.*

The Concluding Prayer of the Church

Lord Jesus Christ, by your death you took away the sting of death: Grant me to so
    follow in faith where you have led the way, that I may at length fall asleep
    peacefully in you and wake in your likeness; for your tender mercies' sake.
    Amen.✝

The Vespers Office   **To Be Observed on the Hour or Half Hour**
                                       Between 5 and 8 p.m.

The Call to Prayer

Glory in his holy Name;* let the hearts of those who seek the LORD rejoice.

Psalm 105:3

The Request for Presence

Send forth your strength, O God;* establish, O God, what you have wrought for us.

Psalm 68:28

The Greeting

The LORD is my strength and my song,* and he has become my salvation.

Psalm 118:14

The Hymn

> Fairest Lord Jesus, Ruler of all nature,
> O you of God and man the Son,
> You will I cherish, you will I honor,
> You, my soul's glory, joy, and crown.
>
> Fair are the meadows, fairer still the woodlands,
> Robed in the blooming garb of spring:
> Jesus is fairer, Jesus is purer,
> Who makes the woeful heart to sing.
>
> Fair is the sunshine, fairer still the moonlight,
> And all the twinkling, starry host:
> Jesus shines brighter, Jesus shines purer,
> Than all the angels heaven can boast.

German

The Refrain for the Vespers Lessons

Keep watch over my life, for I am faithful;* save your servant whose trust is in you.

based on Psalm 86:2

The Vespers Psalm   *He Put a New Song in My Mouth*

I waited patiently upon the LORD;* he stooped to me and heard my cry.
He lifted me out of the desolate pit, out of the mire and clay;* he set my feet upon a
   high cliff and made my footing sure.
He put a new song in my mouth, a song of praise to our God;* many shall see, and
   stand in awe, and put their trust in the LORD.
Happy are they who trust in the LORD!

Psalm 40:1–4

The Refrain

Keep watch over my life, for I am faithful;* save your servant whose trust is in you.

The Small Verse

My help is in the Name of the Lord who made the heavens and the earth. What
   then shall I fear, of what shall I be afraid?

Traditional

The Lord's Prayer

The Prayer Appointed for the Week

O God, who wonderfully created, and yet more wonderfully restored, the dignity
   of human nature: Grant that we may share the divine life of him who humbled
   himself to share our humanity, your Son Jesus Christ; who lives and reigns
   with you, in the unity of the Holy Spirit, one God, for ever and ever. *Amen.*

Concluding Prayers of the Church

Almighty God, who has promised to hear the petitions of those who ask in your
   Son's Name: I beseech you mercifully to incline your ear to me who have made

my prayers and supplications to you; and grant that those things which I have faithfully asked according to your will, I may effectually obtain, to the relief of my necessity, and to the setting forth of your glory; through Jesus Christ my Lord. *Amen.*

May the souls of the faithful departed, through the mercy of God, rest in eternal peace. *Amen.*

The Morning Office   To Be Observed on the Hour or Half Hour
Between 6 and 9 a.m.

The Call to Prayer
Sing to the LORD a new song;* sing to the LORD, all the whole earth.
Psalm 96:1

The Request for Presence
I call with my whole heart;* answer me, O LORD, that I may keep your statutes.
Psalm 119:145

The Greeting   *Te Deum*
Glory to you, Lord God of our fathers; you are worthy of praise; glory to you.
Glory to you for the radiance of your holy Name; we will praise you and highly exalt you for ever. Glory to you in the splendor of your temple; on the throne of your majesty, glory to you. Glory to you, seated between the Cherubim; we will praise you and highly exalt you for ever. Glory to you, beholding the depths; in the high vault of heaven, glory to you. Glory to you, Father, Son, and Holy Spirit; we will praise you and highly exalt you for ever.

The Refrain for the Morning Lessons
Righteousness shall go before him,* and peace shall be a pathway for his feet.
Psalm 85:13

A Reading
Jesus answered them: "In all truth I tell you, it was not Moses who gave you bread from heaven, it is my Father who gives you bread from heaven, the true bread; for the bread of God is the bread which comes down from heaven and gives life to the world. I am the living bread which has come down from heaven. Anyone who eats this bread will live for ever; and the bread that I shall give is my flesh, for the life of the world."
John 6:32–33, 51

The Refrain
Righteousness shall go before him,* and peace shall be a pathway for his feet.

The Morning Psalm   *He Has Shown Me the Wonders of His Love*
How great is your goodness, O LORD! which you have laid up for those who fear you;* which you have done in the sight of all for those who put their trust in you.

You hide them in the covert of your presence from those who slander them;* you
keep them in your shelter from the strife of tongues.
Blessed be the Lord!* for he has shown me the wonders of his love in a besieged city.

Psalm 31:19–21

The Refrain
Righteousness shall go before him,* and peace shall be a pathway for his feet.

The Gloria

The Lord's Prayer

The Prayer Appointed for the Week
O God, who wonderfully created, and yet more wonderfully restored, the dignity
of human nature: Grant that we may share the divine life of him who humbled
himself to share our humanity, your Son Jesus Christ; who lives and reigns
with you, in the unity of the Holy Spirit, one God, for ever and ever. *Amen.*

The Concluding Prayer of the Church
Lord God, almighty and everlasting Father, you have brought me in safety to this
new day: Preserve me with your mighty power, that I may not fall into sin, nor
be overcome by adversity; and in all I do direct me to the fulfilling of your purpose; through Jesus Christ my Lord. *Amen.*†

The Midday Office
**To Be Observed on the Hour or Half Hour
Between 11 a.m. and 2 p.m.**

The Call to Prayer
Bless our God, you peoples;* make the voice of his praise to be heard;
Who holds our souls in life,* and will not allow our feet to slip.

Psalm 66:7–8

The Request for Presence
Let your ways be known upon earth,* your saving health among all nations.

Psalm 67:2

The Greeting
How great is your goodness, O Lord! which you have laid up for those who fear
you;* which you have done in the sight of all for those who put their trust in you.

Psalm 31:19

The Refrain for the Midday Lessons
Your love, O Lord, reaches to the heavens,* and your faithfulness to the clouds.

Psalm 36:5

A Reading
I am coming to gather every nation and every language. They will come to witness
my glory. I shall give them a sign and send some of their survivors to the nations:
to Tarshish, Put, Lud, Meshech, Tubal and Javan, to the distant coasts and islands

that have never heard of me or seen my glory. They will proclaim my glory to the nations, and from all the nations they will bring all your brothers as an offering to YAHWEH, on horses, in chariots, in litters, on mules and on camels, to my holy mountain, Jerusalem, YAHWEH says, like Israelites bringing offerings in clean vessels to YAHWEH's house. And some of them I shall make into priests and Levites, YAHWEH says. For as the new heavens and the new earth I am making will endure before me, declares YAHWEH, so will your race and your name endure.

Isaiah 66:18–23

The Refrain
Your love, O LORD, reaches to the heavens,* and your faithfulness to the clouds.

The Midday Psalm   *The Word of the LORD Is Sure*
Rejoice in the LORD, you righteous;* it is good for the just to sing praises.
Praise the LORD with the harp;* play to him upon the psaltery and lyre.
Sing for him a new song;* sound a fanfare with all your skill upon the trumpet.
For the word of the LORD is right,* and all his works are sure.
He loves righteousness and justice;* the loving-kindness of the LORD fills the
    whole earth.

Psalm 33:1–5

The Refrain
Your love, O LORD, reaches to the heavens,* and your faithfulness to the clouds.

The Small Verse
My help is in the name of the Lord who made heaven and earth and all that is in
    them. Thanks be to God.

Traditional

The Lord's Prayer

The Prayer Appointed for the Week
O God, who wonderfully created, and yet more wonderfully restored, the dignity
    of human nature: Grant that we may share the divine life of him who humbled
    himself to share our humanity, your Son Jesus Christ; who lives and reigns
    with you, in the unity of the Holy Spirit, one God, for ever and ever. *Amen.*

The Concluding Prayer of the Church
O God, the source of eternal light: Shed forth your unending day upon all of us
    who watch for you, that our lips may praise you, our lives may bless you, and
    our worship may give you glory; through Jesus Christ our Lord. *Amen.*†

The Vespers Office   **To Be Observed on the Hour or Half Hour**
Between 5 and 8 p.m.

The Call to Prayer
Behold now, bless the LORD, all you servants of the LORD,* you that stand by night
    in the house of the LORD.

Psalm 134:1

The Request for Presence
My soul waits for the LORD, more than watchmen for the morning,* more than
watchmen for the morning.

Psalm 130:5

The Greeting
You, O LORD, are my lamp;* my God, you make my darkness bright.
With you I will break down an enclosure;* with the help of my God I will scale any
wall.

Psalm 18:29–30

The Hymn
We would see Jesus, lo! His star is shining
Above the stable while the angels sing;
There in a manger on the hay reclining;
Haste, let us lay our gifts before the King.

We would see Jesus, Mary's son most holy,
Light of the village life from day to day;
Shining revealed through every task most lowly,
The Christ of God, the life, the truth, the way.

We would see Jesus, on the mountain teaching,
With all the listening people gathered round;
While birds and flowers and sky above are preaching
The blessedness which simple trust has found.

We would see Jesus, in his work of healing,
At eventide before the sun was set;
Divine and human, in his deep revealing
Of God made flesh, in loving service met.

We would see Jesus, in the early morning,
Still as his fold he calls, "Follow me!"
Let us arise, all meaner service scorning,
Lord, we are yours, and give ourselves to Thee.

J. Edgar Park

The Refrain for the Vespers Lessons
I lie down and go to sleep;* I wake again, because the LORD sustains me.

Psalm 3:5

The Vespers Psalm   *For God Alone My Soul in Silence Waits*
For God alone my soul in silence waits;* truly, my hope is in him.
He alone is my rock and my salvation,* my stronghold, so that I shall not be
shaken.
In God is my safety and my honor;* God is my strong rock and my refuge.
Put your trust in him always, O people,* pour out your hearts before him, for God
is our refuge.

Psalm 62:6–9

The Refrain

I lie down and go to sleep;* I wake again, because the Lord sustains me.

The Cry of the Church

O Lamb of God, that takes away the sins of the world, have mercy upon me.
O Lamb of God, that takes away the sins of the world, have mercy upon me.
O Lamb of God, that takes away the sins of the world, grant me your peace.

The Lord's Prayer

The Prayer Appointed for the Week

O God, who wonderfully created, and yet more wonderfully restored, the dignity
of human nature: Grant that we may share the divine life of him who humbled
himself to share our humanity, your Son Jesus Christ; who lives and reigns
with you, in the unity of the Holy Spirit, one God, for ever and ever. *Amen.*

The Concluding Prayer of the Church

Almighty God, who after the creation of the world rested from all your works and
sanctified a day of rest for all your creatures: Grant that I, putting away all
earthly anxieties, may be duly prepared for the service of public worship, and
grant as well that my Sabbath upon earth may be a preparation for the eternal
rest promised to your people in heaven; through Jesus Christ our Lord. *Amen.*†

The Morning Office To Be Observed on the Hour or Half Hour
Between 6 and 9 a.m.

The Call to Prayer

Be glad, you righteous, and rejoice in the Lord,* shout for joy, all who are true of
heart.

Psalm 32:12

The Request for Presence

May God be merciful to us and bless us,* show us the light of his countenance and
come to us.

Psalm 67:1

The Greeting

Out of Zion, perfect in its beauty,* God reveals himself in glory.

Psalm 50:2

The Refrain for the Morning Lessons

Let the words of my mouth and the meditation of my heart be acceptable in your
sight,* O Lord, my strength and my redeemer.

Psalm 19:14

A Reading

Indeed, from his fullness we have, all of us, received—
one gift replacing another,
for the Law was given through Moses,
grace and truth have come through Jesus Christ.
No one has ever seen God:
it is the only Son, who is close to the Father's heart,
who has made him known.

John 1:16–18

The Refrain

Let the words of my mouth and the meditation of my heart be acceptable in your
sight,* O LORD, my strength and my redeemer.

The Morning Psalm   *I Will Establish Your Line For Ever*

"I have made a covenant with my chosen one;* I have sworn an oath to David my
servant:
'I will establish your line for ever,* and preserve your throne for all generations.' "
The heavens bear witness to your wonders, O LORD,* and to your faithfulness in
the assembly of the holy ones;
For who in the skies can be compared to the LORD?* who is like the LORD among
the gods?
God is much to be feared in the council of the holy ones,* great and terrible to all
those round about him.
Who is like you, LORD God of hosts?* O mighty LORD, your faithfulness is all
around you.

Psalm 89:3–8

The Refrain

Let the words of my mouth and the meditation of my heart be acceptable in your
sight,* O LORD, my strength and my redeemer.

The Small Verse

Blessed be the Lord God of Israel for he has visited and delivered us. Alleluia,
alleluia, alleluia.

Traditional

The Lord's Prayer

The Prayer Appointed for the Week

Father in heaven, who at the baptism of Jesus in the River Jordan proclaimed him
your beloved Son and anointed him with the Holy Spirit: Grant that all who
are baptized into His Name may keep the covenant they have made, and
boldly confess him as Lord and Savior; who with you and the Holy Spirit lives
and reigns, one God, in glory everlasting. *Amen.*†

The Concluding Prayer of the Church

Lord God, almighty and everlasting Father, you have brought me in safety to this
new day: Preserve me with your mighty power, that I may not fall into sin, nor

be overcome by adversity; and in all I do direct me to the fulfilling of your purpose; through Jesus Christ my Lord. *Amen.*✝

The Midday Office   To Be Observed on the Hour or Half Hour
                                     Between 11 a.m. and 2 p.m.

The Call to Prayer
In the temple of the LORD* all are crying, "Glory!"
                                     Psalm 29:9

The Request for Presence
Fight those who fight me, O LORD;* attack those who are attacking me.
. . . say to my soul, "I am your salvation."
                                     Psalm 35:1, 3

The Greeting
Blessed be the Lord GOD, the God of Israel,* who alone does wondrous deeds!
And blessed be his glorious Name for ever!* and may all the earth be filled with
   his glory. Amen. Amen.
                                     Psalm 72:18–19

The Refrain for the Midday Lessons
Blessed be the LORD God of Israel,* from age to age. Amen. Amen.
                                     Psalm 41:13

A Reading
Moses taught the people, saying: "The day you stood at Horeb in the presence of
   YAHWEH your God, YAHWEH said to me, 'Summon the people to me; I want
   them to hear me speaking, so that they will learn to fear me all the days they
   live on earth, and teach this to their children.' So you came and stood at the
   foot of the mountain, and the mountain flamed to the very sky, a sky darkened
   by cloud, murky and thunderous. YAHWEH then spoke to you from the heart of
   fire; you heard the sound of words but saw no shape; there was only a voice.
   He revealed his covenant to you and commanded you to observe it, the Ten
   Words which he inscribed on two tablets of stone. YAHWEH then ordered me to
   teach you the laws and customs that you were to observe in the country into
   which you are about to cross, to take possession of it. Hence, be very careful
   what you do. Since you saw no shape that day at Horeb when YAHWEH spoke
   to you from the heart of the fire, see that you do not corrupt yourselves by
   making an image in the shape of anything whatever . . . When you raise your
   eyes to heaven, when you see the sun, the moon, the stars—the entire array of
   heaven—do not be tempted to worship them and serve them. YAHWEH your
   God has allotted these to all other peoples under heaven, but YAHWEH has chosen you, bringing you out of the iron-foundry, Egypt, to be his own people, his
   own people as you still are today."
                                     Deuteronomy 4:10–20

The Refrain

Blessed be the LORD God of Israel,* from age to age. Amen. Amen.

The Midday Psalm   *I Will Confess You Among the Peoples, O LORD*

My heart is firmly fixed, O God, my heart is fixed;* I will sing and make melody.

Wake up, my spirit; awake, lute and harp;* I myself will waken the dawn.

I will confess you among the peoples, O LORD;* I will sing praises to you among the nations.

For your loving-kindness is greater than the heavens,* and your faithfulness reaches to the clouds.

Exalt yourself above the heavens, O God,* and your glory over all the earth.

So that those who are dear to you may be delivered,* save with your right hand and answer me.

Psalm 108:1–6

The Refrain

Blessed be the LORD God of Israel,* from age to age. Amen. Amen.

The Cry of the Church

Lord, have mercy on us. Christ, have mercy on us. Lord, have mercy on us.

The Lord's Prayer

The Prayer Appointed for the Week

Father in heaven, who at the baptism of Jesus in the River Jordan proclaimed him your beloved Son and anointed him with the Holy Spirit: Grant that all who are baptized into His Name may keep the covenant they have made, and boldly confess him as Lord and Savior; who with you and the Holy Spirit lives and reigns, one God, in glory everlasting. *Amen.*†

The Concluding Prayer of the Church

O God, you make me glad with the weekly remembrance of the glorious resurrection of your Son my Lord: Give me this day such blessing through my worship of you, that the week to come may be spent in your favor; through Jesus Christ our Lord. *Amen.*†

The Vespers Office   To Be Observed on the Hour or Half Hour
Between 5 and 8 p.m.

The Call to Prayer

Let my mouth be full of your praise* and your glory all the day long.

Do not cast me off in my old age;* forsake me not when my strength fails.

Psalm 71:8–9

The Request for Presence

Let your loving-kindness, O LORD, be upon us,* as we have put our trust in you.

Psalm 33:22

The Greeting

To you I lift up my eyes,* to you enthroned in the heavens.

As the eyes of servants look to the hand of their masters,* and the eyes of a maid to the hand of her mistress,

So my eyes look to the LORD my God,* until he shows me his mercy.

based on Psalm 123:1–3

The Hymn

All praise to you, O Lord,
Who by your mighty power
Did manifest your glory forth
In Cana's marriage hour.

You speak, and it is done;
Obedient to your word,
The water reddening into wine
Proclaims the present Lord.

Oh, may this grace be ours:
In you always to live
And drink of those refreshing streams
Which you alone can give.

So, led from strength to strength,
Grant us, O Lord, to see
The marriage supper of the Lamb,
The great epiphany.

Hyde W. Beadon

The Refrain for the Vespers Lessons

In truth God has heard me;* he has attended to the voice of my prayer.

Psalm 66:17

The Vespers Psalm   *Look Upon Him and Be Radiant*

I will bless the LORD at all times;* his praise shall ever be in my mouth.

I will glory in the LORD;* let the humble hear and rejoice.

Proclaim with me the greatness of the LORD;* let us exalt his Name together.

I sought the LORD, and he answered me* and delivered me out of all my terror.

Look upon him and be radiant,* and let not your faces be ashamed.

I called in my affliction and the LORD heard me* and saved me from all my troubles.

The angel of the LORD encompasses those who fear him,* and he will deliver them.

Taste and see that the LORD is good;* happy are they who trust in him!

Psalm 34:1–8

The Refrain

In truth God has heard me;* he has attended to the voice of my prayer.

Psalm 66:17

The Cry of the Church

O Lord, hear my prayer and let my cry come unto you. Thanks be to God.

THE SHORT BREVIARY

The Lord's Prayer

The Prayer Appointed for the Week

Father in heaven, who at the baptism of Jesus in the River Jordan proclaimed him your beloved Son and anointed him with the Holy Spirit: Grant that all who are baptized into His Name may keep the covenant they have made, and boldly confess him as Lord and Savior; who with you and the Holy Spirit lives and reigns, one God, in glory everlasting. *Amen.*†

The Concluding Prayer of the Church

Lord God, whose Son our Savior Jesus Christ, triumphed over the powers of death and prepared for us our place in the new Jerusalem: Grant that I, who have this day given thanks for his resurrection, may praise you in the City of which he is the light, and where he lives and reigns for ever and ever. *Amen.*†

The Morning Office   To Be Observed on the Hour or Half Hour
Between 6 and 9 a.m.

The Call to Prayer

Bless the LORD, O my soul,* and all that is within me, bless his holy Name.
Bless the LORD, O my soul,* and forget not all his benefits.

Psalm 103:1–2

The Request for Presence

Protect me, O God, for I take refuge in you;* I have said to the LORD, "You are my Lord, my good above all other."

Psalm 16:1

The Greeting

I love you, O LORD my strength,* O LORD my stronghold, my crag, and my haven.

Psalm 18:1

The Refrain for the Morning Lessons

Purge me from my sin, and I shall be pure;* wash me, and I shall be clean indeed.

Psalm 51:8

A Reading

It was at this time that Jesus came from Nazareth in Galilee and was baptized in the Jordan by John. And at once, as he was coming up out of the water, he saw the heavens torn apart and the Spirit, like a dove, descending on him, And a voice came from heaven, 'You are my Son, the Beloved; my favor rests on you.'

Mark 1:9–11

The Refrain

Purge me from my sin, and I shall be pure;* wash me, and I shall be clean indeed.

The Morning Psalm   *Awesome Things Will You Show Us*

You are to be praised, O God, in Zion;* to you shall vows be performed in Jerusalem.
To you that hear prayer shall all flesh come,* because of their transgressions.
Our sins are stronger than we are,* but you will blot them out.
Happy are they whom you choose and draw to your courts to dwell there!* they will be satisfied by the beauty of your house, by the holiness of your temple.

Awesome things will you show us in your righteousness, O God of our salvation,*
O Hope of all the ends of the earth and of the seas that are far away.

Psalm 65:1–5

The Refrain

Purge me from my sin, and I shall be pure;* wash me, and I shall be clean indeed.

The Cry of the Church

O Lamb of God, that takes away the sins of the world, have mercy upon me.
O Lamb of God, that takes away the sins of the world, have mercy upon me.
O Lamb of God, that takes away the sins of the world, grant me your peace.

The Lord's Prayer

The Prayer Appointed for the Week

Father in heaven, who at the baptism of Jesus in the River Jordan proclaimed him
your beloved Son and anointed him with the Holy Spirit: Grant that all who
are baptized into His Name may keep the covenant they have made, and
boldly confess him as Lord and Savior; who with you and the Holy Spirit lives
and reigns, one God, in glory everlasting. *Amen.*†

The Concluding Prayer of the Church

Lord God, almighty and everlasting Father, you have brought me in safety to this
new day: Preserve me with your mighty power, that I may not fall into sin, nor
be overcome by adversity; and in all I do direct me to the fulfilling of your purpose; through Jesus Christ my Lord. *Amen.*†

The Midday Office

*To Be Observed on the Hour or Half Hour
Between 11 a.m. and 2 p.m.*

The Call to Prayer

Sing to the LORD a new song,* for he has done marvelous things.

Psalm 98:1

The Request for Presence

Remember me, O LORD, with the favor you have for your people,* and visit me
with your saving help;
That I may see the prosperity of your elect* and be glad with the gladness of your
people, that I may glory with your inheritance.

Psalm 106:4–5

The Greeting

Your righteousness, O God, reaches to the heavens;* you have done great things;
who is like you, O God?

Psalm 71:19

The Refrain for the Midday Lessons

I will sing to the LORD as long as I live;* I will praise my God while I have my being.

Psalm 104:34

A Reading

Blessed be God the Father of our Lord Jesus Christ . . . Such is the richness of the grace which he has showered on us in all wisdom and insight. He has let us know the mystery of his purpose, according to his good pleasure which he determined beforehand in Christ, for him to act upon when the times had run their course: that he would bring everything together under Christ, as head, everything in the heavens and everything on earth.

Ephesians 1:3, 7–10

The Refrain

I will sing to the Lord as long as I live;* I will praise my God while I have my being.

The Midday Psalm   *Come, Let Us Shout for Joy*

Come, let us sing to the Lord;* let us shout for joy to the Rock of our salvation.
Let us come before his presence with thanksgiving* and raise a loud shout to him with psalms.
For the Lord is a great God,* and a great King above all gods.
In his hand are the caverns of the earth,* and the heights of the hills are his also.
The sea is his, for he made it,* and his hands have molded the dry land.

Psalm 95:1–5

The Refrain

I will sing to the Lord as long as I live;* I will praise my God while I have my being.

The Cry of the Church

Even so, come, Lord Jesus!

The Lord's Prayer

The Prayer Appointed for the Week

Father in heaven, who at the baptism of Jesus in the River Jordan proclaimed him your beloved Son and anointed him with the Holy Spirit: Grant that all who are baptized into His Name may keep the covenant they have made, and boldly confess him as Lord and Savior; who with you and the Holy Spirit lives and reigns, one God, in glory everlasting. *Amen.*†

The Concluding Prayer of the Church

Direct me, O Lord, in all my doings with your most gracious favor, and further me with your continual help; that in all my work begun, continued, and ended in you, I may glorify your holy name, and finally, by your mercy, obtain everlasting life; through Jesus Christ my Lord. *Amen.*†

The Vespers Office   To Be Observed on the Hour or Half Hour
                                      Between 5 and 8 p.m.

The Call to Prayer

Tell it out among the nations: "The LORD is King!* he has made the world so firm
that it cannot be moved; he will judge the peoples with equity."

Psalm 96:10

The Request for Presence

Restore our fortunes, O LORD,* like the watercourses of the Negev.

Psalm 126:5

The Greeting

Whom have I in heaven but you?* and having you I desire nothing upon earth.

Psalm 73:25

The Hymn

The King of love my shepherd is, whose goodness fails me never,
I nothing lack if I am his, and he is mine forever.

Where streams of living water flow, my ransomed soul he leads;
And where the verdant pastures grow, with food celestial feeds.

Perverse and foolish, oft I strayed, but yet in love he sought me;
And on his shoulder gently laid, and home, rejoicing, brought me.

In death's dark vale I fear no ill, with you, dear Lord, beside me;
Your rod and staff my comfort still, your cross before to guide me.

You spread a table in my sight; your unction grace bestows;
And oh, what transport of delight from your pure chalice flows.

And so through all the length of days, your goodness fails me never;
Good Shepherd, may I sing your praise within your house for ever.

Sir Henry W. Baker

The Refrain for the Vespers Lessons

Those who sowed with tears* will reap with songs of joy.
Those who go out weeping, carrying the seed,* will come again with joy, shouldering their sheaves.

Psalm 126:6–7

The Vespers Psalm   *Let Them Give Thanks for the Wonders He Does*

Give thanks to the LORD, for he is good,* and his mercy endures for ever.
Let all those whom the LORD has redeemed proclaim* that he redeemed them from
the hand of the foe.
He gathered them out of the lands;* from the east and from the west, from the
north and from the south.
He sent forth his word and healed them* and saved them from the grave.

Let them give thanks to the LORD for his mercy* and the wonders he does for his children.
Let them offer a sacrifice of thanksgiving* and tell of his acts with shouts of joy.

Psalm 107:1–3, 20–22

The Refrain
Those who sowed with tears* will reap with songs of joy.
Those who go out weeping, carrying the seed,* will come again with joy, shouldering their sheaves.

The Cry of the Church
Be, Lord, my helper and forsake me not. Do not despise me, O God, my savior.

THE SHORT BREVIARY

The Lord's Prayer

The Prayer Appointed for the Week
Father in heaven, who at the baptism of Jesus in the River Jordan proclaimed him your beloved Son and anointed him with the Holy Spirit: Grant that all who are baptized into His Name may keep the covenant they have made, and boldly confess him as Lord and Savior; who with you and the Holy Spirit lives and reigns, one God, in glory everlasting. *Amen.†*

The Concluding Prayer of the Church
May Almighty God grant me a peaceful night and a perfect end. *Amen.*

The Morning Office   To Be Observed on the Hour or Half Hour
                                       Between 6 and 9 a.m.

The Call to Prayer
God has gone up with a shout,* the LORD with the sound of the ram's-horn.
Sing praises to God, sing praises;* sing praises to our King, sing praises.
For God is King of all the earth;* sing praises with all your skill.
God reigns over the nations;* God sits upon his holy throne.

Psalm 47:5–8

The Request for Presence
Let all who seek you rejoice and be glad in you;* let those who love your salvation say for ever, "Great is the LORD!"

Psalm 70:4

The Greeting
Out of Zion, perfect in its beauty,* God reveals himself in glory.

Psalm 50:2

The Refrain for the Morning Lessons
When the LORD restores the fortunes of his people, Jacob will rejoice and Israel be glad.

Psalm 14:7b

A Reading

From the sermon of St. Paul to the people of Antioch: "To keep his promise, God
has raised up for Israel one of David's descendants, Jesus, as Savior, whose
coming was heralded by John when he proclaimed the baptism of repentance
for the whole people of Israel. Before John ended his course he said, 'I am not
the one you imagine me to be; there is someone coming after me whose sandal
I am not fit to undo.' My brothers, sons of Abraham's race, and all you godfear-
ers, this message of salvation is meant for you."

Acts 13:23–26

The Refrain

When the LORD restores the fortunes of his people, Jacob will rejoice and Israel be
glad.

The Morning Psalm   *He Has Dealt with Me Richly*

How long, O LORD? will you forget me for ever?* how long will you hide your face
from me?

How long shall I have perplexity in my mind, and grief in my heart, day after
day?* how long shall my enemy triumph over me?

Look upon me and answer me, O LORD my God;* give light to my eyes, lest I sleep
in death;

Lest my enemy say, "I have prevailed over him,"* and my foes rejoice that I have
fallen.

But I put my trust in your mercy;* my heart is joyful because of your saving help.

I will sing to the LORD, for he has dealt with me richly;* I will praise the Name of
the Lord Most High.

Psalm 13

The Refrain

When the LORD restores the fortunes of his people, Jacob will rejoice and Israel be
glad.

The Gloria

The Lord's Prayer

The Prayer Appointed for the Week

Father in heaven, who at the baptism of Jesus in the River Jordan proclaimed him
your beloved Son and anointed him with the Holy Spirit: Grant that all who
are baptized into His Name may keep the covenant they have made, and
boldly confess him as Lord and Savior; who with you and the Holy Spirit lives
and reigns, one God, in glory everlasting. *Amen.*†

The Concluding Prayer of the Church

Lord God, almighty and everlasting Father, you have brought me in safety to this
new day: Preserve me with your mighty power, that I may not fall into sin, nor
be overcome by adversity; and in all I do direct me to the fulfilling of your purpose; through Jesus Christ my Lord. *Amen.*†

The Midday Office   To Be Observed on the Hour or Half Hour
                                     Between 11 a.m. and 2 p.m.

The Call to Prayer
Hallelujah! Sing to the LORD a new song;* sing his praise in the congregation of the
    faithful.

Psalm 149:1

The Request for Presence
Hear, O Shepherd of Israel, leading Joseph like a flock;* shine forth, you that are
    enthroned upon the cherubim.

Psalm 80:1

The Greeting
The Lord is in his holy temple; let all the earth keep silence before him. Amen.

Traditional

The Refrain for the Midday Lessons
The LORD shall watch over your going out and your coming in* from this time
    forth for evermore.

Psalm 121:8

A Reading
You see, God's grace has been revealed to save the whole human race; it has
    taught us that we should give up everything contrary to true religion and all
    our worldly passions . . . waiting in hope for the blessing which will come with
    the appearing of the glory of our great God and Savior Christ Jesus. He offered
    himself for us in order to ransom us from all our *faults and to purify a people to be
    his very own* and eager to do good.

Titus 2:11–14

The Refrain
The LORD shall watch over your going out and your coming in,* from this time
    forth for evermore.

The Midday Psalm   *I Will Perform My Vows in the Presence
                                     of Those Who Worship Him*
Praise the LORD, you that fear him;* stand in awe of him, O offspring of Israel; all
    you of Jacob's line, give glory.
For he does not despise nor abhor the poor in their poverty; neither does he hide
    his face from them;* when they cry to him he hears them.
My praise is of him in the great assembly;* I will perform my vows in the presence
    of those who worship him.
The poor shall eat and be satisfied,* and those who seek the LORD shall praise him:
    "May your heart live for ever!"
All the ends of the earth shall remember and turn to the LORD,* and all the families
    of the nations shall bow before him.
For kingship belongs to the LORD;* he rules over the nations.

Psalm 22:22–27

The Refrain

The LORD shall watch over your going out and your coming in,* from this time
forth for evermore.

The Gloria

The Lord's Prayer

The Prayer Appointed for the Week

Father in heaven, who at the baptism of Jesus in the River Jordan proclaimed him
your beloved Son and anointed him with the Holy Spirit: Grant that all who
are baptized into His Name may keep the covenant they have made, and
boldly confess him as Lord and Savior; who with you and the Holy Spirit lives
and reigns, one God, in glory everlasting. *Amen.*†

The Concluding Prayer of the Church

Let us bless the Lord God living and true! Let us always render him praise, glory,
honor, blessing, and all good things! Amen. Amen. So be it! So be it!

St. Francis of Assisi

The Vespers Office   To Be Observed on the Hour or Half Hour
                                      Between 5 and 8 p.m.

The Call to Prayer

Give thanks to the LORD, for he is good;* his mercy endures for ever.
Let Israel now proclaim,* "His mercy endures for ever."
Let the house of Aaron now proclaim,* "His mercy endures for ever."
Let those who fear the LORD now proclaim,* "His mercy endures for ever."

Psalm 118:1–4

The Request for Presence

Show me the light of your countenance, O God,* and come to me.

based on Psalm 67:1

The Greeting

But you, O LORD, are gracious and full of compassion,* slow to anger, and full of
kindness and truth.

Psalm 86:15

The Hymn

Spirit of God, descend upon my heart;
Wean it from earth, through all its pulses move;
Stoop to my weakness, mighty as you are,
And make me love you as I ought to love.

I ask no dream, no prophet ecstasies,
No sudden rending of the veil of clay,
No angel visitant, no opening skies;
But take the dimness of my soul away.

Have you not bid me love you, God and King?
All, all your own, soul, heart, strength and mind.
I see your cross; there teach my heart to cling.
O let me seek you, and O let me find!

Teach me to feel that you are always nigh;
Teach me the struggles of the soul to bear.
To check the rising doubt, the rebel sigh,
Teach me the patience of unanswered prayer.

Teach me to love you as your angels love,
One holy passion filling all my frame;
The kindling of the heaven-descended Dove,
My heart an altar, and your love the flame.

George Croly

The Refrain for the Vespers Lessons
Remember me, O Lord, with the favor you have for your people,* and visit me
with your saving help.

Psalm 106:4

The Vespers Psalm   *You Have Clothed Me with Joy*
While I felt secure, I said, "I shall never be disturbed.* You, Lord, with your favor,
made me as strong as the mountains."
Then you hid your face,* and I was filled with fear.
I cried to you, O Lord;* I pleaded with the Lord, saying,
"What profit is there in my blood, if I go down to the Pit?* will the dust praise you
or declare your faithfulness?
Hear, O Lord, and have mercy upon me;* O Lord, be my helper."
You have turned my wailing into dancing;* you have put off my sack-cloth and
clothed me with joy.
Therefore my heart sings to you without ceasing;* O Lord my God, I will give you
thanks for ever.

Psalm 30:7–13

The Refrain
Remember me, O Lord, with the favor you have for your people,* and visit me
with your saving help.

The Small Verse
The Lord is my shepherd and nothing is wanting to me. In green pastures He hath
settled me.

The Short Breviary

The Lord's Prayer

The Prayer Appointed for the Week
Father in heaven, who at the baptism of Jesus in the River Jordan proclaimed him
your beloved Son and anointed him with the Holy Spirit: Grant that all who

are baptized into His Name may keep the covenant they have made, and boldly confess him as Lord and Savior; who with you and the Holy Spirit lives and reigns, one God, in glory everlasting. *Amen.*†

The Concluding Prayer of the Church

O Lord my God, to you and to your service I devote myself, body, soul, and spirit. Fill my memory with the record of your mighty works; enlighten my understanding with the light of your Holy Spirit; and may all the desires of my heart and will center in what you would have me do. Make me an instrument of your salvation for the people entrusted to my care, and grant that by my life and teaching I may set forth your true and living Word. Be always with me in carrying out the duties of my faith. In prayer, quicken my devotion; in praises, heighten my love and gratitude; in conversation give me readiness of thought and expression; and grant that, by the clearness and brightness of your holy Word, all the world may be drawn into your blessed kingdom. All this I ask for the sake of your Son our Savior Jesus Christ. *Amen.*†

The Morning Office	To Be Observed on the Hour or Half Hour
	Between 6 and 9 a.m.

The Call to Prayer

Taste and see that the LORD is good;* happy are they who trust in him!

Psalm 34:8

The Request for Presence

Gladden the soul of your servant,* for to you, O LORD, I lift up my soul.

Psalm 86:4

The Greeting

With my whole heart I seek you;* let me not stray from your commandments.

Psalm 119:10

The Refrain for the Morning Lessons

I will bear witness that the LORD is righteous;* I will praise the Name of the LORD Most High.

Psalm 7:18

A Reading

Jesus taught us, saying: "Do not worry; do not say, 'What are we to eat? What are we to drink? What are we to wear?' It is the gentiles who set their hearts on all these things. Your heavenly Father knows you need them all. Set your hearts on his kingdom first, and on God's saving justice, and all these other things will be given you as well."

Matthew 6:31–33

The Refrain

I will bear witness that the LORD is righteous;* I will praise the Name of the LORD Most High.

The Morning Psalm   *The Lord Has Become My Salvation*

It is better to rely on the Lord* than to put any trust in rulers.

All the ungodly encompass me;* in the name of the Lord I will repel them.

They hem me in, they hem me in on every side;* in the name of the Lord I will
repel them.

They swarm about me like bees; they blaze like a fire of thorns;* in the name of the
Lord I will repel them.

I was pressed so hard that I almost fell,* but the Lord came to my help.

The Lord is my strength and my song,* and he has become my salvation.

There is a sound of exultation and victory* in the tents of the righteous:

"The right hand of the Lord has triumphed!* the right hand of the Lord is exalted!
the right hand of the Lord has triumphed!"

Psalm 119:9–16

The Refrain

I will bear witness that the Lord is righteous;* I will praise the Name of the Lord
Most High.

The Small Verse

Let me seek the Lord while he may still be found. I will call upon his name while
he is near.

Traditional

The Lord's Prayer

The Prayer Appointed for the Week

Father in heaven, who at the baptism of Jesus in the River Jordan proclaimed him
your beloved Son and anointed him with the Holy Spirit: Grant that all who
are baptized into His Name may keep the covenant they have made, and
boldly confess him as Lord and Savior; who with you and the Holy Spirit lives
and reigns, one God, in glory everlasting. *Amen.*†

The Concluding Prayer of the Church

Lord God, almighty and everlasting Father, you have brought me in safety to this
new day: Preserve me with your mighty power, that I may not fall into sin, nor
be overcome by adversity; and in all I do direct me to the fulfilling of your purpose; through Jesus Christ my Lord. *Amen.*†

The Midday Office   To Be Observed on the Hour or Half Hour
                                     Between 11 a.m. and 2 p.m.

The Call to Prayer

Let Israel rejoice in his Maker;* let the children of Zion be joyful in their King.

Psalm 149:2

The Request for Presence

Make me understand the way of your commandments,* that I may meditate on
your marvelous works.

Psalm 119:27

The Greeting
How deep I find your thoughts, O God!* how great is the sum of them!

Psalm 139:16

The Refrain for the Midday Lessons
Keep watch over my life, for I am faithful;* save your servant whose trust is in
you.

based on Psalm 86:2

A Reading
People who long to be rich are a prey to trial; they get trapped into all sorts of foolish and harmful ambitions which plunge people into ruin and destruction.
'The love of money is the root of all evils' and there are some who, pursuing it,
have wandered away from the faith and so given their souls any number of
fatal wounds.

1 Timothy 6:9–10

The Refrain
Keep watch over my life, for I am faithful;* save your servant whose trust is in
you.

The Midday Psalm   *You Are My Helper and My Deliverer*
Be pleased, O God, to deliver me;* O LORD, make haste to help me.
Let all who seek you rejoice and be glad in you;* let those who love your salvation
say for ever, "Great is the LORD!"
But as for me, I am poor and needy;* come to me speedily, O God.
You are my helper and my deliverer;* O LORD, do not tarry.

Psalm 70:1, 4–6

The Refrain
Keep watch over my life, for I am faithful;* save your servant whose trust is in
you.

The Cry of the Church
Lord, have mercy on us. Christ, have mercy on us. Lord, have mercy on us.

The Lord's Prayer

The Prayer Appointed for the Week
Father in heaven, who at the baptism of Jesus in the River Jordan proclaimed him
your beloved Son and anointed him with the Holy Spirit: Grant that all who
are baptized into His Name may keep the covenant they have made, and
boldly confess him as Lord and Savior; who with you and the Holy Spirit lives
and reigns, one God, in glory everlasting. *Amen.*†

The Concluding Prayer of the Church
Lord Jesus Christ, you have prepared a quiet place for us in your Father's eternal
home. Watch over our welfare on this perilous journey, shade us from the
burning heat of day, and keep our lives free of evil until the end. *Amen.*

THE *LITURGY OF THE HOURS, VOL. III*

The Vespers Office   To Be Observed on the Hour or Half Hour
                                                          Between 5 and 8 p.m.

The Call to Prayer
Sing to the LORD, you servants of his;* give thanks for the remembrance of his holi-
ness.
For his wrath endures but the twinkling of an eye,* his favor for a lifetime.

                                                                    Psalm 30:4–5

The Request for Presence
Show us the light of your countenance, O God,* and come to us.
                                               based on Psalm 67:1

The Greeting
Your statutes have been like songs to me* wherever I have lived as a stranger.
I remember your Name in the night, O LORD,* and dwell upon your law.
This is how it has been with me,* because I have kept your commandments.

                                                                    Psalm 119:54–56

The Hymn
   Jesus, Savior, pilot me over life's tempestuous sea;
   Unknown waves before me roll, hiding rock and treacherous shoal.
   Chart and compass came from thee; Jesus, Savior, pilot me.

   As a mother stills her child, you can hush the ocean wild;
   Boisterous waves obey your will, when you say to them, "Be still!"
   Wondrous sovereign of the sea, Jesus, Savior, pilot me.

   When at last I near the shore, and the fearful breakers roar
   'Twixt me and the peaceful rest, then, while leaning on your breast,
   May I hear you say to me, "Fear not, I will pilot thee."

                                                                    Edward Hopper

The Refrain for the Vesper Lessons
Righteousness shall go before him,* and peace shall be a pathway for his feet.
                                                                    Psalm 85:13

The Vespers Psalm   *Cast Your Burden Upon the LORD*
But I will call upon God,* and the LORD will deliver me.
In the evening, in the morning, and at noonday, I will complain and lament,* and
   he will hear my voice.
He will bring me safely back from the battle waged against me;* for there are
   many who fight me.
God, who is enthroned of old, will hear me . . .
Cast your burden upon the LORD, and he will sustain you;* he will never let the
   righteous stumble.

                                                                    Psalm 55:17–20, 24

The Refrain
Righteousness shall go before him,* and peace shall be a pathway for his feet.

The Cry of the Church
O God, come to my assistance! O Lord, make haste to help me!

The Lord's Prayer

The Prayer Appointed for the Week
Father in heaven, who at the baptism of Jesus in the River Jordan proclaimed him
    your beloved Son and anointed him with the Holy Spirit: Grant that all who
    are baptized into His Name may keep the covenant they have made, and
    boldly confess him as Lord and Savior; who with you and the Holy Spirit lives
    and reigns, one God, in glory everlasting. *Amen.*†

The Concluding Prayer of the Church
May Almighty God grant me a peaceful night and a perfect end. *Amen.*

The Morning Office   To Be Observed on the Hour or Half Hour
                                       Between 6 and 9 a.m.

The Call to Prayer
Sing with joy to God our strength* and raise a loud shout to the God of Jacob.
Raise a song and sound the timbrel,* the merry harp, and the lyre.
Blow the ram's-horn at the new moon,* and at the full moon, the day of our feast.
For this is a statute for Israel,* a law of the God of Jacob.

Psalm 81:1–4

The Request for Presence
Teach me your way, O LORD,* and I will walk in your truth; knit my heart to you
    that I may fear your Name.

Psalm 86:11

The Greeting
My mouth shall recount your mighty acts and saving deeds all day long;* though I
    cannot know the number of them.

Psalm 71:15

The Refrain for the Morning Lessons
And they will say,* "Surely, there is a reward for the righteous; surely, there is a
    God who rules in the earth."

Psalm 58:11

A Reading
The woman said to him, 'I know that Messiah—that is, Christ—is coming; and
    when he comes he will explain everything.' Jesus said, 'That is who I am, I who
    speak to you.'

John 4:25–26

The Refrain
And they will say,* "Surely, there is a reward for the righteous; surely, there is a
    God who rules in the earth."

The Morning Psalm   *Establish, O God, What You Have Wrought for Us*
Send forth your strength, O God;* establish, O God, what you have wrought for
    us.
Kings shall bring gifts to you,* for your temple's sake at Jerusalem.
Rebuke the wild beast of the reeds,* and the peoples, a herd of wild bulls with its
    calves.
Trample down those who lust after silver;* scatter the peoples that delight in war.
Let tribute be brought out of Egypt;* let Ethiopia stretch out her hands to God.
Sing to God, O kingdoms of the earth;* sing praises to the Lord.
He rides in the heavens, the ancient heavens;* he sends forth his voice, his mighty
    voice.

Psalm 68:28–34

The Refrain
And they will say,* "Surely, there is a reward for the righteous; surely, there is a
    God who rules in the earth."

The Gloria

The Lord's Prayer

The Prayer Appointed for the Week
Father in heaven, who at the baptism of Jesus in the River Jordan proclaimed him
    your beloved Son and anointed him with the Holy Spirit: Grant that all who
    are baptized into His Name may keep the covenant they have made, and
    boldly confess him as Lord and Savior; who with you and the Holy Spirit lives
    and reigns, one God, in glory everlasting. *Amen.*†

The Concluding Prayer of the Church
Lord God, almighty and everlasting Father, you have brought me in safety to this
    new day: Preserve me with your mighty power, that I may not fall into sin, nor
    be overcome by adversity; and in all I do direct me to the fulfilling of your pur-
    pose; through Jesus Christ my Lord. *Amen.*†

The Midday Office   To Be Observed on the Hour or Half Hour
                                     Between 11 a.m. and 2 p.m.

The Call to Prayer
Come, let us sing to the Lord;* let us shout for joy to the Rock of our salvation.
Let us come before his presence with thanksgiving* and raise a loud shout to him
    with psalms.
For the Lord is a great God,* and a great King above all gods.

Psalm 95:1–3

The Request for Presence
Let the peoples praise you, O God;* let all the peoples praise you.

Psalm 67:3

The Greeting
You have made me glad by your acts, O Lord;* and I shout for joy because of the
works of your hands.

Psalm 92:4

The Refrain for the Midday Lessons
Yours are the heavens; the earth also is yours;* you laid the foundations of the
world and all that is in it.

Psalm 89:11

A Reading
I urge you, then, brothers, remembering the mercies of God, to offer your bodies
as a living sacrifice, dedicated and acceptable to God; that is the kind of worship for you, as sensible people. Do not model your behavior on the contemporary world, but let the renewing of your minds transform you, so that you may
discern for yourselves what is the will of God—what is good and acceptable
and mature.

Romans 12:1–2

The Refrain
Yours are the heavens; the earth also is yours;* you laid the foundations of the
world and all that is in it.

The Midday Psalm   *I Shall See the Goodness of the* Lord
                                      in the Land of the Living!

Hearken to my voice, O Lord, when I call;* have mercy on me and answer me.
You speak in my heart and say, "Seek my face."* Your face, Lord, will I seek.
Hide not your face from me,* nor turn away your servant in displeasure.
You have been my helper; cast me not away;* do not forsake me, O God of my
salvation.
Though my father and my mother forsake me,* the Lord will sustain me.
Show me your way, O Lord;* lead me on a level path, because of my enemies.
Deliver me not into the hand of my adversaries,* for false witnesses have risen up
against me, and also those who speak malice.
What if I had not believed that I should see the goodness of the Lord* in the land
of the living!

Psalm 27:10–17

The Refrain
Yours are the heavens; the earth also is yours;* you laid the foundations of the
world and all that is in it.

The Gloria

The Lord's Prayer

The Prayer Appointed for the Week

Father in heaven, who at the baptism of Jesus in the River Jordan proclaimed him
your beloved Son and anointed him with the Holy Spirit: Grant that all who
are baptized into His Name may keep the covenant they have made, and
boldly confess him as Lord and Savior; who with you and the Holy Spirit lives
and reigns, one God, in glory everlasting. *Amen.*†

The Concluding Prayer of the Church

Let us bless the Lord God living and true! Let us always render him praise, glory,
honor, blessing, and all good things! Amen. Amen. So be it! So be it!

St. Francis of Assisi

The Vespers Office　　　　　　　　**To Be Observed on the Hour or Half Hour**
　　　　　　　　　　　　　　　　　　　　　Between 5 and 8 p.m.

The Call to Prayer

Blessed be the LORD, the God of Israel, from everlasting and to everlasting;* and
let all the people say, "Amen!" Hallelujah!

Psalm 106:48

The Request for Presence

Send forth your strength, O God;* establish, O God, what you have wrought for us.

Psalm 68:28

The Greeting

My heart is firmly fixed, O God, my heart is fixed;* I will sing and make melody.

Psalm 57:7

The Hymn

O sing a song of Bethlehem, of shepherds watching there,
And of the news that came to them from angels in the air.
The light that shone on Bethlehem fills all the world today;
Of Jesus' birth and peace on earth the angels sing always.

O sing a song of Nazareth, of sunny days of joy;
O sing of fragrant flower's breath, and of the sinless Boy.
For now the flowers of Nazareth in every heart may grow;
Now spreads the fame of his dear name on all the winds that blow.

O sing a song of Galilee, of lake and woods and hill,
Of him who walked upon the sea and bade the waves be still.
For though like waves on Galilee, dark seas of trouble roll,
When faith has heard the Master's word, falls peace upon the soul.

O sing a song of Calvary, its glory and dismay,
Of him who hung upon the tree and took our sins away.
For he who died on Calvary is risen from the grave,
And Christ, our Lord, by heaven adored, is mighty now to save.

Louis Benson

The Refrain for the Vespers Lessons

I trust in the mercy of God for ever and ever.

I will give you thanks for what you have done* and declare the goodness of your
     Name in the presence of the godly.

Psalm 52:8–9

The Vespers Psalm   *I Would Make Known to This Generation Your Power
     and Your Strength*

O God, you have taught me since I was young,* and to this day I tell of your
     wonderful works.

And now that I am old and gray-headed, O God, do not forsake me,* till I make
     known your strength to this generation and your power to all who are to come.

Your righteousness, O God, reaches to the heavens;* you have done great things;
     who is like you, O God?

You have showed me great troubles and adversities,* but you will restore my life
     and bring me up again from the deep places of the earth.

Psalm 71:17–20

The Refrain

I trust in the mercy of God for ever and ever.

I will give you thanks for what you have done* and declare the goodness of your
     Name in the presence of the godly.

The Cry of the Church

Even so, come, Lord Jesus!

The Lord's Prayer

The Prayer Appointed for the Week

Father in heaven, who at the baptism of Jesus in the River Jordan proclaimed him
     your beloved Son and anointed him with the Holy Spirit: Grant that all who
     are baptized into His Name may keep the covenant they have made, and
     boldly confess him as Lord and Savior; who with you and the Holy Spirit lives
     and reigns, one God, in glory everlasting. *Amen.*†

The Concluding Prayer of the Church

Almighty God, whose loving hand has given me all that I possess: Grant me grace
     that I may honor you with my substance, and, remembering the account which
     I must one day give, may be a faithful steward of your bounty, through Jesus
     Christ our Lord. *Amen.*†

The Morning Office   To Be Observed on the Hour or Half Hour
     Between 6 and 9 a.m.

The Call to Prayer

Search for the LORD and his strength;* continually seek his face.

Psalm 105:4

The Request for Presence
O Lamb of God, that takes away the sins of the world, have mercy upon me.
O Lamb of God, that takes away the sins of the world, have mercy upon me.
O Lamb of God, that takes away the sins of the world, grant me your peace.

The Greeting
O God, you know my foolishness,* and my faults are not hidden from you.

Psalm 69:6

The Refrain for the Morning Lessons
Our sins are stronger than we are,* but you will blot them out.

Psalm 65:3

A Reading
Jesus taught us, saying: "Why do you observe the splinter in your brother's eye
and never notice the great log in your own? How can you say to your brother,
'Brother, let me take that splinter out of your eye,' when you cannot see the
great log in your own? Hypocrite! Take the log out of your own eye first, and
then you will see clearly enough to take out the splinter in your brother's eye."

Luke 6:41–42

The Refrain
Our sins are stronger than we are,* but you will blot them out.

The Morning Psalm   *Forgive My Sin for Your Name's Sake*
Remember, O LORD, your compassion and love,* for they are from everlasting.
Remember not the sins of my youth and my transgressions;* remember me
according to your love and for the sake of your goodness, O LORD.
Gracious and upright is the LORD;* therefore he teaches sinners in his way.
For your Name's sake, O LORD,* forgive my sin, for it is great.

Psalm 25:5–7, 10

The Refrain
Our sins are stronger than we are,* but you will blot them out.

The Cry of the Church
O God, come to my assistance! O Lord, make haste to help me!

The Lord's Prayer

The Prayer Appointed for the Week
Father in heaven, who at the baptism of Jesus in the River Jordan proclaimed him
your beloved Son and anointed him with the Holy Spirit: Grant that all who
are baptized into His Name may keep the covenant they have made, and
boldly confess him as Lord and Savior; who with you and the Holy Spirit lives
and reigns, one God, in glory everlasting. *Amen.*†

The Concluding Prayer of the Church
Lord God, almighty and everlasting Father, you have brought me in safety to this
new day: Preserve me with your mighty power, that I may not fall into sin, nor

be overcome by adversity; and in all I do direct me to the fulfilling of your purpose; through Jesus Christ my Lord. *Amen.*†

The Midday Office   To Be Observed on the Hour or Half Hour
                                    Between 11 a.m. and 2 p.m.

The Call to Prayer
Ascribe to the LORD the honor due his Name;* bring offerings and come into his
    courts.

Psalm 96:8

The Request for Presence
Let your countenance shine upon your servant* and teach me your statutes.

Psalm 119:135

The Greeting
I will give thanks to you, O LORD, with my whole heart;* I will tell of all your marvelous works.

Psalm 9:1

The Refrain for the Midday Lessons
Among the gods there is none like you, O LORD,* nor anything like your works.

Psalm 86:8

A Reading
Woe to those who call what is bad, good, and what is good, bad, who substitute
    darkness for light and light for darkness, who substitute bitter for sweet and
    sweet for bitter. Woe to those who think themselves wise and believe themselves enlightened. Woe to those whose might lies in wine bibbing, their heroism in mixing strong drinks, who acquit the guilty for a bribe and deny justice
    to the upright. Yes, as a flame devours the stubble, as the straw flares up and
    disappears, their root will be like decay and their shoot be carried off like dust,
    for having rejected the law of YAHWEH Sabaoth, for having despised the word
    of the Holy One of Israel.

Isaiah 5:20–24

The Refrain
Among the gods there is none like you, O LORD,* nor anything like your works.

The Midday Psalm   *You, O LORD, Will Bless the Righteous*
Lead me, O LORD, in your righteousness, because of those who lie in wait for me;*
    make your way straight before me.
For there is no truth in their mouth;* there is destruction in their heart;
Their throat is an open grave;* they flatter with their tongue.
Declare them guilty, O God;* let them fall, because of their schemes.
Because of their many transgressions cast them out,* for they have rebelled
    against you.
But all who take refuge in you will be glad;* they will sing out their joy for ever.

You will shelter them,* so that those who love your Name may exult in you.
For you, O LORD, will bless the righteous;* you will defend them with your favor
     as with a shield.

Psalm 5:8–15

The Refrain
Among the gods there is none like you, O LORD,* nor anything like your works.

The Cry of the Church
Even so, come, Lord Jesus!

The Lord's Prayer

The Prayer Appointed for the Week
Father in heaven, who at the baptism of Jesus in the River Jordan proclaimed him
     your beloved Son and anointed him with the Holy Spirit: Grant that all who
     are baptized into His Name may keep the covenant they have made, and
     boldly confess him as Lord and Savior; who with you and the Holy Spirit lives
     and reigns, one God, in glory everlasting. *Amen.*†

The Concluding Prayer of the Church
Almighty God, who has promised to hear the petitions of those who ask in your
     Son's Name: I beseech you mercifully to incline your ear to me who have made
     my prayers and supplications to you; and grant that those things which I have
     faithfully asked according to your will, I may effectually obtain, to the relief of
     my necessity, and to the setting forth of your glory; through Jesus Christ my
     Lord. *Amen.*†

The Vespers Office   **To Be Observed on the Hour or Half Hour**
                                      Between 5 and 8 p.m.

The Call to Prayer
I will call upon God,* and the LORD will deliver me.
In the evening, in the morning, and at noonday, I will complain and lament,* and
     he will hear my voice.
He will bring me safely back . . .* God, who is enthroned of old, will hear me.

Psalm 55:17ff

The Request for Presence
You are the LORD; do not withhold your compassion from me;* let your love and
     your faithfulness keep me safe for ever.

Psalm 40:12

The Greeting
I remember your Name in the night, O LORD,* and dwell upon your law.

Psalm 119:55

The Hymn

> There's within my heart a melody
> Jesus whispers sweet and low:
> "Fear not, I am with thee,
> Peace, be still, in all life's ebb and flow."
> Jesus, Jesus, Jesus, sweetest name I know,
> Fills my every longing, keeps me singing as I go.

> All my life was wrecked by sin and strife,
> Discord filled my heart with pain;
> Jesus swept across the broken strings,
> Stirred the slumbering chords again.
> Jesus, Jesus, Jesus, sweetest name I know,
> Fills my every longing, keeps me singing as I go.

> Feasting on the riches of his grace,
> Resting beneath his sheltering wing,
> Always looking on his smiling face,
> That is why I shout and sing.
> Jesus, Jesus, Jesus, sweetest name I know,
> Fills my every longing, keeps me singing as I go.

> Soon he's coming back to welcome me
> Far beyond the starry sky;
> I shall wing my flight to worlds unknown;
> I shall reign with him on high
> Jesus, Jesus, Jesus, sweetest name I know,
> Fills my every longing, keeps me singing as I go.

Luther Bridgers

The Refrain for the Vespers Lessons
. . . he gives to his beloved sleep.

Psalm 127:3

The Vespers Psalm   *The LORD Sustains Me*

But you, O LORD, are a shield about me;* you are my glory, the one who lifts up my head.

I call aloud upon the LORD,* and he answers me from his holy hill;

I lie down and go to sleep;* I wake again, because the LORD sustains me.

Deliverance belongs to the LORD.* Your blessing be upon your people!

Psalm 3:3–5, 8

The Refrain
. . . he gives to his beloved sleep.

The Small Verse

Open, Lord, my eyes that I may see. Open, Lord, my ears that I may hear. Open, Lord, my heart and my mind that I may understand. So shall I turn to you and be healed.

Traditional

The Lord's Prayer

The Prayer Appointed for the Week

Father in heaven, who at the baptism of Jesus in the River Jordan proclaimed him your beloved Son and anointed him with the Holy Spirit: Grant that all who are baptized into His Name may keep the covenant they have made, and boldly confess him as Lord and Savior; who with you and the Holy Spirit lives and reigns, one God, in glory everlasting. *Amen.*†

Concluding Prayers of the Church

Lord Jesus Christ, by your death you took away the sting of death: Grant me to so follow in faith where you have led the way, that I may at length fall asleep peacefully in you and wake in your likeness; for your tender mercies' sake. *Amen.*†

May the souls of the faithful departed, through the mercy of God, rest in eternal peace. *Amen.*

The Morning Office   To Be Observed on the Hour or Half Hour
                Between 6 and 9 a.m.

The Call to Prayer

Let us bless the LORD,* from this time forth for evermore. Hallelujah!

based on Psalm 115:18

The Request for Presence

I cry out to you, O LORD;* I say, "You are my refuge, my portion in the land of the living."

Psalm 142:5

The Greeting

I will confess you among the peoples, O LORD;* I will sing praises to you among the nations.
For your loving-kindness is greater than the heavens,* and your faithfulness reaches to the clouds.

Psalm 108:3–4

The Refrain for the Morning Lessons

For the LORD God is both sun and shield;* he will give grace and glory.

Psalm 84:10

A Reading

He came to Nazara, where he had been brought up, and went into the synagogue
on the Sabbath day as he usually did. He stood up to read, and they handed
him the scroll of the prophet Isaiah. Unrolling the scroll he found the place
where it is written: *The spirit of the Lord is on me, for he has anointed me to bring the*
good news to the afflicted. He has sent me to proclaim liberty to captives, sight to the
blind, to let the oppressed go free, to proclaim a year of favor from the Lord. He then
rolled up the scroll, gave it back to the assistant and sat back down. And all
eyes in the synagogue were fixed on him. Then he began to speak to them,
'This text is being fulfilled today even while you are listening.' And he won the
approval of all, and they were astonished by the gracious words that came
from his lips.

Luke 4:16–22

The Refrain

For the Lord God is both sun and shield;* he will give grace and glory.

The Morning Psalm   *You Are the God of My Salvation*

To you, O Lord, I lift up my soul; my God, I put my trust in you;* let me not be
humiliated, nor let my enemies triumph over me.

Let none who look to you be put to shame;* let the treacherous be disappointed in
their schemes.

Show me your ways, O Lord,* and teach me your paths.

Lead me in your truth and teach me,* for you are the God of my salvation; in you
have I trusted all the day long.

Psalm 25:1–4

The Refrain

For the Lord God is both sun and shield;* he will give grace and glory.

The Gloria

The Lord's Prayer

The Prayer Appointed for the Week

Father in heaven, who at the baptism of Jesus in the River Jordan proclaimed him
your beloved Son and anointed him with the Holy Spirit: Grant that all who
are baptized into His Name may keep the covenant they have made, and
boldly confess him as Lord and Savior; who with you and the Holy Spirit lives
and reigns, one God, in glory everlasting. *Amen.*†

The Concluding Prayer of the Church

Lord God, almighty and everlasting Father, you have brought me in safety to this
new day: Preserve me with your mighty power, that I may not fall into sin, nor
be overcome by adversity; and in all I do direct me to the fulfilling of your purpose; through Jesus Christ my Lord. *Amen.*†

The Midday Office To Be Observed on the Hour or Half Hour
Between 11 a.m. and 2 p.m.

The Call to Prayer
Open my lips, O Lord,* and my mouth shall proclaim your praise.
Psalm 51:16

The Request for Presence
Look well whether there be any wickedness in me* and lead me in the way that is
   everlasting.
Psalm 139:23

The Greeting
O Lord, I am your servant;* I am your servant and the child of your handmaid;
   you have freed me from my bonds.
Psalm 116:14

The Refrain for the Midday Lessons
Unless the Lord builds the house,* their labor is in vain who build it.
Psalm 127:1

A Reading
This is what I shall keep in mind and so regain some hope: surely Yahweh's mercies are not over. His deeds of faithful love are not exhausted: every morning
   they are renewed; great is his faithfulness! 'Yahweh is all I have,' I say to
   myself, 'and so I shall put my hope in him.'
Lamentations 3:21–24

The Refrain
Unless the Lord builds the house,* their labor is in vain who build it.

The Midday Psalm *In the Full Assembly, I Will Bless the Lord*
Do not sweep me away with sinners,* nor my life with those who thirst for blood,
Whose hands are full of evil plots,* and their right hand full of bribes.
As for me, I will live with integrity;* redeem me, O Lord, and have pity on me.
My foot stands on level ground;* in the full assembly I will bless the Lord.
Psalm 26:8–12

The Refrain
Unless the Lord builds the house,* their labor is in vain who build it.

The Cry of the Church
Even so, come, Lord Jesus!

The Lord's Prayer

The Prayer Appointed for the Week
Father in heaven, who at the baptism of Jesus in the River Jordan proclaimed him
   your beloved Son and anointed him with the Holy Spirit: Grant that all who
   are baptized into His Name may keep the covenant they have made, and

boldly confess him as Lord and Savior; who with you and the Holy Spirit lives and reigns, one God, in glory everlasting. *Amen.*†

The Concluding Prayer of the Church

O God, the source of eternal light: Shed forth your unending day upon all of us who watch for you, that our lips may praise you, our lives may bless you, and our worship may give you glory; through Jesus Christ our Lord. *Amen.*†

The Vespers Office   To Be Observed on the Hour or Half Hour
                                        Between 5 and 8 p.m.

The Call to Prayer

Let everything that has breath* praise the LORD. Hallelujah!
Psalm 150:6

The Request for Presence

O God, you are my God; eagerly I seek you;* my soul thirsts for you, my flesh faints for you, as in a barren and dry land where there is no water.
Therefore I have gazed upon you in your holy place,* that I might behold your power and your glory.
Psalm 63:1–2

The Greeting

Your loving-kindness is better than life itself;* my lips shall give you praise.
So will I bless you as long as I live* and lift up my hands in your Name.
Psalm 63:3–4

The Hymn

You servants of God, your Master proclaim,
And publish abroad his wonderful name;
The name all victorious of Jesus extol,
His kingdom is glorious and rules over all.

"Salvation to God, who sits on the throne!"
Let all cry aloud and honor the Son;
The praises of Jesus the angels proclaim,
Fall down on their faces and worship the Lamb.

Then let us adore and give him his right,
All glory and power, all wisdom and might;
All honor and blessing with angels above,
And thanks never ceasing and infinite love.
Charles Wesley

The Refrain for the Vespers Lessons

The LORD is my light and my salvation; whom then shall I fear?* the LORD is the strength of my life; of whom then shall I be afraid?
Psalm 27:1

The Vespers Psalm　　　　　　*With the Faithful, You Show Yourself Faithful, O God*

With the faithful you show yourself faithful, O God;* with the forthright you show
　　yourself forthright.

With the pure you show yourself pure,* but with the crooked you are wily.

You will save a lowly people,* but you will humble the haughty eyes.

You, O LORD, are my lamp;* my God, you make my darkness bright.

With you I will break down an enclosure;* with the help of my God I will scale any
　　wall.

As for God, his ways are perfect; the words of the LORD are tried in the fire;* he is a
　　shield to all who trust in him.

Psalm 18:26–31

The Refrain

The LORD is my light and my salvation; whom then shall I fear?* the LORD is the
　　strength of my life; of whom then shall I be afraid?

The Cry of the Church

O Lamb of God, that takes away ʾhe sins of the world, have mercy upon me.

O Lamb of God, that takes away the sins of the world, have mercy upon me.

O Lamb of God, that takes away the sins of the world, grant me your peace.

The Lord's Prayer

The Prayer Appointed for the Week

Father in heaven, who at the baptism of Jesus in the River Jordan proclaimed him
　　your beloved Son and anointed him with the Holy Spirit: Grant that all who
　　are baptized into His Name may keep the covenant they have made, and
　　boldly confess him as Lord and Savior; who with you and the Holy Spirit lives
　　and reigns, one God, in glory everlasting. *Amen.*†

The Concluding Prayer of the Church

Almighty God, who after the creation of the world rested from all your works and
　　sanctified a day of rest for all your creatures: Grant that I, putting away all
　　earthly anxieties, may be duly prepared for the service of public worship, and
　　grant as well that my Sabbath upon earth may be a preparation for the eternal
　　rest promised to your people in heaven; through Jesus Christ our Lord. *Amen.*†

The Morning Office　　　　　　　　To Be Observed on the Hour or Half Hour
　　　　　　　　　　　　　　　　　　　　　Between 6 and 9 a.m.

The Call to Prayer

Sing to the LORD a new song,* for he has done marvelous things.

Psalm 98:1

The Request for Presence
Create in me a clean heart, O God,* and renew a right spirit within me.
Psalm 51:11

The Greeting
I am small and of little account,* yet I do not forget your commandments.
Psalm 119:141

The Refrain for the Morning Lessons
Let my mouth be full of your praise* and your glory all the day long.
Psalm 71:8

A Reading
After John had been arrested, Jesus went into Galilee. There he proclaimed the
gospel from God saying, 'The time is fulfilled, and the kingdom of God is close
at hand. Repent, and believe the gospel.'
Mark 1:14–15

The Refrain
Let my mouth be full of your praise* and your glory all the day long.

The Morning Psalm   *May the Lord Rejoice in All His Work*
May the glory of the Lord endure for ever;* may the Lord rejoice in all his works.
He looks at the earth and it trembles;* he touches the mountains and they smoke.
I will sing to the Lord as long as I live;* I will praise my God while I have my
being.
May these words of mine please him;* I will rejoice in the Lord.
Let sinners be consumed out of the earth,* and the wicked be no more.
Bless the Lord, O my soul.* Hallelujah!
Psalm 104:32–37

The Refrain
Let my mouth be full of your praise* and your glory all the day long.

The Cry of the Church
O Lord, hear my prayer and let my cry come unto you. Thanks be to God.
THE SHORT BREVIARY

The Lord's Prayer

The Prayer Appointed for the Week
Almighty God, whose Son our Savior Jesus Christ is the light of the world: Grant
that your people, illumined by your Word and Sacraments, may shine with the
radiance of Christ's glory, that he may be known, worshipped, and obeyed to
the ends of the earth; through Jesus Christ our Lord, who with you and the
Holy Spirit lives and reigns, one God, now and for ever. *Amen.*†

The Concluding Prayer of the Church
Lord God, almighty and everlasting Father, you have brought me in safety to this
new day: Preserve me with your mighty power, that I may not fall into sin, nor

be overcome by adversity; and in all I do direct me to the fulfilling of your purpose; through Jesus Christ my Lord. *Amen.*†

The Midday Office   To Be Observed on the Hour or Half Hour
                                           Between 11 a.m. and 2 p.m.

The Call to Prayer
Blessed be the Lord for evermore!* Amen, I say, Amen.
                                           Psalm 89:52

The Request for Presence
May the graciousness of the Lord our God be upon us;* prosper the work of our
   hands; prosper our handiwork.
                                           Psalm 90:17

The Greeting
Blessed are you, O Lord;* instruct me in your statutes.
                                           Psalm 119:12

The Refrain for the Midday Lessons
"I will instruct you and teach you in the way that you should go;* I will guide you
   with my eye.
Do not be like horse or mule, which have no understanding;* who must be fitted
   with bit and bridle, or else they will not stay near you."
                                           Psalm 32:9–10

A Reading
Then Peter addressed them, 'I now really understand,' he said, 'that God has no
   favorites, but that anybody of any nationality who fears him and does what is
   right is acceptable to him. God sent his word to the people of Israel, and it was to
   them that *the good news of peace was brought* by Jesus Christ—he is the Lord of all.'
                                           Acts 10:34–36

The Refrain
"I will instruct you and teach you in the way that you should go;* I will guide you
   with my eye.
Do not be like horse or mule, which have no understanding;* who must be fitted
   with bit and bridle, or else they will not stay near you."

The Midday Psalm   *In the Temple of the Lord, All Are Crying, "Glory!"*
Ascribe to the Lord, you gods,* ascribe to the Lord glory and strength.
Ascribe to the Lord the glory due his Name;* worship the Lord in the beauty of
   holiness.
The voice of the Lord is upon the waters; the God of glory thunders;* the Lord is
   upon the mighty waters.
The voice of the Lord is a powerful voice;* the voice of the Lord is a voice of
   splendor.

The voice of the Lord breaks the cedar trees;* the Lord breaks the cedars of Lebanon;

He makes Lebanon skip like a calf,* and Mount Hermon like a young wild ox.

The voice of the Lord splits the flames of fire; the voice of the Lord shakes the wilderness;* the Lord shakes the wilderness of Kadesh.

The voice of the Lord makes the oak trees writhe* and strips the forests bare.

And in the temple of the Lord* all are crying, "Glory!"

The Lord sits enthroned above the flood;* the Lord sits enthroned as King for evermore.

The Lord shall give strength to his people;* the Lord shall give his people the blessing of peace.

Psalm 29

The Refrain

"I will instruct you and teach you in the way that you should go;* I will guide you with my eye.

Do not be like horse or mule, which have no understanding;* who must be fitted with bit and bridle, or else they will not stay near you."

The Small Verse

My help is in the name of the Lord who made heaven and earth and all that is in them. Thanks be to God.

Traditional

The Lord's Prayer

The Prayer Appointed for the Week

Almighty God, whose Son our Savior Jesus Christ is the light of the world: Grant that your people, illumined by your Word and Sacraments, may shine with the radiance of Christ's glory, that he may be known, worshipped, and obeyed to the ends of the earth; through Jesus Christ our Lord, who with you and the Holy Spirit lives and reigns, one God, now and for ever. *Amen.*†

The Concluding Prayer of the Church

O God, you make me glad with the weekly remembrance of the glorious resurrection of your Son my Lord: Give me this day such blessing through my worship of you, that the week to come may be spent in your favor; through Jesus Christ our Lord. *Amen.*†

The Vespers Office   **To Be Observed on the Hour or Half Hour Between 5 and 8 p.m.**

The Call to Prayer

Sing praise to the Lord who dwells in Zion;* proclaim to the peoples the things he has done.

Psalm 9:11

The Request for Presence

To you I lift up my eyes,* to you enthroned in the heavens.

Psalm 123:1

The Greeting

I put my trust in your mercy;* my heart is joyful because of your saving help.

Psalm 13:5

The Hymn

King of the martyrs' noble band,
Crown of the true of every land,
Strength of the pilgrim on the way,
Beacon by night and cloud by day:

Hear us now as we celebrate
Faith undeterred by cruel hate;
Hear and forgive us, sinners who
Are burdened by the wrong we do.

Dying, through you they overcame;
Living, were faithful to your Name.
Turn our rebellious hearts, and thus
Win such a victory in us.

Glory to God the Father be;
Glory to Christ, who set us free;
And to the Spirit, living flame,
Glory unceasing we proclaim.

Unknown

The Refrain for the Vespers Lessons

The angel of the LORD encompasses those who fear him,* and he will deliver them.

Psalm 34:7

The Vespers Psalm

Those Who Lie in Wait for My Life
Are Taking Counsel Together

For my enemies are talking against me,* and those who lie in wait for my life take
counsel together.

They say, "God has forsaken him; go after him and seize him;* because there is
none who will save."

O God, be not far from me;* come quickly to help me, O my God.

Let those who set themselves against me be put to shame and be disgraced;* let
those who seek to do me evil be covered with scorn and reproach.

But I shall always wait in patience,* and shall praise you more and more.

My mouth shall recount your mighty acts and saving deeds all day long;* though I
cannot know the number of them.

I will begin with the mighty works of the Lord GOD;* I will recall your
righteousness, yours alone.

O God, you have taught me since I was young,* and to this day I tell of your
wonderful works.

Psalm 71:10–17

The Refrain

The angel of the LORD encompasses those who fear him,* and he will deliver them.

The Cry of the Church

Lord, have mercy on us. Christ, have mercy on us. Lord, have mercy on us.

The Lord's Prayer

The Prayer Appointed for the Week

Almighty God, whose Son our Savior Jesus Christ is the light of the world: Grant that your people, illumined by your Word and Sacraments, may shine with the radiance of Christ's glory, that he may be known, worshipped, and obeyed to the ends of the earth; through Jesus Christ our Lord, who with you and the Holy Spirit lives and reigns, one God, now and for ever. *Amen.*†

Concluding Prayers of the Church

Almighty God, you have surrounded me with a great cloud of witnesses: Grant that I, encouraged by the good example of your servant Peter; may persevere in running the race that is set before me, until at last I may with him attain to your eternal joy; through Jesus Christ, the pioneer and perfecter of our faith, who lives and reigns with you and the Holy Spirit, one God, for ever and ever. *Amen.*†

Lord God, whose Son our Savior Jesus Christ, triumphed over the powers of death and prepared for us our place in the new Jerusalem: Grant that I, who have this day given thanks for his resurrection, may praise you in the City of which he is the light, and where he lives and reigns for ever and ever. *Amen.*†

The Morning Office   To Be Observed on the Hour or Half Hour
                                                      Between 6 and 9 a.m.

The Call to Prayer

Sing to the LORD and bless his Name;* proclaim the good news of his salvation from day to day.
Declare his glory among the nations* and his wonders among all peoples.

Psalm 96:2–3

The Request for Presence

In the morning, LORD, you hear my voice;* early in the morning I make my appeal and watch for you.

Psalm 5:3

The Greeting

Be exalted, O LORD, in your might;* we will sing and praise your power.

Psalm 21:14

The Refrain for the Morning Lessons

Then shall all the trees of the wood shout for joy before the LORD when he comes,* when he comes to judge the earth.

Psalm 96:12

A Reading   *On January 18, the Church celebrates the day of her founding. She recalls with awe the assertion of a Galilean fisherman, "You are the Christ," and the response of the God-among-us, "Upon this rock, I will found my church."*

When Jesus came to the region of Caesarea Philippi he put this question to his disciples, 'Who do people say the Son of Man is?' And they said, 'Some say John the Baptist, some Elijah, and others Jeremiah or one of the prophets.' 'But you,' he said, 'who do you say I am?' Then Simon Peter spoke up and said, 'You are the Christ, the Son of the living God.' Jesus replied, 'Simon son of Jonah, you are a blessed man! Because it was no human agency that revealed this to you but my Father in heaven. So I now say to you: You are Peter and on this rock I will build my community. And the gates of the underworld can never overpower it. I will give you the keys of the kingdom of Heaven: whatever you bind on earth will be bound in heaven; whatever you loose on earth will be loosed in heaven.' Then he gave the disciples strict orders not to say to anyone that he was the Christ.

Matthew 16:13–20

The Refrain
Then shall all the trees of the wood shout for joy before the Lord when he comes,*
when he comes to judge the earth.

The Morning Psalm   *The Lord Has Pleasure in Those Who Court His Favor*
Sing to the Lord with thanksgiving;* make music to our God upon the harp.
He covers the heavens with clouds* and prepares rain for the earth;
He makes grass to grow upon the mountains* and green plants to serve mankind.
He provides food for flocks and herds* and for the young ravens when they cry.
He is not impressed by the might of a horse;* he has no pleasure in the strength of
    a man;
But the Lord has pleasure in those who fear him,* in those who await his gracious
    favor.

Psalm 147:7–12

The Refrain
Then shall all the trees of the wood shout for joy before the Lord when he comes,*
when he comes to judge the earth.

The Cry of the Church
Even so, come, Lord Jesus!

The Lord's Prayer

The Prayer Appointed for the Week
Almighty God, whose Son our Savior Jesus Christ is the light of the world: Grant
    that your people, illumined by your Word and Sacraments, may shine with the
    radiance of Christ's glory, that he may be known, worshipped, and obeyed to
    the ends of the earth; through Jesus Christ our Lord, who with you and the
    Holy Spirit lives and reigns, one God, now and for ever. *Amen.*†

Concluding Prayers of the Church
Almighty Father, who inspired Simon Peter, first among the apostles to confess
    Jesus as Messiah and Son of the living God: Keep your Church steadfast upon

the rock of this faith, so that in unity and peace we may proclaim the one truth
and follow the one Lord, our Savior Jesus Christ; who lives and reigns with
you and the Holy Spirit, one God, now and for ever. *Amen.*

Lord God, almighty and everlasting Father, you have brought me in safety to this
new day: Preserve me with your mighty power, that I may not fall into sin, nor
be overcome by adversity; and in all I do direct me to the fulfilling of your purpose; through Jesus Christ my Lord. *Amen.*†

The Midday Office — To Be Observed on the Hour or Half Hour
Between 11 a.m. and 2 p.m.

The Call to Prayer
Tremble, then, and do not sin;* speak to your heart in silence upon your bed.
Offer the appointed sacrifices* and put your trust in the LORD.

Psalm 4:4–5

The Request for Presence
In your righteousness, deliver me and set me free;* incline your ear to me and
save me.

Psalm 71:2

The Greeting
Exalt yourself above the heavens, O God,* and your glory over all the earth.

Psalm 108:5

The Refrain for the Midday Lessons
"Be still, then, and know that I am God;* I will be exalted among the nations; I will
be exalted in the earth."

Psalm 46:11

A Reading
From St. Peter's address before the Sanhedrin in defense of his healing of a cripple: 'Rulers of the people, and elders! If you are questioning us today about an
act of kindness to a cripple and asking us how he was healed, you must know,
all of you, and the whole people of Israel, that it is by the name of Jesus Christ
the Nazarene, whom you crucified, and God raised from the dead, by this
name and by no other that this man stands before you cured. This is *the stone
which* you, *the builders rejected* but which has *become the cornerstone.* Only in him
is there salvation; for of all the names in the world given to men, this is the only
one by which we can be saved.'

Acts 4:8–12

The Refrain
"Be still, then, and know that I am God;* I will be exalted among the nations; I will
be exalted in the earth."

The Midday Psalm   *God Is the Rock of My Trust*

As often as I said, "My foot has slipped,"* your love, O LORD, upheld me.
When many cares fill my mind,* your consolations cheer my soul.
Can a corrupt tribunal have any part with you,* one which frames evil into law?
They conspire against the life of the just* and condemn the innocent to death.
But the LORD has become my stronghold,* and my God the rock of my trust.
He will turn their wickedness back upon them and destroy them in their own
     malice;* the LORD our God will destroy them.

Psalm 94:18–23

The Refrain

"Be still, then, and know that I am God;* I will be exalted among the nations; I will
     be exalted in the earth."

The Cry of the Church

Michael, Gabriel, Cherubim and Seraphim cease not to cry daily: You are worthy,
     O Lord, to receive glory, alleluia.

THE SHORT BREVIARY

The Lord's Prayer

The Prayer Appointed for the Week

Almighty God, whose Son our Savior Jesus Christ is the light of the world: Grant
     that your people, illumined by your Word and Sacraments, may shine with the
     radiance of Christ's glory, that he may be known, worshipped, and obeyed to
     the ends of the earth; through Jesus Christ our Lord, who with you and the
     Holy Spirit lives and reigns, one God, now and for ever. *Amen.†*

The Concluding Prayer of the Church

Almighty God, who gave to your servant Peter boldness to confess the Name of
     our Savior Jesus Christ before the rulers of this world, and courage to die for
     this faith: Grant that I may always be ready to give a reason for the hope that is
     in us, and to suffer gladly for the sake of our Lord Jesus Christ; who lives and
     reigns with you and the Holy Spirit, one God, for ever and ever. *Amen.†*

The Vespers Office   **To Be Observed on the Hour or Half Hour**
                                                    Between 5 and 8 p.m.

The Call to Prayer

Sing to the LORD and bless his Name;* proclaim the good news of his salvation
     from day to day.
Declare his glory among the nations* and his wonders among all peoples.

Psalm 96:2–3

The Request for Presence

Save us, O LORD our God, and gather us from among the nations,* that we may
     give thanks to your holy Name and glory in your praise.

Psalm 106:47

The Greeting

I will give you thanks for what you have done* and declare the goodness of your
Name in the presence of the godly.

Psalm 52:9

The Hymn

You are the Christ, O Lord, the Son of God most high!
For ever be adored that Name in earth and sky,
In which, though mortal strength may fail,
The saints of God at last prevail!

Oh! Peter was most blessed with blessedness unpriced,
Who, taught of God, confessed the Godhead in the Christ!
For of your Church, Lord, you made known
This saint a true foundation stone.

William How

The Refrain for the Vespers Lessons

Let the faithful rejoice in triumph;* let them be joyful on their beds.

Psalm 149:5

The Vespers Psalm　　　　　*He Has Shown His Righteousness Openly in the Sight
of the Nations*

Sing to the Lord a new song,* for he has done marvelous things.
With his right hand and his holy arm* has he won for himself the victory.
The Lord has made known his victory;* his righteousness has he openly shown in
the sight of the nations.
He remembers his mercy and faithfulness to the house of Israel,* and all the ends
of the earth have seen the victory of our God.
Shout with joy to the Lord, all you lands;* lift up your voice, rejoice, and sing.
Sing to the Lord with the harp,* with the harp and the voice of song.
With trumpets and the sound of the horn* shout with joy before the King, the Lord.

Psalm 98:1–7

The Refrain

Let the faithful rejoice in triumph;* let them be joyful on their beds.

The Cry of the Church

O Lord, hear my prayer and let my cry come unto you. Thanks be to God.

The Short Breviary

The Lord's Prayer

The Prayer Appointed for the Week

Almighty God, whose Son our Savior Jesus Christ is the light of the world: Grant
that your people, illumined by your Word and Sacraments, may shine with the
radiance of Christ's glory, that he may be known, worshipped, and obeyed to
the ends of the earth; through Jesus Christ our Lord, who with you and the
Holy Spirit lives and reigns, one God, now and for ever. *Amen.*†

Concluding Prayers of the Church

I beseech You, O Lord, let the prayers of blessed St. Peter Your disciple and the
foundation of your Church assist me, that those things which by myself I cannot obtain may be granted me by his intercession. Through our Lord. *Amen.*

adapted from The Short Breviary

May the souls of the faithful departed, through the mercy of God, rest in eternal
peace. *Amen.*

The Morning Office   To Be Observed on the Hour or Half Hour
                                              Between 6 and 9 a.m.

The Call to Prayer

Love the Lord, all you who worship him;* the Lord protects the faithful, but
repays to the full those who act haughtily.

Psalm 31:23

The Request for Presence

Early in the morning I cry out to you,* for in your word is my trust.

Psalm 119:147

The Greeting

"You are my God, and I will thank you;* you are my God, and I will exalt you."

Psalm 118:28

The Refrain for the Morning Lessons

I hate those who have a divided heart,* but your law do I love.

Psalm 119:113

A Reading

Jesus taught us, saying: "Whoever holds my commandments and keeps them is
the one who loves me; and whoever loves me will be loved by my Father, and I
shall love him and reveal myself to him."

John 14:21

The Refrain

I hate those who have a divided heart,* but your law do I love.

The Morning Psalm   *In His Holy Name We Put Our Trust*

Rejoice in the Lord, you righteous;* it is good for the just to sing praises.
For the word of the Lord is right,* and all his works are sure.
Behold, the eye of the Lord is upon those who fear him,* on those who wait upon
his love.
Our soul waits for the Lord;* he is our help and our shield.
Indeed, our heart rejoices in him,* for in his holy Name we put our trust.
Let your loving-kindness, O Lord, be upon us,* as we have put our trust in you.

Psalm 33:1, 4, 18–22

The Refrain

I hate those who have a divided heart,* but your law do I love.

The Cry of the Church

Lord, have mercy on us. Christ, have mercy on us. Lord, have mercy on us.

The Lord's Prayer

The Prayer Appointed for the Week

Almighty God, whose Son our Savior Jesus Christ is the light of the world: Grant
that your people, illumined by your Word and Sacraments, may shine with the
radiance of Christ's glory, that he may be known, worshipped, and obeyed to
the ends of the earth; through Jesus Christ our Lord, who with you and the
Holy Spirit lives and reigns, one God, now and for ever. *Amen.*†

The Concluding Prayer of the Church

Lord God, almighty and everlasting Father, you have brought me in safety to this
new day: Preserve me with your mighty power, that I may not fall into sin, nor
be overcome by adversity; and in all I do direct me to the fulfilling of your purpose; through Jesus Christ my Lord. *Amen.*†

The Midday Office   To Be Observed on the Hour or Half Hour
                                          Between 11 a.m. and 2 p.m.

The Call to Prayer

Hallelujah! Give praise, you servants of the LORD;* praise the Name of the LORD.

Psalm 113:1

The Request for Presence

Hear my voice, O LORD, according to your loving-kindness;* according to your
judgments, give me life.

Psalm 119:149

The Greeting

O LORD of hosts,* happy are they who put their trust in you!

Psalm 84:12

The Refrain for the Midday Lessons

With the faithful you show yourself faithful, O God;* with the forthright you show
yourself forthright.
With the pure you show yourself pure,* but with the crooked you are wily.

Psalm 18:26–27

A Reading

. . . We are well aware that all of us have knowledge; but while knowledge puffs
up, love is what builds up. Someone may think that he has full knowledge of
something and yet not know it as well as he should; but someone who loves
God is known by God.

1 Corinthians 8:1–3

The Refrain
With the faithful you show yourself faithful, O God;* with the forthright you show
   yourself forthright.
With the pure you show yourself pure,* but with the crooked you are wily.

The Midday Psalm   *The Eye of the LORD Is Upon Those*
                                           Who Wait Upon His Name
Happy is the nation whose God is the LORD!* happy the people he has chosen to be
   his own!
The LORD looks down from heaven,* and beholds all the people in the world.
From where he sits enthroned he turns his gaze* on all who dwell on the earth.
He fashions all the hearts of them* and understands all their works.
There is no king that can be saved by a mighty army;* a strong man is not
   delivered by his great strength.
The horse is a vain hope for deliverance;* for all its strength it cannot save.
Behold, the eye of the LORD is upon those who fear him,* on those who wait upon
   his love,
To pluck their lives from death,* and to feed them in time of famine.
                                              Psalm 33:12–19

The Refrain
With the faithful you show yourself faithful, O God;* with the forthright you show
   yourself forthright.
With the pure you show yourself pure,* but with the crooked you are wily.

The Cry of the Church
O God, come to my assistance! O Lord, make haste to help me!

The Lord's Prayer

The Prayer Appointed for the Week
Almighty God, whose Son our Savior Jesus Christ is the light of the world: Grant
   that your people, illumined by your Word and Sacraments, may shine with the
   radiance of Christ's glory, that he may be known, worshipped, and obeyed to
   the ends of the earth; through Jesus Christ our Lord, who with you and the
   Holy Spirit lives and reigns, one God, now and for ever. *Amen.†*

The Concluding Prayer of the Church
O Lord, my God, accept the fervent prayers of all of us your people; in the multitude of your mercies, look with compassion upon me and all who turn to you
   for help; for you are gracious, O lover of souls, and to you we give glory,
   Father, Son, and Holy Spirit, now and forever. *Amen.†*

The Vespers Office

To Be Observed on the Hour or Half Hour
Between 5 and 8 p.m.

The Call to Prayer

Come, let us bow down, and bend the knee,* and kneel before the LORD our
Maker.
For he is our God,* and we are the people of his pasture and the sheep of his hand.

Psalm 95:6–7

The Request for Presence

O LORD, watch over us* and save us from this generation for ever.
The wicked prowl on every side,* and that which is worthless is highly prized by
everyone.

Psalm 12:7–8

The Greeting

How glorious you are!* more splendid than the everlasting mountains!

Psalm 76:4

The Hymn

I am thine, O Lord, I have heard your voice,
And it told your love to me;
But I long to rise in the arms of faith
And be closer drawn to thee.
Draw me nearer, nearer, blessed Lord,
To the cross where you have died.
Draw me nearer, nearer, nearer, blessed Lord
To your precious bleeding side.

Consecrate me now to your service, Lord,
By the power of grace divine;
Let my soul look up with a steadfast hope,
And my will be lost in thine.
Draw me nearer, nearer, blessed Lord,
To the cross where you have died.
Draw me nearer, nearer, nearer, blessed Lord
To your precious bleeding side.

O the pure delight of a single hour
That before your throne I spend,
When I kneel in prayer, and with thee, my God,
I commune as friend with friend!
Draw me nearer, nearer, blessed Lord,
To the cross where you have died.
Draw me nearer, nearer, nearer, blessed Lord
To your precious bleeding side.

There are depths of love that I cannot know
Till I cross the narrow sea;
There are heights of joy that I may not reach
Till I rest in peace with thee.
Draw me nearer, nearer, blessed Lord,
To the cross where you have died.
Draw me nearer, nearer, nearer, blessed Lord
To your precious bleeding side.

Fanny Crosby

The Refrain for the Vespers Lessons
Tell it out among the nations: "The LORD is King!"

Psalm 96:10

The Vespers Psalm   *He Shall Keep Me Safe*
One thing have I asked of the LORD; one thing I seek;* that I may dwell in the
    house of the LORD all the days of my life;
To behold the fair beauty of the LORD* and to seek him in his temple.
For in the day of trouble he shall keep me safe in his shelter;* he shall hide me in
    the secrecy of his dwelling and set me high upon a rock.
Even now he lifts up my head* above my enemies round about me.
Therefore I will offer in his dwelling an oblation with sounds of great gladness;* I
    will sing and make music to the LORD.

Psalm 27:5–9

The Refrain
Tell it out among the nations: "The LORD is King!"

The Gloria

The Lord's Prayer

The Prayer Appointed for the Week
Almighty God, whose Son our Savior Jesus Christ is the light of the world: Grant
    that your people, illumined by your Word and Sacraments, may shine with the
    radiance of Christ's glory, that he may be known, worshipped, and obeyed to
    the ends of the earth; through Jesus Christ our Lord, who with you and the
    Holy Spirit lives and reigns, one God, now and for ever. *Amen.*†

The Concluding Prayer of the Church
Blessed be God, who has not rejected my prayer,* nor withheld his love from me.

Psalm 66:18

The Morning Office   To Be Observed on the Hour or Half Hour
                                                      Between 6 and 9 a.m.

The Call to Prayer
But I will call upon God,* and the Lord will deliver me.
In the evening, in the morning, and at noonday,* I will complain and lament,
He will bring me safely back . . . * God, who is enthroned of old, will hear me . . .
Psalm 55:17ff

The Request for Presence
Save me, O God, by your Name;* in your might, defend my cause.
Hear my prayer, O God;* give ear to the words of my mouth.
Psalm 54:1–2

The Greeting
I will offer you the sacrifice of thanksgiving* and call upon the Name of the Lord.
Psalm 116:15

The Refrain for the Morning Lessons
The Lord is near to those who call upon him,* to all who call upon him faithfully.
Psalm 145:19

A Reading
Jesus said to us: "In truth I tell you, anyone who does not welcome the kingdom of
    God like a little child will never enter it."
Luke 18:17

The Refrain
The Lord is near to those who call upon him,* to all who call upon him faithfully.

The Morning Psalm   *Teach Me Your Way, O Lord*
Teach me your way, O Lord, and I will walk in your truth;* knit my heart to you
    that I may fear your Name.
I will thank you, O Lord my God, with all my heart,* and glorify your Name for
    evermore.
For great is your love toward me;* you have delivered me from the nethermost Pit.
The arrogant rise up against me, O God, and a band of violent men seeks my life;*
    they have not set you before their eyes.
But you, O Lord, are gracious and full of compassion,* slow to anger, and full of
    kindness and truth.
Turn to me and have mercy upon me;* give your strength to your servant; and
    save the child of your handmaid.
Show me a sign of your favor, so that those who hate me may see it and be
    ashamed;* because you, O Lord, have helped me and comforted me.
Psalm 86:11–17

The Refrain
The Lord is near to those who call upon him,* to all who call upon him faithfully.

The Cry of the Church
O Lord, hear my prayer and let my cry come unto you. Thanks be to God.
THE SHORT BREVIARY

The Lord's Prayer

The Prayer Appointed for the Week
Almighty God, whose Son our Savior Jesus Christ is the light of the world: Grant
that your people, illumined by your Word and Sacraments, may shine with the
radiance of Christ's glory, that he may be known, worshipped, and obeyed to
the ends of the earth; through Jesus Christ our Lord, who with you and the
Holy Spirit lives and reigns, one God, now and for ever. *Amen.*†

The Concluding Prayer of the Church
Lord God, almighty and everlasting Father, you have brought me in safety to this
new day: Preserve me with your mighty power, that I may not fall into sin, nor
be overcome by adversity; and in all I do direct me to the fulfilling of your purpose; through Jesus Christ my Lord. *Amen.*†

The Midday Office   To Be Observed on the Hour or Half Hour
Between 11 a.m. and 2 p.m.

The Call to Prayer
Open my lips, O Lord,* and my mouth shall proclaim your praise.
Had you desired it, I would have offered sacrifice,* but you take no delight in
burnt-offerings.
The sacrifice of God is a troubled spirit;* a broken and contrite heart, O God, you
will not despise.
Psalm 51:16–18

The Request for Presence
Let your ways be known upon earth,* your saving health among all nations.
Psalm 67:2

The Greeting
I hate those who have a divided heart,* but your law do I love.
Psalm 119:113

The Refrain for the Midday Lessons
I will listen to what the LORD God is saying,* for he is speaking peace to his faithful
people and to those who turn their hearts to him.
Psalm 85:8

A Reading
Thus says YAHWEH, who made a way through the sea, . . . No need to remember past
events, no need to think about what was done before. Look, I am doing something new, now it emerges; can you not see it? Yes I am making a road in the
desert and rivers in the wastelands . . . for my people, my chosen one, to drink.
Isaiah 43:16, 18–20

The Refrain
I will listen to what the LORD God is saying,* for he is speaking peace to his faithful people and to those who turn their hearts to him.

The Midday Psalm   *The Hearts of Those Who Seek God Shall Live*
I will praise the Name of God in song;* I will proclaim his greatness with thanksgiving.
This will please the LORD more than an offering of oxen,* more than bullocks with horns and hoofs.
The afflicted shall see and be glad;* you who seek God, your heart shall live.
For the LORD listens to the needy,* and his prisoners he does not despise.
Let the heavens and the earth praise him,* the seas and all that moves in them;
For God will save Zion and rebuild the cities of Judah;* they shall live there and have it in possession.
The children of his servants will inherit it,* and those who love his Name will dwell therein.

Psalm 69:32–38

The Refrain
I will listen to what the LORD God is saying,* for he is speaking peace to his faithful people and to those who turn their hearts to him.

The Cry of the Church
Lord, have mercy on us. Christ, have mercy on us. Lord, have mercy on us.

The Lord's Prayer

The Prayer Appointed for the Week
Almighty God, whose Son our Savior Jesus Christ is the light of the world: Grant that your people, illumined by your Word and Sacraments, may shine with the radiance of Christ's glory, that he may be known, worshipped, and obeyed to the ends of the earth; through Jesus Christ our Lord, who with you and the Holy Spirit lives and reigns, one God, now and for ever. *Amen.*†

The Concluding Prayer of the Church
Heavenly, Father, in you I live and move and have my being: I humbly pray you so to guide and govern me by your Holy Spirit, that in all the cares and occupations of my life I may not forget you, but may remember that I am ever walking in your sight; through Jesus Christ my Lord. *Amen.*†

The Vespers Office   To Be Observed on the Hour or Half Hour
                                       Between 5 and 8 p.m.

The Call to Prayer
Bless the LORD, you angels of his, you mighty ones who do his bidding,* and hearken to the voice of his word.
Bless the LORD, all you his hosts,* you ministers of his who do his will.
Bless the LORD, all you works of his,* in all places of his dominion;

Psalm 103:20–22

The Request for Presence
Lord God of hosts, hear my prayer,* hearken, O God of Jacob.

Psalm 84:7

The Greeting
Show me your ways, O Lord,* and teach me your paths.
Lead me in your truth and teach me,* for you are the God of my salvation; in you
    have I trusted all the day long.

Psalm 25:3–4

The Hymn
    Every time I feel the Spirit moving in my heart,
    I will pray.
    Yes, every time I feel the Spirit moving in my heart,
    I will pray.
    Upon the mountain, my Lord spoke,
    Out his mouth came fire and smoke.
    All around me looks so shine,
    Ask my Lord if all was mine.

    Every time I feel the Spirit moving in my heart,
    I will pray.
    Yes, every time I feel the Spirit moving in my heart,
    I will pray
    Jordan river runs right cold,
    Chills the body, not the soul.
    Ain't but one train on this track,
    Runs to heaven and right back.

    Every time I feel the Spirit moving in my heart,
    I will pray.
    Yes, every time I feel the Spirit moving in my heart,
    I will pray.

African-American Spiritual

The Refrain for the Vespers Lessons
But it is good for me to be near God;* I have made the Lord God my refuge.

Psalm 73:28

The Vespers Psalm   *You Alone Are God*
Be merciful to me, O Lord, for you are my God;* I call upon you all the day long.
Gladden the soul of your servant,* for to you, O Lord, I lift up my soul.
For you, O Lord, are good and forgiving,* and great is your love toward all who
    call upon you.
Give ear, O Lord, to my prayer,* and attend to the voice of my supplications.
In the time of my trouble I will call upon you,* for you will answer me.
Among the gods there is none like you, O Lord,* nor anything like your works.

All nations you have made will come and worship you, O LORD,* and glorify your
Name.
For you are great; you do wondrous things;* and you alone are God.

Psalm 86:3–10

The Refrain
But it is good for me to be near God;* I have made the Lord GOD my refuge.

The Small Verse
Keep me, Lord, as the apple of your eye and carry me under the shadow of your
wings.

Traditional

The Lord's Prayer

The Prayer Appointed for the Week
Almighty God, whose Son our Savior Jesus Christ is the light of the world: Grant
that your people, illumined by your Word and Sacraments, may shine with the
radiance of Christ's glory, that he may be known, worshipped, and obeyed to
the ends of the earth; through Jesus Christ our Lord, who with you and the
Holy Spirit lives and reigns, one God, now and for ever. *Amen.*†

The Concluding Prayer of the Church
Protect me, Lord, as I stay awake; watch over me as I sleep, that awake I may
watch with Christ, and asleep, rest in his peace. *Amen.*

The Morning Office	To Be Observed on the Hour or Half Hour
	Between 6 and 9 a.m.

The Call to Prayer
Sing to the LORD and bless his Name;* proclaim the good news of his salvation
from day to day.
Declare his glory among the nations* and his wonders among all peoples.
For great is the LORD and greatly to be praised;* he is more to be feared than all
gods.

Psalm 96:2–4

The Request for Presence
Save me, O God,* for the waters have risen up to my neck.

Psalm 69:1

The Greeting
The LORD lives! Blessed is my Rock!* Exalted is the God of my salvation!

Psalm 18:46

The Refrain for the Morning Lessons
He looks at the earth and it trembles;* he touches the mountains and they smoke.

Psalm 104:33

A Reading

Jesus taught the people, saying: "What is your opinion? A man had two sons. He
went and said to the first, 'My boy, go and work in the vineyard today.' He
answered, 'I will not go,' but afterwards thought better of it and went. The man
then went and said the same thing to the second who answered, 'Certainly, sir,'
but did not go. Which of the two did the father's will?" They said, "The first."
Jesus said to them, "In truth I tell you, tax collectors and prostitutes are making
their way into the kingdom of God before you. For John came to you, showing
the way of uprightness, but you did not believe him, and yet the tax collectors
and the prostitutes did. Even after seeing that, you refused to think better of it
and believe in him."

Matthew 21:28–32

The Refrain

He looks at the earth and it trembles;* he touches the mountains and they smoke.

The Morning Psalm   *The LORD Accepts My Prayer*

LORD, do not rebuke me in your anger;* do not punish me in your wrath.
Have pity on me, LORD, for I am weak;* heal me, LORD, for my bones are racked.
My spirit shakes with terror,* how long, O LORD, how long?
Turn, O LORD, and deliver me;* save me for your mercy's sake.
For in death no one remembers you;* and who will give you thanks in the grave?
I grow weary because of my groaning;* every night I drench my bed and flood my
     couch with tears.
The LORD has heard the sound of my weeping.
The LORD has heard my supplication;* the LORD accepts my prayer.

Psalm 6:1–6, 8–9

The Refrain

He looks at the earth and it trembles;* he touches the mountains and they smoke.

The Cry of the Church

O God, come to my assistance! O Lord, make haste to help me!

The Lord's Prayer

The Prayer Appointed for the Week

Almighty God, whose Son our Savior Jesus Christ is the light of the world: Grant
     that your people, illumined by your Word and Sacraments, may shine with the
     radiance of Christ's glory, that he may be known, worshipped, and obeyed to
     the ends of the earth; through Jesus Christ our Lord, who with you and the
     Holy Spirit lives and reigns, one God, now and for ever. *Amen.†*

The Concluding Prayer of the Church

Lord God, almighty and everlasting Father, you have brought me in safety to this
     new day: Preserve me with your mighty power, that I may not fall into sin, nor
     be overcome by adversity; and in all I do direct me to the fulfilling of your pur-
     pose; through Jesus Christ my Lord. *Amen.†*

The Midday Office   To Be Observed on the Hour or Half Hour
                                     Between 11 a.m. and 2 p.m.

The Call to Prayer
God has gone up with a shout,* the LORD with the sound of the ram's-horn.
Sing praises to God, sing praises;* sing praises to our King, sing praises.
For God is King of all the earth;* sing praises with all your skill.
God reigns over the nations;* God sits upon his holy throne.

Psalm 47:5–8

The Request for Presence
Answer me when I call, O God, defender of my cause;* you set me free when I am
    hard-pressed; have mercy on me and hear my prayer.

Psalm 4:1

The Greeting
Deliver me, my God, from the hand of the wicked,* from the clutches of the evil-
    doer and the oppressor.
For you are my hope, O Lord GOD,* my confidence since I was young.
I have been sustained by you ever since I was born;* from my mother's womb you
    have been my strength; my praise shall be always of you.

Psalm 71:4–6

The Refrain for the Midday Lessons
Your love, O LORD, for ever will I sing;* from age to age my mouth will proclaim
    your faithfulness.

Psalm 89:1

A Reading
All of us, with our unveiled faces like mirrors reflecting the glory of the Lord, are
    being transformed into the image that we reflect in brighter and brighter glory;
    this is the working of the Lord who is the Spirit.

2 Corinthians 3:18

The Refrain
Your love, O LORD, for ever will I sing;* from age to age my mouth will proclaim
    your faithfulness.

The Midday Psalm   *We Shall Be Glad All the Days of Our Life*
Satisfy us by your loving-kindness in the morning;* so shall we rejoice and be glad
    all the days of our life.
Make us glad by the measure of the days that you afflicted us* and the years in
    which we suffered adversity.
Show your servants your works* and your splendor to their children.
May the graciousness of the LORD our God be upon us;* prosper the work of our
    hands; prosper our handiwork.

Psalm 90:14–17

The Refrain
Your love, O LORD, for ever will I sing;* from age to age my mouth will proclaim
   your faithfulness.

The Gloria

The Lord's Prayer

The Prayer Appointed for the Week
Almighty God, whose Son our Savior Jesus Christ is the light of the world: Grant
   that your people, illumined by your Word and Sacraments, may shine with the
   radiance of Christ's glory, that he may be known, worshipped, and obeyed to
   the ends of the earth; through Jesus Christ our Lord, who with you and the
   Holy Spirit lives and reigns, one God, now and for ever. *Amen.*†

The Concluding Prayer of the Church
In truth God has heard me; he has attended the voice of my prayer. Thanks be to
   God. *Amen.*

based on Psalm 66:17

The Vespers Office   To Be Observed on the Hour or Half Hour
                                             Between 5 and 8 p.m.

The Call to Prayer
Bless God in the congregation;* bless the LORD, you that are of the fountain of
   Israel.

Psalm 68:26

The Request for Presence
O LORD, watch over us* and save us from this generation for ever.
The wicked prowl on every side,* and that which is worthless is highly prized by
   everyone.

Psalm 12:7–8

The Greeting
One generation shall praise your works to another* and shall declare your power.

Psalm 145:4

The Hymn

"I come," the great Redeemer cries,
"To do your will, O Lord!"
At Jordan's stream, behold!
He seals the sure prophetic word.

"Thus it becomes us to fulfill
all righteousness," he said.
Then, faithful to the Lord's commands,
through Jordan's flood was led.

Hark, a glad voice! The Father speaks
From heaven's exalted height:
"This is my Son, my well beloved
In whom I take delight."

The Savior Jesus, well beloved!
His Name we will profess,
Like him desirous to fulfill
God's will in righteousness.

No more we'll count ourselves our own
But his in bonds of love.
Oh, may such bonds for ever draw
Our souls to things above!

Christian Hymnbook, 1865

The Refrain for the Vespers Lessons
The heaven of heavens is the LORD's,* but he entrusted the earth to its peoples.

Psalm 115:16

The Vespers Psalm   *The LORD Is My Strength*
I love you, O LORD my strength,* O LORD my stronghold, my crag, and my haven.
My God, my rock in whom I put my trust,* my shield, the horn of my salvation,
   and my refuge; you are worthy of praise.
I will call upon the LORD,* and so shall I be saved from my enemies.
The breakers of death rolled over me,* and the torrents of oblivion made me afraid.
The cords of hell entangled me,* and the snares of death were set for me.
I called upon the LORD in my distress* and cried out to my God for help.
He heard my voice from his heavenly dwelling;* my cry of anguish came to his ears.

Psalm 18:1–7

The Refrain
The heaven of heavens is the LORD's,* but he entrusted the earth to its peoples.

The Cry of the Church
Even so, come, Lord Jesus!

The Lord's Prayer

The Prayer Appointed for the Week
Almighty God, whose Son our Savior Jesus Christ is the light of the world: Grant
   that your people, illumined by your Word and Sacraments, may shine with the
   radiance of Christ's glory, that he may be known, worshipped, and obeyed to
   the ends of the earth; through Jesus Christ our Lord, who with you and the
   Holy Spirit lives and reigns, one God, now and for ever. *Amen.*†

The Concluding Prayer of the Church
Grant me, I beseech thee, O merciful God, prudently to study, rightly to understand and perfectly to fulfill that which is pleasing to thee, to the praise and
   glory of thy name. Amen.

St. Thomas Aquinas

The Morning Office   To Be Observed on the Hour or Half Hour
                                       Between 6 and 9 a.m.

The Call to Prayer
Sing to the LORD a new song;* sing to the LORD, all the whole earth.

Psalm 96:1

The Request for Presence
I call with my whole heart;* answer me, O LORD, that I may keep your statutes.

Psalm 119:145

The Greeting *Te Deum*
Glory to you, Lord God of our fathers; you are worthy of praise; glory to you.
Glory to you for the radiance of your holy Name; we will praise you and
highly exalt you for ever. Glory to you in the splendor of your temple; on the
throne of your majesty, glory to you. Glory to you, seated between the
Cherubim; we will praise you and highly exalt you for ever. Glory to you,
beholding the depths; in the high vault of heaven, glory to you. Glory to you,
Father, Son, and Holy Spirit; we will praise you and highly exalt you for ever.

The Refrain for the Morning Lessons
Righteousness shall go before him,* and peace shall be a pathway for his feet.

Psalm 85:13

A Reading
Hearing that John had been arrested, he withdrew to Galilee, and leaving Nazara
he went and settled in Capernaum, beside the lake, on the borders of Zebulun
and Naphtali. This was to fulfill what was spoken by the prophet Isaiah: *Land
of Zebulun! Land of Naphtali! Way of the sea beyond Jordan. Galilee of the nations!
The people that lived in darkness have seen a great light; on those who lived in a country of shadow dark as death a light has dawned.* From then onwards Jesus began his
proclamation with the message, 'Repent, for the kingdom of Heaven is close at
hand.'

Matthew 4:12–17

The Refrain
Righteousness shall go before him,* and peace shall be a pathway for his feet.

The Morning Psalm *The LORD Will Bless Those Who Fear Him*
O Israel, trust in the LORD;* he is their help and their shield.
O house of Aaron, trust in the LORD;* he is their help and their shield.
You who fear the LORD, trust in the LORD;* he is their help and their shield.
The LORD has been mindful of us, and he will bless us;* he will bless the house of
Israel; he will bless the house of Aaron;
He will bless those who fear the LORD,* both small and great together.

Psalm 115:9–13

The Refrain
Righteousness shall go before him,* and peace shall be a pathway for his feet.

The Gloria

The Lord's Prayer

The Prayer Appointed for the Week
Almighty God, whose Son our Savior Jesus Christ is the light of the world: Grant
that your people, illumined by your Word and Sacraments, may shine with the

radiance of Christ's glory, that he may be known, worshipped, and obeyed to the ends of the earth; through Jesus Christ our Lord, who with you and the Holy Spirit lives and reigns, one God, now and for ever. *Amen.*†

The Concluding Prayer of the Church
Lord God, almighty and everlasting Father, you have brought me in safety to this new day: Preserve me with your mighty power, that I may not fall into sin, nor be overcome by adversity; and in all I do direct me to the fulfilling of your purpose; through Jesus Christ my Lord. *Amen.*†

The Midday Office   To Be Observed on the Hour or Half Hour
                                            Between 11 a.m. and 2 p.m.

The Call to Prayer
Let us bless the LORD, from this time forth for evermore. Hallelujah!
                                            based on Psalm 115:18

The Request for Presence
Send forth your strength, O God;* establish, O God, what you have wrought for us.
                                            Psalm 68:28

The Greeting
I will thank you, O LORD my God, with all my heart,* and glorify your Name for evermore.
                                            Psalm 86:12

The Refrain for the Midday Lessons
This is the LORD's doing,* and it is marvelous in our eyes.
                                            Psalm 118:23

A Reading
But God, being rich in faithful love, through the great love with which he loved us, even when we were dead in our sins, brought us to life with Christ—it is through grace that you have been saved—and raised us up with him and gave us a place with him in heaven, in Christ Jesus.
                                            Ephesians 2:4–6

The Refrain
This is the LORD's doing,* and it is marvelous in our eyes.

The Midday Psalm   *He Saves for His Name's Sake*
We have sinned as our forebears did;* we have done wrong and dealt wickedly.
In Egypt they did not consider your marvelous works, nor remember the abundance of your love;* they defied the Most High at the Red Sea.
But he saved them for his Name's sake,* to make his power known.
He rebuked the Red Sea, and it dried up,* and he led them through the deep as through a desert.
He saved them from the hand of those who hated them* and redeemed them from the hand of the enemy.

The waters covered their oppressors;* not one of them was left.
Then they believed his words* and sang him songs of praise.

Psalm 106:6–12

The Refrain

This is the LORD's doing,* and it is marvelous in our eyes.

The Cry of the Church

O Lord, hear my prayer and let my cry come unto you. Thanks be to God.

THE SHORT BREVIARY

The Lord's Prayer

The Prayer Appointed for the Week

Almighty God, whose Son our Savior Jesus Christ is the light of the world: Grant
that your people, illumined by your Word and Sacraments, may shine with the
radiance of Christ's glory, that he may be known, worshipped, and obeyed to
the ends of the earth; through Jesus Christ our Lord, who with you and the
Holy Spirit lives and reigns, one God, now and for ever. *Amen.*†

The Concluding Prayer of the Church

Lord Jesus Christ, by your death you took away the sting of death: Grant me to so
follow in faith where you have led the way, that I may at length fall asleep
peacefully in you and wake in your likeness; for your tender mercies' sake.
Amen.†

The Vespers Office

To Be Observed on the Hour or Half Hour
Between 5 and 8 p.m.

The Call to Prayer

Glory in his holy Name;* let the hearts of those who seek the LORD rejoice.

Psalm 105:3

The Request for Presence

Send forth your strength, O God;* establish, O God, what you have wrought for us.

Psalm 68:28

The Greeting

The LORD is my strength and my song,* and he has become my salvation.

Psalm 118:14

The Hymn

Pass me not, O gentle Savior, hear my humble cry;
While on others you are calling, do not pass me by.
Savior, Savior, hear my humble cry;
While on others you are calling, do not pass me by.

Let me at the throne of mercy find a sweet relief,
Kneeling there in deep contrition; help my unbelief.
Savior, Savior, hear my humble cry;
While on others you are calling, do not pass me by.

Trusting only in your merit, would I seek your face;
Heal my wounded, broken spirit, save me by your grace.
Savior, Savior, hear my humble cry;
While on others you are calling, do not pass me by.

You, the spring of all my comfort, more than life to me,
Whom have I on earth beside you? Whom in heaven but thee?
Savior, Savior, hear my humble cry;
While on others you are calling, do not pass me by.

Fanny Crosby

The Refrain for the Vespers Lessons
Keep watch over my life, for I am faithful;* save your servant whose trust is in you.

based on Psalm 86:2

The Vespers Psalm   *We Shall Be Saved*
Restore us, O God of hosts;* show the light of your countenance, and we shall be
    saved.
Let your hand be upon the man of your right hand,* the son of man you have
    made so strong for yourself.
And so will we never turn away from you;* give us life, that we may call upon
    your Name.
Restore us, O Lord God of hosts;* show the light of your countenance, and we
    shall be saved.

Psalm 80:7, 16–18

The Refrain
Keep watch over my life, for I am faithful;* save your servant whose trust is in you.

The Small Verse
My help is in the Name of the Lord who made the heavens and the earth. What
    then shall I fear, of what shall I be afraid?

Traditional

The Lord's Prayer

The Prayer Appointed for the Week
Almighty God, whose Son our Savior Jesus Christ is the light of the world: Grant
    that your people, illumined by your Word and Sacraments, may shine with the
    radiance of Christ's glory, that he may be known, worshipped, and obeyed to
    the ends of the earth; through Jesus Christ our Lord, who with you and the
    Holy Spirit lives and reigns, one God, now and for ever. *Amen.*†

Concluding Prayers of the Church

Almighty God, who has promised to hear the petitions of those who ask in your
Son's Name: I beseech you mercifully to incline your ear to me who have made
my prayers and supplications to you; and grant that those things which I have
faithfully asked according to your will, I may effectually obtain, to the relief of
my necessity, and to the setting forth of your glory; through Jesus Christ my
Lord. *Amen.*

May the souls of the faithful departed, through the mercy of God, rest in eternal
peace. *Amen.*

The Morning Office   **To Be Observed on the Hour or Half Hour**
                                 Between 6 and 9 a.m.

The Call to Prayer

Search for the LORD and his strength;* continually seek his face.

Psalm 105:4

The Request for Presence

Hearken to my voice, O LORD, when I call;* have mercy on me and answer me.
You speak in my heart and say, "Seek my face."* Your face, LORD, will I seek.
Hide not your face from me,* nor turn away your servant in displeasure.

Psalm 27:10–12

The Greeting

What terror you inspire!* who can stand before you when you are angry?

Psalm 76:7

The Refrain for the Morning Lessons

I sought the LORD, and he answered me* and delivered me out of all my terror.

Psalm 34:4

A Reading

Jesus taught us, saying: ". . . what woman with ten drachmas would not, if she lost
one, light a lamp and sweep out the house and search thoroughly till she found
it? And then, when she had found it, call together her friends and neighbors,
saying to them, 'Rejoice with me, I have found the drachma I lost.' In the same
way, I tell you, there is rejoicing among the angels of God over one repentant
sinner."

Luke 15:8–10

The Refrain

I sought the LORD, and he answered me* and delivered me out of all my terror.

The Morning Psalm   *No Evil Shall Happen to You*

Your eyes have only to behold* to see the reward of the wicked.
Because you have made the LORD your refuge,* and the Most High your habitation,
There shall no evil happen to you,* neither shall any plague come near your
dwelling.

For he shall give his angels charge over you,* to keep you in all your ways.
They shall bear you in their hands,* lest you dash your foot against a stone.
You shall tread upon the lion and adder;* you shall trample the young lion and the
    serpent under your feet.

Psalm 91:8–13

The Refrain
I sought the LORD, and he answered me* and delivered me out of all my terror.

The Cry of the Church
Lord, have mercy on us. Christ, have mercy on us. Lord, have mercy on us.

The Lord's Prayer

The Prayer Appointed for the Week
Almighty God, whose Son our Savior Jesus Christ is the light of the world: Grant
    that your people, illumined by your Word and Sacraments, may shine with the
    radiance of Christ's glory, that he may be known, worshipped, and obeyed to
    the ends of the earth; through Jesus Christ our Lord, who with you and the
    Holy Spirit lives and reigns, one God, now and for ever. *Amen.*†

The Concluding Prayer of the Church
Lord God, almighty and everlasting Father, you have brought me in safety to this
    new day: Preserve me with your mighty power, that I may not fall into sin, nor
    be overcome by adversity; and in all I do direct me to the fulfilling of your pur-
    pose; through Jesus Christ my Lord. *Amen.*†

The Midday Office   To Be Observed on the Hour or Half Hour
                                         Between 11 a.m. and 2 p.m.

The Call to Prayer
Bless our God, you peoples;* make the voice of his praise to be heard;
Who holds our souls in life,* and will not allow our feet to slip.

Psalm 66:7–8

The Request for Presence
Let your ways be known upon earth,* your saving health among all nations.

Psalm 67:2

The Greeting
How great is your goodness, O LORD! which you have laid up for those who fear
    you;* which you have done in the sight of all for those who put their trust in
    you.

Psalm 31:19

The Refrain for the Midday Lessons
Your love, O LORD, reaches to the heavens,* and your faithfulness to the clouds.

Psalm 36:5

A Reading

Do two people travel together unless they have agreed to do so? Does the lion roar in the forest if it has no prey? Does the young lion growl in his lair if it has caught nothing? Does a bird fall on the ground in a net unless a trap has been set for it? Will the net spring up from the ground without catching something? Does the trumpet sound in the city without the people being alarmed? Does misfortune come to a city if YAHWEH has not caused it? No indeed, Lord YAHWEH does nothing without revealing his secret to his servants the prophets. The lion roars: who is not afraid? Lord YAHWEH has spoken: Who will not prophesy?

Amos 3:3–8

The Refrain

Your love, O LORD, reaches to the heavens,* and your faithfulness to the clouds.

The Midday Psalm   *Your Word Gives Light*

Your decrees are wonderful;* therefore I obey them with all my heart.
When your word goes forth it gives light;* it gives understanding to the simple.

Psalm 119:129–130

The Refrain

Your love, O LORD, reaches to the heavens,* and your faithfulness to the clouds.

The Small Verse

My help is in the name of the Lord who made heaven and earth and all that is in them. Thanks be to God.

Traditional

The Lord's Prayer

The Prayer Appointed for the Week

Almighty God, whose Son our Savior Jesus Christ is the light of the world: Grant that your people, illumined by your Word and Sacraments, may shine with the radiance of Christ's glory, that he may be known, worshipped, and obeyed to the ends of the earth; through Jesus Christ our Lord, who with you and the Holy Spirit lives and reigns, one God, now and for ever. *Amen.*†

The Concluding Prayer of the Church

O God, the source of eternal light: Shed forth your unending day upon all of us who watch for you, that our lips may praise you, our lives may bless you, and our worship may give you glory; through Jesus Christ our Lord. *Amen.*†

The Vespers Office   To Be Observed on the Hour or Half Hour
                                              Between 5 and 8 p.m.

The Call to Prayer

Behold now, bless the LORD, all you servants of the LORD,* you that stand by night in the house of the LORD.

Psalm 134:1

The Request for Presence
My soul waits for the LORD, more than watchmen for the morning,* more than
watchmen for the morning.

Psalm 130:5

The Greeting
You, O LORD, are my lamp;* my God, you make my darkness bright.
With you I will break down an enclosure;* with the help of my God I will scale any
wall.

Psalm 18:29–30

The Hymn
Crown him with many crowns, the Lamb upon his throne.
Hark! How the heavenly anthem drowns all music but its own.
Awake, my soul, and sing of him who died for thee,
And hail him as your matchless King through all eternity.

Crown him the Lord of life, who triumphed over the grave,
And rose victorious in the strife for those he came to save.
His glories now we sing, who died, and rose on high,
Who died, eternal life to bring, and lives that death may die.

Crown him the Lord of peace, whose power a scepter sways
From pole to pole, that wars may cease, and all be prayer and praise.
His reign shall know no end, and round his pierced feet
Fair flowers of paradise extend their fragrance ever sweet.

Crown him the Lord of love, behold his hands and side,
Those wounds, yet visible above, in beauty glorified.
All hail, Redeemer, hail! For you have died for me,
Your praise and glory shall not fail throughout eternity.

Matthew Bridges

The Refrain for the Vespers Lessons
I lie down and go to sleep;* I wake again, because the LORD sustains me.

Psalm 3:5

The Vespers Psalm   *You Made Me Glad, O LORD*
It is a good thing to give thanks to the LORD,* and to sing praises to your Name, O
    Most High;
To tell of your loving-kindness early in the morning* and of your faithfulness in
    the night season;
On the psaltery, and on the lyre,* and to the melody of the harp.
For you have made me glad by your acts, O LORD;* and I shout for joy because of
    the works of your hands.

Psalm 92:1–4

The Refrain
I lie down and go to sleep;* I wake again, because the LORD sustains me.

The Cry of the Church

O Lamb of God, that takes away the sins of the world, have mercy upon me.
O Lamb of God, that takes away the sins of the world, have mercy upon me.
O Lamb of God, that takes away the sins of the world, grant me your peace.

The Lord's Prayer

The Prayer Appointed for the Week

Almighty God, whose Son our Savior Jesus Christ is the light of the world: Grant
that your people, illumined by your Word and Sacraments, may shine with the
radiance of Christ's glory, that he may be known, worshipped, and obeyed to
the ends of the earth; through Jesus Christ our Lord, who with you and the
Holy Spirit lives and reigns, one God, now and for ever. *Amen.*†

The Concluding Prayer of the Church

Almighty God, who after the creation of the world rested from all your works and
sanctified a day of rest for all your creatures: Grant that I, putting away all
earthly anxieties, may be duly prepared for the service of public worship, and
grant as well that my Sabbath upon earth may be a preparation for the eternal
rest promised to your people in heaven; through Jesus Christ our Lord. *Amen.*†

The Morning Office   To Be Observed on the Hour or Half Hour
                                       Between 6 and 9 a.m.

The Call to Prayer

Hallelujah! I will give thanks to the LORD with my whole heart,* in the assembly of
the upright, in the congregation.

Psalm 111:1

The Request for Presence

Let them know that you, whose Name is YAHWEH,* you alone are the Most High
over all the earth.

Psalm 83:18

The Greeting

I shall always wait in patience,* and shall praise you more and more.

Psalm 71:14

The Refrain for the Morning Lessons

The same stone which the builders rejected* has become the chief cornerstone.

Psalm 118:22

A Reading

. . . the Pharisees went out and began to plot against him, discussing how to destroy him. Jesus knew this and withdrew from the district. Many followed him and he cured them all but warned them not to make him known. This was to fulfill what was spoken by the prophet Isaiah: *Look! My servant whom I have chosen, my beloved, in whom my soul delights, I will send my Spirit upon him,* and he will *present* judgment to the nations; *he will not brawl or cry out, his voice is not heard in the streets, he will not break the crushed reed, or snuff the faltering wick, until he has made judgment victorious; in him the nations will put their hope.*

Matthew 12:14–21

The Refrain

The same stone which the builders rejected* has become the chief cornerstone.

The Morning Psalm *"I Will Rise Up," Says the* LORD

Oh, that the LORD would cut off all smooth tongues,* and close the lips that utter proud boasts!

Those who say, "With our tongue will we prevail;* our lips are our own; who is lord over us?"

"Because the needy are oppressed, and the poor cry out in misery,* I will rise up," says the LORD, "and give them the help they long for."

The words of the LORD are pure words,* like silver refined from ore and purified seven times in the fire.

O LORD, watch over us* and save us from this generation for ever.

Psalm 12:3–7

The Refrain

The same stone which the builders rejected* has become the chief cornerstone.

The Gloria

The Lord's Prayer

The Prayer Appointed for the Week

Give us grace, O Lord, to answer readily the call of our Savior Jesus Christ and proclaim to all people the Good News of his salvation, that we and the whole world may perceive the glory of his marvelous works; who lives and reigns with you and the Holy Spirit, one God, for ever and ever. *Amen.*†

The Concluding Prayer of the Church

Lord God, almighty and everlasting Father, you have brought me in safety to this new day: Preserve me with your mighty power, that I may not fall into sin, nor be overcome by adversity; and in all I do direct me to the fulfilling of your purpose; through Jesus Christ my Lord. *Amen.*†

The Midday Office   To Be Observed on the Hour or Half Hour
Between 11 a.m. and 2 p.m.

The Call to Prayer
God is the Lord; he has shined upon us;* form a procession with branches up to
the horns of the altar.

Psalm 118:27

The Request for Presence
Open my lips, O Lord* and my mouth shall proclaim your praise.

Psalm 51:16

The Greeting
Let all who seek you rejoice and be glad in you;* let those who love your salvation
say for ever, "Great is the Lord!"

Psalm 70:4

The Refrain for the Midday Lessons
The words of the Lord are tried in the fire;* he is a shield to all who trust in him.

Psalm 18:31

A Reading
'For my part, this is my covenant with them, says Yahweh. My spirit with which I
endowed you, and my words that I have put in your mouth, will not leave
your mouth, or the mouths of your children, or the mouths of your children's
children, says Yahweh, henceforth and forever.'

Isaiah 59:21

The Refrain
The words of the Lord are tried in the fire;* he is a shield to all who trust in him.

The Midday Psalm   *The Lord Is Faithful in All His Works*
The Lord is gracious and full of compassion,* slow to anger and of great kindness.
The Lord is loving to everyone* and his compassion is over all his works.
All your works praise you, O Lord,* and your faithful servants bless you.
They make known the glory of your kingdom* and speak of your power;
That the peoples may know of your power* and the glorious splendor of your
kingdom.
Your kingdom is an everlasting kingdom;* your dominion endures throughout all
ages.

Psalm 145:8–13

The Refrain
The words of the Lord are tried in the fire;* he is a shield to all who trust in him.

The Small Verse
Blessed be the Lord God of Israel for he has visited and delivered us. Alleluia,
alleluia, alleluia.

Traditional

The Lord's Prayer

The Prayer Appointed for the Week
Give us grace, O Lord, to answer readily the call of our Savior Jesus Christ and
proclaim to all people the Good News of his salvation, that we and the whole
world may perceive the glory of his marvelous works; who lives and reigns
with you and the Holy Spirit, one God, for ever and ever. *Amen.*†

The Concluding Prayer of the Church
O God, you make me glad with the weekly remembrance of the glorious resurrection of your Son my Lord: Give me this day such blessing through my worship
of you, that the week to come may be spent in your favor; through Jesus Christ
our Lord. *Amen.*†

The Vespers Office   To Be Observed on the Hour or Half Hour
Between 5 and 8 p.m.

The Call to Prayer
Enter his gates with thanksgiving; go into his courts with praise;* give thanks to
him and call upon his Name.

Psalm 100:3

The Request for Presence
May God give us his blessing,* and may all the ends of the earth stand in awe of
him.

Psalm 67:7

The Greeting
We give you thanks, O God, we give you thanks,* calling upon your Name and
declaring all your wonderful deeds.

Psalm 75:1

The Hymn
Tell me the stories of Jesus I love to hear;
Things I would ask him to tell me if he were here:
Scenes by the wayside, tales of the sea,
Stories of Jesus tell them to me.

First let me hear how the children stood round his knee,
And I shall fancy his blessing resting on me;
Words full of kindness, deeds full of grace,
All in the love-light of Jesus' face.

Into the city I'd follow the children's band,
Waving a branch of the palm tree high in my hand;
One of his heralds, yes I would sing
Loudest hosannas, "Jesus is King!"

William Parker

The Refrain for the Vespers Lessons
I will fulfill my vows to the LORD* in the presence of all his people.

Psalm 116:16

The Vespers Psalm   *The LORD Will Make Good His Purpose for Me*
I will give thanks to you, O LORD, with my whole heart;* before the gods I will sing
    your praise.
I will bow down toward your holy temple and praise your Name,* because of
    your love and faithfulness;
For you have glorified your Name* and your word above all things.
When I called, you answered me;* you increased my strength within me.
All the kings of the earth will praise you, O LORD,* when they have heard the
    words of your mouth.
They will sing of the ways of the LORD,* that great is the glory of the LORD.
Though the LORD be high, he cares for the lowly;* he perceives the haughty from
    afar.
Though I walk in the midst of trouble, you keep me safe;* you stretch forth your
    hand against the fury of my enemies; your right hand shall save me.
The LORD will make good his purpose for me;* O LORD, your love endures for
    ever; do not abandon the works of your hands.

Psalm 138

The Refrain
I will fulfill my vows to the LORD* in the presence of all his people.

The Gloria

The Lord's Prayer

The Prayer Appointed for the Week
Give us grace, O Lord, to answer readily the call of our Savior Jesus Christ and
    proclaim to all people the Good News of his salvation, that we and the whole
    world may perceive the glory of his marvelous works; who lives and reigns
    with you and the Holy Spirit, one God, for ever and ever. *Amen.*†

Concluding Prayers of the Church
Almighty God, by your Holy Spirit you have made us one with your saints in
    heaven and on earth: Grant that in my earthly pilgrimage I may always be sup-
    ported by this fellowship of love and prayer, and know myself to be sur-
    rounded by their witness to your power and mercy. I ask this for the sake of
    Jesus Christ, in whom all my intercessions are acceptable through the Spirit,
    and who lives and reigns for ever and ever. *Amen.*†

Lord God, whose Son our Savior Jesus Christ, triumphed over the powers of death
    and prepared for us our place in the new Jerusalem: Grant that I, who have this
    day given thanks for his resurrection, may praise you in the City of which he is
    the light, and where he lives and reigns for ever and ever. *Amen.*†

The Morning Office   To Be Observed on the Hour or Half Hour
                                                  Between 6 and 9 a.m.

The Call to Prayer
Let my mouth be full of your praise* and your glory all the day long.
                                                  Psalm 71:8

The Request for Presence
Your word is a lantern to my feet* and a light upon my path.
                                                  Psalm 119:105

The Greeting
O God, you have taught me since I was young,* and to this day I tell of your won-
    derful works.

                                                  Psalm 71:17

The Refrain for the Morning Lessons
This is the LORD's doing,* and it is marvelous in our eyes.
                                                  Psalm 118:23

A Reading   *On January 25, the Church celebrates the conversion of St. Paul.*
                     Called by many "the second founder of the Church," Paul was
                     the driving force behind the spread of Christianity into the
                     Greco-Roman world. Tradition says that he, like St. Peter, was
                     martyred by the Emperor Nero.

From St. Paul's defense of himself before King Agrippa: "I consider myself fortu-
    nate, King Agrippa, in that it is before you I am to answer today all the charges
    made against me by the Jews, the more so because you are an expert in matters
    of custom and controversy among the Jews. So I beg you to listen to me
    patiently. As for me, I once thought it was my duty to use every means to
    oppose the name of Jesus the Nazarene. This I did in Jerusalem; I myself threw
    many of God's holy people into prison, acting on authority from the chief
    priests, and when they were being sentenced to death I cast my vote against
    them. I often went round the synagogues inflicting penalties, trying in this way
    to force them to renounce their faith; my fury against them was so extreme that
    I even pursued them into foreign cities. On such an expedition I was going to
    Damascus, armed with full powers and a commission from the chief priests,
    and in the middle of the day as I was on my way, Your Majesty, I saw a light
    from heaven shining more brilliantly than the sun round me and my fellow
    travelers. We all fell to the ground, and I heard a voice saying to me in Hebrew,
    'Saul, Saul, why are you persecuting me? It is hard for you kicking against the
    goad.' Then I said, 'Who are you, Lord?' And the Lord answered, 'I am Jesus,
    whom you are persecuting. But get up and stand on your feet, for I have
    appeared to you for this reason: to appoint you as my servant and as witness of
    this vision in which you have seen me, and of others in which I shall appear to
    you. *I shall rescue you* from the people and from *the nations to whom I send you to*
    open their eyes, so that they may turn *from darkness to light,* from the dominion of

Satan to God, and receive, through faith in me, forgiveness of their sins and a
share in the inheritance of the sanctified.' After that, King Agrippa, I could not
disobey the heavenly vision. On the contrary, I started preaching, first to the
people of Damascus, then to those of Jerusalem and all Judean territory, and
also to gentiles, urging them to repent and turn to God, proving their change of
heart by their deeds."

Acts 26:2–3, 9–20

The Refrain
This is the LORD's doing,* and it is marvelous in our eyes.

The Morning Psalm   *Let Your Saving Ways Be Known, O LORD*
May God be merciful to us and bless us,* show us the light of his countenance and
    come to us.
Let your ways be known upon earth,* your saving health among all nations.
Let the peoples praise you, O God;* let all the peoples praise you.
Let the nations be glad and sing for joy,* for you judge the peoples with equity and
    guide all the nations upon earth.
Let the peoples praise you, O God;* let all the peoples praise you.
The earth has brought forth her increase;* may God, our own God, give us his
    blessing.
May God give us his blessing,* and may all the ends of the earth stand in awe of
    him.

Psalm 67

The Refrain
This is the LORD's doing,* and it is marvelous in our eyes.

The Gloria

The Lord's Prayer

The Prayer Appointed for the Week
Give us grace, O Lord, to answer readily the call of our Savior Jesus Christ and
    proclaim to all people the Good News of his salvation, that we and the whole
    world may perceive the glory of his marvelous works; who lives and reigns
    with you and the Holy Spirit, one God, for ever and ever. *Amen.*†

Concluding Prayers of the Church
O God, by the preaching of your apostle Paul you have caused the light of the
    Gospel to shine throughout the world: Grant, I pray, that I, having his wonder-
    ful conversion in remembrance, may show myself thankful to you by follow-
    ing his holy teaching; through Jesus Christ my Lord, who lives and reigns with
    you, in the unity of the Holy Spirit, one God, now and for ever. *Amen.*†

Lord God, almighty and everlasting Father, you have brought me in safety to this
    new day: Preserve me with your mighty power, that I may not fall into sin, nor
    be overcome by adversity; and in all I do direct me to the fulfilling of your pur-
    pose; through Jesus Christ my Lord. *Amen.*†

The Midday Office

To Be Observed on the Hour or Half Hour
Between 11 a.m. and 2 p.m.

The Call to Prayer

Blessed be the LORD, the God of Israel, from everlasting and to everlasting;* and
let all the people say, "Amen!" Hallelujah!

Psalm 106:48

The Request for Presence

Turn to me and have mercy upon me;* give your strength to your servant; and
save the child of your handmaid.

Psalm 86:16

The Greeting

O LORD, your love endures for ever;* do not abandon the works of your hands.

Psalm 138:9

The Refrain for the Midday Lessons

The fear of the LORD is the beginning of wisdom;* those who act accordingly have
a good understanding; his praise endures for ever.

Psalm 111:10

A Reading

St. Paul wrote to the church of Galatia saying: "Now I want to make it quite clear
to you, brothers, about the gospel that was preached by me, that it was no
human message. It was not from any human being that I received it, and I was
not taught it, but it came to me through a revelation of Jesus Christ. You have
surely heard how I lived in the past, within Judaism, and how there was simply no limit to the way I persecuted the Church of God in my attempts to
destroy it; and how in Judaism, I outstripped most of my Jewish contempo-
raries in my limitless enthusiasm for the traditions of my ancestors. But when
God, who had set me apart from the time when I was *in my mother's womb,
called* me through his grace and chose to reveal his Son in me, so that I should
preach him to the gentiles, I was in no hurry to confer with any human being,
or go up to Jerusalem."

Galatians 1:11–17

The Refrain

The fear of the LORD is the beginning of wisdom;* those who act accordingly have
a good understanding; his praise endures for ever.

The Midday Psalm   *I Have Prepared a Lamp for My Anointed*

For the LORD has chosen Zion;* he has desired her for his habitation:
"This shall be my resting-place for ever;* here will I dwell, for I delight in her.
I will surely bless her provisions,* and satisfy her poor with bread.
I will clothe her priests with salvation,* and her faithful people will rejoice and sing.
There will I make the horn of David flourish;* I have prepared a lamp for my
Anointed."

Psalm 132:14–18

The Refrain
The fear of the LORD is the beginning of wisdom;* those who act accordingly have
a good understanding; his praise endures for ever.

The Gloria

The Lord's Prayer

The Prayer Appointed for the Week
Give us grace, O Lord, to answer readily the call of our Savior Jesus Christ and
proclaim to all people the Good News of his salvation, that we and the whole
world may perceive the glory of his marvelous works; who lives and reigns
with you and the Holy Spirit, one God, for ever and ever. *Amen.*†

Concluding Prayers of the Church
Almighty God, whose will it is to be glorified in your saints, and who raised up
your servant Paul to be a light in the world: Shine, I pray, in my heart that I also
in my generation may show forth your praise, who called me out of darkness
into your marvelous light; through Jesus Christ my Lord, who lives and reigns
with you and the Holy Spirit, one God, now and for ever. *Amen.*†

Heavenly Father, you have promised to hear what we ask in the Name of your
Son: Accept and fulfill my petitions, I pray, not as I ask in my ignorance, nor as
I deserve in my sinfulness, but as you know and love me in your Son Jesus
Christ our Lord. *Amen.*†

The Vespers Office · · · · · · · · · · · · To Be Observed on the Hour or Half Hour
Between 5 and 8 p.m.

The Call to Prayer
Sing to the LORD a new song;* sing to the LORD, all the whole earth.
For great is the LORD and greatly to be praised;* he is more to be feared than all
gods.
Psalm 96:1, 4

The Request for Presence
Give ear, O LORD, to my prayer,* and attend to the voice of my supplications.
Psalm 86:6

The Greeting
Your way, O God, is holy;* who is so great a god as our God?
Psalm 77:13

The Hymn
We sing the glorious conquest before Damascus' gate,
When Saul, the Church's spoiler, came spreading fear and hate.
God's light shone down from heaven and broke across the path
His presence pierced and blinded the zealot in his wrath.

O Voice that spoke within him; O strong, reproving Word;
O Love that sought and held him a prisoner of his Lord;
Help us to know your kingship that we, in every hour,
In all that may confront us, will trust your hidden power.

Your grace, by ways mysterious, our sinful wrath can bind,
And in those least expected, true servants you can find.
In us you seek disciples to share your cross and crown
And give you final service in glory at your throne.

John Ellerton

The Refrain for the Vespers Lessons
He will judge the world with righteousness* and the peoples with his truth.

Psalm 96:13

The Vespers Psalm   *Bless the LORD, All You Servants of the LORD*
Behold now, bless the LORD, all you servants of the LORD,* you that stand by night
   in the house of the LORD.
Lift up your hands in the holy place and bless the LORD;* the LORD who made
   heaven and earth bless you out of Zion.

Psalm 134

The Refrain
He will judge the world with righteousness* and the peoples with his truth.

The Gloria

The Lord's Prayer

The Prayer Appointed for the Week
Give us grace, O Lord, to answer readily the call of our Savior Jesus Christ and
   proclaim to all people the Good News of his salvation, that we and the whole
   world may perceive the glory of his marvelous works; who lives and reigns
   with you and the Holy Spirit, one God, for ever and ever. *Amen.*†

Concluding Prayers of the Church
Heavenly Father, Shepherd of your people, we thank you for your servant Paul,
   who was faithful in the care and nurture of your flock; and I pray that, following his example and the teaching of his holy life, I may by your grace grow into
   the stature of the fullness of our Lord and Savior Jesus Christ; who lives and
   reigns with you and the Holy Spirit, one God, for ever and ever. *Amen.*†

Almighty God, whose beloved Son willingly endured the agony and shame of the
   cross for our redemption: Give me courage to take up my cross and follow him;
   who lives and reigns with you and the Holy Spirit, one God, now and for ever.
   Amen.†

The Morning Office　　　　　　　　To Be Observed on the Hour or Half Hour
　　　　　　　　　　　　　　　　　　　　　　Between 6 and 9 a.m.

The Call to Prayer
Open my lips, O LORD,* and my mouth shall proclaim your praise.
Psalm 51:16

The Request for Presence
Open my eyes, that I may see* the wonders of your law.
Psalm 119:18

The Greeting
I will thank you, O LORD my God, with all my heart,* and glorify your Name for
evermore.
Psalm 86:12

The Refrain for the Morning Lessons
For who is God, but the LORD?* who is the Rock, except our God?
Psalm 18:32

A Reading
Jesus taught the disciples, saying: "Look, I am sending you out like sheep among
the wolves; so be cunning as snakes and yet innocent as doves. Be prepared for
people to hand you over to sanhedrins and scourge you in their synagogues.
You will be brought before governors and kings for my sake, as evidence to
them and to the gentiles. But when you are handed over, do not worry about
how to speak or what to say; what you are to say will be given to you when the
time comes, because it is not you who will be speaking; the Spirit of your
Father will be speaking in you."
Matthew 10:16–20

The Refrain
For who is God, but the LORD?* who is the Rock, except our God?

The Morning Psalm　　　　　　　*Your Servant Holds Your Word to Be Dear*
You are righteous, O LORD,* and upright are your judgments.
You have issued your decrees* with justice and in perfect faithfulness.
My indignation has consumed me,* because my enemies forget your words.
Your word has been tested to the uttermost,* and your servant holds it dear.
I am small and of little account,* yet I do not forget your commandments.
Your justice is an everlasting justice* and your law is the truth.
Trouble and distress have come upon me,* yet your commandments are my
delight.
The righteousness of your decrees is everlasting;* grant me understanding, that I
may live.
Psalm 119:137–144

The Refrain
For who is God, but the LORD?* who is the Rock, except our God?

The Small Verse
O Lamb of God, that takes away the sins of the world, have mercy upon me.
O Lamb of God, that takes away the sins of the world, have mercy upon me.
O Lamb of God, that takes away the sins of the world, grant me your peace.

Agnus Dei

The Lord's Prayer

The Prayer Appointed for the Week
Give us grace, O Lord, to answer readily the call of our Savior Jesus Christ and
proclaim to all people the Good News of his salvation, that we and the whole
world may perceive the glory of his marvelous works; who lives and reigns
with you and the Holy Spirit, one God, for ever and ever. *Amen.*†

The Concluding Prayer of the Church
Lord God, almighty and everlasting Father, you have brought me in safety to this
new day: Preserve me with your mighty power, that I may not fall into sin, nor
be overcome by adversity; and in all I do direct me to the fulfilling of your purpose; through Jesus Christ my Lord. *Amen.*†

The Midday Office   To Be Observed on the Hour or Half Hour
                                      Between 11 a.m. and 2 p.m.

The Call to Prayer
Open my lips, O Lord,* and my mouth shall proclaim your praise.

Psalm 51:16

The Request for Presence
You are my helper and my deliverer,* do not tarry, O my God.

Psalm 40:19

The Greeting
Hosanna, Lord, hosanna!* Lord, send us now success.
Blessed is he who comes in the name of the Lord;* we bless you from the house of
the Lord.

Psalm 118:25–26

The Refrain for the Midday Lessons
. . . You hold me by my right hand.
You will guide me by your counsel,* and afterwards receive me with glory.

Psalm 73:23–24

A Reading
The Lord hates all that is foul, and no one who fears him will love it either. He
himself made human beings in the beginning, and then left them free to make
their own decisions. He has set fire and water before you; put your hand to
whichever you prefer. A human being has life and death before him; whichever
he prefers will be given him.

Ecclesiasticus 15:13–14, 16–18

The Refrain
. . . You hold me by my right hand.
You will guide me by your counsel,* and afterwards receive me with glory.

The Midday Psalm   *How Sweet Are Your Words to My Taste*
Oh, how I love your law!* all the day long it is in my mind.
Your commandment has made me wiser than my enemies,* and it is always
    with me.
I have more understanding than all my teachers,* for your decrees are my study.
I am wiser than the elders,* because I observe your commandments.
I restrain my feet from every evil way,* that I may keep your word.
I do not shrink from your judgments,* because you yourself have taught me.
How sweet are your words to my taste!* they are sweeter than honey to my
    mouth.
Through your commandments I gain understanding;* therefore I hate every lying
    way.
                                                            Psalm 119:97–104

The Refrain
. . . You hold me by my right hand.
You will guide me by your counsel,* and afterwards receive me with glory.

The Small Verse
My help is in the Name of the Lord who made the heavens and the earth. What
    then shall I fear, of what shall I be afraid?
                                                            Traditional

The Lord's Prayer

The Prayer Appointed for the Week
Give us grace, O Lord, to answer readily the call of our Savior Jesus Christ and
    proclaim to all people the Good News of his salvation, that we and the whole
    world may perceive the glory of his marvelous works; who lives and reigns
    with you and the Holy Spirit, one God, for ever and ever. *Amen.*†

The Concluding Prayer of the Church
Direct me, O Lord, in all my doings with your most gracious favor, and further me
    with your continual help; that in all my work begun, continued, and ended in
    you, I may glorify your holy name, and finally, by your mercy, obtain everlast-
    ing life; through Jesus Christ my Lord. *Amen.*

The Vespers Office   **To Be Observed on the Hour or Half Hour**
                                           Between 5 and 8 p.m.

The Call to Prayer
Open my lips, O Lord,* and my mouth shall proclaim your praise.
Had you desired it, I would have offered sacrifice,* but you take no delight in
    burnt-offerings.

The sacrifice of God is a troubled spirit;* a broken and contrite heart, O God, you will not despise.

Psalm 51:16–18

The Request for Presence
Out of the depths have I called to you, O LORD; LORD, hear my voice;* let your ears consider well the voice of my supplication.

Psalm 130:1

The Greeting
You have put gladness in my heart,* more than when grain and wine and oil increase.
I lie down in peace; at once I fall asleep;* for only you, LORD, make me dwell in safety.

Psalm 4:7–8

The Hymn

Savior, like a shepherd lead us,
Much we need your tender care;
In your pleasant pastures feed us,
For our use your folds prepare.
Blessed Jesus, blessed Jesus!
You have bought us, Yours we are.

We are yours, you do befriend us,
Be the guardian of our way;
Keep your flock, from sin defend us,
Seek us when we go astray.
Blessed Jesus, blessed Jesus!
Hear, O hear us when we pray.

You have promised to receive us,
Poor and sinful though we be;
You have mercy to relieve us,
Grace to cleanse and power to free.
Blessed Jesus, blessed Jesus!
We will early turn to thee.

Early let us seek your favor,
Early let us do your will;
Blessed Lord and only Savior,
With your love our bosoms fill.
Blessed Jesus, blessed Jesus!
You have loved us, love us still.

Dorothy Thrupp

The Refrain for the Vespers Lessons
The LORD has sworn an oath to David;* in truth, he will not break it:
"A son, the fruit of your body* will I set upon your throne."

Psalm 132:11–12

The Vespers Psalm   *Our Eyes Look to the LORD Our God*
To you I lift up my eyes,* to you enthroned in the heavens.
As the eyes of servants look to the hand of their masters,* and the eyes of a maid to the hand of her mistress,
So our eyes look to the LORD our God,* until he shows us his mercy.
Have mercy upon us, O LORD, have mercy,* for we have had more than enough of contempt,
Too much of the scorn of the indolent rich,* and of the derision of the proud.

Psalm 123

The Refrain
The LORD has sworn an oath to David;* in truth, he will not break it:
"A son, the fruit of your body* will I set upon your throne."

The Gloria

The Lord's Prayer

The Prayer Appointed for the Week
Give us grace, O Lord, to answer readily the call of our Savior Jesus Christ and
   proclaim to all people the Good News of his salvation, that we and the whole
   world may perceive the glory of his marvelous works; who lives and reigns
   with you and the Holy Spirit, one God, for ever and ever. *Amen.*†

The Concluding Prayer of the Church
Grant, Lord God, to all who have been baptized into the death and resurrection of
   your Son Jesus Christ, that, as we have put away the old life of sin, so we may
   be renewed in the spirit of our minds, and live in righteousness and true holiness; through Jesus Christ our Lord, who lives and reigns with you, in the
   unity of the Holy Spirit, one God, now and for ever. *Amen.*†

The Morning Office   To Be Observed on the Hour or Half Hour
                                               Between 6 and 9 a.m.

The Call to Prayer
Let us make a vow to the LORD our God and keep it;* let all around him bring gifts
   to him who is worthy to be feared.

                                                             Psalm 76:11

The Request for Presence
Let my cry come before you, O LORD;* give me understanding, according to your
   word.
Let my supplication come before you;* deliver me, according to your promise.

                                                        Psalm 119:169–170

The Greeting
I will offer you a freewill sacrifice* and praise your Name, O LORD, for it is good.

                                                             Psalm 54:6

The Refrain for the Morning Lessons
How sweet are your words to my taste!* they are sweeter than honey to my
   mouth.

                                                            Psalm 119:103

A Reading
Jesus taught us, saying: "Again, you have heard how it was said to our ancestors,
   You must not break your oath, but must fulfill your oaths to the Lord. But I say this to
   you, do not swear at all, either by *heaven,* since that is *God's throne,* or by *earth,*

since that is *his* footstool; or by Jerusalem, since that is *the city of the great King,* Do not swear by your own head either, since you cannot turn a single hair white or black. All you need say is, 'Yes' if you mean yes, "No' if you mean no; anything more than this comes from the Evil One."

Matthew 5:33–37

The Refrain

How sweet are your words to my taste!* they are sweeter than honey to my mouth.

The Morning Psalm   *Happy Are Those Who Always Do What Is Right*

Hallelujah! Give thanks to the LORD, for he is good,* for his mercy endures for ever.

Who can declare the mighty acts of the LORD* or show forth all his praise?

Happy are those who act with justice* and always do what is right!

Remember me, O LORD, with the favor you have for your people,* and visit me with your saving help;

That I may see the prosperity of your elect and be glad with the gladness of your people,* that I may glory with your inheritance.

Psalm 106:1–5

The Refrain

How sweet are your words to my taste!* they are sweeter than honey to my mouth.

The Cry of the Church

O God, come to my assistance! O Lord, make haste to help me!

The Lord's Prayer

The Prayer Appointed for the Week

Give us grace, O Lord, to answer readily the call of our Savior Jesus Christ and proclaim to all people the Good News of his salvation, that we and the whole world may perceive the glory of his marvelous works; who lives and reigns with you and the Holy Spirit, one God, for ever and ever. *Amen.*†

The Concluding Prayer of the Church

Lord God, almighty and everlasting Father, you have brought me in safety to this new day: Preserve me with your mighty power, that I may not fall into sin, nor be overcome by adversity; and in all I do direct me to the fulfilling of your purpose; through Jesus Christ my Lord. *Amen.*†

The Midday Office   To Be Observed on the Hour or Half Hour

Between 11 a.m. and 2 p.m.

The Call to Prayer

"Come now, let us reason together," says the Lord.

Isaiah 1:18 (KJV)

The Request for Presence
O LORD, I call to you; come to me quickly;* hear my voice when I cry to you.

Psalm 141:1

The Greeting
In you, O LORD, have I taken refuge;* let me never be ashamed.

Psalm 71:1

The Refrain for the Midday Lessons
Happy are they all who fear the LORD,* and who follow in his ways!

Psalm 128:1

A Reading
YAHWEH spoke to Moses and said: 'Speak to the whole community of Israelites and say: "Be holy, for I, YAHWEH your God, am holy. You will not steal, nor deal deceitfully or fraudulently with your fellow citizen. You will not swear by my name with intent to deceive and thus profane the name of your God. I am YAHWEH. You will not exploit or rob your fellow. You will not keep back the laborer's wage until the next morning. You will not curse the dumb or put an obstacle in the way of the blind, but will fear your God. I am YAHWEH." '

Leviticus 19:1–2, 11–18

The Refrain
Happy are they all who fear the LORD,* and who follow in his ways!

The Midday Psalm   *I Will Lift Up My Hands to Your Commandments*
Let your loving-kindness come to me, O LORD,* and your salvation, according to your promise.
Then shall I have a word for those who taunt me,* because I trust in your words.
Do not take the word of truth out of my mouth,* for my hope is in your judgments.
I shall continue to keep your law;* I shall keep it for ever and ever.
I will walk at liberty,* because I study your commandments.
I will tell of your decrees before kings* and will not be ashamed.
I delight in your commandments,* which I have always loved.
I will lift up my hands to your commandments,* and I will meditate on your statutes.

Psalm 119:41–48

The Refrain
Happy are they all who fear the LORD,* and who follow in his ways!

The Cry of the Church
Be, Lord, my helper and forsake me not. Do not despise me, O God, my savior.

THE SHORT BREVIARY

The Lord's Prayer

The Prayer Appointed for the Week
Give us grace, O Lord, to answer readily the call of our Savior Jesus Christ and
proclaim to all people the Good News of his salvation, that we and the whole
world may perceive the glory of his marvelous works; who lives and reigns
with you and the Holy Spirit, one God, for ever and ever. *Amen.*†

The Concluding Prayer of the Church
Direct me, O Lord, in all my doings with your most gracious favor, and further me
with your continual help; that in all my work begun, continued, and ended in
you, I may glorify your holy name, and finally, by your mercy, obtain everlasting life; through Jesus Christ our Lord. *Amen.*†

The Vespers Office   To Be Observed on the Hour or Half Hour
Between 5 and 8 p.m.

The Call to Prayer
Come, let us sing to the LORD;* let us shout for joy to the Rock of our salvation.
Let us come before his presence with thanksgiving* and raise a loud shout to him
with psalms.
For the LORD is a great God,* and a great King above all gods.
In his hand are the caverns of the earth,* and the heights of the hills are his also.
The sea is his, for he made it,* and his hands have molded the dry land.

Psalm 95:1–5

The Request for Presence
May God be merciful to us and bless us,* show us the light of his countenance and
come to us.

Psalm 67:1

The Greeting
Exalt yourself above the heavens, O God,* and your glory over all the earth.

Psalm 57:6

The Hymn
From all that dwell below the skies
Let the Creator's praise arise!
Let the Redeemer's Name be sung
Through every land, by every tongue!

Eternal are your mercies, Lord,
And truth eternal is your word:
Your praise shall sound from every shore
Till suns shall rise and set no more.

Praise God from whom all blessings flow;
Praise him, all creatures here below;
Praise him above, you heavenly host:
Praise Father, Son, and Holy Ghost.

Isaac Watts
Stanza 3, Doxology

The Refrain for the Vespers Lessons
Those who trust in the LORD are like Mount Zion,* which cannot be moved, but
stands fast for ever.

Psalm 125:1

The Vespers Psalm   *His Mercy Endures For Ever*
Give thanks to the LORD, for he is good,* for his mercy endures for ever.
Give thanks to the God of gods,* for his mercy endures for ever.
Give thanks to the Lord of lords,* for his mercy endures for ever.
Who only does great wonders,* for his mercy endures for ever;
Who struck down the firstborn of Egypt,* for his mercy endures for ever;
And brought out Israel from among them,* for his mercy endures for ever;
Who led his people through the wilderness,* for his mercy endures for ever.
Who remembered us in our low estate,* for his mercy endures for ever;
And delivered us from our enemies,* for his mercy endures for ever;
Who gives food to all creatures,* for his mercy endures for ever.
Give thanks to the God of heaven,* for his mercy endures for ever.

Psalm 136:1–4, 10–11, 16, 23–26

The Refrain
Those who trust in the LORD are like Mount Zion,* which cannot be moved, but
stands fast for ever.

The Gloria

The Lord's Prayer

The Prayer Appointed for the Week
Give us grace, O Lord, to answer readily the call of our Savior Jesus Christ and
proclaim to all people the Good News of his salvation, that we and the whole
world may perceive the glory of his marvelous works; who lives and reigns
with you and the Holy Spirit, one God, for ever and ever. *Amen.*†

The Concluding Prayer of the Church
Protect us, Lord, as we stay awake; watch over us as we sleep, that awake we may
watch with Christ, and asleep, rest in peace. *Amen.*

The Morning Office   To Be Observed on the Hour or Half Hour
                                                      Between 6 and 9 a.m.

The Call to Prayer
Know this: The Lord himself is God;* he himself has made us, and we are his; we
are his people and the sheep of his pasture.

Psalm 100:2

The Request for Presence
For God alone my soul in silence waits;* truly, my hope is in him.

Psalm 62:6

The Greeting
Your testimonies are very sure,* and holiness adorns your house, O Lord, for ever
and for evermore.

Psalm 93:6

The Refrain for the Morning Lessons
Blessed is he who comes in the name of the Lord;* we bless you from the house of
the Lord.

Psalm 118:26

A Reading
Jesus taught us, saying: "The lamp of the body is the eye. It follows that if your eye
is clear, your whole body will be filled with light. But if your eye is diseased,
your whole body will be darkness. If then, the light inside you is darkened,
what darkness that will be!"

Matthew 6:21–23

The Refrain
Blessed is he who comes in the name of the Lord;* we bless you from the house of
the Lord.

The Morning Psalm   *Bless the Lord, All You Who Do His Bidding*
The merciful goodness of the Lord endures for ever on those who fear him,* and
his righteousness on children's children;
On those who keep his covenant* and remember his commandments and do them.
The Lord has set his throne in heaven,* and his kingship has dominion over all.
Bless the Lord, you angels of his, you mighty ones who do his bidding,* and
hearken to the voice of his word.
Bless the Lord, all you his hosts,* you ministers of his who do his will.
Bless the Lord, all you works of his, in all places of his dominion;* bless the Lord,
O my soul.

Psalm 103:17–22

The Refrain
Blessed is he who comes in the name of the Lord;* we bless you from the house of
the Lord.

The Cry of the Church
O God, come to my assistance! O Lord, make haste to help me!

The Lord's Prayer

The Prayer Appointed for the Week
Give us grace, O Lord, to answer readily the call of our Savior Jesus Christ and
proclaim to all people the Good News of his salvation, that we and the whole
world may perceive the glory of his marvelous works; who lives and reigns
with you and the Holy Spirit, one God, for ever and ever. *Amen.†*

The Concluding Prayer of the Church
Lord God, almighty and everlasting Father, you have brought me in safety to this
new day: Preserve me with your mighty power, that I may not fall into sin, nor
be overcome by adversity; and in all I do direct me to the fulfilling of your purpose; through Jesus Christ my Lord. *Amen.†*

The Midday Office   To Be Observed on the Hour or Half Hour
                                         Between 11 a.m. and 2 p.m.

The Call to Prayer
Praise God from whom all blessings flow; praise him, all creatures here below;
praise him, you heavenly hosts; praise Father, Son and Holy Ghost.
                                                                Traditional

The Request for Presence
Hear my prayer, O LORD,* and give ear to my cry; . . .
For I am but a sojourner with you,* a wayfarer, as all my forebears were.
                                                          Psalm 39:13–14

The Greeting
With my whole heart I seek you;* let me not stray from your commandments.
                                                          Psalm 119:10

The Refrain for the Midday Lessons
The LORD loves those who hate evil; he preserves the lives of his saints* and delivers them from the hand of the wicked.
                                                          Psalm 97:10

A Reading
Thus says YAHWEH: At the time of my favor I have answered you, on the day of
salvation I have helped you. I have formed you and have appointed you to be
the covenant for a people, to restore the land, to return ravaged properties, to
say to prisoners, 'Come out,' to those who are in darkness, 'Show yourselves.'
Along the roadway they will graze, and any bare height will be their pasture.
They will never hunger or thirst, scorching wind and sun will never plague
them; for he who pities them will lead them, will guide them to springs of

water. I shall turn all my mountains into a road and my highways will be raised aloft. Shout for joy, you heavens, earth exult! Mountains, break into joyful cries! For YAHWEH has consoled his people, is taking pity on his afflicted ones.

Isaiah 49:8–11, 13

The Refrain

The LORD loves those who hate evil; he preserves the lives of his saints* and delivers them from the hand of the wicked.

The Midday Psalm   *How Excellent Is His Greatness*

Bless the LORD, O my soul;* O LORD my God, how excellent is your greatness! you are clothed with majesty and splendor.

You wrap yourself with light as with a cloak* and spread out the heavens like a curtain.

You lay the beams of your chambers in the waters above;* you make the clouds your chariot; you ride on the wings of the wind.

You make the winds your messengers* and flames of fire your servants.

You have set the earth upon its foundations,* so that it never shall move at any time.

You covered it with the Deep as with a mantle;* the waters stood higher than the mountains.

At your rebuke they fled;* at the voice of your thunder they hastened away.

Psalm 104:1–7

The Refrain

The LORD loves those who hate evil; he preserves the lives of his saints* and delivers them from the hand of the wicked.

The Cry of the Church

O God, come to my assistance! O Lord, make haste to help me!

The Lord's Prayer

The Prayer Appointed for the Week

Give us grace, O Lord, to answer readily the call of our Savior Jesus Christ and proclaim to all people the Good News of his salvation, that we and the whole world may perceive the glory of his marvelous works; who lives and reigns with you and the Holy Spirit, one God, for ever and ever. *Amen.*†

The Concluding Prayer of the Church

Almighty and everlasting God, by whose Spirit the whole body of your faithful is governed and sanctified: Receive my supplications and prayers which I offer before you for all members of your holy Church, that in our vocation and ministry we all may truly serve you through our Lord and Savior Jesus Christ. *Amen.*†

The Vespers Office

To Be Observed on the Hour or Half Hour
Between 5 and 8 p.m.

The Call to Prayer
Come now and see the works of God,* how wonderful he is in his doing toward
all people.
In his might he rules for ever; his eyes keep watch over the nations;* let no rebel
rise up against him.

Psalm 66:4, 6

The Request for Presence
Show us your mercy, O Lord,* and grant us your salvation

Psalm 85:7

The Greeting
Praise God from whom all blessings flow; praise Him all creatures here below;
praise Him above, you heavenly hosts; praise Father, Son, and Holy Ghost.

Traditional Doxology

The Hymn

O Love of God, how strong and true,
Eternal and yet ever new;
Uncomprehended and unbought,
Beyond all knowledge and all thought.

We read you best in him who came
To bear for us the cross of shame,
Sent by the Father from on high,
Our life to live, our death to die.

O wide embracing, wondrous Love,
We read you in the sky above;
We read you in the earth below,
In seas that swell and streams that flow.

We read your power to bless and save
Even in the darkness of the grave;
Still more in resurrection light
We read the fullness of your might.

Horatius Bonar

The Refrain for the Vespers Lessons
You crown the year with your goodness,* and your paths overflow with plenty.

Psalm 66:12

The Vespers Psalm   *Sing the Glory of Our God*
Be joyful in God, all you lands;* sing the glory of his Name; sing the glory of his
praise.
Say to God, "How awesome are your deeds!* because of your great strength your
enemies cringe before you.
All the earth bows down before you,* sings to you, sings out your Name."

Psalm 66:1–3

The Refrain
You crown the year with your goodness,* and your paths overflow with plenty.

The Small Verse
The Lord is my shepherd and nothing is wanting to me. In green pastures He hath
settled me.

The Short Breviary

The Lord's Prayer

The Prayer Appointed for the Week
Give us grace, O Lord, to answer readily the call of our Savior Jesus Christ and
    proclaim to all people the Good News of his salvation, that we and the whole
    world may perceive the glory of his marvelous works; who lives and reigns
    with you and the Holy Spirit, one God, for ever and ever. *Amen.*†

The Concluding Prayer of the Church
Help each one of us, gracious Father, to live in such magnanimity and restraint
    that the Head of the Church may never have cause to say to any one of us, This
    is my body, broken by you.

Prayer from China

The Morning Office   To Be Observed on the Hour or Half Hour
Between 6 and 9 a.m.

The Call to Prayer
Come now and see the works of God,* how wonderful he is in his doing toward
    all people.

Psalm 66:4

The Request for Presence
Show me your marvelous loving-kindness,* O Savior of those who take refuge at
    your right hand from those who rise up against them.
Keep me as the apple of your eye;* hide me under the shadow of your wings.

Psalm 17:7–8

The Greeting
Hosanna, LORD, hosanna! . . . Blessed is he who comes in the name of the LORD;*
    we bless you from the house of the LORD.

Psalm 118:25–26

The Refrain for the Morning Lessons
For God, who commanded the light to shine out of darkness, hath shined in our
    hearts, to give the light of the knowledge of the glory of God in the face of Jesus
    Christ.

2 Corinthians 4:6

A Reading
Jesus said to us: "In all truth I tell you, whoever listens to my words, and believes
    in the one who sent me, has eternal life; without being brought to judgment
    such a person has passed from death to life. In all truth I tell you, the hour is
    coming—indeed it is already here—when the dead will hear the voice of the
    Son of God, and all who hear it will live."

John 5:24–25

The Refrain

For God, who commanded the light to shine out of darkness, hath shined in our
hearts, to give the light of the knowledge of the glory of God in the face of Jesus
Christ.

The Morning Psalm   *What Are We That You Should Care for Us*

Blessed be the LORD my rock!* who trains my hands to fight and my fingers to
battle;

My help and my fortress, my stronghold and my deliverer,* my shield in whom I
trust, who subdues the peoples under me.

O LORD, what are we that you should care for us?* mere mortals that you should
think of us?

We are like a puff of wind;* our days are like a passing shadow.

Bow your heavens, O LORD, and come down;* touch the mountains, and they shall
smoke.

Hurl the lightning and scatter them;* shoot out your arrows and rout them.

Stretch out your hand from on high;* rescue me and deliver me from the great
waters.

Psalm 144:1–7

The Refrain

For God, who commanded the light to shine out of darkness, hath shined in our
hearts, to give the light of the knowledge of the glory of God in the face of Jesus
Christ.

The Gloria

The Lord's Prayer

The Prayer Appointed for the Week

Give us grace, O Lord, to answer readily the call of our Savior Jesus Christ and
proclaim to all people the Good News of his salvation, that we and the whole
world may perceive the glory of his marvelous works; who lives and reigns
with you and the Holy Spirit, one God, for ever and ever. *Amen.*†

The Concluding Prayer of the Church

Lord God, almighty and everlasting Father, you have brought me in safety to this
new day: Preserve me with your mighty power, that I may not fall into sin, nor
be overcome by adversity; and in all I do direct me to the fulfilling of your purpose; through Jesus Christ my Lord. *Amen.*†

The Midday Office   To Be Observed on the Hour or Half Hour
                                                Between 11 a.m. and 2 p.m.

The Call to Prayer

Give thanks to the LORD, for he is good;* his mercy endures for ever.

Psalm 118:29

The Request for Presence

You are the Lord;* do not withhold your compassion from me; let your love and
your faithfulness keep me safe for ever.

Psalm 40:12

The Greeting

There is forgiveness with you;* therefore you shall be feared.

Psalm 130:3

The Refrain for the Midday Lessons

Keep watch over my life, for I am faithful;* save your servant who puts his trust in
you.

Psalm 86:2

A Reading

You must see what great love the Father has lavished on us by letting us be called
God's children—which is what we are! The reason why the world does not
acknowledge us is that it did not acknowledge him. My dear friends, we are
already God's children, but what we shall be in the future has not yet been
revealed. We are well aware that when he appears we shall be like him,
because we shall see him as he really is.

1 John: 1–2

The Refrain

Keep watch over my life, for I am faithful;* save your servant who puts his trust in
you.

The Midday Psalm   *Israel Would I Satisfy with Honey from the Rock*

Hear, O my people, and I will admonish you:* O Israel, if you would but listen to
me!

There shall be no strange god among you;* you shall not worship a foreign god.

I am the Lord your God, who brought you out of the land of Egypt and said,*
    "Open your mouth wide, and I will fill it."

And yet my people did not hear my voice,* and Israel would not obey me.

So I gave them over to the stubbornness of their hearts,* to follow their own
devices.

Oh, that my people would listen to me!* that Israel would walk in my ways!

I should soon subdue their enemies* and turn my hand against their foes.

Those who hate the Lord would cringe before him,* and their punishment would
last for ever.

But Israel would I feed with the finest wheat* and satisfy him with honey from the
rock.

Psalm 81:8–16

The Refrain

Keep watch over my life, for I am faithful;* save your servant who puts his trust in
you.

The Cry of the Church
In the evening, in the morning, and at noonday, I will complain and lament,* and
he will hear my voice.

Psalm 55:18

The Lord's Prayer

The Prayer Appointed for the Week
Give us grace, O Lord, to answer readily the call of our Savior Jesus Christ and
proclaim to all people the Good News of his salvation, that we and the whole
world may perceive the glory of his marvelous works; who lives and reigns
with you and the Holy Spirit, one God, for ever and ever. *Amen.*†

The Concluding Prayer of the Church
Lord Jesus Christ, by your death you took away the sting of death: Grant me to so
follow in faith where you have led the way, that I may at length fall asleep
peacefully in you and wake in your likeness; for your tender mercies' sake.
Amen.†

The Vespers Office   **To Be Observed on the Hour or Half Hour**
Between 5 and 8 p.m.

The Call to Prayer
Behold now, bless the Lord, all you servants of the Lord,* you that stand by night
in the house of the Lord.
Lift up your hands in the holy place and bless the Lord;* the Lord who made
heaven and earth bless you out of Zion.

Psalm 134

The Request for Presence
Look upon me and answer me, O Lord my God;* give light to my eyes, lest I sleep
in death.

Psalm 13:3

The Greeting
O Lord, I am not proud;* I have no haughty looks.
I do not occupy myself with great matters,* or with things that are too hard for me.
But I still my soul and make it quiet, like a child upon its mother's breast;* my soul
is quieted within me.

Psalm 131:1–3

The Hymn
You are the Way, to you alone from sin and death we flee;
And all who would the Father seek, must seek him, Lord, by thee.

You are the Truth, your word alone true wisdom can impart;
You only can inform the mind and purify the heart.

You are the Life, the rending tomb proclaims your conquering arm;
And those who put their trust in you nor death nor hell shall harm.

You are the Way, the Truth, the Life: grant us that way to know,
That truth to keep, that life to win, whose joys eternal flow.

George W. Doane

The Refrain for the Vespers Lessons
Those who are planted in the house of the LORD* shall flourish in the courts of our
God.

Psalm 92:12

The Vespers Psalm   *Be Merciful to Me, O LORD*
You only are my portion, O LORD;* I have promised to keep your words.
I entreat you with all my heart,* be merciful to me according to your promise.
I have considered my ways* and turned my feet toward your decrees.
I hasten and do not tarry* to keep your commandments.
Though the cords of the wicked entangle me,* I do not forget your law.
At midnight I will rise to give you thanks,* because of your righteous judgments.
I am a companion of all who fear you;* and of those who keep your
commandments.
The earth, O LORD, is full of your love;* instruct me in your statutes.

Psalm 119:57–64

The Refrain
Those who are planted in the house of the LORD* shall flourish in the courts of our
God.

The Small Verse
The Lord is my shepherd and nothing is wanting to me. In green pastures He has
settled me.

THE SHORT BREVIARY

The Lord's Prayer

The Prayer Appointed for the Week
Give us grace, O Lord, to answer readily the call of our Savior Jesus Christ and
proclaim to all people the Good News of his salvation, that we and the whole
world may perceive the glory of his marvelous works; who lives and reigns
with you and the Holy Spirit, one God, for ever and ever. *Amen.*†

Concluding Prayers of the Church
Almighty God, who has promised to hear the petitions of those who ask in your
Son's Name: I beseech you mercifully to incline your ear to me who have made
my prayers and supplications to you; and grant that those things which I have
faithfully asked according to your will, I may effectually obtain, to the relief of
my necessity, and to the setting forth of your glory; through Jesus Christ my
Lord. *Amen.*†

May the souls of the faithful departed, through the mercy of God, rest in eternal peace. *Amen.*

The Morning Office   To Be Observed on the Hour or Half Hour
                                                         Between 6 and 9 a.m.

The Call to Prayer
Come now and look upon the works of the Lord,* what awesome things he has done on earth.

                                                     Psalm 46:9

The Request for Presence
O Lord . . . answer us when we call.
                            Psalm 20:9

The Greeting
My eyes are fixed on you, O my Strength;* for you, O God, are my stronghold.
                                        Psalm 59:10

The Refrain for the Morning Lessons
The Lord executes righteousness* and judgment for all who are oppressed.
                                     Psalm 103:6

A Reading
Jesus said: "But I say this to you who are listening: Love your enemies, do good to those who hate you, bless those who curse you, pray for those who treat you badly. To anyone who slaps you on one cheek, present the other cheek as well; to anyone who takes your cloak from you, do not refuse your tunic. Give to everyone who asks you, and do not ask for your property back from someone who takes it."

                                       Luke 6:27–30

The Refrain
The Lord executes righteousness* and judgment for all who are oppressed.

The Morning Psalm   *My Merciful God Comes to Meet Me*
Rouse yourself, come to my side, and see;* for you, Lord God of hosts, are Israel's God.
Awake, and punish all the ungodly;* show no mercy to those who are faithless and evil.
They go to and fro in the evening;* they snarl like dogs and run about the city.
Behold, they boast with their mouths, and taunts are on their lips;* "For who," they say, "will hear us?"
But you, O Lord, you laugh at them;* you laugh all the ungodly to scorn.
My eyes are fixed on you, O my Strength;* for you, O God, are my stronghold.
My merciful God comes to meet me* . . .

                                       Psalm 59:5–11

The Refrain
The Lord executes righteousness* and judgment for all who are oppressed.

The Cry of the Church
Lord, have mercy on us. Christ, have mercy on us. Lord, have mercy on us.

The Lord's Prayer

The Prayer Appointed for the Week
Give us grace, O Lord, to answer readily the call of our Savior Jesus Christ and
    proclaim to all people the Good News of his salvation, that we and the whole
    world may perceive the glory of his marvelous works; who lives and reigns
    with you and the Holy Spirit, one God, for ever and ever. *Amen.*†

The Concluding Prayer of the Church
Lord God, almighty and everlasting Father, you have brought me in safety to this
    new day: Preserve me with your mighty power, that I may not fall into sin, nor
    be overcome by adversity; and in all I do direct me to the fulfilling of your pur-
    pose; through Jesus Christ my Lord. *Amen.*†

The Midday Office   To Be Observed on the Hour or Half Hour
                             Between 11 a.m. and 2 p.m.

The Call to Prayer
Be strong and let your heart take courage,* all you who wait for the Lord.
                                                        Psalm 31:24

The Request for Presence
Give ear to my words, O Lord;* consider my meditation.
Hearken to my cry for help, my King and my God,* for I make my prayer to you.
                                                        Psalm 5:1–2

The Greeting
You are God; we praise you;
You are the Lord: we acclaim you;
You are the eternal Father:
All creation worships you.
To you all angels, all powers of heaven,
Cherubim and Seraphim, sing in endless praise:
    Holy, holy, holy Lord, God of power and might,
    heaven and earth are full of your glory.

The Refrain for the Midday Lessons
Great peace have they who love your law;* for them there is no stumbling block.
                                                        Psalm 119:165

A Reading
When Moses came down from Mount Sinai with the two tablets of the Testimony
    in his hands, as he was coming down the mountain, Moses did not know that

the skin of his face was radiant because he had been talking to him. And when Aaron and the Israelites saw Moses, the skin on his face was so radiant that they were afraid to go near him. But Moses called to them, and Aaron and all the leaders of the community rejoined him, and Moses talked to them, after which all the Israelites came closer, and he passed on to them all the orders that YAHWEH had given him on Mount Sinai. Once Moses had finished speaking to them, he put a veil over his face. Whenever Moses went into YAHWEH's presence to speak with him, he took the veil off until he came out. And when he came out, he would tell the Israelites what orders he had been given, and the Israelites would see Moses' face radiant. Then Moses would put the veil back over his face until he went in to speak to him next time.

Exodus 34:29–35

The Refrain
Great peace have they who love your law;* for them there is no stumbling block.

The Midday Psalm   *How Wonderful Is God in His Holy Places*
Sing to God, O kingdoms of the earth;* sing praises to the Lord.
He rides in the heavens, the ancient heavens;* he sends forth his voice, his mighty voice.
Ascribe power to God;* his majesty is over Israel; his strength is in the skies.
How wonderful is God in his holy places!* the God of Israel giving strength and power to his people! Blessed be God!

Psalm 68:33–36

The Refrain
Great peace have they who love your law;* for them there is no stumbling block.

The Cry of the Church
O Lord, hear my prayer and let my cry come unto you. Thanks be to God.

THE SHORT BREVIARY

The Lord's Prayer

The Prayer Appointed for the Week
Give us grace, O Lord, to answer readily the call of our Savior Jesus Christ and proclaim to all people the Good News of his salvation, that we and the whole world may perceive the glory of his marvelous works; who lives and reigns with you and the Holy Spirit, one God, for ever and ever. *Amen.*†

The Concluding Prayer of the Church
O God, the source of eternal light: Shed forth your unending day upon all of us who watch for you, that our lips may praise you, our lives may bless you, and our worship may give you glory; through Jesus Christ our Lord. *Amen.*†

The Vespers Office   To Be Observed on the Hour or Half Hour
                                                        Between 5 and 8 p.m.

The Call to Prayer
Bless our God, you peoples;* make the voice of his praise to be heard;
Who holds our souls in life,* and will not allow our feet to slip.
                                                        Psalm 66:7–8

The Request for Presence
O God of hosts;* show us the light of your countenance, and we shall be saved.
                                                        Psalm 80:7

The Greeting
As the eyes of servants look to the hand of their masters,* and the eyes of a maid to
    the hand of her mistress,
So my eyes look to you, O Lord my God.
                                                        based on Psalm 123:2–3

The Hymn

Guide me, O you great Jehovah,   When I tread the verge of Jordan,
Pilgrim through this barren land.   Bid my anxious fears subside;
I am weak, but you are mighty;   Death of death and hell's destruction,
Hold me with your powerful hand.   Land me safe on Canaan's side.
Bread of heaven, bread of heaven,   Songs of praises, songs of praises,
Feed me till I want no more;   I will ever give to you,
Feed me till I want no more.   I will ever give to you.

                                                        William Williams
Open now the crystal fountain,
Whence the healing stream does flow;
Let the fire and cloudy pillar
Lead me all my journey through.
Strong deliverer, strong deliverer,
Forever be my strength and shield
Forever be my strength and shield.

The Refrain for the Vespers Lessons
For I am but a sojourner with you,* a wayfarer, as all my forebears were.
                                                        Psalm 39:14

The Vespers Psalm   *Having You I Desire Nothing on Earth*
When my mind became embittered,* I was sorely wounded in my heart.
I was stupid and had no understanding;* I was like a brute beast in your presence.
Yet I am always with you;* you hold me by my right hand.
You will guide me by your counsel,* and afterwards receive me with glory.
Whom have I in heaven but you?* and having you I desire nothing upon earth.
Though my flesh and my heart should waste away, God is the strength of my
    heart and my portion for ever.

Truly, those who forsake you will perish;* you destroy all who are unfaithful.
But it is good for me to be near God;* I have made the Lord GOD my refuge.
I will speak of all your works* in the gates of the city of Zion.

Psalm 73:21–29

The Refrain

For I am but a sojourner with you,* a wayfarer, as all my forebears were.

The Cry of the Church

Even so come, Lord Jesus!

The Lord's Prayer

The Prayer Appointed for the Week

Give us grace, O Lord, to answer readily the call of our Savior Jesus Christ and
proclaim to all people the Good News of his salvation, that we and the whole
world may perceive the glory of his marvelous works; who lives and reigns
with you and the Holy Spirit, one God, for ever and ever. *Amen.*†

The Concluding Prayer of the Church

Almighty God, who after the creation of the world rested from all your works and
sanctified a day of rest for all your creatures: Grant that I, putting away all
earthly anxieties, may be duly prepared for the service of public worship, and
grant as well that my Sabbath upon earth may be a preparation for the eternal
rest promised to your people in heaven; through Jesus Christ our Lord. *Amen.*†

The Morning Office   To Be Observed on the Hour or Half Hour
Between 6 and 9 a.m.

The Call to Prayer

I will sing of mercy and justice;* to you, O LORD, will I sing praises.

Psalm 101:1

The Request for Presence

But as for me, O LORD, I cry to you for help;* in the morning my prayer comes
before you.

Psalm 88:14

The Greeting

Your testimonies are very sure,* and holiness adorns your house, O LORD, for ever
and for evermore.

Psalm 93:6

The Refrain for the Morning Lessons
Happy are they whose way is blameless,* who walk in the law of the LORD!

Psalm 119:1

A Reading
Jesus taught us, saying: ". . . if you are bringing your offering to the altar and there remember that your brother has something against you, leave your offering there before the altar, go and be reconciled with your brother first, and then come back and present your offering."

Matthew 5:23–24

The Refrain
Happy are they whose way is blameless,* who walk in the law of the LORD!

The Morning Psalm   *Open for Me the Gates of Righteousness*
Open for me the gates of righteousness;* I will enter them; I will offer thanks to the LORD.
"This is the gate of the LORD;* he who is righteous may enter."
I will give thanks to you, for you answered me* and have become my salvation.
The same stone which the builders rejected* has become the chief cornerstone.
This is the LORD's doing,* and it is marvelous in our eyes.
On this day the LORD has acted;* we will rejoice and be glad in it.

Psalm 118:19–24

The Refrain
Happy are they whose way is blameless,* who walk in the law of the LORD!

The Gloria

The Lord's Prayer

The Prayer Appointed for the Week
Almighty and everlasting God, you govern all things both in heaven and on earth: Mercifully hear the supplications of your people, and in our time grant us your peace; through Jesus Christ our Lord, who lives and reigns with you and the Holy Spirit, one God, for ever and ever. *Amen.†*

The Concluding Prayer of the Church
Lord God, almighty and everlasting Father, you have brought me in safety to this new day: Preserve me with your mighty power, that I may not fall into sin, nor be overcome by adversity; and in all I do direct me to the fulfilling of your purpose; through Jesus Christ my Lord. *Amen.†*

The Midday Office   To Be Observed on the Hour or Half Hour
                                     Between 11 a.m. and 2 p.m.

The Call to Prayer
Hallelujah! Praise the Name of the LORD;* give praise, you servants of the LORD,
You who stand in the house of the LORD,* in the courts of the house of our God.
Praise the LORD, for the LORD is good;* sing praises to his Name, for it is lovely.

Psalm 135:1–3

The Request for Presence
Let them know that you, whose Name is YAHWEH,* you alone are the Most High
    over all the earth.

Psalm 83:18

The Greeting
. . . My heart sings to you without ceasing;* O LORD my God, I will give you
    thanks for ever.

Psalm 30:13

The Refrain for the Midday Lessons
The LORD will make good his purpose for me;* O LORD, your love endures for
    ever; do not abandon the works of your hands.

Psalm 138:9

A Reading
Some time later, the word of YAHWEH came to Abram in a vision: "Do not be
    afraid, Abram! I am your shield and shall give you a very great reward." "Lord
    YAHWEH," Abram replied, "What use are your gifts, as I am going on my way
    childless? . . . Since you have given me no offspring," Abram continued, "a
    member of my household will be my heir." Then YAHWEH's word came to him
    in reply, "Such a one will not be your heir; no, your heir will be the issue of
    your own body." Then, taking him outside, he said, "Look up at the sky and
    count the stars if you can. Just so will your descendants be." He told him.
    Abram put his faith in YAHWEH and this was reckoned to him as uprightness.

Genesis 15:1–6

The Refrain
The LORD will make good his purpose for me;* O LORD, your love endures for
    ever; do not abandon the works of your hands.

The Midday Psalm   *Open My Eyes That I May See*
Deal bountifully with your servant,* that I may live and keep your word.
Open my eyes, that I may see* the wonders of your law.
I am a stranger here on earth;* do not hide your commandments from me.
My soul is consumed at all times* with longing for your judgments.
You have rebuked the insolent;* cursed are they who stray from your
    commandments!
Turn from me shame and rebuke,* for I have kept your decrees.

Even though rulers sit and plot against me,* I will meditate on your statutes.
For your decrees are my delight,* and they are my counselors.

Psalm 119:17–24

The Refrain

The LORD will make good his purpose for me;* O LORD, your love endures for
ever; do not abandon the works of your hands.

The Gloria

The Lord's Prayer

The Prayer Appointed for the Week

Almighty and everlasting God, you govern all things both in heaven and on earth:
Mercifully hear the supplications of your people, and in our time grant us your
peace; through Jesus Christ our Lord, who lives and reigns with you and the
Holy Spirit, one God, for ever and ever. *Amen.*†

The Concluding Prayer of the Church

O God, you make me glad with the weekly remembrance of the glorious resurrection of your Son my Lord: Give me this day such blessing through my worship
of you, that the week to come may be spent in your favor; through Jesus Christ
our Lord. *Amen.*†

The Vespers Office   **To Be Observed on the Hour or Half Hour**
                                        Between 5 and 8 p.m.

The Call to Prayer

Open my lips, O Lord,* and my mouth shall proclaim your praise.

Psalm 51:16

The Request for Presence

Be my strong rock, a castle to keep me safe,* for you are my crag and my stronghold; for the sake of your Name, lead me and guide me.

Psalm 31:3

The Greeting

O gracious Light, pure brightness of the everlasting Father in heaven, O Jesus
Christ, holy and blessed! Now as we come to the setting of the sun, and our
eyes behold the vesper light, we sing your praises O God: Father, Son and Holy
Spirit. You are worthy at all times to be praised by happy voices, O Son of God,
O giver of life, and to be glorified through all the worlds.

Phos Hilaron

The Hymn

Lift high the cross, the love of Christ proclaim
Till all the world adore his sacred name.
Come, Christians, follow this triumphant sign.
The hosts of God in unity combine.

Lift high the cross, the love of Christ proclaim
Till all the world adore his sacred name.
Each newborn servant of the Crucified
Bears on the brow the seal of him who died.

Lift high the cross, the love of Christ proclaim
Till all the world adore his sacred name.
O Lord, once lifted on the glorious tree,
As you have promised, draw the world to thee.

Lift high the cross, the love of Christ proclaim
Till all the world adore his sacred name.
So shall our song of triumph ever be:
Praise to the Crucified for victory!

George Kitchin and Michael Newbolt

The Refrain for the Vespers Lessons
In God the LORD, whose word I praise, in God I trust and will not be afraid . . .

Psalm 56:10

The Vespers Psalm   *You Are My God*
But as for me, I have trusted in you, O LORD.* I have said, "You are my God.
My times are in your hand;* rescue me from the hand of my enemies, and from
    those who persecute me.
Make your face to shine upon your servant,* and in your loving-kindness save me."
LORD, let me not be ashamed for having called upon you . . .

Psalm 31:14–17

The Refrain
In God the LORD, whose word I praise, in God I trust and will not be afraid . . .

The Small Verse
Into your hands I commend my spirit for you have redeemed me, O God of my
    life. Glory be to the Father, and to the Son and to the comforting Spirit.

Traditional

The Lord's Prayer

The Prayer Appointed for the Week
Almighty and everlasting God, you govern all things both in heaven and on earth:
    Mercifully hear the supplications of your people, and in our time grant us your
    peace; through Jesus Christ our Lord, who lives and reigns with you and the
    Holy Spirit, one God, for ever and ever. *Amen.*†

The Concluding Prayer of the Church
O God, you have brought me near to an innumerable company of angels, and to
    the spirits of just men made perfect: Grant me during my earthly pilgrimage to
    abide in their fellowship, and in your heavenly country to become partakers of
    their joy; through Jesus Christ our Lord, who lives and reigns with you and the
    Holy Spirit, one God, now and for ever. *Amen.*†

The Morning Office   To Be Observed on the Hour or Half Hour
                                      Between 6 and 9 a.m.

The Call to Prayer
Bless God in the congregation;* bless the LORD, you that are of the fountain of
   Israel.

                                                    Psalm 68:26

The Request for Presence
Look upon your covenant;* the dark places of the earth are haunts of violence.

                                                    Psalm 74:19

The Greeting
Deliver me, O LORD, by your hand* from those whose portion in life is this world.

                                                    Psalm 17:14

The Refrain for the Morning Lessons
The fool has said in his heart, "There is no God."* All are corrupt and commit
   abominable acts; there is none who does any good.

                                                    Psalm 53:1

A Reading
Jesus taught us, saying: "If your brother does something wrong, rebuke him and,
   if he is sorry, forgive him. And if he wrongs you seven times a day and seven
   times comes back to you and says, 'I am sorry,' you must forgive him."

                                                    Luke 17:3–4

The Refrain
The fool has said in his heart, "There is no God."* All are corrupt and commit
   abominable acts; there is none who does any good.

The Morning Psalm   *I Have Washed My Hands in Innocence*
Truly, God is good to Israel,* to those who are pure in heart.
But as for me, my feet had nearly slipped;* I had almost tripped and fallen;
Because I envied the proud* and saw the prosperity of the wicked:
For they suffer no pain,* and their bodies are sleek and sound;
In the misfortunes of others they have no share;* they are not afflicted as others
   are;
Therefore they wear their pride like a necklace* and wrap their violence about
   them like a cloak.
Their iniquity comes from gross minds,* and their hearts overflow with wicked
   thoughts.
They scoff and speak maliciously;* out of their haughtiness they plan oppression.
They set their mouths against the heavens,* and their evil speech runs through the
   world.
And so the people turn to them* and find in them no fault.
They say, "How should God know?* is there knowledge in the Most High?"
So then, these are the wicked;* always at ease, they increase their wealth.
In vain have I kept my heart clean,* and washed my hands in innocence.

I have been afflicted all day long,* and punished every morning.
Had I gone on speaking this way,* I should have betrayed the generation of your
    children.
When I tried to understand these things,* it was too hard for me;
Until I entered the sanctuary of God* and discerned the end of the wicked.

Psalm 73:1–17

The Refrain
The fool has said in his heart, "There is no God."* All are corrupt and commit
    abominable acts; there is none who does any good.

The Cry of the Church
Bless the Lord, O my soul, and forget not all his benefits.

The Lord's Prayer

The Prayer Appointed for the Week
Almighty and everlasting God, you govern all things both in heaven and on earth:
    Mercifully hear the supplications of your people, and in our time grant us your
    peace; through Jesus Christ our Lord, who lives and reigns with you and the
    Holy Spirit, one God, for ever and ever. *Amen.*†

The Concluding Prayer of the Church
Lord God, almighty and everlasting Father, you have brought me in safety to this
    new day: Preserve me with your mighty power, that I may not fall into sin, nor
    be overcome by adversity; and in all I do direct me to the fulfilling of your pur-
    pose; through Jesus Christ my Lord. *Amen.*†

The Midday Office **To Be Observed on the Hour or Half Hour**
Between 11 a.m. and 2 p.m.

The Call to Prayer
Be glad, you righteous, and rejoice in the LORD;* shout for joy, all who are true of
    heart.

Psalm 32:12

The Request for Presence
LORD, hear my prayer, and let my cry come before you;* hide not your face from
    me in the day of my trouble.

Psalm 102:1

The Greeting
Into your hands I commend my spirit,* for you have redeemed me, O LORD, O
    God of truth.

Psalm 31:5

The Refrain for the Midday Lessons
My help comes from the LORD,* the maker of heaven and earth.

Psalm 121:2

A Reading

Let the word of Christ, in all its richness, find a home with you. Teach each other, and advise each other, in all wisdom. With gratitude in your hearts sing psalms and hymns and inspired songs to God.

Colossians 3:16

The Refrain

My help comes from the LORD,* the maker of heaven and earth.

The Midday Psalm   *Let My Heart Be Sound in Your Statutes*

Your hands have made me and fashioned me;* give me understanding, that I may learn your commandments.

Those who fear you will be glad when they see me,* because I trust in your word.

I know, O LORD, that your judgments are right* and that in faithfulness you have afflicted me.

Let your loving-kindness be my comfort,* as you have promised to your servant.

Let your compassion come to me, that I may live,* for your law is my delight.

Let the arrogant be put to shame, for they wrong me with lies;* but I will meditate on your commandments.

Let those who fear you turn to me,* and also those who know your decrees.

Let my heart be sound in your statutes,* that I may not be put to shame.

Psalm 119:73–80

The Refrain

My help comes from the LORD,* the maker of heaven and earth.

The Cry of the Church

O God, come to my assistance! O Lord, make haste to help me!

The Lord's Prayer

The Prayer Appointed for the Week

Almighty and everlasting God, you govern all things both in heaven and on earth: Mercifully hear the supplications of your people, and in our time grant us your peace; through Jesus Christ our Lord, who lives and reigns with you and the Holy Spirit, one God, for ever and ever. *Amen.*†

The Concluding Prayer of the Church

May God have mercy on me, forgive me my sins and bring me to life everlasting. In Jesus' name. *Amen.*

The Vespers Office   To Be Observed on the Hour or Half Hour
                                       Between 5 and 8 p.m.

The Call to Prayer

Come now and look upon the works of the LORD,* what awesome things he has done on earth.

Psalm 46:9

The Request for Presence
May God be merciful to us and bless us,* show us the light of his countenance and
   come to us.
Let your ways be known upon earth,* your saving health among all nations.

Psalm 67:1–2

The Greeting
O LORD of hosts,* happy are they who put their trust in you!

Psalm 84:12

The Hymn

In the Father's power	In the Father's power
In the Son's power	In the Son's power
In the Spirit's power	In the Spirit's power
Be this hour	Be this hour
Father be my friend	Father who created me
Jesus be my friend	With thine eye watch me
Spirit be my friend	Savior who redeemed me
To the journey's end	With thine eye look on me
	Spirit who strengthens me
Father be my guard	With thine eye regard me
Jesus be my guard	The eyeing of the Three
Spirit be my guard	For my saving be
When the way is hard	*David Adam*

The Refrain for the Vespers Lessons
Bless the LORD, you angels of his, you mighty ones who do his bidding,* and hearken to the voice of his word.

Psalm 103:20

The Vespers Psalm   *Where Can I Go Then from Your Spirit*
LORD, you have searched me out and known me;* you know my sitting down and
   my rising up; you discern my thoughts from afar.
You trace my journeys and my resting-places* and are acquainted with all my
   ways.
Indeed, there is not a word on my lips,* but you, O LORD, know it altogether.
You press upon me behind and before* and lay your hand upon me.
Such knowledge is too wonderful for me;* it is so high that I cannot attain to it.

Psalm 139:1–5

The Refrain
Bless the LORD, you angels of his, you mighty ones who do his bidding,* and hearken to the voice of his word.

The Small Verse
In the sight of the Angels I praise You. I adore at Your holy temple and give praise to Your Name.

adapted from THE SHORT BREVIARY

The Lord's Prayer

The Prayer Appointed for the Week
Almighty and everlasting God, you govern all things both in heaven and on earth: Mercifully hear the supplications of your people, and in our time grant us your peace; through Jesus Christ our Lord, who lives and reigns with you and the Holy Spirit, one God, for ever and ever. *Amen.*†

The Concluding Prayer of the Church
Blessed be the God and father of my Lord Jesus Christ, who has not rejected my prayer, nor withheld his love from me.

based on Psalm 66:18

The Morning Office   To Be Observed on the Hour or Half Hour
Between 6 and 9 a.m.

The Call to Prayer
Come, let us sing to the LORD;* let us shout for joy to the Rock of our salvation.
Let us come before his presence with thanksgiving* and raise a loud shout to him with psalms.

Psalm 95:1–2

The Request for Presence
Show us the light of your countenance, O God,* and come to us.

based on Psalm 67:1

The Greeting
To you I lift up my eyes,* to you enthroned in the heavens.
As the eyes of servants look to the hand of their masters,* and the eyes of a maid to the hand of her mistress,
So our eyes look to the LORD our God,* until he shows us his mercy.

Psalm 123:1–3

The Refrain for the Morning Lessons
I will bear witness that the LORD is righteous;* I will praise the Name of the LORD Most High.

Psalm 7:18

A Reading
Jesus said: "Whatever you ask in my name I will do, so that the Father may be glorified by the Son. If you ask me for anything in my name, I will do it."

John 14:13–14

The Refrain
I will bear witness that the LORD is righteous;* I will praise the Name of the LORD Most High.

The Morning Psalm   *The LORD Will Not Break His Oath to David*
Arise, O LORD, into your resting-place,* you and the ark of your strength.
Let your priests be clothed with righteousness;* let your faithful people sing with joy.
For your servant David's sake,* do not turn away the face of your Anointed.
The LORD has sworn an oath to David;* in truth, he will not break it:
"A son, the fruit of your body* will I set upon your throne.
If your children keep my covenant and my testimonies that I shall teach them,*
   their children will sit upon your throne for evermore."

                      Psalm 132:8–13

The Refrain
I will bear witness that the LORD is righteous;* I will praise the Name of the LORD Most High.

The Small Verse
Keep me, Lord, as the apple of your eye and carry me under the shadow of your wings.

                      Traditional

The Lord's Prayer

The Prayer Appointed for the Week
Almighty and everlasting God, you govern all things both in heaven and on earth: Mercifully hear the supplications of your people, and in our time grant us your peace; through Jesus Christ our Lord, who lives and reigns with you and the Holy Spirit, one God, for ever and ever. *Amen.*†

The Concluding Prayer of the Church
Lord God, almighty and everlasting Father, you have brought me in safety to this new day: Preserve me with your mighty power, that I may not fall into sin, nor be overcome by adversity; and in all I do direct me to the fulfilling of your purpose; through Jesus Christ my Lord. *Amen.*†

The Midday Office   To Be Observed on the Hour or Half Hour
                      Between 11 a.m. and 2 p.m.

The Call to Prayer
Open my lips, O Lord,* and my mouth shall proclaim your praise.
                      Psalm 51:16

The Request for Presence
Let my cry come before you, O LORD;* give me understanding, according to your word.
Let my supplication come before you;* deliver me, according to your promise.
                      Psalm 119:169–170

The Greeting

How priceless is your love, O God!* your people take refuge under the shadow of
your wings.
They feast upon the abundance of your house;* you give them drink from the
river of your delights.
For with you is the well of life,* and in your light we see light.

Psalm 36:7–9

The Refrain for the Midday Lessons

Mercy and truth have met together;* righteousness and peace have kissed each
other.

Psalm 85:10

A Reading

Paul wrote: ". . . I was made a servant with the responsibility towards you that
God gave to me, that of completing God's message, the message which was a
mystery hidden for generations and centuries and has now been revealed to
his holy people. It was God's purpose to reveal to them how rich is the glory of
this mystery among the gentiles; it is Christ among you, your hope of glory:
this is the Christ that we are proclaiming, admonishing and instructing everyone in all wisdom to make everyone perfect in Christ."

Colossians 1:25–28

The Refrain

Mercy and truth have met together;* righteousness and peace have kissed each
other.

The Midday Psalm   *Sing to the* LORD *a New Song*

Sing to the LORD a new song;* sing to the LORD, all the whole earth.
Sing to the LORD and bless his Name;* proclaim the good news of his salvation
from day to day.
Declare his glory among the nations* and his wonders among all peoples.
For great is the LORD and greatly to be praised;* he is more to be feared than all
gods.
As for all the gods of the nations, they are but idols;* but it is the LORD who made
the heavens.
Oh, the majesty and magnificence of his presence!* Oh, the power and the
splendor of his sanctuary!

Psalm 96:1–6

The Refrain

Mercy and truth have met together;* righteousness and peace have kissed each
other.

The Small Verse

Lord, be merciful to me, a sinner. Christ, be merciful to me, a sinner. Father, be
merciful to me, a sinner. Spirit, be merciful to me, a sinner. Lord, be merciful to
me, a sinner.

Traditional

The Lord's Prayer

The Prayer Appointed for the Week
Almighty and everlasting God, you govern all things both in heaven and on earth:
Mercifully hear the supplications of your people, and in our time grant us your
peace; through Jesus Christ our Lord, who lives and reigns with you and the
Holy Spirit, one God, for ever and ever. *Amen.*†

The Concluding Prayer of the Church
Let us bless the Lord God living and true! Let us always render him praise, glory,
honor, blessing, and all good things! Amen. Amen. So be it! So be it!

St. Francis of Assisi

The Vespers Office — To Be Observed on the Hour or Half Hour
Between 5 and 8 p.m.

The Call to Prayer
Sing to the LORD with thanksgiving;* make music to our God upon the harp.

Psalm 147:7

The Request for Presence
Let your countenance shine upon your servant* and teach me your statutes.

Psalm 119:135

The Greeting
How glorious you are!* more splendid than the everlasting mountains!

Psalm 76:4

The Hymn
'Tis so sweet to trust in Jesus, and to take him at his word;
Just to rest upon his promise, and to know, "Thus says the Lord."
Jesus, Jesus, how I trust him! How I've proved him o'er and o'er!
Jesus, Jesus, precious Jesus! O for grace to trust him more!

Yes, 'tis sweet to trust in Jesus, just from sin and self to cease;
Just from Jesus simply taking life and rest, and joy and peace.
Jesus, Jesus, how I trust him! How I've proved him o'er and o'er!
Jesus, Jesus, precious Jesus! O for grace to trust him more!

I'm so glad I learned to trust you, precious Jesus, Savior, friend;
And I know that you are with me, will be with me to the end.
Jesus, Jesus, how I trust him! How I've proved him o'er and o'er!
Jesus, Jesus, precious Jesus! O for grace to trust him more!

Louisa Stead

The Refrain for the Vespers Lessons
Your love, O LORD, for ever will I sing;* from age to age my mouth will proclaim
your faithfulness.

Psalm 89:1

The Vespers Psalm   *You Make the Darkness That It May Be Night*

The trees of the LORD are full of sap,* the cedars of Lebanon which he planted,
In which the birds build their nests,* and in whose tops the stork makes his
    dwelling.
The high hills are a refuge for the mountain goats,* and the stony cliffs for the rock
    badgers.
You appointed the moon to mark the seasons,* and the sun knows the time of its
    setting.
You make darkness that it may be night,* in which all the beasts of the forest prowl.
The lions roar after their prey* and seek their food from God.
The sun rises, and they slip away* and lay themselves down in their dens.
Man goes forth to his work* and to his labor until the evening.

                                                            Psalm 104:17–24

The Refrain

Your love, O LORD, for ever will I sing;* from age to age my mouth will proclaim
    your faithfulness.

The Gloria

The Lord's Prayer

The Prayer Appointed for the Week

Almighty and everlasting God, you govern all things both in heaven and on earth:
    Mercifully hear the supplications of your people, and in our time grant us your
    peace; through Jesus Christ our Lord, who lives and reigns with you and the
    Holy Spirit, one God, for ever and ever. *Amen.*†

The Concluding Prayer of the Church

Lord Jesus Christ, you have prepared a quiet place for us in your Father's eternal
    home. Watch over our welfare on this perilous journey, shade us from the
    burning heat of day, and keep our lives free of evil until the end. *Amen.*

                                    THE LITURGY OF THE HOURS, VOL. III

The Morning Office   **To Be Observed on the Hour or Half Hour**
                                                Between 6 and 9 a.m.

The Call to Prayer

Worship the LORD in the beauty of holiness;* let the whole earth tremble before him.

                                                            Psalm 96:9

The Request for Presence

Show us the light of your countenance, O God,* and come to us.

                                            based on Psalm 67:1

The Greeting

Seven times a day do I praise you,* because of your righteous judgments.

                                                        Psalm 119:164

The Refrain for the Morning Lessons
Protect my life and deliver me;* let me not be put to shame, for I have trusted in
    you.
Let integrity and uprightness preserve me,* for my hope has been in you.

Psalm 25:19–20

A Reading
Jesus said: "In all truth I tell you, no one can enter the kingdom of God without
    being born through water and the Spirit; what is born of human nature is
    human; what is born of the Spirit is spirit. Do not be surprised when I say: You
    must be born from above. The wind blows where it pleases; you can hear its
    sound, but you cannot tell where it comes from or where it is going. So it is
    with everyone who is born of the Spirit."

John 3:5–8

The Refrain
Protect my life and deliver me;* let me not be put to shame, for I have trusted in
    you.
Let integrity and uprightness preserve me,* for my hope has been in you.

The Morning Psalm   *His Loving-kindness Toward Us Is Great*
Praise the LORD, all you nations;* laud him, all you peoples.
For his loving-kindness toward us is great,* and the faithfulness of the LORD
    endures for ever. Hallelujah!

Psalm 117

The Refrain
Protect my life and deliver me;* let me not be put to shame, for I have trusted in
    you.
Let integrity and uprightness preserve me,* for my hope has been in you.

The Cry of the Church
O Lamb of God, that takes away the sins of the world, have mercy upon me.
O Lamb of God, that takes away the sins of the world, have mercy upon me.
O Lamb of God, that takes away the sins of the world, grant me your peace.

The Lord's Prayer

The Prayer Appointed for the Week
Almighty and everlasting God, you govern all things both in heaven and on earth:
    Mercifully hear the supplications of your people, and in our time grant us your
    peace; through Jesus Christ our Lord, who lives and reigns with you and the
    Holy Spirit, one God, for ever and ever. *Amen.*†

The Concluding Prayer of the Church
Lord God, almighty and everlasting Father, you have brought me in safety to this
    new day: Preserve me with your mighty power, that I may not fall into sin, nor
    be overcome by adversity; and in all I do direct me to the fulfilling of your pur-
    pose; through Jesus Christ my Lord. *Amen.*†

The Midday Office   To Be Observed on the Hour or Half Hour
                                  Between 11 a.m. and 2 p.m.

The Call to Prayer
Come, let us sing to the LORD;* let us shout for joy to the Rock of our salvation.
Let us come before his presence with thanksgiving* and raise a loud shout to him
    with psalms.
For the LORD is a great God,* and a great King above all gods.
In his hand are the caverns of the earth,* and the heights of the hills are his also.
The sea is his, for he made it,* and his hands have molded the dry land.

Psalm 95:1–5

The Request for Presence
Remember not our past sins;* let your compassion be swift to meet us.

Psalm 79:8

The Greeting
Zion hears and is glad, and the cities of Judah rejoice,* because of your judgments,
    O LORD.

Psalm 97:8

The Refrain for the Midday Lessons
I will listen to what the LORD God is saying,* for he is speaking peace to his faithful
    people and to those who turn their hearts to him.

Psalm 85:8

A Reading
If we live by the truth and in love, we shall grow completely into Christ, who is
    the head by whom the whole Body is fitted and joined together, every joint
    adding its own strength, for each individual part to work according to its func-
    tion. So the body grows until it has built itself up in love.

Ephesians 4:15–16

The Refrain
I will listen to what the LORD God is saying,* for he is speaking peace to his faithful
    people and to those who turn their hearts to him.

The Midday Psalm   *Sing to the LORD a New Song*
Hallelujah! Sing to the LORD a new song;* sing his praise in the congregation of the
    faithful.
Let Israel rejoice in his Maker;* let the children of Zion be joyful in their King.
Let them praise his Name in the dance;* let them sing praise to him with timbrel
    and harp.
For the LORD takes pleasure in his people* and adorns the poor with victory.

Psalm 149:1–4

The Refrain
I will listen to what the LORD God is saying,* for he is speaking peace to his faithful
    people and to those who turn their hearts to him.

The Gloria

The Lord's Prayer

The Prayer Appointed for the Week
Almighty and everlasting God, you govern all things both in heaven and on earth:
Mercifully hear the supplications of your people, and in our time grant us your
peace; through Jesus Christ our Lord, who lives and reigns with you and the
Holy Spirit, one God, for ever and ever. *Amen.*†

The Concluding Prayer of the Church
Direct me, O Lord, on all my doings with your most gracious favor, and further
me with your continual help; that in all my work begun, continued, and ended
in you, I may glorify your holy name, and finally, by your mercy, obtain everlasting life; through Jesus Christ my Lord. *Amen.*†

The Vespers Office   To Be Observed on the Hour or Half Hour
                                                Between 5 and 8 p.m.

The Call to Prayer
Come, let us sing to the LORD;* let us shout for joy to the Rock of our salvation.
Psalm 95:1

The Request for Presence
May the glory of the LORD endure for ever;* may the LORD rejoice in all his works.
Psalm 104:32

The Greeting
How great is your goodness, O LORD! which you have laid up for those who fear
you;* which you have done in the sight of all for those who put their trust in
you.
Psalm 31:19

The Hymn

Holy Spirit, Truth divine,   Holy Spirit, Power divine,
Dawn upon this soul of mine;   Fill and nerve this will of mine;
Word of God and inward light,   Grant that I may strongly live,
Wake my spirit, clear in sight.   Bravely bear, and nobly strive.

Holy Spirit, Love divine,   Holy Spirit, Right divine,
Glow within this heart of mine;   King within my conscience reign;
Kindle every high desire;   Be my Lord, and I shall be
Perish self in your pure fire.   Firmly bound, forever free.
                                        Samuel Longfellow

The Refrain for the Vespers Lessons
I am small and of little account,* yet I do not forget your commandments.
Psalm 119:141

The Vespers Psalm   *He Shall Cover Me with His Pinions*

He who dwells in the shelter of the Most High,* abides under the shadow of the
   Almighty.

He shall say to the LORD, "You are my refuge and my stronghold,* my God in
   whom I put my trust."

He shall deliver you from the snare of the hunter* and from the deadly pestilence.

He shall cover you with his pinions, and you shall find refuge under his wings;*
   his faithfulness shall be a shield and buckler.

You shall not be afraid of any terror by night,* nor of the arrow that flies by day;

Of the plague that stalks in the darkness,* nor of the sickness that lays waste at
   mid-day.

A thousand shall fall at your side and ten thousand at your right hand,* but it shall
   not come near you.

Psalm 91:1–7

The Refrain

I am small and of little account,* yet I do not forget your commandments.

The Small Verse

Those who sowed with tears* will reap with songs of joy.

Those who go out weeping, carrying the seed,* will come again with joy, shouldering their sheaves.

Psalm 126:6–7

The Lord's Prayer

The Prayer Appointed for the Week

Almighty and everlasting God, you govern all things both in heaven and on earth:
   Mercifully hear the supplications of your people, and in our time grant us your
   peace; through Jesus Christ our Lord, who lives and reigns with you and the
   Holy Spirit, one God, for ever and ever. *Amen.†*

The Concluding Prayer of the Church

Almighty God, to whom our needs are known before we even ask, Help me to ask
   only what accords with your will; and those good things which I dare not, or in
   my blindness I cannot ask, grant for the sake of your Son Jesus Christ our Lord.
   Amen.†

The Morning Office   To Be Observed on the Hour or Half Hour
                                              Between 6 and 9 a.m.

The Call to Prayer

Rejoice in the LORD, you righteous,* and give thanks to his holy Name.

Psalm 97:12

The Request for Presence
Bow down your ear, O Lord, and answer me,* for I am poor and in misery.
Keep watch over my life, for I am faithful;* save your servant who puts his trust in
you.

Psalm 86:1–2

The Greeting
Blessed is the Lord!* for he has heard the voice of my prayer.

Psalm 28:7

The Refrain for the Morning Lessons
Blessed are they which do hunger and thirst after righteousness: for they shall be
filled.

Matthew 5:6 (KJV)

A Reading
The Word became flesh, he lived among us, and we saw his glory, the glory that he
has from the Father as the only Son of the Father, full of grace and truth.

John 1:14

The Refrain
Blessed are they which do hunger and thirst after righteousness: for they shall be
filled.

The Morning Psalm   *Teach Me Discernment*
O Lord, you have dealt graciously with your servant,* according to your word.
Teach me discernment and knowledge,* for I have believed in your
    commandments.
Before I was afflicted I went astray,* but now I keep your word.
You are good and you bring forth good;* instruct me in your statutes.
The proud have smeared me with lies,* but I will keep your commandments with
    my whole heart.
Their heart is gross and fat,* but my delight is in your law.
It is good for me that I have been afflicted,* that I might learn your statutes.
The law of your mouth is dearer to me* than thousands in gold and silver.

Psalm 119:65–72

The Refrain
Blessed are they which do hunger and thirst after righteousness: for they shall be
filled.

The Small Verse
My soul thirsts for the strong, living God and all that is within me cries out to him.

Traditional

The Lord's Prayer

The Prayer Appointed for the Week
Almighty and everlasting God, you govern all things both in heaven and on earth:
    Mercifully hear the supplications of your people, and in our time grant us your

peace; through Jesus Christ our Lord, who lives and reigns with you and the Holy Spirit, one God, for ever and ever. *Amen.*†

The Concluding Prayer of the Church
Lord God, almighty and everlasting Father, you have brought me in safety to this new day: Preserve me with your mighty power, that I may not fall into sin, nor be overcome by adversity; and in all I do direct me to the fulfilling of your purpose; through Jesus Christ my Lord. *Amen.*†

The Midday Office   To Be Observed on the Hour or Half Hour
Between 11 a.m. and 2 p.m.

The Call to Prayer
Glory in his holy Name;* let the hearts of those who seek the LORD rejoice.

Psalm 105:3

The Request for Presence
Let your compassion come to me, that I may live,* for your law is my delight.

Psalm 119:77

The Greeting
Your righteousness, O God, reaches to the heavens;* you have done great things; who is like you, O God?

Psalm 71:19

The Refrain for the Midday Lessons
Happy are they whose transgressions are forgiven,* and whose sin is put away!

Psalm 32:1

A Reading
. . . "The Lord YAHWEH says this; I am not acting for your sake, House of Israel, but for the sake of my holy name . . . I shall pour clean water over you and you shall be cleansed; I shall cleanse you of all your filth and of all your fool idols. I shall give you a new heart, and put a new spirit in you . . ."

Ezekiel 36:22, 25–26

The Refrain
Happy are they whose transgressions are forgiven,* and whose sin is put away!

The Midday Psalm   *I Will Extol You Among the Nations*
The LORD lives! Blessed is my Rock!* Exalted is the God of my salvation!
He is the God who gave me victory* and cast down the peoples beneath me.
You rescued me from the fury of my enemies; you exalted me above those who rose against me;* you saved me from my deadly foe.
Therefore will I extol you among the nations, O LORD,* and sing praises to your Name.
He multiplies the victories of his king;* he shows loving-kindness to his anointed, to David and his descendants for ever.

Psalm 18:46–50

The Refrain
Happy are they whose transgressions are forgiven,* and whose sin is put away!

The Cry of the Church
Lord, have mercy on us. Christ, have mercy on us. Lord, have mercy on us.

The Lord's Prayer

The Prayer Appointed for the Week
Almighty and everlasting God, you govern all things both in heaven and on earth:
    Mercifully hear the supplications of your people, and in our time grant us your
    peace; through Jesus Christ our Lord, who lives and reigns with you and the
    Holy Spirit, one God, for ever and ever. *Amen.*†

The Concluding Prayer of the Church
Open, Lord, my eyes that I may see.
Open, Lord, my ears that I may hear.
Open, Lord, my heart and my mind that I may understand.
So shall I turn to you and be healed.

Traditional

The Vespers Office   To Be Observed on the Hour or Half Hour
Between 5 and 8 p.m.

The Call to Prayer
God is the LORD; he has shined upon us;* form a procession with branches up to
    the horns of the altar.

Psalm 118:27

The Request for Presence
Hear the voice of my prayer when I cry out to you,* when I lift up my hands to
    your holy of holies.

Psalm 28:2

The Greeting
All your works praise you, O LORD,* and your faithful servants bless you.
They make known the glory of your kingdom and speak of your power . . . * and
    the glorious splendor of your kingdom.

Psalm 145:10–12

The Hymn
> O Sabbath rest of Galilee!
> O calm of hills above,
> Where Jesus knelt to share with thee
> The silence of eternity
> Interpreted with love.
> Drop your still dews of quietness
> Till all our strivings ease;
> Take from our souls the strain and stress,
> And let our ordered lives confess
> The beauty of your peace.
> > *John G. Whittier*

The Refrain for the Vespers Lessons
Those who trust in the LORD are like Mount Zion,* which cannot be moved, but
stands fast for ever.
> > *Psalm 125:1*

The Vespers Psalm   *This Is Comfort in My Trouble*
Remember your word to your servant,* because you have given me hope.
This is my comfort in my trouble,* that your promise gives me life.
The proud have derided me cruelly,* but I have not turned from your law.
When I remember your judgments of old,* LORD, I take great comfort.
I am filled with a burning rage,* because of the wicked who forsake your law.
Your statutes have been like songs to me* wherever I have lived as a stranger.
I remember your Name in the night, O LORD,* and dwell upon your law.
This is how it has been with me,* because I have kept your commandments.
> > *Psalm 119:49–56*

The Refrain
Those who trust in the LORD are like Mount Zion,* which cannot be moved, but
stands fast for ever.

The Small Verse
The earth is the Lord's and all the fullness thereof, the world and we who dwell
within. Thanks be to God.
> > *Traditional*

The Lord's Prayer

The Prayer Appointed for the Week
Almighty and everlasting God, you govern all things both in heaven and on earth:
Mercifully hear the supplications of your people, and in our time grant us your
peace; through Jesus Christ our Lord, who lives and reigns with you and the
Holy Spirit, one God, for ever and ever. *Amen.*†

The Concluding Prayer of the Church
May God himself order my days and make them acceptable in his sight. Blessed is
the Lord always, my strength and my redeemer.
> > *Traditional*

The Morning Office   **To Be Observed on the Hour or Half Hour**
Between 6 and 9 a.m.

The Call to Prayer
Come, let us sing to the LORD; . . .
For the LORD is a great God,* and a great King above all gods.
Psalm 95:1, 3

The Request for Presence
I call upon you, O God, for you will answer me;* incline your ear to me and hear
    my words.
Psalm 17:6

The Greeting
When your word goes forth it gives light;* it gives understanding to the simple.
Psalm 119:130

The Refrain for the Morning Lessons
"I will appoint a time," says God.
Psalm 75:2a

A Reading
Jesus taught them, saying: "Let anyone who is thirsty come to me! Let anyone
    who believes in me, come and drink! As scripture says, 'From his heart shall
    flow streams of living water.'" He was speaking of the Spirit which those who
    believed in him were to receive; for there was no Spirit as yet because Jesus had
    not yet been glorified.
John 7:37b–39

The Refrain
"I will appoint a time," says God.

The Morning Psalm   *You Will Receive Me Afterwards with Glory*
When my mind became embittered,* I was sorely wounded in my heart.
I was stupid and had no understanding;* I was like a brute beast in your presence.
Yet I am always with you;* you hold me by my right hand.
You will guide me by your counsel,* and afterwards receive me with glory.
Whom have I in heaven but you?* And having you I desire nothing upon earth.
Though my flesh and my heart should waste away,* God is the strength of my
    heart and my portion for ever.
It is good for me to be near God;* I have made the Lord God my refuge.
Psalm 73:21–26, 28

The Refrain
"I will appoint a time," says God.

The Gloria

The Lord's Prayer

The Prayer Appointed for the Week

Almighty and everlasting God, you govern all things both in heaven and on earth: Mercifully hear the supplications of your people, and in our time grant us your peace; through Jesus Christ our Lord, who lives and reigns with you and the Holy Spirit, one God, for ever and ever. *Amen.*†

The Concluding Prayer of the Church

Lord God, almighty and everlasting Father, you have brought me in safety to this new day: Preserve me with your mighty power, that I may not fall into sin, nor be overcome by adversity; and in all I do direct me to the fulfilling of your purposes; through Jesus Christ my Lord. *Amen.*†

The Midday Office   To Be Observed on the Hour or Half Hour
                                     Between 11 a.m. and 2 p.m.

The Call to Prayer

O tarry and await the Lord's pleasure; be strong, and he shall comfort your heart;* wait patiently for the Lord.

Psalm 27:18

The Request for Presence

Open my eyes that I may see* the wonders of your law.
Psalm 119:18

The Greeting

My heart sings to you without ceasing;* O Lord my God, I will give you thanks for ever.

Psalm 30:13

The Refrain for the Midday Lessons

Blessed be the Lord for evermore!* Amen, I say, Amen.
Psalm 89:52

A Reading

Besides, you know the time has come; the moment is here for you to stop sleeping and wake up, because by now our salvation is nearer than when we first began to believe. The night is nearly over, daylight is on the way; so let us throw off everything that belongs to the darkness and equip ourselves for the light. Let us live decently, as in the light of day ...

Romans 13:11–13a

The Refrain

Blessed be the Lord for evermore!* Amen, I say, Amen.

The Midday Psalm   *He Gathered Them from the East, the*
                                     West, the North and the South

Give thanks to the Lord, for he is good,* and his mercy endures for ever.

Let all those whom the Lord has redeemed proclaim* that he redeemed them
from the hand of the foe.
He gathered them out of the lands;* from the east and from the west, from the
north and from the south.
He led them out of darkness and deep gloom* and broke their bonds asunder.
Let them give thanks to the Lord for his mercy* and the wonders he does for his
children.

Psalm 107:1–3, 14–15

The Refrain
Blessed be the Lord for evermore!* Amen, I say, Amen.

The Gloria

The Lord's Prayer

The Prayer Appointed for the Week
Almighty and everlasting God, you govern all things both in heaven and on earth:
Mercifully hear the supplications of your people, and in our time grant us your
peace; through Jesus Christ our Lord, who lives and reigns with you and the
Holy Spirit, one God, for ever and ever. *Amen.*†

The Concluding Prayer of the Church
Almighty God, unto whom all hearts are open, all desires known, and from
whom no secrets are hidden: Cleanse the thoughts and desires of my
heart by the inspiration of your Holy Spirit and grant that I may perfectly
love you and worthily magnify your name; through Christ Jesus my Lord.
Amen.†

The Vespers Office   To Be Observed on the Hour or Half Hour
                                            Between 5 and 8 p.m.

The Call to Prayer
Know this: The Lord himself is God;* he himself has made us, and we are his; we
are his people and the sheep of his pasture.

Psalm 100:2

The Request for Presence
For God alone my soul in silence waits;* truly, my hope is in him.

Psalm 62:6

The Greeting
I will thank you, O Lord my God, with all my heart,* and glorify your Name for
evermore.

Psalm 86:12

The Hymn

> The heavens declare your glory, Lord;
> In every star your wisdom shines;
> But when our eyes behold your word,
> We read your name in fairer lines.
>
> The rolling sun, the changing light,
> And nights and days, your power confess;
> But the blessed Volume you have given
> Reveals your justice and your grace.
>
> Sun, moon, stars convey your praise
> Round the whole world, and never stop;
> So when your truth began its race,
> It touched and glanced on every land.
>
> Nor will your spreading gospel rest
> Till through the world its course has run;
> Till Christ shall all the nations bless
> That see the light, or feel the sun.

Isaac Watts, adapted

The Refrain for the Vespers Lessons

Arise, O God, and rule the earth,* for you shall take all nations for your own.

Psalm 82:8

The Vespers Psalm   *The Earth Is the Lord's*

The earth is the Lord's and all that is in it,* the world and all who dwell therein.
For it is he who founded it upon the seas* and made it firm upon the rivers of the deep.
"Who can ascend the hill of the Lord?* and who can stand in his holy place?"
"Those who have clean hands and a pure heart,* who have not pledged themselves to falsehood, nor sworn by what is a fraud.
They shall receive a blessing from the Lord* and a just reward from the God of their salvation."
Such is the generation of those who seek him,* of those who seek your face, O God of Jacob.

Psalm 24:1–6

The Refrain

Arise, O God, and rule the earth,* for you shall take all nations for your own.

The Gloria

The Lord's Prayer

The Prayer Appointed for the Week

Almighty and everlasting God, you govern all things both in heaven and on earth: Mercifully hear the supplications of your people, and in our time grant us your peace; through Jesus Christ our Lord, who lives and reigns with you and the Holy Spirit, one God, for ever and ever. *Amen.*†

The Concluding Prayer of the Church

Defend, O Lord, all your servants with your heavenly grace, that we may all continue yours forever, and daily increase in your Holy Spirit more and more, until we come to your everlasting kingdom. *Amen.*†

May the souls of the faithful departed rest in peace.

The Morning Office   **To Be Observed on the Hour or Half Hour Between 6 and 9 a.m.**

The Call to Prayer
Sing to the LORD a new song;* sing to the LORD, all the whole earth.

Psalm 96:1

The Request for Presence
I call with my whole heart;* answer me, O LORD, that I may keep your statutes.

Psalm 119:145

The Greeting
Your righteousness, O God, reaches to the heavens;* ... who is like you, O God?

Psalm 71:19

The Refrain for the Morning Lessons
Let this be written for a future generation,* so that people yet unborn may praise the LORD.

Psalm 102:18

A Reading
Then as Jesus was teaching in the Temple, he cried out: "You know me and you know where I came from. Yet I have not come of my own accord: but he who sent me is true; You do not know him, but I know him because I have my being from him and it was he who sent me."

John 7:28–29

The Refrain
Let this be written for a future generation,* so that people yet unborn may praise the LORD.

The Morning Psalm   *O Shepherd of Israel, Leading Joseph Like a Flock*
Hear, O Shepherd of Israel, leading Joseph like a flock;* shine forth, you that are enthroned upon the cherubim
In the presence of Ephraim, Benjamin, and Manasseh,* stir up your strength and come to help us.
Restore us, O God of hosts,* show the light of your countenance, and we shall be saved.

Let your hand be upon the man of your right hand,* the son of man you have
  made so strong for yourself.
And so will we never turn away from you:* give us life, that we may call upon
  your Name.
Restore us, O Lord God of hosts;* show the light of your countenance, and we
  shall be saved.

Psalm 80:1–3, 16–18

The Refrain
Let this be written for a future generation,* so that people yet unborn may praise
  the Lord.

The Cry of the Church
Our hearts, O Lord, are restless until they rest in You!

The Lord's Prayer

The Prayer Appointed for the Week
Almighty and everlasting God, you govern all things both in heaven and on earth:
  Mercifully hear the supplications of your people, and in our time grant us your
  peace; through Jesus Christ our Lord, who lives and reigns with you and the
  Holy Spirit, one God, for ever and ever. *Amen.*†

The Concluding Prayer of the Church
Lord God, almighty and everlasting Father, you have brought me in safety to this
  new day: Preserve me with your mighty power, that I may not fall into sin, nor
  be overcome by adversity; and in all I do direct me to the fulfilling of your purposes; through Jesus Christ my Lord. *Amen.*†

The Midday Office   To Be Observed on the Hour or Half Hour
                               Between 11 a.m. and 2 p.m.

The Call to Prayer
Out of Zion, perfect in its beauty,* God reveals himself in glory.
"Gather before me my loyal followers,* those who have made a covenant with
  me* and sealed it with sacrifice."

Psalm 50:2, 5

The Request for Presence
For God alone my soul in silence waits;* from him comes my salvation.

Psalm 62:1

The Greeting
My God, my rock in whom I put my trust,* my shield, the horn of my salvation,
  and my refuge; you are worthy of praise.

Psalm 18:2

The Refrain for the Midday Lessons

The Lord has sworn and he will not recant:* "You are a priest for ever after the
order of Melchizedek."

Psalm 110:4

A Reading

*Melchizedek, king of Salem, a priest of God Most High, came to meet Abraham when he
returned from defeating the kings,* and *blessed him;* and Abraham gave him *a tenth
of everything.* By the interpretation of his name, he is, first, 'king of saving justice,' and also *king of Salem,* that is, 'king of peace'; he has no father, mother or
ancestry, and his life has no beginning or ending; he is like the Son of God. He
remains a priest forever.

Hebrews 7:1–3

The Refrain

The Lord has sworn and he will not recant:* "You are a priest for ever after the
order of Melchizedek."

The Midday Psalm   *I Will Bring Him to Honor*

For he shall give his angels charge over you,* to keep you in all your ways.

They shall bear you in their hands,* lest you dash your foot against a stone.

You shall tread upon the lion and the adder;* you shall trample the young lion and
the serpent under your feet.

Because he is bound to me in love, therefore will I deliver him;* I will protect him
because he knows my Name.

He shall call upon me, and I will answer him;* I am with him in trouble; I will rescue him and bring him to honor.

With long life will I satisfy him,* and show him my salvation.

Psalm 91:11–16

The Refrain

The Lord has sworn and he will not recant:* "You are a priest for ever after the
order of Melchizedek."

The Small Verse

Even so come, Lord Jesus.

The Lord's Prayer

The Prayer Appointed for the Week

Almighty and everlasting God, you govern all things both in heaven and on earth:
Mercifully hear the supplications of your people, and in our time grant us your
peace; through Jesus Christ our Lord, who lives and reigns with you and the
Holy Spirit, one God, for ever and ever. *Amen.†*

The Concluding Prayer of the Church

Almighty and everliving God, let your fatherly hand ever be over all of us your
servants; let your Holy Spirit ever be with us; and so lead us to the knowledge

and obedience of your Word, that we all may serve you in this life, and dwell with you in the life to come; through Jesus Christ my Lord. *Amen.*†

The Vespers Office   To Be Observed on the Hour or Half Hour
                                     Between 5 and 8 p.m.

The Call to Prayer
Come and listen, all you who fear God,* and I will tell you what he has done for me.
Psalm 66:14

The Request for Presence
Show us the light of your countenance, O God,* and come to us.
based on Psalm 67:1

The Greeting
The Lord is in his holy temple; let all the earth keep silence before him.
Traditional

The Hymn

God of truth, O Lord of might,   Grant this, O Father ever one
Disposing time and change aright,   With Jesus Christ Your only Son
Who clothes the splendid morning ray   And Holy Ghost, whom all adore,
And gives the heat at noon of day   Reigning and blessed forevermore.

Extinguish now each sinful fire
And banish every ill desire;
And while You keep the body whole
Shed forth Your peace upon the soul.

adapted from The Short Breviary

The Refrain for the Vespers Lessons
Bless the Lord, O my soul,* and all that is within me, bless his holy Name.
Psalm 103:1

The Vespers Psalm   *One Thing Have I Asked of the Lord*
The Lord is my light and my salvation; whom then shall I fear?* the Lord is the
   strength of my life; of whom then shall I be afraid?
When evildoers came upon me to eat up my flesh,* it was they, my foes and my
   adversaries, who stumbled and fell.
Though an army should encamp against me,* yet my heart shall not be afraid;
And though war should rise up against me,* yet will I put my trust in him.
One thing have I asked of the Lord: one thing I seek;* that I may dwell in the
   house of the Lord all the days of my life;
To behold the fair beauty of the Lord* and to seek him in his temple.
Psalm 27:1–6

The Refrain
Bless the Lord, O my soul,* and all that is within me, bless his holy Name.

The Cry of the Church
O Lord, make haste to help us. O Christ, make haste to save us.

The Lord's Prayer

The Prayer Appointed for the Week
Almighty and everlasting God, you govern all things both in heaven and on earth:
Mercifully hear the supplications of your people, and in our time grant us your
peace; through Jesus Christ our Lord, who lives and reigns with you and the
Holy Spirit, one God, for ever and ever. *Amen.*†

The Concluding Prayer of the Church
Almighty God, who after the creation of the world rested from all your works and
sanctified a day of rest for all your creatures: Grant that I, putting away all
earthly anxieties, may be duly prepared for the service of public worship, and
grant as well that my Sabbath on earth may be a preparation for the eternal rest
promised to your people in heaven; through Jesus Christ my Lord. *Amen.*†

January Compline

Sunday
The Night Office   To Be Observed Before Retiring

The Call to Prayer

May the Lord Almighty grant me and those I love a peaceful night and a perfect
    end. *Amen.*†

The Request for Presence

Our help is in the Name of the Lord; the maker of heaven and earth.

The Greeting

Almighty God, my heavenly Father: I have sinned against you, through my own
    fault, in thought, and word, and deed, in what I have done and what I have left
    undone. For the sake of your Son our Lord Jesus Christ, forgive me all my
    offenses; and grant that I may serve you in newness of life, to the glory of your
    Name. *Amen.*†

The Reading

So you are no longer aliens or foreign visitors; you are fellow citizens with the
    holy people of God and part of God's household. You are built upon the foun-
    dations of the apostles and prophets, and Christ Jesus himself is the corner-
    stone. Every structure knit together in him grows into a holy temple in the
    Lord; and you too, in him, are being built up into a dwelling-place of God in
    the Spirit.

Ephesians 2:19–22

The Gloria

The Psalm   *Tell It Out Among the Nations*

Oh, the majesty and magnificence of his presence!* Oh, the power and the
    splendor of his sanctuary!
Ascribe to the LORD, you families of the peoples;* ascribe to the LORD honor and
    power.
Ascribe to the LORD the honor due his Name;* bring offerings and come into his
    courts.
Worship the LORD in the beauty of holiness;* let the whole earth tremble before
    him.
Tell it out among the nations: "The LORD is King!* he has made the world so firm
    that it cannot be moved; he will judge the peoples with equity."

Psalm 96:6–10

The Gloria

The Small Verse

Into your hands, O Lord, I commend my spirit; for you have redeemed me, O
    Lord, O God of truth. Keep me, O Lord, as the apple of your eye; hide me
    under the shadow of your wings.†

The Lord's Prayer

The Petition

Watch, O Lord, with those who wake, or watch, or weep tonight, and give Your angels and saints charge over those who sleep. Tend Your sick ones, O Lord Christ. Rest Your weary ones. Bless Your dying ones. Soothe Your suffering ones. Shield Your joyous ones, and all for Your love's sake. *Amen.*§

The Final Thanksgiving

Lord, you now have set your servant free to go in peace as you have promised; for these eyes of mine have seen the Savior, whom you have prepared for all the world to see: a Light to enlighten the nations, and the glory of your people Israel. Glory to the Father, and to the Son, and to the Holy Spirit: as it was in the beginning, is now, and will be for ever. *Amen.*

Monday
The Night Office   To Be Observed Before Retiring

The Call to Prayer

May the Lord Almighty grant me and those I love a peaceful night and a perfect end. *Amen.*†

The Request for Presence

Our help is in the Name of the Lord; the maker of heaven and earth.

The Greeting

Almighty God, my heavenly Father: I have sinned against you, through my own fault, in thought, and word, and deed, in what I have done and what I have left undone. For the sake of your Son our Lord Jesus Christ, forgive me all my offenses; and grant that I may serve you in newness of life, to the glory of your Name. *Amen.*†

The Reading

He comes to us as One unknown, without a name, as of old, by the lakeside, He came to those men who knew Him not. He speaks to us the same word: "Follow thou me!" and sets us the tasks which he has to fulfill for our time. He commands. And to those who obey Him, whether they be wise or simple, He will reveal Himself in the toils, the conflicts, the sufferings which they will pass through in his fellowship, and, as an ineffable mystery, they shall learn in their own experience Who He is.

Albert Schweitzer

The Gloria

The Psalm   *Serve the LORD with Gladness*

Be joyful in the LORD, all you lands;* serve the LORD with gladness and come before his presence with a song.

Know this: The LORD himself is God;* he himself has made us, and we are his; we are his people and the sheep of his pasture.

Enter his gates with thanksgiving; go into his courts with praise;* give thanks to him and call upon his Name.

For the LORD is good; his mercy is everlasting;* and his faithfulness endures from age to age.

Psalm 100

The Gloria

The Small Verse

Into your hands, O Lord, I commend my spirit; for you have redeemed me, O Lord, O God of truth. Keep me, O Lord, as the apple of your eye; hide me under the shadow of your wings.†

The Lord's Prayer

The Petition

Watch, O Lord, with those who wake, or watch, or weep tonight, and give Your angels and saints charge over those who sleep. Tend Your sick ones, O Lord Christ. Rest Your weary ones. Bless Your dying ones. Soothe Your suffering ones. Shield Your joyous ones, and all for Your love's sake. *Amen.*§

The Final Thanksgiving

Lord, you now have set your servant free to go in peace as you have promised; for these eyes of mine have seen the Savior, whom you have prepared for all the world to see: a Light to enlighten the nations, and the glory of your people Israel. Glory to the Father, and to the Son, and to the Holy Spirit: as it was in the beginning, is now, and will be for ever. *Amen.*

Tuesday
The Night Office   To Be Observed Before Retiring

The Call to Prayer

May the Lord Almighty grant me and those I love a peaceful night and a perfect end. *Amen.*†

The Request for Presence

Our help is in the Name of the Lord; the maker of heaven and earth.

The Greeting

Almighty God, my heavenly Father: I have sinned against you, through my own fault, in thought, and word, and deed, in what I have done and what I have left undone. For the sake of your Son our Lord Jesus Christ, forgive me all my offenses; and grant that I may serve you in newness of life, to the glory of your Name. *Amen.*†

The Reading   *Pied Beauty*

Glory be to God for dappled things—
For skies of couple-colour as a brindled cow;

For rose-moles all in stipple upon trout that swim;
Fresh-firecoal chestnut-falls; finches' wings;
Landscape plotted and pieced-fold, fallow and plough;
And all trades, their gear and tackle and trim.
All things counter, original, spare, strange;
Whatever is fickle, freckled (who knows how?)
With swift, slow; sweet, sour; adazzle dim;
He fathers-forth whose beauty is past change:
Praise him.

Gerard M. Hopkins

The Gloria

The Psalm   *Your Paths Overflow with Plenty*
Those who dwell at the ends of the earth will tremble at your marvelous signs;*
    you make the dawn and the dusk to sing for joy.
You visit the earth and water it abundantly; you make it very plenteous;* the river
    of God is full of water.
You prepare the grain,* for so you provide for the earth.
You drench the furrows and smooth out the ridges;* with heavy rain you soften
    the ground and bless its increase.
You crown the year with your goodness,* and your paths overflow with plenty.
May the fields of the wilderness be rich for grazing,* and the hills be clothed with
    joy.
May the meadows cover themselves with flocks, and the valleys cloak themselves
    with grain;* let them shout for joy and sing.

Psalm 65:8–14

The Gloria

The Small Verse
Into your hands, O Lord, I commend my spirit; for you have redeemed me, O
    Lord, O God of truth. Keep me, O Lord, as the apple of your eye; hide me
    under the shadow of your wings.†

The Lord's Prayer

The Petition
Watch, O Lord, with those who wake, or watch, or weep tonight, and give Your
    angels and saints charge over those who sleep. Tend Your sick ones, O Lord
    Christ. Rest Your weary ones. Bless Your dying ones. Soothe Your suffering
    ones. Shield Your joyous ones, and all for Your love's sake. *Amen.*§

The Final Thanksgiving
Lord, you now have set your servant free to go in peace as you have promised; for
    these eyes of mine have seen the Savior, whom you have prepared for all the
    world to see: a Light to enlighten the nations, and the glory of your people
    Israel. Glory to the Father, and to the Son, and to the Holy Spirit: as it was in the
    beginning, is now, and will be for ever. *Amen.*

Wednesday
The Night Office   To Be Observed Before Retiring

The Call to Prayer
May the Lord Almighty grant me and those I love a peaceful night and a perfect
    end. *Amen.*†

The Request for Presence
Our help is in the Name of the Lord; the maker of heaven and earth.

The Greeting
Almighty God, my heavenly Father: I have sinned against you, through my own
    fault, in thought, and word, and deed, in what I have done and what I have left
    undone. For the sake of your Son our Lord Jesus Christ, forgive me all my
    offenses; and grant that I may serve you in newness of life, to the glory of your
    Name. *Amen.*†

The Reading
There is no greater proof in the world of our spiritual danger than the reluctance
    which most people always have and all people sometimes have to pray; so
    weary of their length, so glad when they are done, so clever to excuse and
    neglect their opportunity. Yet prayer is nothing but desiring God to give us the
    greatest and best things we can have and that can make us happy. It is a work
    so easy, so honorable, and to so great a purpose, that (except in the incarnation
    of His Son) God has never given us a greater argument of His willingness to
    have us saved and our unwillingness to accept it, of His goodness and our
    gracelessness, of His infinite condescension and our folly, than by rewarding so
    easy a duty with such great blessings.

Jeremy Taylor

The Gloria

The Psalm
O Lord, you are my shepherd;
I shall not want.
You make me lie down
In green pastures;
You lead me beside still waters.
You restore my soul;
You lead me in paths of righteousness
For your name's sake.
Even though I walk
Through the darkest valley,
I will fear no evil;
For you are with me;
Your rod and your staff—
They comfort me.
You prepare a table before me·

In the presence of my enemies;
You anoint my head with oil;
My cup overflows.
Surely, goodness and mercy
Shall follow me
All the days of my life,
And I shall dwell in your house, O Lord,
My whole life long.❖

The Gloria

The Small Verse
Into your hands, O Lord, I commend my spirit; for you have redeemed me, O
   Lord, O God of truth. Keep me, O Lord, as the apple of your eye; hide me
   under the shadow of your wings.†

The Lord's Prayer

The Petition
Watch, O Lord, with those who wake, or watch, or weep tonight, and give Your
   angels and saints charge over those who sleep. Tend Your sick ones, O Lord
   Christ. Rest Your weary ones. Bless Your dying ones. Soothe Your suffering
   ones. Shield Your joyous ones, and all for Your love's sake. *Amen.*§

The Final Thanksgiving
Lord, you now have set your servant free to go in peace as you have promised; for
   these eyes of mine have seen the Savior, whom you have prepared for all the
   world to see: a Light to enlighten the nations, and the glory of your people
   Israel. Glory to the Father, and to the Son, and to the Holy Spirit: as it was in the
   beginning, is now, and will be for ever. *Amen.*

Thursday
The Night Office   To Be Observed Before Retiring

The Call to Prayer
May the Lord Almighty grant me and those I love a peaceful night and a perfect
   end. *Amen.*†

The Request for Presence
Our help is in the Name of the Lord; the maker of heaven and earth.

The Greeting
Almighty God, my heavenly Father: I have sinned against you, through my own
   fault, in thought, and word, and deed, in what I have done and what I have left
   undone. For the sake of your Son our Lord Jesus Christ, forgive me all my
   offenses; and grant that I may serve you in newness of life, to the glory of your
   Name. *Amen.*†

The Reading   *Two Went Up into the Temple to Pray*

Two went up to pray? or rather say
One went to brag, th' other to pray;

One stands up close and treads on high,
Where th' other dares not send his eye.

One nearer to God's altar trod,
The other to the altar's God.

Richard Crashaw

The Gloria

The Psalm   *Eagerly I Seek You*

O God, you are my God; eagerly I seek you;* my soul thirsts for you, my flesh
faints for you, as in a barren and dry land where there is no water.
Therefore I have gazed upon you in your holy place,* that I might behold your
power and your glory.
For your loving-kindness is better than life itself;* my lips shall give you praise.
So will I bless you as long as I live* and lift up my hands in your Name.
My soul is content, as with marrow and fatness,* and my mouth praises you with
joyful lips,
When I remember you upon my bed,* and meditate on you in the night watches.
For you have been my helper,* and under the shadow of your wings I will rejoice.
My soul clings to you;* your right hand holds me fast.

Psalm 63:1–8

The Gloria

The Small Verse

Into your hands, O Lord, I commend my spirit; for you have redeemed me, O
Lord, O God of truth. Keep me, O Lord, as the apple of your eye; hide me
under the shadow of your wings.†

The Lord's Prayer

The Petition

Watch, O Lord, with those who wake, or watch, or weep tonight, and give Your
angels and saints charge over those who sleep. Tend Your sick ones, O Lord
Christ. Rest Your weary ones. Bless Your dying ones. Soothe Your suffering
ones. Shield Your joyous ones, and all for Your love's sake. *Amen.*§

The Final Thanksgiving

Lord, you now have set your servant free to go in peace as you have promised; for
these eyes of mine have seen the Savior, whom you have prepared for all the
world to see: a Light to enlighten the nations, and the glory of your people
Israel. Glory to the Father, and to the Son, and to the Holy Spirit: as it was in the
beginning, is now, and will be for ever. *Amen.*

Friday
The Night Office   To Be Observed Before Retiring

The Call to Prayer
May the Lord Almighty grant me and those I love a peaceful night and a perfect
end. *Amen.*†

The Request for Presence
Our help is in the Name of the Lord; the maker of heaven and earth.

The Greeting
Almighty God, my heavenly Father: I have sinned against you, through my own
fault, in thought, and word, and deed, in what I have done and what I have left
undone. For the sake of your Son our Lord Jesus Christ, forgive me all my
offenses; and grant that I may serve you in newness of life, to the glory of your
Name. *Amen.*†

The Reading   *Litany of Penitence*
Most holy and merciful Father:
I confess to you and to the whole communion of saints in heaven and on earth.
I have not loved you with my whole heart, and mind, and strength. I have not
loved my neighbors as myself. I have not forgiven others, as I have been for-
given.
Have mercy on me, Lord.
I have been deaf to your call to serve, as Christ served us. I have not been true to
the mind of Christ. I have grieved your Holy Spirit.
Have mercy on me, Lord.
I confess to you, Lord, all my past unfaithfulness: the pride, hypocrisy, and impa-
tience of my life,
I confess to you, Lord.
My self-indulgent appetites and ways, and my exploitation of other people,
I confess to you, Lord.
My anger at my own frustration, and my envy of those more fortunate than I,
I confess to you, Lord.
My intemperate love of worldly goods and comforts, and my dishonesty in daily
life and work,
I confess to you, Lord.
My negligence in prayer and worship, and my failure to commend the faith that is
in me,
I confess to you, Lord.
Accept my repentance, Lord, for the wrongs I have done: for my blindness to
human need and suffering, and my indifference to injustice and cruelty,
Accept my repentance, Lord.
For all false judgments, for uncharitable thoughts toward my neighbors, and for
my prejudice and contempt toward those who differ from me,
Accept my repentance, Lord.

For my waste and pollution of your creation, and my lack of concern for those
who come after us,
Accept my repentance, Lord.
Restore me, good Lord, and let your anger depart from me,
Favorably hear me for your mercy is great.
Accomplish in me and all of your church the work of your salvation,
That I may show forth your glory in the world.
By the cross and passion of your Son our Lord,
Bring me with all your saints to the joy of his resurrection.†

The Gloria

The Psalm   *Teach Us to Number Our Days*
Our iniquities you have set before you,* and our secret sins in the light of your
countenance.
When you are angry, all our days are gone;* we bring our years to an end like a
sigh.
The span of our life is seventy years, perhaps in strength even eighty;* yet the sum
of them is but labor and sorrow, for they pass away quickly and we are gone.
Who regards the power of your wrath?* who rightly fears your indignation?
So teach us to number our days* that we may apply our hearts to wisdom.

Psalm 90:8–12

The Gloria

The Small Verse
Into your hands, O Lord, I commend my spirit; for you have redeemed me, O
Lord, O God of truth. Keep me, O Lord, as the apple of your eye; hide me
under the shadow of your wings.†

The Lord's Prayer

The Petition
Watch, O Lord, with those who wake, or watch, or weep tonight, and give Your
angels and saints charge over those who sleep. Tend Your sick ones, O Lord
Christ. Rest Your weary ones. Bless Your dying ones. Soothe Your suffering
ones. Shield Your joyous ones, and all for Your love's sake. *Amen.*§

The Final Thanksgiving
Lord, you now have set your servant free to go in peace as you have promised; for
these eyes of mine have seen the Savior, whom you have prepared for all the
world to see: a Light to enlighten the nations, and the glory of your people
Israel. Glory to the Father, and to the Son, and to the Holy Spirit: as it was in the
beginning, is now, and will be for ever. *Amen.*

Saturday
The Night Office   To Be Observed Before Retiring

The Call to Prayer
May the Lord Almighty grant me and those I love a peaceful night and a perfect
end. *Amen.*†

The Request for Presence
Our help is in the Name of the Lord; the maker of heaven and earth.

The Greeting
Almighty God, my heavenly Father: I have sinned against you, through my own
fault, in thought, and word, and deed, in what I have done and what I have left
undone. For the sake of your Son our Lord Jesus Christ, forgive me all my
offenses; and grant that I may serve you in newness of life, to the glory of your
Name. *Amen.*†

The Reading   *The Apostles' Creed*
I believe in God, the Father almighty,
Maker of heaven and earth;
And in Jesus Christ his only Son our Lord;
Who was conceived by the Holy Ghost,
Born of the Virgin Mary,
Suffered under Pontius Pilate,
Was crucified, died and was buried.
He descended into hell.
On the third day he rose again from the dead.
He ascended into heaven,
And sits on the right hand of God the Father almighty.
From thence he shall come to judge the quick and the dead.
I believe in the Holy Ghost,
The holy catholic Church,
The communion of saints,
The forgiveness of sins,
The resurrection of the body,
And the life everlasting. *Amen.*†

The Gloria

The Psalm   *What Our Forefathers Have Told Us*
                                                 We Will Not Hide from Their Children
Hear my teaching, O my people;* incline your ears to the words of my mouth.
I will open my mouth in a parable,* I will declare the mysteries of ancient times.
That which we have heard and known, and what our forefathers have told us,* we
will not hide from their children.
We will recount to generations to come the praiseworthy deeds and the power of
the LORD,* and the wonderful works he has done.

He gave his decrees to Jacob and established a law for Israel,* which he
  commanded them to teach their children;
That the generations to come might know, and the children yet unborn;* that they
  in their turn might tell it to their children;
So that they might put their trust in God,* and not forget the deeds of God, but
  keep his commandments;
And not be like their forefathers, a stubborn and rebellious generation,* a
  generation whose heart was not steadfast, and whose spirit was not faithful to
  God.

Psalm 78:1–8

The Gloria

The Small Verse

Into your hands, O Lord, I commend my spirit; for you have redeemed me, O
  Lord, O God of truth. Keep me, O Lord, as the apple of your eye; hide me
  under the shadow of your wings.†

The Lord's Prayer

The Petition

Watch, O Lord, with those who wake, or watch, or weep tonight, and give Your
  angels and saints charge over those who sleep. Tend Your sick ones, O Lord
  Christ. Rest Your weary ones. Bless Your dying ones. Soothe Your suffering
  ones. Shield Your joyous ones, and all for Your love's sake. *Amen.*§

The Final Thanksgiving

Lord, you now have set your servant free to go in peace as you have promised; for
  these eyes of mine have seen the Savior, whom you have prepared for all the
  world to see: a Light to enlighten the nations, and the glory of your people
  Israel. Glory to the Father, and to the Son, and to the Holy Spirit: as it was in the
  beginning, is now, and will be for ever. *Amen.*

Index of Authors

Acknowledgments

"The Angels Will Deliver Us" from *An African Prayer Book* by Desmond Tutu. Copyright 1997 by Doubleday. Used by permission.

"Come Holy Dove" from *Edge of Glory* by David Adam. Copyright 1985 by Morehouse Publishing. Used by permission.

"God, You Have Prepared in Peace the Path" from *An African Prayer Book* by Desmond Tutu. Copyright 1997 by Doubleday. Used by permission.

"He Comes as One Unknown" by Albert Schweitzer from *Gospel: the Life of Jesus as Told by the World's Greatest Writers,* compiled by Constance & Daniel Pollock. Copyright 1998 by Word Publishing. Used by permission.

"Help Each One of Us, Gracious Father/Prayer from China" from *Another Day: Prayers of the Human Family,* compiled by John Carden. Copyright 1986 by Church Missionary Society.

"In the Father's Power" from *Edge of Glory* by David Adam. Copyright 1985 by Morehouse Publishing. Used by permission.

"Late Have I Loved Thee" from *An African Prayer Book* by Desmond Tutu. Copyright 1997 by Doubleday. Used by permission.

"A Mind to Know You" from *Speaking to God* by Nancy Benvenga. Copyright 1993 by Ave Maria Press. Used by Permission.

"New Day" from *Edge of Glory* by David Adam. Copyright 1985 by Morehouse Publishing. Used by permission.

"O Lord You Are My Chosen Portion" from *Awake My Heart* by Fred Bassett. Copyright 1998 by Paraclete Press. Used by permission.

"O Lord, You Are My Shepherd" from *Awake My Heart* by Fred Bassett. Copyright 1998 by Paraclete Press. Used by permission.

"The Privilege Is Ours to Share in the Loving" from *An African Prayer Book* by Desmond Tutu. Copyright 1997 by Doubleday. Used by permission.

"Two Went Up into the Temple to Pray" by Richard Crashaw from *Gospel: The Life of Jesus as Told by the World's Greatest Writers* compiled by Constance & Daniel Pollock. Copyright 1998 by Word Publishing. Used by permission.

"You Are the Future" from *Rilke's Book of Hours: Love Poems to God,* translated by Barrows and Macy. Copyright 1996 by Riverhead Books. Used by permission.

Excerpts from *Creative Prayer* by Brigid Herman. Copyright 1998 by Paraclete Press. Used by permission.

Excerpts from *The Doubleday Christian Quotation Collection* selected and arranged by Hannah Ward and Jennifer Wild. Copyright 1997 by Doubleday. Used by permission.

Excerpts from *The Doubleday Prayer Collection* selected and arranged by Mary Batchelor. Copyright 1997 by Doubleday. Used by permission.

Excerpts from *Holy Living* by Jeremy Taylor. Copyright 1988 by Paraclete Press. Used by permission.

Excerpts from *The Hours of the Divine Office in English and Latin* prepared by the staff of Liturgical Press. Copyright 1963 by The Liturgical Press. Used by permission.

Excerpts from *Imitation of Christ* (Thomas à Kempis) edited by Hal M. Helms. Copyright 1982 by Paraclete Press. Used by permission.

Excerpts from *The Joy of Full Surrender* (Jean-Pierre de Caussade) edited by Hal M. Helms. Copyright 1986 by Paraclete Press. Used by permission.

Excerpts from *Liturgy of the Hours, Vol. III* by International Commission on English in the Liturgy. Copyright 1974 by International Commission on English in the Liturgy. Used by permission.

Excerpts from *New Companion to the Breviary.* Copyright 1988 by the Carmelites of Indianapolis, Indiana. Used by permission.

Excerpts from *The Oxford Book of Prayer* edited by George Appleton. Copyright 1985 by Oxford University Press. Used by permission.

Excerpts from *Praying with Mary* by Janice Connell. Copyright 1997 by HarperCollins Publishers. Used by permission.

Excerpts from *Sacred Poems and Prayers of Love* edited by Mary Ford-Grabowsky. Copyright 1998 by Doubleday. Used by permission.

Excerpts from *A Short Breviary* edited by The Monks of St. John's Abbey. Copyright 1949 by St. John's Abbey. Used by permission of The Liturgical Press.

All verses, other than Psalms, are excerpted from *The New Jerusalem Bible* unless otherwise noted.

All verses from Psalms are excerpted from *The Book of Common Prayer* unless otherwise noted.

KJV refers to verses excerpted from the King James Version of the Bible.